SHIFTER NATION: EAST COAST BEARS COLLECTION

MEG RIPLEY

Disclaimer

This book is intended for readers age 18 and over. It contains mature situations and language that may be objectionable to some readers.

CONTENTS

RANGER KNOX

SHIFTER NATION: WEREBEARS OF ACADIA

1

HANNAH

I PULL INTO THE SPOT WHERE MY AIRBNB HOST SAID I COULD LEAVE MY CAR and look around me. It's my first time in Bar Harbor, and though my surroundings look more beautiful than anything I've ever seen on the Travel Channel, I'm not here to admire the foliage: I have an ulterior motive. Sure, the magazine could force me to use my vacation time, but they couldn't keep me from writing while I did.

I've been trying to work my way up to a full-time editorial position with *New World* for about a year, and when HR told me that I had to either take my vacation time or lose it, I hatched a plan to work on something while I was away. The magazine has its one-thousandth issue coming out in a month, and I figured--I hoped--that an exposé on the controversial history behind the National Park Service would put me in a better position to get ahead. So, I scheduled my vacation time and booked an Airbnb in Bar Harbor, a quaint little tourist town right outside of Maine's Acadia National Park, and started to plan my research.

I'd gotten the idea from a piece I'd read recently, which delved into how the National Park Service came into existence. Of course, there had always been green spaces that rich people bought up and set aside as conservation areas, but there was something in the article about the founders--something I couldn't put my finger on--that struck me as a little odd. Aside from that, I'd come across these wacko conspiracy theory websites claiming the national parks were actually set up for some kind of nefarious purpose. The theories I'd read speculated they were being used as reserves for fossil fuels or gold and other precious metals; the most interesting and least likely to be true theory was that the lands had been set aside by freemasons and other occult groups in power for the sake of performing secret ceremonies.

I grab my laptop case and backpack off the passenger seat and check my phone to make sure I'm on time. Mary, the woman whose house I'm staying in, seems to be a fairly accommodating host, based on the messages we've been exchanging, anyway. Her place is more accessible than the hotels in Bar Harbor, and considering it's the height of foliage season, much cheaper. I lock my car out of habit, even though I can't imagine anyone on the sleepy little street stealing from me.

It's chillier than I thought it would be, so I hurry up to the front door of the little house, pulling my denim jacket tight around me. I knock on the door and wait, fidgeting as I look around. Maine is one of those places that's stunning when you're looking at it in pictures or video, but if you're standing outside in late September, it's chilly and damp, making it hard to appreciate the beauty of the yellow, orange, and red leaves on the trees.

"You must be Hannah!" Mary looks like someone's mom: gray-streaked chestnut hair, wrinkles at the corners of her eyes, wearing a matching pink sweatsuit with 80s-era floral appliques stitched on the chest and pant legs. "Quick, come inside, dear; it's getting cold out there."

I follow her through the door and make small talk about my drive up as she gives me a tour of the house. The kitchen has plenty of cast iron and a gas-powered stove--according to Mary, it's more reliable than electric in the winters. Mary leads me upstairs to my room, explaining about the bathroom and how she got a tankless, gas-powered water heater installed so that she'd never have to wait for hot water.

She shows me to the guest room, giving me the chance to unpack and get settled, but instead, I pull out my laptop and search for the Acadia National Park website. I chose it as the place for my work-cation because Acadia was one of the first national parks established by the NPS; I'd hoped it would be a good place to start.

I look over the material I've already assembled about the park, thinking about how I'll kick off my investigation. *Well, the first thing to do would be to get there and check the place out,* I decide as I examine the maps of the area. Mary's place is about two miles away--close enough that, in theory, I could walk there, but if I did, I may not have enough energy left to explore the place. It's taken me all day to get up to Maine and it's already late afternoon; I should probably wait until the morning, but if I want to get a real feel for the place, I'm going to need to check it out when there aren't as many visitors there. I change into some warmer clothes--a thicker pair of jeans, a turtleneck sweater and a beanie--and I tell Mary that I'm off to run some errands.

I get back into my car and pull up the directions to the park. I've got about another hour or so before it's too dark to really see, but I've got a heavy flashlight with me, so I'm not too worried.

As I pull into the park a few minutes later, I fumble through the glove compartment in search of the one-week pass I'd ordered online before my trip and hand it to the ranger at the gate. I take a second look and have to admit he's pretty hot; he fills out that uniform really well with those broad shoulders of his. His deep brown hair and beard are cut short, and he's got strikingly bright green eyes.

"Just to let you know, the visitor center is closed for the day, but the park is open twenty-four hours," he tells me. "If you need any help, there are signs posted just about everywhere telling you how to get in touch with the rangers."

"Thanks," I tell him, taking back my visitor pass. Maybe I can interview him about Acadia, or at least get an official quote.

"I'm on duty for the rest of night, so I'll be checking to make sure that everyone gets out. If you plan on staying late, give me a call up here at the gate and I'll keep folks from coming after you to make sure you're not dead or lost," he says with a little smile.

I grin back at him. "That seems normal," I say, not quite sarcastic. "Give me the number, and I'll be sure to let you know that I'm okay." I program the number into my phone and the ranger passes me through the gate, heading back to the warmth of the guard house while I pull forward.

I don't see many cars in the lot, but that makes sense; it's starting to get dark, and it's chilly, too--enough so that I'm glad I thought to change into warmer clothes. I grab my flashlight and make sure I've got my phone and a few other things in my purse, and climb out of the car.

As I'm walking towards one of the hiking trails, I have to admit, the park is genuinely beautiful. It's almost the end of the foliage season, and I could see why outdoorsy people would come to the park at the peak of it. I step onto the path and breathe in the scent of dried leaves, loamy soil, and the shoreline, trying to get a feel for everything around me.

I start wandering, falling into a kind of rhythm that helps me to think. It'll be easier to get more intel when it's daylight, but as night begins to fall around me, there's something about the quiet of the place that makes it a little easier to understand why people might conjure up all these bizarre theories.

Right then, something shifts in the air, and I get the sense that I'm being watched, but I can't see anyone when I look around to prove it to myself. Even though I've been a journalist for a few years, I've never really been in any kind of dangerous situation before; there's no reason anyone would be after me, anyway. Right?

The deeper I get into the wooded areas around the hiking trail, the more the eerie feeling starts to weigh on me. Maybe it's just campers or rangers working, but a primal part of me feels like there's something else at play.

Something predatory.

I try to remain calm by reminding myself there aren't all that many predators in this area; black bears and coyotes are out here, but they're shy, and I have to assume they're not all that interested in attacking humans.

"Shake it off, they're more afraid of you than you are of them," I tell myself, looking around. I realize that I'm on a loop, and decide that instead of branching off onto one of the more remote trails, I'll just move ahead and make my way back to the parking lot.

Just then, I hear the distinct sound of a stick breaking behind me, followed by what sounds like a growl.

My heart starts pounding in my chest. "Probably just a coyote going after a rabbit or something," I tell myself as I start to move a little faster on the path, trying to get back to my car as quickly as possible.

I hear something else, something I can't even name; a sound I don't even know the word for, and that's enough to make me launch into a steady jog. It's dark, and though my flashlight is shaking uncontrollably in my hand, there's still enough light for me to see the path ahead of me. I hear more movement behind me, and despite telling myself that it's probably nothing, or that I'm just overreacting to the darkness and the creepy silence of the woods, I start sprinting outright.

"Get her!"

That is something I absolutely can't mistake for being some coyote or bobcat going after prey in the underbrush. I can't be certain it's directed at me, but it seems like the best idea is to just get the hell out of there as fast as I can, no matter who it's actually directed at.

I nearly make it to the trail's entrance when I hear the heavy footfalls right behind me, faster than I would have imagined possible, and I stumble over some uneven patch of the trail and land on the damp ground below with a thud.

"Fuck!" I mutter, struggling to get back on my feet to flee. I can't lie to myself for a second longer; there's someone--or some*thing*--chasing me, and I need to get to my car. What the hell ever possessed me to think it was a good idea to visit this park and hike these trails alone at night?

2

KNOX

Some of those new assholes are chasing after a park visitor!

The words ring out in my brain almost like a shout, and I recognize the mental "voice" of one of the members of my clan, Cassidy Powers. I put her on trail duty for the night, and when I reach out to her mind, I can place her close to one of the easier hiking paths.

I've been waiting for those bastards to do something I can call them out on for the last three weeks. Since Acadia is neutral territory for shifters, I can't kick them out--even as an Alpha--unless I have good reason to, and catching them committing a crime should be reason enough. I start heading in the direction I can feel Cassidy's signal coming from, and I keep my ears open for any hint of what the pricks might be doing.

I slow down a bit once I get onto the right trail, taking a few moments to catch my breath. Just ahead of me, I catch the tail end of one of them running along the trail. My heart beats faster in my chest for reasons that have nothing to do with running and I growl to myself, thinking of how I'd like to call those fucking pissants out formally and take them down.

Instead, I have to deal with the situation at hand. I vaguely catch the scent of a human female overlaid by the mark of the four bears chasing her. If these guys are going after a *human* park visitor, that's a big problem, and one I'm going to have to take care of as neatly as possible. They didn't even bother shifting into their bear forms; at least if they had, I could publicly dismiss it as a random wildlife incursion.

As I pursue the group and their prey, I start thinking of how I'm going to handle brushing this incident aside. There was some chick from a magazine calling the park a week or so before, and based on her questioning, I have a feeling she was priming the pump to uncover some things that are better left alone. And if word gets out that there's been an attack on someone visiting the park, there's no way she'll keep it out of whatever bullshit article she's working on.

I catch up to the group just before the entrance to the trails, and I hear the woman, who's now shouting.

"Don't think you're going to get anything from me--not without a goddamn fight!"

I can't help but be a bit impressed by her feisty spirit, and as I try to sneak up on them, I catch little glimpses of her as they follow her deeper into the woods. I assume they're probably planning to steal whatever valuables she's got on her--or maybe, do worse.

The woman must have taken some kind of self-defense classes; she stopped running and is now kicking and throwing punches, turning her head to bite as viciously as any cornered animal would, making it tough for her would-be attackers to get what they want from her.

"Let's take her to the campsite. Knock her out, Kevin."

"What the fuck? This was supposed to be a quick grab, Shawn. Let's just get her purse and get out of here, man. Right, Harris? Jamie?"

Shawn leers at the woman, "Yeah, but she's a hot little piece..."

I let them hear me approach, crunching hard on some underbrush and sticks to announce myself.

"You have two seconds to get the hell out of here," I say, letting the Alpha growl reverberate through my voice. There's one benefit to these interlopers not being part of my clan: they couldn't hear me coming, since they aren't tuned into the same telepathic channel.

"Oh, shit," I hear one of them mutter.

"Uh, we were just *helping* this young lady find her way back to her car," Jamie stammers, but he knows I'm not buying any of his bullshit.

"Did I stutter?" I get in his face and roar, "Get the fuck out of here. Now!"

Shawn, their Alpha, tries to posture a bit, but after a moment, with a low growl, they slink away into the woods. In the distance, I recognize the faint sounds of them shifting into their bear forms as they proceed to lumber off and sulk.

My focus shifts to the next priority: taking care of the woman, who is now sitting on a nearby boulder.

"You okay? I tried to get here before they could do anything," I say.

"Just got a good scare," she says. I move closer to her and see that she's managed to hold onto her purse; points for that, I guess. During the chase, I'd been too obsessed with getting to her before the outsiders could do anything, but now that we're close--and the adrenaline is starting to ebb out of my system--I can actually appreciate the scent of her; it reminds me of lavender honey, fresh out of a hive deep in the woods, and I recognize it as the scent of the visitor I'd just given the office phone number to an hour or so ago. I inhale once again; my mouth begins to water, but as I start to pick up on the sharper smell of her fear and anger, I have to remind myself she was almost the victim of an attack; one that could jeopardize the secrecy of Acadia.

"Here, let me help you up," I offer, reaching out to give her a hand. Even with my keen eyesight, in the dark, it's hard to make out too many particulars, but I can tell she's got an incredible body beneath her clothes: full breasts and round hips with a little padding along her thighs that triggers vivid images of what it'd be like to have those sexy legs wrapped around me. She doesn't accept my hand, but instead, rises from her seat on the huge chunk of granite and dusts herself off.

"Thanks for coming to my rescue," she says blandly.

"Just doing my job," I tell her, giving her a smile that I'm pretty sure her human eyes can't see in the darkness of the forest. "Please, let me walk you to your car to make sure you get out of here alright."

"I guess you could do that," the woman says, shifting her purse on her shoulder.

"What are you up to, wandering the woods at night, anyway?" We take off in the direction of the trail out to the parking lot, and I'm doing my best to get answers, while seeming to make small talk along the way.

"I know--I was actually heading back to my car when they started chasing me," the woman says. "I guess I just wanted to do a quick trip through a bit of the park before I settle further into my research."

"Research? Are you a scientist?" I haven't received any petitions for studies, but sometimes students do trips on their own, without grants or funding, for papers. The woman I'm walking with doesn't look like she's much older than the average grad student, so that could be the case.

"I'm a journalist, actually," she tells me. "I'm investigating the history of the National Park Service for an article, and I wanted to get a feel for one of its parks before starting to delve deeper, so I planned a little trip up here to Acadia."

I nearly stop dead in my tracks.

"A journalist?" *Great. Of course those assholes chose literally the worst person to attack.* This is going to make things even more complicated.

"Yeah—I'm working with *New World* magazine," she says. "The name's Hannah Grant." She holds out her hand for me to shake it, and I oblige, in spite of the multiple distractions raging for control of my mind.

"Knox Bernard," I tell her. "We've spoken before." I see her eyes widen as we pass into the lighted area surrounding the parking lot.

"You're the administrator for this park," she says, looking at me sharply. "We talked on the phone."

"We did," I agree. *God could this situation get worse?*

"You're...much more attractive than you sounded on the phone," the woman says, smiling a little awkwardly.

"I don't know if I should be offended or flattered," I tell her. She laughs, and it's like someone's run a finger down my spine in the best way possible.

"No, I didn't mean it as an insult at all," she says, shaking her head. "I'm just surprised that you're the one who came to my rescue, I guess." She shakes her head again and rummages through her purse. "I should probably head back to my Airbnb before I embarrass myself even more."

"Let me just check you over before you leave," I suggest, partly because I want to make sure she's actually okay, but also because I want an excuse to linger. The scent rolling off her is enough to drive me mad; aside from that, I have to set some ground rules about this article she's working on. I can't be having a scandalous investigation into the park underway.

"I guess," Hannah says, looking at me warily. I hold up my flashlight and wave the light over her hands, up her arms and down her legs, checking her over. I don't really need it--there's enough light from the moon and the safety lamps set out in the parking lot for me to see clearly--but it gives me an excuse to take my time, and besides: she doesn't need to know that I can already see her as plain as day.

"I hope that little incident didn't give you a bad first impression of the park," I say, playing the light over her back. Her denim jacket must have gotten snagged on something; but thankfully, it's not torn through.

"Well, it certainly gave me a good first impression of the park *rangers*," Hannah says playfully. "Rushing to help this stupid damsel in distress."

"It could've happened to anyone," I tell her. "I've been trying to run those campers out of here for a couple of weeks, but they're paid up and I haven't had anything I can use as leverage 'til now. Hopefully this changes things."

"You know who they were?"

"I know this park inside and out," I point out with a little smile. "Well, you look like you're all in one piece, but you should check yourself over for ticks once you get back home."

"I will," Hannah says. And then we're just standing there in the parking lot, awkwardly, with maybe a foot and a half of space between us. "Are you on duty tomorrow? I was hoping I could get a tour...in the daylight, of course."

"I'm off duty, technically," I reply, thinking fast. "But if you want to get a tour of the park, I'd be more than happy to show you around."

"That would be great," Hannah says.

"Think you can get here at about two? It should be warm enough, and we can make good time along the shoreline and through the wooded areas."

"You realize I'm going to be interviewing you," Hannah says, making it not quite a question.

"I expected as much," I say, grinning at her. "Two?"

"That works," she tells me, smiling back. "Thanks again. For...you know."

"Just doing my job," I insist. I turn away from her, stepping back to watch the gentle swaying of her hips as she walks the rest of the way to her car. I'm not sure whether I'm looking forward to tomorrow because it'll give me a chance to run interference, or to be around that lingering, sweet scent of hers, but I can only hope I can get enough sleep to be functional before I have to meet up with her.

I watch as her car pulls away and then head back onto the trail, towards the part of the woods where the interlopers disappeared to. I'm going to have to discuss the incident with the members of my clan, and if I expect to be able to expel these bastards from the neutral, sacred lands of the park, I'll need some solid evidence to present to the conclave of shifters.

3

HANNAH

THE MORNING AFTER MY ILL-FATED TRIP TO ACADIA NATIONAL PARK, I'M up early, scanning through some of the research I've already done, trying to put together a cohesive strategy for interviewing Knox Bernard later in the day.

As I look through my records, there's something odd I keep coming across, and while it doesn't make me feel like I'm becoming a full-on conspiracy theorist, it does set off some red flags. Like many of the national parks that exist in the US, Acadia was made possible through lots of advocacy and generous contributions from wealthy men--but the donations were made by the same handful of families repeatedly.

Most well-off families do benevolent things to get their names in history books. But a lot of the people involved in the establishment of Acadia, and the National Park Service as a whole, seemed to not want any credit at all. I decide by around eleven that I'll ask Knox what he knows about the history of the park itself, and start getting ready for our meeting. I've got a few bumps and bruises from falling on the trail, but I'm actually surprised at how unafraid I am to venture back into the woods. Of course, that could just be because I won't be alone, and especially because the ranger who'll be taking me around is actually pretty hot.

I weave my hair into a french braid and pull an old cap from my university over my head to keep the sun out of my eyes. It's cool enough that it makes perfect sense to wear hiking boots, my other pair of thick jeans, and a heavy pullover sweater. I find myself hoping that I at least look halfway decent; not that I should be worried about how I look, other than needing to come across as professional.

"Headed out to the park? It looks like a beautiful day for a hike," Mary says as I clomp downstairs from my room.

"Yeah. I'm even getting a special tour," I tell her. I'd mentioned I was going to be in town to work on an article for *New World*, but I hadn't given away any details about what I was actually investigating, just that the piece is about national parks in general.

"Oh really? Well a cute young thing like you is bound to get some special treatment," Mary says, pouring herself another cup of coffee. "Want me to fix you up some of this in a thermos? It'll help to keep you warm out there."

"I'd love some. Thanks," I say, smiling at her.

I check over everything in my bag as she's hustling about the kitchen to get my thermos ready: I've got my recorder, a spare microphone, a notepad with some preliminary questions written out, a heavy-duty flashlight, a full bottle of water, my phone, maps and guides of the park--everything I need for the day's trek and for the interview I lined up with Knox.

I wonder absently about the guys who tried to attack me, and what's become of them, but I know I'm not going to include that detail in the article unless I absolutely have to--that's not the kind of incident I want to have my name next to, if only because it makes me look like a total idiot for putting myself in that predicament in the first place.

In no time flat, I'm pulling through the gate at Acadia. I spot Knox waiting for me, and I have to admit: in full daylight--even without his uniform--he looks super hot. He's in a pair of relaxed jeans that fit snug in all the right places, along with a shirt that looks a little light for the weather, a leather jacket, and rugged hiking boots.

I find an empty parking spot--there are a lot fewer of them now, since it's daylight--and pull into it, checking my hair and making sure I collected everything I'd need. I climb out of my car and by the time I've got it locked up and my bag slung over my shoulder, Knox is only a couple of yards away. I see him looking me over and realize that I'm not the only one who likes what they see.

"Good day for a hike," he says, giving me a smile. For a second, something vaguely primal flashes in his eyes, and I have to wonder if I imagined it somehow.

"You do know that I'm going to spend the entire time trying to pry information out of you, right?" It only seems fair to give him warning, but I give him a little smile to go with it. I'm not usually coy or all that flirty with people I'm interviewing, but there's something about Knox that makes me blush and flutter my eyelashes.

Up close, he's more muscular than I realized the night before; I can almost make out his pecs against the fabric of his shirt. He's definitely more ripped than I would imagine a park ranger to be, and I can't help, just for a second, imagining what he would look like naked.

Shit! You stop that right now, Hannah Grant. I take a quick breath to try and stifle the heat that seems to be coursing through my veins, heading just south of my hips. *What is* wrong *with me?*

"I expected as much," Knox says, keeping that little grin on his face. I notice something secretive in his eyes, and begin to wonder if maybe I'm onto something; perhaps some of the bizarre claims I've read about the NPS aren't so outlandish after all. I can't think of what else he could feel the need to hide, but I'll play along for now.

"Well, shall we get started?" I open the thermos and take a swig of coffee. "I've got all day, but the sooner we start..."

"The sooner we'll have it done and over with," Knox finishes for me. "Let me show you my favorite trail."

We start off in that direction and I fall into step with the ranger, running the questions through my head and trying to figure out where to begin.

"So, I'm assuming that as the manager of the park, you're pretty well-versed in its history," I say. "Oh! I almost forgot. Do you mind if I record this?"

"Not at all, go right ahead," Knox replies. I take the recorder out of my bag and rattle off my standard disclaimer, holding the machine a few inches from Knox's face for him to confirm his agreement to being recorded.

"So, as I was saying, I assume you're pretty knowledgeable about the park's history," I begin again.

"It comes with the territory," Knox says. "Is there something specific you want to know?"

"While I was doing my research, I came up sort of...confused, I guess, about some of the founders," I say. "Obviously, the main people involved were Christopher Ellsworth, his father Christopher B. Ellsworth, and Theodore Davis, but there were others too, right?"

"Of course," Knox nods. "What about them?"

"A lot of them don't seem to have much in the way of public records," I say. "I mean, there are notations that they contributed or lobbied to the cause, but when I tried to find some of their birth certificates, for example, I came up empty."

Knox shrugs. "It was nearly a century ago, so keep in mind, many of the records might be a little shoddy."

I frown at that, but I can't think of a way to press the point further. "So, Knox, you've probably heard the strange rumors about Acadia, and the National Park Service in general. What are your thoughts?" I hurry a bit to keep up with him as we head up a little incline. I have to admit it's beautiful out, even if it's a bit chilly.

"The conspiracy wackos?" Knox gives me a sardonic grin. "Don't tell me you're doing some hit piece about how the people who created the national parks were all warlocks and freemasons."

"No, no; I'm trying to do as straightforward a piece as possible," I say quickly. "But it does come up, you know."

"I know," Knox nods. "It's just always seemed so ridiculous to me--doesn't it seem that way to you?"

"Well, we know a lot of the founding fathers were masons, or members of other fraternities," I counter; I'm not even sure why I'm pressing the point at all, because a day ago, I found the whole idea ridiculous. "But obviously, the idea of building a bunch of parks to make it easier to sacrifice goats in private is a bit much to believe."

"Glad to hear you think so," Knox says, his voice rippling with amusement.

We come to a stopping point and I mention I need to sit down for a bit; I offer Knox some coffee and he waves me off. "I've actually got a picnic basket with some snacks hidden for us down the trail a bit," he tells me. "Did you bring water, too, or just coffee?"

"I have a water bottle, and it's full," I tell him, and he nods his approval.

"Do you do much hiking, Hannah?"

I shrug off the question. "Some, but my job doesn't leave me much time to."

"How did you end up in this line of work, anyway?"

"Kind of by accident," I explain. "I always liked asking questions, and I enjoyed writing back in school, so when it came time to pick a major, journalism sounded like the perfect path. By the time I graduated, I had honed my skills...and well, here I am." I take another sip of my still-warm coffee and look at Knox speculatively. "How about you? When did you decide to become a park ranger?"

"I've wanted to be one since I was a kid," Knox says. "I've always loved the outdoors; hunting, camping, fishing. I even took foraging classes when I was young. My parents liked living off the land, and when I turned twelve, we did a tour of the different national parks; that's when I decided."

I try to picture Knox as a twelve-year-old boy, foraging in the woods for mushrooms, berries or whatever, but it's impossible. He's far too masculine and fully-grown for me to imagine him any other way.

"Ready to move on?" he asks, gesturing toward the next leg of the trail.

4

KNOX

"What can you tell me about Theodore Davis?"

I had hoped that Hannah would give up the line of questioning about the park's early history after what I'd said before, but she's obviously intent on digging deep. Of course, I can't tell her much about Davis; only the official history.

"He was a major conservationist, and a wealthy guy," I say, turning a corner and glancing back to look at Hannah.

I've been trying to stay downwind of her the entire time we've been hiking. I nearly forgot just how good she smells, and how much her scent--lavender honey, and now, after some hiking, a deeper musk that drives my animal instincts into overdrive--makes me want nothing more than to carry her off into one of the more isolated areas and explore every inch of her body. *She's not even your kind. Get your head out of the clouds.*

"He was one of several people involved in the establishment of the park. Davis donated a bunch of his land and convinced some of his rich buddies to do so as well. He was one of the guys who was able to get the area protected by the feds. The government eventually agreed to preserve the space as a monument, but it didn't get its status as a national park until after the National Park Service was formed a few years later."

"Have you heard any anecdotes explaining what spurred his interest in conservation to begin with?"

I glance at her again; Hannah's keeping pace with me pretty well, even without the advantage of having the preternatural speed that comes with being a shifter.

"Lots of rich people back then made it their pet cause, and they still do today. It's a way to preserve beautiful landscapes, and add some credit to their names. You know?"

"I guess that makes sense, but why not...I don't know. Why not build hospitals, or something like that?"

I shrug. "Some of them did that, too," I tell her. "But a lot of them liked to be in the great outdoors in their downtime, and the best way to make sure they could enjoy it was to set up parks like this one."

Of course, the real reason behind why many of the conservationists were so devoted to the cause is a very different story. One that Hannah could never know.

Davis and a handful of the other founders--his comrades--were shifters.

Around the turn of the twentieth century, the industrial revolution began to encroach on our normal safe spaces, the same way it had been pushing out other wildlife. We needed areas where we could shift at will or during the full moon; to be ourselves and embrace our dual natures while being shielded from the public eye. So, while Davis and his associates were rallying for the designation of a preserved space for us here in Maine, other wealthy shifters with political prowess infiltrated the federal government and made their case for forging the National Park Service as a whole, which would establish preservation areas for shifters across the nation.

As for Hannah, hopefully, if I keep repeating the story that's on the official record, I can get her off this line of questioning altogether. I'm pledged--as every shifter is--to keeping our kind and its history secret. Because of my position as the administrator of Acadia, as well as the Alpha of my clan, I have the responsibility of making sure no outsiders know about the real purpose behind the national parks. Hannah is most definitely an outsider, no matter how much the ursine part of my brain keeps insisting that she should belong to me.

"I guess maybe the fact that it was mostly a bunch of super-wealthy people is why some folks are so keen on the idea that they were free masons, or Elks, or whatever," Hannah says.

"People are always going to say weird things like that about rich people," I agree. *Thank god. That's an answer she can deal with.*

I'm about to change the subject when I hear the voice of one of my clan-mates, Jack, in my mind.

No one's been able to track down the four of them. We're combing the woods, but they've done something to cover their scent trail.

I almost groan out loud at the news; after I saw Hannah safely out of the park last night, I'd sent the word out to track down and capture the bears who'd tried to attack her. Since they were outsiders, no one could track them by their mental signature--they weren't attuned to the rest of us--and if they were somehow managing to cover their scent-trails, that made it even harder.

"Something wrong?" I look around and see that I've slowed down to a near-stop, and Hannah is looking up at me, concerned.

"I just remembered something," I say, shaking my head. With her so close, I can't avoid breathing in her scent, and it drives any worry about the bastards completely from my mind, replacing it with the bone-deep need to touch her. I make myself step back, away from her, and fill my lungs with some of the crisp air of the surrounding forest. "Let's keep going; the basket of food I put together for us is just ahead."

I can feel the heat flowing through my body, and just from being around Hannah, and breathing in her scent, I can already feel myself getting hard. This is disastrous. I need to get away from her as soon as I can; not just because she's distracting as hell, but because I need to find a way to deal with the bears that almost attacked her.

I send a signal to the members of my clan, telling them they need to comb back through the woods, and if they have to, raid the camp the interlopers set up for themselves amongst the cabins and find whatever they need to get a good scent-mark to go by.

We get to the spot where I put the basket off to the side and I lead Hannah out to a clearing; it's one of those places that the hikers and tourists almost never get to, because it's off the trail and a little under cover, and it's one of my favorite places in the park to visit when I'm by myself. I can't say for sure why I've brought Hannah here specifically, except that it's quiet and well-lit during the day.

"So," she says, once she's settled on the blanket over the grass, "what's the craziest rumor you've ever heard about the park?"

I laugh while I'm taking out the sandwiches, salad and fruit. "There was one floating around for a while that the government uses national parks to grow super-potent weed to get kids hooked on it," I tell her. "That one occasionally gets the alt-right prayer groups out here looking for hidden marijuana to report."

"And probably some potheads looking to score some premium product, too," Hannah adds.

"Yeah, that too," I chuckle. I start in on some of the salad I made, and Hannah takes a swig of water before taking a bite of her sandwich.

"I wouldn't think a big tough guy like you would be interested in having a picnic in the woods," she says, raising an eyebrow.

"Hey--I love being in the woods, and I love to eat. What's not to like?" I ask, shaking my head.

Hannah laughs. "Well, what's keeping Yogi Bear and Boo-Boo from coming to steal your picnic basket, Ranger?" she asks with a flirty grin.

I chuckle at that. "Bears aren't usually interested in well-hidden picnic coolers," I tell her. "Generally, if they're going to bother to raid something, it'll be out in the open, like if someone leaves the remains of a campfire feast out."

"Good to know," Hannah says. For a few minutes we eat in silence, but I can see the gears turning in her mind, the way she's looking off into middle-distance, thinking about what she's going to ask me next.

The clan keeps checking in occasionally, but I'm able to keep that in the back of my mind, like I always do. Now that I have a little time to sit here and relax, I can't help but scan my eyes over Hannah's curves. I'd checked her out the night before, of course, but the sunlight does something special to her light brown hair and makes her hazel eyes sparkle. I keep finding myself glancing at the way her tits strain at the fabric of her sweater, or thinking--almost against my will--about how she must taste, what it would be like to feel her thighs close against my head as I devour her.

The grapes I'm eating don't taste half as sweet as I'm sure she would, and as I let my mind wander a bit more, I can feel my dick getting hard--not enough to be embarrassing, but enough to make my pants feel uncomfortably tight; enough to make me sweat a bit.

"So," I say, plucking another cluster of grapes out of a plastic container, "what else do you want to know about the park?"

"I'm really just trying to get to the bottom of what's behind its creation," Hannah says with a shrug. "Like any journalist, if I see something vague that doesn't quite add up, it's like some switch in my brain flips; I have to know what the answers are."

I smile at that, but I can only hope that Hannah isn't as good at her job as her questions lead me to believe.

"There's nothing sketchy going on," I say matter-of-factly. "Davis was a great man, and most of the conservationists--including Rockefeller--were pretty decent, beyond the whole 'super-capitalist' thing they had going on."

Hannah snorts. "But those people seem to have always had shadowy personal lives," she points out. "I mean, just take the Kennedys, for example. There was that Kennedy sister whose dad sent her to get a lobotomy because she was, I guess, mildly mentally ill and disobedient, and she ended up pretty much becoming a zombie. And no one talks about it when they're talking about JFK."

"So, what's your pet theory? What skeletons do you think are lurking in the closets of the people who wanted--shockingly--to save some of this beautiful land from being turned into factories and strip malls?"

Hannah shrugs. "I have no idea," she admits. "Not *yet,* anyway."

"Well, I wish you luck in getting to the bottom of it," I say. "I can't help you tease out these fringe theories; I only know the official story."

"Of course, you do," Hannah says. She grabs a ripe plum out of the cooler and takes a bite. Watching her, seeing the juice dribble down her chin onto the front of her shirt; noticing the look of pure pleasure on her face at the flavor turns me on beyond belief.

I want nothing more than to pin Hannah down on the blanket and taste the plum on her lips, tear her clothes off and make her understand that she belongs to me.

Down, boy! Fuck! I push my primal instinct to the back of my mind and try to get back the control I've prided myself on.

"I'll be happy to show you around a little more," I tell her. "There are some great bird-watching spots around the park, and maybe we'll be lucky enough to get a look at some of the other wildlife from a safe distance."

"I'd like that a lot," Hannah says, nodding her approval.

Before I can suggest that we pack up the remains of our little feast and move on, I hear the unmistakable sound of bears approaching, growling, telling me once again, the politics of my life as a bear are about to collide with my professional life.

5

HANNAH

I SEE KNOX GO TENSE, AND MY HEART STARTS BEATING FASTER. "WHAT'S wrong?" He's been a little on edge most of the day, but it's obvious to me that he's alert to something I haven't noticed.

"Bears," he says, hardly above a whisper.

"*Bears?*" I look around; I thought I'd heard something a moment before, but I didn't think anything of it.

"Bears, and they're close," Knox murmurs.

My heart isn't just beating faster in my chest--it's pounding, my blood is rushing in my ears, and I have no idea what to do with myself.

"What do we do?" Knox rises to his feet in one quick movement; it's almost too fast for me to see, in fact. One moment, he's lounging on the blanket next to me, and in the next, he's heading towards the tree line.

"Stay here," he whispers. "I'll take care of this." I watch him move through the grass in near-silence, and while part of me is pretty sure that of the two of us, he must be the one to know what to do--but another part of me is imagining what would happen next if he gets himself killed by a bunch of bears.

Knox disappears into the woods, and I'm stuck sitting on the blanket with the remainder of the food he brought, wondering what the hell to do if his plan falls apart. I hear movement in the woods and I shiver, thinking of Knox going up against however many bears there are out there.

Aren't bears solitary? They don't wander around in groups, other than, obviously, mother bears with their offspring, right? I couldn't remember ever hearing anything about bears working as a group towards some common goal, but apparently, they did.

After a while, my curiosity got the best of me, and I couldn't resist rising and making my way toward the tree line. I must be out of my mind; it's crazy to think of walking into the woods when there are bears within a short distance of me, but I can't stand not knowing what's going on.

I try to move as quietly as possible through the grass and it occurs to me how strange it was that Knox was able to get into the woods without making a single noise; but then, I remind myself, he's a park ranger; he's used to doing stuff like that.

I slip past the trees and it feels like every inch of my skin is crawling with anticipation. As I step in the direction Knox went in, I start hearing some of what's going on: growls, groans, and the unmistakable sound of foliage being trampled and crunched under enormous feet. I can't hear any sign of Knox, and a terrifying thought occurs to me.

Oh god, what if they got him? What if he's dead?

And then it occurs to me to wonder what the hell I think I'm going to accomplish by going after him, when I don't have any training in dealing with bears *at all.*

I see a blur of dark fur and crouch down, hoping I'm downwind of the huge beasts. I crawl forward, enough to be able to see what's happening, and I'm completely confused: three bears thunder off in the opposite direction of the clearing, muzzles coated in foamy saliva, while two more continue to wrestle. I can't see Knox anywhere, and I lift myself up a bit--still trying to remain hidden--to look for him. Where the hell could he have gone? I thought he was supposed to be taking care of the situation so the bears wouldn't come after us--or more accurately, *me*?

The two bears still fighting are going at it harder than I would have imagined possible, tumbling and growling and even roaring every few moments, and I can't help but just sit there, fascinated and afraid, watching them.

I have no idea what to do. At first, the two bears look almost identical, but as I stare at the fight going on between them, I notice slight differences: one is definitely bigger than the other, even if it's hard to tell from all the movement. One of them has patches of bare skin showing through the fur--maybe from some kind of infection, or mange? I'm not sure. But I definitely feel like the bigger bear is somehow familiar, and somehow comforting. It keeps putting itself between the other bear and the path to where Knox and I had been having our picnic before.

The smaller bear manages to slip past the bigger one, and then looks straight at me. I want to believe that it can't see me, but it's hard to keep that belief up when it licks its chops and starts heading in my direction. Panic washes over me, and before I even know what I'm doing, I get to my feet. My legs prickle with pins and needles from the circulation rushing through them again, and I turn around and begin to run, crashing through the woods.

As I'm heading back in the direction I've come, I spot something: Knox's jacket, on the ground, half-tucked behind a log. That only makes me feel more panicked, reminding me that the one security I have against the bears fighting in the woods is nowhere to be seen. I run past the blanket in the clearing, not even bothering to grab my purse: all I care about is getting away before the bear can catch me.

It isn't until I'm a good half mile down the trail that I realize I don't even know where I am, or where I'm headed. I'm totally lost, and as that realization dawns on me, a sharp, pointed catch lights up along my ribs, and I have to stop running. I slow down and look behind me; the bear either got distracted by the picnic or the other bear caught up to it--whatever the case, it isn't chasing me.

I stop, panting and gasping for breath, and bend forward until my hands are on my knees. My head spins and I feel myself wavering, my knees going rubbery from so much running all at once along with the fear of being chased by at least one bear. I sink down onto my knees and wince at the impact on my hands as I try to catch my breath and--at the same time--figure out what I should do.

"Hannah! Hannah, are you okay?" I scramble up onto my feet just in time to see Knox jogging towards me; his jacket is gone, and there are some scratches across his face and his hands, but otherwise, he looks just fine.

"Where the hell did you go?" I dust my hands off on my jeans and look Knox up and down quickly. It definitely looks like something happened to him, but I can't wrap my head around the fact that he somehow disappeared, and then reappeared, not as harmed as I would have thought for a guy who had a run-in with four bears.

"I lured a few of the bears away, and then the remaining ones were fighting it out," Knox tells me.

"One of them chased after me," I say.

Knox nods. "I had doubled back by then. When I saw it going in your direction, I headed it off and sent it back into the woods, away from the trail," he says.

I look at him for a long moment. Other than his jacket, I'd seen no sign of Knox while I was running from the bear. *He probably took it off and tossed it aside when he started fighting with the bears,* I tell myself, but the whole situation seems so endlessly bizarre.

"Is it safe to go back to the picnic? I left my bag back there," I say.

Knox nods. "I got rid of all of them; they won't be bothering us anymore," he tells me as I look him over. He's obviously been scratched up, but it looks more like the work of being whipped in the face by branches and vines rather than claws. Of course, there's no way for me to know what really happened between the time he left the blanket and when he reappeared on the trail, coming to me; something about the whole situation just doesn't add up.

"I guess I have to thank you again," I say as I start back in what I hope is the right direction.

Knox falls into step next to me. "Oh?"

I grin at him. I don't want him to think I doubt his story, but in the back of my mind, I'm trying to piece together a scenario that would both explain what I saw and validate his story.

"Yeah, you've saved me twice," I point out.

"Just doing my job," Knox says. He moves a little closer to me, and I catch a whiff of some kind of deep, earthy musk clinging to him; it doesn't smell bad exactly, but very--*very*--primal. It must be something from the bears, I decide, putting it out of my mind. But even as we finally get back to the blanket, I find the smell clinging to Knox is actually kind of appealing in a strange way.

"Wow, that must get the adrenaline pumping," I say absently. "Chasing off bears, I mean."

"It definitely makes me feel manlier than--say--having a picnic," Knox admits.

I have to chuckle at that. I glance over at him as I'm gathering up my things from the blanket, and I can't help but notice there's a definite bulge at the front of his jeans. The sight of it makes the blood rush to my face and I look away quickly. Either Knox is turned on by me, or he's turned on by fighting bears; I'm not sure which one is more concerning.

"So...I guess that effectively derailed our interview," I say, reaching into my bag and turning off the recorder.

"We can start back up if you want," Knox suggests.

I shake my head. "Nah...although, if you're free later in the week, I might circle back and get some more quotes from you," I say. Suddenly, everything catches up with me, and I feel like I can't get up from the blanket and move another step. My legs feel like they're weighed down with lead, and my heart's only just started to slow down in my chest. "I think I could happily take a nap right here," I tell Knox wryly.

"Not used to running for your life, I take it," he says with a little grin.

"Not really, no," I admit. I lay back on the blanket while he finishes clearing up the remainder of the food, putting it in the cooler. I take a swig of my water and watch him. *God, he's hot.*

"If you want, I can give you a leg rub," Knox suggests. "Might help."

I raise an eyebrow, but I can't think of an actual reason to say no. "Okay," I say, after thinking it through for a moment.

What could possibly go wrong?

6

KNOX

I couldn't resist offering to give Hannah a leg massage. It popped into my mind and the words instinctively rolled off my tongue. I had to touch her.

Do you have the trail for those assholes?

I project the thought out to the rest of my clan, who are scattered around the park. As soon as I'd realized they were in the woods near where Hannah and I sat, I'd sent out a call to let my clan know. Even though three of the four bears had fled, I was fairly certain they'd be tracked down this time. The last bear, Harris, the one I'd been fighting when Hannah had come upon us, was unconscious several yards away, about to be secured by my clan. I'd drawn a considerable amount of blood from each of the outsiders, which is much harder to hide than other scent-marks.

Don't worry, Boss, we're closing in on them, Cassidy projects to me.

I turn my attention back to Hannah. "Why don't I start at your ankles," I suggest.

I can't back down from the offer now--not when she's accepted it.

Hannah looks up at me for a moment, "Really, you don't have to--"

"I insist."

She blushes, but I settle myself at her feet, kneeling there. I pick up one of Hannah's ankles and begin kneading it slowly, working from the

Achilles tendon up toward her calf. Hannah moans, and the sound of her--mingled with her irresistible scent--is almost more than I can stand. I try to take shallow breaths, mostly through my mouth, but I can still feel the tension in her body as I switch to her other ankle and then start moving up to massage her calf.

Even through her jeans, I can feel the strength in her legs; the heat of her body. After changing into my animal form to protect her--and get rid of the punks that have no business in this territory--my bear consciousness is still partly in command of me, and hard to push back. The feeling of her body, the smell of her, is driving me crazy.

She should be mine. Except she's not a bear--she's not *any* kind of shifter. How could I want her? How could she smell like something that belongs to me? Is it possible that a human...could be my *mate*?

She moans again when I get up to just above her knee, and I look up at her face. "You're enjoying yourself," I murmur, smiling a bit at her. Hannah's cheeks flush; she looks away and then quickly back at me, and I can see the rosiness spread across the little slice of her chest that's visible at the neck of her sweater. Breathing in deeply, I can actually *smell* her arousal, rolling off her in waves which makes it impossible to focus on anything but my ever-growing desire for her.

"Maybe we should stop," Hannah says, her voice cracking. "I mean, I don't want to be inappropriate. I don't want there to be any questions about whether my article is objective or not."

I chuckle. "Can't have that, can we?"

I lean in a little closer to her. I can't help it, it's like her body itself is drawing me in, and I can feel her pulse quickening; I can smell the way her arousal is deepening as my thumbs work at the muscles of her thighs, kneading and rolling.

"No one would ever have to know," I say. No one in my clan needs to find out that I want to devour this human female whole; that I want to gorge myself on the honey I can smell between her thighs and feel her body wrapped around me.

"Someone could see us," Hannah whispers.

I laugh again. "Other than the wildlife, not many people are going to head this far away from the trail," I point out. "If you can tell me that you don't *want* me to fuck your brains out right here and now, I'll stop, and I'll even apologize for coming onto you."

I hold her gaze. We both know she can't honestly say she doesn't want it.

"I do," she admits. "I just don't think I should get involved with someone who's a source for my article."

I lean in and brush my lips against hers, letting my fingers stop exploring her thighs and instead move up to cup the full tits I've wanted to get my hands on all day. She murmurs something against my mouth, but it doesn't sound like a protest at all; more like a moan of pleasure.

I deepen the kiss and brush my thumbs against her hardening nipples, straining at the fabric of her bra under her sweater. There's no question she's turned on, and I'm so hard that I ache, my cock throbbing in my jeans.

Hannah presses up against me and the feeling of her body against mine is so perfect--the feral consciousness that controls half my mind roars with pleasure, and all I want is to rip her clothes off and unleash my wild urges without restraint. But the human part of my mind comes to the forefront just in time to remind me Hannah isn't ready for that--she might never be.

I pin Hannah on the blanket, barely holding myself over her, and probe her mouth with my tongue; I can taste the fruit she ate last, and the lingering sweetness of her own natural flavor, spurring me to taste her elsewhere, waking the hunger that gnaws at my bones. I drop down to her throat, nuzzling her there, inhaling the sweet-musky scent of her pheromones.

"If you want me to stop, say the word and I will, immediately," I tell her as I lick the spot just under her jaw where I can feel her pulse fluttering.

"Don't...stop," she says breathlessly, and no two words have ever been better in the history of language. I start pawing at her clothes, trying to find the hem of her sweater. The only thing in the entire world I want right now is to see her fully naked--and then, after that, I want to eat her until she gushes in my mouth.

Hannah manages to pull my shirt over my head and her hands dance over my back, pausing when she finds the scratches and scrapes from my fight with the other bears. They've already almost healed completely, but hopefully, she won't notice.

I somehow get her sweater off, and then her bra, freeing her gorgeous tits from their prison, and I take a second to just admire them. "God, Hannah," I say, shaking my head at how fucking hot she is, laid on her back, her chest flushed, the pale skin of her breasts ending in two pale pink areolas with nipples as hard as pebbles.

I dip down and grab both of them, bringing first one and then the other up to my mouth. Hannah's skin tastes as good as her lips, with a little salt mingled in from her sweat and the faintest leftover traces of her fear from when she'd been running away from one of the bears earlier. I suck each of her nipples and swirl my tongue around the sensitive little nubs, and the sound of Hannah moaning out, her breath catching in her throat as her body heats up under me, is like a drug. I want to make this woman come harder than she's ever come before in her life.

I spend a little time on her tits and then work my way down along her abdomen, reaching for the fly of her jeans. I can't possibly wait another second; I can't hold myself back. I get her jeans and panties down over her hips and she squirms beneath me, kicking them the rest of the way down her legs.

With her finally naked, I can hold back enough to appreciate the view in front of me: Hannah's tits rise and fall, shaking a bit from how hard and fast her breaths are coming, and as my gaze wanders down over her body, I notice she's got a little tattoo of a heart on the inside curve of her hip. But that's less important than the sight of her pussy, her light brown hair trimmed down to a little patch, her folds wet with her fluids. The scent of her arousal makes my mouth water, and all I can think about is devouring every last bit of her.

I spread her legs wide and dive between them, barely giving Hannah a chance to realize what's happening before I bury my face against her soaking wet folds. I lap up every last bit of her fluids, tasting every inch of her; Hannah's hips buck against me, but my arms have her pinned right where I want her. She tastes every bit as good as I could have imagined, her sweet flavor coating my tongue, dripping down my chin as she gets more and more turned on.

I slow down to take my time with her, teasing her, bringing the tip of my tongue up to the firm little bead of nerves and then back down to her inner folds. I suck as much of her into my mouth as I can, like eating an overripe peach, swallowing and worshipping her, probing her, devouring her while she moans, cries out and writhes underneath me.

I keep her right on the razor's edge, reading her body, bringing her right up to the moment before she could come, and then back off just enough to keep her from reaching her peak. Hannah gets hotter and hotter, her hands grabbing at my head and shoulders, her fingernails digging into my skin, her thighs tightening around me the second, then the third time I bring her to the edge.

All the while, I can feel myself getting more and more turned on, my dick hard as a rock, hot as molten metal, trapped in my pants. I can't wait to feel her wrapped around me; I can tell she's tight, and she's so hot and wet that even before she comes, my face is soaked.

I finally give her what I know she needs, sucking her clit between my lips, swirling my tongue around it as Hannah gasps, shakes and almost screams with pleasure as she comes. Her fluids gush against my chin and I suck as much of her into my mouth as I can, alternating between keeping enough pressure on her clit to keep her climax going and swallowing down her fluids, lapping them up eagerly.

I feel her climax starting to ebb and I gradually slow down, pulling back bit by bit. By the time I'm hovering inches away from Hannah's pussy, she's panting and gasping, trembling all over.

"That...was amazing," Hannah says, opening her eyes and tilting her head just enough to look down at me between her legs. I laugh, planting a wet kiss on her tattoo before making my way up her body to kiss her lips.

"That can't have been the first time someone's gone down on you," I say, rubbing myself against her leg. If I don't get inside of her soon, the animal side of my consciousness is fairly sure I'll die.

"No, but it was definitely the first time someone did it that...enthusiastically," Hannah says. I laugh again, kissing along the column of her throat and bringing my hands up to her tits to tease her nipples.

"You taste good enough that I could eat you all night," I tell her.

"That could get in the way of getting anything else done, like sleeping," Hannah points out playfully. "And from the hard-on I feel in your pants, you're about to pop; eating me all night wouldn't help you in that department."

"You're right about that, I suppose." I sigh, and then moan as Hannah reaches down to rub me through my pants. The animal part of my brain wants me to roll Hannah over and take her, filling her up hard and fast.

I'm teasing Hannah's nipples all the while, and I can see and feel her starting to get turned on all over again. *Imagine what it would be like if you* could *mate her. Imagine making her yours and having her waiting for you every night.*

Hannah gasps as I twist one of her nipples a little harder than I intend to, but the half-moan at the back of her throat tells me she likes it, nonetheless. "You seem pretty eager," I tell her.

"Your fault," she says, grinning up at me, "for getting me all hot like this."

Somehow, she's managed to get my fly open without me noticing, and when her hand begins to stroke my cock, I reach the point of no return. I *need* to feel her.

"So, you're really okay with this?" I ask, as soon as I can actually talk.

"I'm definitely okay with it," Hannah says. I lick my lips, still able to taste her, and then pull back, giving into the instincts taking control of my mind.

I turn Hannah over onto her stomach and pull her up by the hips, and she scrambles to get into the position I clearly want her in, holding herself up on her elbows with her ass in the air. The view from behind is every bit as amazing as it is from the front, and I push my jeans down over my hips, my boxers going with them, taking in the sight of Hannah's delicious curves.

I guide the tip of my cock against her and hold onto her hip with one hand, keeping her right where I want her. I thrust into her from behind all at once, too turned on to take my time; Hannah moans out and her body squeezes me, flexing and then relaxing around my aching cock. It feels so goddamn good, I almost lose it right then and there. I have to stay still for a few seconds, breathing to push down the instinct to come right away. After a few moments, I've got control of myself again and start moving inside of her, pulling almost all the way out and thrusting back in, finding my rhythm.

Hannah feels so good--hot, wet and tight around my cock--and from the sounds leaving her throat, she feels the same way about me. I reach around the curve of her hip and find her clit, and begin to stroke it in time to my thrusts.

"Fuck, Hannah!" I lean over her, moving faster as the feeling of her body turns me on more and more, pounding into her from behind. She moans and cries out, pushing her hips back to take me deeper and deeper, falling into my rhythm, her body flexing around me in tight little spasms.

I manage to hold back long enough to bring her to another climax, and then I give up control again, pounding her hard and fast as the tension deep down in my balls hits a fever pitch right before it unravels. It feels so good--so right--to come buried deep inside her, and I let out an involuntary roar, the animal part of me laying claim to the woman under me, as wave after wave of pleasure temporarily blots out everything else that was ever on my mind.

We collapse together on the blanket and I roll over to my side, wrapping my arm around her tightly, pulling her close to my chest. I feel my heart pounding against her back as I nuzzle in her ear and whisper, "I could certainly get used to this."

I really could; I just have to be careful. I have a lot to protect and a lot at stake.

7

HANNAH

THERE WAS SOMETHING ABOUT THE COMBINATION OF RUNNING FOR MY LIFE, the way Knox's massage felt, and something I can't quite put my finger on that just threw my inhibitions--and perhaps, better judgement--completely out the window. I can't deny the tenderness between my legs is pretty damn satisfying, but I might have jeopardized my own article by getting too close to a source. It's totally not like me; I've never done anything like this before in my entire life.

Knox just walked me to my car, and I'm getting my gear secured in the passenger seat, ready to go back to Mary's place and start transcribing the interview. *He's hot, and that was definitely the best sex I've ever had--but was it worth fucking up my career?*

"Hey, you!"

I jump as I hear someone tapping on my window, and at first, I feel defensive; I'm expecting the woman standing there to say she saw me and Knox having sex. Her jet-black hair is pulled back into a messy ponytail, and she's dressed in a pair of shorts and a long-sleeved t-shirt that says "Question Authority." *Seems a little chilly for the weather to me. Must be a local,* I assume.

"Can I help you?" I cautiously begin to put my window down, stopping after a few inches.

"You were talking to the administrator, right? Just a little while ago?"

I nod, wondering what that has to do with anything, but at least it seems like this chick doesn't know what he and I were just up to at the other end of the park.

"Yeah, I was interviewing him about an article I'm working on about the history of Acadia and the National Park Service," I tell her. "I'm a journalist with *New World* magazine." The woman looks me up and down quickly and then comes to some kind of decision.

She peeks over her shoulder and then turns back to face me. "This place has secrets, you know," she tells me. "I live around here, and I know it's Knox Bernard's job to keep those secrets under wraps."

I raise an eyebrow at this. "What *kind* of secrets?"

I'm expecting her to say something about Masons, Sons of Columbus, or Pagans, or maybe Knox's favorite crazy theory that the government is growing super-potent pot at the state and national parks.

"Well, this is gonna sound crazy, but he's," she peeks over her shoulder again, then whispers, "some kind of *supernatural creature*."

Okay, well that's not what I would have thought. It sounds even more bizarre than anything else I've heard associated with Acadia, but the woman is telling me this with absolute seriousness.

"Every month, right around the full moon, Acadia issues special alerts to campers, advising them to avoid leaving the trails at night."

"I'm sorry, but that just sounds..." I shrug. I don't even know how to finish that sentence without being rude or potentially offensive.

"The full moon is in two days," the woman points out. "You can find out for yourself. Whatever it is they're doing here, that's the best time to see it with your own eyes."

I cross my arms over my chest and look at the woman for a moment, and ponder what she's telling me. I didn't really believe any of the conspiracy theories I'd read, but if it checks out that this woman is, in fact, a local, and even *she* thinks there's something going on here, it would be worth investigating, wouldn't it? And it's not like it would be outside of the scope of what I'm working on.

"I have to admit, this is one of the strangest things I've ever heard. I don't mean to come across as rude, but why should I believe you?" I look around; people are starting to leave the park as it's beginning to get dark and the air is getting colder. "How do I even know you're a local? You don't have the same accent as everyone else."

"Here, look at my ID," the woman says. "I moved up here about five years ago." She takes a wallet out of her shoulder bag, which is covered with all sorts of anti-establishment pins, and fumbles with it for a moment before handing me a Maine driver's license. This is definitely her picture; the license reads: *Jessica Durand, date of birth August 24, 1980. Female, 5'7",* and the address is a place in Bar Harbor, not far from Mary's.

"Okay, so you're a local," I concede. "How do I know you're not just putting me up to this because you have something against Mr. Bernard?"

Jessica leans in a bit toward me. "Look, believe it or don't believe it, but I want answers. Something's up, and Knox and his other freaky buddies at the park are trying to keep it quiet." She gives me a hard look. "You're with the press; you could blow this thing wide open."

Before I can ask her another question, Jessica backs off and calls out to someone who's apparently a friend of hers, leaving me all by myself to contemplate the news.

At first, I reject the idea altogether; after all, this sounds like it's just another rumor; there's probably nothing to it. Jessica--whoever she is--might just be someone who's got a crush on Knox; maybe she's just trying to make things difficult for him because she suspects that I'm into him or something.

I look over toward Jessica again, and it seems that whoever she's speaking to doesn't want to take what she's dishing out. The woman's holding her hands up, waving her off and shaking her head as she walks in my general direction. I see Jessica lumber off down the road, seemingly talking to herself.

I decide to hop out of my car and flag down the other woman. "Hey, do you know her?" I ask, pointing in Jessica's direction.

She stops, turning her head my way and rolls her eyes. "God, it's like you can't come here without being trapped in a verbal headlock by that freak."

I cross my arms and lean back against my car, furrowing my brow. "I just met her for the first time. She's got some...strange ideas about this place; that's for sure."

"She's got some strange ideas about *everything*," she replies. "If I were you, I'd steer clear of her. That is, unless hashing out nonsense with an eccentric weirdo for hours is your cup of tea."

"Good call," I say. "Thanks for the heads up."

She waves and continues down the path, heading deeper into the park, and I hop back in my car and turn the ignition, wondering what the hell just happened as the car sputters to life. But even as I drive out of the park, passing Jessica on the way, I feel that little tingle that comes along with a good story; that little itch to figure something out and get to the bottom of it.

Before Knox and I hooked up, I'd definitely noticed that he seemed to stonewall questions about the founding of the park and the people involved in it. That could be nothing--or it could be that Jessica was on to something after all, and that Knox is, in fact, trying to cover something up.

If there *is* something going on during the full moon, what would it hurt to find it out? I could come by the park at night, and see for myself.

8

KNOX

"We've got three of the four, that should be enough," Trent says to me as we head back to the park offices.

I shake my head; as long as Shawn is out there, everything that Acadia stands for is in danger of being exposed.

"If he gets caught doing something stupid, we're fucked," I point out.

"He's got to be smart enough to not want to draw attention to himself while he's alone," Trent counters.

I shrug. "He and the other three tried to attack *a fucking journalist* the other night," I insist. "None of those pricks seem to have any common sense or regard for Acadia whatsoever."

"They couldn't have known she was a journalist," Trent says.

"They didn't, but they shouldn't be going after *any* humans. Who knows how long they've been putting us all at risk, and for all we know, those dicks could have been shifting right in front of the park visitors." I shake my head and start taking my radio and other gear off as we step into the office together. "They're just sloppy. And lazy."

"Well, we've got the clan looking for him; he can't stay hidden forever," Trent says.

"Tomorrow's the full moon, the first night of it, anyway," I tell him. "I don't want anyone here to be under threat from that asshole."

"I'm less worried about our kind than any human bystanders that might be lurking," Trent says. "We can more or less take care of ourselves."

Because it's neutral territory, every month during the full moon, Acadia plays host to dozens of shifters from the surrounding area. We gather in an incredibly remote section of the park, spacious enough to allow our kind to run, hunt, forage and express our full primal nature--something that most shifters around the country would rarely get to experience otherwise.

My clan has always been known for being a gracious host. As the Alpha, it's my job to make sure that there's nothing tainting Acadia as neutral territory; I can't allow anyone to try and claim it as a domain for their own pack or clan. Shawn, along with his buddies Harris, Kevin, and Jamie, are proving to be a sizeable threat to maintaining our neutrality.

I'm confident that I can convince the shifters' conclave to agree that they have to be expelled from the grounds, at the very least. If they decide their transgressions are severe enough, I might even have clearance to execute them, but I'm not going to count on it. But in order to get their opinion, I need to have all four of these degenerates in custody. They won't hold a tribunal otherwise.

"We need to track Shawn down before tomorrow night," I say. "The members of the conclave will be here for the full moon anyway, and we can get them to decide on a verdict."

Trent nods his agreement with me. "The clan has the park cordoned the best they can. I'm sure we'll find him in time."

I send a mental signal to each of the members of my clan, taking note of their whereabouts, touching each of their minds in turn. It's trickier than just calling out to them, but it's something I've worked out over the years of being an Alpha; it's a skill that comes in handy at moments like this.

Trent's right: as I hone in on each of their minds, I can tell the clan is as close as it can be to having the whole park cordoned off. If Shawn tries to leave, then there's a good chance he'll run into someone, or at least pass close enough to be pursued. For the time being--while I'm on official duty--I can't personally do much more.

I sit down and Trent heads out to make his usual rounds. In the back of my mind, I can't help but think about the nosy reporter, Hannah Grant. With these outsiders treating Acadia like their own personal criminal hunting grounds, her arrival couldn't have possibly come at a worse time.

But right now, I'm not really thinking about how her presence complicates the situation with Shawn and his clan; I'm thinking about how good it felt to be inside of her, and how much I want to taste her again.

She's made herself scarce for the past couple of days since then, but she's been at the forefront of my mind ever since. I sit back in my desk chair and stare up at the ceiling. *She suspects you're covering something up, something you know but that isn't common knowledge--that much she made clear to you before the two of you hooked up.* That should be a red flag right there; I shouldn't try to pursue Hannah any further, unless I'm willing to risk exposing everything my kind has worked so hard to keep secret, but the bear within has been calling out for her ever since our little tryst in the park. I try to shake off the thought, but then remember that she'd promised to circle back to finish our interview, which she hasn't done yet.

"That's as good of an excuse as any to stop by wherever she's staying," I muse to myself. I should be able to pick up on her scent trail and figure out her location; then I can check on her, see if she's got some more questions for me, and hopefully put any ideas she's had regarding conspiracy theories to rest for good. *Maybe then, we could pick up where we left off the other day.*

I wait until my shift is over and change into some street clothes: a pair of jeans, a t-shirt and a thick flannel, along with what I consider to be my off-duty boots. I get onto my bike and gun the engine, checking to make sure it's in peak shape, and then start heading down the main road out of the park.

I don't know exactly where Hannah's staying, so as I pull off the grounds, I slow down, sampling the air as I head towards Bar Harbor.

After a few minutes, I finally catch a hint of that unmistakable scent and begin to follow its trail. There are several different spots in the park's proximity where I can tell she's been: first a gas station, then a gift shop; I pick it up again at a greasy spoon a little further east up Route 233, heading closer to Bar Harbor.

I finally manage to track the scent to a house in a residential neighborhood downtown and spot Hannah's car parked on the street. This is definitely where she's staying; her mark is stronger along the sidewalk and the grass leading from her car to the front door. I park my bike and walk up to the house.

Almost as soon as I knock, a middle-aged woman answers, looking me up and down with interest. "How can I help you?"

"I'm looking for Hannah Grant. She's staying here, right?"

The woman looks me up and down again--a little doubtfully--and then gives me a polite smile. "She's sitting on the porch out back," she says. "You can go around, or I can get you something to drink if you want to cut through the house."

"I'll go around, thanks," I say with a wave. The woman gives me the vibe that she's going to talk my ear off, given half a chance to, and I've got a lot on my mind. I don't want any distractions.

As I head around back and open the gate to the back yard, I spot Hannah sitting at a little patio table with her feet up on another chair, and a laptop in front of her along with a cup of coffee. She's got headphones on and she's typing away, and I have to admit that she looks every bit as good as she ever has: her hair's down, falling to her shoulders, and she's wearing a sweater dress that hugs her curves perfectly, along with a pair of leggings and some knee-high boots. She looks both adorable and hot all at the same time, and I feel like somehow, I haven't been remembering her right at all; the reality is so much better than my memories.

She looks up as I get a bit closer and jumps, almost dropping her laptop. "Whoa! Where did you come from?" She takes her headphones off, carefully sets her laptop down on the table and sits up in her seat, looking at me more intently.

"I remembered you'd wanted to get around to interviewing me again, and I figured now would be as good a time as any," I say.

"Oh! Right. I wrote that down, but I've been diving deeper down the rabbit hole, so to speak, and spaced out on following up with you," Hannah says. "Wait, how did you know I was here?"

I think fast; I couldn't exactly tell her I followed her scent. "Oh, I was just passing through town and I recognized your car on the street, so I decided to stop by and see if you had a little free time to finish things up."

She looks away from me for a second and starts playing with her hands, then smiles at me. *She's hiding something.* "Well, I'm free right now if you are," she says.

"Cool. If you want, I can take you to my favorite bar in town."

"Now that you mention it," Hannah says, shifting a bit in her seat, "I'm technically supposed to be on vacation. I'd love to."

"You are? Then why are you working on an article?" I sit down across from her, and Hannah takes a sip of her coffee.

"They made me take vacation time or I'd lose it," Hannah says. "And I thought that getting out of town for a few days to work on this in a leisurely fashion would be as good as an actual vacation."

I shake my head in disbelief, but admittedly, I'm almost as bad when it comes to vacations; when I take time off, I usually visit other parks, and it isn't as though I'm just visiting as a tourist.

"You need to learn to *actually* take some time off," I tell her. I find myself grinning almost before I realize it, and then I add, "maybe I can help you with that."

"I didn't think you were interested in seconds," Hannah says, and I get a little flash of pleasure at the sight of color lighting up her cheeks.

"Oh, I'm definitely interested; I just figured you wouldn't be in town all that long," I say.

"I was planning on being here a little over a week," Hannah says. "I figured, for the piece I wanted to write, that would be a long enough stay."

"So, there's another, what, five days before you go back?"

I'm torn between feeling relieved and disappointed. On one hand, it's a good thing. I can clear up any misconceptions she might have about the park and she'll finally be out of my hair. But on the other hand, the bear within keeps telling me that Hannah should belong to me and only me. I need her in my cabin, where I can claim her as my mate; where she can bear my cubs for years to come.

I shake the thought from my mind, focusing on the most dire task at hand: protecting the secrets of Acadia. "Alright, then, let's go to the bar and grab a drink, and you can pick my brain a bit more," I suggest.

Hannah nods and stands up, looking around her. "Give me a couple of minutes to put on my jacket, grab my purse and put my stuff away, and I'm game," she says.

"Do you want to ride with me?" I lift my helmet and raise an eyebrow. "I've got a spare helmet."

"Sounds like fun," Hannah says, and once again I see that high, hot color in her cheeks. It's obvious that she's still attracted to me, even if there's something else going on that she's trying to keep to herself.

Maybe after a drink or two, I can get it out of her.

9

HANNAH

Knox's favorite bar is somehow both exactly what I would have expected and nothing like I would have thought it would be.

I make mental notes for my article: it's obviously been around for a long time, evidenced by its ancient-looking exposed chestnut beams, not to mention, the dated furniture scattered around the place. The guy behind the bar is an elderly man, wearing an old-fashioned dress shirt and vest combination, and I almost want to ask if he pictures himself as being some character in an old-school Western.

There are a handful of booths along one wall, which is decorated with driftwood, fishing nets and old lanterns, and Knox steers me in that direction. As we sit, I notice the benches are upholstered with an old, but well-maintained fabric, and the table is made of heavy, solid mahogany.

I notice, too, that there's only one TV in the entire bar, off in the opposite corner, away from where we're sitting. There are maybe five patrons watching it, not looking particularly interested as they slowly nurse the beers in front of them.

"So, what else did you want to ask me?"

That's a good question, and I've been trying to figure out what I can do to cover for dropping the ball on that part of my investigation. The ride on the back of Knox's bike was thrilling--enough so that any practical thoughts that had been in my head even seconds before the engine got started just vanished.

"I've been doing some more research, talking to a few locals and some frequent visitors," I explain. "I'm still just trying to piece together whatever I can to explain what doesn't seem clear--in general--about the history of the park and some of the...*events* going on there right now."

"How far have you gotten?" Knox's voice sounds casual, but I pick up on a weird tension underneath.

"I've eliminated a lot of dead ends," I say cheerfully, giving him a wry smile. A waiter comes to the table and Knox orders an Imperial IPA; apparently, the brewery is local.

"And what would you like, ma'am?" I realize I haven't even given any real thought to what I'm going to drink.

"I guess...a Jack and Coke?" It seems like a safe enough drink, as long as I don't have more than maybe one or two. The waiter nods and leaves.

"So, you were saying you've run into a lot of dead ends," Knox says, once we're alone again.

"Yeah," I admit. "I still haven't been able to find the birth certificates for some of the founders, and haven't come up with anything to explain a few of the other gaps. It's actually kind of troubling."

I'm not about to tell him I'm planning on being in the park tomorrow night to spy on whatever freak show might possibly be going on there.

"And you've been interviewing some of the locals? Anything interesting come up there?"

I shrug off Knox's question. In reality, I've been talking to as many people as possible, trying to do everything I can to either confirm or deny what Jessica told me. But if Knox *is* involved in some kind of a cover-up, I can't tell him anything--not yet, anyway.

"There are a lot of people who really love the park, but they don't know much about its history," I say wryly.

The waiter brings us our drinks and I try to think of a way to get more information out of Knox without revealing the angle of my investigation. We raise our glasses to each other in a wordless toast and I rack my brain for how to phrase my next question.

"It must be really disappointing to have come all this way, only to meet so many dead ends," Knox says.

"It's not too unusual," I tell him. "You win some, you lose some."

"You don't strike me as the kind of woman who accepts losing without a fight," Knox says. "I was actually wondering if you were avoiding me because...well, you know."

"Because we got down and dirty in the woods?" I shake my head. "I mean, that was probably the least professional choice I've ever made, but the real reason is I've been trying to track down as many leads as possible."

"You sound more like a detective than a reporter," Knox suggests.

I laugh. "The two things aren't all that different."

I have to admit, I really like Knox. I feel so comfortable around him, even though my mind is spinning with the notion that he could be involved in some weird secret society.

"That must explain why there's so much crossover," Knox says.

I take another sip of my drink. "So, I've been thinking I might want to wander the park again a bit."

"Well, you'll be happy to hear that we've rounded up all but one of the guys who tried to attack you the other day," Knox tells me.

"Oh! I've been so busy that I totally forgot about it." It's a lie; I've thought about the incident at least once a day since it happened, but I've been working hard not to let it overshadow my investigation.

"The last one's still loose in the park, but the rangers will easily be able to track him down," Knox says.

"So, I'm guessing that you'd want me to be on my guard if I'm in the park on my own," I suggest.

"I'd be happy to chaperone you, if you want, or I can get one of the other rangers to accompany you."

"I don't think that'll be necessary," I say quickly. "It's not all that dangerous; I mean, he's probably trying to avoid anyone's attention, right?"

"True, but I would hate for you to run into him," Knox insists.

"I'll let you know," I say. "In the meantime, what can you tell me about some of the odd layout discrepancies in the park?" That, I hope, should keep his mind occupied for a while.

"Layout discrepancies?" Knox frowns in confusion and takes a sip of his beer.

"There are some spots on maps dated before the opening of the park that have never appeared on any official park maps. It's as if the locations have been intentionally omitted," I say. It's as close as I can come to admitting that I've actually found some information suggesting that something's amiss.

"Well, a lot of those old maps probably aren't all that accurate," Knox says with a shrug.

"These were created by surveyors who were contracted by the government," I point out. "I would hope they'd be accurate."

"If you want to come back to the park with me after this, I can show you some of the documentation we have in the office," Knox says. "I'd be happy to show you the most recent surveys we have on file."

"I'd really appreciate that," I say.

We change the subject for a while and I find out that Knox has worked his way up the hierarchy at Acadia the old-fashioned way, getting his degree and then following it up with conferences and certifications. I have to admit: I had no idea how much work it took to become a national park ranger.

Knox offers to pay for our drinks. He's had two beers and I've had two Jack and Cokes; not enough to get drunk, but enough that there's a bit of a buzz going on in my head, relaxing me a little more. I point out that I can just expense the charge once I get back home, but he insists and settles the bill.

Then I'm on the back of his bike again, and he's driving us to the park, where he has permanent quarters. The vibration of the motorcycle between my legs, along with the fuzziness and warmth of the alcohol in my system, has a predictable effect: instead of being scared that I'm going to fall off the iron horse, or that Knox is going to get hit, I can feel my nerves starting to tingle. I'm only too aware of the feeling of Knox's back pressed against my chest as we make our way out of Bar Harbor.

It's too easy for me to remember how good the sex was, even if having it was a total mistake. The vibration between my legs is almost right up against my crotch, and it's easy for me to see why girls are so into riding motorcycles with good-looking men. It's like having a relatively low-speed massager up against me; it's not enough to make me climax on its own, but definitely enough to get me hot all over and make me wish I could abandon professional scruples to suggest that he pull over and take me back into the woods and have me again. Especially paired with Knox's warm, muscular body and the musky scent of his cologne.

We park outside of his cabin, and as I get off the bike, I attempt to compose myself. *What the hell is wrong with me?* I've been attracted to plenty of guys before, but the intense way my body responds to Knox is unlike anything I've ever experienced.

"Something wrong?"

I shake my head and follow Knox's lead as he heads toward the park's office, not too far from his cabin. As we enter, he tells one of the other park employees that he's going to show me some of the surveys and elevation reports. The ranger shrugs and tells me he hopes I have a good afternoon, and then he's gone. And Knox and I are all alone.

Suddenly, I feel like this was a terrible idea, but in spite of that thought, I can't deny that there's still a damp warmth between my legs, and that I'm replaying--in my mind--how good it felt to have Knox deep inside of me. Over the past couple of days since we hooked up, I've had to get myself off with my fingers a few times, remembering our little tryst in vivid detail.

"Okay," Knox says, unlocking a cabinet. "I think I've got the latest ones here; these are official documents. You can even see the surveyors' notes about where they went and how they made their determinations."

"Do you think I could get copies of these? Or maybe take pictures?" Knox takes a thick folder out and sets it down on his spartan desk.

"Sure, if you'd like. I'll have to fill out a form for your request, but there's no reason why you can't include it in the documentation for your article," he says, sounding oh-so-helpful.

I sit down and start looking through the paperwork; it looks, right off the bat, like everything is above-board and meticulously documented.

After a few moments, I sit back, and see Knox watching me intently. "Any particular reason you're staring at me?" I feel the blood rush into my cheeks and I reach up to smooth my hair against my scalp nervously.

"I found the form you need, but I was waiting until you decided to take a break," Knox says. "And then I noticed how cute you look sitting at my desk."

In spite of the focus I've had on the paperwork in front of me, the humming, simmering arousal that I worked up on the motorcycle never quite went away. I sit back a bit from the desk and look Knox up and down. He's just as hot as ever in his street clothes, and I can't help but think how satisfying it would be to tear them right off him.

"Thanks," I say, blushing even harder. I don't know what to do with my hands, my mouth or any part of my body; I'm tingling all over, hot and cold flashes of sensation dancing through my nerves, and I've almost completely forgotten about the survey reports. "I guess I should go ahead and fill that paperwork out," I say, looking down at the desk.

Knox sets the sheet of paper down on the desk, but instead of stepping away from me, he lingers, and I think--though I can't be sure--I hear and feel him sniff the top of my head. *Did he really just do that?*

I begin filling out the paperwork and Knox leans over me, watching my hand move, and touches my shoulder. Just that little bit of contact is enough to make it even harder to focus, enough to turn me on even more.

Fuck it. You've already rung the bell; there's no reason not to ring it again. I look up at Knox, turning to face him. "Maybe you could show me that cabin they set up for you," I suggest.

Knox smiles slowly. "The office is closed," he points out. "I could lock that door, and no one would come in here. No one would know what's going on."

I feel a little jolt of heat at that suggestion, and I notice the wetness between my legs again, hotter than ever. The idea of having a little fun with the park administrator in his office is just too tempting.

"Go lock it, then," I suggest, my heart beating faster in my chest at the thought.

I watch as Knox crosses the room almost faster than I could imagine possible, and in near silence. He locks the door and then, just as quickly, he's back at the desk, lifting me out of his chair and tilting my chin up to kiss me on the lips.

I reach up and wrap my arms around his broad shoulders, pressing myself against his body; up close to him like this, kissing him back eagerly, it's even easier for me to remember how good our first time together was.

Knox's hands move over my body, touching, caressing and teasing me, and I moan against his lips, gripping him tighter as I get more and more turned on. He cups my breasts in his palms, giving them a careful squeeze, and I shudder, catching his bottom lip between my teeth and nibbling at it playfully.

Then, all at once, we're both pawing at each other's clothes; I fumble a bit with Knox's shirt before I can get it off, but I'm finally rewarded by the sight of his chest. I slowly slide my fingertips over its firm planes and valleys, downward to the fly of his jeans, and my mouth is positively watering, knowing what's inside.

Then Knox lifts me up onto the desk and ducks down, his lips capturing my right nipple. He sucks and licks me, moving from one breast to the other, worshipping me with his mouth; I temporarily forget about the erection I know is standing at attention for me, too wrapped up in the sensations coursing through me to think.

Knox works my breasts with his mouth for what seems like ages, sucking hard enough to make me gasp as his tongue swirls around the hardened nubs. His tongue feels strange; I noticed it the first time we hooked up, but I notice it even more now, how rough it feels against my skin, but it's thrilling all at the same time, sending little jolts of sensation coursing through my body.

Knox reaches down and hooks his fingers under the waistband of my panties, tugging them downward. I push my butt up off the desk to help him, and then, all at once, I'm naked. My hands wander until I find the fly of his pants, and once I manage to figure out where the button and zipper are, I'm somehow getting them open, reaching inside and finding--to my surprise--that he's wearing nothing at all underneath. His hot, rock-hard cock twitches in my hand as I stroke him, and when I get back up to the tip of his erection, I feel the slickness of his precum coating my fingers.

Knox breaks away from my breasts and looks down at me, flushed and panting slightly, a faint, almost-growling sound in his throat, and he looks like a starved animal as he begins to plant his face between my legs.

"As much as I love the idea of you going down on me for hours, I don't think that's necessarily a good idea right here," I say breathlessly.

Knox laughs. "I take your point," he says, kissing me quickly on the lips as I reach for his shaft again. His hand slips up between my legs and he starts stroking me, swirling his fingertips around my clit, falling into the same rhythm I'm using on him until I moan. "God, you're already so wet... and you smell so good..."

"Can we get to the main event?"

I'm so turned on it almost hurts, but at the same time, I don't entirely trust Knox's promise that no one would come barging into his office at any moment. Even though he locked the door, I feel like there's a good possibility that someone could come looking for him or hear us through the wall, but somehow, that makes the whole situation even hotter, even though it makes me worry.

"God, yes," he groans, shoving his pants down to the floor and pushing my hand away from his cock, guiding himself up against me as I squirm to get into the best position, perched on his desk. I love the way the tip of his cock feels against me, and my hips move almost as if they've got a mind of their own, trying to take him inside of me all at once.

Knox thrusts into me and I grab his hips, pulling him closer to take him in as deeply as I can. I reach up for Knox's shoulders, hooking my hands behind his neck, and we start moving together. It feels every bit as good as it did the first time; absolutely perfect, in fact. The heat and hardness of Knox's cock fills me completely and the pacing of his thrusts is exactly what I've been craving. It's almost magical, the way we fit together, and I love it more and more by the moment.

I kiss his lips, his neck, along his shoulders and down onto his chest, licking and nibbling at him playfully, and I hear that somewhat strange low growl again as I feel Knox's body tense up the closer he gets to his peak.

He reaches down and begins stroking and rubbing me as we move together, sending little crackling jolts of pleasure through my body. I cry out and try to muffle it against his shoulder, so wrapped up in the pleasure tingling through my nerves that I can't even think about where we are anymore.

Knox guides me down onto my back and begins slamming into me, hard and fast, looking down at me intently, and I'm helpless in the trap of how good it feels. He unwraps my legs from around his hips and grabs me by the ankles, lifting them onto his shoulders; the shift in position is almost more than I can take, feeling the thickness of him rubbing along my inner walls, pushing deeper than ever inside of me.

I twist my hips to meet his thrusts, trying to hold back, but Knox starts rubbing my clit as he pounds into me and I can't stop myself anymore. I bring my hand up to cover my mouth as the tension deep down between my hips gives away with a snap, and pleasure floods through me. Spasms of sensation ripple through my body and I give into it, writhing on the top of Knox's desk, not caring if I knock anything over or if someone hears me.

I'm so wrapped up in my own pleasure that I barely feel the twitching of Knox's cock inside of me or the way his body tenses. He reaches his climax in the middle of mine, and I'm only just starting to come down when I feel the hot gush of his seed deep inside me. I hear him let out a short, guttural roar as he pounds into me a with few more hard, fast thrusts, almost hitting my cervix, bringing my orgasm back with all new force. Even after Knox finishes, he keeps rubbing my pleasure center, milking my second climax for all it's worth, until I'm limp on his desk, panting and gasping for breath.

"That was even better than the first time," I say as soon as I'm able to talk again.

"It was," Knox agrees. I open my eyes; my head's almost tilted off the desk, and I can still feel him inside of me. I want more, but I know it's a bad idea.

"I should probably get back to Mary's," I say reluctantly.

"Why? I can give you a ride home later," Knox says. I feel him hardening inside of me once more and he starts moving slowly, rocking his hips against mine. "Besides, you're on vacation. You don't have a deadline."

I want to say no--I want to do the right thing, the professional thing--but I have to admit that the idea of round two is *more* than a little appealing...

10

KNOX

I WANT TO BELIEVE THAT I CAN JUST HAVE MY FUN WITH HANNAH AND THEN say goodbye to her when she has to return home, but the animal instinct dominating my brain demands that I convince her to stay--that I need to make her mine; make her understand she should be mine--now, more strongly than ever.

"Hey, you hungry?"

Hannah perks at that suggestion and I feel like a champ for coming up with a good, valid reason to keep her around me for a little while longer.

"I could eat," she says. "But don't I kind of owe it to you to take care of dinner? You made lunch for us the other day and paid for our drinks."

"If being square bothers you so much, why don't you just help me cook something back at my place?" I ask. For a second, it looks like Hannah is going to try and argue the point further, but she shrugs it off.

"I guess that'll work," she says, smiling wryly.

"We'll eat and then I'll take you back to your place," I suggest. *And then I'll convince you to stay the night.*

As we walk from the office over to my cabin, I try to remember whether it's clean enough to be seen when I feel Cassidy's mind reaching out to me. It's the worst timing I can imagine, but as the Alpha, it's something I have to deal with.

Knox! Someone let the other three out!

I get a vivid mental picture of the place where members of my clan have been holding Jamie, Harris and Kevin, the guys who had been working with Shawn, and it's empty. I bite back a groan; I have to assume it was either Shawn or someone else working with him, and that somehow, they made it past the two members of my clan who'd been watching over the assholes until we could have the conclave decide their fate.

I have to figure out what to do; I can't just take off and leave Hannah at my cabin without telling her what's going on, or at least giving her a valid excuse.

Call my cell; I'm with a human right now and I need to excuse myself without making her suspicious. Cassidy agrees to my request, and a moment later, my phone rings.

"I should get this," I tell Hannah. She nods and I tap 'accept' and bring the phone to my ear. "What's going on?"

"Are you with that journalist again?"

Cassidy knew about my fling with Hannah because Hannah's scent was still clinging to me when Cassidy and I quartered the woods after Shawn and his crew came after me.

"Yeah," I say, keeping my voice neutral.

"Fun time's over. Tell her, I dunno, that there was another sighting of those bears you dealt with the other day. It's the truth."

I have to admit she has a point. I acknowledge and end the call, and turn to Hannah.

"I need to step out for a bit," I say. "Those bears that almost crashed our picnic the other day got out of the observation area, so I need to head out and see what's going on right now."

"If you want," Hannah suggests, as I switch into my work boots, "I could do the cooking while you're out. That would even things out between us, anyway."

"Sounds good," I say with a grin. At least if she's making dinner, I can count on her being occupied enough not to try and snoop. I give her a quick kiss on impulse and then I'm out the door, headed for the scene of the problem.

I try not to think about Hannah, back in my cabin, as I'm walking towards the holding area where Jamie, Harris and Kevin escaped from.

The rest of the clan is operating according to an automatic system we put in place for situations like this; the best trackers in the group are already combing through the woods, following whatever scent trail the bears might have left behind, trying to locate them.

"What do we know?"

Trent's waiting for me at the site, and he's looking like his usual, irritable self. "We think that Shawn busted them out somehow," Trent says.

"How did he get past security? How did *they*, for that matter?"

That's the biggest issue: there should have been someone watching to make sure the guys we already had in custody didn't break out.

"Matilda and Harold were on duty, and they're nowhere to be found," Trent says. "We don't know if someone took them out, or if they were helping *with* the breakout, for whatever reason."

Matilda and Harold are a much older than me, ages 70 and 75, respectively, and they'd been living in the area much longer than I have. They've always been pretty rank-and-file; I've had no problems with them betraying my trust, but there's always the possibility that Shawn or one of the others found a way to tempt them.

"So, we have some people looking for Shawn and his crew, and others looking for Matilda and Harold?"

I cross my arms over my chest and sample the air with my nose. Even in my human form, my nose is keen, but it would be better if I shifted into the bear that makes up the other half of my identity.

"Yeah, I've been running the coordination from here until you arrived," Trent says, nodding.

I reach out to the rest of my clan, projecting my thoughts as loudly as possible. *Report back every ten minutes. If I have to, I'll call in some Feds, but I'd rather not get them involved.*

Nobody, least of all me, wants to get the FBI involved, but if it means we'll have better chance of capturing these assholes, that might be our best bet. I have to do whatever I can to keep things quiet, and the sheer risk that the four rogue bears bring about to all of us can't be ignored. We can't have them running loose tomorrow night; I've seen firsthand how reckless they are, and there's too great of a risk that they'll stir up a shitstorm with the other shifters that will be here for the full moon.

Even though I have complete confidence in my clan, being the

Alpha, I have to be at the forefront of the efforts, so I start to head out in search of the bastards.

Found Shawn! The mental voice of Alex suddenly cuts out as quickly as it popped into my brain, and I feel my adrenaline starting to rise. Obviously, Alex is going to have to fight Shawn to bring him in. With any luck, his fellow instigators will be close by, and we can have the whole situation wrapped up in a matter of an hour or so.

I feel Alex's mind again a few minutes later, and I can sense he's been hurt. He's definitely been in a fight, but I can sense his victorious surge as well, so hopefully, he'll be bringing Shawn in right away. *Got him down for the count. Cass is coming to help me bring him in. The son of a bitch knocked me around pretty good.*

The reports I'm receiving from the others aren't as promising, and after about an hour of searching--with Shawn unconscious, cooling his heels in the containment shed--I have to go back, or Hannah will suspect something's gone wrong and might come looking for me. There's no way I'll have her roaming around out here with those jackasses on the loose.

I mentally project a message to my clan, all twenty of them: *Everyone keep me posted; I have to run interference with a human. If anything changes, I'll be on the scene within five minutes.* Everyone agrees to that and I start to head back to my cabin.

It bugs the hell out of me to hear that no one knows what happened to Matilda and Harold. Are they on my side and injured badly enough that their minds can't respond? Or, for some reason, have they defected and that's why they can't be found anywhere?

I reach out to Trent just as I get to my cabin: *Have one of the younger ones check Matilda's and Harold's houses.* Trent tells me that he's on it, and I clear out the issue from my mind, keeping one little thread of my thoughts open for someone to get to me. Now isn't the time to have mental shields up.

I decide that I'm going to have dinner with Hannah and then immediately take her home. No matter how much I want to have her again tonight--in my own bed, at that--I have to get her back to her place. This goes beyond the fucking article at this point; she needs to be out of harm's way, and I need to be able to focus on the park and what my clan needs from me.

I have to make phone calls to the members of the conclave, asking them to get here early tomorrow so they can decide how to handle these idiots trying to muck up our neutral territory. I kick the mud off my shoes and make a quick mental list of who I'm going to need to call; the list isn't all that extensive, but it's going to be like pulling teeth to get them all to agree on a final verdict.

I open the door to my cabin and the scent of Hannah's cooking is enough to make my mouth instantly water. Quick sniffs tell me she's made rainbow trout--my favorite--with a lemon butter sauce, roasted broccoli and rice pilaf, and as I inhale again, I pick up on something sweet for dessert; for just a second, the animal and human parts of my consciousness both agree that I *need* to convince her to stick around. Anyone who can whip up a meal that smells this good in a short time frame, who's also as good in bed as Hannah is, needs to be mine--and it's about damn time that she knows it. I take a deep breath and push that thought completely out of my mind for the time being; I need to focus.

11

HANNAH

THE WHOLE TIME WE'RE EATING, KNOX SEEMS DISTRACTED, BUT EVERY TIME I mention it, he just says he's thinking ahead to what he has to do the next day around the park.

"Because of that incident with the bears, there's some complicated paperwork I have to fill out."

"You were able to catch them and get them contained again?"

Knox shakes his head. "We got one of them; I've got trackers out after the others, so I decided to come back here and have a solid meal," he says, smiling at me in that charming way he has. "Besides, I wouldn't want all your hard work to go to waste."

"And then you're going to drop me off back at Mary's, right?"

I don't think that's actually what I want, though. There's a very strong part of me that's begging for Knox to invite me to stay, wrapped in his muscular arms all night, but the rational side of me knows I need to be working on my article. More importantly, I need to look over the maps and survey reports to figure out the right places to check out tomorrow night.

"If that's what you want, then I'm happy to take you home," Knox says, and based on the tone of his voice, it seems like that's exactly what he wants to do. *That's weird. I could have sworn--right when he walked in, at least--that he definitely wanted me to stay.* But I push the weirdness of the situation out of my mind. I should be relieved that he wants to take me home; I should be planning to expose him, after all. *This is why journalists aren't supposed to get too close to their subjects. Or sources. Or whatever Knox is.*

"Yeah, that's probably the best idea," I admit, even though it pains me a little bit.

Why am I getting so attached to this guy? It can't just be the great sex, though that's a *major* point in his favor; it's not like I haven't ever had good sex before. And we haven't interacted enough to justify me having any kind of emotional connection with him, although I have to admit, having him rescue me from a potential attack and chasing off those bears probably accelerated things, from an attachment standpoint.

We finish eating and I start to gather up the plates. "I whipped up a couple of chocolate lava cakes while I was waiting," I say, blushing a bit. "Do you like chocolate?"

"Who doesn't," Knox laughed.

"I figured it would be a good way to use my time that wouldn't include snooping around your house."

"Well, I appreciate you not snooping," he says, sitting back from the little table.

After he'd left, I had actually gotten a chance to appreciate the place; it's cozy, comfortable and clean, which I'm not sure if I should have expected or not. He's got an overstuffed, distressed leather couch in the living room, and when I peeked into the bedroom, I saw a plush, sprawling bed that I bet I'd sleep really well in--especially after another tumble between the sheets with him.

But I know better. I'm only here for a few more days, and I'm better off keeping my mind off any opportunity to have sex with Knox again, no matter how satisfying it would be.

I grab a butter knife and slide it around the edges of the two lava cake ramekins, putting a plate on top of them so I can flip them over and portion them out onto two dessert plates. I grab a tub of vanilla ice cream from the freezer, and after dropping a generous scoop next to each little cake, I place the plates down on the table. I watch Knox drag a spoon through his cake, allowing the liquified chocolate to ooze from its center. He eats it with gusto, and I feel a kind of pride I haven't felt in ages: the pride that comes along with seeing someone you have feelings for enjoying something you made. It's been a couple of years since I cooked for anyone; I'd almost forgotten how much I enjoy it.

"So, what's your schedule like for the next few days? If it's okay with you, I might need to ask you a few more questions." In truth, I need to know when he'll be occupied so I can sneak off to the park during the full moon to complete my investigation.

"Well, I'm going to be really busy for the next two days. Lots of paperwork, on top of a seasonal check of different sites around the park to make sure the wildlife populations are doing what they should." He gives me a little grin. "This cake is amazing, by the way."

"Just something I learned from my mom," I tell him, shrugging off the compliment. Although it feels really good, I need to stop opening myself up to opportunities for Knox to praise me, if I'm going to maintain any kind of objectivity.

"Please thank her for me," Knox says.

I laugh, "I will. So, I guess maybe I'll meet up with you again in three days?"

If I can get a little more detail out of him, I can make sure that I'm not going to end up running into him on the park grounds.

Then, too, I remind myself that the full moon is going to be over the next two days; that's pretty telling that Knox is going to be super busy. *He gave you a perfectly rational reason for that,* I tell myself, but at the same time, I can't help but hope that I'll find something out. By now, I'm convinced that there's *something* to uncover.

"I'd be happy to meet up with you for lunch in three days," Knox says. "I can cook something for you...to even the score."

I roll my eyes. "I used *your* groceries; I'm pretty sure we're even," I say. "There's no need for you to one-up me."

"I'm kind of a traditionalist, I guess," Knox says. "I like to provide for someone I'm sleeping with."

"We're not sleeping together," I point out. "We've had sex a couple of times, but we haven't actually slept in the same bed."

Knox laughs. "If you want to spend the night, then, I'll be free that evening," he suggests with a little grin.

I'm about to respond to that when a troubled look comes over his face for just a second; it's gone before I can even fully see it, but the brief little flicker is enough to derail my train of thought.

"Yeah, maybe we'll see if we'd be compatible bed mates. Do you hog the covers?" I ask.

I know I shouldn't have said that. The last thing I need to do is encourage this kind of banter, but I can't help myself. There's just something about Knox that overrides all my sense of professionalism.

"I don't think you'll have to worry about being cold when you're in *my* bed," Knox says.

I shake my head, rolling my eyes as I blush. "We'll see about that; I might still be focused on getting the last details of the article together by then," I say.

"It still seems like kind of an odd way to spend a vacation," Knox tells me. "When are you going to learn how to relax?"

"*Relaxing* didn't get me where I am today. Besides," I counter, "I'd say I've been relaxing plenty." In fact, in a certain light, I'm probably relaxing far too much.

Our cakes are gone and I can't think of any real reason to maneuver Knox into letting me stay; he insists that he'll do the dishes when he comes back from dropping me off, and that *he* has to be the one to take care of them, because I did the cooking. It's actually a refreshing attitude.

"Do you want to borrow a jacket? It's gotten colder since we rode out here," Knox says.

I accept his offer and he drapes one of his jackets around me. It smells like him--deeply--and I get a little thrill of pleasure at the scent and the warmth of it. It's so nice, and for a few seconds, as I get onto the bike behind Knox, I really wish I could spend more time with him. And maybe just not tonight. I want to forget about my article altogether and just ride out our passions until we both fall asleep.

But throughout the entire ride back to Mary's place, I'm busy pushing my mind to focus on the real reason I'm in Bar Harbor. It isn't for the leaves, it isn't for the beauty of the park, and it isn't to fool around with tough, good-looking park rangers. It's to get a good story about Acadia and the National Park Service.

The vibration between my legs is distracting, but I manage to keep my mind where it is, and before I know it, Knox is coming to a stop outside of Mary's place, turning off the engine to his bike and putting down the kickstand. I feel almost disappointed; in the back of my mind, I've kind of been hoping that he would turn around at some point. But he didn't, and if I have to get down to work, then so does he, and it's for the best that we both stay on our own pages.

But when he walks me up Mary's front steps, both of us have a crisis of resolve. "Why don't you hold onto the jacket until we meet up again? It looks nice on you," Knox says, as we step up to the door.

"I appreciate it; it's really warm."

It sounds terrible, but I have no idea what to say--or even what I *should* say--to the man who I'm becoming so attached to, but obviously won't have any contact with after the next few days.

Before I can come up with something a little more compelling, Knox leans in and brushes his lips against mine, and any thought I have about how much better it is for me to make sure I get my work done dissolves instantly. I instinctively wrap my arms around his neck and press against him, hoping that he'll pick me up and carry me back to his bike, telling me he's taking me to his place.

We stand like that for what seems like ages, and Knox deepens the kiss, plunging his tongue past my lips, tasting me and letting me taste him. It feels so good, and I can't deny that I feel like I belong in his arms, that his lips feel perfect against mine and I want nothing more in the entire world than to just keep going.

But I make myself do the responsible thing. I pull back just as Knox's hands are slipping up under my hem to get at the bare skin underneath and shake my head. "We both have a lot of work to do," I say shakily.

"You're right," Knox says, but I can hear he doesn't want to say it any more than I want him to. Neither of us wants to break apart, but we both know we have to; I can feel it in the way he holds my body against his just a little bit tighter for another second before letting me go. "I'll see you in a couple of days, and we can see about whether we're both free to spend the night, okay?"

I nod, too breathless and too turned on to trust myself to make the right response if I try to speak. Knox grins as if he knows exactly what's on my mind, and reluctantly steps back.

"Good night," I manage to say, and then I force myself to turn around and get my key in the lock. The first night that I got here, Mary told me that she locks up as soon as it's dark, even though her neighborhood isn't dangerous, just as a matter of practice.

"Good night," Knox calls to me from across the yard.

I force myself to open the door, walk through it, and close it behind me. I take a deep breath and decide that before I get down to work, I'll take a shower.

12

KNOX

I LOOK AROUND AND TRY TO PUSH THE RESTLESS, ANXIOUS FEELING FROM MY mind, but it's impossible to. It's only minutes before the moon will rise, and my clan only managed to capture the last of the escaped bears an hour ago. During the search, we'd all been devastated to pick up on a signal from Trent, alerting us that he'd found the remains of Matilda and Harold in the underbrush near the tail end of Richardson Brook: *They were attacked, and they've got Shawn's mark all over them. I can tell they didn't go down without a good fight, though.*

How fucking pathetic is Shawn, anyway? Going after a couple of elderly bears? My blood begins to boil, but I force myself to pause and take a deep breath. *Justice will come soon enough*, I remind myself. Waiting for the members of the conclave to arrive--now, more than ever--is like waiting for the axe to fall.

The rest of my clan has already started assembling in our usual meeting spot in the park: the most remote end of Jordan Pond. The spot we meet at is secluded, and other shifters acknowledge it as *our* spot, too--even though it's within the neutral territory of the national park.

Once we've shifted, as a group, we'll be meeting with the conclave. Shawn, Harris, Kevin and Jamie won't have the ability to change into their bear forms since we've got them all locked up in the shed and out of sight of the full moon.

It's getting darker and I feel the change beginning to crackle through my bones. At any other time, I have to consciously call it up, but during the full moon, it happens almost without my will; any shifters outside, under the moon, are the affected the same. The full moon change is always a big one: apart from being nearly involuntary, it feels like the purest of transformations, where we're more truly aligned with the animal parts of our consciousness.

The rest of my clan is beginning to look as restless as I am. I can feel their expectations; I can hear it in their minds. We need to resolve this issue and restore harmony to Acadia--and honor the lives of Matilda and Harold by bringing these assholes to justice once and for all.

I spot the members of the conclave approaching my clan's territory, all of them looking appropriately cautious about entering. There are five of them: Jeremy, an older bear; a mountain lioness named Vanessa; Leonard, a wolf who's only a few years older than I am; a she-wolf named Priscilla, and Nathan, a fox. Every five years, the shifters in the area surrounding our neutral territory hold an election to appoint a new conclave, which is meant to represent as many of the different shifter groups as possible.

"Good evening, Knox," Jeremy says as they approach, stopping just outside the border of our territory. "You asked us to oversee an issue with some outsiders disrupting the peace?"

"Yes, I did," I say, beckoning them to enter. They cross over the scent-marked boundary of our clan's territory, which distinguishes the area from the rest of the park, and advance towards our group.

"Tell us what the situation is, and then we will hear from the accused," Vanessa says.

"There are actually several incidents I'd like to recount for you. A few days ago, these bears--who have been causing trouble regularly for weeks, since the last full moon when they arrived--were on the verge of attacking a human visiting the park before I caught them and sent them on their way. The person was a journalist; their acts could have exposed us all if she was able to get away from them and they weren't able control their feral sides."

"This is serious, indeed," Jeremy agrees.

I nod. "They tried to attack again the following day in their bear forms. I got into a brawl with one of them in an attempt to keep them from going after a nearby human."

"I see," says Jeremy. "Is there anything else you'd like to add?"

"I would, and this is the worst offense of them all." I motion to Trent, who's standing to my left, "He found evidence that at least one of the four did, in fact, murder two bears from my clan, Matilda and Harold. Shawn, the alpha of their crew, left his scent-marks all over their bodies, which Trent found a ways north of here tonight."

The members of the conclave nod, looking grave.

"We'd like to extend our sincere condolences to each of you," Nathan says, as the rest of the conclave bows their heads in agreement. "We need to speak to the accused now, and we must do it quickly. Where are they being detained?"

"They're in a shed nearby, over on the edge of our territory," I tell them, gesturing in the direction of the trail leading to where the delinquents are.

"Very well. We'll head down to hear their pleas, and we should be back shortly to discuss the verdict," Nathan says.

I nod. "We appreciate your help very much."

As they leave, I look up at the sky, feeling the tingling through my body intensify. The moon will be out within a matter of minutes, and we will all need to transform into our other forms. I take a deep breath, holding the change at bay by force of will. I sniff the air--I can almost smell the magic that makes the change possible, dancing through the little secluded spot by the pond.

The members of my clan begin to prepare themselves for the change as soon as the moon rises. I hold off, not wanting to commit to the shift until I hear from the conclave, and I look around, taking deep breaths.

My focus shifts to Hannah for a moment as I await their return. *I'm 35 years old; at this point in my life, I need to get serious about finding my mate; someone to settle down and have cubs with,* I tell myself. *But if Hannah finds out what I really am, there's zero chance of having a future like that with her. Not to mention she isn't even from around here; it'd be hard to convince her to move up to these parts and abandon everything she's been doing with her life up until now.*

I'm plucked from my thoughts as I my ears pick up on rustling within the tall grass nearby. The conclave is making their way back toward the pond, and their expressions are somber. Behind them, Shawn, Harris, Kevin and Jamie trudge along, bound in silver chains; we made sure to take that precaution once we'd managed to track them down for the second time, not wanting to risk having them escape again.

"We've come to a decision," Vanessa says, looking first at me, then over to the rest of the clan. "This is neutral territory, and it's indisputable that these four have violated the terms of being on this land, and what it means to all of us. But one of the tenets of our society is that even wrong-doers are allowed to attempt to defend themselves in combat."

This isn't the result I was hoping for, but I know I have to abide by it. "So, what has the conclave concluded?"

As I look at the five members, Jeremy is the one to speak up. "At moonrise, the four guilty members will shift, and they will be given a twenty-minute head start, at which point, they will be fair game. If they can escape the territory before the Alpha can reach them, they'll earn their freedom. If they are able to successfully conquer the Alpha, they'll receive their freedom as well. But, let it be known, any confrontation will be fought to the death. If they manage to earn their freedom and attempt to re-enter the territory at any given time, execution sentences will be carried out without hesitation."

"To make our point clear, absolutely no one may intervene," Vanessa adds. "It is between the Alpha, Knox Bernard, and these four."

The verdict is better than what I had been dreading, but not by much. I'll have to chase down four separate bears; if they have any sense at all, they'll take off in different directions. I'll have to take them all out separately if I want to make sure that they will never threaten me, my clan, or Hannah again.

"I accept," I say, because frankly, I don't have a choice.

"Take the chains off these four, and we will oversee the challenge," Jeremy says.

Trent and Cassidy step forward and begin to remove the chains binding Harris, Shawn, Jamie, and Kevin.

I move closer to Shawn and a low growl escapes from my throat. "Why? Why did you do it?"

Shawn smirks, still bound by his chains. "Do *what*, pussy boy?"

I level my eyes with his. "You know damn well what I'm talking about, jerk-off!" My growl is now a deep roar at this point.

"Oh, those old geezers? Please, I was doing you a favor." He spits in my face. "Survival of the fittest, motherfucker."

I lunge for his throat, but Trent and Alex pull me back.

"You'll have plenty of time to settle this in a few minutes," Trent reminds me.

Shawn laughs maniacally, shaking so violently from his hysterics that his chains clatter through the night air. "We'll see about that," he snickers as Alex steps behind Shawn and frees him.

I breathe deeply, trying to calm myself as I start stripping out of my clothes. I feel the magic of the change intensifying in me, the animal instincts rising up to take control of my mind more completely than they do at any other time of the month. I give into it, closing my eyes, letting the transformation course through my whole body, from head to toe.

I feel my heart nearly push through my ribcage as I'm taken over by the seismic change. Tremors ripple through my limbs as my joints and bones begin to crack and morph violently. I feel my face elongate, stretching into a broad snout as I begin to taste iron-rich blood, my razor-sharp ursine teeth now emerging from my jaws. My eyes involuntarily roll to the back of my skull as equal doses of pain and ecstasy flow through my entire being. My skin tears and gives way to accommodate the lengthening of my bones, and tufts of thick, black fur force their way to the surface in its place. A moment later, I've made my full transformation.

When I open my eyes again I'm a black bear, surrounded by the other black bears of my clan, and the members of the conclave in their animal forms: a fox, a mountain lioness, two wolves, and a grizzly bear.

The grizzly, Jeremy, lets out a deep bellow, and I see Shawn and his accomplices lumber off into the woods next to the pond, dispersing to take advantage of their twenty-minute head start. Despite my animal form, there's just enough of my human mind still persisting for me to hold back and keep myself from automatically chasing after the four.

I wait impatiently, counting the seconds in my mind. Before I can hunt or forage for the foods I love, before I can commune with the rest of my clan, I have to take care of this problem. At least it'll all be over soon;

one way or another, the four shitheads will be out of my life for good by the end of the night.

To pass the time, I sniff the night air, reading the scents painted through it. There's a new hive of bees not far from the lake, and I look forward to raiding it sometime soon after dark when they'll be less defensive. I also want to make sure to get the last berries of the season to share with Hannah.

It's almost time, and I'm sniffing the air again to try and determine which path to take first when I catch her scent. It's unmistakable: lavender honey with a deeper musk underneath; delicious, magnetic and so fresh that it has to mean that Hannah is close by, right now. It's not an old scent from her possibly tromping through the area earlier in the day; I would have noticed it before.

Adrenaline shoots through me and the entire situation immediately becomes drastically more complicated. I have to wonder if she saw me--and the clan, and the conclave--change forms. These four reckless deviants pose a serious threat to Hannah if I can't get to them in time. I lower my head and let out a bellow. My human mind wants to take over--this situation is too complicated--but my animal mind maintains control. The simplest thoughts I have dominate my brain: protect the female, and remove the threat.

I take off after one of the scent trails, keeping part of my mind on the fact that Hannah is in the woods, too; I need to keep away from her, if I can. What is she even doing in this part of the woods at night? *Not important. Get the assholes taken down first and worry about that later.*

I follow Harris' trail, keeping myself aware of the others; as I suspected, they seem to have all gone off in different directions. At least, if I can track them down and take out two of them, the other two will be barred from the park for the rest of their lives. That would be a start.

Just as I'm getting close to Harris, though, I catch Hannah's scent again, and then, as I'm sniffing the air and the ground, I realize that Shawn's scent has crossed into this area of the woods, too; he's been through the trail in the last fifteen minutes, to judge by the freshness of the scent. I hear a scream, and my animal and human brains identify it immediately.

It's Hannah.

I quickly abandon any thought of going after Harris. Instinct takes over. I have to protect Hannah, whatever she's run afoul of; I can only suspect that it's Shawn.

I sniff the air and I find the direction Hannah is headed in, and a moment later, I find her, just yards away from me. She screams again, and I'm running towards her before I realize what I'm doing.

13

HANNAH

I DON'T KNOW WHAT I WAS EXPECTING TO SEE WHEN I HIKED OUT TO ONE OF the suspicious sites I'd noticed while cross-referencing the maps, but it definitely wasn't *this*.

A group of people--including my most recent sex partner, Knox--stripped naked, and then somehow, violating every natural law, disappeared into the bodies of a bunch of bears, along with a fox, two wolves, and of all things, a goddamn mountain lion.

Whatever other plans I had for the night evaporate from my head completely as I watch four of the bears shuffle off into the woods in a hurry. One of the others chases after him and I fumble with my phone, doing my best to capture this all on video while still trying to get over the initial shock of what I'd seen. I decide that it would be a moot point to try and check out whatever other sites I'd mapped out. Jessica was right after all; there's some fucking freaky shit happening in these parts, and there's no way I'm going to stay in the park with these roaming bands of human-animal creatures running around.

But then, as I attempt to find my way back toward my car, I lose the trail, and then get lost in the park altogether, with my phone now out of range of a cell tower.

It's bad enough to be wandering through the woods, unable to find my way out as the temperature continues to drop, but when I hear a growl from a few yards away and the barely-there sound of leaves and sticks crunching, I somehow know--immediately--that I'm the target of the animal in question.

My heart pounds in my chest as I try to figure out what to do about the situation. I hear myself screaming, one high, loud yelp escaping my throat, but I almost don't know how it could be me; I'm so removed from my own body.

I can't stop moving, but I force myself to slow down to avoid tripping over something and leave myself sprawling in the scrub, a perfect little bundle of tasty human meat that's just waiting to be devoured.

Is it one of the people that turned into an animal? Is it Knox? Something tells me that it's definitely not Knox; he wouldn't be chasing after me...frightening me...would he? How much humanity stays in the mind of the animal after he or she transforms?

I get a mental flashback of the sight of about thirty or more humans, standing stark naked near a lake in the woods, almost seeming to dissolve as more and more animalistic characteristics come over them. *As for the wolves, I guess you'd have to call them werewolves, wouldn't you? But what would you call a human that changes into a mountain lion, or a bear?*

I try to shake off the panic and shock I'm feeling when I hear the telltale sounds of a heavy, large predator behind me. I scream again without even realizing it until my strained throat forces me to cough. It's moving fast and I need to figure out what I'm going to do; I can't just keep walking like an idiot. I reach into my bag; I have a hunting knife that Mary gave me when I told her I was going to be checking out a few different parts of the woods at night. She'd pointed out that while it's technically a crime to kill animals in the park, I could maim one in self-defense and not get charged, and more to the point, it would be better to deal with criminal charges than to die a gruesome death.

I take the knife out and turn around to face the animal coming toward me. There's enough moonlight for me to catch a few glimpses of the creature as it descends on me: it's a huge bear with tattered, mangy fur. *Okay, so that bear from the other day...* My brain does rapid calculus as the bear barrels down on me and I realize that the massive, glorious-looking bear that I'd seen fighting with this other one--when I hadn't been able to find Knox--had to have *been* Knox. That explains the bear fight from the other day, the missing jacket and, more importantly, how quickly Knox had gotten back to me. Everything fell into place.

But before I have time to make sense of that revelation, the bear is within fighting distance. I take the knife and hold it up threateningly. "I know you're a human, or part human," I say. I try to stand as strong as I can and attempt to make eye contact with the leering, growling beast. "If you come at me, I'm going to do my level best to kill you." Surely, these shapeshifting, human-animal people aren't protected by the park's regulations. What happens to *them* when they die? Do they remain in their animal forms, or turn back to humans?

The bear hesitates for a moment, seems to size me up, and then lunges at me. I lash out with the knife, but before I can even get at the bear, I hear crashing and a roar nearby. I hear someone--or something--coming at us, and then the bear that was about to attack me is on his side, bowled over by another bear.

I stagger back, stunned at what I'm witnessing. The two bears go at it immediately, swiping at each other, snapping their teeth and growling, wrestling on the ground as each of them struggles to gain the upper hand.

It takes me a few moments to realize that the bear who's come to my rescue is actually Knox; he must have recognized my scream and came running. I'm torn between relief and new fear, and once again, I have to wonder how much of humanity is in the bear that's pounding on the one that would have attacked me in a few seconds? Is it the human inside that made Knox come to my rescue, or some animal instinct based on my scent and the sound of my voice?

I suddenly lose my bearings and fall to the ground, hard enough to make my teeth click and my jaw hurt from the impact, and I see the battle continue to rage on. It's like a weirdly-tinted deja vu from the other day, and while part of me is aware of the possibility that I might still get attacked, my body's frozen as my mind is working through the surrealness of the situation. Reality slaps me in the face as it fully occurs to me that yes, I truly did see Knox--a man I'd had sex with, and more than once--transform into a fucking bear. And now that bear is protecting me from another bear, who apparently wants to attack me, for reasons of its own.

All at once, I come back to myself as I hear a sickening crunch and a roar. I look around and spot the two furry forms on the ground, and for a second, I don't know what happened. I've been in a state of complete shock, so enveloped in my own thoughts that I totally lost track of what was going on in front of me.

The larger of the two bears--Knox, in his other form--rises, and the other bear doesn't move at all. I realize, with a sickening feeling in my stomach, that Knox killed the other bear. I should be grateful, and a part of me is, but I'm also horrified.

Knox-bear lumbers towards me slowly, snuffling and making low noises in his throat. I have no idea what to say. I have no idea what to even *think*. Is Knox even really in there? The bear stops short of me and lets out a groan, and I stagger back on my ass, scrambling on the ground with my hands, unable to even muster the mental capacity to stand up and run.

Before my eyes, Knox-bear seems to shrink, shift and move, and I realize that he's transforming back into a human, albeit very slowly. It seems almost painful; the sound of bones cracking and joints popping back into place send a chill down my spine.

Then, finally, Knox is standing in front of me, fully naked but fully human, streaked with blood but with only a handful of scratches over him.

"So," he says, his voice low. He coughs. "I take it you saw something."

"You're...some kind of...bear...shapeshifter," I say, shaking my head. "But that's impossible."

"It's obviously possible," Knox counters. "You just saw me shift with your own eyes." He gives me a wry grin. "I'd hoped you didn't see the first change, but when I heard you tell Shawn here..." he kicks at the bear, which seems to be melting into a human, which is somehow even more unnerving than Knox's transformation, "that you knew he was human, I figured if I could get rid of him, that would be a good time to come clean."

"Thanks, I guess," I say, still numb and stunned from the whole ordeal.

"It's a lot to take in." Knox looks worried.

I smile weakly. "Yeah...it is," I agree. "I just found out that not only are shapeshifters actually a thing, but that I've had sex with one more than once without even knowing."

"Who knows, you might have slept with one before me," Knox says. "We're sworn to secrecy about it."

I mentally scan through the last few guys I've dated. "Nope. I highly doubt it."

"You'd never know..."

I furrow my brow at that. "So... this is why you wanted to wait a couple of days to see me again," I say, remembering that tidbit. "*This* is why you were going to be busy." I'd figured on any number of outlandish scenarios, but this is one I never could have foreseen. "So, what, is the park some kind of hunting ground for your group?"

"It's not only for my group, but any shifter who wants to come here. As long as they're willing to obey the rules." Knox gestures absently to the dead bear-man, who now looks completely like a man, and a naked one at that. "He and three others broke the rules when they tried to attack you, and when they tried to fight me on the premises. This one here even killed a few of my friends."

"He...and three others..." It hits me then: the four men who tried to attack me on my first visit were all part bear. More of the whole crazy story falls into place in my mind. They were also the bears that had interrupted my picnic with Knox the second time I came to the park. And now at least one of them was dead.

"I...I think I need to get back to Mary's," I say. "I have a lot to think about."

"Will you come see me before you leave? And I think--I hope--you're not going to write about this, are you?" Knox looks more worried than ever. "It would put my entire kind in jeopardy."

"I need to think this through before I decide what I'm going to do."

I give myself a shake. Questions start up in my brain; on and on, the significance of what I've just learned in the last hour or so renders itself to a bunch of trivial nonsense.

"So, can we meet up like we were originally planning to? How about that?"

I think about it, and in spite of the shock I feel about what I've learned, I have to admit that I'm curious. Knox didn't hurt me, after all; he saved my life.

"It's a deal," I say. "Now if I can just get the hell out of here..."

"I'll show you the way, but then I'll have to get back to hunting the other bears down," Knox says. The phrase sends a shiver down my spine, but I don't ask any more questions.

14

KNOX

I'M NOT SURE THAT I'M EXACTLY HOLDING MY BREATH, BUT AT THE SAME time, I'm determined not to be disappointed if Hannah doesn't show up.

I'd hoped to keep her from finding out about my bear side--for the time being, anyway--but now that she knows, I need to find a way to keep her from spilling our secret. Above and beyond that, though, I need to see her again. The way I reacted to knowing she was in danger, in my animal form, told me a lot. The fact that I was able to shift back to human form during the full moon told me even more. With Shawn now dead and the other three bears off the territory for good, I finally felt it was safe to have Hannah back here.

When I see her walking towards my cabin from the front of the park, I feel a wave of relief. If nothing else, she's agreed to see me, and she looks interested instead of frightened or shocked. I take a deep breath and steady myself. Just because she agreed to come, just because she's willing to talk to me, doesn't mean that she's interested in anything more. And I have to be prepared for that.

"Hey," Hannah says as she steps up to me.

"How have you been?"

Hannah raises her eyebrows. "I've had a lot to process," she admits. She kicks at some loose mulch on the trail leading up to my cabin and looks up, meeting my gaze. "I've given it a lot of thought. It's unethical for me to not publish the truth, but sometimes in this field, you have to balance ethics with what is truly the right thing to do," she says. "I mean, if I published the truth, most people would just think that I've lost my mind. But, if even a fringe element ended up actually believing me, surely a witch hunt would ensue that would put you and your kind in grave danger. I can't and won't take that risk." She shakes her head. "I'll just have to write something else."

"Well, you could still write about the park," I suggest. "Just not about the angle that includes people like me."

Hannah chuckles. "Let's go inside and talk," she tells me, and I'm only too ready to agree.

We go into my cabin and I offer her something to drink. "I'll have a cup of coffee," she says, and I pour one for her, bringing milk and sugar to the table to go with it.

"Well, I'm sure you have a lot of questions. Where should we start?"

It seems so stilted, so awkward between us now, and I hate it.

"Can... can you turn someone else into a bear, or whatever you are, by biting them?"

I shake my head. "No, it's something you're born with," I reply.

"I see," she says, stirring a little more sugar into her coffee. "So... is a shifter baby born as a human, or an animal?"

"Really, it could go either way," I tell her. "If the mother is a shifter and she's in her animal form as she gives birth, the baby will be born in his or her animal state. If she's in her human form, she'll give birth to an infant in his or her human state," I explain. "It also depends on whether or not one of the parents is a full-blooded human."

"Wait a second, so humans and shifters are capable of producing offspring together?"

"They can. Their children would have at least a 50% chance of becoming shifters. Even if they didn't end up becoming shifters, they would carry the gene. If they mate with other shifters one day, they'd have children who could shift," I explain.

"Wow, sounds complicated." She takes another sip from her mug before asking, "Have...you ever had sex in your bear form?"

I nod. "Only with another werebear, never with a human or an actual bear," I say.

"Okay, so *werebear* is the term you like to use. Well, what is the connection between your status as a human and your status as a werebear?"

"I became the Alpha male of the bear pack that is technically the host for this territory when I became the administrator," I say.

"Do you have to have a partner to be an Alpha male?"

I shake my head. "No, but it helps," I admit. "I've been waiting to meet the right person before I choose my mate."

I pause for a moment and decide that now's as good of a time as any to cut the bullshit and tell her what's on my mind; what's *been* on my mind for days now. "If I'm being honest..." I say, taking her hands in mine, "I think that person is you."

Hannah's eyes widen for a moment. "What makes you think I'd be a good *mate*?"

I gently take her face in the palms of my hands and look into those gorgeous hazel eyes of hers. "Hannah, I knew I wanted you from the first time I met you," I tell her. "Every time we got together after that, I knew it even more strongly. And the other night, well, that confirmed it."

"How do you know for sure?" she asks.

I smile slowly. "My bear side tells me you smell like something that should be mine," I tell her. "Like something I should protect and devote myself to; something I should take care of."

She stares out the window for the next few minutes, pondering over it all, but then she cracks a small smile.

"You know, I'd be lying if I told you I haven't felt something between us; something strong that's more than just..." She looks down for a moment, but then her gaze returns to mine. "It's like I *need* you, Knox, and no matter what the rational side of my brain screams out to me, there's something inside that tells me..."

"That we're meant to be together?"

"Yes," she says. "I know that, in many ways, we're so different, but if I just go home and try to forget this ever happened--that *we* ever happened—I know I'll regret it." She reaches over to the table to grasp my hands, "I have to see where this will go."

This is promising indeed, but I try to press her further to make sure we're on the same page. "Do you mean in terms of me living here and you living back in Boston?"

Hannah shrugs. "It would depend, I guess. It's probably against the rules for an Alpha to get involved with someone who's not...like you, right?"

"We Alphas make a lot of our own rules," I say.

"Isn't that going to piss off some of the others?" Hannah looks dubious.

"Everyone knows and respects that the Alpha lives by his or her own rules, so no. Besides, I've never heard of any Alpha being tried by a conclave for choosing a human as his or her mate."

She looks at me for a long moment. "All I ask, for the time being, is for you to be patient with me, Knox. This is a lot to take in, and there's a lot to adjust to."

I think about it; in all my musings, in all my hopes, I haven't thought through what I would do if Hannah would actually entertain the thought of being with me.

"I'm willing to do whatever it takes to make this work," I say.

I keep looking at her for a long moment. Being so close to her again, breathing in her scent, I think about what it would be like to be with her--to have her as my mate--for the rest of my life, and it makes my heart feel like it could explode right out of my chest. *I just have to make sure to give her a little breathing room.*

"Well, I'll have to head back home in a few days," she says. "Why don't I get clearance from my boss to work remotely, and I'll come back up and we can spend a little more time getting to know each other here in the cabin? That's one of the perks of my job; I can pretty much work wherever there's a Wi-Fi signal. How does that sound?" Hannah sits back slightly in her chair and raises an eyebrow.

"That sounds like a perfect start," I say with a grin. "No matter how much time you need back home, I'll be here waiting for you."

All the awkwardness leaves us then, and we're talking about the future like nothing strange at all stands in our way. The idea of lunch goes out the window completely. When Hannah gets up to put her coffee mug in my sink, I grab her and pull her into my lap, kissing her, tasting the sweetened coffee on her lips.

We immediately begin working at each other's clothes, almost tearing them, and I know--deep down--that it's only a matter of time before she'll be living up here with me in my cabin.

I put my mouth to work, dipping down to Hannah's tits and claiming them, worshipping them with my lips and tongue as I manage to get her panties off and toss them across the room.

Hannah squirms in my lap, and I can feel her wet heat against my throbbing, aching cock, like our bodies are doing everything they can to merge as one. I fall completely into instinct, getting the last of Hannah's clothes off and lifting her up onto the kitchen table. I work my way down from her tits to her pussy, and it's so deliciously soaking wet, so hot and ready for me, that I can't even bring myself to wait or to tease Hannah. I push her gently onto her back and bury my face against her slick folds, sliding my tongue up and down, tasting her hungrily.

Hannah moans out and the sound is like music to my ears, spurring me on as I work her with my lips and tongue. I spread her legs wide and bring the tip of my tongue up to her clit, swirling it in tight circles before dipping down to her entrance, sucking as much of her into my mouth as I can. I bring her to the edge of climax in a matter of moments and then back off, slowing down just enough to let her cool down. Over and over again, I get her so hot that I know she can barely stand it and then I stop just short of letting her get what she really wants, until I know she thinks she's going to die if I don't let her come.

I pull back finally and look at her face; she's flushed and panting, looking almost like an animal herself, and I love her more than I ever thought possible, but I know it's not the time to tell her. I have to wait for her to feel the same way; for her to feel comfortable saying it.

The animal in me wants to flip her onto her stomach, but I know I need to be as human as possible around her--for now, at least. I wrap her legs around my waist and guide the tip of my cock against her soaking wet folds, and thrust into her, taking her all at once.

We fall into a rhythm immediately, with Hannah pushing her hips down, twisting them in reaction to my movements, and it feels so completely perfect that I know she has to feel it, too. I start slow and then gradually build up speed, holding myself back as I bring Hannah to the edge yet again--but this time I let her tumble over it and ride through her orgasm, kissing her face everywhere and dipping down to her tits. I manage to hold my own climax back throughout Hannah's, and slow down while she's recovering, moving just enough to keep her going while I maintain my own arousal.

Then we're moving together again, speeding up, and the feeling of Hannah's muscles clenching around me in little spasms is almost more than I can take, in a matter of mere moments. But I keep it together, working up her arousal, turning her on more and more. I take advantage of the lull to worship her tits, her lips, to touch her sensitive little clit, working her until she's so turned on it must be killing her and then slamming into her with all I've got when my need gets the better of me.

The second time I feel her body clench around me in orgasm, I tumble into my own climax, coming harder than I ever have with anyone else. I groan against Hannah's chest, against her shoulder, and kiss her as wave after wave of pleasure washes over me, and I feel that connection between us, that bond that I know only happens when a bear--or any shifter--has found his or her mate.

I sag against Hannah, panting for breath, and I feel her body fluttering around me in erratic little post-orgasmic spasms as aftershocks work through her.

"Weren't...weren't we going to get lunch?"

I laugh at Hannah's question. "Feeling hungry?"

Hannah nods. "I could eat a horse," she tells me. I breathe in the smell of her; just knowing that gorgeous, intoxicating scent is going to be in my life permanently--even if Hannah doesn't fully realize it yet--is enough to make me want to shift and run through the park's grounds, roaring my triumph.

I pull myself back and grin down at the woman I've fallen for. "I'm all out of horse, but I do have a fresh wild duck and some fingerling potatoes and carrots that I'd love to roast up for you," I say with a wink. "My family has a recipe that's been handed down for generations that I've been dying to make for you. Let me get that started, then afterwards... maybe we could move the party to the bedroom."

"That sounds amazing," Hannah says. "I vote yes."

I slip on my boxers and start preparing our meal. Fifteen minutes later, just as I'm putting the duck in the oven, Hannah's just gotten out of the shower and joins me, wearing nothing but one of my flannels.

"Hey, I just thought of something...something about the research I'd been doing."

I laugh, "Does your mind ever stop?"

Hannah gives me a playful shove. "No seriously," she says. "So, remember how I wasn't able to find the birth certificates for some of Acadia's founders?"

I look up from the cutting board, where I'd been chopping garlic to add to the gravy. "Yeah?"

"Well, how long have shifters been gathering in Acadia for?"

I pause mid-chop. She'd seen my clan and the concave shift right there before her eyes, so there was no denying the *existence* of shifters. But the histories of Acadia and the NPS? I took a sacred oath, vowing to never reveal the true reason behind how they came to be.

"Shifters have been around just as long as humans have."

"You should be a politician," she says, crossing her arms as she laughs. "I asked how long have they been *gathering in Acadia* for."

"Oh, I don't know. A long time."

"Well, I put two and two together and had the thought that perhaps some of those founders were shifters themselves," she says.

"Is that so?" I stiffen, trying to act as nonchalant as possible, but then remember that I hadn't let her in on the secret; she's a smart woman, and was able to piece the puzzle together herself.

"Am I right, or am I right?" she asks, grabbing a piece of carrot from the cutting board to munch on.

I grin. "Well, what makes you think that?"

"I concocted the idea that if, say, one of the founder's mothers gave birth in her animal form, the founder would have been born as an animal...and what wild animal would have a birth certificate?"

I hand her another piece of carrot. "That's pretty farfetched, don't you think?"

She laughs. "Um, if you'd asked me last week about the concept of a bunch of naked humans morphing into animals under the full moon, I would have told you *that's* farfetched. So, am I on to something here?"

I turn around, grabbing her by the waist as I pull her in close for a kiss. "I'll never tell."

"Well, what if I phrase it this way: am I crazy, or am I smart?"

"*You*," I say, planting a trail of kisses down her neck, "are the smartest person I've ever known."

And she *is*. How I got so lucky to find a woman as irresistible as

Hannah, I'll never know. For the first time in my life, I notice the unrelenting drive of my inner bear relax, creating harmony between my dual sides like I've never experienced. It knows I've found my destined mate, and even though things between Hannah and I are just getting started, at this rate, my instincts tell me that she'll be pregnant within the year.

RANGER TRENT

SHIFTER NATION: WEREBEARS OF ACADIA

1

TRENT

This does NOT look good...

I was standing over a body. Not just *any* body either. The body of Danielle Peterson of *Danielle's Destinations*, a well watched show on Maine's Travel Channel.

Only this time, it didn't look like she would be 'signing off from this destination.'

I ran my hand through my shortly cropped black hair and reached out to Sophia with my mind, urging her to come quickly. I looked around for any sign that anyone had been present at the scene before my arrival, trying to find any clues that could tell me what had happened.

Danielle's small, plump body was contorted in ways limbs should never bend. Her chocolate-brown eyes were wide, yet empty and her black curls were matted into a knot with leaves and branches caught in them. She was sprawled out on the ocean shoreline of Acadia's most well-known beach, Hunters Beach, located in the south-eastern region of the park; it was usually far outside of my normal hiking area, but I had wanted to look at the ocean that day.

And instead, I had found a body.

If I didn't know any better, I would have thought that maybe she had slipped on one of the rocks, hit her head and was just unconscious. Rocky beaches were always difficult to navigate—and extremely slippery.

The rocks were glistening, which told me that the Atlantic had risen enough that day to coat the stones with a beautiful shine that reflected against the sunlight. So, it could have been possible. And I would have thought that were the case, had there not been blood everywhere.

There were lacerations and puncture wounds all over Danielle's body. She didn't slip and hit her head: it was an attack, and judging by the damage, my mind went to only one explanation.

"What seems to be the pro—*Oh no*! I know who that is: it's Danielle, from *Danielle's Destinations*! What the hell happened?" Sophia Ross, our emergency manager, rushed up to the body laying before me, checking for any signs of life. She was carrying a basic medical kit, which definitely would not be enough to aid the fallen celebrity.

"Has she moved at all?" Sophia asked while checking Danielle's pulse at both her neck and her wrists, her brunette ponytail bobbing as she worked over the body quickly. Her hazel eyes looked up at me waiting for an answer.

"No signs of movement. When I found her, she was just lying there," I said, snapping out of my daze and crouching down next to her while trying to stay out of her way. She pulled out a stethoscope and listened for a heartbeat.

She didn't seem to find one.

Sophia started doing chest compressions and breathing into Danielle's mouth, but quickly jumped back. As her breath had entered Danielle's lungs, blood splattered out from her wounds.

"These lacerations went deep and punctured her lungs. She's gone," she admitted, looking down at the body sadly. She started scanning around just like I did, trying to find the person who could have done this.

"What do you think happened?"

"Well, someone attacked her, obviously. Judging by the contorted limbs, she put up a pretty good fight. These lacerations, though...I would say it was probably—"

"A bear...Right?" I made direct eye contact with her, knowing the answer before she even agreed.

"Yeah. A bear, for sure," Sophia nodded.

"Dammit!" I stood and threw my fist into the nearest rock, causing it to crumble at my feet. I stared down at the ground, wondering how this could have happened.

"Now you know Cassidy isn't going to be happy about that." Sophia shook her head, putting away her stethoscope.

Cassidy was our park planner, and she had each rock meticulously placed on the beach. My gaze rose to Sophia, who was looking down at Danielle. "So, do you think it was one of us?"

Sophia's eyes met mine and they were filled with worry. I could tell we were sharing the same thoughts.

Could a bear shifter have done this?

Was he or she one of our own?

Why would anyone have done something like this?

Well, it was my job to find out.

"I don't know. There was no one here when I arrived. If one of us did this to her, I can't pick up any incriminating scents with all this blood here. We're going to have to get this cleaned up so I can try to track down whatever it is."

"You know Knox is going to want to hear about this. Should I tell him?"

"You clean this up; I'll handle Knox."

I started walking away toward the woodlands, reaching out to our Alpha, Knox, with my mind.

What?

I could already sense the annoyance in his thoughts.

Sorry to bother you man, we—

I'm trying to enjoy my day off, and you're cockblocking me.

He was not going to like this.

Sorry, Boss...

Just tell me what it is!

I winced at the urgency that came off as Alpha authority. It was a little hard to discern the emotions, but I decided there was a little of both mixed in there.

We found a body, Knox. Out on Hunters Beach.

A local? Knox's thoughts were serious now.

Worse. It's Danielle Peterson. I winced as I delivered the news.

The travel guide? Are you serious? Knox's thoughts were loud and echoed in my head.

And we think it was a bear...

Don't move. I'll be right there.

But Sophia is here cleaning up the b—

DON'T TOUCH THE BODY! I'll be there in a few minutes.

And with that, the connection was gone. I ran back to Sophia, who was just about to drop the corpse into the water of the Atlantic.

"Whoa! What the hell are you doing?" I closed our distance, my long legs allowing me to cover the ground separating us quickly.

"What do you mean what am I doing? She's famous! We have to get rid of her!" Sophia sounded a bit panicked, and I could hear her heart hammering away in her chest.

"We can't just throw her into the ocean and hope she turns up somewhere!" I grabbed the body from her.

"So, what are we supposed to do?" she asked with frantic eyes.

"Knox demanded the corpse no longer be touched until he gets here."

"Why? What's going on?" Sophia looked confused, which I supposed was better than panicked. Maybe.

However, I was just as unsure. We didn't usually get human deaths in Acadia. If someone from our clan died, we buried them and had a ceremony with all members present. We couldn't just bury Danielle Peterson. She was famous, and people would recognize her disappearance.

"I'll just put the body back where we found it and we'll wait for Knox. He was very insistent and not in a good mood."

"Was he with Hannah?" Sophia teased, her skinny shoulders doing a little shimmy. Her ability to switch from one mood to another had always astounded me.

Hannah had come to the park a couple months ago to write a story on the history of Acadia and our national parks in general. Knox was skeptical of her at first; after all, if the media were to find out that our national parks were established as safe havens for people who could *shapeshift into animals*, our kind would be in for a one hell of a shitstorm. Luckily, the two of them really hit things off and our secret has been safe.

Since then, it hasn't been hard to find Knox on his days off—although god help you if you tried to bother him. Almost every time, he'd be in his cabin with Hannah—all day—and you wouldn't see him again until it was time for his next shift. He'd never really showed much interest in the women around here, so I was glad to finally see him settling down with someone.

"I honestly will never understand how you can joke in times like these, Soph. We're handling a dead body here and you're behaving like a high schooler." I shook my head and placed Danielle back where we found her. I tried to align her body the way I remembered it being, in the same grotesque position that had stopped me cold in the middle of my hike.

Whatever the reason was for Knox wanting to see her and handle this personally, I was going to find out what happened to this woman.

No matter what.

SOPHIA and I sat on the rocks waiting for Knox to arrive in silence while my brain kept working through what could have happened.

Could Harris, Jamie, or Kevin have come back, despite their ban from the park? They already risked exploiting our existence once by trying to attack a reporter—who turned out to be Hannah—a few months ago. I was glad when their Alpha, Shawn, was destroyed by Knox for killing Matilda and Harold, two of the elders from our clan. Shawn's three cronies had been spared, but Shawn had been given exactly what he deserved.

Could there be a new rogue out there? Could someone from our clan have done this? I shook my head at the last thought. There was no way one of us could have committed such a crime. I grew up with everyone and I couldn't imagine anyone hurting a harmless person. Besides, no one wanted to feel Knox's wrath if they were caught even thinking about doing something like that. And I didn't want to imagine what it would be like to have to lock up one of our own.

Knox stormed out from the trees, marching right towards the beach and interrupted my thoughts. "What the hell?" he muttered as he walked over, kneeled and examined the body. "Well, this is Danielle Peterson, alright."

I could hear low rumbling coming from Knox's chest.

"What's the problem? Shouldn't I go about the investigation as usual? It could just be one of Shawn's punks returning for revenge for their Alpha or something."

"This is out of our hands now…" Knox stood up and looked to the sky, seeming deep in thought.

"What? What do you mean?" Sophia asked. She and I exchanged confused looks once more.

"Danielle Peterson is famous. Famous enough that her death will be noticed by the media. We have to call it in." Knox took a tired breath.

"Call it in?" I didn't like where this was going. I'd been the law enforcement ranger of Acadia National Park for two years and I'd never had to call anything in. If anything ever happened in Acadia, I handled it.

"The FBI. We have to get the feds involved."

"The feds? No way; this is my jurisdiction! *I* make the arrests. *I* investigate crimes around here."

I couldn't believe my ears. He wanted to get the feds involved? Why? I felt my blood boil at the thought of some stuck-up asshole spouting off about rules and regulations.

"You have to remember, we're on federal land; this is beyond our jurisdiction," Knox glared at me, probably sensing my anger, "and you *will* cooperate with them, understood?"

"But this was clearly a bear shifter attack! No wild bear around these parts would do this. We could be risking exposing our existence publicly over some travel guide?"

Pure-blooded black bears killed less than one person a year and there were at least a million of them in North America—I knew it couldn't have been one of them. It was a shifter, and Knox was trying to get us all killed over whoever the idiot was.

"I'm calling it in. End of discussion. You both are ordered to not touch the body until they get here to examine it." Knox commanded, marching back into the woods.

"So, we're just supposed to sit here and wait while whoever did this could be getting away?" I shouted after him. It was getting more and more difficult to control my anger. I should have been out there looking for the killer.

"You will do as I say!" I felt the overwhelming pressure of the Alpha authority wash over me and I became silent, my body rippling from confined anger.

Knox said nothing else and walked away.

Sophia stepped closer to me. "Hey…I know you don't want someone coming in and telling you what to do, but it's the law. And you know it better than any of us. It would have been great if we went along protecting this park ourselves and never had to get the feds involved, but we all knew there was a chance that it could happen one day. I'll admit, I didn't think it would happen this soon, especially after that crew of rogue bears caused all that trouble a few months ago, but who knows! Maybe it won't be so bad?"

Sophia looked at me and shrugged. She wanted me to accept this, but it was just too hard of a pill to swallow.

"It's going to be a real shit show, I just know it. Some guy with a pole up his ass coming here, acting like he knows this place? It's just bad news. Not to mention having them sticking their nose in our business? Everyone will have to be on their toes, including the person who did this. And we have no way of controlling that because we have no idea who it is that did this! There is literally no way this can go well."

"Wow, Trent, so optimistic! No wonder Knox keeps you around!" Sophia said sarcastically. She patted my shoulder and then went to sit on a rock near the body. "Might as well take a seat and get comfortable; we might be here for a while. In fact, we'll *definitely* be here for a while."

She sighed and looked out at the ocean.

"I don't know who I'd rather deal with, them or you," I said, shaking my head and sitting on a rock near hers.

She laughed and nudged me playfully. Sophia had always been like a sister to me and was always there to lighten the mood. Even still…

I was not looking forward to this.

Not one bit.

2

BLANCA

"We are now flying over Acadia and will be touching down momentarily." I heard the pilot's voice in my ears through the headset.

I looked out the window of the FBI emergency helicopter to see at least twenty mountains and lakes. My gaze widened in awe, taking in everything I could with long sweeps of my eyes.

It was beautiful. I wasn't sure what I expected, but I found the view absolutely breathtaking. The lakes looked crystal blue, sparkling as the sun shone on them. The mountains were tall and all I could think was that if I got any down time before I left, I wanted to hike one, for sure.

"I know you guys aren't here for pleasure or anything, but we are just passing over Acadia's Eagle Lake, and I would highly recommend visiting if you get the chance after your investigation is over," the pilot said. I looked out and saw a giant lake; it looked so inviting, like its waters were beckoning to us with its cerulean fingers.

"And just over there, you can see Cadillac Mountain. If you're out early enough, it's a beautiful place to watch the sun rise."

I kind of liked this pilot.

"How do you know so much about the park?" I asked into my headset.

"I took my wife here for our 10-year anniversary. She's really into nature and we loved it."

Once I thought about it, it seemed like a fantastic place to spend a few days, but I wasn't there for a vacation. I wouldn't be doing much mountain climbing, swimming, hiking or anything like that.

I was there to investigate a death and possible murder.

I wasn't given much information about the case, only that there had been a death in Acadia National Park. I was in shock when I had heard Danielle Peterson was the victim, as she was one of the most well-known TV personalities at the time. If people watched the Travel Channel, it was for her. What could have possibly happened?

I wasn't sure, but I was there to find out.

Investigations involving national parks were usually handed off to the Department of the Interior, but due to the high case volume they were experiencing, my team had taken over. With everyone else working on their own assignments, I was the lucky one chosen to hop on the next helicopter out to Acadia.

I didn't mind; it wasn't like I had a case to work on at the time. Plus, it was just the kind of investigation I was often picked for. Any assignments involving thieves, murderers and terrorists were usually handed off to me. If someone asked, I'd tell them that those people had no place on this earth and I was glad to put them behind bars. People who broke the law deserved to be punished and I was happy to help exact justice whenever I could. Some people hated their jobs, but I looked forward to every case.

However, I didn't have enough information to tell if the case would involve a murderer and I sure as hell wasn't going to make assumptions. I went by the facts, and there was little for me to go on, so I would have to wait.

I was lucky that my supervisor had found two agents from other teams to assist me. I would need some help, especially if we ended up catching a person responsible for the death. He or she would be detained until we could take the individual back to headquarters for questioning, and I would need people from our side to watch over the suspect. I didn't know anyone at the park, and until I cleared them all of suspicion, I didn't trust a single one of them.

Jesus himself could work there and I would make sure to check out his background file and alibi.

The file for this case contained several sheets of paper. The first outlined the call that was made to the FBI by the Deputy Park Manager, reporting that he found the body of Danielle Peterson dead in his park. The rest of the meticulously printed papers were outlines of the individuals who held jobs at Acadia. The reports didn't contain too much detail, other than names, races, ages, and how long the person had held his or her position at the park. Or was it a wild life preserve? I couldn't remember and I supposed it didn't matter. The last of the stack included two files that had large X marks on them with the word "Deceased" stamped across their fronts. I wondered if those positions had been refilled yet and what had been the cause of their deaths. If so, those were variables that I didn't have the appropriate information on, and I would need to gather that as quickly as I could.

Just try to focus on the death you were sent here to investigate, I told myself, taking a deep breath. I felt adrenaline start to pump through me as we descended onto Acadia's helicopter pad. The Acadia Air Tour helicopter was parked to the side and three people were standing just outside of range waiting for us.

Once we touched down, I grabbed my briefcase and removed my headset. "Get ready," I said to the agents behind me. "We need to be prepared for anything, starting right now."

I looked out the window and the three people were walking towards the helicopter. I could see them clearly and they were only a couple of feet away from the safety range. There were two men and one woman, a pair of them in similar outfits and one dressed in a much more casual outfit.

The woman was brunette sporting a shoulder-length ponytail. She wore a green bomber jacket with ranger patches all over it, a white tee shirt, and grey pants. She looked fit, but not overly-muscular or anything. She probably hiked through the park often, especially by the looks of her boots. I guessed she must be Hispanic or mixed as my eyes passed over her caramel complexion.

The tallest guy had a buzzed, military-style cut and was very muscular. He looked serious, but his posture was open. His peachy complexion was mostly covered by a navy blue long sleeve shirt and slightly loose jeans.

Seems a little too casual if you ask me, I snorted. If only the FBI allowed casual days. I didn't mind the business suits, but jeans and a tee shirt just seemed so comfortable. I guessed no one would take me seriously though, so I quickly decided that the suits were better anyway.

The last guy did not give the impression he was happy to be there. He wasn't even looking at the helicopter and seemed to be purposely avoiding acknowledging it. The man donned what appeared to be a ranger police uniform. He was wearing a grey button-down long sleeve shirt, a dark green tie and, appropriately, forest green pants. The guy was also sporting hiking boots and his badge was displayed prominently on his chest, probably clipped to his breast pocket. He was tall and tanned from the sun with a football player's build, complete with broad, muscular shoulders. His brow was furrowed, and his hands were hidden in his pockets.

The pilot gave the okay for us to exit the helicopter and I opened the door, ready to officially meet the welcoming trio.

It was a chilly mid-November day—but warm for Maine—another plus for wearing a pantsuit. It was about forty degrees and very breezy, causing my black blazer to whip around me. It was a good thing I decided to wear a black camisole under my white button-up shirt; I was thankful for the small extra layer. My legs, however, felt the chill of the wind under my black dress pants. It was also a good thing I decided to wear flats and not heels; after four days of wearing them in the office, I had decided I needed a break.

Because of my short legs, I had to jump down from the helicopter; it must have looked *so* professional, like a kid leaping off a tall stool. One of the agents had offered me a hand, but I refused it; I wanted these people, whoever they were, to take me seriously.

I got my badge ready as I walked up to them, using my briefcase to block some of the wind, and the other two agents followed close behind me. Once I was clear, the helicopter took off, thank god; I didn't like having to yell at people over the loud noise of the engine and whirring blades above our heads.

As I walked up to the group waiting for us, the man with the buzz cut approached me directly.

"Hello, I'm Knox Bernard, the Deputy Park Manager. I apologize for my casual appearance; this was supposed to be my day off." He then motioned to the brunette woman and she smiled, seeming very friendly,

"This is Sophia Ross, our Emergency Manager." She pulled on one side of her bomber jacket to show me her medic badge.

"And this is our Law Enforcement Ranger, Trent Bailey." Knox motioned to the man beside him, who seemed to study me for a bit and then gave a curt nod. Trent didn't motion to his badge or anything; not that I needed him to, it was just common courtesy in this business. He obviously wasn't happy to be there, and it showed in his introduction and body language.

I inwardly rolled my eyes. Men in law enforcement never liked for women to be higher in rank than them. And judging by his behavior, he wasn't happy that his boss had called me in to handle this case.

I didn't care. I wasn't there to coddle his ego; I was there to find a possible murderer. He could either help me or not; it would be his choice.

Looking at him again, he would be kind of hot, if it wasn't for the attitude.

Oh well, I wasn't going to try to butter him up. I didn't mix business with pleasure, anyway.

"And you are?" Knox asked, raising an eyebrow. He obviously wasn't going to start talking about anything until I introduced myself. Knox was wary, but he had friendly eyes and I could tell he was going to be as cooperative as I needed him to be. I got the same vibe from Sophia, but I knew Trent was going to be a piece of work.

"Blanca Gianni, FBI. I'm the agent assigned to this case." I showed my badge to all three of them, and they each examined it and nodded, accepting its legitimacy. Trent seemed to inspect it more closely than the other two, his brow furrowing, which I tried especially hard not to roll my eyes at.

Of course, he would do that.

I'm here, and there's nothing you can do about it until this case is solved. So, lose the attitude and get with the program, I thought, getting a bit annoyed that I was going to have to deal with him for the entirety of the investigation, most likely. I, of course, didn't say those words out loud, but made a mental note to remember them in case he needed his ego checked sometime in the next few days.

"This is Alex and Gerard; they are here to assist with my investigation." I motioned to the guys behind me who also showed their badges.

"Now, please fill me in. Where was the body found? Who found her? Who examined her? I need as many details as possible."

"Why don't we fill you in once we take you to see the body? Seeing it might answer some questions on its own. It's less than a ten-minute walk and you can draw your own conclusions. We tried to leave the body where it was in case it would help you get some clues for the investigation. If you will just follow us," Knox started walking off, with Sophia and Trent right behind him.

"Stay close." I whispered to Alex and Gerard. I didn't like the fact that they didn't answer my questions initially. They seemed legit, but I didn't quite trust them just yet. I needed to see the body first; until then, I wasn't going to take any chances.

With Alex and Gerard following closely, we trailed after the three rangers to Danielle's body.

3

TRENT

You've got to be kidding me...

The feds could have sent anyone in their entire agency, and they chose *her*?

I watched as she examined the body silently, moving around it slowly, taking in every detail as she jotted notes down on a small pad. She was about five feet tall, a foot shorter than me. She looked younger than me, mid-twenties, but her height made her seem even more adolescent in my eyes. She had jet black hair tied tightly in a bun, but there were a few wavy strands loose from the wind. On top of being short, she was pear shaped, thinner on top, with wide hips and thick thighs.

*Those hips look perfectly built for bearing children...*I rolled my eyes at my inner bear's primal thoughts and pushed back the surge of heat that began to spread through my body. There was no way I was looking at her like that. She was here to tell me what to do; to take over my job. I just wanted her out of here. Hopefully, she summed this up to a bear attack and not an actual murder; then, we could conduct our own investigation to find the shifter who was responsible.

Once she was done examining the body, she walked back up to Knox, Sophia, and I, who were standing together off to the side, trying our best to stay out of her way.

"Now that I've seen the body, are you going to answer my questions?" she asked bluntly, her pen at the ready.

She doesn't waste any time, does she? I clenched my jaw and looked at Knox to see how he would respond.

"Well, I'm sure seeing the body has answered where it was found. It was discovered by Trent here, who contacted Sophia immediately to confirm the victim's death. If she'd been alive, Sophia would have provided medical attention immediately. She's our medic as well as our search and rescue specialist," Knox said, nodding to Sophia who returned his gesture.

But Blanca wasn't looking at them.

Her eyes were on me.

"So, it was you who found the body, huh?"

"Yes." My response was clipped. I was ordered to be cooperative, but that didn't mean I had to be friendly. I felt Knox studying me.

Blanca continued her line of questioning, "Were there signs of anyone around when you came upon the body?"

"No." I tried to remove any trace of irritation from my voice as to not anger Knox, but the lady was pushing it. Obviously, I did my job and scoped out the perimeter.

"No footprints?" She looked at me suspiciously with her crystalline blue eyes.

Oh shit... My eyes widened slightly. I hadn't even thought to check for footprints. I had been so quick to call Sophia to see if there was any chance of saving the body, and when I had looked around initially, I didn't see anything. I would have noticed if there had been footprints.

"I don't remember seeing any footprints when I scoped the area," I admitted. It was the truth; I hadn't noticed any. I spotted Knox's brow furrow in my peripheral vision.

Did you check for footprints, Trent? I heard Knox's voice echo in my head. I sighed, not wanting to lie to him, but also not wanting to have to deal with his reaction.

Not exactly. I didn't see anything when I looked around, but I also didn't actively search for them. I was so focused on getting Sophia here to examine the body... I winced at the angry look Knox was giving me.

As soon as her initial inspection is over, you are to scout the area and look for footprints that might lead us to the shifter, understood? There was that

Alpha authority again, pushing down on me and making me nod quickly. Knox usually didn't have to impose his leadership ability often, but having the FBI there must have had him on edge.

You're not the only one stressed... I thought, then shifted my gaze to Blanca, who was looking back and forth between me and Knox. *Shit, this chick is observant.*

"I'm sorry, did I miss something?" she asked. I could hear the interest in her voice as she studied us.

"Nope," I shrugged, trying to hide the slight panic I felt. There was no way she could know about our intra-clan telepathy, but it made me uneasy that she could possibly guess anything close to it. The way her eyes looked at—no, *through*—me was more than a little bit uncanny.

It looked like she either accepted that nothing just happened, or she decided to let it go because she began to jot down some notes before moving on to Sophia.

"Upon initial inspection of the body, what did you discover?"

Now listen closely, you two. We're playing this off as a bear attack. We want her out of here as quickly as possible and that's the only way of doing it. I heard Knox's order ring out quickly and sternly.

"When I approached her, I noticed her bones were broken in several different places." Sophia walked up to the corpse with Blanca following her; Knox and I were close behind. "Her neck, arms and legs appear to be broken based on their angles. I checked for a pulse at both the neck and wrist, but found none. I attempted CPR and noticed that the lacerations on her chest and abdomen had gone deep enough to puncture her lungs. They were filled with blood and I pronounced her dead at 9:23 this morning." Sophia seemed quite proud of herself to be spouting off to the agent. Knox gave her a nod.

If only everyone's reports could be as detailed... I stiffened when I heard Knox's mental mutter.

"And what did you make of these lacerations?" Blanca asked after jotting down a few more notes.

"Usually when things like this happen, it's an animal attack. We have a lot of people who bother the local fauna, thinking they are used to interacting with humans, when they are not. The lacerations look like they came from bear claws to me. I surmise that Danielle must have been with her camera crew, because I doubt she'd be out here alone with a microphone, and they probably spotted a bear and tried to approach it. Surely, the bear felt threatened and chased them through the woods, and she ended up here. I imagine this deep laceration along her chest was the final blow. She must have bled out and died." Sophia shrugged at the end to indicate there was nothing more to it in her opinion.

"If there was a camera crew, where are they?" Blanca asked, scanning the area.

"I just assumed they must have run in a different direction when the bear came after them," Sophia stated.

"We don't make *assumptions*. Someone will have to find them if they are lost in the woods." Blanca gave the woman a hard look before her eyes returned to the battered body of Danielle, seemingly deep in thought. "Do you have a sign at the entrance of the park indicating that animals should not be disturbed?"

"Yes, we do. If you drove in, you would have seen it. I'd be happy to show it to you if you'd like," Knox replied in a friendly manner, but I could tell that he didn't like being questioned.

"We find that not everyone reads the signs or listens to the warnings when it comes to the animals. This is a clear example of that." I said, backing up my Alpha.

"Hmm...possibly..." Blanca looked deep in thought as she continued to stare at the body.

Knox, Sophia, and I exchanged concerned expressions.

"What are you implying?" Knox asked sternly after a beat.

Blanca didn't address him and instead, looked up at Sophia. "Could these injuries have been caused by a human?"

"What? What makes you think that?" Sophia looked completely perplexed by the question; perhaps overly so. Goodness knew the woman wasn't going to get nominated for an Academy Award anytime soon.

"Is it possible?" Blanca asked sternly. "Please answer the question."

Sophia looked at Knox, her lips firmly pressed together. Knox gave a curt nod.

"I mean...yes, it's possible. A human couldn't deal this kind of damage with just his or her hands alone. The suspect would need a weapon of some sort."

"A weapon like what?" Blanca's expression grew much more interested and I felt a rumble of foreboding travel through me.

"I don't know. Maybe a large fishing hook if used the right way, like a kind used for deep sea fishing? Or those ones with multiple points, treble hooks? There aren't many things that could cause the type of damage we're seeing, honestly."

"But if the person was trying to make it *look* like a bear attack, they would pay special attention to something like that..." Blanca's face was still clouded over by her intense thinking. I could practically see theories as they dashed across her mind.

What the hell? Is this chick crazy? Sophia's voice echoed.

Come on Knox, now she's just making stuff up. We know this was a shifter in bear form. There's no way a human did this! I was on the same page as Sophia, for once.

"You've all gone quiet, so I guess you think I'm insane or something, but this is my job: to speculate. So, until more evidence is found and this is confirmed *by me* to be a bear attack, I will continue to speculate that this could possibly be a murder. I'll be conducting a week-long investigation here, and if nothing points to a murderer in that time, I'll leave. If something *does* turn up that could indicate anything else—anything at all—then that's what I'll pursue in my investigation." Blanca looked at each of us, and lingered on me especially, narrowing her eyes.

Why does she keep looking at me like that? I squinted my eyes in return.

"I expect everyone's *full cooperation* during my investigation. If any other information about the case turns up, you are to report directly to me, including you, Mr. Bernard."

I took a broad step forward, bristling. "Who the hell do you think you—"

"Stand down, Trent!" Knox glared at me, holding an arm out in front of me to prevent my advance. My blood was boiling. I wasn't about to let this lady step onto our territory and take over. I only answered to Knox, period.

"You will have our full cooperation, I assure you." Knox addressed Blanca directly, who was glaring at me intensely. Our gazes pierced through each other's and my anger rose. I felt my body start to shake, threatening to explode with energy at any moment.

Knox grabbed my arm tight enough that would hurt a normal

human, but was just enough to snap me out of my thoughts. *I said to stand down.*

I took a deep breath and swallowed, hoping my anger would dissipate.

"I have rounds to do," I growled before I turned to leave.

"If someone is found responsible, I'll need you to show me the holding quarters for criminals," I heard Blanca's voice call out as I started to walk away, but I didn't turn around to acknowledge her.

"I can help you with that," Knox replied; I heard the smile in his voice and it made the fire in me burn that much hotter.

Who was he kidding? I knew he wasn't happy, but whatever; he could put on a show for the feds if he wanted to. That wasn't in my job description and way above my pay grade. He asked me to be cooperative and I was. I told her everything I knew about finding the body.

Except the footprints...

I hope you're going out to catch this guy, whoever he is, so we can keep him out of sight until she is gone. Knox didn't seem angry at me for walking away, just adamant about what I should be spending my time doing.

I'm on it.

I really hoped this guy was stupid and just carelessly left a trail of his footprints out in the open for me to follow straight to him. But once I found him, maybe I would get really lucky and he would put up a fight.

Because hell, I was certainly in the mood for one.

4

TRENT

AFTER ABOUT HALF AN HOUR, I PICKED UP ON A TRAIL OF FOOTPRINTS. They were oddly arranged, however, with uneven weight distribution and sporadic gait length. It looked like the person had tried to retrace their steps backwards a few times, but had wobbled and lost their place more than once. Then, the prints grew deep, like the shifter had been running as quickly as he or she could.

I considered changing into my bear form to find the assailant more quickly, but decided against it; I wasn't sure if Blanca had Alex and Gerard doing their own patrolling and I didn't need them thinking I was the culprit.

I continued to follow the footprints as best I could through the woodlands and then, I saw it.

A huge puddle of blood.

I looked around quickly, trying to find the source, and I spotted drops of crimson liquid heading west. I started walking slowly, following the trail, and moments later, my boot collided with something. I had been so deep in thought that I nearly gave myself a heart attack. Looking down, I saw what I had stubbed my foot on and heaved the mightiest sigh I had ever uttered.

Two men were sprawled out in front of me, still and lifeless. One was a skinny guy with shoulder-length blonde hair; the other was a chubby ginger. Cuts and bites were apparent all over their bodies, staining the ground with a sticky pool of their blood. They didn't seem to have as many broken bones as Danielle did, but they obviously hadn't needed a grand, dramatic fall to end their lives.

Dammit, the shifter had struck again.

I examined the corpses to see if I could figure out who they were. I noticed a tripod and camera lying in the dirt a few feet from the bodies, as well as a boom mic, so I assumed they were Danielle's camera crew.

In that moment, I realized why I was having so much trouble following the footprints: I was following two pairs of human feet coupled with the shifter's, and they were all scrambled together from the chase that had taken place.

"Who the fuck is doing this shit?" I growled out loud. It had become personal. Whoever the shifter was, he was making more trouble for me.

Knox, we've got two more by Eagle Lake. Looks like Sophia was right: the camera guys ran, and the shifter went after them, too. They're both dead.

You've got to me kidding me! Knox seemed as fed up with the situation as I was. *I'm with the agent now, so I need you to call me to deliver the news. Pretend like you didn't tell me because I have a feeling she'll be listening very closely. I can take her to the bodies and hopefully that will stall her long enough for you to be able to find this asshole! We need to catch him before this gets even more out of hand.*

I whipped out my cellphone and pressed 1.

"Bernard," Knox answered apathetically.

"Hey Knox, it's Trent. I think I found the bodies of Danielle's camera crew. You might want to come take a look with the agent."

"What? More bodies? This is getting ridiculous. Where did you find them?"

"Out here on Eagle Lake. Should I wait here for you two to arrive?" I really didn't want to have another encounter with Blanca if I didn't have to, so I was really hoping he was going to say no to that last part.

"No, you don't have to stay there. Call Sophia and have her come examine the bodies so Agent Gianni here can have some more information by the time she gets there."

Phew.

"Will do sir."

I hung up the phone and started walking again, reaching out to Sophia.

Hey Soph, I left a present for you on the western part of Eagle Lake. Follow the blood trail and you can't miss it.

More bodies? I could sense her excitement. She really enjoyed her job, as gruesome as it could be. We didn't see dead bodies often, so three in one day must have been like a party for her—a macabre, headache of a party that threatened our entire clan.

Your favorite, I snorted.

I'll be right there!

Just try to get here before the agent does. You know she's going to want information. She didn't answer me, but I figured she was on her way to the location.

During the conversation, I'd been looking around the bodies for either bear or human prints that could have lead me to the shifter, but it proved extremely difficult to see beyond the blood to sort out anything that could have been mixed in with the footprints of the camera guys. I knew the shifter's tracks were there, though, so I kept going.

A few minutes later, I found them. They were bear prints, alright.

Boy, were they bloody, too. I imagined the bastard was tracking the red trails from his victims on his paws, which just made things easier for me to be able to find them.

"Still here?" Sophia startled me as she came upon the scene, running up to the bodies to examine them quickly.

"Just found the shifter's prints and I'm going after them. Have fun with your corpses." I started walking away without even looking at her, focused on discerning the bear prints from the human ones.

"Oh, you know I will," she called out after me and I snickered.

IT TOOK me about ten minutes to find him. I took in a long, deep whiff of the cool forest air as I spotted him.

Based on his pheromones, the shifter's most definitely a male.

He was still in bear form and hunched over the water, trying to catch some fish. His fur was coated in blood and I wondered why he hadn't bothered to jump in the lake and wash himself off.

Why is he still in bear form? Maybe he figured he could blend in with the park's bear population and not be noticed? Whatever his reasoning, it pissed me off that he had killed three people and was looking for something to eat like nothing had happened.

I walked out from the tree I was hiding behind until the bear could see me clearly.

"My name is Trent Bailey and I'm the Law Enforcement Ranger of this park. I am a shifter as well and ask that you please return to your human form so I can ask you some questions." I really hoped he didn't listen. I was holding my anger off for the moment, but I could feel it bubbling underneath the surface.

The bear glared at me and then let out a roar, standing on his two hind legs.

He wasn't going to come easily. The bear wanted to play hard ball, but I was ready for it. I removed my clothes quickly, not taking my eyes off him; I needed my uniform intact since I didn't have any spares nearby.

The change ripped through me, shredding my human form and snapping my bones as a towering black bear rose where I had once stood. In my bear form, I was taller than most and brawly, which meant I won almost all the fights people were stupid enough to challenge me to.

The battle awaiting me would be no different.

The beast charged at me with full force, swiping his claws at my head, making me jump back. I dodged a bit too late and the bear's claws grazed my chest.

I growled and threw my weight onto the bear, crashing down on him and clawing away until his breath was ragged. I unleashed all the pent-up anger that had been building as the day progressed with no pausing and no mercy.

It didn't take long for the shifter to stop fighting back. He shuddered and sank to the ground, bleeding. He was nowhere near as bad as his victims had been, but I wanted him alive for questioning.

Where was he from? Why had he killed those people?

I guessed it didn't matter too much, because once the conclave was presented with the overwhelming evidence against him, he would be executed on the spot.

I grimaced as I thought of what had happened the last time they had met. The conclave was the shifters' counsel and they handled all crimes within the shifter community of the region. Evidence was presented to them and they decided the verdict they felt was best punishment for the crimes committed. With three humans dead, they weren't going to be lenient in any way, shape or form.

I honestly couldn't wait to see that.

Due to his injuries, the shifter's body was no longer able to hold his bear form and he began to morph back to his human state. He had dark brown spiked hair, a lanky frame and was average height for a guy who weighed no more than 200 pounds. He was naked and covered in semi-dried as well as fresh blood; a mix of his victims' and his own.

I'm going to have to find him some clothes. Quickly. People would most definitely have noticed if I was dragging around a naked man in handcuffs, and I sure as hell I didn't need the attention.

His breathing was rough, but he was still alive, and that's all that mattered to me. He didn't even deserve that much, of course, but we had trials for a reason. I guessed his injuries would be fully healed in about an hour and he would be fine.

I shifted back to human form and began to dress myself, the scratches on my chest already scabbed over.

Good. The last thing I needed was blood on my shirt to make Blanca think I was the culprit. I quickly put the rest of my uniform back on, keeping my eyes on the shifter. I removed the pair of handcuffs I kept clipped to my belt and snapped them around the guy's wrists; he struggled a little, but obviously didn't have enough strength to fight me.

Like mine, his wounds were already beginning to heal. They weren't scabbed over like mine, but he'd stopped bleeding. I needed to hurry if I wanted to take advantage of his weakened state for transport.

"You are in so much trouble. I can't wait to see what they do with you," I growled into his ear as I lifted him up. I reached out to Knox with my mind again.

Found him. I started walking toward the lodges to find some clothes for the asshole. *Are you guys still at Eagle Lake with the bodies?*

Yeah, we just got here a few minutes ago. Take him to the holding area.

What are we going to do with him?

She's not going to be able to close the case without questioning him, obvi-

ously, so we have no choice but to allow Agent Gianni to proceed with her interrogation of the suspect.

But Knox, shouldn't he be presented to the conclave for—

He should be, seeing as how he's taken three lives, but remember, Acadia is technically federal property, so we have to let the feds investigate. But that doesn't mean we can't make it look like the crime was committed by a human; we have to protect the clan, after all. Take him into holding. I'm going to need you to head over to the fishing lodge and dig up a deep-sea treble hook or two that you can say you found on him; we're going to go with that as the murder weapon. Oh, and don't clean him up. It'll look better if he still has the victims' blood all over him. It's evening; I doubt the agent will want to question him now, so I'll tell her that a suspect has been found and will be kept in our holdings for her to question in the morning. You are to personally keep an eye on him in the meantime.

Understood. After the day we had, I didn't have the energy to argue with Knox anymore. He was irritated enough, with the worst crime in our recorded history taking place on his day off.

When we finally reached the holding lodge, I grabbed a shirt and sweatpants from my office for the shifter, then removed his handcuffs and pushed him into the cell. He still hadn't said a word, but his wounds were almost completely healed, so I knew he would be conscious enough to talk in a short while.

"Guess who you get to spend the night with?" I sneered. "And don't bother trying to change again. These bars are specially made to withstand bear strength. You're not going anywhere."

5

BLANCA

This case is turning into a handful.

I was staring down at the bodies of Danielle's camera crew, which Sophia was examining.

"Do you guys usually have this many deaths in one day?" I raised an eyebrow at Knox, who was also studying the bodies with a serious expression.

"I can assure you, this is the first time anything of this magnitude has happened and I am just as eager as you are to find the culprit."

He didn't look at me when he spoke, but it was then that I decided to trust him. He seemed shook up by the whole ordeal; I was good at reading people and I could tell he wasn't behind the killings.

So that made one of them I felt I could trust.

I wasn't too sure about Sophia yet; she was so nonchalant about the bodies and something about that bugged me. Maybe she had so many years in practice, she was immune to it. I could relate, though; some would say the same about me and I'd only been with the FBI for three years.

I thought back to the pilot's words and wished I was there on vacation as I looked out at Eagle Lake. *Man, this lake is beautiful.* It was at least fifteen miles wide and I could only see mountains in the distance. The view was amazing.

Or at least, it would have been, if it weren't for the pair of corpses and the flies they were beginning to attract.

Sophia stood up. "Alright, I'm not finding a pulse or heartbeat on either. Definitely dead. Judging by the injuries, I'd say these two line up completely with Danielle's death. Whatever killed her got these guys, too."

"I was afraid you'd say that."

So not only did I have to deal with Danielle's death, I had two more on my hands. "So, either we're dealing with a rogue bear on a killing streak, or a murderer trying to make his kills look like bear attacks."

I wasn't used to murder cases in nature. Usually, homicides occurred in buildings or parking lots and there was a weapon close by, fingerprints on the bodies or some other kind of surface. But there were no fingerprints on any of the corpses other than Sophia's. I checked myself and dusted Danielle's entire crime scene. There was nothing else to get fingerprints on that millions of other people hadn't touched before. We were surrounded by nothing but lakes and the Atlantic, wet rocks, mountains, trees, flowers, grass and dirt.

I had nothing to go on and it irked the hell out of me.

"So, what do you think the story is so far, Sophia?"

She was looking at the bodies and then glanced back in the direction of Danielle's remains, trying to piece it together with me.

"Well, I do think you were right about a couple of things, for sure. Whoever killed Danielle also murdered these two guys. Your hypothesis about it killing Danielle first and the camera guys running away seems to line up as well. Based on the blood trail we found leading up to this point, it's safe to say, whatever it was, chased these men to this point and did them in, too."

So, I knew the 'what,' 'when,' and 'where' of the story. There were two possible 'hows.' 'Who' and 'why' were still left to be uncovered, and I had no idea where to start.

For the first time ever, I was completely stumped, but I refused to accept it. There was always a clue, somewhere, somehow. If it was a wild animal, there would be clues to lead us to it. If the killer was human, surely, he or she wasn't skilled enough not to leave *any* shred of evidence behind.

Right?

I looked at Alex and Gerard who were still studying the bodies. Alex had his hand to his chin like he was thinking very hard. He glanced up at me and shrugged.

"Ughhhhh!"

I cried out my frustration before I even realized it and stomped my foot. It was a childish move, but I hated when things weren't going according to plan. Things always went my way. When they didn't, I *made them* go my way.

"It's getting a bit late; the sun is setting," Sophia said as she looked into the distance. When my gaze followed her, I saw that she was right.

6pm already? I was shocked when I looked at my watch. It felt like we had only been there for a couple of hours.

"Maybe we should pick up the search tomorrow, Blanca, and just get these bodies taken care of for today?"

Gerard appeared concerned and tired. Alex looked exhausted as well; we *all* were.

"I'm sorry, guys, but you know I can't do that. Tracks could be covered, evidence could be moved. This is nature, where animals roam free. They could bury the murder weapon themselves if there is one. The killer, whether human or bear, could be long gone by now. We have to keep looking." I gave them both pleading expressions and they nodded.

"Sophia, will you help me take care of the bodies?" She nodded. "Alex and Gerard, I want you guys to scout the area. I know Trent is out there, but having three people looking is better than one. Call me if you find *anything*."

Frankly, I still didn't trust Trent. He was probably out brooding about someone taking over and making him feel like less of man.

Although I can't imagine why with looks like that...

I shook my head. *Business, Blanca*. Besides, what would I want with a guy like that? It wasn't like he was devastatingly handsome with a strong jaw and—

Focus!

Sophia and I each started toward a body while Alex and Gerard were about to head into the woods.

"Actually, that won't be necessary."

Knox's voice stopped us in our tracks. I looked over to see him close his phone with an overly emphasized 'click.' I had been so preoccupied with what I should do next, I hadn't been paying much attention to him. He was a couple feet away, so I guessed he must have walked over to take a phone call while we were talking.

"What's up?" I asked. I was done with the formalities at this point. I was exhausted and there was a lovely hotel room in Bar Harbor waiting for me. It had a pool and that was the first place I was going after my shower.

"Trent found the murderer."

My mouth dropped. "What?"

"Looks like you were right, Ms. Gianni. He was about to jump into one of our lakes to wash himself off, when Trent was able to tackle and handcuff him. He is covered in blood and Trent found some treble hooks with him. It looks like he cleaned those off already, though."

"So, where is he? Let's go to him now. Alex and Gerard can take care of the bodies." I nodded to my agents and they started toward the corpses.

"I'm sorry, Ms. Gianni, but I'm going to have to call this one. I think you should get some rest. We have the murderer in custody and Trent is perfectly capable of holding him overnight. The suspect will be waiting for you in the holding area in the morning and you can question him then." Knox's voice didn't seem evasive. He looked genuinely concerned.

I thought about it for a moment. I really wanted to talk to the suspect, but even once I figured it all out, I'd have to call a pilot to bring us back to headquarters. I knew the chances of us being picked up tonight would be slim because only the emergency ones were left on duty for the day. And this was hardly an emergency.

I also kind of wanted to enjoy my hotel room for at least one night.

"Okay, fine. I will question him in the morning, but I want my own agents guarding him. No offense or anything. I am very grateful to Trent for finding the guy and I would appreciate if you could tell him that, but I would feel more comfortable with Alex and Gerard guarding the suspect."

Knox thought about it for a moment and then nodded.

"Okay. I'm sure that can be arranged."

"Thank you." I walked over to Alex and Gerard. "I'm sorry, guys. I know you're exhausted, but I just don't trust that Trent guy enough to leave him alone with the suspect."

"It's okay, we understand. We'll guard him like a hawk until you get there." Alex said, and Gerard nodded.

"I'll be there to relieve you in the morning and then you guys can go rest while I conduct the interrogation. Make sure you take shifts during the night."

"Sophia, why don't you drive Ms. Gianni to her hotel? I'll take the guys over to the holding area and relieve Trent for the night."

Sophia nodded and smiled at me. Knox motioned for my agents to follow him and they did.

"Come on, Blanca, my Jeep is back at Hunters Beach."

I followed her as we walked back to where Danielle's body was found. Sophia seemed friendly and good at her job. After some thought, I decided that I trusted her after all. She was very thorough in her reports to me and I saw a bit of myself in her work ethic.

"Hey, so what's the story behind this Trent guy? Does he usually have problems with authority?" I asked jokingly to test the waters with the woman. It helped that I also wanted the scoop on the guy and she seemed like the best person to ask.

"Not necessarily. He just doesn't like people messing with his job. He's pretty serious about it." Sophia shrugged.

"He just seems so edgy around me," I said, moving branches out of my way while we walked through the trees, the forest thick and lush all around us.

"Oh, he's edgy around *everyone*. Don't take it personally," Sophia laughed. "He doesn't like to get close to people; he had a rough childhood. It took me a year and half to even get him to have a normal conversation with me. But, once he gets to know you, he can be a really sweet guy."

Sophia talked about Trent like they were close. "Are you two…a couple?" I asked, trying to sound casual.

"Me and Trent? No way! More like brother and sister!" Sophia was laughing again, and I felt at ease. She was surprisingly calming to talk to, which was certainly refreshing after the long day we had.

"So, what happened to him? Trent, I mean." I asked curiously. Part of my question was just small talk, but the other part wanted to know more about him. He was so reserved and seemed so angry all the time—or at least around me. He was like a puzzle that I wanted to solve and tuck away so I would never have to think of it again.

"His dad abandoned him and his mom when he was a kid. When they moved, there was a police officer who was very friendly towards him and seemed to be getting close to his mother very quickly. He basically adopted the kid, but without the paperwork. Trent really liked the guy and wanted to be just like him when he grew up. One day, the officer got gunned down in the line of duty. When Trent and his mother found out, they were devastated. Trent doesn't seem to have ever gotten over it." Sophia sounded sad, her voice dropped and she wasn't smiling anymore. Her pace had slowed as well.

"I'm sorry, I didn't mean to pry." I touched her arm and she looked up at me and smiled.

"It's okay. I just worry about him sometimes...Oh, look! The Jeep is just beyond these trees here."

Sophia started sprinting toward her vehicle and I followed, sorting out my thoughts at this new revelation.

Maybe I had been a little too hard on Trent. He was obviously good enough at his job that he found the murderer when I didn't have a clue what to do next. I decided that when I saw him in the morning, I would be a little nicer to him.

Maybe.

If he lost the attitude.

"You getting in?" Sophia called from the driver side.

I didn't realize I had stopped walking. "Oh yeah, sorry!" I hopped in the Jeep, just a little more prepared for the next day than I had been earlier.

6

TRENT

Can you just wake up already?

I was sitting in front of the cell housing our new suspect with my arms crossed, waiting for him to wake up. He was still unconscious, just lying on the floor.

I know I didn't beat him up that badly, I thought, rolling my eyes and sighing. It was going to be a long night if he didn't wake up.

It appeared I spoke too soon, because at that moment, he started to twitch. He was lying on his side, facing the back of the cell. As he slowly sat up, I could see his head turning from side to side, noticing walls in each direction. Then, he rotated his body towards me.

I could see the confusion working its way through his facial expression. His brow furrowed as he studied me and the office around us. Something told me he didn't like what he saw because that confusion quickly shifted to anger as he bared his teeth.

"Whoa! Hold on there, sir!" I said calmly, raising my hands up in surrender. I wanted him to know that I wasn't going to hurt him—not because I didn't want to, but because I wasn't allowed to.

The shifter's expression didn't change.

"What's your name?" I asked, seeing if I could get him talking, but he just growled and glared at me angrily, as if I was threatening him in some way. "You're detained because you were found covered in blood after three bodies were discovered. You are being held as the primary suspect in these murders and I would appreciate your cooperat—"

The shifter unleashed a mighty roar and slammed his fists against the bars. His eyes were crazed, bloodshot, and his pupils had almost dilated completely, giving the appearance of sclera lens.

My eyes widened in horror. *What the fuck is this guy's problem?*

I stood and walked over to my desk, my eyes glued to the detainee. I'd never seen a shifter behave like that before; it was almost like the bear's mind had taken over completely and it no longer mattered what form he took.

No, it was more than that. Bears weren't notorious for being angry creatures, especially within the shifter community. Our inner bears tended to react to our human emotions; our minds and bodies have been one and the same. What one felt, the other felt.

This one, however, seemed to have no connection with his human conscious. The bear mind was ravenous and enraged like it was in constant fight mode.

And what's wrong with his eyes? They're only supposed to get like that during the full moon. I was completely clueless; the full moon was weeks away.

Just then, I swore I saw something. The banging had stopped, and the shifter was just holding onto the bars of the cell with the same angry expression—only I could have sworn I saw paws holding the bars, not human hands.

Oh, come on, man. He couldn't have shifted that quickly without you noticing!

I brushed off the thought with a shake of my head. It had been a long day, and surely, I was just getting tired. I slapped myself a bit to wake up; I had to watch the guy all night and I didn't want to doze off, so I decided to keep trying to engage him.

As I walked back over to the chair in front of the shifter's cell, his eyes followed my every move with a look of menace, like he would leap on me at any moment if he got the chance to.

I lowered myself into the seat slowly, keeping my eyes in contact with his the entire time. "Let's try this again, huh? Are you ready to tell me your name?" I raised an eyebrow at him and rested my elbows on my knees. I wasn't afraid of the guy and I wanted him to know that.

Then, it happened. It was only for a brief second, but this time, I was sure. I wasn't just tired, and I wasn't seeing things.

The shifter's snarl had briefly morphed into a bear snout right before my eyes. It was quick, gone again when I blinked, but I saw his nose elongate as it shifted, and when I had opened my eyes again, it was back to a human nose.

I stared at him in complete, wide-eyed wonder. My brain couldn't register this partial shift; I'd never seen anything like it. Was this of his own volition?

"And here's Trent's office, which is also where the holding cells are located." I jumped out of my seat, startled by Knox's voice as he entered the room with Alex and Gerard following him. Knox gave me a look of concern when he saw me; he must have sensed that I was surprised by their entrance.

"Agent Gianni requested that her men be the ones to guard the suspect overnight and I accepted. I am here to relieve you for the night—"

"They can't!" I shook my head wildly, starting to panic. After what I just saw, there was no way I was letting the agents near the cell.

"Now is no time to be possessive over your office, Trent. You've been on duty since 8am and you could use the rest." Knox motioned for me to follow him outside. I looked from the agents to the cell frantically. There was nothing I could say in that moment as an excuse for why I didn't want them guarding the cell that wouldn't completely give our kind away, so I reached out to Knox with my mind.

I'll go outside with you, but we need to talk.

Knox nodded, and I quickly walked out the door, hoping that after I told him what I saw, he would be able to come up with an excuse as to why the agents couldn't guard the cell.

As soon as we got outside, I told Knox everything I had seen and heard: the dilated pupils, the roars, the growls, the bear paws and the snout. My arms were gesturing wildly, and I could feel myself talking a mile a minute, but I couldn't slow down. I had to get those agents out of there. And Knox had to help me.

"Okay, Trent. I need you to calm the fuck down." Knox grabbed my shoulders and shook me once—hard. I hadn't realized I was almost hyperventilating from the panic I felt at the thought of the agents seeing a fraction of what I just saw. We *had* to get back in there.

"Now you see why I can't just leave them in there! We have to go back!" I struggled to try and release myself from Knox's grip, but he had always been stronger than me. It was why he was Alpha, and I was his Beta.

"I'm not letting you go until you calm down. Take a deep breath."

I drew in a deep gulp of air, holding it in for a couple of seconds and then released it, channeling all my panic and thoughts.

"Good. Now, this is very alarming. I don't want you to think I'm not taking you seriously; I am. But there is no way I can ask those gentlemen to leave. I already accepted the request to have them guard the suspect for the night and we must allow them to do that. I don't want us *both* under investigation for not honoring her request."

I opened my mouth to interject, but Knox raised a hand to stop me.

"Those agents are very tired. And I imagine when I bring them coffee lightly tainted with sleeping meds, the only things they'll be seeing are the backs of their eyelids."

I nodded slowly. Knox made sense, but I was still concerned.

"So, what are we going to do about the shifter? We can't just hand him off anymore."

Knox nodded and looked deep in thought for a few moments.

"Okay. What I need you to do is contact Ramon. Sneak him in with some excuse and get him to test the shifter's blood. We need to find out what's wrong with him."

Ramon Marquez was our Resource Manager who came to us from Cabo Pulma National Park in Mexico. He oversaw biology, botany, aquatics, soil science and geology for the park as well as for the clan—specifically when it came to biology. He was working on genetic research that would create stronger traits in our clan, which was why he was brought to Acadia.

I agreed with Knox: he was the best person to help figure out what was going on.

"Alright, I'll wait here for him."

"Good. I'm going to go get those fellows their coffees and head back to the lodge with Hannah. She's been blowing up my phone all day. As soon as you and Ramon learn anything, reach out to me immediately.

And don't take anything into your own hands." Knox gave me a very serious look and I nodded.

"I've got this. Go to Hannah before she decides to come looking for you." I smiled a little, still concerned about the situation, but I didn't want Knox to see that.

His phone rang, and he sighed as he answered the call.

"Yes, babe? I'm coming home right now. I'm sorry I couldn't pick up earlier; you won't believe the day I've had…." Knox's voice trailed off as he headed back to the detainment area.

I watched him close the door behind him and then found a good place to hide: a crowd of trees close to the holding lodge. I didn't want Alex or Gerard to come out for fresh air or something and see me watching them. Once I felt secure in my surroundings, I reached out to Ramon.

Aye, Trent. My man. What's up, amigo? I could tell Ramon was happy to hear from me. Once I thought about it, I hadn't talked to him in almost a week. I was glad to hear his voice too, but there wasn't much time to catch up.

Hey man, we've got a problem. I need you to come to the holding lodge with a testing kit as soon as possible.

What am I going to be testing? I could hear the interest in Ramon's voice.

Blood, I believe. You might need to get some hair samples, too.

I'll be right there. Ramon's voice was serious, and I could tell he'd be ready when he arrived.

All I had to do was wait and hope nothing freakish happened until he came.

7

TRENT

I SPOTTED RAMON APPROACHING THE DOOR OF THE LODGING AREA.

"Pssstttttt..." I whispered with my hands cupped over my mouth. Ramon whipped his head around quickly, trying to find the source of the sound. I threw a stone in his direction. "Over here!"

He finally saw me and walked over to the trees with a confused expression.

"What the hell you are you doing over here, man?" Ramon looked through the trees at me, brushing some branches out of the way and crouched down beside me.

"I figured I'd just explain things when you got here, because it's kind of a long story."

I told him about finding Danielle's body, the two camera guys and the shifter who we knew was responsible for it all. When I started describing the odd things I witnessed when observing the shifter in his cell, Ramon's eyes went wide, and his gaze panned from me to the holding lodge repeatedly.

"*Diablo*, man. That's crazy!" I nodded, and Ramon shook his head. He knew this wasn't good. "So how are you getting me in there?"

"I have a plan," I said, motioning for him to follow me as I stood up and walked through the doors of the holding lodge.

Alex and Gerard were reading some papers and taking the first few sips of their coffees when we entered. They looked up when they saw me walk in and seemed confused by my presence.

"What brings you back?" Alex asked, putting down his magazine and sizing up Ramon who was standing beside me.

"Yeah, weren't you relieved for the night? We can handle this." Gerard appeared a little agitated.

"I'm here to help Agent Gianni. I figured it would save her a lot of work in the morning if I brought someone in to test the dried blood on the suspect's body—you know, to see if it matches the victims'." I held my hands up, showing I meant no harm.

Alex kept his eyes on me for a long time and finally decided I must be telling the truth, so he nodded at Gerard to step aside and let us through.

"We were due for a smoke break anyway, right Alex?" Gerard pulled out a pack of Marlboro Reds and I scrunched my face, slightly disgusted. I never liked cigarettes, and was glad they were stepping outside to smoke. I would not have been happy to smell the cancerous stench in my office in the morning.

Ramon and I watched them leave, and once we heard the door close behind them, we headed straight for the cell. The shifter took one look at us and jumped toward the bars with the same pitch-black eyes that I saw before.

"*Mierda*!" Ramon exclaimed, taking a step back from the cell as the shifter tried to push his mouth between the bars, gnashing and gnawing at the air. Ramon looked mostly surprised, but I could sense a hint of fear as well.

"I told you something was wrong with him. We don't have much time to do this, so I'll go in there and restrain him. You grab the blood and hair samples, and then we'll run back out and test it. Make sure to grab some dried blood samples, too, so we have something to show the agent in the morning. Got it?"

Ramon's eyes moved from me to the shifter and back. His expression reflected his worry, but he finally nodded and started to fumble through his kit for his armamentarium.

I grabbed the keys to the cell, "Just let me know when you're good." I glanced back at him, key at the ready. Ramon held up a few vials, a knife, a needle and a tourniquet.

"Ready."

With that, I took a deep breath and shoved the shifter's face back through the bars and opened the cell door with my other hand. I pounced on him, grabbing both his arms, pinning them to his back with one hand and held his face down with the other. Ramon was just staring at us as I fought to keep the bastard still.

"Hurry up, man! What are you standing there for?" I yelled through gritted teeth. I was using almost all my strength to keep this guy held down and I wasn't sure how long I'd be able to do it.

My voice seemed to have snapped Ramon out of whatever shock he was experiencing. It wasn't hard for him to find a vein; as he stuck the needle into the shifter's arm, our eyes widened a bit as we watched his blood flow into the vial.

"Isn't it—"

"Blacker than it should be? Yes." Ramon's voice was serious now. His brow furrowed as he studied the ebony liquid filling the tube in his hands. "I'm going to need more than one. How much longer can you hold him?"

"A minute. Tops." The suspect was kicking his legs wildly and I didn't have enough hands to hold those down, too.

Ramon filled the next two vials in seconds. "That's all I'll need." Grabbing his knife, he cut a piece of the shifter's hair, placed it in a separate vial and hauled ass out of the cell. "Okay, but now how are you getting out of there?"

"I'm going to count to three. On three, I want you to close the cell door and turn the key."

"What? *¿Estás loco?* I'm not leaving you in there with Chupacabra!"

"Just do it! Trust me! There's no more time!" I yelled. Ramon nodded, and I started counting. "One...Two..."

"Three!" I used the last of my energy to push my strength to its limit, allowing me to exit the cell in one second, slamming the door behind me. I heard the lock click as I knelt down and caught my breath. I was breathing heavily and looked up to see Alex and Gerard returning to their post.

"Too much for you to handle, Mr. Bailey?" Alex joked, and Gerard chuckled before letting out a yawn.

The meds must be starting to kick in. I rolled my eyes and stood up slowly, trying not to show my exhaustion.

Ramon was staring at the cell, watching the suspect just sitting on the floor, glaring in our direction.

"Well, did you get the blood samples?" a sleepy-eyed Gerard asked.

We both looked at him and nodded. Little did he know, they weren't the blood samples he thought we got.

"I have to get them back to the lab to test, but the results should be ready in the morning, before Agent Gianni returns," Ramon said as he started walking towards the door, "now, if you'll excuse us..."

"You boys have a great night and make yourselves at home," I added, motioning around my office with a forced smile and walked out after Ramon.

"Hey, man. Wait up!" I called, trying to catch up to him as he made a beeline for his lab.

"*Lo siento*, but I have to get this back to the lab, Trent. I know that *pendejo* killed a bunch of people, but he's obviously very sick."

"What do you think it is? There aren't many things that can do us in." It's not like we were taught shifter biology in school; everything we knew was passed down by our parents and the rest of the clan, and I'd never learned anything about what I'd just witnessed in the cell.

"You're right. There aren't very many things that can infect us—not viruses like the common cold or the flu, at least, but we're susceptible to HIV/AIDS. We can develop cancer, too, but I've never seen any illnesses like this. I have to figure out what's going on with him and more importantly, figure out if it can spread to our clan in any way." Ramon's face was filled with worry and as he explained how the information could affect the clan, I felt his same concern.

"Is it okay if I come with you? Knox asked me to report anything we find back to him."

"Of course, *amigo*! Your company is always welcome." With that, Ramon's worry seemed to have vanished for the moment and was replaced by a smile—one I had missed for a while.

The tragedy at Acadia was causing a lot of trouble, but I couldn't help but think that it was bringing the clan closer together as well.

RAMON WAS MUNCHING on some microwave pizza in one hand and adjusting his microscope with the other. I was sitting across the room laughing hysterically at the sight.

"Won't that cause cross contamination or something?" I shook my head at him.

"The only contamination happening here is your breath polluting the air!" Ramon joked, using a dropper to apply a solution to the blood on the slide. I couldn't see what it was, but even if I could, I wouldn't be able to tell what he was using. I was never really into science; there were too many exact measurements and calculations for me. The law was simple, and I liked it. Everything was there in black and white, plain as day, and all I had to do was enforce it. Plus, spending my day in a stuffy lab was not my idea of fun.

Ramon squinted over the eyepiece and all went quiet for a bit. I had already watched him test the dried blood samples and there was no surprise there. We found the blood of all three victims on him and Ramon was able to give me a report stating that, so I could pass it on to agent Gianni in the morning.

I looked around his lab and realized there wasn't much there: a desktop computer in one corner of the room, some lab coats along the wall, a sink, some supply cabinets, and a big table in the middle of the room that currently had a bunch of science crap on it. I had no idea what most of it was or what he used them for.

"Trent, you've gotta see this, man!" Ramon's voice sounded both panicked and excited as he looked into his microscope. I jumped out of my seat, walking over to him quickly.

"What's up?"

"Take a look." Ramon stepped aside.

At first, I didn't know what I was looking at. It looked like a bunch of black and dark red dots just floating around on a lighter red background. Then something started to happen. The black dots were drifting closer to the red ones and once they reached their targets, it was like they were swallowing the red dots whole.

"What the hell..." I guessed the red dots were the shifter's blood cells, but what were the black ones?

"Exactamente." Ramon was shaking his head and I could tell he was thinking the same thing. "That is no cancer I have ever seen."

"So, what do you think it could be?"

"I have no idea, but I'm definitely going to have to do more testing on this blood. Whatever that guy is infected with is swallowing his cells whole, which is why the sample is almost completely black. It has obviously affected the neurons controlling his shifting abilities, because he can't even function as a human *or* a bear. Something is taking over his body, and I have to find out what it is." Ramon looked worried—yet determined—and his eyes returned to the microscope. "I'll tell Knox about what I found. You look tired, man; you should go home and get some rest." Ramon slapped his hand onto my shoulder.

"And something to eat. Not all of us can survive on microwave pizza," I chuckled, and Ramon rolled his eyes.

He seemed pretty concerned about whatever had infected this guy and it was starting to make me a little nervous, too. The situation was getting serious. All I knew was that when Agent Gianni came to interrogate the suspect in the morning, I was going to be there.

I JERKED awake as I heard my cell phone going off. I looked at my clock and it was 3:00am.

Who the hell is calling me?

I groaned and checked the caller ID; it was Knox, so I answered immediately.

"What's up, Boss?" I yawned and rubbed my eyes. I probably wouldn't have answered if it was anyone else.

"Ramon just filled me in on what you two discovered, and I'm very concerned. We've found an unknown infection with unknown ramifications from an unknown source—and all those things need to get *known*, right fucking now. I think whatever we find at this point should be gathered and presented to the conclave." Knox's voice was serious.

"I agree completely, but what are we going to do about the FBI?"

"That's why I'm calling you. Agent Gianni reported what happened here today and everything she found to the FBI, and they want the suspect to be transported back to their headquarters. They think it's useless to hold the investigation here when the evidence is so overwhelming. They want to proceed first thing in the morning—"

"What?"

"—And I need you to convince Agent Gianni to keep the suspect here for further questioning." Knox finished with a stern tone. He did not like being cut off.

"How the hell am I supposed to do that?" Right then, I didn't care about his attitude. He was asking the impossible of me. It wasn't like Blanca and I were best buddies or anything; in fact, we were the opposite: two stubborn egos housed in incompatible personalities.

Even if those curves of hers *did* call out to my ursine mind.

"I don't know? Tell her the blood samples you got have not been confirmed to belong the victims yet, so we still aren't 100% sure if he killed those people. She lives by the facts, and if that guy committing a trio of murders isn't a fact, she'll want to make sure of it before she leaves."

"Okay, I'll head over to her hotel in the morning and offer her a ride here to see if she can call them off." I sighed. It wasn't going to be easy; Agent Gianni and I had definitely gotten off on the wrong foot, so I was going to have to smooth things over if I had any hope of having her on my side.

"Hey, being a little nicer could help, too. Make sure you work your charm; flirt a little," Knox teased as he hung up. I shook my head and sighed as I ended the call. I threw my phone on my nightstand and fell back onto the bed. Wouldn't she have been suspicious if I suddenly tried to be nice?

Maybe my inner bear will be getting his way after all, I thought. *Hell, it's been awhile. And she* is *pretty cute...*

Either way, if I didn't already have a tough day waiting for me, it had certainly just gotten tougher.

8

BLANCA

Do I have to leave today? I thought, still lying in bed. My alarm had just gone off and the clock read 7:00am.

After getting back to the hotel, I made my report to the FBI. They decided to have the suspect transferred to headquarters immediately because of the overwhelming evidence against him. I didn't exactly agree with that; I wanted to make sure we had the right guy before we brought him in, and I hadn't even gotten a chance to meet him yet.

Alex had called me earlier that night as well to tell me that Trent had been by to pick up some blood samples for testing. I was surprised; he seemed to be going above and beyond for this case, but maybe that's how he treated all his assignments and I'd misjudged him. Either way, I'd hoped he would have those blood sample results for me in the morning, so I could confirm we had the right man and feel better about taking him to HQ.

I spent the remainder of the night alternating between the hotel pool and jacuzzi. I cursed the fifteen-minute timer that alerted you to get out of the hot tub to regulate your temperature; if there wasn't a lifeguard present, I probably would have spent the whole hour in there. It felt good to finally get a chance to relax after such a tense day.

It was then that it dawned on me: I was actually dreading leaving.

I hadn't been on a vacation in a long time, and the perks of my accommodations made me feel so relaxed. I was staying in a room at Bar Harbor Inn's Oceanfront Lodge with a plush king-sized bed, and the scene from my windows was spectacular. It was decorated in gorgeous beige and pale blue colors, with rustic furniture that was surprisingly comfy. I wasn't ready to let go of that. The hotel room was paid up until the end of the week and I really wished I had an excuse to stay. But, the orders were given, and I had to follow them.

I didn't want to jump back into investigating three murders, but it wasn't like I could leave it to Trent.

Come on, you said you would be nice to him today.

I did say that.

With that, I took a deep breath and rolled out of bed. I had my outfit ironed and laid out already: another black suit with a white shirt. The ensemble was a little different, since I decided to go with a skirt instead of pants that day, and I wondered if I should wear heels to look more professional when picking up the suspect. I would probably be in an office until the helicopter arrived, so I didn't see any harm in wearing them, but decided to bring flats in my handbag, just in case. I'd be in a national park, after all.

I grabbed my handbag and briefcase, slipped into my heels, and headed out of the hotel room. I was glad the elevator was just around the corner and made my way to it, deciding that I would ask the receptionist for the number of a local taxi service.

Once the elevator opened to the lobby, I spied Trent.

Is he waiting for me? I stopped in my tracks and looked around. He was wearing his ranger officer uniform, checking his phone; I had to admit, I never noticed just how good he looked in it. It fit in all the right places, with just the right amount of wear to make him look more rugged. His shortly cropped black hair looked damp, as if he'd just showered and the thought of him scrubbing himself down made my thighs clench together. I felt a blush sweep across my cheeks.

Oh god, I must be so red right now! I looked away quickly, taking deep breaths to calm myself. *What the hell is wrong with me? No pleasure with business, Blanca!*

Well...the case was potentially wrapping up soon...

I shook my head. *It's not like you have time for that! Focus!*

"Good morning, Agent Gianni. I hope you slept well." Trent was walking up to me with a bright, genuine smile and I immediately went on guard. Why was he being so friendly suddenly?

I cleared my throat. “Good morning, Mr. Bailey. Are you waiting for someone?” I asked, a bit more coldly than I wanted.

“Yes, I was waiting for you, actually. I thought you might like a ride up to Acadia. The taxis in Bar Harbor can be pretty expensive.” He chuckled, running a hand through his hair. When he laughed like that, his eyes almost closed completely.

God, he is so hot...

“Ms. Gianni?”

“Huh?” I blinked and realized I had been staring at him again. “Sorry! Just spaced out for a moment. I had some trouble sleeping last night.”

“Yeah, me too. It was a rough night,” he responded. When I said it, I was lying, but I could tell he was serious.

“Bad dreams?” I asked, trying to soften the conversation.

“Nah, just other stuff...Anyhow, can I give you a lift to the park? My Jeep’s just outside.” Trent’s smile was back, but I could tell there was something hidden behind it. He was being secretive, and I didn’t like that; I told myself I’d be nice to him to him, though, so I let it slide for the time being.

“Sure, lead the way!” I returned his smile and followed him out to his Jeep.

When we stepped outside, Trent’s two-passenger army-green vehicle was parked right out front. Its tires were covered in dirt, as was much of the rest of the vehicle.

Just as we stepped up to his Jeep, Trent paused and turned to face me. “Hey,” he started, nervously running his hand through his hair again, “so...I realize I haven’t been the most...*cooperative*, Agent Gianni, and I wanted to apologize. After thinking about it, the bottom line is we both want the same thing: for this case to be solved and justice to be served. I know I’ve been a jerk, and I’m sorry...so...” He cocked an eyebrow and gave me a half smile. “Truce?”

I certainly wasn’t expecting *that*, but I had to admit, it was always a pleasant surprise when a man could admit to his faults. I extended my hand out to his for a shake, “Alright, then. Truce.”

Trent nodded and opened the door for me, offering his hand to help me up.

"My lady..."

"Why thank you, kind sir." I made a bowing gesture towards him and laughed as I got in. Something was definitely different about Trent today —and whatever it was, I liked it.

He got into the driver's side and started the Jeep, steering us toward Acadia.

"Any particular reason you decided to come pick me up this morning? Wanted to celebrate me leaving today?" I asked after a few moments of silence.

"Well, I was actually supposed to deliver the blood results to you before you left, but I decided to pick you up after our resource manager, Ramon, told me he couldn't confirm the blood was from the victims. He said he was having a difficult time separating the properties of four different people."

"*Four* different people?" I was confused. There had only been three victims. Was there a fourth that we didn't know about?

"He was able to identify the suspect's DNA among the others'. His victims must have injured him in some way."

"Oh, I see." I thought about it for a bit. It changed things for me, to not have the blood results confirm we had our killer. I had been counting on them to ease my conscious. What if we had the wrong guy? "How long do you think it will take for Ramon to decipher the blood samples?"

Trent shrugged. "He didn't give me a time frame; he just said it was taking him longer than he thought, and he wasn't sure when he'd have the results ready." It was hard to read him because he wasn't looking at me. His eyes were firmly planted on the road.

Must be a ranger thing.

Either way, I decided he must be telling the truth. What reason would he have to lie? That complicated things, though. I didn't want to bring the suspect to headquarters without knowing for sure he was at fault. That would be completely unjust.

"Mr. Bailey, would you mind pulling over somewhere? I need to make a phone call." I was all business again. I believed only in the facts, and the agency would just have to accept that.

"Sure thing. Everything okay? We're still about five minutes from the entrance of the park." Trent's voice sounded a bit concerned as he pulled off to the side of the road for me.

"Of course, it should only take a moment." I smiled at him as we made eye contact and got out of the car.

I pressed the number one on my phone and tapped my foot, waiting for someone to respond.

An apathetic voice finally answered, "FBI. Caulwell speaking." The man had been with the FBI for a long time and you could tell he was ready to retire.

"Good morning, Chief. This is Agent Gianni."

"Have you secured the suspect? Our pilots are a little busy right now, but they should be heading to you in less than two hours for sure." Chief Caulwell sounded dismissive, as if he had more important things to do.

"Well, that's actually why I'm calling. I was supposed to secure evidence today confirming whether or not our suspect is the murderer, but the labs weren't able to be obtained this morning." I winced. I hated delivering bad news to the chief. He was just like me: he expected things to go according to plan.

"What do you mean?" Caulwell's tone shifted to what sounded almost like annoyance. Whether it was at me for delivering the news, or at the situation, I wasn't sure.

"There are three victims, and the park's scientist found four different blood samples on the suspect. He was only able to positively identify the suspect's blood, and not the other three because the samples were so mixed together. He says he can separate things out, but it will take him some time. I'm calling to ask if it's possible to hold off on transport until those test results are secured, sir." I recoiled at the last bit, hoping not to annoy the Chief any further.

"Hmmm...okay. Go ahead and wait, but I'll only give you an extension for one week. If the results are not in by then, you are to return with the suspect and the investigation will be continued here. Understood?"

My jaw dropped. Caulwell was *never* this amicable; I was completely caught off-guard. I was so prepared to fight to stay in Maine, I hadn't even thought of how I would respond if the Chief had agreed.

"Uh—understood! Thank you, Chief. I won't let you down and will do my best to expedite those results so we can move forward with the investigation."

Yes! One more week in that awesome hotel!

"You get on that, Gianni." The Chief hung up and it took every fiber of my being to not to jump up and down in excitement. I had wanted an excuse to stay in Maine and now I had one. I just had to make sure there was no rush on those blood samples.

I composed myself, and as I headed back to Trent's Jeep, I'm fairly certain I caught him checking me out. His eyes were moving slowly over my body and once our eyes met, he gave me a bright smile and my breath was stolen. He really was something to look at.

Well, since I'm here for another week with not much else to do, maybe I can have some fun...

I returned his smile and got back in the car.

"You like what you see, Mr. Bailey?" I teased, testing out my best flirty laugh.

"Caught me." Trent's voice was a little lower now; huskier. His expression looked hungry, but I couldn't tell what for. He was looking me over again, and my skin was getting warm. "So, what now, Ms. Gianni?"

"Well...um...my Chief has agreed to keep the suspect here until we have the test results, so I may be spending the rest of the week here." I fiddled with my hands. His stare was so intense, I couldn't look anymore. When he didn't say anything, I glanced in his direction, catching his tongue gliding across his lips.

*The things he could do with that...*I felt a shudder jolt through me. I licked my own lips nervously and pressed my legs together tightly.

"So, what can I do for you now?" Trent asked, tentatively placing a hand on my thigh. I could tell he was still testing the waters with me because his hand hovered for a couple for seconds before making contact, as if he was waiting for me to object. When I didn't, he rested his hand there, his touch soft and light.

I was surprised. I expected his hands to be firm and deliberate like he had been when we first met, but this touch showed that he was beginning to open up to me. The Trent I was seeing was the real deal. I had no idea what brought him out suddenly, but I was thankful I decided to wear a skirt.

I closed my eyes as his thumb slid across my thigh and back with the same consistently light touch. It tickled something deep inside me and I flushed, biting my lip to hold back a moan that was dangerously close to escaping. His hand began to move slowly upward, carefully, only inch by agonizing inch. My skin was burning, reflecting the flames erupting within me.

I wanted him. He was feeling me out, and all I could do was hope he could read my signals loud and clear.

And then his lips descended over mine. His lips were soft, full, and slightly wet, and my eyes opened wide, completely shocked. I didn't know what I had expected, but it certainly wasn't a kiss—not just yet, at least. His hands moved higher up my thigh, under my skirt and I sunk into the kiss, diving into the delicious feeling of him touching me. I cupped my hand against his cleanly shaven cheek, the other hand twisting into his hair as I threw myself into it. Our lips danced together, and he slid his tongue against mine, begging for entrance. I granted, parting my lips slightly, and as he slid inside, tasting me, and I couldn't help but release the moan I'd been trying so desperately to hold back.

That must have been the sound he was waiting for. He reached behind my head with his free hand, releasing my dark tresses from the tightly-wound bun I wore. His hands were intertwined in my thick waves the next moment, pulling my head closer to deepen the kiss.

His hand moved from underneath my skirt and I almost let out a whimper until it found its new destination in seconds. He cupped his hand over my breast and pressed his thumb against my bra, pinpointing my nipple.

Another moan escaped me, causing our lips to part and he used that opportunity to travel down my neck. He planted soft, wet kisses against the column of my throat and I could have just melted in his arms. He smelled of freshly-mowed grass and rain, his scent wrapping around me like a warm breeze. I pressed my chest into his palm, wishing our bodies could just fuse together.

Knock, knock.

My eyes snapped open and I gasped at what I saw. A man in a police uniform was looking through Trent's window at us with a very serious expression. I tapped Trent, who seemed to have completely froze at the sound.

"Uh...you might want to handle this..." I was instantly nervous. Was making out on the side of the road a crime? I mean sure, in a literal sense it was, but we were in the middle of nowhere. It wasn't like anybody was going to see.

Well, except for the cop. Just my luck.

Trent slowly untangled himself from me and looked at his window. I could see his smile reflected through his sideview mirror, and it was just as charming as one might expect.

Huh? When the officer outside saw Trent's face, he also smiled. *Do they know each other?*

"Wait here, I'll be right back." Trent said, kissing my cheek and exiting the vehicle, leaving me sitting there, stunned. I scanned the area to see if anyone else was around, but the road was clear. Leaning over into the driver's seat to look out Trent's window, I tried to see if I could snoop a little. What could I say? It was in my nature as a detective.

Trent was talking to the officer with his back to me, obscuring the man from my view so that I couldn't see either of their facial expressions to determine what was going on.

I can't be arrested for public indecency or something like that while I'm on the job! How will I explain this to the Chief? I started to panic a little as the reality of the situation sank in.

I sat back in my seat, fiddling with my hands again—a nervous habit that I was trying to break. Under any other circumstance, I might have straightened myself, exited the Jeep and asked the officer what the problem might be. But I was supposed to be working and I didn't need anything getting back to headquarters that might make it seem like I wasn't doing my job.

I mean, *I wasn't,* but they didn't need to know that.

I heard the door handle and looked up to see Trent getting back into the car, laughing.

"What happened? Were we doing something wrong? Did I get you in trouble? Am *I* in trouble?"

"Calm down, Blanca!" Trent put a finger to my lips and smiled. "You know you do a lot of talking with that thing. I wonder what else it can do."

I rolled my eyes.

"Can you just tell me what happened, please?" I folded my arms, hoping to give the impression that I meant business and I wasn't playing anymore.

"It's fine, trust me. That's Al, the sheriff of Bar Harbor. He was patrolling the road to Acadia and saw my Jeep on the side of the road and got worried. He thought we might have been out of gas or something. He even apologized for knocking! He didn't realize what we were doing until he had already startled us." Trent was laughing as he spoke, and when he finished, I couldn't help but smile a little, too. I breathed a sigh of relief. "So, no, we're not in trouble and he hardly saw anything."

"Good." I nudged his shoulder.

"Is that nudge for us to pick up where we left off?" Trent smiled, leaning over to me. I put a finger to his lips this time.

"Actually, since we're keeping the suspect here, I would like to get some kind of work done. Can you take me to the holding cell so I can ask him some questions?"

"You really are a workaholic, huh? You'd rather interrogate that douchebag than spend your day making out with a stud like me?" Trent laughed and shook his head as he turned the ignition.

"I never said I'd rather do one more than the other, but maybe a *stud like you* would like to pick this up later after a bit of dinner back at my hotel?" I asked, trying to sound confident and flirtatious. I wanted him to think I had control of the situation, but by the way my heart was beating, I knew I didn't.

"Oh, are you asking me out on a date, Ms. Gianni? That's a first!" Trent seemed taken aback.

"A girl has never asked you out before?" I was shocked. How could someone so hot never be approached by the opposite gender? It was completely impossible in my mind.

"I tend to chase women. They don't chase me." Trent said confidently, his eyes back on the road again as we drove along.

"Well, you'd better be ready to run, because I have the reputation of being quite the chaser," I joked.

"Alright, pretty lady. I'll be sure to grab my running shoes." He stole a glance and winked at me. A light blush spread across my cheeks and I was suddenly deep in thought.

How did we get like this so quickly? One minute, we couldn't stand each other and the next, we couldn't keep from laughing and smiling. What happened? What changed? I just couldn't put my finger on it, but if we were only going to be around each other for less than a week, I'd much rather have us like this than at each other's throats.

Besides, I would need someone to show me around Acadia this week, especially those places the pilot had mentioned on my helicopter ride. After this interrogation, I was going to make this my vacation after all.

"We're here." Trent's voice snapped me out of my thoughts; we were indeed at the entrance to Acadia National Park. I looked out my window and saw the sign warning people not to approach the animals. Knox was waiting by the gate, wearing a ranger uniform that closely resembled Trent's.

"I have to talk to Knox for a second, and then I'll take you up to the holding lodge."

He'd gotten out of the Jeep without so much as a glance at me; *did I say something wrong?* Trent didn't seem mad or upset, just not as playful as he had been moments before. Maybe coming back to the park put him back in business mode?

I straightened myself, *You should be doing the same.* Just as I got into the proper mindset, Trent was hopping back into the Jeep.

"Alright. Off we go," he smiled at me as Knox opened the gate to let us in. I wondered what time the park opened.

"Is the park usually gated off in the mornings?"

"No, not usually. The park is open 24/7, but with the murders, Knox is taking extra precautions and monitoring each person that comes in today."

"That's probably a good idea." I nodded, glancing out the window again. Everywhere I looked, there was something. Trees, mountains, lakes and the shoreline; Acadia seemed to have everything you could want in nature all rolled into one.

"Hey, would you be up for giving me a tour of the park sometime before I leave?" I asked, not bothering to turn my face to as I spoke. If he didn't want to be all flirty and stuff at work, I respected that and agreed completely, so I tried to keep my tone casual.

"Sure. I know plenty of places I could take you. People usually love Cadillac Mountain. It's one of the first places you can see the sunrise in the morning."

"Really? I'd love to see that." My face brightened as I looked at Trent.

He glanced at me and smiled. “Two dates planned in one week already. You really are going to make me run, huh?” Trent chuckled.

“Like the wind.” I joked. I could see a building coming up in front of us.

“Alright, well, here’s the holding lodge.” Trent said, pulling up to the facility. “Let’s go check on your boys.”

9

BLANCA

Trent and I walked into his office to find Alex sleeping while leaning against the wall, a magazine over his face. Gerard had his head down on Trent's desk, and I could hear a light snore coming from his throat.

You've got to be kidding me...

I glanced at Trent, who was trying his damnedest to hold back his laughter.

"And you didn't trust *me* to keep watch overnight, huh?"

"Shut up!" I rolled my eyes. "Guys, wake up!"

Both agents jumped out of their sleep at the sound of my voice, and the magazine Alex had covering his face fell to the floor as he looked around wildly.

I put my hands on my hips. "So, this is how you two keep watch? Way to show how serious the FBI is about their work!" I scolded.

Not like you were doing any better... I rolled my eyes at my inward thought. I wouldn't have been in a car making out with a hot guy if I had a suspect to watch.

"We're so sorry, Agent Gianni. We were awake most of the night, I swear!" Gerard exclaimed, slightly panicked.

"Yeah! We only fell asleep the last hour or so," Alex chimed in.

"I can check the cameras for you if you want..." Trent glanced at me, clearly enjoying the moment.

"That won't be necessary, Mr. Bailey. I trust my boys. They had a long night and must have needed a moment of rest. I just wish they would have waited until I got here, like I asked." I gave my two agents stern looks and they winced. "I'll be including this in my report. You're relieved for the day; go get some sleep."

"Wait, isn't HQ sending a helicopter for us today to bring the suspect in?" Alex seemed confused. They must have gotten called about the pick-up for today as well, but it appeared no one filled them in on the change. The Chief must have figured I would let them know.

"Plans have changed. We're waiting for the blood results before we bring the suspect back to HQ. I will still conduct an interrogation today as planned and we'll go from there." I nodded at them both as a dismissal; they returned the gesture and started to head out.

"Hey, wait up! I'll drive you guys to the gate and call Knox on the way to send someone to take you to your hotel." Trent went after them, leaving me in the office alone.

Then, I heard shuffling.

How could you forget what you came here to do? I rolled my eyes again. I was being pretty hard on myself after the whole car thing with Trent.

I grabbed a chair from the side of Trent's desk and slid it up to the cell, pulling a pad and pen from my briefcase as I looked up at the suspect. He was just sitting on the floor, glaring at me. I sat in the chair and returned his intense stare; I wasn't afraid of him.

"Hello. I am Agent Gianni of the FBI and I'm investigating three murders that took place here in Acadia yesterday morning. You have been arrested as the primary suspect for said killings and I would like to ask you some questions. Let's start with your name."

The man's gaze did not falter once while I spoke. He just kept glaring.

"We can do this the easy way or the hard way. We've already lifted blood samples off you, and when they are confirmed to be the victims', we'll be taking you to FBI headquarters. So, you can tell me your name and what happened, or you can just wait for the investigation to take its course. Either way, unless you really didn't do it, you're screwed. And I highly doubt you didn't do it."

The man bared his teeth at me and I heard a low growl escape his lips.

"Oh, so you can make animal noises, but you can't speak?" I folded my arms in frustration. I was getting nowhere with this guy.

Just then, I could have sworn I saw something.

It was only for a second, but while I was staring at him, I saw brown fur sprout all over his hands. When I blinked, it was gone.

I closed my eyes for a moment, and opened them again. The man was normal, still baring his teeth like a threatened dog.

I figured it must have just been my imagination. Why would a man have fur growing from his skin?

"This isn't getting anywhere." I stood up, shaking my head as I turned away from the cell and walked toward Trent's desk. But once my back was turned, I heard a loud roar behind me and something hit the bars.

Clank!

I whipped my head around at the sound and what I saw, I could not believe. I gasped and tried to take a step back, but my ankle caved and I lost my balance on my heels. I fell to the floor, pushing myself backward with my hands.

In the cell, a brown bear was towering over me, its mouth jutting out from between the bars as it snapped, its claws swiping wildly in my direction. I heard it growl in frustration, not being able to reach me, and I cried out for help, closing my eyes tightly.

It's just a dream! It's just a dream!

"Oh shit! Blanca? Blanca, are you okay?" I felt hands on my shoulders and I screamed, only thinking of claws ripping through me. "Blanca, open your eyes! It's me!"

Trent?

I opened my eyes, hyperventilating as I looked around. My eyes met with the bear's and I cried out again in horror.

"It's okay, Blanca! You're okay! It's locked up. He can't hurt you."

WHY IS HE SO CALM? THERE'S A GODDAMN BEAR IN HIS OFFICE!

"It-It's a bear! How did he get in here? Where's the suspect?" I was terrified, and I tried to slow my breathing, but my body was in full-on panic mode.

"I was hoping it wouldn't come to this, but the bear...*is* the man,

Blanca." Trent was shaking his head in disbelief. "I fucking knew this would happen!"

The animal released another roar from its prison and Trent glared in its direction.

"You'd better shut up before I come in there."

I looked from the bear in the cell to Trent and back.

Why is he talking to it like it can understand him?

I stared at the animal long and hard, and as I watched in disbelief, it started to change. The bear shrunk and shed its hair until it became the suspect. My eyes widened as I observed the transformation, shaking from fear of the unknown.

What...the...hell is going on here?

"Look, Blanca. I'm going to explain some things to you. I need you to promise to let me get it all out before you decide what to do next. It's a bit heavy, though; you might want to stay seated for this." Trent looked worried and heavy, like he was about to drop a bomb on me, and I was afraid I wasn't ready for it. I knew I wouldn't be able to move, though, so I nodded and took a deep breath.

"The man in that cell is a bear shifter. This means that he can turn into a bear at will. There are other kinds of shifters, too; ones that are able to transform into many different types of animals. When I found Danielle's body this morning, I knew a shifter was at fault because of the damage. Actual wild bears hardly chase after humans or kill people, and when I saw the corpses of the cameramen, I realized we had a rogue on our hands.

I did my best to track him down, and when I did, I wrestled him into cuffs and brought him here. Thing is, he's not supposed to shift the way he did in front of you. I've also seen parts of his body change while the rest of him stayed in human form; this is also not supposed to happen. It seems like something has caused his human brain to lie dormant while his bear runs rampant whenever it pleases, even when he's in human form. He doesn't speak, he only growls and roars. Something is wrong with him and I have to find out what. And I might...need you to help me." Trent winced at the last part.

He was breathing a little heavier now, after talking at the speed of light to try and get everything out. I just stared at him, only blinking.

Bear shifters? What the hell? Is this guy nuts? Did I just make out with someone who needs to be tied up in a strait-jacket? Damn, I sure know how to pick 'em...Wait a minute...

Something dawned on me in that moment. Trent seemed to know a lot about this, as if it wasn't his first time encountering this problem. In fact, he seemed extremely familiar with this information.

No...

"H-how do you kn-know all this?" I stuttered, feeling the fear and panic rising again.

Please don't say it. Please don't say it. Please don't—

"I'm a bear shifter as well, Blanca..." Trent gazed deep into my eyes. When I looked back, I could see worry and a little fear there. He was scared, too.

Shit...

"We aren't supposed to discuss our existence with those outside our community, so that's why we couldn't tell you about him when you first arrived. Making it seem like it was either a human or an actual bear was our top priority. We thought we would be able to reason with him if we found him, but he doesn't respond to anything." Trent glanced back to the man in the cell.

"Wait, *we*? Who's *we*? How many of you are there?"

"Knox, Sophia, even Ramon. We're all shifters. There are others as well, and Acadia is our clan's home."

"Your *clan*? There's a whole clan of—of...*shifters*?"

This was impossible. There was no way this was real. People who could change into bears at will? That sounded like something straight out of the fantasy books I read in high school. How could people like that exist?

"I-I...need some time to process this..." I said finally. I was still shaking as I tried to get up. Trent reached out a hand to help me. "Don't touch me!"

The exclamation sounded worse than I wanted it to. I didn't mean to scream at him; fear was still coursing through me and he'd just told me he could shift into a fucking *bear* whenever he wanted to.

He wasn't human, and I wasn't ready to accept that yet. Having him touch me would make this all real.

"I'm sorry...I just—I should leave..." I said, looking away from Trent's defeated face. I used the desk as leverage to help me to my feet and started to walk out of the office. Trent's voice made me stop, although I almost didn't want to hear anything else he had to say.

"Blanca, I need you to promise not to tell anyone. We could all be in danger if the public were to find out about us. I know you need to do your job with this guy, but maybe we can find a way to make this work out for everyone? It might be too much to ask of you right now, but please. Promise me you won't say anything for now..."

I could hear the pleading in Trent's voice. But, how could he ask me to promise something like that? Who would I be able to sort out my thoughts with if I didn't tell anyone?

I couldn't make that promise, so, I didn't. I continued to walk out of his office, and I didn't look back.

"This is Agent Gianni reporting from Acadia. May I please speak with Agent Caulwell?"

I didn't know who answered the phone when I called, but it was no one I recognized and it was definitely not the person I wanted to talk to. I was briskly walking away from the holding lodge toward the main gate and thanked the heavens the ground wasn't muddy; I hated when my heels sunk into dirt.

"One moment, Mrs. Gianni."

The receptionist was transferring me to the chief. My mind was racing, and I had no idea what to do. The thoughts in my head were screaming at me to tell him everything I just heard and to let the FBI sort out the situation.

I felt an overwhelming sense of duty rush through me. *They deserve to know about this unknown species.*

My heart was fighting my mind though, begging me to keep silent. Trent was still a person—sort of. He deserved a chance at a normal life just like everyone else, right? Even with the whole 'turning into a bear' thing.

Who was I to destroy their lives? And is that precisely what I'd be doing if I told the chief?

"Chief Caulwell speaking." The chief sounded annoyed again, which must have meant I was interrupting him. "Hello?"

Oh crap... What do I tell him?

"Hey Chief, this is Agent Gianni. I was...um...I was just calling to let you know that... uh..." The words wouldn't come out. I couldn't do it.

"Yes, Agent Gianni? What is it?"

"Sorry, Chief. I was actually just calling to let you know that I conducted an interrogation this morning with the, uh, suspect. He was very unresponsive and did not confess to the murders, so we'll have to wait for the test results before proceeding."

"Whatever. Keep me posted." The chief hung up and I breathed a sigh of relief. I felt like I'd been holding my breath during the whole conversation.

What am I going to do now?

I decided to just head back to my room. The hotel had a spa and maybe a massage would help me sort through my thoughts.

Oh shit! I never asked the receptionist at the hotel for the taxi number. I hope I have enough service to find it! I checked my phone and noticed I had one frigging bar, but luckily, I was able to find the taxi number—even though it took forever. They told me they'd meet me at the gate in 10 minutes. I had Knox's number and knew I could call him for a ride, but after hearing everything I just heard, I didn't want to be around *anyone* at the park.

10

TRENT

KNOX HAD CALLED ME IN EARLY TO HELP HIM TEAR OUT SOME INVASIVE weeds that were encroaching on the trails. The main Acadia trail that went around the entire park was 50 miles long and the job would take us all day, for sure.

"Is something wrong, man? You look like someone stole your puppy." Knox didn't say it jokingly; he was seriously concerned.

I hadn't told him about what happened with Blanca yet, and I was honestly dreading it. She took off the day before and neither she—nor her agents—had retuned since. I panicked; what if they had gone back to the FBI and told them everything? They could be sending people to infiltrate Acadia at any moment.

I didn't think Blanca went back and told them—or, at least I hoped with every fiber of my being that she didn't. I wanted to believe that my plea to her carried some weight, especially after the time we spent together in the Jeep. I knew I was told to flirt like hell with her, so I did, but I couldn't deny that my inner bear had begun to surface again that day. Desire—deeper than I'd ever known—surged through my body, blazing through *all* my extremities, and as my lips crashed against hers, I knew my bear had chosen his mate.

Like it or not, I knew it was time to tell Knox; I couldn't keep it from him any longer.

"Knox, there's something I have to tell you." I could hear the dread in my voice and I knew Knox could, too.

"Yes?" His tone sounded like a parent whose child was about to admit to something.

"Agent Gianni...yesterday in the holding cell...She...The shifter, he..."

"Spit it out, Trent." Knox's voice was stern now.

"Agent Gianni knows about us. About shifters." I held my breath, waiting for a response. He was silent at first.

"She *what*?" Knox roared; his expression was livid. "How did this happen?!"

"Before you get angry, let me explain. The suspect shifted in front of her, right there, plain as day! And while I was trying to explain things to her, he changed back. There was no denying it! What was I supposed to tell her? She was just hallucinating?"

"Wait, he full blown shifted in front of her? Who the hell does that in front of a human?" Knox still seemed infuriated, but his anger appeared more directed towards the shifter now and not me.

"I don't think he's *trying* to do anything. Knox, something is seriously wrong with that guy, and when Ramon saw him, he agreed. At first, we thought that maybe the bear had completely taken control over his mind and body, but after watching him closely yesterday, it's much more than that. He's wild, almost rabid. He doesn't speak and doesn't respond to anything; he just growls and snarls. If you try to talk to him, he bares his teeth and lashes out. I've never seen a shifter act the way he does, and neither has Ramon."

"What about the blood sample? Have we heard anything else about it?" Knox seemed to be calming down slowly. He definitely wasn't as angry as he'd been previously, thank god.

"I haven't heard anything from Ramon yet. He must be hard at work trying to unravel what's going on. Seeing the shifter seemed to make him worry that whatever was affecting that guy could possibly spread to the rest of us. I personally think it's a stretch, since he scratched me when I was trying to bring him in and nothing seems to be wrong with me."

"I'll have to check with him for an update." Knox's voice seemed concerned and he reached out to Ramon with his mind as he went back to whacking weeds. I followed suit; the air seemed tense after the conversation and I'm sure Knox was thinking about how to handle the situation now that the FBI knew about our existence.

After a few moments of silence, Knox groaned. "Fuck, nothing solid yet from Ramon. So, about when did all of this happen yesterday?"

"Maybe 10am?" I winced. I knew he would be pissed that I waited so long to tell him about it. It had been over a day, but I needed the day to figure out what to do. I met Knox's eyes to notice him glaring back at me.

"So, you decided to wait over a day to tell me this because...?"

"I'm not going to give you an excuse. I'm sorry; I should have told you earlier," I responded. "So, how do you think we should handle this?"

"That's a good question. I don't know. This isn't going to be as easy as it was when Hannah found out about us. I was lucky she fell in love with me, but I doubt Blanca is going to be that smitten with you any time soon." Knox rolled his eyes.

"Well...you never asked me how that things went..." I smirked a little, hoping he knew what I was talking about. He caught my eye and returned the smile.

"I'm guessing from that face you were able to work your charm after all?"

"You could say that..."

"So, what happened? Did you get some ass?" Knox chuckled, seemingly back to his normal self.

"Not everyone can be as lucky as you are," I laughed. Knox looked at me as if he was waiting for the details. "We kissed."

"That's it? Hardly anything to brag about. You think she's sweet on you just because you had a little make out session? You'll have to do better than that, Trent. *Much* better." Knox was shaking his head in disappointment.

"It wasn't just a kiss, okay? I felt something, and I know she did, too. Things would have gone further if we weren't interrupted." I rolled my eyes, remembering the moment we heard a knock on the window of my Jeep. "Bar Harbor's sheriff caught us on the side of the road, but I was able to laugh it off with him."

"Your fault for getting caught," Knox snickered. "Okay, so you had her, but you lost her due to the interruption. Do you think she'd give it another try?"

"I highly doubt it after the whole shifter thing. You should have seen her face. She wouldn't even let me touch her when she found out I was one, too." My gaze fell to the dirt; I didn't want to remember the look in Blanca's eyes when she pulled away from me. "How did you handle it? When Hannah found out?"

I looked up at Knox, searching for some kind of direction from my Alpha, my friend. I knew if anyone could help me, Knox would know what to do.

"Hannah was different, Trent. She saw me shift and confronted me about it; you know how she is. Blanca seems to put up a tough front, but learning this information shook her world. She found out the guy she was making out with moments ago can turn into a bear at will. That's not an easy thing to take in, especially when it was thrown in her face like that. I think you should give her some time. Let her process things. If she was going to tell the FBI about us, she would have done it already and Acadia would be swarming with agents. But we're not, which means she probably hasn't said shit. Let her come to you. And if the kiss was as intense as you think it was, I'm sure she thought it was, too. Just wait for her."

Knox's words seemed sincere and they resonated with me. Maybe he was right. This wasn't just a fling now; I *needed* things for us to work out, more than just for satisfying my inner bear's carnal needs.

This had to work for the sake of the clan.

"Alright, I'll wait. But, what if she never comes?"

"You'd better hope she does. This is our only way out right now until I think of something else. I'm lucky you two started to hit it off; otherwise, we'd have nothing to go on. I'll try to think of another solution in the meantime in case this doesn't pan out, but Trent, you know how you're always joking about being happy that Hannah came around for me because I needed someone? Well, you do, too. And this could be your turn. She could really be the one and I'd love to see you just as happy as I am."

Knox smiled and I could feel a love one can only feel from their Alpha. It was almost fatherly, coming from someone who watches over and protects you, who wants the best for you. I felt a tinge of heartache when I remembered Officer Davidson, the man who almost took my mom and I in all those years ago. I felt the same kind of love from him, and then he was gone.

Nodding at Knox, I returned his smile. He seemed to always know exactly what to say or do when faced with a sticky situation. He was a great Alpha, and in that moment, I was thankful to be in Acadia.

"Now, let's get these weeds taken care of! The sooner we finish, the sooner we'll be done," Knox said, adding more gusto to his hacking.

Having a night off sounded great, and who knew? Maybe she would come by that night.

I certainly hoped so.

11

BLANCA

I FELT SO MUCH BETTER AFTER AN HOUR-LONG, FULL-BODY SWEDISH massage at the hotel; it was just what I needed to help cope with the stress of it all.

Bear shifters? How could creatures like that even exist? How did they come to be? Not to mention Trent is one. Great choice, Blanca!

I shook my head at my thoughts as I opened the door to my room. I still wasn't sure what I was going to do with the news, but after the massage, I decided it was time to get back to work. I needed to go visit Knox to get more information about Acadia, but I was stalling. Surely, Trent had told him I knew their secret by then.

I honestly just wanted to go back to being ignorant about bear shifters and pretend they didn't exist.

Maybe that's what I should do for now. Act like I don't know their secret. I honestly feel like that's the only way I could handle a talk with Knox. Hopefully, Trent won't be there...I'm just not ready to face him yet. I sighed. *Why does everything have to be so complicated?*

I just needed Knox to answer some general questions about Acadia for the paperwork, and then I could return to the comfort of my room. *Hey, it's a start.* With that realization, I grabbed my suitcase and pulled out a pair of black dress pants and a white blouse; there was something about the contrast and uniformity that made me feel powerful, and I could have certainly used an extra boost that day.

When I was ready to go, I called the taxi company, figuring they would arrive at the hotel soon after I made my way downstairs. And I was right. By the time I got to the lobby and outside, the taxi pulled up two minutes later.

WHEN I ARRIVED AT ACADIA, Knox was not at the entrance. He'd told me where his office was located back when we were examining the bodies, so I decided to head there to see if I could find him.

It was a short walk, maybe ten minutes from the gate, but when I got to Knox's office, there wasn't a car outside.

Is he not here either? Maybe I should knock or something, just to check.

I banged on the door.

"Mr. Bernard? It's Agent Gianni. Are you in there?" I yelled, looking through the windows. I was sure I saw a light on.

"Oh, come in!" I heard a female voice call out to me and I was immediately confused.

His secretary, maybe? Whoever she was, she probably knew Knox's whereabouts.

I entered the office to see walls covered with papers, a filing cabinet and a desk with a computer. A woman with light brown hair and hazel eyes peeked out from behind the machine; if her complexion hadn't been so fair, I would have thought she was Sophia. She smiled and motioned for me to come closer.

"Are you Mr. Bernard's secretary?" I asked, still not sure of who she was.

The woman erupted in laughter. "Ha, he wishes! I'm Hannah Grant, Knox's girlfriend."

"Oh, I'm sorry! I'm Blanca Gianni. I'm an FBI agent who was assigned to investigate the serial murders that took place here." I stretched my hand across the desk to shake hers and she returned the gesture.

"Pleased to meet you. I'm glad you guys were able to catch the culprit!"

"Possible culprit. We're waiting for blood samples to confirm," I corrected.

Does Knox tell his girlfriend everything?

"Gotcha. Well, is there something I can help you with?" Hannah asked as she returned to her typing.

"Um, yes, actually. Do you happen to know where Mr. Bernard is at the moment? I have some questions about Acadia for the paperwork and I'm assuming he's probably the best person to ask." I held up the forms.

"And you would be correct about that. He actually went with Trent to clear some weeds on the trail. It's a pretty tough job that usually takes them all day. It's only 3pm, so I would imagine they'll be at it for at least a few more hours."

"Oh, well, okay then..." I wasn't sure what to do. "Maybe I'll just try again tomorrow."

I began to turn away and her voice stopped me.

"Hey, are you okay, Ms. Gianni? You seem like you have a lot on your mind or something."

She was right. I *did* have a lot on my mind. In fact, she might just be the person to talk to, but I would have to play it cool.

Bring it up vaguely to see if she has a reaction that signals she knows what you're talking about. If she's confused, let it go and walk away.

I took a deep breath and turned around; I wanted to make sure I could read her facial expression.

"Um, yeah. Trent told me something about the suspect—and himself—yesterday. Something that makes them...change. Would you happen to know anything about that?" I tried to sound as nonchalant as possible, but I heard my voice tremble a bit. I was nervous. I didn't want to give too much away, in case she had no idea that her boyfriend could turn into a goddamn bear at any moment.

I watched Hannah's eyes grow wide. She walked to the door and locked it, and I immediately went on guard.

Why is she locking the door?

Hannah walked back to the desk but didn't return to her seat. She stared at me, almost as if she was looking through me, and then finally spoke.

"Yes, Ms. Gianni. I know about bear shifters," she said finally, making direct eye contact with me. "How did you find out?"

"The suspect changed in front of me while I was interrogating him, so Trent told me about everyone here. Why did you lock the door?" I asked, my eyes moving from hers, back to the exit. "Are you a bear shifter, too?"

"Oh, no. I'm sorry, I just didn't want us to have to worry about someone interrupting us and I thought you might feel better talking if it was more private. If it makes you uncomfortable, I can open it for you." Hannah looked very apologetic and moved closer to the door.

"That's okay. You're right, I think I'd feel more comfortable knowing that we won't be interrupted. Thinking about it now, you're the only person I can talk to about this..." I looked down and started twiddling my fingers.

"I know the feeling; I've had to keep it a secret for the past few months myself. None of the other shifters have human girlfriends. It kind of sucks; I feel like an outsider most of the time."

"How did you find out?" I glanced up and Hannah was moving back towards the desk, motioning for me to sit in the chair in front of her. I sat, while she perched herself on the corner of Knox's workstation.

"I heard from a local, who was deemed crazy, that something freaky was happening in the park during the full moon. Being a reporter and all, I just had to see for myself. I happened to be close by and watched when Knox shifted." Hannah shrugged, but her demeanor didn't seem as nonchalant; I could tell this secret had been wearing on her. "But I felt something with Knox, and after some time, I warmed up to the whole bear thing. It took me a while, but I was able to see past it so I could be with him. Things happened so fast with us, and before I knew it, I was in love."

It looked like talking about all of this was taking a huge load off her shoulders; seemed like she needed this conversation just as much as I did.

"So, what are you going to do now that you know?" Hannah asked in a worried tone. "You aren't going to tell the FBI, are you?"

"I don't know, honestly. It's my duty to tell them, but I know it would be wrong of me to do so. Who knows what they would do with this kind of knowledge. They could be just as alarmed as I was when I first found out and try to eliminate all shifters or destroy Acadia. I don't want that to happen. Acadia is such a beautiful place and everyone I have met here is so nice. And Trent..." I stopped.

What about him? I was still so unsure of my feelings. We only kissed, but in that one moment, I had been willing to give up everything for him. And I have never felt that with anyone before. It had to count for something, right?

"Do you like him? I heard you guys didn't start off on the right foot."

"We didn't. He obviously has a problem with women in authority, but he warmed up to me eventually. Then, he picked me up from the hotel the other day and things just...clicked. I felt like a googly-eyed teenager all over again." I blushed, thinking back to our hot and heavy moment in the car.

"It was like that for me as well. I was here doing a story on Acadia and Knox swept me off my feet before I even knew it was coming." Hannah chuckled.

"I like him, but I just don't know if I can deal with the whole...shifter thing." I admitted, looking up at Hannah. Her expression held nothing but understanding.

"I know what you mean; I needed some time to get there, too. I had Knox shift in front of me a bunch of times until it seemed as normal as it could. It's still quite magical for me to experience, and I'm not frightened by it anymore. In time, we moved to hanging out while he was in bear form. I would stroke his fur and lay with him sometimes. Getting to know his bear as well as his human side really helped me become more comfortable with everything. But you have to understand, even though the animal is a part of them, it's not the main part. They are not bears who play human, they're people just like us who, for some reason, can turn into bears for as short or as long as they wish. Some shifters choose not to change form at all except for during the full moon. So, I don't want you to think that if, say, you wanted to be with Trent, you would have to deal with him being a bear all the time. It would only be every once in a while. And if you wanted," Hannah grabbed my hand and smiled at me, "I could help ease you into the whole thing."

She really made me feel comfortable for some reason. I had just met her only moments ago, but I felt perfectly safe being locked in a room with her and having her hold my hand. Her presence was so soothing, and she made me feel like I could possibly do this.

No. I can do this.

"Yeah, I think I'll keep our little secret here from the FBI. And I'd love to get in touch with Trent to tell him about my decision...and to see where things stand between us. In fact..." I checked the time. My watch said 5:30pm. "They should be getting back soon, right?"

I looked up at Hannah and she was smiling. I could have sworn I saw tears pooling in her eyes as well.

"I'm sorry, I'm just so happy. Thank you so much for doing this for us —for the clan. I'm sure it will mean a lot to Knox, and Trent, even if things don't work out between you two. I really hope they do, though. Trent needs someone. And I think you'd be perfect for him."

"You really think so?" I could feel myself tearing up a little, too. She didn't know this, but I think I needed someone myself. I've spent years focused on my work and trying to establish myself among the ranks. I long abandoned the thought of relationships or even just enjoying time with someone. That's why the moment in the car felt so nice. It had been so long since I allowed myself to be with someone like that, and I was ready to see where this could go.

"I do." Hannah nodded and at that moment, her phone rang. She wiped her eyes quickly and answered. "Hey, honey, how's it going? Uh huh...okay, I'll see you soon then!"

She hung up the phone and gave me a huge smile.

"They're on their way back now!"

"What should I do?" I gave Hannah a slightly panicked look. I thought I'd have a little more time before I saw Trent.

"Maybe you could head over to Trent's cabin and meet him there? I can give you directions; your walk over will give you some time to put your thoughts together."

"That would be perfect."

Hannah started jotting some notes down. "And I'll tell Knox you had some questions for him, but that you'll be back tomorrow. I'm sure he won't mind. I'll keep him occupied," Hannah handed me the directions and winked.

"Thank you so much. For everything," I said, hoping my eyes showed her how grateful I was for the talk and for her help.

"You're welcome. Now go, before they see you!" Hannah shooed me away, giggling. I ran to the door, unlocked it, and headed out into the wilderness, hoping I could reach Trent's cabin unnoticed.

12

TRENT

I HIKED BACK TO MY CABIN, WIPING THE SWEAT FROM MY FOREHEAD WITH A bandana I had tucked in my pocket. My shirt was drenched, and I needed a shower—badly. As I got closer to the cabin, I noticed someone sitting on the front steps. The individual was looking at the ground, so I couldn't see his or her face at first, but as I got closer, I could see that it was a woman fiddling with her hands.

And there was only one person I knew with that nervous habit.

Shit! I reek and I'm covered in sweat... I looked around quickly and jumped behind a tree, taking a whiff of my shirt and coughing at the stench. *Ugh, gross!*

It wasn't like I had another clean shirt on me that I could just change into, so I decided taking it off was probably the best option. I pulled its hem over my head and rubbed it all over my chest and neck, trying hard to scrub the stench and sweat from my body. I took a deep breath and stepped out from behind the tree, continuing to approach my cabin. A branch crunched under my boot as I approached Blanca and she snapped her head up, looking directly at me. She seemed startled at first, but her eyes lowered to my chest, I could see a blush spread across her cheeks.

"Hello, Ms. Gianni. Were you waiting for me?"

Of course, she was waiting for you, dipshit. Why else would she be here?

"Um, yes, I was. I, uh…I'm ready to talk…if you are, that is…" She was looking down at her hands again.

"Sure. I might have to take a shower first, if that's okay?" She glanced back up at me and her eyes widened a bit as she nodded, appearing even more red than before.

"Why don't you come inside? It's getting a little chilly out here." I stepped up to my door and turned the lock, allowing her to step inside first. I watched her look around my cabin and I saw a smile spread across her lips.

"Wow, this is really nice. Not quite what I expected, honestly."

"What did you expect?"

"I just thought it'd be more like a frat house. All sporty, you know?" She shrugged.

"Well, I can't take any credit for the decorating. The cabin was fully furnished when I started working at Acadia."

I really liked my cabin, which had been designed to match the environment outside, decked out in earth tones. The front door opened to the living room, which had a wide window to the left, covered by beige curtains. The walls had a stained-oak finish and there was a small cherrywood dining table by the window with two chairs. In one corner of the room sat an overstuffed recliner, and on the other side, there was a fireplace with a matching couch facing it.

The cabins didn't have televisions because they were designed for people who enjoyed the outdoors and wanted to be away; I never liked watching TV, anyway.

"Well, it's lovely," she said, turning to me with a smile.

God, she's so beautiful…

Our eyes locked and her face told me everything. I knew why she had come without her uttering a single word, and my heart almost leapt out of chest.

"Trent, I—"

"Kiss me." I quickly closed the distance between us, my eyes pleading for her. There was that blush again, but she looked up at me, her arms reaching up to lock around my neck and her lips met mine. The kiss was tentative at first, our lips testing each other, finding a rhythm, but when we found one, it was like a waltz, slow and passionate. One of my hands intertwined in her hair while the other drifted to her waist. She placed a palm on my chest and I shivered; her hands were cold against the heat of my skin.

The kiss deepened, our tongues exploring each other wildly. I felt starved; I wanted more of her, but I didn't want to rush this. She came to me and I didn't want her to regret it.

Her palm moved along my torso, feeling her way around me. One of my hands slid past her waist to her hip, then around back, cupping one fleshy cheek. The gesture lifted her slightly on her toes and she released a light moan. I smirked into the kiss, happy with her response, but when her hand drifted down my stomach to my belt, I stopped her there.

"Would you like to accompany me in the shower, Ms. Gianni?" I whispered against her lips. She nodded, and when she pulled back from the kiss, her face was flushed.

I led her up the stairs, our hands linked. The hallway only had two doors: the one on the left was to my bedroom, while the door on the right was to the bathroom. I veered right, and once we were both inside, I gently tilted her chin up, keeping her gaze locked with mine as I pulled the hem of her blouse over her head. I felt my manhood twitch at the sight of the lace bra cupping her perfect C-cup breasts.

I allowed my gaze to leave hers and bent down to unbutton her black dress pants. She ran her hands through my hair and started kissing my neck as I unzipped them, letting them fall down over her hips and pool on the floor, allowing her matching lace panties to greet me. She stepped out of her pants and slipped off her shoes and I saw her behind was bare —she was wearing a thong. Just like that, I felt my girth swell, pressing against the zipper of my jeans.

I could see that she noticed the bulge in my pants when I followed her eyes, which were wide with wonder.

"Aren't you going to help me out, too?" I asked playfully. Her cheeks flushed even more deeply, but she walked over to me confidently. She fumbled with my belt and fly, but finally got them open and pulled my jeans and boxers down in one fell swoop, exposing my member. It stood at full attention, seven inches long. It wasn't the most impressive size, but I knew how to work with it.

I was surprised to see shock in her eyes. "Is something wrong?" I asked, running my hands through my hair.

"You're just...so big..." She flushed as she spoke, trying hard to look somewhere else. "I'm sorry, I just haven't been with anyone in a long time..."

She seemed embarrassed, too, and I felt even more of a connection.

"It's been a while for me, too."

"Really?" She seemed relieved to hear me say that.

"Really." I said, pressing my body against hers. "We'll take it slow."

I was thankful at how easily I was able to unclip her bra. It wasn't exactly my greatest skill, but I tried really hard to get it right. Her breasts were perky and full, hardly moving as I released them. I could feel her body tremble as my hands moved down to her hips. She seemed nervous about me removing her panties, so I decided to kiss down from her ribs to distract her. Her breathing picked up a little and I looked up to see her eyes closed. I nibbled on her hips as I hooked her thong over my thumbs and pulled them down. And then it hit me.

Her scent filled me, and I felt my need grow stronger. She was completely shaven and looked delicious. I was throbbing, and I wasn't sure how much longer I could hold out.

"I'll go in and start the water. It takes a bit to get warm and you seem cold enough already."

"I'm warming up now..." There was that voice again, the seductive one I remembered from our moment in the car, and I almost exploded right there.

I couldn't bring myself to say a word. In mere seconds, she had the ability to shift from shy, timid and flushed to a sexy, confident goddess. It amazed me and made me want her even more.

I turned the water on and stepped into the shower, taking a deep breath before I peeked out and held out my hand to her. She smiled and my heart skipped a beat; I couldn't believe this beauty was not only in my house, but stark-naked right there in front of me.

She placed her hand in mine and I pulled her into the shower, allowing her to soak herself while I poured some body wash and worked it into a lather.

"May I?" I asked, and when she gave me that sly grin with a nod, I started at her shoulders, working the soap down her arms, then back up, gliding over her breasts. I spent a little more time there, kneading them softly and stroking her nipples lightly. I heard her gasp and push her chest into my hands, her hands tangled in my hair. Her lips were by my ear now and I enjoyed hearing her quickened breathing against it. I moved my hands down over her stomach and back, gliding my fingertips through the suds, making her shiver.

"I thought you were supposed to be warming me up?" she teased.

Oh, I can warm you up alright... I thought, needing no further invitation. My hands moved over her hips, down her thighs and back up toward her center. As my hands made their way between her thighs, she spread them slightly, allowing me entrance. The closer I got, the warmer I felt and the more my need grew.

I finally reached her womanhood, making the area slick with soap, causing my hand to slip and slide against her. I allowed my finger to explore a little, gently caressing her folds and then slipping into them. Finding her little pleasure nub, I let the suds guide my finger over it in a tight, circular motion. She released a load moan against my ear, moving her hips along with my fingers. When I felt her speed against my finger quicken, I moved my hand, grabbing more body wash from the bottle. I heard her whimper and chuckled.

"Soon."

I soaped-up her ass and moved down her thighs to her legs until she was completely lathered.

"Your turn," she said as I stood up straight again. Her eyes weren't meeting mine though, they were much lower. I watched her grab the shower gel and instead of lathering it in her hands, she poured some on my chest, allowing it to drip down to my legs. She smirked and seemed to be pleased with herself, rubbing the soap into my torso, moving it upwards to my shoulders and arms. She kneaded the muscle there, and I groaned; all the weed whacking had made me tense and I could feel it release as she massaged me for a while longer.

After working some of the soap over my back and pulling me closer to her as she lathered it, her breasts pressed against me. I could feel her hardened nipples against my chest and she was kissing my neck again; I closed my eyes, enjoying the feeling. My manhood was pressed against her stomach, and as one of her hands moved down to hold it, my breath caught in my throat.

She began to lather my cock, stroking me. Her pace picked up as it became slippery, and my breathing became ragged. Just when I thought I would explode into her hand, she released me and began to soap-up my legs.

I allowed her to step under the water first, the suds running off her, and my eyes followed their journey down her luscious curves. With her ass pressing against my length, I couldn't hold back any longer, so I guided her toward the wall, my hands moving down to her entrance as I plunged a finger into her. She gasped and threw her head back, her hair whipping onto my shoulder. I moved my finger slowly inside her, caressing her walls until they loosened enough for me to insert a second finger. She kept her head against my shoulder, her eyes closed, and she was biting her lip, moving her hips along with my ministrations.

I growled, taking her by the shoulders and maneuvering her against the opposite wall so the water wouldn't get in our way. As I pulled her hips back towards me, she spread her legs on her own and I knew she was most definitely ready.

I positioned myself at her entrance and thrusted in deep. *Fuck...* I could have exploded right there inside her—her walls gripped my cock so perfectly. The feeling was intoxicating, and I felt I could have stayed there forever.

I guessed I was taking too long because she bucked her hips against me, begging me to move.

"Please..." Her voice was barely a whimper.

I complied, grabbing her hips and rocking them with each and every thrust. A symphony of moans erupted from her lips as we picked up speed, her ass slamming against me as we found our rhythm. My hands moved up to her chest, cupping her breasts and massaging her nipples as I pumped into her. As I felt her insides start to tremble, I knew she was getting close.

One of my hands moved down to her sensitive pearl, massaging her there while the other hand stayed at her breast. Her moans grew louder, and as I quickened my pace, I wasn't sure how much longer I could last.

I didn't have to wait long.

"Oh, Trent!" she screamed as her climax erupted throughout her body. She was scrambling against the wall, grabbing for something to hold onto as she trembled against my chest, moaning and shaking as she grinded against my length.

Her walls spasmed around me and I exploded with a roar, my hands at her hips again as I pumped into her wildly, spilling my seed into her. She threw her head back and moaned, another wave flowing through her as she reached her peak a second time. She wobbled and I thought she might fall over, so I stepped forward and wrapped my arms around her.

She was still shaking a little as she hugged my arms and sighed happily. I kissed her cheek and could see a smile.

"*That* was amazing..." she said in a dreamy voice, laying her head against my arm. Our hearts were beating rapidly, and eventually, I could have sworn they shared the same rhythm. I turned her around and kissed her slowly, wrapping a thick towel around her before carrying her into my room.

"You look like you could use some rest," I said, laying her down on my king-sized bed. Just as I crawled in next to her, my phone rang. I groaned, and Blanca looked like she didn't want me to answer, but when I saw the caller ID, I knew I had to.

It was Knox.

"Hey, Boss, what's up?"

"I got in touch with Ramon and we're having a meeting in 15 minutes to discuss his findings. Can you meet us at my office?"

"Um, yeah. But I have Blanca with me."

"Oh, do you?" Knox teased. "Where are you?"

"At my cabin." I said flatly, rolling my eyes.

"Do you need more time, or—"

"I'm fine. I'll be there." I said, getting ready to hang up. I didn't want Blanca to overhear him joking around about us.

"Wait, bring her with you. She should know about the infection as well since it affects her suspect. We have to figure out what we're going to do about him."

"Got it, she'll be there." I said, hanging up and making eye contact with Blanca. She looked confused and I guessed she realized that 'she' meant *her*.

"We have to go. Knox and Ramon are having a meeting about the blood samples and Knox wants you to be there, so we can plan what to do about the suspect."

"Alright."

And just like that, we were both back in business mode.

13

BLANCA

I WASN'T SURE WHAT I WAS ABOUT TO HEAR IN THAT CONFERENCE ROOM, but everyone at the table looked extremely serious, so I surmised the news couldn't have been good.

"Okay, let's start by filling Blanca in on what she doesn't know," Knox began.

"I'll do that," Trent volunteered, turning toward me as he took a deep breath. "Bear shifters don't usually kill humans. We can be hot-tempered in bar fights and things of the like, but murderous rampages aren't really what we're known for. So, when we saw the three murders, we knew we were dealing with a problem. When I captured the shifter, he didn't respond to anything; he only exhibited aggressive behavior."

"It was the same when I tried questioning him and then he started transforming back and forth," I said, trying to work things out in my head as they were presented to me.

"Yeah, about that: it's not supposed to happen that way. We can't change only one part of our body; it's full-form or nothing for us. I couldn't make my hands bear paws even if I tried, but somehow, he can. That was when I knew something was wrong. So, I called in Ramon here to have his blood tested."

"So, you weren't really testing for the victims' blood?"

"No, *lo siento*. I actually tested those as soon as we got them and identified all three victims. This shifter definitely committed the murders. But we had to stall somehow to keep him here, so I could figure out what was going on with him," Ramon interjected. He looked apologetic; they all seemed to, but I understood. I knew they didn't want to keep all this from me, but they had to for the sake of their clan.

"So, have you figured it out yet?" I asked.

"*Es complicado.* I know what's wrong, but I don't know what *it is.* Whatever has infected this guy is destroying him. His blood cells, his brain cells, they're all turning black. Trent even watched in my lab as whatever this infection is, literally started eating the shifter's blood cells. It looks like the infection is taking over his body by devouring his cells and reproducing its own. I've never seen anything like it before. *Es increíble;* also, scary." Ramon sighed heavily as if telling us his findings released a weight off his shoulders.

"Do you have a hypothesis about where this infection might have come from or how he got it?" Knox asked. He looked very concerned and I guessed even he must be afraid of this unknown infection.

"The only thing I can think of right now is that it's something he picked up in the environment; maybe a new type of virus? He has no wounds that would make me believe he was bitten or stung by something, but he's a shifter, so his body probably healed the infection site quickly, if that was the case. Perhaps it was an airborne pathogen and it traveled through his respiratory tract? I could keep examining him, but..."

"But what?" Trent, Knox and I all asked at the same time.

"We would have to kill him. He is unresponsive at this point, aggressive, and overall dangerous, but if he is dead, I can perform an autopsy and maybe I can gain more information about the infection," Ramon responded bluntly.

"We can't kill him; he's one of us. Only the conclave can grant us that permission. If we do it and they find out, we will be put to death ourselves." Knox said, shaking his head.

"But we can pretend he died!" I exclaimed. "I could tell the FBI that he killed himself. Bashed his head into the wall without anyone realizing? I could tell them that I left disposing of the body to you guys and that the blood samples revealed that he was indeed the killer. I fill out the paper work and case closed. Acadia gets to keep the shifter here and you can observe him that way."

"Hmm...she has a point," Trent said, looking to Knox for his opinion.

"It could definitely work. And once we have more information on the infection—as much as can possibly be obtained—we can present him and everything we've learned to the conclave for final judgement. If this is something that has the potential to affect our community, they should know about it."

"The conclave?" I interjected.

"The conclave is the council of elders of all shifters. They adjudicate issues that arise within the clan." Trent responded.

"It will be difficult to do all this testing while keeping him alive. We'll need a two-person team assisting me every time I go in for more samples." Ramon was considering the possibility at first, and then he finally agreed. "But yes. It could work"

"Then it's settled. Ramon will give Agent Gianni the blood sample paperwork proving the shifter to be the murderer. She will fill out the case work as if he died and present it to her chief. And we'll bring this to the conclave to get their take on things," Knox repeated the plan back to everyone to make sure we were all on the same page, and we were. We all nodded in agreement and Knox pronounced the meeting adjourned.

Ramon turned to Knox and started discussing plans for the shifter, while Trent turned to me with a forlorn look.

"So, what does that mean for us?" he asked, his eyes to the floor.

"Don't worry, I have a plan for that, too. I'm going to step outside and make some phone calls," I whispered and got up, exiting the room and stepping out into the cold, crisp air.

I dialed 1 on my phone.

"Chief Caulwell."

"Hey Chief, it's Agent Gianni. I have news about the Acadia case. The suspect is deceased; he bashed his head into the holding cell and collapsed. By the time anyone noticed, he was already gone." I tried to make myself sound as believable as possible.

"Weren't Alex and Gerard supposed to be watching him?" The chief sounded angry and I didn't want my boys to get in trouble for this.

"They were tired, so I sent them to their hotel rooms to get some sleep. It was me who was supposed to be watching him and when I heard the banging, I thought he was just banging on the bars and trying to get someone to let him out. I apologize, sir." The only way I could think of making this go smoothly was for me to take the blame.

"I can understand that, Agent Gianni. Well, you know what to do. Just fill out the paperwork and I'll have a helicopter there for you tomorrow."

"Actually sir, I was wondering if I could take my vacation days now?" I winced, hoping it wasn't an absurd question after what I just told him.

"You? A vacation? You've never taken a vacation before!" The chief sounded genuinely surprised.

"All the more reason to take one now. I have sort of fallen in love with Acadia. And with the investigation, I wasn't really able to enjoy it very much. I would very much like to do that now, sir. If it's okay with you, of course."

The line was silent at first, but then the chief spoke up.

"I'll see you in three weeks." Was all he said and hung up.

"Yes!" I exclaimed, jumping up and down.

"What's all the excitement for?" I heard Trent approaching and immediately stopped.

"That was me getting three weeks of paid vacation to stay here with you in Acadia!" I smiled brightly, running into his arms and hugging him tightly.

"Awww, only three weeks?" he teased, but I heard a smile in his voice as well.

"Well, we'll see how things go. Don't push it." I warned with a smile.

"Three weeks sounds amazing." Trent whispered and tilted my chin up to kiss him.

I just knew that those were going to be the best three weeks of my life.

14

TRENT

EPILOGUE: THREE MONTHS LATER

"What do you think I should get her?" I asked Knox as we drove around the trail doing our late evening patrol before he watched over the gate that night. It was the Friday before Valentine's Day, and I had the next day off. I wanted to do something special for Blanca, but our relationship was still so new that I was stumped on what to get her for the occasion.

"It's tomorrow and you still haven't gotten her anything? You won't have a girlfriend for much longer if she finds that out. That's how you thank a girl for leaving the FBI to join local law enforcement for you?" Knox chuckled, and I winced.

He was right: I had procrastinated too long. After everything Blanca did to be with me—and to preserve the secrecy of our clan—she deserved better. She'd worked closely with Ramon and the conclave over the last few months, and after all that time, they concluded the pathogen must have been a mutation of the rabies virus, based on the similar antibodies they were able to isolate from the shifter's serum and spinal fluid. Without her hard work and devotion to the case, who knows how long it would have taken the clan to make this discovery.

"She's just always with me; I hardly have time to myself when I'm not working. Not that I'm complaining or anything..." I winked at Knox.

"Yeah, getting all that ass must keep you pretty preoccupied," Knox laughed.

"Okay, enough about our sex life; I need ideas, man," I pleaded with him.

"Well, it's a little too late to go out and buy something. All the stores in Bar Harbor probably closed at 6, as usual."

Shit, he's right...What am I going to do?

"So, you could take her somewhere, or make something for her? We both know you're not that good with your hands, though," Knox snickered.

"That's not what *she* thinks," I joked. "Alright, so crafts are out of the question. I *could* bring her somewhere...hmmm..."

I thought long and hard about a romantic place I could take her to. Picturing Bar Harbor in my head, I couldn't really think of any places that she would really love except the beach, but I doubt she would want to go there at that time of year. Being February in Maine, every inch of the area was completely covered in snow and ice. I wanted to light up her day and make it really special.

That's it!

"I know what I'm going to do."

"Where are we going?" Blanca asked in a sleepy voice, a blindfold over her eyes. She would have fallen asleep in my Jeep if I hadn't been driving so fast. It was a little after 6am and I was flying through Acadia, trying to get to the location I had painstakingly set up only hours ago.

We have to make it there before first light... I thought, checking my watch. *Okay, we have about 10 minutes to get there and get settled.*

I could see the base of the Cadillac Mountain trail in front of me and I knew I had to slow down a little. There were a lot of twists and turns on the path and falling off a mountain for Valentine's Day was not my idea of romantic.

I checked my watch again.

6:20am. Come on...Only 8 more minutes...

And there was the spot. I pulled over and jumped down from the Jeep, rushing over to the trunk to grab a duffel bag. I was glad I was bundled up in my flannel-lined jeans, a thick, navy-blue sweater, a fleece neck-warmer, gloves, and my ranger bomber. It was thirty degrees out, and I was sure to tell Blanca to dress warmly when I woke her up. I walked over to the other side to help her down, and she jumped out of the Jeep, sporting an outfit that closely resembled my own: a black turtleneck sweater, skinny jeans, fur-lined boots, mittens, and a parka. I watched her put her hood up and then grabbed her by the hand, leading her to the site.

I took a final scan of the area, making sure everything was perfect.

"Can I take the blindfold off now?" Blanca was shivering a little and sounded slightly annoyed. She didn't really like the cold, but I was about to help with that.

"Not yet. I'm going to help you sit down, okay?"

"Sit down? In the friggin snow?"

"Just trust me, Blanca." I said, reassuringly.

I helped her down onto a blanketed area that she couldn't see. I had laid out two comforters on a patch of ground that I cleared the snow from so it wouldn't melt under us as we sat. I watched her feel around her.

"It's soft, but not wet. So, it's not snow..."

"You're right; it's not snow," I laughed, sitting next to her. I pulled two more comforters out of the bag I brought from the Jeep and wrapped one around her. She snuggled into the blanket and I thought it was the cutest thing I'd ever seen. I smiled and pulled out two thermoses, guiding one into her hands.

"It's so warm!" She seemed intrigued. "What is it?"

I opened hers and positioned it at her lower lip.

"Blow." Just when I thought she couldn't get any cuter, she let out small breaths against the cup, almost completely missing the opening. I hoped it wouldn't be too hot for her. "Okay, drink."

She tentatively placed the thermos against her mouth again and sipped it slowly.

"Peppermint hot chocolate, my favorite!" A huge smile spread across her face as she took another sip of the sweet, creamy drink.

I checked my watch. *Oh shit! I almost missed it!*

I quickly removed her blindfold and she opened her eyes, blinking rapidly. Once her eyes adjusted, she looked in front of her and that's when it happened.

In the distance was Hunters Beach, the water crashing against the rocks. The sun had just burst into the sky, rising almost as if from underneath the water. I glanced over to her and her mouth was open in amazement, her eyes lighting up as the sun shone on them.

"Oh my gosh, Trent; it's breathtaking!"

"Yeah...and so are you..." I whispered. Seeing the sunrise against her face was the most beautiful thing I had ever seen. She looked over at me with a loving smile and threw her arms around my neck, her lips against mine. We shared a deep and passionate kiss, warming me from the inside out. She didn't seem to mind that the blanket had fallen off her.

"Thank you..." she said, finally pulling back. I saw tears pooling in her eyes.

"Happy Valentine's Day, baby. Every day, I'm so grateful you decided to stay up here with me," I said, pecking her lips. She settled into my arms and I wrapped the blankets around us, making a mini fort. She sipped her hot chocolate and I grabbed mine, planting a kiss on the side of her head.

"I love you, Blanca." I whispered into her ear.

"I love you too, Trent." She turned her head to kiss me again, beaming, and she turned back to the sunrise. We watched as the sunlight spread across Acadia, over us, lighting up the whole world, and I smiled, thinking of how we got to see it first that day.

RANGER RAMON

SHIFTER NATION: WEREBEARS OF ACADIA

1

MIN

When I had been called to meet with someone from the National Center for Preparedness, Detection, and Control of Infectious Diseases (NCPD-CID,) I had been a little more than surprised.

What could they possibly want with me?

They were a smaller faction of the Centers for Disease Control and Prevention (CDC) who were there to protect the general population from outbreaks of any infectious disease by making the world aware of how to be prepared for such events.

I was working as an entomologist for the CDC at the time, specializing in infectious diseases that could be transferred to humans through insects. I studied how they were able to pass along illnesses so that the CDC could figure out how to prevent them from being transmitted in the first place.

I loved my job. I always wanted to go into a field that would better the greater good of mankind and I was pretty sure I had found the perfect job. I was a bug freak as well, so that was a bonus.

My father, born in France, was a scientist; he'd always let me assist with dissections of animals when I was in middle school. I remembered telling him about performing a procedure on a cow's eye in biology class in the seventh grade and how intrigued I was about the process.

"Dad, it was so cool! I got to peel back the sclera and cut the cornea out, and this liquid jelly stuff came out. They even let us use the lens to look at each other! Everything was upside down and backwards; I could have even used it as a magnifying glass!" I remembered telling him, so excited, I had practically been jumping.

"What ever happened to the good old frog dissection, eh *minou*?" he had asked, closing the book he was reading and taking off his glasses. "I ought to show you how it was done back in my day."

My dad had a penchant for calling me by all sorts of French pet names when I was younger. *Minou* and *Minette* were my favorites because they had my name in them and meant 'kitty,' and I really had a soft spot for cats. My name was actually Korean, given to me by my mother. It meant 'quick,' 'clever' or 'sharp:' all the things she hoped I'd be, and I appreciated those meanings even more as I grew older.

That very same day, my dad had let me sit in on a frog dissection with him. He instructed me on everything to do as I nervously held the utensils. He first let me remove the skin on its legs to show me the frog's muscles, then I cut through the abdominal muscle to expose its insides. He explained the different names of the frog's organs as I opened the flaps, and from that point on, I was a total science nerd.

I wanted to be just like him when I grew up. He never told me which field of science he studied when I was younger, but I was actually glad for that because it wasn't until we performed the operation on a cicada that I knew I wanted to study insects. I had just graduated eighth grade and was on my way to high school, and it was the first dissection my dad had let me do completely on my own. I had decided to cut the cicada clear in half, and I remember being amazed at the sight of its pink back muscles, used to power its wings. I was so fascinated by the differences between insect innards and those of animals that I was hooked. I never dissected another animal again and I would head out almost every day, hunting for new insects to dissect.

I later found out my father worked for The European Federation for Animal Science, or EFAS, trying to improve farming methods with domestic animals. He studied different conditions and how they played a part in the animals' well-being, which was nothing remotely near what I wanted to pursue, so I probably wouldn't have wanted to follow his footsteps either way.

So, there I was, doing what I loved and being singled out for a project because of it. When the NCPD-CID had asked for me personally, I was completely shocked; usually, they pretty much kept to themselves and didn't enlist help from other departments. I, in fact, was hardly ever requested for any projects, unless I was the only entomologist on call that day.

Being French-Korean had always singled me out, but not in a good way. In France, where I did most of my schooling up until college, I was one of only about thirteen thousand French-Korean people, living in a country with a population of about sixty-seven million. I was a minority and most people didn't know how to deal with me. I had mostly Korean features, but my nose was more bulbous, in my opinion. My lips were full, which I thanked the heavens for often, but my eyes were small, and my ebony hair was bone straight. My face was not as rounded as Koreans' often were: I had a strong jawline, and that, along with the nose, is what usually threw people off.

I went through the normal Asian stereotypes in school while living in France. People automatically assumed I was 'smart' without proof and picked me first to do group projects with, but I was always the last person picked for physical activities. My thin frame did make me fragile, but I saw skinnier white kids picked before me. I never took it to heart, though. I was, indeed, smart and lacking in my athletic abilities, but I just wished people didn't automatically assume these things of me. I wanted to be stupid and agile for once—not to get picked first in gym class or anything, just to prove everyone wrong and watch their dumbfounded expressions when I kicked ass on the basketball court, but failed all my tests. I could've pretended with my exams, but that would have only hurt me, so I quickly learned to just focus on myself.

It was no different in the CDC office. Everyone assumed I was the best entomologist in the office—even though they had never worked with me—but nevertheless, I was always passed over for field work opportunities. So, color me suspicious when I had been called in for this project, which was revealed to me over the phone to involve field work.

But, I wanted in. This was my chance to prove I could do it and I was determined to show everyone.

The NCPD-CID was located in the same building, so thankfully, all I had to do was take the elevator down from the eleventh floor to the fourth. I was told to pass all the cubicles and head straight for the main office, which I did. Through the glass, I spied a man sitting behind the desk; he was round and heavy set, with dark hair and a very bushy mustache. There was a blonde woman on the other side with an empty chair next to her, which I assume was reserved for me.

I knocked on the door and the man motioned for me to enter the office.

"You must be Min Dupont!" he exclaimed, standing up and shaking my hand.

"Yes, that's me," I nodded, hoping my hand shake hadn't been too soft. I really wanted to make a good impression.

"I'm Eric Hanson, the head of the department," he smiled, motioning for me to sit down.

I looked to the woman on my left, who didn't say a word to me. *Is she only here to witness the meeting?* I wondered.

"I'm sure you are wondering what project I have called you here to take part in," Mr. Hanson continued.

"I am." That came off more clipped than I wanted it to. I was trying to go for a more blunt, direct approach, and I hoped he didn't take it wrong, but he didn't seem phased.

"Before I give any details, I must have you know that anything said during this meeting is to be held in complete confidence. You can't even tell anyone in your own department. In fact, if you accept, you will be on the next plane to a national park in Maine."

Maine? That's a random location...What could possibly be there? I pondered.

"You have my word that I will not disclose any information you reveal, even if I should decide not to take part in the assignment."

"Not like you have much of a choice," the woman snickered next to me.

Eric gave her a stern look and the woman was quiet.

"My apologies, Ms. Dupont," he regarded. "I'm about to reveal to you some classified information. Hardly anyone outside this department knows about this and we would like to keep it that way for now to avoid a panic."

Panic? What exactly have I gotten myself into...? I decided to hear him out before I passed any judgement, so I nodded in response and he continued by pushing his chair aside, exposing the projector screen behind him.

"This footage was taken via satellite during a full moon over Acadia National Park. Try not to be alarmed."

This is most definitely ***not*** *sounding good...*

Eric started the footage and I wasn't sure what I was looking at. At first, there were just a bunch of people standing around gazing up at the moon. Then, they started shaking as if an earthquake was happening, but the ground wasn't moving. Suddenly, everyone's bodies were... lengthening. Gaining mass. And...

Bursting with *fur?*

What the hell is this? Is this some kind of joke? My eyes were wide, and my jaw dropped as I witnessed the changes happening on the screen.

Where people were once standing, bears had replaced them. They all ranged in height and weight, and just like that, they were walking up to each other, some nuzzling and sniffing, others braking off into a run, headed for the dense forest. With that, the footage ended and there was silence. I looked to both Eric and the woman beside me, who seemed completely unfazed by the footage.

"What exactly did I just watch?" I asked in disbelief.

"The individuals you've just seen are what are called bear shifters. They're people who can turn into different species of bears at will, and are forced to make the transition during the full moon," Eric responded bluntly.

How can he be so matter-of-fact about this discovery?

"So, like werewolves? Only bears?" This had to be a joke.

"Yes. I have another piece of footage I need you to see before I tell you why I need your help," Eric said, pressing a button to roll some new footage.

I watched as a bear attacked a woman on the screen. She was waving her arms frantically trying to stop it, while running towards what appeared to be a rocky beach. I covered my mouth in horror as the bear chased her and shredded her with its claws until she lay among the stones, unconscious and bleeding. The bear sniffed her for a moment, spotted something in the trees, and ran towards it.

Eric seemed to notice my fear.

"What you just witnessed was the death of Danielle Peterson, the host of the Travel Channel's *Danielle's Destinations*."

Wait, what?

"I remember hearing about her death on the news. She was killed by some guy with huge deep-sea fishing hooks, wasn't she?" I asked, confused.

"That's the information that was released to the public, yes."

"So, a bear killed her? Why not just say it was an animal attack then?"

"Because that was a bear *shifter*, not just a wild bear." This was the second time the woman beside me spoke up.

"An FBI report by a woman named Blanca Gianni was submitted about the murder with the information that was released to the general public. The information in it didn't completely line up, so we looked into it personally. That's how we found the satellite surveillance of what actually happened," Eric revealed.

The woman made eye contact with me and had piercing green eyes. "Shifters do not injure humans. They have fully aware consciousness and control. What you just saw is a shifter infected with a form of a mutated rabies virus."

I whipped my head toward Eric to see if this was true and he nodded.

"That's where you come in," he said.

"I don't understand. What am *I* supposed to do about this? How do they even get this 'mutated' form of rabies?"

"We don't know. We imagine they contracted it the same way other creatures in the wild get it: from a bite of an infected animal," Eric shrugged. "The point is, we need to help them. And to help them, we need you to help us."

"By doing what?"

The woman reached to the left of her and picked up a clear glass box. "With these."

I looked inside and saw what appeared to be fully grown ticks. However, they were unlike any I had ever seen: they had a distinct letter H on their backs.

"Ticks? How are these going to help with a rabies outbreak within a group of shifting bears?" I snorted. They couldn't be serious. This all had to have been a joke.

"These aren't your everyday ticks," she started. "They hold the antibodies that will help prevent the virus from spreading among the shifters, like we have for dogs."

"So, like a vaccine?"

"Yes. We can't cure the virus once an individual has become infected, however, we can vaccinate the entire shifter population using these ticks to prevent an outbreak. To our knowledge, since the shifter you saw in the video died, we have not detected anyone else with the virus. We would like to handle this before someone else contracts it," the woman explained.

"So, you want me to go to this national park, unleash these ticks, and do what? Just leave and hope for the best?" I wasn't really sure about the merit of this project. It seemed valiant enough, but had the ticks had a trial run? Was *this* a trial run?

"Well, we would want you to stay there for observation. See if anyone develops the virus or has any negative side effects to the vaccine," Eric answered. His hands were folded over his desk and he was hunched over.

"Is this a trial run?" I finally asked.

"Not exactly. I myself have already conducted two trials and have found the ticks to be effective at inoculating their hosts. We think Acadia is the perfect location for this since the infected shifter was there," the woman answered. She seemed irritated that she had to explain these things to me, but hell, I wasn't thrilled to learn them in the first place. This project seemed sketchy and I wanted to cover all the bases to make sure of what I'd be getting myself into.

"What if someone already has the virus?" I asked.

"No one does," Eric answered sternly.

I folded my arms. "How can you be sure?" I wasn't convinced by the answers I was being given.

"I know because I have the test results of everyone who works in that park. I sent a phlebotomist there to test everyone's blood for the virus under the guise of a routine federal blood test. The park had been quarantined after the incident to both make sure the scenes were completely cleaned up as the shifter killed multiple people, and to implement some safety precautions. It was found to be in the park's best interest to close down for a while until the public felt safe again.

None of the staff have the virus, so they make perfect vaccine candidates."

"May I see the paperwork?"

"Of course." Eric passed the results of the blood tests my way and I looked them over carefully. He was correct: every single person tested negative for the virus, and the blood tests had only been done two days prior.

"So, everyone at this park is a shifter? All of the staff? What about the people in town?" I was a little wary. How would I know who was a shifter and who wasn't?

"No, not everyone is a shifter over there. Shifters travel to different parks, so the footage you saw was a gathering featuring some from different areas. We can't exactly pinpoint which individuals are shifters when they're in their human forms, but as I said previously, they wouldn't attack you either way. I know the video was unnerving, but keep in mind that you will be going there to help these people," the woman urged.

I wasn't sure how I felt about learning of the existence of shifters. After watching that video, it was hard to believe they wouldn't hurt me. Knowing it was the virus that caused the particular incident only comforted me slightly.

But, I had gotten into the CDC to help people, and these people clearly needed help.

"Okay. I'll do it," I agreed.

"Perfect!" Eric exclaimed. "We want to get these released as soon as possible while the park is still closed off to the public for safety renovations. Therefore, I will need you to go home and pack immediately."

Immediately? Boy, they weren't wasting any time.

"I'll pick you up with our flight tickets shortly." The woman stood with Eric and I followed suit.

"You'll be coming with me?" I couldn't say I was thrilled; I didn't exactly need a babysitter.

"I work there," she said bluntly as she exited the room.

"Don't worry about her; she's just very invested in the project. She'll be giving you your orders as well, so if anything happens, go to her first. I'm sure she'll acquaint herself with you more on the plane. For now, though, she asked that I not reveal her identity until she felt she could trust you," Eric informed, shaking my hand and motioning me towards the door. "You'd better get home and start packing."

I thanked him for the opportunity and sprinted towards the elevator, noticing the woman was nowhere in sight.

It'll take me ten minutes to get home and at least half an hour to pack, so hopefully, I have at least an hour. Boy, this will be interesting, I sighed.

2

RAMON

"Well, *amigo*, it's just you and me now."

I was staring down at a dead body. The shifter that had been infected with the mutated rabies virus that had killed Danielle Peterson was now lying on my autopsy table.

I had watched his health deteriorate and his behavior become even more aggressive—if at all possible—since his capture. It had gotten to the point where he was permanently in bear form and seemed unable or unwilling to change back. The last day, he was just lying on the floor of his cell, his breath ragged and labored. I had known he would die soon. I had been intrigued to see if the virus also affected whether he would shift back to human form after his death, which usually happened in healthy shifters. Or would he remain in bear form because the virus had taken over so much?

My question had been answered by his naked human frame lying before me. I already knew the cause of death, so a forensic autopsy was not necessary, but a clinical one was imperative to figuring out what the virus had done to this man's insides. I never had to do an autopsy while working at the national park in Mexico, but I had the training and knew what I was doing.

"*¡Empecemos!*" I exclaimed, grabbing my knife. The first thing I noticed, was that the body was covered in bug bites. The shifter had been out in the wild for who knows how long with no clothes on and I couldn't be sure he hadn't brought any with him into his cell where they continued to feast on him.

"Maybe that's why he was always in such a bad mood," I laughed to myself.

I made the first incision going straight down from his chest to his pubic bone. The shifter bled black, but I had been expecting that. His blood had gotten darker and darker each time I drew it for testing.

The body didn't have much fat tissue, so it was a little tough to cut through the muscle to get to the ribs, but I finally managed. I cut through the rib cage as well, cracking it open so his organs were fully exposed, and I was completely shocked by what I saw.

"It looks exactly the same," I spoke aloud, regarding each organ in my hands. The shifter's stomach was small and empty. He wouldn't eat anything, no matter how hard I had tried to get him to. His intestines were barren. His liver was intact, and his lungs were perfect.

Then, I saw the heart.

It had to be the heart; it just didn't look like one anymore. Now, it resembled a giant piece of coal, hardened and completely black.

"Huh...*interesante...*" I examined it a bit longer and set it aside, picking up the camera to snap a photo of it, along with the other internal organs to document how the virus had seemingly not affected anything else.

That seems nearly impossible. With the virus taking over the blood cells, what was fueling bodily organs to continue to function? There was no way the virus was smart enough to be able to allow them to function like blood could. Maybe the organs shut down once the virus took over completely?

This virus had me doubting almost everything I knew about science.

I decided to examine the brain next, cutting along the shifter's hairline and pulling his scalp back, exposing his skull with a noticeable crack in it.

"*¿Que demonios?*" A crack in the skull would have caused a massive bleed out to the brain and the shifter would have died. I could tell that it had been there for a while; it was not a fresh injury. Why was his skull cracked in the first place?

I used my medical saw to cut through the skull and make an opening big enough where I could remove the brain.

"*¡Dios mio!*" I exclaimed after almost cutting straight into the brain.

Why is it so close to the skull? It shouldn't be... I thought, removing the window of bone I cut out and I couldn't believe my eyes.

The shifter's brain had swollen to the point where it had almost taken up the entire skull. Removing the piece had only caused the swelling to bulge out from the opening.

How long has this guy's brain been like this? Any human would have died instantly from brain swelling of this magnitude...

I had to break the cranium completely open to extract the brain. Other than the massive swelling, it was perfectly normal.

"Ah!" I shrieked, dropping the brain onto the table and grabbing my shoulder. I opened my lab coat and pulled the sleeve of my shirt up to see a small bug bite.

"And now you've brought them with you? Come on! I didn't even see anything!" I cursed, checking the area. I still didn't see an insect, so I just assumed I had killed it when I grabbed my shoulder. Nevertheless, it made me want a shower. Badly.

I decided to wrap up the autopsy; there wasn't much more I could do anyway, so I took a few more shots of the enlarged brain and stitched up the body.

Hey, man. Still locked up with your boyfriend? I heard Trent's voice calling out in my head and rolled my eyes. I had been spending so much time on research regarding the shifter, Trent kept making jokes about the number of hours and effort I was putting into it. *The guy is dead, you can move on now!*

I focused my thoughts to telepathically respond. *Well, someone has to figure out how he might have picked up the virus from the environment and how it affected his body. Just in case we encounter it again.*

Yeah, yeah, yeah. Blah, blah, blah. You're all work and no play these days, man. You need a break.

I'll take a break when I feel like I have done all I can and found out everything there is to know about this.

Did you finish the autopsy? Knox's voice joined their channel.

Yes, sir. I have the pictures of all the abnormalities. I was going to head home and shower and then request a meeting with you to discuss my findings.

That can wait until tomorrow morning. When you get home, you can still shower and get dressed, but Trent and I will be by to pick you when you're done.

Pick me up for what?

We're having a bros' night out, man! Going to Leary's for a few drinks! Trent sounded loud and excited.

Yo no se...It's pretty late guys...

What are you? An old man? It's only 9pm!

Don't make me have to order you. Knox's voice was stern. I sure as hell didn't want to get our Alpha all riled up, so I finally gave in.

Fine. I'll need at least an hour to get ready, though.

No one said anything else, and I imagined they were just happy I finally caved.

I loved going out for beers with Trent and Knox, but I just hadn't felt like it that night. Not like I had a choice anymore, though. I removed my lab coat, pulled on my hoodie, and headed out into the chilly spring night.

When I got back to my place, I felt a headache setting in and I was feeling a bit nauseous. I pounded a glass of water, which was helping, but not enough to make it completely disappear.

Just as I was turning off my shower, I heard a banging at my door.

"Aye, man! You ready yet?" I heard Trent's voice booming through my lodge and rolled my eyes. I grabbed a towel, wrapped it around my waist and went to open the door.

"Of course, I'm not ready yet. That was hardly even a half hour," I groaned. They always rushed me when it came to going out. I mean, yes, I was always the last one ready, but that was mainly because I was usually the last one to know about our bros' nights out in the first place.

"You really need to cut down on your prep time, man. You're a guy. Guys are supposed to get ready quickly."

"Yeah well, I'm not feeling too good all of a sudden. I have a headache and my stomach's a little queasy."

"You're just saying that to try and get out of going."

"I'm serious!"

"It's supposed to be chicks like Hannah and Blanca who take forever to get ready." Trent rolled his eyes, ignoring my statement, and plopped himself onto my couch.

"Speaking of Hannah and Blanca, what are they going to be up to tonight?" I asked, heading back to my room to get dressed. Hannah was Knox's girlfriend and Blanca was Trent's, and they were just as good of friends as Trent and Knox were to me.

"Chick flick movie marathon or something. They practically threw us out." Trent laughed. "Hey! Make sure you wear something presentable!"

"Why?" I yelled from my room, examining a grey short-sleeved shirt. I heard Trent come into the room, followed by Knox; good thing I already had my boxers on. I laid the grey shirt on the bed and towel dried my cropped deep brown hair.

"Because we are going to find you a lady tonight!" Trent proclaimed.

"Oh no. Not another one of those nights!" I complained. Trent liked to set up these bro nights to try to get me to approach women. I always felt so much pressure that I'd up saying something awkward, or I'd be a complete clutz. And then they'd ultimately laugh at any of my dismal attempts to recover and never let me live down any of my mishaps.

"Oh, come on, last time was hardly a try. You slipped on a spilled drink before you even got to the last girl," Trent said with a smirk.

Here we go...

"And there was no way for us to tell that the first girl was waiting for her boyfriend to come meet her. Who goes to the bar to meet their boyfriend, anyway? And the other girl? Well, she just wasn't all that hot, honestly. Must have been a case of beer goggles in the first place."

"I'd really rather not have another night of misfortune, *hombres*. If there happen to be any girls there that catch my eye, let *me* handle it," I warned, pulling the grey shirt over my head and grabbing a blue and red flannel to wear over it. I decided it would be enough to keep me warm in the forty-degree March weather, and besides, we'd be in Knox's Jeep—not to mention, shifters had higher body temperature than humans. I still liked to pretend I would be cold, so I didn't get weird looks walking around in frigid temperatures with a tank top on.

"Alright, fine, I'll stop giving you advice. I'm just happy your coming out, honestly. But for real, you need to find a girlfriend. You're the only one of us who hasn't settled down yet and even Knox is getting a little worried about you." Trent pointed at Knox who nodded in agreement.

"You're drowning yourself in your job, leaving no time for yourself, Ramon. You have an amazing work ethic, but you also need to stop and enjoy the simple things in life."

"Like a woman!" Trent exclaimed, and I rolled my eyes. Sometimes, he acted like such a frat boy, just like the stereotypes played out on TV and in movies. Trent would be the one chugging a beer keg and getting wasted every night, failing all his classes except anything that involved physical activity. Knox would probably have been in the ROTC program. I don't even think we would all have been friends if we had gone to the same college.

"I just don't like to rush things like that. If there is a woman out there for me, she'll come. I'd rather not force the universe. It all worked out for you guys in ways I'm sure you least expected." Knox and Trent looked at each other and both nodded in agreement. "Maybe the same will happen for me."

After saying those optimistic things, I really believed them. It wasn't like I didn't want a girlfriend or anything. I did. But, I would know when there was a girl who was worth it. I just hadn't found her yet. I couldn't say I was optimistic that tonight would be the night that I would find her, but who knew? The night was still young, after all.

"Hurry up, man!" Trent and Knox had headed back into the living room and I sighed, taking one last look at myself in the mirror.

It'll do. I didn't look particularly well put together or anything, but whatever. We were going to a bar and I doubted the girl of my dreams would be found at a lowly pub.

3

MIN

Our flight arrived at 8pm and had been three hours long. The woman next to me hardly said a word; when I asked her to tell me about the park, "You'll see it when you get there," was her tight-lipped response.

She wasn't a very chatty—or friendly—so, I decided to get a little shut eye for the rest of the flight. And when I woke up, I felt great. I wasn't sure if it was such a good thing, because I realized I would probably be awake all night because of it.

"When we get outside, there will be a car waiting for you. It'll be yours for the duration of your stay, so you'll have a means for getting to and from the park," the woman said as we disembarked from the plane.

"So, where will I be staying?"

God, I hope it's not some shitty motel or something, I thought, grabbing my forest green suitcase as it finally came down the conveyor belt. She didn't have any luggage, so when I grabbed mine, she started walking toward the exit and didn't answer my question. When we got to the street, she led me to a sleek black car.

"An Audi?"

"2016 A8. I don't need to remind you that this is a classified mission. You can disclose to people what your job at the CDC is, but nothing about the mission or the information that was revealed to you. You can disclose that this is a government vehicle being loaned to you for your job. If anyone asks why you are visiting Acadia, however, you are to say that you are there to collect the aquatic insect data that's supposed to be recorded every 5-10 years. We are within the time frame, so it will make for a valid excuse." She handed me a folder. "Here's some paperwork to validate this if anyone needs further confirmation. In there are also some pages that you'll have to fill out, indicating when the ticks were released and if you see anything out of the ordinary happen afterward."

This just seems weird. Why are we keeping this such a secret if we're supposed to be helping these people? Can't we just reveal that we know about them and offer our help? I thought, but then I wondered how open these shifters were to being known. They might have a completely negative reaction to the government knowing of their existence and go into hiding or reject the help. *I guess it might be best to just handle it without their knowledge...*

"There's a black suitcase that was already placed in your trunk that contains a case of the ticks. Oh, and to answer your question, you will be staying at the Bass Cottage Inn, here in Bar Harbor. The address is already plugged into the GPS in your car; all you have to do is follow its directions."

A man got out of the driver's seat, grabbed my bag and hoisted it into the trunk. "She's all yours," he said, just before he and the woman walked off together.

I squealed in excitement as I took another look at the car. The shit box I was driving back home was a 2016 silver Chrysler 200, which was probably the lowest rated sedan in all the US at the time. But, it was all I could afford when I started my big government job and I thought I would get a better car once I started racking up paychecks. Chrissy, as I called her, ended up growing on me after all, so, until she died, I drove her. But, I couldn't say I wasn't thrilled to drive an Audi.

I practically ran to the driver's side of the car, eager to get in. Once I sat and closed the door, I examined the insides.

A sunroof, back up cam, button to heat the seats, built in GPS, Bluetooth, and USB ports? This is amazing! I immediately plugged in my phone and started singing along to New Order.

"Every time I see you falling / I get down on my knees and pray / I'm waiting for that final moment / You say the words that I can't say..." I sang aloud, bouncing in my seat a bit. I'm not sure why I was so happy, but the car had put me in a good mood. I revved the engine as I pulled the car onto the road and hit the start button on the GPS.

Now, I just need the hotel to be just as awesome and this night will be perfect!

"YOU'VE *GOT* to be kidding me," I said to myself, pulling up to the Inn. The place was practically a mansion. There seemed to be at least three floors and I counted fourteen windows on the second and third floors alone. When I got out of the car, there was a man waiting for me wearing black slacks, a white button-down shirt and a black vest. He was older and bald, with a full white beard.

"You must be Ms. Dupont. Welcome to Bass Cottage Inn! Let me help you with your bags." He walked over to the trunk that I had popped open and grabbed my suitcases. "My name is Frank, and I will be showing you to your room."

This man was probably the most chipper person I'd ever met in my life.

"You will be staying in the Verbena room, which is located on the second floor in the left wing," he said, walking up to the beautiful stained-glass doors. As we passed through the doorway, I peered around the gorgeous foyer as he continued, "To your left and right are several sitting areas for you to enjoy. Feel free to help yourself to any of the books we have on display over here on the left. Look past the shelves and you'll notice a grand piano. Do you play?"

"Um, no," I responded, too caught up in my surroundings. Everything was decorated in rich shades of mahogany and taupe with gorgeous ornate designs; I couldn't wait to see my room. We climbed one flight of stairs, heading to the left side of the building. He led me past several sets of doors, all the way down to the far end of the corridor.

"Well, here we are!" he exclaimed, opening the door to the room and setting my luggage on the rack. When I entered, my jaw hit the floor. The room was decorated in the same colors as downstairs, but with navy and slate accents. There was a generously-sized leather sofa, a regal armchair, and a king-sized canopy bed with a gas fireplace next to it.

"Although it seems you have come alone, your bathroom features a two-person jetted tub which will be through that door." He gestured to the right of the room. "Breakfast is served from 8 to 10am, should you wish to join us, and it is complimentary with your stay. Feel free to order anything you'd like."

Free breakfast—not just continental crap—and a jacuzzi? This place is unreal.

"And with that, I'll leave you to enjoy your accommodations. Do ring us downstairs if you need anything," Frank smiled and left the room, leaving the keys on the coffee table.

As soon as he left, I ran straight for the bed and threw myself onto the plush down duvet.

"Wow," I said aloud, gazing around the room in awe. *Is this what getting field work is like?*

Just then, my phone rang. *Who could that be?*

I grabbed my phone and didn't recognize the number on the caller ID, but decided to answer.

"Hello?"

"Is your room to your liking?" I heard the woman's voice from earlier on the other line.

"It's amazing. How long can I stay here?"

"As long as you want, honestly. The government will pay for it until your job is done, as long as you keep me updated on your progress," she replied bluntly.

"You're kidding, right?"

"Not at all," she said flatly. "I will submit a report stating that you have arrived here safely. I expect your next update in one week's time. That should be plenty for you to at least plant the ticks."

"Understood," I replied. I was beginning to realize I was never going to get on this woman's good side—if she even had one. As I opened my mouth to ask one more question, I heard the woman end our call without as much as a simple goodbye.

"Rude," I said aloud, throwing the phone down onto the bed beside me. I stared at the ceiling, feeling even more awake than before and checked my watch. It was 9pm.

Well, it's still so early, and it's Friday night. Maybe I should check out the night life here in Bar Harbor?

With that, I grabbed my phone and began searching for bars in the area. Leary's Landing Irish Pub popped up and it had the best reviews, so I decided to go there. Spotting a full-length mirror in the corner, I padded over to it, wondering if I should change my outfit. *Eh, it's good enough. Besides, I just want to grab a couple of drinks and scope out the locals,* I thought as I tucked my phone in my back pocket and headed for the door.

When I pulled up to the pub, it looked pretty dead inside and I wasn't sure if I wanted to venture in, but I decided to roll the dice.

When I walked in, everyone's eyes turned to me. There were only about eight people inside: three girls sat at the bar, looking to be in their twenties. A couple of older guys were hanging out at the other end of the bar, then, in the back corner, three relatively young guys in their mid to late twenties were gathered around a table. One had a buzzed, military-style cut and was tall and muscular. The other guy had the same build but had shortly cropped black hair and had a tan. The guy in between them is who captured my attention, though.

He had beautiful bronze skin, with short dark hair that I wanted to run my fingers through. His features were strong, and he was cleanly shaven, just how I liked 'em. He was of Hispanic descent for sure, I just couldn't tell from exactly where. His eyes were a light brown, almost hazel.

And they were staring directly at me.

I blushed and looked away immediately, heading toward the bar. There was a chalk board fixed to the wall featuring a list of four specialty cocktails, and my eyes scanned over the options.

"What can I get for you?" the bartender asked.

"Uh…I'll have the Fresh Whiskey Smash," I decided. It was described as a shot of Irish whiskey with a shot of fresh lemon juice and a mint sugar cube in it. Sounded pretty delicious to me. If it was good, I would stick with it; I didn't feel like dealing with a hangover in the morning.

The bartender presented the drink to me in a margarita glass, oddly; I decided to stir the drink until the ice cube melted and then took a cautious sip.

I had to admit, it was pretty delicious. I was usually a wine person, but I liked to try signature drinks when I felt adventurous. And with all that had happened that day, I was definitely feeling it.

"Um, hi there." I heard a voice next to me and almost spit out my drink.

The gorgeous guy from the corner table had decided to come to say hello.

4

RAMON

I HAD ALL BUT GIVEN UP ON THIS BROS' NIGHT.

"Come on, man; you can't be *everyone's* type. That doesn't mean you're ugly or anything." Trent was trying to cheer me up after a humiliating rejection from the girls at the bar.

I had gone up and tried my hand at a little small talk, asking how they were doing, what they were drinking. When I offered to buy them a round, one of them snorted, "No thanks. You're not my type," as the other cackled loudly.

Things like this always happened. Either the girl wasn't interested in me, or got bored when I started talking about my interests—science, mostly. I was at the end of my rope.

"*Mira*, there's no more *chicas* here tonight, so can we just drink and hang out? Let's leave the matchmaking shit for another night," I said, raising my glass of Guinness.

"Alright, my friend. But if another girl walks in and you're interested, you should say something," Trent said, raising his drink in return. Knox clinked glasses with us and we all took long pulls of our drinks.

I paused, looking around quickly. "Do you guys hear that?" I asked, trying to read everyone's lips in the bar. I couldn't figure out where that sound was coming from.

"Hear what, man?" Trent and Knox were on guard now, sweeping the bar as well.

"Whistling. Someone's whistling." I tried focusing really hard on the sound, but no one had their lips pursed or anything.

"I don't hear anything," Knox said, staring at me.

Trent laughed, slapping me on the back. "The booze getting to you already, bud?"

"Haha. Yeah, maybe." I laughed nervously. The whistling grew fainter and then it disappeared.

Did I just imagine it?

My eyes swept around the bar idly, and that's when I spotted her. She had a black, bone-straight, shoulder length bob with dark eyes to match. She was pale with full lips and a slender frame. She was Asian, I was sure, I just couldn't tell from where. There was something else in there...

She had captured my attention completely. And when my eyes moved back to hers, we connected, and I felt a jolt of electricity run through me as her lips parted and her checks flushed. She turned around quickly and practically ran up to the bar. My eyes followed her every step, peeping a nice round bottom that would fit into my hands perfectly. She ordered a drink and took a sip.

*I wish those were my lips instead...*I thought. There was something about her that was just so goddamn sexy.

"You should go talk to her," Knox said, nudging me. He must have caught me checking her out.

"Nah, I couldn't. She's way out of my league, *hombre*," I responded, shaking my head and waving his words away. There was no way that girl would talk to me. But every fiber of my being wanted to say something to her.

"She could be thinking the same thing, Ramon. I saw her blush when you made eye contact," Knox teased.

"The worst she can say is she isn't interested," Trent shrugged.

"Like I need anyone else telling me *that* tonight."

Trent slapped me on the back. "Don't be a punk, man."

"Fine," I agreed finally, getting up from my bar stool and downing the rest of my beer. The girl was still standing by the bar and seemed to be considering the drink she had just tasted.

What do I say to her? I thought, milling over a million and one greetings in my head. *Do I say something Spanish? No, you idiot. What if she doesn't know Spanish? Everyone knows 'hola,' though. Nah, better not risk it.*

I went back and forth in my head as I walked up to her and she didn't even notice me approach.

"Um...hi, there," I finally said, running a hand through my hair nervously.

She looked up at me and her eyes widened.

"Um, hi." I watched a deep flush blossom over her cheeks and realized that maybe she was just as nervous as I was.

"I saw you walk in and my friends hyped me up to come talk to you," I chuckled, trying to be honest. If she was shy, I wanted to show her that I wasn't that confident in talking to people, either.

"Do your friends *make* you talk to women often?" She raised her eyebrows at me. I wasn't sure how to take the question, but I decided to be truthful.

"Yeah, they think something's wrong with me," I chuckled.

"Ah...*cherchez la femme...*" she said, taking a sip from her drink.

"You speak French?" I asked, bewildered. I hadn't been expecting that at all.

"*En effet*. That's right. I lived in France until I was seventeen. I lived with my father who was French, and he sent me to English schools. He said only knowing French would hinder my future, so he wanted me to learn in English." She took a long swig of her drink, "I came to America for college ten years ago and I've been here ever since."

Wow, she's so open about herself, I thought, and I admired that.

"So, what does it mean?"

"What?"

"I'm not sure if I can pronounce it. *Cherchez la femme,* was it?" It came out with a heavy Spanish accent and I cringed, fairly certain I had pronounced it incorrectly.

"That was perfect!" She giggled, and my heart skipped a beat. It was a lovely soft chime and I hoped I would be hearing it more. "It's a saying we used to have in France. Literally, it would translate as 'looking for women.' The saying itself is meant to describe when a man is acting out of character. The French believe that a woman will solve his issues, so he must go out and find one. Like how your friends are doing. Who also seem to be looking over here to check on you."

When I turned to look back the table, Trent and Knox raised their glasses to me. She raised her own in return and I chuckled.

"Yeah, that's pretty spot on," I agreed, as she finished her cocktail. "You happened to be in a good spot, since I needed another drink. I see you've finished yours, too; may I buy you another?"

Please say yes, please say yes...

"Sure!" She smiled, and my breath caught.

She is gorgeous...

"What are you drinking, might I ask?"

"The Fresh Whiskey Smash," she said, proudly.

"Ooooh, whiskey! That's my kind of girl!" I joked, calling the bartender over with a wave. "Can I get another Fresh Whiskey Smash for the lady and I'll have some Jack on the rocks, please."

"Hmmm, so you're a Jack kind of guy?" She seemed intrigued.

"Yeah, I used to drink a lot of tequila back in Mexico, so when I got to the states and found whiskey, it grew on me. I still love tequila, though. It'll always have a special place in my heart." I smiled, remembering all the times I went to the bars in Mexico and they had hundreds of different tequilas. I would swear I had tried them all.

"So, you're Mexican?"

"*¡Nacido y criado!*" I exclaimed, proudly. "Born and raised!"

She laughed, and I was glad she found me funny. She was enchanting—and so attractive. I hoped she was feeling the same.

"I wouldn't have assumed you were born in France, just by looking at you."

"My mother is Korean."

"Can you speak Korean, too?" I asked as our drinks arrived. She grabbed hers and sipped it immediately, so I felt like I had to follow suit. As the whiskey trickled down my esophagus, it felt like a fire bursting in my chest. Man, I loved that feeling.

"No, actually. I only know what my name means. My parents are divorced, and I only lived with my dad. My mother is a diplomat and I never got to see much of her as a child."

Mierda...Things are turning dark...Turn it around, man.

"I'm sorry to hear about your parents," I started. "Speaking of names, I just realized that we haven't even introduced ourselves yet. I'm Ramon Marquez. I work for Acadia National Park as their Resource Manager."

I reached out my hand and she shook it.

"Pleased to meet you, Ramon. I'm Min Dupont and I work for the CDC as an entomologist."

"An entomologist? You study *bugs*? That's amazing!" This woman just got more interesting with every moment. And the fact that she was into science was such a turn on.

"And what does a resource manager such as yourself do?" She flashed that beautiful smile again.

"Well, my job entails a lot of things. I mostly focus on the biology, botany, aquatics, soil science, and geology of the park," I stated proudly, hoping she would find my job interesting as well.

"Wow, that's a mouthful," she giggled. "I've dabbled in several different areas of science, but alas, bugs are my one true love."

"There's nothing wrong with having a specialty. I spent all six years of school taking every science class I could sign up for and could never settle on just one thing. I can be pretty indecisive," I admitted.

"I don't think there's anything wrong with that either. Your job must never get boring."

"Not for one minute," I smiled.

"Yeah, me neither. There's always new insects to discover and interesting things to learn about them."

"So, you mentioned you know what your name means?" I asked, eager to know more about her. I didn't want the conversation to end.

"Quick, clever, and sharp," she said, laughing before taking another sip of her drink. "At least that's what my parents told me."

"Would you consider yourself to be those things?"

"Maybe...what do you think?"

Is she trying to seduce me now? Not like she had to try hard; I was already thinking about what she might look like sprawled over my bed.

"Clever, for sure. Quick and sharp? You'll have to show me," I responded, hoping to send a signal.

She smirked and downed her drink instantly, setting the glass on the bar. She hopped off her bar stool and started walking towards the door.

"You coming?" She turned back to look at me and my jaw dropped. This woman went from shy to a confident seductress in minutes and I was hooked. I looked over at Trent and Knox. Trent was giving me the thumbs up and Knox was motioning for me to go with her. I nodded, downed the rest of my Jack and followed her out the door.

"An Audi A8 GT? What year is this?" I gushed as we reached her car. I wasn't sure what I expected her to drive, but it sure as hell wasn't a sleek sports car.

"2016. Get in. I'm about to show you how quick and sharp I can be," she declared, taking the driver's seat. I raised my eyebrow.

Fuck yeah! I got into the passenger's side, and it was just as sweet as I imagined it to be. *How can this chica have a better car than me, man?*

And sure enough, she could drive the shit out of that bad boy. We were back to her place in less than five minutes and she pulled into the parking space in one fell swoop. It looked effortless, and I was turned on immensely.

Nothing sexier than a girl who can drive a sports car, I thought to myself as I felt my member begin to harden in my pants. *Down boy. Let's get inside first.*

"Quick and sharp enough for you?" she smirked.

Oh, so you're cocky too?

"I don't know...I might need some more examples..." I flirted. She arched a thin, black eyebrow and I chuckled. And then, without warning, her lips were pressed to mine.

My eyes widened at her sudden forwardness, but I sure as hell wasn't complaining. I kissed her back fervently, hoping not to come off as overly eager, while also making it clear that I very much wanted more. She brought a hand up to my cheek and I was thankful I had decided to shave earlier today.

My hand went to the nearest thing it could find—her hip—and I pulled her closer toward me. Our tongues danced, and she sucked on my bottom lip. I squeezed my hand and she let out a light moan.

"Wanna come upstairs?" she breathed against my lips. I nodded, but inside, I was screaming

FUCK YES.

How's it going over there, Casanova? I heard Trent's voice in my mind.

Amigo, we're sitting in her 2016 Audi A8 GT.

WHAT? Yo, my man!

I know, right?

You'd better hit that tonight, bro. See if she'll let you drive it in the morning. I could hear the laughter in Trent's voice.

She actually just invited me up.

Say no more, man! Call me tomorrow with the details.

"Are you coming?" Min was already out of the car and had her door open, waiting for me to get out.

Shit. I hopped out the car and followed her up to the doors of the building.

"Bass Cottage Inn, eh? Someone's fancy." I laughed as we walked through the doors and she led me upstairs.

"*Pftt.* Company's paying for it," she snorted as we walked down the hallway. We reached the last room at the end and she opened the door.

"Wow, this place is nice," I remarked, stepping into the opulent room. Judging by her two zipped suitcases, I guessed she had arrived that day; she hadn't even unpacked anything yet. "Did you just get here?"

I didn't get an answer. Instead, her lips were on mine once again, and she was peeling off my flannel shirt.

I liked girls that got down to business.

I helped her take off the shirt and lifted the grey one with it, and within seconds, her hands were exploring my chest as our kiss deepened. I wanted to return the favor, so I felt for her jacket, but then I opened my eyes to see it already lying on the floor.

*She does work quickly...*I admired her eagerness.

I decided it made no sense to hold back at this point. I grabbed her blouse and lifted it over her head, revealing a lacy pale blue bra.

"Yeah, they're kind of small..." she joked, looking down at her breasts and then back up at me.

"They're perfect." I grabbed her and pulled her body against mine. I bent down and started kissing and nibbling at her neck, while at the same time, working to open her bra clasp. She laced her fingers behind my head and moaned a little with each bite, sending blood straight into my shaft, which was now pressing against her. She kissed the only place she could reach at the moment, my shoulder, but it felt good just the same to feel her soft lips anywhere against my skin.

Her bra opened fairly easily, and I patted myself on the back. It had been a while since I had been with a woman, but so far, so good.

I pulled away, taking her bra with me. Her breasts were the perfect handful, perky, and her nipples were the softest pink. They almost blended into her flushed skin.

"You're staring again," she said, crossing her arms over her chest. I grabbed both of her arms and pulled her toward me again, pressing her breasts against my bare chest. They were soft and caved at the contact.

"*¿Puedes culparme?*" I whispered in her ear seductively, brushing my lips against it.

"I have no idea what you just said, but fuck, it was sexy…" She grabbed my face and pulled it back down to kiss me again, and I smiled inwardly. That was definitely the effect I had been going for. Seconds later, her hands were unbuttoning my jeans, and instead of pulling them down on their own, she yanked my boxer briefs down with them.

Since we're playing that game… I did the same to her, taking off her jeans and thong at the same time, our naked bodies now facing one another.

Her womanhood was covered in very fine hair; so fine, that from afar, it would be unnoticeable. All I wanted was to part her legs to see more.

Her eyes were on my member, and I knew without looking that it was standing at attention. Her eyes were wide, and I could tell immediately what she was thinking without her having to say a word.

5

MIN

"It's just so *thick*," I murmured. I was staring at his rock-hard shaft, trying to imagine how he could possibly get inside me with that thing.

Nevertheless, I wasn't afraid to try; in fact, I was determined to make it work. I got down on my knees and hungrily approached his cock, grabbing it with both hands. It was about seven inches long, but it had to be close to two inches wide.

I was both excited and nervous as I placed my lips on the tip at first and then opened my mouth to take it in. I heard him sigh with pleasure as my tongue started working around it. When I coated it completely with my saliva, I started to bob my head up and down over his shaft, using one hand to pleasure him at the base. The more I moved along his length, the easier it got to close my mouth more tightly over it and he started to moan.

I used my free hand to reach down and fondle myself; with his size, I would need all the lubrication I could get. He tasted a mix of sweet and salty and I wanted more; it was turning me on to no end and I had to stop pleasuring myself to keep from releasing. As his moans grew louder, I could feel myself dripping with need.

Oh no, not yet, you don't... I told myself, standing up from the floor. He groaned, and his eyes were darker now, a deep brown, and half lidded with desire. He lifted me up and carried me to the bed with no effort at all.

Could this man possibly get any hotter? I thought as he laid me down, but I got my answer quickly when he threw my legs open and dove between them. A moan immediately escaped my lips as I felt his tongue invade my slit. He knew exactly where to lick, zoning in on my pleasure center, slowly at first, but then he started to pick up speed. My hips bucked against his mouth and soon I was grinding against his tongue, wanting more and more. I felt one of his fingers slip inside me easily, and soon, another finger joined it. He sucked my pearl between his lips softly and I gasped, my mind going blank. Him and me, that's all there was, and I was soaring towards my climax. And then he stopped. I whimpered as he climbed on top of me.

I was so close...

"Not yet, *mi dulce*..." he whispered. I could feel his member pressing against my inner thigh and I wanted it more than anything in that moment.

"Please..." I begged.

I didn't have to wait long until I felt his manhood rubbing against my entrance, coating itself in my wetness.

I gasped as I felt him thrust into me, my nails digging into his shoulders, and I heard him wince. It wasn't particularly painful, but he filled me completely, throbbing against my walls and it was a delicious feeling. He waited there for a moment, giving me time to expand around him and I was thankful for it. When I felt comfortable, I moved my hips, giving him the cue that I was ready.

He moved slowly at first, pulling himself almost completely out and then pushing his full length into me. I whimpered again, wanting him to move faster, and he complied, his hips pumping faster into me. He moved down and took one of my nipples into his mouth as he thrusted, flicking his tongue over its firm peak. Pleasure was bouncing through my entire body, ricocheting from my nipple to my clit and throughout the rest of me. I wrapped my legs around his waist as he moved to my other nipple, teasing it and driving me crazy with need.

"Faster... Deeper..." I breathed, wanting to feel more of him more quickly. I wrapped my arms around his neck tightly, pressing my body against his as he slammed into me repeatedly, releasing a symphony of moans from my lips. The flame within me was swallowing me whole, enveloping me in scorching flames. The fire was growing and growing as his member assaulted my g spot repeatedly, pounding into me. My climax hit me like a wave, crashing over me intensely as my body stiffened. My nails instinctively dragged down his back, and I heard a growl rip through him. He was breathing heavily, and I guessed his climax was near as well. With each thrust, my orgasm rippled through me further and just when I thought I would explode, he released a thunderous roar, his seed spilling into me. I moaned as he filled me, warmth flooding through me. I squeezed my walls around him, milking him, but also wishing he could just stay within me. I whimpered as his shaft slid from my body and he chuckled, collapsing next to me.

"I want more," I pouted, curling up against his chest and nuzzling his neck.

"That good, huh?" he joked, stroking my hair.

"God...*so* good..." I responded sleepily. Even though I yearned for him, my body had other plans as a yawn escaped my mouth.

"I don't think you could handle more, Sleeping Beauty," Ramon laughed.

"Wanna bet? Try me again in the morning," I challenged, throwing a leg over him and wrapping an arm around his waist.

"Holding me hostage?" he whispered against my head, kissing my forehead and I nodded against his chest.

And the last thing I heard before sleep claimed me was his soft chuckle and the click of the lamp light going off.

I DON'T wanna wake up... I thought, feeling the warm sunlight against my face, but not wanting to open my eyes. I knew it was morning, but I was not ready to face the day just yet. I tried burying my face into the nearest thing and realized I was laying on something heated.

"Awake finally?" I heard a man's voice ask.

Or someone.

Oh shit! I thought, remembering meeting a guy at the bar last night. *What was his name again? Roman? No, that's not right...Ramon. That was it! Wait, why does he feel so hot? Does he have a fever or something?*

"Why are you so hot? You're burning up!"

"Maybe it's having you next to me?"

I smiled remembering the mind-blowing sex he had delivered to me last night.

"Good morning..." I smiled. He was grinning at me in all of his sexy naked glory, and he was indeed glistening with a sheen of sweat.

"Maybe it got cold last night and they turned the heat up or something?" I decided to get up and shifted my legs. I winced, feeling how sore I was from the night before.

He noticed and chuckled lightly. "I remember someone requesting morning sex, but I don't think you have it in you," he joked as I propped myself up on one elbow.

"Yeah, I might have been a little overzealous," I laughed. "I'll definitely need some time to recover."

Gazing over his body, I really wish I didn't need to recuperate. But, I knew sex right now would be more painful than enjoyable. The soreness I felt was satisfying, though; it was a reminder of his large member inside me, stretching my walls. And that was a memory I wanted to relive and remember for a long time.

"Did you sleep well?" he asked.

"I did. Did you?"

"Not really. I actually hardly slept at all, but I feel fine. I just watched you sleep."

"Creep," I snickered, peeking over him to look at the clock. "Shit, it's already 11am!"

"Was there something you had to do before now?" he asked, confused by my sudden disappointment.

"Not particularly. But this place serves free breakfast until 10 and I missed it. I'm sure the food here is to die for."

"Well, how long are you staying? I'm sure you can catch it another day."

I wasn't quite sure how long I would be there for, so I decided not to answer and to just focus on the last part of what he said.

"But I want breakfast *now*," I whined. I was mostly joking, but I really was pretty hungry.

"There's always Jordan's," he shrugged.

"Jordan's?"

"Yeah. Usually most places in Bar Harbor close for breakfast early, but Jordan's serves breakfast until 2pm. They're usually closed in March and don't open until April, but they announced that they were opening early this year because of the good weather. Usually it's still pretty cold at this time of year, but with temperatures in the forties, that's pretty good for March. They specialize in everything blueberry."

"Sounds perfect. Let's go!"

I hopped out of bed and immediately regretted it, the soreness very prevalent between my legs. I did my best to ignore it as I bent down to open my suitcase.

"Need a toothbrush? I packed two by some miracle," I laughed, turning to see that he had already slipped into his boxers and was just buttoning his jeans.

Boy, he looks good just like that.

"That's how you should go to breakfast," I said, biting my lip and checking him out. Hard.

"Oh yeah? You'll keep me warm?" He walked over to me, sliding his hands from my hips to my bottom. He cupped me there and squeezed, lifting me slightly off the ground and I closed my eyes, releasing a soft moan.

"More like you'll keep me warm, doing things like that…"

"Oh, trust me. It's working for me, too," he chuckled, taking my hand and placing it on his crotch. His cock was engorged, and a thrill shot through me.

Fuck…

And then my stomach growled. We both burst out laughing at the timing.

"I mean I'm hungry for that, too, but it seems my stomach is demanding food at the moment," I giggled.

"Alright, why don't you get dressed, then, and I'll take you up on that toothbrush," he said, taking one from my hand and disappearing into the bathroom. "Holy shit!"

"What?" Thinking there was something wrong, I ran to the bathroom.

"You have a jacuzzi in here?"

"He wasn't kidding when he said it could fit two people," I snorted and Ramon gave me a puzzled look. "Oh, the guy who showed me to my room. Old guy. Nothing to be worried about."

"And who's to say I'm worried?" he laughed.

"You never know," I smiled and shrugged, leaving the bathroom to go get dressed. I heard the water at the sink start.

I pulled out a yellow V-neck long sleeve shirt and a pair of navy blue leggings, and after getting dressed, I brushed my hair and thanked the heavens I wasn't a make-up person.

*I wonder if he likes girls who wear make-up, though...*I thought, heading to the bathroom so I could brush my teeth. He was just zipping his pants and flushing the toilet.

"Oh sorry! I guess I should have said I was coming in," I giggled as he put the toilet seat down and went to wash his hands.

What a gentleman.

"It's okay. Nothing you haven't seen, eh?" He chuckled, drying himself with the hand towel. He bent down to kiss me, but I put a finger to his lips.

"I have this thing where I can't kiss people until we have both bushed our teeth."

"That's understandable." I was happy he took the small rejection easily, and I would be sure to make it up to him as soon as I was done brushing my teeth. As I turned the water on, he disappeared from the bathroom to finally put his shirt on.

What a shame.

When I was done brushing my teeth, I headed back into the bedroom and grabbed my leather jacket that was still on the floor. I thought about picking up the other clothes that were scattered about, but decided to handle it when I got back.

"Ready to go?" He smiled. "You look great."

I beamed as I grabbed both sets of keys. "Now I'm ready," I said, as I reached up for his face and pulled it closer to mine, engaging his lips in a deep kiss. Handing him the keys to the Audi, I told him, "Your turn to drive."

His face lit up and his jaw dropped. "Really?"

"Yeah. I figured it'd be faster for you to drive than to have me put it into my GPS," I shrugged. He kissed me again and practically ran down the stairs like a kid on Christmas morning, and it was the most adorable thing I had ever seen. I locked the room behind me and headed down the stairs to my car. When I got there, he was already in the driver's side with a huge grin on his face. I laughed to myself as I got into the passenger side.

"Now, let's see what this baby can do."

6

RAMON

She's letting me drive her car? I HAD MY FINGERS CURLED AROUND THE steering wheel and I still couldn't believe it. *This chica is amazing!*

I couldn't wait to brag to Trent about it as we took off toward Jordan's. We got there in two minutes flat; I was both disappointed and proud.

"Seems like you could show me a thing or two about how to handle a car like this," Min smirked. She seemed to have enjoyed the ride, even though it had been a quick one.

"Well, after the show you put on last night, Mario Andretti, I tried to deliver," I wiggled my eyebrows at her and she giggled.

She has to be the cutest and sexiest thing on Earth.

We got out of the car and headed into Jordan's, and as we ascended the front steps, I noticed it looked exactly the same as it did last year with its red counter stools and wooden booths. I requested a booth for us and we were seated immediately. Mugs were placed in front of us featuring the Jordan's logo and the waitress returned with a fresh pot, pouring us each a cup.

"Blueberry blend?" I asked.

"As always," the waitress smiled. Her name tag read 'Georgina.'

"Oh, may I have an Old Soaker too, please?" I asked before she could walk away.

"Sure thing, hun!"

"What's an Old Soaker?" Min asked, searching the menu for it.

"It's a blueberry soda you can only get here in Bar Harbor. You *need* to try it."

"Sounds yummy. In fact, so does everything on this menu."

"Well, how about you order whatever you want, and we'll split the plates half way?"

"That sounds perfect! But I hope you're hungry because I want to try it all—and I really love blueberries."

I laughed. Too bad she didn't know I was a shifter, because we can have one hell of an appetite. The waitress returned to the table, setting the blueberry soda down before me.

"So, what can I get for you guys?"

"We're going to have whatever *she* says we're having," I smiled, nodding in Min's direction as I put down my menu.

"We will have a short stack of blueberry pancakes with real maple syrup, an order of extra-crispy home fries, two eggs sunny side up, a side of bacon, a blueberry Belgium waffle with vanilla whipped cream, a blueberry cinnamon-granola yogurt parfait, and a blueberry streusel muffin, please," Min finished and smiled up at the waitress who was scribbling furiously.

"Will that be all?"

"Yes ma'am. Thank you," Min said as the waitress took our menus and walked off to place our order.

"Damn girl, you're going to put me in a blueberry coma after this," I laughed.

"I told you to prepare yourself."

"Okay, ready to try this?" I asked, passing her the blueberry soda. The waitress had already uncapped it for us and Min eagerly took a swig.

"*God,* that's delicious! I'll have to bring a whole case of those back with me."

I tried to take a sip myself, but I found the fizzy drink difficult to swallow.

That's odd. I've never had a problem drinking soda before... I forced the beverage down my throat and tried to hide my discomfort. *Maybe I'm getting a sore throat or something...*

We idly chatted until our food came out slowly, plate by plate. We were both glad that it didn't come out all at once; it would have been so overwhelming, and to be honest, I wasn't sure it would all fit on the table. Georgina brought the muffin and parfait out first and Min immediately grabbed the muffin.

"I call the top half!"

"That's not how these things work," I chuckled. "You're supposed to cut it in half."

"I *am* cutting it in half," she said, ripping the top off the muffin and putting it on her plate. "You never said which top it had to be."

I groaned. She was right, living up to that clever part of her name. And before I could get to the parfait, she grabbed that too.

"Aw, come on; not the parfait, too..."

"Well, a parfait isn't a parfait without the yogurt, so I'll play fair," she smiled, and I watched her divide it down the middle and slide it across the table toward me.

The pancakes and waffle came out next, the home fries and eggs coming out shortly after. We each ate half the waffle, one pancake and one egg. I found the pancakes and waffles extremely hard to get down, but I forced myself through it, and I picked at the home fries in between.

I groaned, sitting back and holding my stomach. "*Dios mio*, I'm so full."

"Yeah, I'm pretty sure I overdid it," she breathed, doing the same. "Do you have anything going on today?"

I'm supposed to meet up with Knox to review the autopsy findings, but I'm sure he won't mind if I come by later after telling him I was with a girl.

"No, not really. How about you?" She paused for a moment and then shook her head.

"Want to come back to my place and take a nap? Because I need one after this meal," she laughed. "And then maybe we can relax in the jacuzzi afterwards?"

"That sounds perfect," I smiled. I could definitely go for a nap after eating all those carbs.

I'll have Sophia check my throat when I get back to the park...

WE GOT BACK to her room and immediately fell onto the bed. I closed my eyes, and just as I was about to drift off, I felt a sharp pain in my stomach, like someone had just punched me. I winced and tried not to wake Min, who was curled up against me, snoring softly. I detangled myself just as I felt a heave, and I practically sprinted to the bathroom.

Everything I had just eaten came up violently. I didn't know what had come over me; I was fine one minute, and the next, my stomach was beating itself up.

Could this be food poisoning?

"Hey, are you okay?" I heard a knock at the door and a sleepy voice.

"Uh, yeah. I guess I just ate too much. I'll be right out," I replied after clearing my throat and flushing the toilet; thank god I'd made it there in time. I stumbled over to the sink and brushed my teeth, rinsing my mouth out and gargling a bit as well. When I finally felt stable enough to do so, I left the bathroom and noticed Min had been standing outside waiting for me with a concerned look on her face.

"You sure you're alright? Can I get you anything?"

"I'm sure I'll be fine. Let's get back to bed; we could both use a little more shut eye." I grabbed her hand and led her back to the canopy bed; she curled right up against me and was sleep in minutes.

I felt much better after getting the food out of my stomach, but now I was starting to worry. I wasn't sure what was wrong with me, but I could feel that something was most definitely *off*. Shifters usually had higher temperatures than humans, but I was starting to feel my core temperature rise. It was settling through me like a furnace.

Maybe I just need to sleep it off...

MIN WOKE up first this time, nuzzling me awake. I opened my eyes to see her smiling face looking back at me.

"Feel better?" she asked, running her fingers through my hair and then pressing her palm against my forehead.

"Still hot," I moaned, noticing how sweaty my shirt had become.

"We can hop in the jacuzzi and fill it with cooler water. I'm actually feeling pretty warm myself and could use some cooling down," she smirked.

A cold soak in the jacuzzi sounded so refreshing to me in that moment. "*Si, por favor*," I replied eagerly, getting up from the bed and padding over to the bathroom. Min followed me, stripping off her clothes and I did the same.

"Do you know how to work it?" she asked as I examined the temperature gauge.

"Looks just like a thermostat. I turned the temperature down to 68, which was the lowest it would go." I was slightly disappointed; forty or fifty would have been better, but I set the jacuzzi to fill itself, which it did miraculously quickly. Min smiled wide as I turned on the jets.

"*Despues de ti, mi querida.*" I motioned for her to get in first. She slipped in, her beautiful slim body disappearing under the water.

"Oh, it's definitely cold!" she shrieked, holding herself as she sat in the water. I climbed in after her, welcoming the frigid water that wrapped around my heated skin, and sank my shoulders beneath the surface.

"This feels amazing," I sighed, relaxing into the cool bath.

Min drifted toward me, sitting in my lap. "I actually need your warmth; this might be a little too cold for me." She wrapped my arms around her and settled in. "Ah...that's much better."

I closed my eyes, stroking her arms.

"Think you'll stay the night with me again?" I heard her ask.

"Would you like me to?"

"Maybe. I can't lie; it would be nice."

"Well, I'll have to call my boss because I was supposed to meet with him tonight. I'll see if we can to meet tomorrow instead."

"Oh, I don't want to intrude on your work." I could hear the disappointment in her voice, though.

"My boss was one of the guys trying to push me to talk to you last night," I laughed. "I'm sure he'll be more than happy to postpone if he knows I'm with you."

"Well, I am honored. You must not hook up with a lot of women, I guess?" She turned to look up at me.

"Not since moving here, no; I've been pretty focused on my work. As you said, many things fall into my lap with my job title, so I'm always busy. The only time I ever go out is when I'm dragged out by those two, and they're always trying to set me up with women, but it never works out. I'm either not their type, or they immediately get turned off because they think I'm a science nerd."

She flashed a genuine smile. "I just so happen to like science nerds."

"That's because you *are* one," I laughed, nuzzling her nose.

Laying there with her felt like I was exactly where I needed to be. I was glad I went out with the boys last night; I would have missed her.

And she was perfect.

Now all you've gotta do is tell her you're a bear shifter, I groaned inwardly.

How was I going to break the news to her? I'd never had to reveal my true nature to a woman before; no girl in Mexico had made me feel so at home with her in my arms, like I'd felt right at that moment.

I loved her witty sense of humor; no woman had made me laugh as much as she had. And with her wanting me to stay, I knew we would be spending a lot of time together. It had been almost a full day and all I could think about was showing her all the beauty of Bar Harbor and Acadia, then bringing her back to my cabin and making love all night long.

And as long as I didn't get angry, I knew I could hide my bear long enough; the full moon wasn't for another three weeks. But, depending on how this went, I would need to tell her, eventually.

"I really like you, Ramon. I'm not sure how long I'll be here in Maine, but I would like to spend as much time as I can with you—if that's okay, of course." She was gliding her fingertips along my arms, making goosebumps pop up along my skin.

"Of course," I replied, kissing the top of her head. "I really like you, too, Min."

I squeezed my arms around her tightly, and a part of me never wanted to let go.

7

MIN

BEFORE I KNEW IT, I HAD SPENT AN ENTIRE WEEK WITH RAMON.

He ended up taking time off of work to show me around the park; we hiked over nearly fifty gravel trails to one of the park's granite bridges one day, passing numerous crystalline lakes and ponds. Towering mountains surrounded us, and dense woodlands stretched as far as the eye could see. It was beautiful, and I could have sworn I saw every bird species known to man there. Another day, he took me to Eagle Lake for a picnic, and the last time we went, we hiked up Cadillac Mountain and watched the most breathtaking sunset I have ever witnessed in my life.

And all three times, I had forgotten the ticks.

Well, truth be told, I hadn't necessarily *forgotten* them. I'd tried to think of some way to discreetly carry them along without having him notice, but I couldn't; the case holding the top-secret ticks was far too large to fit into my travel bag.

It was Friday evening, and I decided that the following day, I'd finally tell Ramon that I had to get to work and that we could hang out later that night if, he wanted to. If all else failed, he'd be back at work on Monday, so I would have been able to go then, too.

Ping.

Is that my phone? I grabbed it to see what the notification was. Ramon and I were eating dinner at Havana, a Latin-American restaurant in Bar

Harbor, and while Ramon got up to use the restroom, I tapped the screen.

'Your period started today' was the most recent notification my phone received from the My Days app.

Hmm...no, it didn't. I narrowed my eyes, staring at my phone. Ramon had returned to his seat, so, not wanting to be rude, I stuffed my phone back into my purse and took a forkful of my seafood paella. *Maybe it'll come tomorrow.*

ANOTHER WEEK WENT BY, and no one from the NCPD-CID had called for an update on my mission. The woman told me she'd touch base with me in a week, but it had been two weeks without contact; I'd also been instructed to not call anyone.

Had they forgotten about me? Had they expected me to fail? Maybe this was all a joke. Bear shifters weren't real, and I was stupid enough to believe they could actually get a vaccine to be viably transmitted by ticks. This was all a test, and I was failing miserably.

I suppose it was a good thing, though, because, dammit, I still hadn't released the ticks.

It was Friday morning, and once again, Ramon and I had spent another week together. He had taken more time off, telling his boss that he hadn't been feeling well. And in fact, that wasn't a lie; I'd been taking care of him the entire week. He had a fever, didn't want to eat or drink anything, and he hardly wanted to sleep. When I finally got him to eat something, he couldn't keep it down for more than a few hours. He told his boss that he had the flu, but if he did, I felt like he would have been sleeping much more than he was. It was like his body was shutting down, but his mind was on high alert.

I actually thought I was getting sick as well. I didn't have a fever or anything like that, but I had to use the restroom at least twenty times a day, even if I hadn't had anything to drink in a couple of hours. I was also nauseous and vomiting, but not after every time I ate, like what Ramon was experiencing, and I was utterly exhausted, no matter how long I had slept for. *Probably just a stomach bug*, I thought.

The night before, I had the most bizarre dream, too. I'd woken up to use the bathroom, and when I turned to Ramon, I could have sworn I saw the face of a bear instead of his. Strangely, I remembered feeling his arm wrap around me—which felt much heavier than usual—and when I touched it, I felt thick fur over his forearm. I jumped, and when I snapped my eyes open, it looked completely normal. I figured my subconscious must have been revisiting the videos that I saw back at the office, allowing them to invade my nightmares because I hadn't completed the task yet.

I had hoped that whatever we'd come down with would be gone soon so I could go to the park to plant the ticks, but I wasn't sure if that was going to happen.

Ramon was sleeping soundly beside me, and I was glad he was finally getting some much-needed rest. Just then, my phone buzzed quietly on the nightstand; I reached for it and noticed another notification from the My Days app.

'Your period has ended.'

Wait, what? My period hasn't even come yet.

I tapped the icon for the My Days app and remembered that my period was supposed to have come last week.

And it still isn't here? That's odd...My period is never late...

That's when it hit me.

Nausea, vomiting, fatigue; peeing like crazy...

I scrambled out of bed, threw on a pair of sweats and grabbed my keys, quietly slinking out the door as I bolted to the car. I asked my phone where the nearest pharmacy was, and luckily, it mentioned there was one close by in Bar Harbor. I pressed the navigate button and careened my way into town, my mind racing. Thankfully, I was easily able to find parking—and, once inside, a pregnancy test—so I quickly headed back to my room and tiptoed into the bathroom. Ramon hadn't moved a muscle, it seemed.

When I reached inside the box and pulled out the stick with a shaking hand, I stared at it and took a deep breath.

It's going to be fine. There's a first for everything. This could just be the first time your period is late, no big deal, I tried to convince myself, but it wasn't really working.

I sat on the toilet, staring at the stick, waiting for the result.

And then after a few minutes—which seemed more like an eternity

—it was there, just like that: a pink plus sign was staring right back at me. There was no denying it now. A part of me wanted to take another test, a third even, just to be sure, but deep down, I knew that the test was correct.

I was pregnant.

I sat on the toilet with my head in my hands.

How am I going to tell Ramon? Will he want to keep it? Do I want to keep it? I can't tell him while he's sick. Maybe I should just wait until he's feeling better...That'll at least give me time to decide what I want to do...

I took another deep breath and wrapped the stick in toilet paper, sneaking it out of the bathroom, and hid it in my suitcase.

"What are you up to, *bella*?" I heard Ramon's sleepy voice and quickly zipped up my luggage.

"Oh, just checking to see how many outfits I had left. Turns out I didn't pack as many as I thought I did. Good thing this place has a laundry room. I'll have to go down and do some." I smiled and walked over to the bed, checking his temperature with the back of my hand; he was still extremely hot. "How are you feeling?"

"Same as the past couple of days, honestly. I might go to the park and have Sophia check me out, just to make sure it's nothing serious."

"Who's Sophia?"

"El medico del parque." I took enough Spanish in college to know that meant the park medic.

"You should've done that when you first got sick instead of assuming it was the flu. You're a scientist, not a doctor," I chuckled. "Why don't we put you in another cold soak in the jacuzzi? You said it helped last time and maybe it'll get your fever down."

"Si, seguro."

I noticed that Ramon seemed to speak more Spanish now that he was sick; it was like his brain didn't have the will power to translate his sentences to English as easily. I didn't mind; if I didn't understand him, he usually told me what he meant. I watched him take off his drenched white V-neck and was instantly distracted by his chest.

Oh, come on, the guy is sick! I shook my head to try and focus and then I saw something. It looked like some sort of an arachnid, and it had its head buried into Ramon's skin.

"Is that...?" I moved my face closer to examine the insect. Sure enough, it was an engorged tick, but when I examined its body more closely, I noticed a marking resembling the letter H on its back. "That's impossible!"

"*¿Que?*" Ramon was looking up at me with a confused expression. He then tried to peek at his shoulder, too, but the tick was too far back for him to see.

How the hell could one of these ticks be on Ramon? Could one of mine have escaped? Did they send someone else to disperse another batch? Wait a minute...This tick shouldn't be on Ramon like this...When these particular ticks bite humans, they're genetically engineered to recognize that they aren't shifters and detach. So why is this one buried underneath Ramon's skin like this? Unless...no...no...NO!

"You're a shifter?" I shrieked, stumbling backwards away from the bed. I didn't need him to answer me to know the truth. The dreams I'd been having weren't dreams at all; they actually happened.

Ramon wasn't looking at me, and that was all I needed to confirm my suspicions. "Min, let me explain."

"Explain *what*? Why you didn't tell me? How could you hide this from me?"

"What? I can't just run around telling people I'm a fucking shifter!"

I just stared at him in disbelief. *How could this happen?*

"*Espera un minuto...* How do you know about us? And more importantly, how did you know *I* was shifter?" Ramon was looking at me suspiciously. "Who are you, really? You're not an entomologist, are you? Is your name even Min?" He was getting angry, but I refused to go on trial.

"Everything I said to you is true!"

"So, do some explaining! How do you know about shifters? *¿Qué está pasando?*" Ramon was still trying to look at his shoulder, seeming to realize there was something there that revealed his true identity. "What are you looking at back there?"

"If you sit down, I will explain," I said finally, walking over to my luggage. I pulled out two things: the box of ticks and a pair of tweezers. I walked back over the bed where Ramon had sat down; his eyes were locked with mine, his brow furrowed in anger.

I checked the box for any cracks where ticks could have escaped from, and there were none. It was still completely sealed.

"Did you go in my suitcase at any point and open this box?" I asked, holding it up.

"No, I didn't. What the fuck are those? You brought *bugs* with you?"

"They're not just any bugs. They're ticks." I took a deep breath as I set the box on the bed and walked over to Ramon with the tweezers.

"What are you doing with those?"

"They're part of my assignment. Here, hold still; this is going to hurt." I grabbed the tick carefully by the head with the tweezers and twisted it around, dislodging it from Ramon's skin.

"Damn!" Ramon exclaimed, his shoulder flinching. "What the fuck was that?"

I held the tick in front of his eyes. It was still moving and engorged with Ramon's blood.

"I had a tick on me?" Ramon looked from the insect to his shoulder and back again. "Must have been from the last time I was at the park, I guess."

"Well, not necessarily."

"*No entiendo.*"

I drew in a deep breath, "Let me explain. What I'm about to tell you is top secret government information. As far as I know of, only three people know about this operation." Ramon's eyes grew wide as I continued, "A small faction of the government known as the NCPD-CID became aware of the real cause of death associated with Danielle Peterson. When the FBI report was filed, it seemed fishy, so they looked into it. They found satellite surveillance of the attack and therefore became aware of bear shifters."

"So, you work for this department?"

"I guess you could say that. I work for the CDC, and the NCPD-CID is a sub department. They hired me to come to Acadia on a special assignment."

"And I'm guessing it wasn't to collect *aquatic insect data*?" Ramon crossed his arms over his chest.

"No, it wasn't," I sighed. "Well, about this bear shifter who attacked Danielle Peterson...based on what you've told me about your job responsibilities, I'm guessing that you're the most qualified to study him."

"*Si*," Ramon nodded.

"And were you able to detect anything?"

"We concluded that he was affected by some sort of rabies mutation that he picked up somewhere." Ramon seemed hesitant to disclose this data to me.

"Well, they know that, too, and they wanted to help. With *these* guys," I said, grabbing a vial from my bag and sealing the engorged tick I removed from Ramon in it.

"How were these ticks supposed to help us?" he asked as I placed the vial in his hand for him to examine more closely.

"They contain the vaccine for the mutated virus. They used the rabies vaccine to create one that could combat the mutation as well, and they conducted two trials and found it effective in preventing infection. Due to the attack happening here, they wanted to make sure no one else would contract the virus by vaccinating everyone. They would rather have bear shifters living in secret, than have to deal with the ill effects of infected rogue bears running around," I shrugged. It actually wasn't as hard to talk about this as I thought it would be.

Ramon seemed very interested. "So, they sent you here to...*vaccinate* us?"

"Yes. But something is wrong," I admitted, and Ramon's eyes met mine with more confusion. "See the marking on its back? I didn't release any of these particular ticks here in Acadia."

"That's not possible; you just found one on me. Maybe one escaped from the box?"

"I just checked and it's still completely sealed. Unless you opened it, I don't know how this ended up on you."

Just then, my stomach dropped. I paused for a moment, worrying my lip as I recalled the virus' symptoms from the NCPD-CID's files: fever, headache, nausea, vomiting, hallucinations, insomnia... I started to put two and two together, and wasn't sure if I should even suggest this, but I felt it was the right thing to do.

"Another thing is, well...Ramon, I think you might have contracted the virus somehow."

"What?"

I walked over to the file I was given by the woman and showed it to Ramon. The first page outlined the symptoms of the mutated virus, and Ramon shook his head in disbelief at what he was reading. "I don't understand. If the tick was on me, that means it administered the vaccine to me, so I shouldn't have the virus. Right?" His eyes bore into mine with sheer panic.

Just then, if only for a split second, Ramon's hand turned into a bear paw; when I blinked, it had transformed back to a human hand. I covered my mouth, staring at him in disbelief.

"*Dios mío,*" Ramon's eyes were worried when they met mine and my heart sank. He didn't deserve this.

"I don't know...I don't even know how to explain this or what's going on..." I choked out as tears pricked the corners of my eyes.

He let out a long sigh, "Well, when I have questions that need answering, I always go to my lab."

"I think we definitely need to dissect the tick and see what's going on." I grabbed the vial from him and the case filled with ticks, putting them back in the suitcase. "Come on! Let's go!"

Ramon put his sweaty shirt back on and slipped into his boots, and we were out the door in no time.

8

RAMON

MIN HAD PINNED THE TICK DOWN WITH HER TWEEZERS AND HELD IT UNDER my microscope as I picked up a fine scalpel.

"Okay, so make an incision in its belly. A few drops of blood should come out, which will be yours, but we'll have to examine it under the microscope as well to see if anything other than the virus is in it."

I nodded. This whole thing was crazy, though. How could I possibly have the virus?

I made a small incision along the tick's belly, and just as Min said, a few drops of dark red blood spilled onto the slide.

"Is it supposed to be that dark?" Min asked.

"The virus itself is black, and when it attacks blood cells, those turn black as well. The further the virus progresses, the darker the blood becomes."

Min removed the insect so only the blood was left, and I placed a cover slip on top of it to spread the blood more thinly. I peered closely through the eyepiece to examine its contents.

"There it is." I could see the virus attacking my blood cells, turning them black, and as I scanned for anything else, nothing was noticeable. I stepped aside and let Min take a look.

"Yeah, I don't see anything except the virus attacking your blood cells." Min stepped back and looked around, thinking. "Maybe we should open up one of my ticks to see what we should be looking for?"

"Sure."

Min went over to her luggage and opened the case of ticks. She delicately removed one with the tweezers and placed it on the table before opening its belly with the scalpel. Taking a bit of its gut contents and smearing it onto a slide, she placed it under the microscope for me to examine.

As I viewed the specimen, I shot a confused look to Min. *Why are the innards of the ticks carrying the vaccine the same color as the live virus?*

My eyes widened. "*Mierda...*"

"What? What is it?" Min pushed me aside to look through the eyepiece and looked up at me in horror. "They *lied* to me; they're the ones spreading the virus! And they conned me into helping them! I can't fucking believe this."

"Are they trying to make us into monsters, and then expose us as such to freak everyone out?"

"Or worse...Maybe they're trying to wipe you out..."

She was right; in fact, her thoughts were probably more likely. Exposing our kind to the world would cause an uproar and panic. If the government simply wiped us all out instead, they could just pretend we never existed. Problem solved.

"So, that's what happened to the rogue bear who killed Danielle Peterson. He was infected with the virus."

"Did he die recently?" Min asked.

I couldn't answer her right away. A sharp, intense pain shot through my temples and I was blinded for a moment. I screamed in pain and held my head; it felt like my skull was splitting in two.

"Ramon! Are you okay?" Min rushed over and pressed the back of her palm against my forehead once again. Her hand felt cold against my burning, sweat-drenched skin, and it was more than welcomed.

Just as quickly as it came, the pain had dissipated. I blinked repeatedly until my vision returned.

"Yeah, sorry about that. It must have been some kind of passing tension headache." I smiled to reassure her, but I could tell she was not convinced. "What did you ask me before?"

"I asked if the rogue shifter had died recently."

"Yes, actually. He died the morning of the night we met. I had just finished his autopsy hours before I came to the bar."

"Then that's when you were infected; the tick must have detached from the corpse during the autopsy and latched onto you."

"How can you be sure?"

"I read in the file that if the tick administers the 'vaccine' successfully, it leaves the shifter in search of another host. So, I'm guessing once the virus kills the host, they move onto the next shifter."

"Un-fucking-believable!" I slammed my fist on the table, trying to control my anger, but I could feel it bubbling inside me. I already felt like a furnace and the pounding in my head wasn't helping.

"Do you guys spray for ticks?"

"No; it would be cost-prohibitive. Acadia is so large and would need to be sprayed several times per year to be effective. We just don't have that kind of funding. Not only that, spraying could potentially impact the ecosystem in other ways."

"I'm not even sure it would have worked on these ticks, anyway. Who knows what other mutations they have?" Min shrugged, trying to console me, but it was hard to think of anything else.

I had been infected, and certain death was just around the corner.

Beyond myself, I had to let Trent and Knox know. As the disease progressed, I'd become a serious threat to the clan and park visitors.

And Min.

In that moment, my fear turned to anger. And then, resolve.

"If those *putas* think they can take us down, they've got another thing coming. We've got all those ticks carrying live specimens of the virus; surely, if the two of us put our heads together, we can come up with an antidote and beat this."

Min's eyes lit up as she looked into the glass box and counted the ticks. "We only have fifteen ticks left, so we'll need to be careful. That's fifteen attempts at an antidote."

"I'll have to notify my boss immediately, so we can get started. You said the government put you up to this; do you remember the names of the people you are taking orders from?"

"Yeah, it was a man Eric Hanson, and a woman, I think her name was Cassidy Powers."

"*Cassidy Powers*? *¿Estás seguro?* Positive? That's impossible!" I was pacing back and forth in disbelief after Min had revealed that she was taking orders from a shifter—from our clan.

"I'm fairly positive that was her name. She only mentioned it once and probably hoped I would forget it, honestly." Min rolled her eyes. "She was not a very nice person; *that* much I know for certain."

What? Cassidy was one of the nicest people I knew!

"That sounds so unlike her..." I continued to pace, trying to wrap my head around this shocking news.

"So, you know her? I mean, she told me she worked in Acadia, but I'm not sure how close you all are."

"Well, I wouldn't say we're close friends or anything, but being a part of the clan, I would consider her family—but certainly not anymore."

"Wait, she's part of your clan? So, she's a shifter, too?"

I nodded slowly as rage burned in the pit of my stomach. "I wonder how the guy who killed Danielle Peterson became infected. He was long gone by the time we got to him; we couldn't even get a name out of him."

"Well, Cassidy did say she administered the first two trials herself. That was obviously one of the incidents, but did you have any other run ins with malicious shifters?"

"Yeah, last fall, my boss' girlfriend was cornered by three rogue bears who came to Acadia, and one of them in particular was such an asshole that he ended up getting himself killed. Maybe he was the subject of the first trial? It's all coming together now..."

"So, what are we going to do first?"

"We are going to tell my boss and the law enforcement ranger of the park and have Cassidy detained for questioning; hopefully, she'll give us more information about the ticks, and then we can work on the antidote."

I reached out to Knox with my mind. *Boss? We've got a problem. A HUGE problem.*

Fuck, what's going on, Ramon?

Where is Cassidy right now? I did my best to keep my thoughts calm, but between my rage and my worsening symptoms, it wasn't easy.

Surveying the landscape of the park for safety improvements. If we want to make visitors feel safe in the park again, we have to do everything we can to make sure it's secure.

Well, about that rogue bear I did the autopsy on two weeks ago...

Yeah?

Remember we ruled it as a mutated rabies virus infection?

Yeah?

Cassidy planted it.

What the...? That's a very serious accusation, Ramon. Do you have any proof to back this up?

Tons. If you have Trent detain her, I can bring all the proof to the holding lodge, and you can see it for yourself.

You'd better be right about this. I don't usually arrest clan members without seeing solid proof firsthand.

Knox, there's no way she didn't do it.

Trent is on his way to pick her up. I'll see you at the holding lodge.

"Alright, let's go to the holding lodge," I said, carefully placing the blood and virus slides in a small carrying case so they wouldn't become tainted on the way over.

"I thought you were going to call your boss?"

"I did."

She gave me a sideways glance. "What?"

"We have intra-clan telepathy. Anyone in the clan can be reached by thought, but only if by another clan member."

"So, you used you *mind* to contact your boss?"

"Yes. He just deployed our law enforcement ranger, Trent, to detain Cassidy."

I looked up to see Min staring at me, her eyes wide. "I have to admit, that's pretty cool."

I shook my head and chuckled. "Come on, we have to bring every bit of proof we have. Knox, my boss, is not going to be easily convinced that Cassidy is conspiring against us unless we have a ton of proof to back us up. You're an outsider, so I would say the less talking you do, the better. It'll be more effective if Knox hears everything from me, but he may have some questions for you, so be prepared to be under interrogation as well. Knox will protect his own before he puts his trust in you."

It was sad, but it was true. I was reluctant to believe Min at first, too, but seeing how she reacted to everything, I knew she had nothing to do with this.

We just had to prove it to Knox and Trent.

"Alright, I'm ready."

WHEN WE GOT to the holding lodge, both Trent and Knox's Jeeps were parked outside. Cassidy was detained, and I highly doubted she would confess upon seeing Min, so we both had to be prepared to present our case.

And we were.

We walked into the holding lodge and Min and I exchange looks. Trent and Knox were standing by the desk talking in low voices, while Cassidy was behind bars screaming at them.

"Come on boss, what the hell is this about? You've got me locked in here for what?" She heard the door open and froze when she saw Min. That was all the confirmation I needed to know she was guilty, but I wasn't sure if Trent and Knox had caught it.

"Hey, guys. This is Min Dupont. She's an entomologist for the CDC."

"What the hell is she doing here at a time like this?" Knox asked angrily.

"She knows, Knox. About us. I can explain everything."

"You guys have got to stop telling your girlfriends about us! This is the third woman in a year, all because you guys can't keep your mouths shut."

"Well...to be fair...You couldn't, either." Trent shrugged and smiled at Min. "Nice to meet you Min, I'm Trent."

"Pleasure." She reached out her hand and he shook it. Knox gave her a nod and wasn't fully ready to accept her with open arms just yet.

"Are you going to tell me what all this is about now?"

"*Si.*" I started unpacking my microscope and the case of ticks as well as the slides showing my blood and the tick's innards.

"What the fuck are those?" Trent asked, his face disgusted.

"Ticks. And they are the source of our problem."

"We're listening," Knox said.

"Okay, so the night we went out to the bar, I had just finished the autopsy of the infected shifter. I told you guys I wasn't feeling well and had a headache. I was also feeling queasy."

"Yeah, then you took two weeks off to spend with your girlfriend here." Knox rolled his eyes.

"Well, actually, she spent most of that time taking care of *me*. I was vomiting all over the place, pure stomach acid and I couldn't bring myself to swallow anything, not even liquid. I still have a headache, nausea, and I've hardly slept in days."

"Yeah, you have the flu, right? You told me."

"That's what I thought. Until Min pulled one of these guys out of my shoulder," I said holding up the case of ticks. "These things carry our end. They were genetically engineered to kill us."

"What are you talking about, Ramon?" Trent asked, exchanging confused expressions with Knox.

I took a deep breath. "I have the mutated rabies virus as well. I'm infected," I admitted.

"You're not shifting uncontrollably, though, and you're perfectly conscious. The other shifter kept changing into a bear and he couldn't even tell us his name."

"Yeah, but he must have been dealing with the infection for a while when we found him. I have been infected for two weeks, so at some point, I imagine I will get to that state. Before Min and I tested the ticks and my blood, I had a random shift moment, where my hand turned into a bear paw for a brief second."

"How do you know that you got sick from the tick? How did you find out it was carrying the disease?" Knox asked.

I looked at Min.

"Through me." She stepped forward.

"And how do you know all this?" Knox seemed suspicious now.

"I was called in for some field work and was shown several videos regarding shifters. They knew about a rogue killing Danielle Peterson and they knew about the mutated rabies virus. They handed me these ticks and told me they held a vaccine that would prevent all shifters in Acadia from getting the virus."

"So, you did as you were told and unleashed these bugs into our park?" Knox accused.

"No, sir. All the ticks in this box have remained there. I haven't released a single one, except for the one that Ramon and I killed to confirm that they were carrying the virus."

"Which leads me to the microscope," I said placing the slide with my blood sample under it. "This is my blood, extracted from the tick that Min pulled off my shoulder."

Knox and Trent took turns looking into the microscope.

"Shit, it's just like when you tested that rogue shifter's blood," Trent agreed.

"Now this slide shows what was extracted from a fresh tick." I replaced the first slide with the new one.

"It's the virus..." Knox's voice was filled with concern. He looked from the microscope to Ramon. "And you have it. Does this mean you are going to die? Can we get it from you?"

"I don't know. But Min and I have decided to work long and hard to find an antidote." I nodded and so did Min.

"But what does this all have to do with Cassidy?" Knox turned to the cell. Cassidy was looking around frantically at them.

"She's the one who gave me the ticks in the first place. She works with the government, too," Min said, glaring at Cassidy with her arms crossed.

"What the hell is she talking about? I've never seen her a day in my life. Who are you, anyway?"

"Oh, don't play dumb now!" Min spat, starting toward the cell bars, but Trent stopped her.

"You gave all the proof we needed to confirm that these ticks hold a deadly virus that can kill us, but nothing that links Cassidy other than your words. You must forgive me for being a more than a little cautious. We don't know you, but we know her. I must consider her innocent until you provide proof otherwise."

Min looked to me for help. I shrugged; I had no idea how she was going to prove that it was Cassidy who gave her the ticks and the file. Something seemed to dawn on Min and she whipped out her cellphone.

"If I can prove she is lying about not knowing who I am, is catching her in a lie enough to make you believe me?" Min asked as she scrolled through her phone, trying to find something.

"Hmmm...I suppose. Lying is hugely against our clan code," Knox nodded.

Min handed him her phone. "She called me when I first arrived in Acadia to make sure I got to the inn safely. She said she would call me for an update with my progress, but she never did."

Knox pulled out his phone and checked the numbers aloud. "That's your number, Cassidy. I thought you didn't know her?" His look turned to a glare quickly.

"Are you sure? You should check them again!" Cassidy seemed panicked at this point.

"I tried to give you the benefit of the doubt, but now you have lied to me. You will tell me the truth. *Now!*" Knox ordered. I could feel his Alpha authority ringing through the room, rippling through me, and I could tell from Trent's wince that he could feel it, too.

"Fine! It's true!" Cassidy admitted, sitting slowly on the floor of her cell. "I'm helping the government eradicate bear shifters. When they found out about our existence, they tried to scout me since I've been here in Acadia for the least amount of time. At first, I refused, but they told me I could either go down with everyone, or help them take you all down. If I helped, I would be spared as long as I aided them with experiments. So, I agreed. My first job was to set up phone and computer taps on all staff devices, which I did. Anything that you have texted, called, or emailed about is known by the government. Their goal is to rid the world of shifters without exposing them to the public and causing a panic. So, this was their attempt at genetic warfare. The rogue shifters that attacked Hannah were from the first trial. They were captured by the government and promised that the ticks would administer a drug that would increase their abilities. They agreed to partake in the experiment and the ticks were placed directly on them. They were placed here for testing where they got into trouble with you and you killed their leader, Shawn. You asked me and Hank to take care of Shawn's body and I was able to kill the tick before it could move on to the next host. The rogue shifter who killed Danielle Peterson was our second test. I was able to infect him while he was visiting for the full moon. And I see that tick found Ramon, here, during the autopsy." Cassidy was smiling deviously now. "I may not have gotten all of you, but I got one of you. Once the government finds out that you know of their plans, they'll take care of you. They'll know something is wrong if they stop getting updates from me."

"You betrayed the whole clan just so you can become one of their guinea pigs? How do you know they won't just kill you too?" Trent asked, banging on the bars.

"I don't know, but if you all found out, I would be dead, if I didn't help them I would be dead. This is the only way I had a chance, but no matter what I chose, I could die. What's the big difference anyway?" she shouted back.

"The difference is that we would have died together—as a clan! And we would have fought to the very end!" Knox roared, his anger blazing through his words and his chest rose and fell. He was very clearly livid. We all fell silent, looking down at the ground. He was right. I stole a glance at Cassidy, and even she couldn't make eye contact with anyone.

"Tell us everything you know about the virus and the ticks," Knox ordered.

"The virus was created to alter our genetic makeup and make us feral. The more times we shift while we are infected, the harder it becomes to shift back to our human states. The ticks only jump to find new hosts when their shifter host dies, so that's how Ramon got infected. The ticks were engineered to identify shifters based on the taste of their blood; they can identify a DNA strand in shifters that is not present in humans. If they determine the blood is human, they abandon the host to find a shifter. The human is left with a tick bite, but no deadly symptoms. This is how they are trying to keep the virus contained to just shifters."

"Genius..." I said aloud without realizing. Everyone's eyes fell on me. "Sorry, but you have to admit that's pretty cool. They really pulled out all the stops." I obviously wasn't happy about dying from this virus, but I found it fascinating how much thought they put into their plan to kill us off.

"And it would have worked, had Min here not screwed everything up." Cassidy rolled her eyes.

"Looks like *you're* the one who screwed up," Min scowled.

Knox started barking out orders. "Trent, stay here and watch Cassidy.

Ramon, Min, go start on that antidote. If you need anything, and I mean anything, call me immediately. And Min?"

"Yes?"

"There will come a point in time where Ramon will no longer be able to speak or think like himself if you both don't find the antidote in time. He'll begin to shift at random times and he may or may not shift back. If this happens, call Trent and I immediately—and run. We will come and get him, and he'll be moved to a cell here where he can't hurt anyone."

"If that happens, could I move the lab here. I want to stay with him." Min was looking at me worriedly.

"That shouldn't be a problem," Trent nodded.

"Alright, everyone, get to it." Knox slapped me on my arm and gave me a reassuring squeeze before he turned to leave, and I started to pick up my things and follow after him.

The sooner I got started on the antidote, the sooner I could recover.

9

MIN

I TURNED TO LEAVE RIGHT BEHIND RAMON.

"Hey Min, can I talk to you for a second?" Trent asked, watching Ramon exit the building.

"Sure, what's up?" I asked. I recognized him as one of the guys at the bar who had urged Ramon to talk to me.

"So...when are you going to tell him?" Trent's arms were crossed over his chest.

"Tell who what? If you guys still think I'm hiding something, I'm not. I told Knox everything I know." I felt immediately offended that Trent still didn't trust me, even when his Alpha had accepted the truth.

Trent burst out laughing.

"What is so funny?" I glared. *Now he's making fun of me? What the hell is wrong with this guy?*

"I believe you, okay? I wasn't talking about this situation. I was talking about that one." Trent pointed his finger at my belly.

"What the hell are you talking about?"

"Now look who's playing dumb."

"I really have no idea what you're trying to get at."

"The *baby*, Min."

I gasped, and for a split second, my heart stopped beating.

"H-how do you know? I...I haven't told anyone yet." A slight panic started to build inside me; with all that had happened today, taking the test seemed like a distant dream.

"Your pheromones. They're intensely strong in the beginning to let us shifters know that our mates are with child. They become faint after the first month and then spike again when the baby is close to being delivered so that we can prepare to bring it into this world," Trent informed me.

"If that's the case, then why hasn't Ramon noticed?" I questioned. If all shifters could detect it, did that mean Knox knew, too? And even Cassidy? I looked over at her and she was still on the floor, her eyes to the ground.

"With all the symptoms he's experiencing from the virus, his body is probably under too much stress. If he starts to recover, though, he *will* notice."

"And if he doesn't get better?" I choked on my words, feeling tears well up in my eyes.

"If I were going to die, I would be honored to know that I had a child entering this world to carry out my legacy." Trent nodded and placed a hand on my shoulder. I smiled, but my heart wasn't in the moment when I walked away. My mind was elsewhere.

Could he have passed the virus along to the baby, too?

WHEN I GOT OUTSIDE, Ramon was there waiting for me, holding his microscope and other supplies.

"What took you so long?" Ramon asked as I walked alongside him.

"Trent just wanted to firm up a plan in case you...you know..."

"Try to kill you or something?" Ramon looked defeated and my heart fell to my stomach. I wasn't afraid that he would hurt me, even if he went rogue; I would be there for him every step of the way, no matter what.

"Ramon..."

"Let's just get to working on the antidote. Not just for my sake, but for the sake of the clan. Just in case someone else could be infected."

I stopped walking and took a deep breath.

"Like your child." I winced, preparing myself for the worst. Ramon stopped dead in his tracks and everything in his arms tumbled to the ground.

"Ramon?" I ran up to him, examining his body to make sure he was okay. His eyes were wide, and his mouth was open.

"*What* did you just say?"

I looked him directly in the eyes. "I'm pregnant." I grew teary, but I didn't want to break our eye contact; I wanted him to know I was serious. His mouth widened into a grin, and before I knew it, he grabbed me by the waist and lifted me into the air, laughing.

"You're pregnant? I'm going to be a *dad*?" He lowered me to the ground and held me in his arms. I could see tears welling in his eyes, too, and I nodded, smiling up at him. He bent down, holding me tightly against him and kissed me as tears cascaded down my cheeks, and in that moment, I knew.

I knew he was happy.

And I was going to keep this baby, no matter what.

"Wait...the virus..." Ramon's eyes were panicked through his tears.

"I don't know if the virus can be transmitted that way, but we can't take any chances."

"Now, more than ever, we need to do this—not just for me and the clan, but for our child. We *will* come up with an antidote. But I need you to promise me something."

"Anything."

"If I die or become rabid before we find the antidote, you'll continue to test for it without me."

"Yeah," I nodded, fighting a new wave of tears, "I promise."

I didn't want to think of life without Ramon. In merely two weeks, he'd managed to capture my heart completely. I realized I hadn't known true love before I met him; he had blessed me with a new life, and now, the life of a child.

How could I raise a child without him or her knowing his love; instant and unconditional, and felt for someone who hadn't even been born yet?

It reminded me of my father. And in that moment, I vowed that I would do everything I could to make sure our child would know Ramon's love firsthand. I would make it happen, somehow.

A WEEK WENT by and we still hadn't found an antidote for the virus. We worked around the clock and took naps when one or both of us were tired. Knox had us under constant supervision, worried that Ramon would lose consciousness and go rogue at any moment. He came by occasionally to check on us himself, but he mostly had Trent watching over us while he kept an eye on Cassidy.

There were a few scares. There were times where we'd have to stop working because a part of Ramon's body would shift, and towards the end of the week, Trent and I grew worried as he began to growl in his sleep.

"I'm not sure how much longer he's going to be able to hold this back. I can tell he's fighting it, but the virus will take over completely at some point," Trent admitted as we watched Ramon snarling and twisting in his sleep; his symptoms always seemed to be the worst at night.

"We'll just have to be on guard. The second he fully shifts or stops responding to us, we'll have to take him in." My heart ached with every word that escaped my lips. I didn't want Ramon behind bars, but I knew once the infection progressed to the point where we would have to secure him, he wouldn't be 'Ramon' anymore. He would just be his bear, rabid and ferocious.

The next day only made me more afraid.

Ramon and I were extracting some fresh samples of the virus from a new tick for our next round of testing. Ramon was holding the scalpel, ready to make an incision into the tick's belly, when his hand began to shake. At first, it was a slight tremble, but it quickly advanced into a violent vibration.

"Ramon?" I looked up at him and he was just staring at the tick, shaking uncontrollably. "Ramon! Are you okay?"

He didn't answer me, but his eyes met mine, and they were pitch black. His pupils had fully dilated, and a low rumble began emanating from his chest, growing to a terrifying growl seconds later.

"Min, back away." I could hear Trent's voice, but I couldn't take my eyes off Ramon. He was looking at me, but his eyes went *through* me. "Min, you're going to want to start back up...*Now!*"

In the blink of an eye, Ramon was gone, and a bear stood where he once did; growling, snarling and towering over me. I screamed and immediately scampered back.

Suddenly, another bear came from the side and tackled the one in front of me, pinning it to the ground. I watched as Ramon's bear struggled against Trent's, but Trent's bear was much larger and just had to lay on top of Ramon's to overpower him.

I watched the bear below Trent's submit, and Trent's bear rose, holding his paw against the smaller bear's back.

Slowly, before our eyes, Ramon appeared again, unconscious; Trent used that as a cue to return to his human form as well.

"It's time, Min."

I could feel my chin quivering as I nodded. I knew he meant it was time to have Ramon locked up, and tears trickled down my cheeks.

"I don't know if he'll still be himself when he comes to, so I think you should be prepared for that." Trent's voice was grim; I could tell he felt my pain. I was losing a mate, but he was losing a good friend.

I was suddenly overwhelmed.

"Do you think if I talk to him, he can hear me? Or understand me?" I choked through my tears, holding back a sob.

"Who's to say? It's worth a shot. Just let me get him in cuffs, just in case he experiences another setback." Trent seemed very tentative to handcuff Ramon. He was hesitant, but his sense of duty seemed to overpower any other thoughts as the he restrained his friend.

I walked over to them slowly and knelt down by Ramon's head. I reached out my shaking hand to touch his hair, terrified that he'd glare at me with those eyes again. But, he didn't stir as I stroked his sweat drenched head. I touched his forehead and his fever was worse than ever. A sob finally escaped me, and Trent padded over to console me, rubbing my back.

"Ramon...I don't know if you can hear me, but I want you to know—I *need* you to know—I love you! And I will keep working on this antidote day and night until it clicks. I will *not* let you die...but you have to fight, too, okay, baby? I know you can't promise me, but I need you to fight this until the very last second. If not for me, for our child."

I was not much of a crier; in fact, I couldn't remember the last time I cried. But in that moment, I was sure I sobbed more than I ever had in my life. I wanted Ramon to survive; I *needed* him to.

"Alright, I'm going to take him to the holding cell. I know you said that you'd want to work on the antidote at the lodge if he's locked up, and I want you to know that's still okay. Behind bars, he can't harm you; they're specifically designed to withstand bear strength, so there's no way he could escape and hurt you. Either way, I will be there to make sure of it. So, if you'd like to go there, you're still welcome to." Trent rested a hand on my shoulder and gave me a reassuring look.

I tried to wipe my face and nodded. "You go on ahead. I'll take my car; I remember the way."

"Okay, I'll see you soon. Try not to take too long or I'll worry you ran for the hills or something." Trent smiled, but I couldn't find it in me to return the gesture. I appreciated his effort, but all I could think about was never being able to talk to Ramon again, never hearing his adorable Spanish phrases and smart-ass jokes.

I watched Trent lift Ramon's naked body and carry him out. My eyes followed them until they disappeared out the door and a whole new wave of sobs crashed over me.

How can I raise a bear shifter? I hardly know anything about them! I need Ramon. He has to make it through this!

I wasn't particularly religious, but in that moment, I prayed as hard as I could. I prayed to anyone listening, whoever was up in the sky, to give me the guidance to find the antidote for Ramon, for our child. And I kept repeating that prayer, hoping that the more I said it, the higher it would reach. If I could speak it into existence, it would happen. I just had to keep praying, keep saying it. I could will it to happen if I tried hard enough.

Or at least, that's what I kept telling myself.

10

MIN

A few days had gone by and I was hard at work on the antidote in the holding lodge. I had grown anxious; I was down to only two ticks and I had just opened the first of the two to try out the latest version of the antidote. I knew I was close. I had finally gotten to the point where I could stop the virus from attacking the blood cells by applying the antidote to the samples in a petri dish, but I needed it to be stronger. I needed it to remove the virus not only from the cells, but also from the body completely. I kept increasing the dosage, but it still wasn't enough. It was missing something. I needed to add something else to it, but what?

I heard a low growl; I was distracted by Ramon snarling at me through the bars of his cell. Ever since the day he shifted in the lab, he'd remained in the same state of mind. He would randomly shift and maintain his bear form longer every time it happened. He would roar and bang on the cell bars, pounding on the walls—luckily, Knox had brought me sound proof headphones for moments like those. I felt terrible tuning Ramon out, but I had to, for his sake; I couldn't concentrate with his bear making a ruckus. I knew it wasn't his fault, but I always felt guilty, as I had in that moment, when I slipped them on over my ears.

Trent and Knox had some protocols to go over for the new safety project Acadia was implementing, so I had told them I would be okay working by myself. I knew Ramon couldn't hurt me from within the cell, so I wasn't too worried. In the next cell over, Cassidy never spoke a word to anyone either, and seemed to have accepted her fate. Either way, I wouldn't have shown her an ounce of sympathy; that bitch was ready to throw me under the bus.

When Ramon would shift back into a human, his body was always so exhausted that he would just lie there on the floor, not moving a muscle; in times like that, I would go over to the cell and attempt to speak with him. I thought it highly unlikely that he could hear me or understand me at this point; with how quickly the infection was setting in, once he was incoherent, I knew most of his brain had been taken over by the virus.

But it was his heart that I was worried about. Once the virus would infiltrate that, he would surely die.

I had no idea how much time I had left. It was hard to gauge based on their experience with the rogue shifter, since Cassidy couldn't remember when she infected him. So, we were playing a game of chance.

I had to be extremely careful with that particular round of testing; I needed to be sure I could test the last tick with the final iteration of the antidote.

Just then, I was distracted by something waving in front of me.

A sandwich?

I looked up to see two women standing in front of me. One was average height with a slim, fit build and the other was short, plump and pear-shaped. Their lips were moving, but I couldn't hear a word they were saying.

I removed the headphones from my ears. "Excuse me?"

"Oh, sorry; I didn't realize you couldn't hear us. We thought you'd be hungry, so we brought you a bite to eat. We've been sending things along with Knox and Trent, but we wanted to stop by and say hello ourselves." The slender woman smiled at me and handed me the Ziploc bag with the sandwich inside. "Do you like peanut butter and jelly? We also brought you some water and snacks. We heard you're eating for two, so we wanted to make sure you were taken care of."

The woman was talking to my belly with the last bit. It took me a moment to realize who they were.

"Oh, you two must be Hannah and Blanca."

"Sorry, we should have at least introduced ourselves!" The shorter of the two laughed. "I'm Blanca and this is Hannah. I'm Trent's girlfriend, and she's Knox's."

"Pleased to meet you both." I smiled, trying to be happy for the company. A part of me was, but mostly, I just wanted to get back to working on the antidote. I looked over to Ramon's cell to see him lying on the floor again, in naked human form. I tried to push it from my mind as I turned back to Blanca and Hannah.

"How are you holding up, hun? Any cravings yet? Morning sickness?" Hannah asked me, looking concerned.

"My, uh, breasts, have been a bit swollen, but that's all," I answered, nervously tucking my hair behind my ear. This seemed a bit personal for a first-time conversation, but I knew they were just trying to check in on me and I didn't want to be rude and send them away.

"I don't really think we can help with that, but cravings? We've got you, girl." Blanca gave me a thumbs up.

They both looked to Ramon's cell.

"How is he?" They almost seemed to regret asking.

"Worse. I'm honestly not sure if he has much time, so I'm working as hard as I can."

"Well, the work you're doing here is nothing short of amazing." Blanca was the one who spoke, but Hannah nodded in agreement. "If you ever need a hand with anything or want to chat, don't hesitate to reach out."

"Yeah, us girls have to stick together, you know?" Hannah smiled.

"Thank you; I appreciate that. And I am grateful for all the food and water you've been sending; you both have been such life savers. I honestly probably wouldn't eat if you hadn't been passing it along. I've just been so focused on the antidote. If my eyes didn't need sleep, I probably wouldn't go to bed at all, either." I chuckled lightly, hoping that I seemed likeable. I wanted us all to be friends—and women with shifter boyfriends seemed exactly like the friends I needed right then.

Now if only I could keep mine alive long enough to still *have* a boyfriend.

"Well, you're very welcome. We're more than glad to help," Blanca said. "We also heard about *her*."

Hannah and Blanca were glaring at Cassidy in her cell. Cassidy returned the gesture, but didn't say anything, as usual.

"Anyway, we're heading into town to grab a few things, but we wanted to stop by and check on you first. Is there anything we can pick up for you while we're out?" Hannah asked.

"Someone to help me with this antidote would be nice, but I doubt you'd be able to find someone who can," I laughed.

"How far along are you with your findings?" Blanca seemed slightly interested. Trent had told me that she was the one who filed the FBI report on Danielle Peterson.

"I have gotten the virus to stop spreading, but that isn't enough. If I gave this version to Ramon now, the symptoms alone would kill him. The virus is keeping his body strong because *it* is strong. But once it overtakes his heart, he will die. I need the antidote to completely wipe out the virus and replenish the affected cells. Right now, it's just enough to protect cells that haven't been touched by the virus."

"So, you've created sort of a vaccine?" Hannah looked impressed.

"Yes, but that isn't what we need. It *would* protect everyone else from getting infected, though, and I have set aside a few vials of it in case the government decides to release the ticks themselves without me or Cassidy. I'm not sure if the batch they gave me was all they had; at this point, I highly doubt it."

"You're probably right," Blanca said. "Let me think here...My grandmother actually helped with the first trials of penicillin back in the forties. One of the things they did was try to use different viruses against each other, seeing if they could cancel each other out. Maybe you could try that with this virus? Or somehow break it down on a molecular level so that you can harness its strength and pair it with the vaccine that you have already created?"

"Hey...you might actually be on to something. I'll have to play around with it, but I'm fairly certain I could get that to work. I was actually going to try the virus vs. virus approach, but I think breaking down the mutated virus on a molecular level would give us a much better shot. Thank you so much for the idea!"

I was so happy they had come to visit, because honestly, I don't think I would have thought of that approach until it was too late. But, now that I had a new course of action, I was eager to get back to work. I started preparing the chemicals for breaking down the virus, feeling positive for the first time in weeks.

"Well, we'll let you get back to work," Hannah offered, and after they each gave me a hug, they waved goodbye and left the lab.

"IT WORKED! Oh my god, it actually worked! It's perfect!" I felt tears welling in my eyes as I watched the diseased black cells transform. They were repairing themselves right before my eyes at an extremely rapid pace. Combining the strength of the virus with the vaccine gave it the push it needed to overtake the diseased cells.

It was game time.

I pulled off my headphones and looked over to Ramon's cell to see his bear lying on the floor, completely still.

"Ramon?" I hurried over to him. The bear's face was close to the bars and one of his paws was stretched outside the cell. His eyes were closed, and when I pressed my ear close to the bars, I couldn't hear him breathing. "Oh no...no, no, no, no, no! Don't do this to me, Ramon, come on, baby!"

I reached inside the cell and pressed my hand against the bear's chest, doing my best to feel for a heartbeat, but I couldn't find one.

"Oh, god. Ramon? Ramon? Can you hear me? Ramon! Wake up!" I shook the bear's paw. It was heavy and gave no resistance.

This can't be happening! He can't... I refused to accept it. Hyperventilating and shaking, I grabbed a syringe and filled it with some of the antidote. I'd made enough for 3 doses: one for Ramon, one for the baby, and one to duplicate in case anyone else were to contract the virus.

I ran back to the cell, "This better work." I reached through the bars for his chest once more; I still couldn't detect a heartbeat, so I found where his heart would be in relation to a human's and emptied the contents of the syringe there. I hoped that the closer the antidote was to his heart, the quicker it would work. "Don't die on me, Ramon...Please..."

I sat against the cell bars, holding his bear paw in my hands, rocking back and forth, willing him to wake up.

Please wake up...Please wake up...Please wake up... I chanted over and over again, tears streaming down my face. Minutes passed and there were no changes. After fifteen minutes, I was sobbing and crying, shouting at him to wake up.

"You can't do this us! I told you to fight! Fight for us, Ramon! Wake up!" I let go of the bear's paw and brought my face right up against the cell bars. "I love you, Ramon..."

After minutes more of staring at him, I was sure he was gone. But, before I could turn away, I swore I saw his bear form falter for a split second. I kept my eyes on him, and sure enough, his body was flitting between its bear and human forms.

His body was fighting the infection.

"Yes! Come on, Ramon! You can do this!"

I watched as his bear form disappeared completely, replaced by his handsome face once again. A whole new wave of emotion washed over me. And then he opened his eyes.

"M-Min?" His voice was raspy, and thirst deprived, but it was his, and happiness flooded through me.

"Ramon! You're back!" I smiled at him through my tears, wishing the bars would vanish so I could collapse into his arms.

"Am I in a holding cell?" Ramon looked around, confused.

"Yes. I'll go call Trent and Knox to come let you out." I ran to get my phone, not taking my eyes off of him.

"Hello? Min? Is everything okay?" Trent's voice was filled with worry and I couldn't help but laugh.

"Everything's actually fantastic, Trent. I did it! Ramon's back with us!"

"What? Seriously? Knox and I will be right there!" The phone hung up immediately, and I padded back over to Ramon, who was smiling at me from within the cell.

"I must have gotten pretty bad, huh?" Ramon ran his hand through his hair.

"We didn't let it get too crazy before we locked you up. You didn't hurt anyone, so you don't have to worry."

"You did it, Min. I'm so proud of you." Ramon reached through the bars to stroke my cheek. Tears just kept falling and I couldn't say anything. I couldn't believe he was there in front of me. All my hard work and faith paid off.

"Ramon?" I heard Trent's voice as he ran into the room, and Knox was right behind him. Trent rushed up to the cell and opened the door, immediately hugging Ramon before he could even step outside.

"Don't you ever scare us like that again. You hear me?" Trent warned.

When Trent finally let him go, Knox shook Ramon's hand.

"We didn't think you were going to make it, buddy. I'm happy to see you're back with us."

"Well, then let me through to thank the woman responsible!" Ramon joked, stepping past Knox.

I laughed through my tears. "You almost died and you're still joking?"

He pulled me into a tight embrace and I held him just as firmly, burying my face in his neck. I didn't care that he hadn't showered in days and he was covered in sweat. He was there, in front of me, holding me, and that was all that mattered. I just wanted to melt into him. And just when I thought I would, he pulled away slightly and captured my lips in a passionate kiss.

It felt as if I'd found an oasis after walking through the desert. It was as if we had never kissed before, spreading warmth through every part of me that seeped into my bones. Our lips danced wildly, and we had almost forgotten we weren't alone.

Almost.

"Ahem," Knox coughed, interrupting our intimate scene. We pulled away reluctantly and Ramon gave him a look.

"I can't have a moment with my lady?" Ramon asked.

"You most certainly can, but for starters, you're buck naked, bro, and as good of friends as we are, I would prefer to not have to look at you for too long," he chuckled. "Also, we've got some business to take care of. The conclave called to answer my request for Cassidy's trial; they've arrived and are ready to adjudicate her case."

"The conclave?" I asked, confused.

"They are a special council of shifters, representing all kinds, not just bears. Their duty is to pass judgement on clan-related incidents," Knox informed me.

"Are they going to kill her?"

"Conspiring to eliminate the whole clan and teaming up with the government? It's fairly likely," Trent snorted.

I looked over to Cassidy, who was staring at the ground. I knew what she did was wrong, but was punishment by death really necessary?

"I don't want to go," I admitted. I couldn't watch her execution. I knew I had no say in their affairs, but that didn't mean I had to witness the results of their decision first hand.

"You kind of have to, with your amount of involvement," Trent winced.

"We can leave before the execution—if there is one," Ramon assured me, and I nodded at him in agreement.

"Alright, let's get Ramon some clothes and then we can meet the conclave at the clearing."

When we arrived, there were five others standing there waiting for us.

"Hello, Knox." The oldest man of the group addressed Knox, stepping forward. He was short with a grey beard and balding.

"Have you been waiting long, Jeremy?" Knox bowed and so did Trent. Trent shoved Cassidy, who finally did the same. I guessed that I should have probably bowed as well, so I did.

"Is everyone involved present?" a man of average height with closely cropped chestnut hair spoke up. He only looked a few years older than Knox.

"Yes, Leonard. Everyone is here."

"I sense a human among us..." One of the two women—a blonde—was sniffing the air, and her blue eyes landed on me. "Someone explain this."

Ramon stepped forward to defend me. "Her name is Min Dupont, and she is my mate. She's the one who brought Cassidy's treason to light."

"And was proof presented to back up claims?" The other woman asked. She was older, and her silver hair was tightly pulled back into a high ponytail.

"Yes," Knox stated simply.

"Okay, then; let us begin," Jeremy announced. He beckoned Trent forward, who brought Cassidy along with him, and knelt her in front of the conclave. "Cassidy Powers, you are being charged here tonight with treason, conspiracy, and attempted murder of the entire clan. How do you plead?"

"Guilty. Just get it over with." She rolled her eyes in contempt.

Leonard raised an eyebrow, "Well, there it is."

"I, for one, would like to hear what she did." The final man—a tall ginger—walked up to Cassidy and looked her over in disgust.

"She conspired with the government to initiate genetic warfare against us by using ticks. They genetically engineered a species that could carry a mutation of the rabies virus which can only affect shifters, causing us to shift against our will and become rabid...before it kills us," Knox informed the conclave.

"Yes, Nathan. And the virus attacks all cells in the body. The beginning symptoms resemble the rabies virus, but then random shifts begin," Ramon added.

"So, how is the human involved?" The blonde woman asked.

"Well, Vanessa, she was hired by the government to distribute the ticks here in Acadia, but once I was infected with the virus, she created an antidote for it," Ramon said.

"You were infected?" The older silver haired woman was concerned.

"Yes, Priscilla. Up until about an hour ago when Min here gave me the antidote." Ramon smiled at me and I returned the expression. I was happy he was doing all the talking, because to be honest, the conclave scared me. They seemed so intimidating. And to top it off, they wouldn't even address me as anything other than a human.

"I see," Jeremy nodded.

"Cassidy is also behind the rogue shifters from the last trial here in Acadia. When you came to judge Shawn, Harris, Kevin and Jamie, they were infected with the virus; it just hadn't advanced to the more serious stages yet. Cassidy informed us that the government dealt with the three who managed to escape the park," Knox continued.

"I think we have enough information to understand her guilt," Nathan said. "There is no need to deliberate. She has already admitted her guilt and there is more than enough evidence against her."

"Why did you do it?" Vanessa turned to Cassidy.

"I didn't want to die."

"You have made quite a mess. You could have died with your clan, but instead, you will die alone in shame."

Cassidy didn't respond.

"I would like to ask for my mate and I to be excused from witnessing the execution. I don't think she needs to see this." Ramon stepped in front of me.

"Granted. You may be excused. We only need two people as witnesses to the trial, so Trent and Knox are enough."

With that, Jeremy waved us away. Ramon grabbed my hand and we headed back to my car.

"What are we going to do about the government? The people who hired me and Cassidy?"

"Well, we could have Hannah or Blanca call them using Cassidy's phone and pretend to be her? She could tell them that the ticks were located by the clan and destroyed before you could distribute them. She could also tell them that she no longer wants to partner with them and would rather take on the government with her clan than be their guinea pig." Ramon shrugged.

I nodded. That actually sounded like a great plan.

"Alright, then. I'll have Knox grab Cassidy's phone after the execution."

"Thank you, Ramon." I smiled and kissed him. He pulled me in and deepened the kiss, catching me slightly off guard.

But he was kissing me, and he was alive, and I couldn't have been more grateful.

11

RAMON

EPILOGUE

I AWOKE TO LIGHT KISSES BEING PLANTED ON ALONG MY NECK. THE KISSES moved to my chest and I smiled.

"*Buenos días, mi amor,*" I whispered. I opened my eyes to see my beautiful mate looking up at me seductively.

"Good morning. The baby's *finally* asleep." Min had moved down to my boxers and was reaching inside; I hadn't realized they looked like a tent. "Looks like *someone* is awake..."

She pulled my shaft out and started to stroke it slowly. I moaned; if I hadn't been awake before, I certainly was at that moment.

"Are you sure you're ready for that?" I asked.

"Please. It's been two months since I gave birth, and as good as your tongue is, I want this, too..." She stopped stroking me to pull her long T shirt over her head, and her bare, full breasts bounced before me.

"Oh, my tongue is good huh?" I joked.

"So good..." She said coming up to kiss me. I used my tongue to part her lips and explore her mouth and she moaned, grinding against my member. I could feel her nether lips folding around my manhood through her panties.

I felt her reach down and I moaned as I suddenly felt her warm, velvety walls fully encase my length.

"Wait, I thought you were wearing panties?" I asked between kisses.

"I just pulled them to the side; stop talking."

Min's lips pressed firmly against mine as she started riding me. She moved up and down along my length and I grabbed her hips, guiding them. She started off in a slow grind, but she quickly picked up her speed. Before I knew it, I was slamming her hips down, loving the sound of her loud moans. She began to quiver and I thrusted upward, making sure to bury myself as deep as I could inside her. She screamed as she hit her peak, trembling as she rode out her orgasm, her nails digging into my shoulders.

When I felt her calm, I flipped our positions so that she was lying down.

"My turn," I growled.

She giggled as I pulled her to the edge of the bed, lifting one of her legs. I entered her once again, slamming into her in one thrust. She gasped, and I didn't give her time to breathe as I started pumping into her wildly. I reveled in the feeling of my length moving within and her walls tightened around me. Her facial expressions were so incredibly hot when she looked up at me, it just fueled my fire, which was rising quickly. I could feel her body begin to quake beneath me again, and I smiled inwardly. She was ready for round two.

I focused on the burning within me and it spread throughout my whole body, wrapping around me like a blanket until I thought I would explode from the heat. And I did, my seed spilling into her with each thrust.

"Ramon!" She called my name loudly as I watched her orgasm rip through her. She was shaking again, and I smirked as I slammed my length back into her one last time, just to hear her scream again.

"Ramon..." she whimpered when I pulled out.

"Oh, you want more?" I joked.

"Maybe..." She licked her lips.

"You can go more than twice?"

"I can go as long as you want." And now she was biting her lip.

Mierda... She was so unbelievably hot sometimes, I just couldn't handle it. She knew just what to do, just what to say to drive me crazy. And I loved every minute of it.

Just when I went to climb on top of her again, I heard the faint cry of our baby.

"Looks like all your screaming woke our son," I laughed.

"Shut up!" Min slapped my shoulder and got up, pulling her long T shirt back over her head and fixing her panties.

"Awww...I liked you like that." I made a pout at her and she rolled her eyes.

"Yeah, well your son doesn't need to see his mom like that," she laughed.

"I suppose you're right."

"Do you want to come with me, now that you're awake?"

"I don't know...I'm feeling pretty tired again after all that exercise," I joked. Min picked up a pillow and threw it at me before she disappeared into the baby's room.

"I'll be right there," I laughed as I rolled out of bed. I walked into the next room and there was Min, holding our son, his lips suckling her left breast. She was facing me, and when I entered the room, she looked up and smiled.

"Look sweetie, it's daddy!"

"Hey, Jorge. How's my little man?" I said, walking up to them both. Jorge unlatched from his mother's breast at the sight of me and reached his arms up towards me.

"He always wants his daddy. Even my milk isn't enough to keep him away from you," Min chuckled, passing him over to me, and I held him securely.

I thought Min was the most beautiful thing I had ever seen, until she had Jorge. He was a gorgeous baby; he had to be, because he was hers. He had eyes and hair just like Min's, but in his complexion and other features, I saw myself. Thank God we were able to have the antidote administered to him while he was still in the womb, and he responded to it like a champ. Now there he was, the most precious creature on Earth, strong, thriving and full of life.

"Are we still going to Trent and Blanca's barbeque?" Min asked.

"We already promised we would," I said, giving her behind a tender squeeze.

"Alright, well I'm going to get in the shower. Here, you can watch him until I get back." Min started towards the door.

"Can't I just come with you?" I wiggled my eyebrows at her and she laughed.

"Only if you can get him preoccupied," she said as she drifted into the hallway.

I watched her ass sway from side to side as she left the room. After having our child, she had put on a little more weight in all the right areas. Her hips were wider, her bottom was larger and more firm, and her breasts had filled out. Her stomach somehow shrunk right back to normal—the doctor said breastfeeding would help in that department—but even if her belly was still soft, I would still find it sexy. Thick or skinny, she was gorgeous, and I couldn't imagine being with another woman.

Thinking about her body reminded me about showering with her and I put Jorge back in his crib.

"Listen, Jorge. Daddy wants to spend some quality time with mommy; it won't take long. You think you could watch this and behave until we come back?" I started the wildlife animal mobile above his crib and he cooed as he smiled widely. "That's my man."

"Min, Ramon; it's so good to see you! Thanks for coming." Blanca gave us each a hug and kissed us both on our cheeks. "And look at little Jorge here; what a cutie! He couldn't possibly have merged you both more perfectly."

Blanca bent down and spoke to Jorge.

"Hi, little Jorge. How are you, buddy?" Blanca gave him a bright smile and Trent walked up to me.

"You still want to go through with this?" he whispered in my ear.

"Hell yeah, *amigo*. Is everything set for it?"

"We're all set, just grab it from Knox and you're good to go."

"Are you guys hungry?" Blanca winked at me.

"Starving!" Min exclaimed. "It seems like I always am these days. Breastfeeding will do that to you."

"Well, Knox is over there with the food. Please, everyone, help yourselves."

"I'll get our food, *mi amor*. Why don't you go sit over there?" I pointed to an empty chair in the middle of where everyone had congregated. We had told the group to leave this seat empty for her.

"Okay, hun. Make sure to pile on some extra potato salad." Min didn't seem suspicious of anything and headed toward the chair. I waited until she was seated with the baby next to her and then I made my way over to Knox.

"Aye, *hombre,* is it ready?" I asked.

"It is," he said, handing me a warm churro. We'd been practicing making them recently and I thought that one looked pretty authentic.

"This looks great!"

"Yeah, I actually had a lot of fun making these. Hannah loves them, so I'll probably be making them for her now, too. You think it's skinny enough?"

"*Si, amigo*. It's perfect!" Knox laughed. "Hey man, were you able to get Hannah to handle that Cassidy thing?"

"With the government? Yeah. If Cassidy was alive, it wouldn't have gone well for her. They were not very forgiving of her backing out of their deal. They threatened to find her and kill her and the rest of us."

"Well, they'll need a lot of luck finding her," I laughed. "I guess we can expect someone else from the government to show up soon."

"Yeah, they canceled Min's room in Bar Harbor and said they'll be sending someone for her car, so I'd imagine that person will ask to speak to Cassidy."

"You don't think she got fired, do you?" I was slight worried by the government's response.

"Well, she said it was a sub department of hers, so I doubt they have the power to fire her. I'm sure they also don't want her to spout off about what they did. She wouldn't even have to reveal us; she could just say they tried to eradicate a whole group of people and show the proof. I'm sure they would get in quite a bit of trouble."

"Yeah, I think you're right."

"Alright, it's all you. Good luck, man!"

I pressed a small object into the tip of the churro and slowly walked toward Min.

"Here you go, *mi amor*. Something sweet for someone sweet." I smiled as I got down on one knee in front of her.

"They made churros?" She smiled as she broke in half, and as she raised the sugary confection to her lips to take a bite, a glimmer caught her eye. "Wait—what? What's this? Oh my god!" Min's eyes widened, and she covered her mouth with both hands.

"Min Dupont, you are the love of my life. Will you marry me?" I asked, grinning wide. Everyone surrounded us and Min looked around with tears in her eyes.

"Yes! A million times, yes!" she shouted, throwing her arms around my neck.

"I hope those are happy tears," I whispered into her ear, holding her tightly, trying not to get sugar from the churro in her hair.

"Of course they are," Min laughed, pulling away and wiping her eyes. I pulled the ring off the end of the churro and dusted the sugar off of it. She extended her left hand to me, beaming as I placed the ring on her finger and smiled back at her brightly. Pulling me up to meet her face, she kissed me, and I smiled against her lips.

I almost forgot it wasn't just the two of us until I heard the enormous round of applause around us. People were cheering and clapping, shouting our names. I decided to kiss her like no one was there; I wanted her to know how overcome with joy I was that she had agreed to become my wife.

I was going to marry the mother of my child.

I heard whistling and figured that she got the idea.

"Wow," she breathed when I pulled away. "Tell me how you really feel!"

I laughed. She was perfect; always a wise ass, just like me.

I felt two slaps on my back and Trent and Knox were on either side of me.

"Congrats, man! I knew she would say yes." Trent wore a wide grin on his face.

"There wasn't a doubt in my mind." Knox shook my hand. "Congrats!"

I watched as Hannah and Blanca surrounded Min, inspecting her ring. I had gotten her an eighteen-carat white gold band, fully-set with diamonds with a large, square-cut diamond set in the middle. I wanted a ring men could see from a mile away. I want them to know she was mine before they even had the thought to walk up to her.

"You did good, man," Knox said, nodding.

"The three musketeers and our three ladies. Who knew?" Trent exclaimed, wrapping his arms around me and Knox.

"I sure didn't. I didn't even think Knox would find someone. He's so fucking serious all the time," I laughed.

"What can I say? Hannah was too hot to pass up," Knox shrugged.

"So, when are you guys going to pop the question? I was the last one to get a lady, but the first to engaged. How'd you guys let that happen?" I joked.

Trent and Knox pulled two small boxes from their pockets and opened them to show me the rings nestled inside.

"Are those for Hannah and Blanca?" I asked, surprised.

"Yeah, what do you think about a triple wedding? Are you cool with it?" Trent asked.

"That sounds incredible! I mean, we would have to ask the ladies, but look at them over there." I pointed to the girls standing a few feet from us. They were laughing and smiling together like they'd been best friends for years. "They already get along so well. I doubt they'll have a problem with that."

"Well, hopefully we don't steal your spotlight or anything!" Trent said, starting towards the girls, and Knox followed.

"Good luck!" I shouted after them. I watched as they knelt down in front of Hannah and Blanca at the same time, asking for their hands in marriage. They both squealed and looked at each other, nodding eagerly. There wasn't a moment of doubt in my mind that they would say yes.

And just like that, we were all engaged. I watched as the girls compared rings and thought of how amazing the next year was going to be. The clan was becoming stronger the bigger it got, and we were ready for anything the world could throw at us.

RANGER DREW

SHIFTER NATION: WEREBEARS OF ACADIA

1

KATHLEEN

The National Center for Preparedness, Detection, and Control of Infectious Diseases, or the NCPD-CID, probably thought that I would be thrilled with the accommodations they'd be providing me with while traveling to Bar Harbor, Maine just because I was a poor little bottom feeder in their eyes. I was sure they figured I would be grateful for an economy class plane ticket, a shoddy room in a two-star hotel, and a car deemed the worst model to have ever come out in 2008.

And they were right.

I actually hadn't been on a plane since I was thirteen, when I came to the United States from Ireland. I didn't remember too much about that plane ride; surely, I had slept through most of it. I couldn't say I'd been excited to fly all those years ago, but that day, I was over the moon. Flying sure beat hitch hiking or backpacking, which is how I had become accustomed to getting around.

I always made it a habit to travel light because I was always on the move. But America was such a vast, overwhelming country for me; before that day, I'd never traveled outside the state. West Virginia technically had everything I needed anyway, but it sure as hell wasn't a vacation land in any way, shape or form.

The semi-comfortable seats in coach were welcomed, as were the movies and music. It was only about a five-hour flight from Atlanta, Georgia, where the NCPD-CID's main office was located, to Bar Harbor, Maine—just enough time for me to watch *Hancock* and *You Don't Mess with the Zohan*—so I pulled out my earbuds and plugged them into my seat's audio jack. I didn't get to the movies much, but I had no issues pirating or streaming movies when I had some down time—which was hardly ever.

I didn't have proper luggage, but my backpack was roomy enough to carry my laptop and seven outfits. Lucky for me, it was July, the warmest month of the year for Bar Harbor, and I had packed mostly tank tops and shorts. The temperatures were supposed to be between sixty and eighty degrees, so I had brought one light sweater to throw over my tank tops when the temperature was on the lower side. I only brought the old, beat up navy blue sneakers that I wore on the plane ride, and a slightly nicer black pair for when I'd have to infiltrate Acadia National Park. I was told to bring at least one nice outfit, but the best piece of clothing I could find in my wardrobe was the black ruffled shirt that I usually saved for dates —which were extremely few and far between. Pair that with shorts and my black semi-decent sneakers and I had a not-so-professional outfit, but it was the best I could come up with on such short notice. I wasn't exactly sure *why* I needed an outfit like that in the first place, but I'm sure if I had shown them what I had, it wouldn't have been up to par.

Okay, who was I kidding. Those were the only clothes I owned.

If all else failed and I needed something better, I hoped that Bar Harbor would have a cheap boutique where I could grab something. The guy who hired me had mentioned they'd be providing me with funds for my meals, but that he'd have to authorize payment for other things, like gas for the car; if they wanted me to have a professional outfit, I would think they wouldn't mind footing the bill for one.

The guy from the NCPD-CID who had hired me, Eric Hanson, told me that when I got off the plane, there would be someone waiting for me, holding a sign with my name on it, and that person would be handing a car off to me. I had kept my composure well when he'd told me this at first, but inwardly, I had been flipping out.

My very own car? I barely had my license, even though I was in my early twenties at the time.

I didn't want him to think I was excited about the trip, the car, or anything else, for that matter. Hanson had found me after one of his technicians intercepted a hacking I was conducting on their file inventory.

A client from a hacking site I received work through was going to pay me to search through the NCPD-CID's private records for anything of interest. Any experienced hacker probably wouldn't have taken the job. Hacking into government files was difficult alone; private files were a whole different level of hell. The person who requested this job probably knew that someone like me would be checking out the wanted section, though; someone willing to do anything for any amount of money. Getting a thousand dollars would have been like winning the lottery, and would have helped me get by for a long time. But, hacking was a competitive job market—and also illegal. So, between dodging the feds and doing my damndest to score the most attractive jobs, it was hard to keep a decent amount of funds in the bank to cover food and day-to-day expenses.

I had been so eager to get paid, however, that I failed to take extra precautions for security purposes. When shutting down a hack, I could usually clear my computer and the interceptor wouldn't have enough time to get information on me to act. But that day, just enough time had passed for the individual to be able to track my IP address.

At the time, I'd been using the Couchsurfing app, where you could plan to stay with someone for up to three days, completely free of charge. When I found out about the app after I turned eighteen, it changed my entire life. I had done the research: with 29,643 hosts in West Virginia, where I lived, there were enough places for me to stay over the span of 247 years. My plan was to stop couch surfing in a few years, though; I hoped I would be able to save enough money to get my own apartment by then.

To participate, I had to bring a small gift, or treat my host to dinner whenever I changed places. Dining out with others could get pretty expensive, and I never had that kind of money to spare, so I usually just picked up the nicest trinket I could find at the dollar store closest to the host's place. Apparently, other couch surfers didn't do that as often because my hosts were always thrilled to receive a gift and gave me great reviews because of it; thank god, because I needed reviews like those to keep me going. Too many poor reviews would mean hosts wouldn't welcome me into their homes, and my master plan would fall through completely.

Anyway, I was surprised the NCPD-CID found me because my entire Couchsurfing profile was fake: fake name, fake address, everything. The only real thing was my picture and I had made sure other people were in it; it was blurry, and you couldn't get a good look at my face. Most people thought it was something artsy I was trying to do, but whatever made me inconspicuous was fine with me.

So, how were they able to nab me?

Apparently, when they mapped out my IP address, they used surveillance to watch me flee my host's place, taking a snapshot of my face and cross referencing it. They found my foster care info and learned who I was, then they hacked my Couchsurfing profile to find out where I was going to stay next. All of this happened within the span of ten minutes, because in the fifteen minutes it took me to get to the new host's house, the police were there waiting for me.

And all I could think was how much this was going to hurt my Couchsurfing reviews.

I thought I was going to be hauled off to jail for sure, no questions asked. They had too much proof against me, and even I knew it wasn't smart to fight them. However, instead of being sent to prison, I was handcuffed and taken in a van to Atlanta, Georgia, to the office of the NCPD-CID. It had been a long nine-hour trip in the van with no food or drink, and I wondered if it was legal to do that. I was basically a prisoner, but even prisoners had rights.

Upon arriving at the office and being locked in a room with Hanson, I was uncuffed and offered a tuna melt sandwich and a bottle of water. I ignored it for a bit, but my growling stomach gave me away and I ate it in silence.

"Good, now that you are fed, we can get right down to it. My name is Eric Hanson; I'm the head of this department. Your name is Kathleen Boland and you tried to hack into our system, but we caught you. What were you trying to get?"

"I was hired to do it."

"By whom?"

"I have no idea. The site I was contracted through is anonymous; I don't know the person who requested the job. The clients pay the site, who holds the funds in escrow until the individuals they hire complete their jobs. If your IT guys could track me down that quickly, they should have the person who requested the job in no time." I shrugged, taking another bite of the sandwich. It was pretty delicious, actually; the tuna was flavorful and not smothered in mayonnaise, like I hated.

"We will need the username of the person as well as the website you use, then." Hanson had remained standing since I arrived, and it made me uncomfortable.

"Why? So, you guys can shut it down? People have to make a living somehow."

"It's illegal!" He slammed his fist on the table. I stared blankly at him.

Okay...try to go through this smartly, Kathleen. If you cooperate, it could make things easier for you.

"I will reveal it if it will get time off my sentence," I said firmly. Hanson stared at me for a moment and then chuckled, finally sitting down.

"You're not going to jail."

"Wait, what?" I looked around, confused by the sight of the two police officers standing just outside the room. They hadn't looked at me, though. They stood at attention and kept their eyes straight ahead.

"You are going to work for me now. As an informant."

"You're hiring me after I tried to hack you? I didn't know the government was in the habit of hiring criminals to do their bidding," I snickered. There was no way he was for real.

"The difference is, I'm not necessarily going to pay you to do it. You will do it, or you will go to jail. It is your choice." Hanson narrowed his eyes, leaning back in his chair.

"Pffft. I'd rather go to jail. I'd probably be detained for what? Six months? Who knows how long you will want me to work for free." I folded my arms over my chest.

"Actually, I could get you for first degree computer crime. When you hack into equipment costing over ten thousand dollars, which our computer systems are most definitely worth, you warrant yourself twenty years in prison and a fine of fifteen thousand dollars." Hanson smiled deviously.

Shit.

"Listen, Kathy—"

"Don't call me Kathy." I glared at him. He knew I wasn't ready to do twenty years in jail. And then to pay a fifteen thousand dollar fine when I got out? There was no way I could afford that. "How long would I have to work for you?"

"It depends on how you do on this project. If you do well, I'll keep you on."

"And if I don't, you haul my ass to jail?"

"Not exactly…"

"What do you mean?" I didn't like his tone. It sounded like I didn't actually have a choice after all.

"If you take this job and anything goes wrong, as in, if you decide to not finish your duties, or if someone finds out about it, or anything like that, then you will be terminated." Hanson's eyes did not leave mine and they were blank.

"Terminated? I'm afraid I don't understand."

"I will have to get rid of you. Your parents are already dead, and you have no close relatives, so that makes things fairly simple. You don't seem to have any friends or anyone who might notice your disappearance, either. So, I would wipe your existence from the face of the Earth. Kathleen Boland would have never existed. I will frame it to look like you died in that gas explosion with your parents back in Ireland."

What the fuck?

"You can't do that!"

"Yes, I can. And I will. But you won't have to worry about that if you don't fail." Hanson folded his hands over his stomach, with a smug look on his face.

I had been right: this wasn't much of a choice. Either I go to jail for a quarter of my lifespan and then spend at least two years doing hacking jobs to pay for a job gone wrong, and that's if I didn't get caught again. There was no way I could get a job doing anything else; I was on the move way too much. And, at that point, would anyone even let me into his or her home? I could only imagine the review Ms. Lorraine left on my profile.

So, do I take the job, or go to jail? I can't do twenty years in prison; there's just no way. Maybe I could get out early on good behavior or something? But isn't that only when most of your sentence has been served? I don't think I could last that long, either.

"Before I decide, what's the job?"

"I can't tell you. It's top secret government information that will only be revealed to you once you accept the position."

"Well, are there any perks? You're not exactly selling me on this here."

"Perks? I guess there are some. I will pay for your stay and transportation in the state I need you to visit, and I will provide you with a car. The car will have a tracking device on it, though, and if you try to leave without prior authorization, you will be stopped. I will give you a $60 daily budget for meals, which will be placed on a card that only I have access to. You will not be able to withdraw money or use it for anything other than food or gas. If you try to make an unauthorized purchase, the card will be declined. If the car needs gas, you are to text a number and $40 will be transferred to the card, which you must use for gas that day, or it will be removed. You will never have more than $100 on the card at any one time. Again, as I said, this is not a paid job. The perk is that you'll be doing this instead of going to jail."

My own car? Sixty bucks a day for food?

"Okay, I'll do it," I said in the most composed voice I could muster at the time. On the inside, I was extremely excited.

"Good. To start with, your job is simple. You are to go to Acadia National Park in Maine and gain information about the staff who work there. Once you feel like you have all the information you can collect, I want you to report back to me. I will give you the next step in your assignment at that time."

"Wait, that's it? You're paying for my food and lodging, and giving me a car, to get some info on a group of staff members that you could probably get yourself?"

"There is a difference between information collected on paper and seeing something firsthand. Take you, for example. I thought you would be difficult about this based on the information that was provided about you, but I must say, you've handled this much better than I anticipated. Besides, like I said, this is only the first part of your mission. The boys will escort you to the airport now. I'm guessing whatever you have with you is all you have?" Hanson's eyes shifted to my backpack, which was lying at the feet of the officer outside the door. "I had it searched and it seems that you are all packed up for the trip. I put a tracker on your laptop as well."

Pfft, like I can't disable that and destroy it in a heartbeat.

"If the signal goes dead, so are you."

Shit.

"If you are caught doing anything illegal on it, you will also be terminated."

"God, you're ready to kill me at any moment. Might as well put a detonator in my chest," I sneered as the police officer entered to escort me out.

Before getting on the plane, I had been handed my backpack and a folder that had all the details that Hanson had collected on the park's staff. Each person had 'Shifter' written on his or her profile.

Shifter? What the hell does that mean? That they're shifty people? My eyes had settled on a muscular man with light brown eyes. *Well, he's cute.*

Hanson had told me that I was to disguise myself as a tourist who was just there to see Acadia.

And that's how I ended up on Flight 369 to Bar Harbor, Maine. When the plane finally touched down, there was indeed a man with a sign with my name on it standing next to a Toyota Corolla.

It was nothing special, just a plain silver sedan; it looked used enough, but without scratches or dents. It didn't have that brand-new shine to it, but in my eyes, it was sparkling.

I had been told that I'd be staying at the Holiday Inn. I knew that since it was a hotel chain, I couldn't expect anything fancy, but it beat looking for new places on Couchsurfing, that's for sure.

Damn...this car does not do well with inclines... I thought, struggling up the hill to the inn. I had gone from sixty-five miles per hour right down to twenty-five miles per hour and I couldn't get the car back up to speed without slamming the gas pedal to the floor. Even then, I only climbed the hill at thirty miles per hour. It was very obviously built for reliability, but even that was questionable.

Great. They gave me a fucking mom car.

When I arrived at the inn, it seemed like a regular chain hotel with flowers on the balconies. In the parking lot, I noticed a van sporting the inn's logo, but no other visitors seemed to be in sight—it was 11pm, though.

I parked the car and proceeded into the hotel lobby, where I spotted a large sitting area with a beige tweed sectional and an L-shaped front desk with stations for two receptionists. I couldn't imagine when it would ever get busy enough for there to be more than one receptionist needed; the town was so small. You could probably drive around the whole thing in an hour tops judging by the look of it on the drive there.

"Hi. I'm here to check in."

"Name please?" The receptionist had wire-framed glasses over her hazel eyes and a shoulder length brunette bob. She wore what I assumed to be the hotel uniform, but I could only see the top half. It was sort of bougie, like a uniform I would think a higher-rated hotel would have their employees wear, but I guess that had to get their ratings up somehow. It was a whimsical buttoned top with vertical stripes, a tied scarf and a chocolate-colored vest, and at first, I thought it was quite ugly, but the longer I looked at it, the more I thought it was kind of cute. Her gold name tag showed that her name was Nancy.

"Kathleen Boland."

"Ah yes, you will be just down the hall to your left. Room forty-nine." She handed me a key to the room and I took it graciously. When I arrived at my room, I was taken aback by how nice it looked. There was a queen-sized bed by the large sliding glass door with a white leather headboard and crisp sheets with sky blue accents. Two Cherrywood nightstands saddled each side of the bed and a painting of boats in Bar Harbor hung above it. Blue and beige curtains cascaded from either side of the glass door, which opened onto a small balcony with a pair of Adirondack chairs.

"Thank god there's air conditioning in here," I said aloud, flipping it on and programming it to seventy degrees. It was seventy-eight at the time, and it was going to get as warm as eighty degrees as the week progressed, so I was definitely going to need a way to cool down.

I checked the closet and noticed an iron and ironing board inside. *Pfft. Like I'll need those.*

I peeked into the bathroom and ignored the hairdryer, which I also had no use for; I doubted it would work well with my curls. The mini fridge was stocked with water bottles, and I grabbed one, taking a healthy swig from it. A coffee/tea maker sat on top of the mini fridge along with a basket of assorted packets of each, and I was thankful for that. I would definitely need a hit of caffeine in the morning before I drove over to the park.

But what am I going to do? I couldn't log on to the hacking site because there was a chip in my laptop, and I imagined there was also one on my phone, so there wasn't much I could do on those without Hanson analyzing everything. But if I didn't touch either of them, he wouldn't be able to gain more information on me as well. *I guess I could watch some television.*

Just then, the phone in the room rang. My head shot in its direction.

Maybe there was an issue at the front desk? I've barely been in here for ten minutes...

I thought about not answering, but my politeness won over.

"Hello?"

"I hope the room and car are to your liking." I heard Hanson's smug voice on the other line.

"They are adequate, thank you." There was no way I was going to tell him how happy I was to have a room like the one I would be staying in. I was happy about the car, but after driving it, I realized it was not much to get excited over.

"Well, you can't expect five-star treatment for a first-degree criminal." I could hear the shrug and amusement in his voice. I was really starting to hate him. I didn't answer him and waited for a while. He never said anything, so finally, I broke the silence.

"Is there any reason you're calling?"

"Yes. I mostly just wanted to make sure you got to the room safely."

Yeah, right.

"Well I have, thank you, and I'm quite tired. I'd like to go to bed, so if that's—"

"Just make sure you go to the park tomorrow to start your research."

"Will do." I almost slammed down the receiver. I had just spoken with him that very same day; I certainly didn't need to be reminded of the task. If he called in the morning, I decided I wasn't going to answer. I didn't need a baby sitter.

I turned on the television and was happy to see the hotel provided HBO and Showtime. The first season of *True Blood* was playing as the late night special and I had been meaning to stream it when I had time, but I could at least watch the first episode and see if I liked it. That was if I didn't fall asleep while watching it.

I was enjoying it, but after half an hour, my eyes grew heavy and I drifted off in the middle of the episode.

2

KATHLEEN

I WOKE UP THE NEXT MORNING AT 9AM. SLEEPING FOR EIGHT HOURS WAS not a luxury I was accustomed to; usually, I was only able to sleep in three-hour intervals. I would be on the hacking site until I couldn't keep my eyes open, doze off for a few hours, and repeat. I couldn't afford to sleep for long; all I could think about were the jobs I was missing out on.

Usually, most hackers hungrily scanned through the job listings for gigs they were willing to take on, and by the time I would get through the list, the only jobs left would be the ones no one in their right mind would want.

Like the one I got caught doing.

Anything government-related was something most hackers wouldn't touch with a ten-foot pole, especially if the payment wasn't worth the hassle. So that usually left the lower-budget and/or less desirable jobs for me.

For once, I didn't have to stress over job hunting, and it felt pretty damn good.

I spotted a notepad on the nightstand, saying there were three restaurants on site.

No continental breakfast? That sucks.

La Bella Vita had flatbread pizzas and wine, which was hardly a breakfast. Stewman's Lobster Pound had seafood sandwiches and salads which seemed promising until I noticed that they were only open for dinner. And then there was pool bar. *There's a pool here, too?*

It must have been around the back of the building because I hadn't seen it when I drove up to the inn. Unfortunately, I didn't have a swimsuit, so I made a mental note to pick one up on the drive back to the hotel if I saw one. I couldn't remember the last time I had been in a swimming pool and, god, it sounded relaxing. *If they're paying for it, I might as well enjoy it.*

So, it seemed the options for breakfast were nil. The notepad gave suggestions on places you could order from, but I figured since I was getting up anyway, I would just grab something on my way to the park. If I were lucky, maybe there'd be a little donut shop on the way.

I grabbed my phone and looked for some places nearby on Yelp. The Log Cabin restaurant offered a decent menu, despite its three-and-a-half-star rating. It looked cheap, and that was enough for me, so I rolled out of bed, showered, and got dressed in twenty minutes. I headed out the door and raced to the restaurant, feeling some hunger pains, realizing I hadn't eaten anything since the tuna melt sandwich the day before.

When I got to the restaurant, it was semi-busy, but I was seated quickly. My waitress swung right over to get me a drink. She had a brunette ponytail and looked in her mid-forties, and her name tag read 'Patricia.'

"What can I get you to drink, honey?"

"I'll have a hot chocolate, please."

"Whipped cream?"

"No, thank you." I thought about getting coffee, but I felt pretty well rested. I flipped over the one-page menu and noticed a meal in red text that caught my eye.

Maine Logger's Plate, a favorite! This will get you ready for a day in Acadia National Park! It seemed like the best deal on the menu. *Who am I to ignore fate?*

The waitress returned with the hot chocolate.

"Have you decided?"

"Yes, I'll have the Maine Logger's Plate, please." I handed her the menu.

"Great choice! How would you like your eggs?" She started scribbling onto her notepad.

"Omelet style, please, with ham, onions, peppers and cheddar cheese."

"Sausage or Bacon?"

"Bacon, please."

"White, wheat, or rye toast?"

"White, please. And could you add cheddar to my home fries as well?" I smiled.

"Absolutely! I'll put this right in for you and it should be out in a jiffy." She returned the gesture and scurried away to hand the order to the cook.

I didn't have to wait long for the food to come. After ten minutes, Patricia was placing two plates in front of me: a small one holding the two pancakes, and another large plate with the bacon, home fries, and omelet piled on top. The food looked amazing, and when I took my first bite, it was pretty damn delicious. I decided that I would probably have breakfast there every day, if I was feeling in the mood for it; Hanson was giving me a daily sixty-dollar allowance for meals, so why the hell not. After I practically licked the plates clean, I paid the bill and left the restaurant, heading off for my first visit to Acadia.

Pop. Pshhhhhhhhhhhh... Two miles down the road, the car skidded hard to the right side of the road and I did my best to straighten the wheel before it came to a complete stop.

"What the fuck was that?" I got out of the car and walked around its perimeter, then, I saw it: a scrap of sheet metal was lying a few yards back on the road, and my right two tires were completely slashed. "You've *got* to be kidding me."

It would be just my luck to get two flat tires in the middle of an open stretch of road with no cars. *Isn't this the height of tourist season, though?* I assumed some family in an SUV with kayaks secured to its top would be driving by soon, so I waited. Within a few minutes, I spotted a several cars on the horizon, and then tried to wave them down.

Not one of them stopped for me. I couldn't tell if it was because they knew they couldn't help me or they were just in a rush, but no one could know what I needed help with; the slashed tires were on the other side of the vehicle, facing away from the road. Maybe they could just see how the car was leaning to the right side as they drove by.

The rush of traffic ended and I still couldn't get anyone to help me, so I just leaned against the car and waited.

Hopefully, someone will notice me standing here and stop to check if I'm okay...

The universe must have been listening, ready to answer my prayers —for once—because two minutes later, a red pickup truck, a 2008 Chevrolet Silverado, pulled over in front of my car. My eyes widened. *Oh, thank god; someone stopped!*

I watched as the perfect picture of tall, dark and handsome strolled over to me. His skin was glistening with sweat on that hot, summer day, and he wore a fitted, white t-shirt and low hanging, tattered blue jeans with combat boots. He was extremely muscular and I couldn't help but ogle his strong biceps, which were straining the arms of his tee. For some reason, he looked extremely familiar, but I couldn't put my finger on where I would know him from.

But I most certainly knew I wanted to lay a finger on him.

"Are you okay?" he asked, walking over to me after closing the door to his truck. "Your car looks a bit lopsided."

His mouth spread into a grin, revealing a friendly smile and his voice was like molasses, deep and smooth. I almost melted on the spot.

"My right tires...Some scrap metal..." I struggled to formulate a coherent sentence, but he didn't seem to mind. He walked around me to inspect the damage on the other side of the car. I followed behind him to be welcomed by the sight of his nice, firm ass just barely hidden beneath the waist of his jeans. I licked my lips and tried to control myself.

What the hell is wrong with you, girl? You avoid men like the plague, and then this guy comes along and you're wetting your panties. Get over yourself. I rolled my eyes inwardly. I wasn't sure why I was so overtaken by this man, but there was something about him that sent a hot jolt of electricity right through my body.

And he was the only person to stop and try to help me.

"Yeah, these are done. Lucky for you, I happen to have two fifteen-inch tires in the back of my pick up to help the locals in cases like these. I drive this truck for patrol and then the fire truck, when you know, there's a fire." He chuckled and shrugged, walking back to his truck.

*He's a firefighter? That's so...sexy...*My mind immediately went to him wearing an open fireman's jacket with the pants and hat to match, going up to the fire truck and getting the hose, ready to wet me down. I almost started drooling before he started to speak again.

"We'll need a jack to get these tires changed, so let me grab that as well." He grunted as he hoisted up both tires and looped them onto his shoulders, then dropped each next to its respective flat. Sauntering back to the truck, he grabbed the jack and headed back to my car, where he knelt by my front tire first.

He placed the jack just under my car and began to crank it up. I watched the muscles of his forearm and biceps ripple as they moved back and forth with each pump of the handle, and I could feel myself getting wet. If his shirt had been just a smidge tighter, it would have surely ripped.

"So, you're a firefighter, huh? Do you guys get fires in town often?"

"There is a town fire station, but I don't work for them. I work for the park."

Just then, I realized why he looked familiar: he was the guy with the light brown eyes that caught my attention in the NCPD-CID's files. The picture had not done him justice, though; he was far more attractive in person.

I wonder if he knows what the shifter tag means...Not like I could show him, anyway.

When he finally had the car jacked up off the ground, he stood and inspected the tire's lock nuts. My gaze shifted from him to the car and I wasn't sure what he'd be doing next. I knew nothing about cars, so I certainly didn't know the first thing about changing a tire.

"I'll need a tire iron, so let me go grab that," he said finally, heading back to his truck.

"You weren't kidding when you said you had everything," I giggled.

"Well, everything except the key to get these wheel locks off," he laughed.

Wheel locks? "Wait, what are those?"

"People install them to help prevent theft of their rims and tires. Do you know where the key is?"

"I'm not sure, but let me check the glove compartment." I headed into the car and fished around in the glove box; thankfully, I found a faded, opened package that read 'McGard Cone Seat Lug Nut Wheel Locks' with a small, metal object inside. "I guess we both lucked out on this one. It was in there!"

"Did you not put it there in the first place?" he chuckled.

"Nah, this car is a loaner from a friend. She's just letting me borrow it while I visit Acadia." I handed him the wheel lock key. Our fingertips brushed for a moment, and another electrical current of desire ran straight to my nether regions. I suppressed a shiver.

"Is that what brought you to the area? I knew I had never seen you around. I figured you were either new here or just visiting."

If he had felt the current, too, he showed no sign of it. It was slightly disappointing, but to be honest, I was trying to cover it up as well.

"The latter. Just visiting. Acadia sounded beautiful, and I love hiking, so I thought I would come up and check it out."

As he proceeded to loosen the wheel locks, the key broke off inside the nut. He nodded to the lifted car and laughed to himself. "Well, I think this is a sign that today might not be your day."

"Then, what else should I do with my time?"

"Your car seems to think your time is better spent with me." He flashed me another broad grin and I couldn't help but smile back.

"My car sure knows how to pick 'em! The guys with all the right parts, but no process," I teased.

"Oh, really? Well, I guess I can't argue much with that," he laughed, grabbing his phone to search for tips on how to remove a tire with a broken wheel lock key stuck inside and scrolled through the results.

"Maybe you need two pairs of eyes." I approached him and he tipped to the side, allowing me to read over his shoulder. I resisted the urge to rest my hand on his bicep as his thumb flicked over the screen. We searched for about ten minutes and didn't find anything—even on YouTube—but I didn't mind; as the sun rose higher in the sky, he began to sweat even more, and the scent of his body spray was intoxicating. I usually didn't like them; I always thought they were too strong, but whatever scent he had, paired with his own, created a perfection that I could bask in all day.

"Alright. Since that was a bust, I'll just have to wing it," he shrugged. He grabbed the tire iron and a few other tools from his truck and went to work on the 'lug nuts' of the wheels—I learned that term from the few tutorials we just watched. He seemed to have to put his full body weight into loosening them, and for a few minutes there, it seemed like they would be nearly impossible to remove. But after about ten minutes—and a lot of sweat—he had managed to extract all of the nuts from the first wheel. He pulled the wheel off and replaced it with one from his truck, using the tire iron to screw the lug nuts back in; tightening them seemed almost as tough as removing them had been. He repeated this process on the other wheel, then lowered the jack and removed it, standing back to admire his handy work.

"You'll probably need to go to the in-town mechanic to have them tighten those more with a power wrench because I wouldn't trust my strength." He rubbed the back of his head.

"Oh, you look plenty strong to me." I winked with a laugh.

"Well, I wouldn't want your wheels rolling off while you're driving or something." He chuckled.

I was extremely grateful for his help, and I wasn't exactly sure what came over me, but I ended up throwing my arms around his delicious, sweat-drenched body. "Thank you so much for stopping to help me. I had been waiting for so long and tried waving people down, but no one would stop."

"You're welcome," he said softly, returning the hug. When we pulled apart, our eyes met, and I thought he might kiss me, but instead, he smiled.

"You know, I didn't catch your name. Mine is Andrew. Andrew Williams." He reached out his hand for me to shake and I thought about the NCPD-CID.

Can I tell him my real name? I figured there was no harm.

"Nice to meet you, Andrew. My name is Kathleen Boland." I shook his outstretched hand. "I can't believe we went all that time without even introducing ourselves."

"Yeah, do you usually hug strangers?" he teased.

"No!" I slapped his shoulder playfully.

"Do you go by Kathleen, or do you like Kathy? Most people call me Drew, for short."

"I *hate* when people call me Kathy. Please don't," I spat, a little more irritated than I intended to sound, but I really despised the name. There used to be a girl in my foster home named Kathy and she would always pester me. Our foster parents would call us twins even though we looked nothing alike and weren't even the same age. The name hosted a part of my teenage years that I'd preferred to forget.

"Anyway, I'd like to pay you back for this. Can I treat you to dinner tonight?"

I didn't usually ask men out. In fact, I couldn't remember the last time I had. Guys asked me on dates from time to time, but I always declined. I never had time for relationships or dating, but with this new government assignment, I figured that as long as I got the job done, I could do whatever I wanted.

"Hmm...I've never had a girl ask me out before. Or hug me without telling me her name first. You are full of surprises, aren't you? Sent from the heavens to test me." He laughed.

"I guess so! Now, is that a yes, or a no? Don't you know you aren't supposed to keep a lady waiting?" I teased.

"Kathleen, I would *love* to go to dinner with you. I can't promise I won't try to pay anyway, though," he warned playfully. "Why don't you leave this amazing car of yours in the parking lot, and I can pick you up. You'll probably want to have dinner in Bar Harbor, which is most likely closer to where you're staying because I live on the park grounds. What hotel are you staying at?"

"The Holiday Inn."

"Okay, how about we go to the Looking Glass. It's pretty close to you. May I pick you up later tonight?"

"Okay, sure." I smiled.

"Alright, then, great," he grinned. "Well, I'm going to head off, and I'll be by to pick you up at 7pm sharp."

"Sounds perfect."

"Well, I definitely should get to work, I'm running pretty late and I'm honestly surprised my boss hasn't called me yet."

"Okay, Drew, I'll see you tonight. And really, thanks again."

"Anytime."

I watched him walk back to his truck and sighed. He drove away, waving and I returned the gesture.

When I got back into the car, I thought about continuing on to the park and meeting the rest of Acadia's staff. If all the guys looked as good as Drew did, I was going to have a hard time containing myself.

I almost went, but I was worried about something Drew had mentioned. He was most definitely strong, but what if he hadn't been strong enough to tighten the lug nuts all the way? It dawned on me that I should probably go to the mechanic to get the car checked out as he suggested. I was already nervous enough to drive again, but once I made it there and had the lug nuts evaluated, I knew I would feel better. I would have to call Hanson to have him cover the expenses.

Oh shit! What am I going to wear on my date? I can't just wear the crap stuffed in my friggin' backpack... I really wanted to wow him. It had been a long time since I had gotten all dressed up and I owed it to myself to feel pretty at least one day out of the year. *Well, they did ask me to get a nice outfit...*

I decided I would tack some extra funds for a professional outfit onto the cost of the mechanic when I called Hanson. I would just try to get something I could both wear professionally and look hot on my date.

3

DREW

I CHECKED MYSELF OUT IN THE MIRROR ONE LAST TIME BEFORE I HEADED out the door.

You look good, man. I had been worried that I was dressed too casually, but I didn't own a dress suit, so I had to make do with what I had. Besides, I didn't think Bar Harbor was a suit-wearing kind of town anyway, and especially not at a restaurant like The Looking Glass.

I had decided on a white polo shirt, black slacks and black dress shoes. I didn't want to layer up too much because the temperature had only dropped about two degrees in five hours, so I assumed it wouldn't be too chilly that night.

I walked out to my garage and thought about taking the pick-up truck as a joke, or even the fire truck, but I didn't think Knox, my boss, would appreciate that very much. And I kind of wanted to wow her with my Cadillac, anyway. It was a 2008 CTS and the second-best car to come out during its year. It had a sharp muscular style which I was trying to emulate, so I decided it would be a perfect match.

I punched the Holiday Inn as the destination in my GPS system and headed toward Bar Harbor. I didn't know her room number, and she didn't know what I was driving, so it was probably going to be a little hard to find her. And my smart ass had forgotten get her number.

Those curves of hers had made it easy to forget *a lot* of things.

My dashboard said 6:58pm when I pulled up to the front of the building. I noticed her car was parked in the back of the lot, and I only had to wait for a minute before I saw her exit the automatic doors. She was wearing a white camisole, a black ruffled skirt that fell just above her knees, and black flats. I wished I had brought a jacket or something in case she got cold throughout the night, because it didn't look like she had brought one. I guessed she had thought the same thing that I did. With the temperatures barely moving, it was probably going to be a warm night; I sure hoped so.

She stood there peering around, looking for me and I honked my horn to let her know where I was. She smiled and waved when she saw me, and padded over to the car.

"You drive a Black Caddy?" she asked, seemingly surprised when she got in. She looked gorgeous. Her curly, ginger hair cascaded past her shoulders and down her back. Her eyes were a vibrant green, stunning me with their piercing gaze. Her skin looked smooth and creamy and her legs went on for miles. As she sat in the car with me, her skirt had slightly risen, exposing her thigh and I fought hard to resist the urge to place my hand there.

Not yet...

"It was one of the best cars of its year, second only to the BMW, so I had to have it. Also, I think it matches my personality pretty well."

"Slick and handsome?" she smiled seductively, obviously flirting with me.

"You don't look so bad yourself." I flashed her a smile and selected The Looking Glass as our next destination in the GPS.

"I went to the mechanic like you recommended. Ten dollars later, my wheels are perfectly safe from falling off," she said proudly.

"Good to hear at least someone listens to me every now and then," I chuckled.

It only took us a couple of minutes to get there and we continued to make small talk during the ride. When we arrived at the restaurant, it was moderately busy. It was a Friday night, so I had anticipated that there would be some traffic, but I hoped we would be able to get seated quickly. I walked over to the usher.

"Table for two please?"

"Certainly, sir. Right this way."

Yes!

The usher brought us to a very quaint corner of the restaurant. All the tables were candle lit by tea lights in mason jars and had miniature vases of flowers as centerpieces. There were no walls by the seating area, just open, thick glass windows with a stunning night view of the sparkling Atlantic; I supposed that's how they got their name. I had never been there before, but honestly, I hadn't been on a date with anyone since I had moved to Acadia. I felt pretty proud of my choice in that moment, though.

I pulled out a chair for Kathleen to take a seat. She smiled brightly at the gesture and sat, scooting the chair closer to the table.

Now I'll just have to keep impressing her...

The waiter came over and introduced himself.

"Good evening, my name is Oliver, and I'll be your waiter tonight." He bowed before asking, "May I start you off with a bottle of wine?"

Kathleen seemed surprised by this and just stared at him.

"Um. We'll have the 2010 Geyser Peak Sauvignon Blanc." I chose the second wine on the list because the first one was a dry Riesling, which I hated. I wasn't much of a wine drinker in general, but I had a little pep talk from Ramon and Trent, the biologist and law enforcement officer of the park, and they had assured me that most women loved wine and it would help us both break the ice and relax more into the evening. I hoped they were right because I was trying really hard not to sweat through my shirt; I was so nervous. Also, the Sauvignon Blanc was about thirteen dollars a bottle, whereas the Riesling was twenty-four dollars. If I was going to make it seem like she was paying, I didn't want to order expensive things and make her anxious.

Then, I looked at the menu.

Fuck! Look at these prices! It wasn't like I couldn't afford them, I was concerned that perhaps she would think I picked an expensive place on purpose just because she was treating me. And I really didn't want her to think that. I looked up to check her reaction to the menu and her eyes were wide. Was it because of the menu selection? The prices? I couldn't really tell what that meant. *So much for my plan to surprise pay. I should probably say something now.*

"Hey, when I picked this place, I'd actually never been here before, and I could never justify having you spend this much to treat me for barely fixing your car. Please, allow me to treat you. Your company is enough repayment." I flashed her a smile and hoped I charmed her into letting me pay. She stared at me for a moment and then put the menu down.

"You did this on purpose, didn't you?" She looked at me suspiciously and I was slightly taken aback. "You picked an expensive restaurant so you could convince me to let you pay."

"No, that wasn't my intention at all; I really haven't been here before—"

"I'm just kidding!" She laughed. "I must admit, though, it is a little out of my price range."

"Oh. Haha." My heart was racing, and I took a breath to steady it. "Well, then please, allow me."

"Sorry if my joke was too serious. You looked a little tense, so I figured I'd scare you a little." She winked at me playfully and my heart stopped beating altogether. She really was beautiful.

We went back to consulting the menu, and since we had agreed on me paying, I thought about changing the wine, but I decided not to.

"Would you like to order an appetizer?" I asked her.

"The lobster rangoon sound delicious!"

"It does. I'm still not sure what I want for my entrée, though. What are you thinking of having?"

"I thought the gnocchi and mushrooms sounded great."

"Well, I won't be having that, that's for sure. I hate mushrooms," I laughed.

"Well, that's one thing you can cross off then," she winked.

"Have you both decided?" Oliver had returned with our wine and two glasses. He opened the bottle and poured a sample for each of us, while looking back and forth between us, waiting for an answer.

"May we please have the lobster rangoon to start, and I'll have the gnocchi and mushrooms. I'm not sure if he knows what he wants yet, though."

I was surprised by her forwardness. I had never had a woman order before and be so assertive, and I found it quite sexy. But, she had put me on the spot.

"I'll have the maple miso glazed salmon, please," I said curtly, taking her menu and handing them both to the waiter. Kathleen had already started on her glass of wine.

"Do you like it?" I asked.

"It tastes kind of like grapefruit and...grass. But I like it!" She laughed as she spoke, and I chuckled as I took a sip from my own glass. I could see where she was picking up those flavors, but it tasted more tropical to me. "So, have you ever saved a kitten from a tree?"

I almost spit out my wine.

"Oh, so we're doing firefighter jokes now, huh? No, I haven't, and even if there was a kitten stuck in a tree, the park has a search and rescue person for that kind of thing. That's one of Sophia's duties at Acadia."

"Have you ever slid down a pole?" She wiggled her eyebrows at me.

"Yes actually, but not for anyone's entertainment."

"Have you ever had to pose for a calendar?"

"Is that really a thing?" I was genuinely surprised. I had never heard of firefighters having to do that in real life, only models.

"Where I live, they did it to raise money for guide and therapy dogs. Needless to say, they raised *a lot* of money," she laughed.

"Well, I guess I've been lucky enough not to have to do that. Not sure how I would feel about having all the women in the area gawking at me as I hung on their refrigerators. It's too small of a town and I feel like I'd be easily recognizable." The thought alone made me shudder.

"Yeah, but you'd be a local celebrity. All the girls would want a picture with you and for you to autograph their calendars! And it would be for a good cause." She shrugged. And she was right. I wasn't sure about the celebrity bit, but if it was for a good cause, maybe I could take a picture covering my face with my hat or something.

"Any more firefighter questions you're dying to ask me?" I chuckled.

"Oh, if you open the hose to full blast, is it really strong enough to lift you off the ground if you're holding it?" She looked intrigued and took a sip of her wine. It was a silly question, but not one I got asked often.

"Well, it depends. A fire hose can only lift about two hundred pounds on its own at full blast, but it would have to be pointed at the ground. We usually have people who weigh at least two hundred and fifty pounds man the hose because they can't be lifted by the water pressure. They also have to be able to lift someone who is two hundred pounds because that will help them control the hose at that pressure. We usually never have to open the hose to full blast, though. It can do more harm than good at that power level in most situations."

Oh great, Drew, you're going on one of your fireman rants again. She probably zoned out halfway through.

"So, I'm guessing you're the one who mans the hose, huh?"

Nope. She's listening. Just has a two-track mind.

"Yes, actually, I do."

"I can tell." She was flirting hard. I couldn't believe this gorgeous girl wanted me. It couldn't be because she thought I was rich or something because she hadn't seen my car until now. And I most definitely wasn't rich; I just had acquired a lot of assets. When you work for a national park, the government pays for your lodging to make up for the four thousand dollars month they pay us. That adds up when you live by yourself and only have to buy groceries and provisions for one person. I saved up for seven months to get the Caddy that I had, and it felt good to buy it. It was really the only expensive item I owned, but I was incredibly proud to have it.

But she seemed to really like me and that was a great boost to the ego. I just had to get through dinner to see how far it could go.

The waiter returned with our appetizer of eight fried wontons. I waited for her to grab one first, but I didn't have to wait long. She reached for one and bit into it immediately, blowing air from her lips and fanning herself.

"Are you okay?"

"Yah juh haw!"

"Huh?" I watched her swallow the bite and sip some wine.

"I said it was hot!" We laughed. "I guess I shouldn't have just dove in like that."

"Was it good at least?"

"Oh, it's incredible. I'm just lucky I didn't burn my mouth on it!"

"What a shame that would be..." I had decided to flirt back. What did I have to lose?

She smiled, but didn't respond. I decided to try a wonton myself and transferred it over to one of the small plates the waiter had provided us with. To avoid the unpleasant experience she had, I cut mine in half and blew on the center before taking a bite. I could taste the lobster and scallion, but there was a sauce. I think I remembered the menu it saying it was cream cheese and blueberry, which surprisingly went quite well with the seafood and I was floored by how delicious it was.

Our entrees came out shortly after, and hers actually looked better than I had imagined it would. The gnocchi had been seasoned with cracked black pepper and freshly shaven parmesan, nestled on top of a white bean puree with a red pepper sauce. There was also a small serving of beet and carrot slaw piled near the corner of the plate.

But I wouldn't have passed mine up for hers any day. The salmon was pan seared over a vegetable soba noodle salad. I thoroughly enjoyed the flavors of Asian dishes and it definitely quelled my hunger. We ate in mostly silence, which I took as a good sign that the food was to her liking.

"How was it?" I asked when she seemed to have finished.

"Fantastic! But I'm always up for dessert..."

"I don't think they have dessert here," I joked.

"Well, you'll just have to come up with something, won't you?" I felt her shoe graze my thigh and my eyes widened.

Quick guys, I need your help! I reached out with my mind to telepathically reach Trent and Ramon, hoping one of my clan-mates would answer quickly.

How's the date going? I heard Trent ask me smugly.

She's rubbing my leg with her shoe and says she wants dessert! What do I do? My voice sounded a little more panicked than I would have liked, but I was more worried about time at that point.

Aye, amigo! You'd better take her back to your place. That's a very clear sign that she wants the D. There was laughter in Ramon's voice, but I realized he was right. I ended our communication before they said something else embarrassing.

"I might have some whipped cream and strawberries in my refrigerator if that would do?" I stroked the top of her foot.

"Here is the check whenever you're ready. I hope everything was to your liking."

"It was, thank you." I didn't even look at him. I was too focused on Kathleen biting her lip in front of me. I glanced at the check to see the total was eighty dollars. I had anticipated a hundred, so I just left the hundred-dollar bill on the table and grabbed Kathleen's hand, escorting her out of the restaurant. We barely made it to the car before

I pushed her right up against the hood and kissed her. My lips were powerful and dominant over her soft, supple ones. It had been a while since I'd last kissed a woman, and it felt damned good. I crushed my body against hers, feeling her well-endowed chest press firmly against mine; I couldn't wait to fondle those gorgeous breasts of hers. I let one hand tangle in her lovely ginger curls, and it was as if I was touching a cloud. Her hands were on my back and I grabbed her left thigh and lifted it to wrap around my hip which exposed quite a bit of her leg to my touch. I took advantage of it and ran my hand up to her bottom, cupping and squeezing it in my palm. It was a generous handful and I couldn't help but be pleased with myself when a moan escaped her lips.

Then, I heard a whistle and my head whipped around to find it. There was a group of guys heading to a nearby bar who were cheering and looking in our direction. I glared and growled, but quickly realized she might think that was a bit uncharacteristic of me, so I tried to clear my throat to mask it.

"Your place?" She sounded breathless, her chest rising and falling. Her eyes were hooded and dark green in the moonlight, filled with lust and desire. I nodded, and gently placed her leg down, opening the passenger side for her. I got in and drove us quickly back to my cabin, my hand stroking her thigh throughout the entire drive. She squirmed under my touch.

"Shouldn't you have both hands on the wheel?" she half asked, half moaned.

"I like to live dangerously," I smirked, squeezing her upper thigh, making her back arch. My manhood had grown, bulging against my pants, which were growing uncomfortable more and more by the moment. I rejoiced inwardly when I saw the indent of my road up ahead.

The car swerved slightly, and my heartbeat raced when I felt a hand in my lap, stroking my member through my pants. She laughed at my surprise.

"I, too, like to live dangerously," she admitted with a sly smile.

I could've exploded in my pants right there. *Jesus, she's hot...*

I tried to concentrate on pulling into my driveway and parking the car, which was a little hard with her trying to unzip my pants.

"Whoa, there. Let's get inside first." I laughed, grabbing her hand and kissing it. She practically ran out of the car and I shook my head. By the time I reached the door, she was already there, waiting for me to open it.

"Time to see if you are the homey type or the bachelor pad type," she giggled.

I wasn't sure which category I fit into, but maybe a little bit of both? I let her be the judge as I unlocked the door and swung it open.

We entered my living room, which had a blue and beige color scheme with stained oak-paneled walls and a fireplace. There were two sets of rustic chandelier style lights hanging from the ceiling. I had a leather sofa, a matching arm chair and oak shelves full of records, which stood next to an end table with my record player on top of it.

"No way, you have records?" She ran to the shelves and checked out my selection. "And you like classical music? And here I was thinking you'd play country music from your iPod or something."

"And why's that? Do you think I'm some backwoods kind of guy who only cares about cars and putting out fires?" I joked.

"What? Oh, no. Come on—" She feigned obliviousness for a moment and then smiled. "Of course, that's not why. I personally love country music. But I like classical, too."

"Would you like me to pick something out for us to relax to?" I asked, heading toward the shelf, but she grabbed me instead.

"I don't really feel like relaxing just yet." She whispered in my ear and then licked the edge of it. I shivered; it was an oddly pleasing sensation, and I'd never had anyone play with my ears before. "So, how about you show me where the bedroom is, and I can show you a good time?"

She didn't have to ask twice.

I led her up the spiral staircase to my bedroom, which housed a queen-sized bed with a mahogany headboard and matching nightstands on either side. I really loved the warmth that wood could bring to a living space, and my home certainly showed it.

"Odd that you like to decorate with wood, one of the most flammable materials, and yet, you're a firefighter. Aren't you afraid of this place burning down?" She eased onto the bed, kicking off her shoes by the nightstand.

"Actually, I have everything coated in a fire-proof stain, so my house could never burn down. I re-coat it every year just to be on the safe side."

She reached out her hand and pulled me toward her.

"I guess you don't need those strawberries after all, huh?"

"Not when I have *this*..." She smirked up at me, stroking my rod through my pants again. She unzipped my fly and reached in, pulling my cock from my boxer briefs. Her eyes widened when it sprung from the fly of my pants.

I smiled and playfully threw her back onto the bed, climbing on top of her.

"Why don't we see what you're working with..." I grinned and moved down to her hips, snaking my hands under her skirt. I felt the waistband of her panties and pulled them slowly down her legs. They were black lace and completely soaked; I held them up and raised an eyebrow. She bit her lip and smiled, and I shook my head and lifted her skirt just enough to expose her womanhood.

"Nice to see that the carpet matches the drapes," I laughed, doing my best to get her back for all her jokes.

"I deserve that," she giggled, pulling down her skirt. "Well, I *am* Irish..."

"You'll have to tell me more about that later when I'm a little less distracted," I said, my eyes connecting with hers.

"Oh yeah? And what could possibly be distracting you?"

"This."

And I dove between her legs, going straight for her pleasure center, my nose buried in her soft, ginger curls. My tongue lapped at her juices, which only made them flow more freely into my eager mouth. I teased her, flicking over to her entrance and thrusted inside, grabbing her hips and coaxing her further along the length of my tongue. She gasped and squirmed, but I held her firmly, quickly moving in and out. She soon moved along with me, riding my tongue as I dove deeper inside of her. I dragged my tongue up slowly toward her sensitive bundle of nerves, sucking it into my mouth, flicking my tongue over it, making her writhe and moan at my onslaught. I felt her shiver slightly and stopped immediately, which really made her whimper.

"Please...don't stop," she whispered.

"But I have something better," I assured her, standing up to reveal my shaft at full attention. I lifted her legs onto each of my shoulders and pressed her knees to her chest. Unbuckling my pants, I let them fall to the floor with my boxer briefs and kicked them across the room before I positioned myself at her entrance and slid into her slowly.

"Ah!" She threw her head back and moaned in ecstasy as my length filled her, pulsating as it plowed more deeply into her core. I felt the soft flesh of her cervix caress the tip of my member and heard a sharp intake of breath as I pressed against it, which made me even harder.

I pulled out just as slowly, making her squirm before entering her the same way once again. I continued to tease her, thrusting in and out at an excruciating pace. I wanted her to feel every inch of me as it exited and filled her; I wanted the feeling to be burned into her memory forever.

When I felt she had become best adjusted to having my rod inside her, I decided to pick up the pace a little, then a lot until I was plowing into her, the head of my cock ramming into her cervix each time. It wasn't long until I felt her shudder beneath me, exploding in spasms of pleasure and screams.

I sucked down her neck, leaving a trail of wet kisses as I let her screams push me over the edge, spilling my seed deep within her with a growl. I clenched the sheets as my shaft twitched deep within her walls, body seizing against hers. After the spasms subsided, I finally withdrew myself and released her legs, slumping on top of her. I could feel her chest heaving from fatigue and exhaustion and mine was no better.

"Hey."

"Hmmm?" I answered, ready to slip off to sleep.

"You're heavy," she giggled, squirming beneath me.

I smiled and rolled off of her. "Well, I suppose if we're going to sleep, we should sleep the proper way, anyway," I admitted. We were laying horizontally across the bed instead of with our heads at the headboard. Kathleen adjusted herself and slid over to the left side of the bed, while I took off my soaked shirt, throwing it onto the floor.

"Are you usually this messy when you have a girl over, Drew?" she teased.

"Only after extraneous activities," I joked. I laid next to her and she curled up against my chest.

"So, you're Irish, huh? Were you born there?" I asked, stroking her curls.

She groaned. "I was hoping you forgot."

"Nope."

"It's not a pleasant story." Her voice sank lower; pained, it seemed.

"You don't have to tell me if you don't want to. I just want to know more about you."

"It's fine; I have no problem telling you. Honestly, I've grown mostly numb to it over the years. Yes, I was born in Ireland. I'm from Kinsale, a little town of only about five thousand people. Mom and Dad were making dinner one evening when I was thirteen and there was a gas leak no one knew about. There was a huge explosion and my dad threw me out the window to save me. By the time the town was able to put the fire out, my parents had been burnt to cinders, and I was left with gashes from the broken glass. I still have the scars from where the glass cut me."

She lifted the side of her shirt and showed me the section between her ribs and hip. I sat up to have a better look, and there were definitely at least three large scars going straight down. I reached out my hand to touch them, but she grabbed it.

"Please don't touch them."

I nodded and laid back down. "So, did you stay with relatives or something?" I decided to continue the conversation so things wouldn't get awkward.

"I had no living relatives. Ireland doesn't exactly have the fostering or adoption system that the United States has, and apparently, Irish children are wanted here, so I was flown here and put into foster care. But I must have been too old or something, because I stayed at that foster home until I was eighteen. The day after my birthday, I left and have never gone back."

I could feel her shrug. I wasn't really sure of what to say after her story. "Where do you live now?"

"West Virginia. But I don't have an apartment or anything. There's this really great app called Couchsurfing where people offer free lodging to strangers for up to three days. There's close to three hundred thousand people in the state on it, so I sort of just hop from place to place. Unfortunately, I don't have a stable income, so I can't really afford to get my own place right now. And with no family..."

"But you can afford a vacation to Acadia?" I was merely teasing, but it did sound pretty odd.

If she's broke, what's she doing here?

"I...uh.... Actually, one of the hosts gave me the vacation. I had given her some shitty gift from the dollar store and she was so in love with it. She was sick and said she wouldn't be able to come and asked me if I would come enjoy it on her behalf. Her only request was that I take lots of pictures and send them to her when I get back."

She seemed a little *too* nervous for such a simple question. Something told me she probably wasn't telling the whole truth, but I decided to let it slide. What did I care?

"Well, then you should get to the park and start taking those pictures! You should have taken some last night, so you could tell her about meeting a handsome stranger here," I joked.

"You're totally right, I should've. I would take one now, but I don't think that little old lady could handle your super-hot bod."

I heard the laughter in her tone and it made me smile. I hadn't had someone I could joke around with in a while that wasn't Trent or Ramon, so it felt nice.

"Well, since you have to go to the park anyway, maybe you can come with me tomorrow and meet everyone? I can take you to see all the great sights it's so famous for, so you can really give this woman a look at Acadia."

"I'd love that." She cuddled closer to me. "How about you, though? Where are you from?"

"Me? I was born in Detroit, Michigan. My parents had me late in their lives, when they were both almost forty and they're both gone now. My dad died of prostate cancer when he was sixty-five and my mom died of a broken heart shortly after. They'd been inseparable since they were teenagers, so a life without him was just a life she couldn't live, it seemed. I was old enough to be on my own by then, and they had left me the house, but I couldn't live there with the both of them gone, so I sold it and moved to California. I've always wanted to be a firefighter, ever since I was a kid, so I made it happen. I originally worked for the Santa Monica Mountains National Recreation Area in Los Angeles, but I felt like I wasn't really needed there. They had to have a firefighter on hand and it was easy money to just patrol and get paid four thousand a month, but I wanted to go where I was needed. Acadia had a lot of random fires when I was hired on, so I was able to place safety precautions and take care of the fires which sort of restored my purpose. I've been here ever since. There aren't many fires these days, but I really like it here; it's become my home."

"Want to hear something funny?"

"Sure."

"When I was younger, I used to wave at fire trucks that passed by. And they would always wave back if they saw me. I always thought of how nice they were and every time I think of firemen, I picture them as the nicest people in the world. Isn't that silly?" She turned and looked up at me.

"I don't think that's silly at all. I'm happy my brothers have given our occupation a good reputation." I kissed her head. "So, you know what I do, but you haven't told me what *you* do. You said you're not making a stable income, right? Are you a freelancer of some sort?"

"I'd rather not say, if you don't mind." She tensed in my arms and I figured it must be a touchy subject.

"That's fine; we don't have to talk about it if you don't want to."

That's odd...

"I'm getting pretty tired, Drew. I think I'm ready to go to sleep, if that's alright."

Great, Drew. Look what you did. I scolded myself, but just kept holding her. She was such a fascinating, yet mysterious person; I just wanted to know everything about her. But she'd dealt with a lot of pain in her life and I knew I had to let her open up to me at her own pace. I decided I would make our day in Acadia a special one for her.

4

KATHLEEN

When I woke the next morning, Drew had prepared breakfast for us. I was pleasantly surprised, and it was absolutely delicious. The Log Cabin had some fierce competition nearby.

Drew said he had went out earlier and picked up some clothes for me to change into since I didn't have any at his place. He figured that since he lived on park grounds, driving back to my hotel just to have me change clothes would be a little much. It was such a nice gesture, but a little odd.

"You bought me undergarments?" I laughed.

"Okay, I lied. I actually sent that girl Sophia I told you about, our medic and search and rescue specialist. She picked out the outfit and gave me an earful of teasing, so be prepared today."

I shook my head and headed back up to the bedroom to change, and I arrived just in time to catch my phone ringing. I checked it and saw that I didn't recognize the number, but I answered the call anyway.

"Hello?"

"How's the project going?"

Oh boy. This clown again.

"I'm going to the park today to meet the staff."

"Why didn't you go yesterday?"

"I got two flat tires on my way there. Someone stopped to help me, but I had to go to the mechanic to make sure the spares were on securely. Took all day."

"And the secretary of the hotel informed me that you did not sleep at the hotel last night. Where were you?"

What? You've got to be kidding me. Nancy was a snitch!

"That's none of your business, frankly. As long as I get the job done, you have no say in what else I do."

"We know where you are. You shouldn't get too close to those people."

"Why?"

"You'll learn..." And the line went dead. Could he be any more ominous? It wasn't like Acadia was going to blow up any time soon. And what the hell did he mean by 'those people'? What was wrong with people in Maine?

"Something wrong?" Drew arrived at the top of the stairs wearing only jeans. "I came up to get a shirt. Did you not like the clothes?"

"Oh, it's not that; I haven't even had the chance to look at them yet. I just got a phone call from Mrs. Q."

Did he hear me?

"Mrs. Q?" He looked confused but went over to his closet and pulled out a red tee shirt.

"Yeah, the old lady who let me take her vacation. She has a really weird name, so she lets me call her Mrs. Q."

Damn, is this lie getting elaborate.

"Oh, okay. Well, I'll be downstairs whenever you're ready to head out." He kissed my forehead and left the room, and I breathed a sigh of relief.

I hated lying to him. He seemed like such a nice guy and I just knew this was going to end up biting me in the ass; I just didn't know how else to go about the situation. It's not like I could tell him I was a hacker who got in trouble with the government and was now working for them as an informant. Lying to him was better than being killed in front of him, which, according to Hanson, would happen in a heartbeat if I decided to tell anyone anything.

I opened the bag Drew had given me. Sophia had picked out an orange tank top, a pair of jean shorts and a pair of combat boots—along with a lacey bralette and matching thong. I rolled my eyes at the undergarments; I could see what Drew meant about her being a jokester. Regardless, surely, he'd be enjoying the looks of them later.

I got dressed quickly and headed downstairs. We arrived at the park in minutes and a man waiting at the gate gave us a friendly wave, so we parked and walked over to meet him.

"Hey, Boss," Drew greeted the man. "This is Kathleen. I'm here to have her meet everyone and then I'm going to show her around."

"Nice to meet you, Kathleen. I'm Knox, the Head Ranger here at Acadia. Drew knows his way around, but if you have any questions he can't answer, feel free to ask." Knox was likeable and handsome, but not really my type. He had a military style cut, happy eyes, and a fit physique. He sounded genuine and I couldn't pick up on anything sketchy about him. I made a mental note to jot down everything I observed about each Ranger so I could report back to Hanson later.

There was nothing to report, though. When the day ended, I had met everyone, and I had nothing ill to say about a single one of them.

Drew had taken me to the holding lodge to meet Trent Bailey, the Law Enforcement Ranger of the park. He was kind of a hard ass, but still playful, and I could see why he and Drew got along so well. He had short hair and it seemed that all the men in Acadia were muscular. And then there was Ramon. Ramon had been a sweetheart and told me how beautiful I was when he knelt to kiss my hand. He had cropped black hair and was quite handsome; his Spanish accent was thick and I liked it. I felt like my Irish one had mostly disappeared, but at times—or if I'd been drinking—people said they could hear it in certain words.

I got to meet Sophia, who definitely was suggestive, to say the least. I remember her mentioning something about marriage and children, but I laughed off most of that conversation. She was gorgeous, though, with her flawless caramel skin, a long deep brown ponytail, and hazel eyes with a fit body. I guessed that all park Rangers had to stay in shape. Maybe it was part of the job description, or you just got fit from all the hiking.

I got to meet Hannah, Knox's fiancé; Blanca, Trent's fiancé; and Min, Ramon's fiancé, completely by chance. They were having a picnic by Eagle Lake when Drew was showing it to me, discussing their upcoming triple wedding. They were all gorgeous women and I felt a bit intimidated by meeting them all at the same time.

"Maybe you'll be one of us soon." Hannah had winked at me.

That was a nice thought. The park was lovely, and I enjoyed being shown around. I took lots of pictures to support my Mrs. Q lie, and next thing I knew, Drew was dropping me off at the inn.

"I hope you enjoyed our day at the park. I'll have to go back to work tomorrow along with everyone else, but maybe we can have dinner afterward?"

"I had a great time and I would love to." I gave him a soft kiss and smile.

"I'll see you tomorrow then. Oh, could I possibly get your number? I realized the other night that I didn't have it."

"Sure!" He handed me his phone and I added myself as a contact before I headed to my room.

I glared at Nancy as I walked past the reception desk and she seemed to cower slightly.

Yeah, bitch. You'd better be afraid. I don't need a fucking babysitter.

When I got to my room, I decided to call Hanson immediately to get the conversation over with. He had provided his number on the first page of the profiles he had sent me, and I punched it onto the screen.

"Hanson."

"It's Kathleen."

"Did you go to the park and meet everyone?"

"Yes."

"Anything out of the ordinary? Anyone seem suspicious? Like they were hiding something?"

"Honestly, I get more of that impression from *you*. I didn't notice anything at all that was off about them. They seem like genuinely nice people."

"Well, they're not."

"What do you mean?"

"On your laptop is two videos. I had my team download them and place them on an encrypted file on your desktop. The password is *b-e-a-r*, although I'm sure you could've figured it out eventually. Doesn't look like you've had much time to look at your computer, though. You'll wish you had seen them sooner."

Seriously? Nice secure password, douchebag. And only four letters? Pfft.

"What the hell are you talking about?" I was so confused by everything he was saying, and his tone was so hateful towards these people that were nothing but pleasant to me. I didn't like it one bit.

"Just watch the videos." And with that, he hung up.

I threw my phone down in frustration and grabbed my backpack, pulling out my laptop. My usually blue password screen came up, and when I got in, I scoured the desktop screen for the encrypted folder and found one titled 'Evidence' that hadn't been there before.

Evidence of what?

I opened the folder with the lame password Hanson had provided and noticed there were two videos in the folder. After a few minutes into the first one, I gasped in shock, covering my mouth in horror. There was a bear on the screen, slashing through a woman's body while she was fighting against it until her body went limp. The bear licked the woman once and I thought it was going to eat her, but it didn't. Instead, there was a sound in the distance. The bear growled and followed it. At the end, there was a note stating it was footage of Danielle Peterson's death, who was the host of *Danielle's Destinations*. I recognized the name from the Travel Channel which one of my hosts watched avidly. But I felt like I recalled them proclaiming it as a murder and that they found the guy who did it, but that he died somehow. I was very confused, and I didn't understand. I recognized the clearing from the rocky beach Drew had shown me that day.

So, what? There's bears in Acadia? I'm not surprised. It's not like the staff had anything to do with her death.

I clicked the second video hesitantly, hoping I wouldn't have to watch anyone else's brutal death. What I saw was a group of people standing around under the moonlight, staring up at the night sky. It had a really eerie feeling and I didn't really understand it. Then, the people started to change.

Into bears.

What?! How is this possible?

I played the video again from the beginning, but nothing was different. They were really shifting into bears.

Wait. That's it. Shifting. Shifters! That's what it meant on the profiles. Wait, so is Hanson saying that one of these people killed Danielle? Wait, so everyone in the profiles he sent are...shifters?

I got out my folder and looked through all the sheets and it was true. Knox, Ramon, Trent, and...

No.

There was no way it was possible. I replayed the video once again, zooming in closer to see their faces, and that's when I saw him.

I watched Drew turn into a bear.

5

DREW

I NEED EVERYONE TO REPORT TO THE GATE IMMEDIATELY. *S*TOP WHATEVER *you're doing and don't ask any questions. I expect everyone here in ten minutes.*

I heard Knox's voice echo in my head and I immediately pulled over. *What could possibly be happening?* He hardly ever called a surprise meeting for the clan, and based on the weak connection I was sensing, he was reaching out to all of us.

I sighed and made my way to the gate, wondering all the while what news waited there.

When I arrived, it seemed that most of the clan was already there. I had been on the opposite end of the park, so it took me a good ten minutes to get to our meeting spot. The clan had formed a semi-circle around the gate and I pushed my way through the crowd, trying to get to the front so I could see what was going on. I spotted Knox first and he was trying to quiet the chatter of the crowd; everyone was staring, and I finally saw why.

Kathleen was standing in the middle of the semi-circle, trembling. She was wearing the same outfit she wore on our first date and my eyes widened as I watched her scan the crowd. Her gaze met mine and she immediately looked away; all I could see in her eyes was fear. I could almost hear her heart beating from where I stood and I wanted to reach out to her, but that seemed like the last thing she wanted.

What is she doing here? Why does she look so scared? My eyes never left her, and Knox finally got everyone to be silent.

"This woman is here on behalf of a certain faction of the government and says she has an urgent message to deliver from them. I'd like you to listen carefully." Knox nodded toward the clan and then joined the semi-circle, turning his attention to Kathleen. It seemed even he didn't know what the message was yet.

I watched her eyes flit around the crowd in panic and my heart twinged. All I wanted to do was hold her.

"I was sent by the National Center for Preparedness, Detection and Control of Infectious Diseases. They are a sub department of the Centers for Disease Control and have asked me to deliver a message to you all." She seemed to gain her bearings the more she spoke. "The NCPD-CID knows your secret. They know about...bear shifters. They've been watching you all since the Danielle Peterson incident via satellite and they witnessed you all change during the full moon."

Gasps and whispers erupted in the crowd, and some of the men began to shout in anger.

Knox turned towards them to quiet them down. "Let her finish!" he yelled. Everyone quieted as his Alpha authority rang over us. I was in too much shock to say or do anything. I also wanted to hear what else Kathleen had to say.

"They have a proposition. They want you all to turn yourselves into the government where you will be housed in cells for testing and observation."

"What the fuck?" Trent shouted. "Hell no! We're not going to become anyone's lab rats!"

The clan murmured in agreement and Knox held up one hand in an attempt to silence everyone once again. I could tell he was irritated and angry, but he was trying extremely hard to contain it. His lips were tightly pressed together, and his muscles were tense.

"What is our other option?" was all he asked.

"They said if you do not turn yourselves in, in one week, they will set Acadia ablaze and destroy your home. And all of you along with it."

"WHAT?!" Trent exploded, heading toward a trembling Kathleen. Knox had to grab him, but I could see Knox's grip was shaky as well. They were fighting their anger to prevent provoking a shift.

Kathleen looked like she was ready to bolt in the opposite direction. The crowd now resembled an angry mob and I just stood there, stunned.

She lied to me...She said she was here as a tourist, and all along, she knew. She was scoping out the area. I can't believe this! Anger began to surge through my veins.

Knox raised his arm again to silence us, taking a few moments to formulate his thoughts.

"I speak on behalf of my entire clan and I am sure we are unanimous in this decision. We refuse to turn ourselves in for testing. If the government wishes to eradicate us, they will just have to try."

Shouts of approval resounded through the crowd and I just stared at Kathleen. I wanted her to look at me and see the betrayal, hurt and anger I was feeling. But she didn't; she seemed too preoccupied with the crowd of angry bear shifters glaring at her. I turned to Knox and caught him nodding to Trent, who started to head toward Kathleen. I instinctively moved to stop him, but Knox gave me a stern look. Kathleen's eyes widened, and she stumbled backwards, but Trent caught her, placing her hands behind her back.

"What are you doing? Let go of me!" Kathleen struggled against Trent and I could see the panic on her face.

Despite all the negative feelings I felt towards her in that moment, my body seemed to want to move on its own volition. My gaze shifted to Knox again, and his eyes had moved to me. He had noticed my slight advances towards her and was glaring me down. I sighed and held myself in position, looking on with a mix of feelings.

"Don't kill the messenger!" Kathleen yelled.

"On the contrary, we aren't going to kill you. But if you think we're just going to let you go back to them, you have it all wrong." Knox's tone was stern; he meant what he said. He would hold her hostage, but I didn't understand what good it would do. Was he hoping that holding her captive would stall the fire?

The crowd didn't seem to follow my mind's path. They erupted into cheers as Kathleen was carried away by Trent to what I imagined would be the holding lodge. Was he just doing this to appease the clan's bloodthirst? I'm sure if he had asked for her punishment, people would have wanted her killed, but Knox was a fair leader. All she had done was deliver a message from people who wanted to kill us. She had made no moves to harm us in any way and Knox wouldn't just take someone out for no good reason.

"She is a traitor. Whatever feelings you had for her, bury them. We trusted her in our park and among our staff, and she was an enemy all along." My eyes left Kathleen and Trent and turned to Knox, who was now standing before me.

"I'm not so sure she's the enemy—"

"She's working for a faction of the government that wants to kill us all. How does that *not* make her the enemy?"

"There could be more to the story. I just...I don't know..." I sighed. I wanted so badly for this to all be just a bad dream.

"I need you to pull it together. They're sending fire and I need you to set up the safety plan. I want Acadia fire proof by next Monday. You can have as many workers and other resources as you need, but you have to make it happen."

By next Monday? That was going to be a stretch, even if I had the entire clan working with me and all the money in the world, but I knew better than to say that to Knox. He was obviously counting on me and I wasn't about to let him down—I couldn't. The whole clan and the entire park were on the line. I had so many lives in my hands and I had to try my hardest to get the park secure.

"I can get it done," was all I said, and Knox nodded. His eyes lingered on me for a moment. "I'll be fine. Seriously."

"You don't have much of a choice." With that, Knox walked away. Most of the clan had already dispersed and Kathleen's shouts for freedom were long gone. I stood there, alone, forcing down the feelings for someone I felt that I no longer knew. Who was Kathleen, really? How much of what she told me was actually true?

I had no answers for those questions, but there were more pressing issues to contend with. I had to figure out how to get fifty thousand acres of land fire-safe in one week.

THE EXECUTION of my safety plan began immediately. I got all the financials approved for securing enough sand bags to cover the entire perimeter of the park and had planned on sectioning off each area. I was sure to get enough extras to disperse randomly as well. I also lined up extra digging supplies, since the park's tool shed only had enough for three workers. The last items on my list were water tanks. I was able to acquire enough two hundred seventy-five-gallon water tanks to disperse throughout the park, one for each area. I made sure each tank had three openings for hoses and obtained enough hoses to attach to them all.

The bill for this safety plan racked up quickly. In fact, I was sure the bill for everything totaled nearly two million dollars. I wasn't sure how the administrator found it in the park's budget, but the following day, the supplies were delivered. Ironic that the government was paying for our safety measures against its own plan for destruction.

As soon as all the supplies arrived on park grounds, I put everyone to work.

The plan was to set up the sand bags and station three people in each area on the day that the fire was supposed to break out. They would start their watches at 12:01am on Monday and remain on duty until the last of any fires had been completely put out.

Whoever caught sight of the fire first would send out a mass telepathic message to the clan as an alert, and everyone would move to act. Each area would have a water tank with three hoses and its perimeter outlined with sand bags. After the alert, each person would grab a hose, open the valve enough to wet the sand bags, then kill the water and wait. If fire broke into the area, he or she would use the hoses to fight it off with the remainder of the water in the tank. The sand bags, however, would prevent the fire from entering their domain. If it somehow encroached, the sand bags would prevent the fire from spreading further and any flames that escaped would be weaker with each wall of sand they hit. It would take two days to set up the sand bags alone and another two days to set up the water tanks and hoses.

As an added precaution, I planned to have trenches dug around the sand bags. It would take three days to do all that digging, but the trenches would significantly slow down the fire and buy more time for us to put it out.

I didn't know how the NCPD-CID was going to initiate the fire, but I had to be prepared for the worst. Forest fires have killed hundreds of people and eliminated millions of acres of land, but if I did my job correctly and everyone payed close attention to my directions, we would lose several trees, but nothing that couldn't be replanted and regrown in ten or so years. Depending on how quickly everyone responded, and if the fire could be contained to one area, we could probably save all but a few trees.

My crew and I got to work on the plan, starting with the sand bags. After a full day's work, I decided I would go visit Kathleen; it was hard to concentrate, and I needed to talk to her. I needed to know if there was any truth to everything she and I shared, and unfortunately, she was the only one who could tell me.

6

KATHLEEN

I WAS SITTING IN THE HOLDING CELL, CLUTCHING MY KNEES TO MY CHEST, while Trent sat at his desk, rifling through some papers.

I took this job to escape jail, yet here I am.

Life sure knew how to lay the irony on thick. I had hoped Drew would come see me and bail me out; the sting of his absence was something I couldn't ignore. Even though I knew bear shifters were killers based on the footage I saw, a little voice in my head kept telling me Drew was different. He couldn't be a killer. Maybe he was one of the nice ones. But still, it had been almost two days and he hadn't shown his face.

How could I blame him, though? The government had chosen to use fire to eliminate the bear shifters of Acadia National Park, and he was their lead firefighter. It was like fate had separated us.

However, there was something about the way the clan of bear shifters had banded together that resonated with me. I had never seen a group of people with such camaraderie, that they were willing to die to protect each other. It was a kind of bravery that was rare, and it touched me. When I first uttered the message I had been sent to deliver, I thought I would have been mauled and torn to shreds. They were indeed angry, but no one had physically attacked me whatsoever. Trent was a little rough while detaining me, but I would have probably reacted the same way. He wasn't growling or snarling at me like a wild animal. In fact, I had seen no shifting; not one person had turned into a bear.

I hadn't understood this at first. From the videos I'd been sent, it seemed like they were these ravenous monsters housed in human bodies. But, all the bear shifters I had encountered had been kind and welcoming, even though they knew I was a human. And even when I had told them their entire clan and home was in danger, they had behaved civilly; instead of killing me for working with the government, they had just locked me up.

Something didn't fit in this story. I wasn't sure what it was, but something was wrong. There was no way these people were the hideous beasts the government tried to make them out to be. I had been so terrified by the videos, I was ready to believe anything.

I needed Drew. I needed him to come and tell me the truth about the clan. Only he could tell me what was really going on.

But I couldn't blame him if he felt betrayed. I was sure he must have thought I was a pathological liar or a con artist. He was probably thinking nothing was real between us. But if that was what he thought, he was so wrong.

I wished he would visit me so I could let him know. I would tell him everything, anything he wanted to know. I closed my eyes as they pooled with tears, but I fought them back; I didn't want anyone to see me cry.

"I hope you're thinking about all the trouble you're causing us."

I knew that voice all too well. My eyes snapped open to see that Trent was gone; I had been so deep in thought, I hadn't heard him leave. To my surprise, Drew was sitting on the floor on the other side of the bars. My eyes widened at the sight of him and I scrambled on my knees toward the bars, holding onto them.

"You're here! You came!"

"You wanted me to?"

"Of course I did. I need to talk to you!" I pleaded. "No one will listen to me, but I know you will."

"Are you going to tell me how you got into this mess?" I nodded. "How do I know I can trust you? You've already lied so much."

"I know, but I had to! I was advised that if I told anyone about the reason I was sent here, I would be killed instantly. They have people watching me, but I don't think they have an insider in the park because they needed me to infiltrate."

"Well, I guess their work here wasn't finished after all."

I was completely caught off guard. "Wait, this isn't their first time attacking you guys?"

"A couple months ago, they sent my friend Ramon's girlfriend, Min, here to infect us with a mutated rabies virus hidden in genetically-engineered ticks. Ramon got infected by a stray one, but Min was able to spot it. They're both scientists, so they were able to work on a cure just in time to prevent Ramon from succumbing to the virus. The ticks were destroyed before they could infect anyone else and an antidote is still kept here, just in case someone else happens to go rabid. Two trials were run here prior to that incident, and that's when the virus first reared its ugly head around these parts to begin with. The first time, an alpha and his pack killed two of our staff members. Knox killed the alpha himself, but the others got away. We later found out that the government eradicated them and considered it a failed experiment. The second time resulted in the death of Danielle Peterson. The rogue bear who attacked her died in the holding cell to your right."

"Wait, so it was a rogue bear with rabies who killed Danielle Peterson? Not one of you guys?"

"Did you really think we did that?" Drew seemed a bit hurt.

"No, I mean, the government tried to make me believe that, and I was so afraid."

I sank onto my heels and sat back on the floor. I knew the government had played me. They had tried to convince me that these bear shifters were monsters, but they weren't.

I decided that I wanted to help the clan. But how?

I wasn't Drew. I couldn't put out fires and I didn't exactly know how to prevent them, either. I couldn't even give them a heads up about the NCPD-CID's plans, other than what they already told me.

But I could find out...

"Hey, do you have a laptop at home?"

"Yeah, I have one. What for?"

"I'm going to hack into the NCPD-CID's communication signal and listen for their plans."

"Wait, you're a *hacker*?"

"Oh yeah, we haven't gotten into that..."

"Yeah, so before I get anything, you're going to tell me exactly who you are and how you got involved in this." Drew did not move from his sitting position and had his eyes fixed on me.

I was feeling antsy; I wanted the computer as quickly as possible. The longer we weren't listening to their conversations, the less information we would have. But he was right. He had been honest with me, and to build back our trust, I had to come clean.

I sighed.

"Kathleen Boland is my real name—and I really do hate being called Kathy. I'm Irish, and the story I told you about my parents is true. I did move here when I was thirteen. I was in a foster home and it's true that I moved out when I turned eighteen. I really do couch surf every three days throughout West Virginia. While I was in foster care, I had parents who were hardly home, and the older kids looked after the younger ones. I found their computer one night and found my way into a hacker chatroom, where the members taught me everything I know. I learned enough to be able to complete jobs successfully without being caught. I started by doing good. The hacker chat room I was a member of dealt with taking down sex trafficking auction sites, and I had been happy to help with the cause. I wasn't paid for my work, but it was rewarding. The job never ended, though, because when one site went down, another five would pop up. I used that to gain experience, and when I turned eighteen, a fellow hacker referred me to a site where people would post jobs for individuals, organizations and websites they want hacked.

If you are caught, you don't get paid. If you don't complete the hack, you don't get paid. When I moved out, hacking was my only source of income and the money always got transferred to me through PayPal with made up names and emails. I wouldn't be surprised if even the accounts were made up or prepaid to avoid tracking." I snickered.

"As for how I got involved in this particular clusterfuck, one day, I noticed a posting for a government hacking of the NCPD-CID. The client was looking for a hacker to infiltrate their private encrypted files and look for anything strange. The person just wanted the findings reported back, and he or she was willing to pay a thousand dollars, which is pretty low for encrypted private government files. I really needed the money, though, so I decided to go for it.

I usually take extra precautions when hacking into government files, but for some reason, I was cocky that night—too cocky because I got caught and erased the info a couple of seconds too late. They were able to trace me and caught me. But instead of being brought to jail, I was brought to the NCPD-CID, where they gave me this job. I just had to infiltrate Acadia, scope you guys out, and report back to them. Then, they showed some surveillance videos of Danielle Peterson's death and your clan shifting under a full moon."

"They were trying to make you think we killed Danielle Peterson."

"Yeah, I realize that now. Then, they gave me the message to deliver to you. So, no, I am not here on vacation, and the name of the Couchsurfer host I gave you is actually the woman who's home I got arrested in." I laughed.

"Well, I bet you got a good review for that, huh?" Drew chuckled. "So, that's it? That's your story? The full truth?"

I nodded and gave him a half smile, hoping my honesty would help win back his respect for me. He paused for a moment, but then returned the gesture.

"You know, I was fully prepared for more lies. It would have made it so much easier to just let you rot in here." I winced at his harshness, but I understood where he was coming from. "Now, I just want to bust you out of here."

"And risk getting yourself in trouble? I've caused you enough headache." I shook my head.

"If only there was a way to get you in Knox and Trent's good graces..." Drew was thinking and so was I.

"Wait! The hacking; we can have them here when it happens! You would have to set it all up, but as long as your computer has speakers, they'll be able to hear the information, too, and verify that it's genuine." I immediately perked up. That was my way out.

"That won't be as easy as it sounds. Knox all but told me to just let you go. He really believes you betrayed us, and he is *not* one who forgives easily. It will take some convincing to get him and Trent here, but I'll do my best."

"I'm sorry I've caused you guys so much trouble. I was just doing as I was told; they threatened to kill me if I didn't cooperate."

"I know." Drew reached through bars and stroked the side of my face. I melted into his hand, rubbing my cheek against it.

"How are the fire preparations going?"

"They're coming along. All the supplies have been ordered and we are putting everything into place. But enough chit chat; I'm going to go grab my laptop and then I'm going to have Knox and Trent meet me just outside the holding lodge so I can talk them into coming."

I nodded again, and Drew finally rose from his sitting position. With one last look at me, he ran towards the door and disappeared.

7

DREW

I WAS AT MY HOUSE IN MINUTES AND I RACED UP THE STAIRS TO GRAB MY laptop, which I kept in my nightstand. I hardly ever used it, and because it was a newer model, I was hoping it could handle the hacking Kathleen was planning on.

I briefly wondered if the porn I had watched on it not too long ago was still up on it, but decided not to think too much about it. Besides, there was no time to go in and delete the evidence.

Whatever, everyone watches porn. I'm pretty sure if I looked through her internet history, it would show some freaky stuff, too. Unless she's worried like I am and deletes her history after every time. I chuckled to myself. It would be hilarious to see her reaction if I had forgotten to erase my history after the last time I used it. Sometimes I got lazy, but I would just have to hope that I remembered and could save myself from some serious embarrassment.

I rushed back to the car, and as I drove back to the holding lodge, I reached out to both Knox and Trent with my mind.

Guys. I need you both to meet me at the holding lodge.

What? You need supervision while you go visit your traitor girlfriend? I could hear the snark in Trent's tone when he answered.

She's not a traitor, man.

Did she spout off more lies to you? She already admitted she's working for the government. What more is there to it?

Easy, Trent. What is this all about, Drew? Knox's voice was calm.

I'll explain everything; just get here.

I had arrived at the holding lodge and raced inside. Kathleen had been looking down when I entered, but her head shot up when she heard me approaching the cell.

"Did you get it?"

I nodded and held up the thin, black laptop and then slipped it to her through the bars.

"Ooooh, a Lenovo. Not bad." She raised her eyebrows at me as she opened the laptop.

I shrugged. "The guys at Best Buy picked it out for me, so I can't really take any credit for picking it out."

"Where are Knox and Trent?" she asked, her eyes scanning the room.

"They're on their way." Or at least, I *hoped* they were.

"Good, I'll set everything up. I doubt you have any hacking software on your laptop, so I'll have to download a couple of things. But, first things first." She closed the laptop and seemed to give it a thorough look over. She checked all the ports and the keyboard when she opened it. "Does Trent have any tape over there?"

I walked over to Trent's desk and spotted some masking tape. I grabbed it and slid it through the bars of the cell to her, watching her rip off a few thin strips, which she used to cover the webcam.

"If I am intercepted, which I doubt I will be, they'll only be able to track me if I don't power down the laptop fast enough, just like before. It only takes a couple of seconds for them to locate the source of the hack, but even if I'm not that fast, you'll have nothing to worry about. What are they going to do to you? Take away your laptop?" Kathleen rolled her eyes and asked for the password to log in. "Let me guess, is it something to do with fire?"

"Yeah, it's *inferno.*" I rubbed the back of my head and looked away.

"You are so predictable; I could've hacked that in seconds." Kathleen chuckled and, moments later, asked for the password to Trent's office. "I bet it's something dumb like *trent69.*"

"That's exactly what it is," I winced.

"I bet a lot of people get free Wi-Fi around here," she joked.

Please no porn...please no porn...please no porn... I waited a couple of seconds, and if there had been porn on the screen when she loaded it, she hid it well. There was no reaction, so I breathed a sigh of relief.

While she downloaded the software she needed, I stood against the cell in silence, wondering what this meant. So what if she hacked into the NCPD-CID's communication line and got Trent and Knox to believe she was with us now. Would they let her go? Would the NCPD-CID try to get her out in time for the fire, or would they just leave her there? I wasn't sure of the answers to any of these questions, but I hoped she'd be off the hook after all this. If Kathleen was really on our side now, she didn't need to be locked up.

"Alright, I'm all set up, just waiting for—"

"You interrupted my meal, so this had better be good." Trent walked into the office, with Knox right after him. Neither looked pleased to be there.

"What's going on?" Knox's eyes were on the laptop in Kathleen's hands.

"Long story short, Kathleen's a hacker who tried breaking into the government's files, but they caught her and made her work for them; that's why she had to deliver that message. But now, she's going to work for *us* and is going to hack into the NCPD-CID's communication line to see if we can get any information on their plans against us."

"How do we know we can trust her? She could be contacting them right now to get them to bust her out of here or something!" Trent was immediately on the defense, but I was prepared.

"I trust her. And she already has the laptop, so you'll just have to deal with it." I looked to Knox to make sure I wasn't overstepping his authority. If he ordered me to take the laptop from her or anything like that, I would do it. But I would still try to convince him. He just nodded, though, and I felt relieved. Trent stood silently but was obviously pissed off. I could tell he wasn't ready to trust Kathleen, but I couldn't really blame him.

"So how exactly are you going to do this, Kathleen?" Knox addressed her directly.

"I'm going to hack their message board. Every organization has a secret message board where they discuss plans for the group that only a select few can sign into. It's usually just the higher-ups that have access, but I would bet the NCPD-CID's board is shared with every single person involved in this bear shifter execution plan. I don't see how else they would find time to discuss it during work hours. If we find nothing there, I can always hack their emails, but I feel like emails take too long for responses. This plan would need immediate contact at any moment and an instant message board would be the best line of communication."

"Can you do it?" Knox asked.

Kathleen nodded. "Getting in is going to be a piece of cake. Staying undetected is the issue. But I can do it and I'm about to. I'm going to place a reader on as well so that it will dictate their messages out loud, so we can all hear them."

Trent and Knox gathered around me against the cell bars as we waited to hear anything.

"What's taking so long?" Trent asked impatiently, but Kathleen answered before I could say something.

"They've beefed up security since my last hack, but I can still get in." Kathleen was typing away furiously, her eyes glued to the laptop screen. "Yes! Alright, I'm in."

Everyone stood in silence as we listened.

"**Is everything set for Monday?**" A robotic voice emitted from the speakers of the laptop.

"Is that the highest the volume can go?" I asked. It was a little hard to hear, but I could still make out the words.

"Yeah, sorry, the speakers aren't all that great." I laughed inwardly, *That's why I usually listen to porn with my headphones on.*

The computerized voice continued, "**Yes, everything is set. He will be paid once the job is completed.**"

"Who's *he*?" I asked.

Kathleen looked at the computer screen and shrugged. "No sign of a screen name. It's usually that way, though."

"**When can he have it completed by?**"

"**He said 5pm...**"

"That's it," Kathleen proclaimed. "That's the time the attack will happen—well, sometime a little before that."

She had been ready to shut down the laptop, but Knox held a hand up to her. "Let's wait to see if they reveal who is going to do it or how it will be done."

"The longer we stay logged in, the longer we are at risk of being discovered. You realize that, right? We already know the general timing of when they plan to initiate the fire, so we can be prepared." Kathleen was treading lightly; I could tell she was nervous about confronting Knox.

"Look, I'm very grateful that you're putting yourself at risk, Kathleen, but the timing isn't enough. We need more information, if we can get it," Knox responded.

Kathleen nodded; we silently waited for any further details to be shared over the next two minutes, but nothing came through.

"Okay, I'm closing the connection. Either something's wrong or they're busy, but we should be hearing correspondence if the communication lines are open." Kathleen scrambled with the laptop and then closed it quickly. "I shut down the hack and deleted everything related to it from your computer, Drew."

"So, we know they're planning on attacking us sometime before 5pm because they hope to have us eliminated by then." Knox seemed deep in thought.

"Well, at least that means we'll be done with work for the day at our normal time," Trent joked.

Just then, someone's phone began to ring. Trent and Knox checked their pockets, but the sound wasn't coming from either of their devices. I knew it wasn't mine just by the ringtone alone, but I checked anyway. It sounded like it was coming from Trent's desk, so he padded over to it and opened one of the drawers. The sound grew louder.

"It's hers. It's coming from the phone we took from her when we arrested her."

"What does the caller ID say?" Kathleen asked suspiciously.

"Unknown."

"It's Hanson. Eric Hanson. He's the head of the NCPD-CID and the one who forced me to do this job. He's probably calling to find out how you guys responded to the ultimatum."

"He probably already knows we're not standing down and that's why he's setting up the plan for the fire," I said, shaking my head.

Trent gave Kathleen the phone, which had started to ring a second time.

"Answer it," he said.

"I don't know, guys; this is weird. We just hacked them and now he's calling me?" Kathleen seemed very nervous.

"If you don't answer, who knows what they will think. They could come here searching for you tonight and set this place ablaze in the meantime," Trent argued.

Knox and I nodded; he was right. The best thing for her to do was answer the phone.

"Hello?" Kathleen spoke shakily. "Yes, I did...They have chosen to stay and fight, but I am trying to convince them...Understood..."

She gulped and pressed the screen to end the call.

"What happened?" I asked, rushing over to the bars. "What did he say?"

"He asked about your decision, and after I told him I was trying to convince you all otherwise, he said I had until Sunday morning to get you on board, or he will proceed with the plan."

"Whatever, it's not like we're changing our minds, anyway," Trent snickered.

"It's going to be okay, Kathleen; you did everything you could possibly do for us. My plan will work, and our clan and the park will be fine," I assured her, but it just didn't feel like enough. I turned to Trent. "Can we get her out of here now?"

Trent looked at Knox, who was silent for a moment, but finally nodded. When Trent unlocked the cell, I rushed in to hold Kathleen, who had started to cry, but she pushed me off.

"Listen, I want to help. Let me help you prepare the park for the fire; it's the least I can do." There was determination in her eyes, and if she hadn't been crying, I might have found myself turned on.

"Well, there is no time to lose. Everyone go home and get your rest," Knox advised. "Tomorrow, the execution of the plan resumes."

Everyone nodded, and Knox and Trent headed out of the office.

I turned to Kathleen, "Do you want me to take you to the hotel?"

"Can I stay with you?" Her eyes were pleading, but she looked away quickly. "You know, since I'm going to come help out tomorrow. You live right here, so it just makes sense..."

I gave her a quick squeeze and helped her to her feet. "Of course, you can stay with me."

THE NEXT FEW days were a blur.

The sand bags were set. The trenches had been dug. The water tanks and hoses were mounted and put into place. Everyone in the clan was aware of their assigned areas. One hundred people were needed to execute this plan, and it was a good thing that there were at least that many members in the clan.

It was Saturday night, and I was driving home after setting up the hoses. The following day would be the last day I had before everyone assumed their positions and the fire was supposed to strike. I had spent the entire day driving around Acadia, making sure everyone had completed their jobs and that each area was prepared. Thankfully, everyone had finished their tasks a day early, so I was able to double-check our work for good measure.

I felt confident and prepared. My plan was fool-proof; I couldn't foresee any possible failures. Kathleen was still worried, but I kept reassuring her.

"Everything will be fine. Maybe you just need something to take your mind off it, huh?" I snickered, pulling into my driveway. She had been staying at my cabin all week to help with the setup, but we hadn't really had much energy for sex. Lifting sand bags and digging trenches made for a hard day's work, and by the time we had gotten home each day, we had passed out almost immediately upon reaching the bedroom.

Well, I had different plans that night.

"What I need is a shower." Kathleen rolled her eyes at me, but I caught a playful smile spreading across her lips.

"What for? So I can get you all hot and sweaty again?" I asked, leaning toward the passenger seat, cupping her face. She parted her lips as I drew closer and I lightly kissed them, suckling her bottom lip. She kissed me back eagerly and, to my surprise, grabbed the firm bulge forming at the front of my pants.

"Race you to the door..." She whispered with a grin. Next thing I knew, we were both running full force toward the steps.

"That wasn't fair; you had a head start because you thought of it. And you were kissing me! I was still in kissing mode. I needed at least ten seconds to switch to running mode," I teased, catching my breath on the porch. She had beat me to the door, no surprise, but I had the key, so she had to wait for me to unlock the door. She just stood there grinning, hardly out of breath, bouncing up and down.

"Come on, slowpoke! Open the door!" she implored, and I chuckled. She seemed awfully excited and I wondered why. As I opened the door, she rushed inside, running up the stairs. I heard the shower start and laughed to myself.

"Beat you!" she yelled down to me and I heard the bathroom door close.

"I thought the race was only to the door!"

Cheater.

I thought about going in to join her, but I decided that I'd rather have a moment to relax and gather the strength I'd be needing in a few minutes; my body was exhausted. I walked over to the living room and plopped down on the couch, sinking into its softness—which was more than welcomed after the labor-intensive week I'd had.

I closed my eyes and let my thoughts drift. I was so happy that everything had fallen into place the way I had hoped. I only wished we had more of an idea about how the fire would start so I could better plan for it, but no matter what, I was certain my strategy would work, and Acadia would be saved. I was sure of it.

I felt delicate hands glide over my shoulders, massaging me as I slumped in gratification.

"Mmmm...That was a quick shower," I murmured through my daze. Her hands were deliberate in their motions as they worked through my muscles, kneading out my tension. I sighed and fought to keep my eyes open. Her heavenly hands left my shoulders and I groaned.

I opened one eye to see her walking around the couch and she straddled me, completely naked.

"Well, what do we have here? What did I do to deserve this treat?" My eyes widened as I drank in her gorgeous curves. Her hourglass figure was perfect to me and her ginger hair was slightly damp, cascading down her chest and back, hiding her nipples from my view.

"You lost, which means I *won*. Which also means I get whatever I want for winning." Kathleen smirked and ran her hands up and down the tired muscles of my arms.

"I don't remember agreeing to that," I teased with my eyebrow raised.

It was a little hard to concentrate with her light touches brushing my skin and her naked warm body on my lap.

"Losers don't have a choice," she said, leaning in to kiss me. Her lips were soft and wet, just like the rest of her body, which I wrapped my arms around. Her bottom was slightly lifted, and I took advantage by cupping her cheeks and squeezing, making her moan against my lips. I pulled away slightly, just enough for our lips to separate, and we were both panting.

"Let me go shower first. I've been sweating all day and I probably smell terrible."

"And you're covered in dirt," she giggled.

"Exactly. You got a chance to get cleaned up, so let me do the same. I'll only be a couple of minutes," I assured her.

"Nope. I'm not going to let you."

"Why not?"

"Because I think it's...kind of hot. I've been watching you all week. Your muscles rippling every time you picked up the shovel or a sand bag, you wiping the sweat from your forehead with that rag...I watched it all, and it got me so wet...I'm getting turned on just thinking about it."

And I could tell. One sniff of the air and my bear was ravenous. He could smell her arousal, and I could read her face. She wanted me, badly.

"Maybe you should feel for yourself." She took one of my hands and brought it to her folds, and that was all it took for my rod to fully engorge. It strained against my jeans once again as my fingers explored her dripping cave. She was most definitely ready, a moaning mess in my arms.

My two thick fingers slipped inside her easily, and I growled as her walls tightened around them. Throwing her head back, she began to grind against my hand, and I wrapped my free arm around her waist and pushed against her, ramming my fingers into her. I enjoyed how she held onto me, digging her nails into my shoulders as we found a steady, hard rhythm.

My cock was becoming increasing uncomfortable as it tried to force its way out of my jeans, and I couldn't hold out any longer, releasing it from its prison, allowing it to bounce out at full attention. In one fell swoop, I slipped my fingers out and slid my length inside Kathleen, plunging straight in. She gripped me tightly and moaned with her lips right against my ear, the sound rippling through me, making my hair stand on end. She had the sexiest moans I had ever heard in my life.

I grabbed her hips and started slamming her down onto my throbbing shaft. She gripped the couch behind me as the sound of our bodies colliding together and the screams of my length reaching deep inside her echoed throughout the room. I could feel her moving with me, even though I controlled her hips. Her moans were getting louder, and a tingling sensation rose from deep within my core, reaching my head, my fingertips and my toes. It shot straight to my body, searching for release.

"Oh god, Drew!" Kathleen screamed my name in the sexiest way possible, her legs trembling on my lap, and I lost it. My seed erupted into her as her velvety walls tightened around me, milking my seed and stretching my orgasm until she finally slumped against me, her slight shivers still vibrating through her. My head fell back against the couch and hers nestled into my neck as we both tried to calm our heavy breathing. When I had finally caught my breath, Kathleen's had become even and steady.

"Kathleen?"

She didn't reply, and her breathing stayed the same.

She fell asleep, I chuckled to myself and tried my best to slide out of her without waking her. She groaned and whimpered as I pulled myself from her body, quickly placing my member back in my jeans and then wrapping her arms around my neck; I decided to bring her upstairs and place her in my bed while I went to shower.

When I started carrying her up the stairs, I heard her whisper something.

"Do you think...I'll ever get to meet...your bear?"

"Only when you're ready." I smiled.

Once I had set her down to sleep and felt the water running down my skin, serious thoughts about Kathleen flooded my head.

If we survive these next two days, I need to convince her to stay with me a while longer...

8

KATHLEEN

I CAN'T BELIEVE I FELL ASLEEP ON HIM! LEAVE IT TO ME... AT LEAST DREW had been nice about it.

Drew was driving Knox's Jeep around the park, checking to make sure that everything was set for everyone to take action the following day. His crew was stationed at their positions because Knox wanted to initiate a drill once Drew had finished checking on all the areas. I had told Drew that I would walk around, following the sand bags, making sure I was within safe parameters. He had tried to get someone to come along with me, but I assured him I would be fine.

Besides, the attack is tomorrow, not today. I followed the sand bags through the trees, checking to make sure that there were no breaks in the wall. I passed many members of the clan stationed at their areas who waved to greet me, and I smiled in return.

The NCPD-CID had been utterly wrong about these people. They were by no means monsters; in fact, they were friendlier than most of the people I had ever met. They welcomed me with open arms, even after I betrayed their trust. Knox had spread the news I had gathered and mentioned how I'd decided to help them fight against the government. I wasn't sure if it was the Alpha authority or the majority effect, but everyone had gone back to being pleasant with me, as if nothing happened.

I mean, I wasn't complaining; it just seemed weird. Kind of cultish, but I didn't want my impression to warp my idea of bear shifters, especially after it was so warped to begin with. I hadn't seen a single bear since I'd set foot in Acadia, and other than the initial anger of the clan when I'd delivered the government's message, everyone had been so amicable.

And Acadia was beautiful. I had never seen such gorgeous scenery. Before I visited, I had assumed Acadia was mostly made up of woodlands, but I had been pleasantly surprised by its varied landscape. The more I thought about Acadia, the more I realized there was so much more I wanted to experience. I wanted to climb all of its mountains; to lay on the rocky shore, breathing in the crisp, salty air. If trees were damaged during this operation, I wanted to help plant new ones. But more importantly, I wanted to watch them grow.

I wanted to stay.

And, if everything worked out between Drew and I, I'd love to ask to stay with *him*, at least long enough for me to rack up enough hacking income so I could lock down my own place, anyway.

I haven't even talked with Drew about how he feels about my hacking. Of course, he didn't say anything about it when I was doing it to help him and his clan, but what if he has an issue with it because it's illegal? I mean, I'm not even sure if I still want to do that anyway; it's not like I'm looking forward to dodging the law for the foreseeable future or getting arrested again.

But hacking was all I knew. What else could I do?

I had wandered off without taking in my surroundings, so I'd lost track of my whereabouts. I was on a gravel trail and I could see a granite bridge in the distance; there were lots of birds around the area, and they all looked the same: a mix of ducks, hawks and falcons.

Wait, are these peregrine falcons? I wasn't sure how I knew, but they just seemed so familiar. I decided I must have come across a picture of them sometime. *What are so many of them doing in Acadia?*

I thought about calling Drew to ask him, but I figured I should save the worry for something a little more serious than a bunch of birds. As I walked down the narrow gravel path, I could see little indentations.

Are these their nests? I looked around in shock; most parks would close off the areas where birds were nesting. I wasn't sure if peregrine falcons were something the world was in short supply of, but I surmised as much.

Suddenly, I heard movement among the trees. At first, I was fully ready to pass it off as one of the birds, and then a man stepped out from behind the brush. I gasped, covered my mouth, and ran behind the nearest tree.

Just then, my phone decided it would be a great time to ring. I grabbed it quickly, hoping I could get to the call before the man noticed me hiding. The caller ID read 'Unknown.'

Oh god, it's Hanson again. Probably calling to get the final answer before he decides to attack...

I thought about ignoring the call, but I figured that if I didn't answer then, Hanson would keep calling to try and get ahold of me.

"Hello?" I whispered, hoping I didn't need to be louder.

"I see you've met my friend."

My eyes widened and I looked around; I noticed the guy was lugging around a jug of some sort. "What are you talking about?"

"You're looking at him right now. It looks like your little boyfriend forgot to set up his supplies around the peregrine falcon nesting area." Hanson's voice was menacing, and made my skin crawl. But he was right: while there were sand bags, no water tanks or hoses were nearby. "Did you forget that we were already watching them via satellite surveillance? We saw all the preparations being done and it was easy to pinpoint the flaw in their plan."

Oh no, I have to call Drew right now! But if I hang up on Hanson, he'll probably initiate the attack! What do I do? I was inwardly freaking out.

"To be honest, it is you who will be Acadia's downfall today. You can blame yourself for their eradication now."

"What? How? All I've done is help them!"

"And that's how you will cause its demise. We know about the hack. Ever since your previous stunt, I hired a computer technician to monitor the security systems around the clock. We ensured that if someone were to try and hack us again, an alarm would go off, prompting the technician to alert us and figure out how to best take action on the matter. It took merely seconds for him to find out it was coming from Acadia, so I immediately knew it was you. We pretended to stick to the old plan and feed you false information. We had already pinpointed this spot to start the fire, and you just happened to waltz right into it." Hanson laughed and my hair stood on end, making me shiver in a terrifying way.

False information? I looked up at the man I had spotted, who had a clean-shaven face and square glasses with a lean build. He was smoking a cigarette and pouring some liquid onto the sand bags in the perimeter. *What the hell is he doing?*

"We're not attacking Acadia tomorrow, Kathleen. Acadia will go down in flames *today*. Right now, in fact."

My eyes flit up to the man again in panic, my heart racing.

Right now? How? The man was looking directly at me, his cigarette dangling from his lips as he gave me a wry smile. I was in complete shock; all I could do was stand there, trembling.

"Goodbye, Kathleen." With that, Hanson ended the call and I brought the phone down from my ear. The man took one last pull from his cigarette and dropped it onto the sand bags that had become saturated with a chartreuse-colored liquid.

Flames erupted immediately in front of me and I watched the arsonist bolt in the opposite direction. The flames spread quickly, igniting all of the sand bags from the surrounding areas. I thought about chasing the burning trail, but it was too fast.

Before I knew it, I was trapped in a ring of fire.

I looked in every direction, searching for a way out. The flames were too high to jump over and there were no trenches to slow it down. The flames had spread so quickly, there were no gaps in the fire between the sand bags.

And the flames were closing in. Trees were catching fire and the peregrine falcons were screeching as they flew into the air and fled the fiery scene.

Call Drew! What are you waiting for?

In my panic, I had forgotten to contact the one person who could help me. I was hyperventilating and tried to calm my breathing, but it was useless.

"Hello?"

"Drew? There's fire! I'm trapped!"

"What? What are you talking about? Where?"

"The nesting area for the peregrine falcons. I'm the only one here and there's no water tanks or hoses and the flames are closing in fast!"

The smoke was already so thick that I was coughing. I tried to move to the center of the area to be the furthest away from the flames as possible.

"Fuck! A tank couldn't fit there without disturbing the nesting area, so we didn't set one up. I never thought they would stoop so low as to start the fire there! Shit!" I released another round of coughs. "I've already sent out a message for everyone in the surrounding area to pull all of their hoses in that direction. Everyone else is heading nearby to help. I'm on my way, but I need you to stay on the phone with me. Take off your shirt and use it as an air filter over your mouth."

"Okay, hold on." I put my phone in my pocket for a moment and removed my tank top. When I tied it over my face, I found that I could breathe easier. "Okay, it's on."

"Alright, your voice is muffled, but I can hear you and that's all that matters. Now, I need you to tell me what happened."

"It was Hanson; he called me. He said that he knew about the hack and fed us false information. Because of the hack, they changed the plan to attack a day early. He knew about our efforts, though; he was still watching Acadia through satellite surveillance."

And with that, the tears began to fall. Hanson was right. It had been all my fault. Maybe if I hadn't hacked them, Acadia would have been more prepared. Maybe they would have stuck to the original plan of attack. Maybe Drew's plan would have still worked.

"Listen to me, Kathleen. That man is evil. Anyone who would try to eradicate an entire population is completely sick. He probably would have attacked a day early even if you hadn't hacked him. It was never in their plan to give us a chance. They just wanted us to think that we had one."

He was right, but I couldn't shake the guilt. And now I was being punished. I was going to die first.

"Kathleen? I need information, so I can know how to put out the fire effectively. How did it start?"

"There was a man who poured a greenish-yellow liquid on the sand bags and lit the fire with a cigarette."

"Oh, shit..." Dread filled Drew's voice and it began to flood into me. If Drew was worried, that wasn't a good sign.

"What? What's wrong?"

"How fast is the fire spreading?"

"Fast; too fast for me to chase it, and it's too high for me to jump over."

"Sounds like they must have combined the gasoline with an additive. They really weren't trying to give us a chance..." Drew's voice sounded defeated and it did nothing for my nerves.

"What? How can you tell there's an additive?"

"Certain additives can cause gasoline to burn through the sand bags, to a degree, and can make fire spread much more quickly."

I could hear the engine revving through the phone; he was speeding to get to me.

"Drew, am I going to die?" The tears were back. Even Drew said it was bad and he couldn't even see it yet—or maybe he could have, and that's why he was racing there. Flames engulfed at least a third of the trees in the area, and they continued to close in at rapid speed.

My whole world was on fire, and there was no way out.

"No, Kathleen, I'm coming for you; you're not going to die! Don't give up on me now. I need you to stay on the phone and keep talking unless it hurts. If it starts to hurt to talk, put the phone by your mouth so I can hear you breathe and know you're okay."

"Please hurry..." I was sobbing by that point. I knew he was going to try, but I couldn't think of any way he'd be able to put that fire out. The hoses could only reach one hundred feet and that was only thirty yards in each direction. They would have to be at the edge of the fire, and even then, I was sure the fire had travelled further than that.

"I'm at the closest site to you and everyone is ready with their hoses. If anything happens on your end, tell me. Okay, everyone, go!" Drew initiated the order and then I heard screams. "Fuck!"

"What's going on? What happened? Drew?!" My heart was beating what felt like a million times per second and it was making it increasingly difficult to breathe.

"Kathleen, I'm going to need you do your best not to panic. But I can't put out the fire with the hoses we have, or at such a close distance."

"What?!"

"Water just made the flames erupt in this direction and, because of the additive, some kind of gas was released that just...melted someone's eyes...We all had to run away from the area."

Oh my god...oh my god...oh my god...I really am going to die... The hyperventilating started again and I was wheezing.

"Kathleen, I need you to slow your breathing. I don't know if it was only the water that formed this gas, and I want to minimize how much of it gets in your lungs, okay? I need you to calm down. How far are the flames from you?"

"Maybe two hundred yards? I don't know. The flames have covered half the area already." I sobbed. That much ground had been covered in a mere ten minutes.

"So, we have about—"

"Ten minutes. Yeah, I know..." I stifled my sobs and tried to calm myself. If those were going to be the last ten minutes I had, I didn't want to spend it crying on the phone with Drew. "Drew, I need to tell you something."

"No, Kathleen. Whatever it is, you can tell me when I get you out. I know what you're trying to do; you're not going to die. Knox is sending a helicopter to you. It *will* make it." His voice was shaky, and I knew that he was only trying to comfort me. But I couldn't blame him for lying.

"I love you, Drew. I've felt strongly for you since our first date and this week has made that feeling grow even stronger. I've never loved someone other than my parents before they died, but I know that I love you. I just need you to know that, okay?" My voice choked on the last part, but I fought it; I was not going to die crying. I was going to die strong, standing my ground until the last moment. "Drew?"

Then, the phone line went dead. I slowly looked at the phone and my assumption wasn't wrong.

He had hung up.

I don't understand...Why would he hang up? Does he not love me back? If not, it's okay, but I needed him! He said he would be here for me! And I couldn't fight the tears any longer. My sobs rocked through me until I was shaking all over, tears streaming down my face and soaking the tank top that covered my mouth. *I'm going to die alone...*

"Kathleen! Kathleen!"

Just then, I heard someone calling my name. I opened my eyes, but all I could see were the colors of the fire blurring through my tears.

"Kathleen! Look up! Grab my hand! Hurry!" I tilted my head up and saw Drew, dangling from a ladder. I somehow hadn't heard the sound of the helicopter in the sky above me, but it suddenly filled my ears. He was holding his hand out. "Come on, grab me! We have to get out of here before the ladder burns!"

I wasted no time and jumped to reach for his hand. We were immediately lifted out of the flames, high into the sky and carried beyond the fire. Drew had pulled me up to hold me and I buried my face in his neck, crying again.

"You came for me," I sobbed.

"Right after your little confession, Knox arrived with the helicopter and I immediately got on. I closed my phone without thinking about it, but I knew I would be with you in an instant so I could tell you face to face. I love you, too, Kathleen." His lips were right by my ear, so there was no mistaking it. Another round of tears erupted from me and I coughed for a long, nasty minute. "You must have gotten a lot of smoke in your lungs. Don't worry, we're almost there."

"Where are we going?" I asked as he squeezed me tightly against his chest.

"Everyone had to evacuate the park. All we can do now is douse it with water from the sky, since attacking it from the ground produced those toxic fumes, and we can do it with a 747 Supertanker. A massive amount of water can be held in its pressurized tanks, which will atomize it and allow it to extinguish the forest fire more effectively. I'll just have to call the base and have one deployed as quickly as possible." His words comforted me. At first, I thought Acadia would be doomed, but knowing that there was a way to put out the fire made me relax a bit. I hoped everything worked according to plan.

When we were completely clear from the fire, someone started to pull the ladder up into the helicopter. Drew hoisted me up onto the ladder when we were close to the entry point so I would be let in first, and then climbed in after me. It was Knox who had pulled us up.

"I thought you were flying it for some reason!" I shouted, taking the tank top from my mouth.

"Thankfully not. We have a pilot for that." He said nodding to the man operating the aircraft; I couldn't see him, but I made a mental note to thank him when we touched down. I had been too scared to look around when Drew was carrying me on the ladder, but at that point, I decided to peer out the window. My heart sank as I watched the fiery destruction of Acadia fade into the distance as we headed toward Bar Harbor. I didn't know exactly how, but I vowed to help the clan rebuild its home, no matter how long it took.

9

DREW

On the ride over to Bar Harbor, I radioed the fire department base to explain the situation we were up against, and they immediately approved the use of the 747 Supertanker. They issued an order for it to be filled up and they'd send it over as soon as it was ready.

"So, what makes this 747 Supertanker equipped for the job of taking out a 3-mile-wide fire?" Knox asked when I ended the call.

"The 747 Supertanker can carry up to twenty thousand gallons of water. It's probably the only aircraft in the world that could hold enough water to put out a blaze like that."

"Wow. That's impressive," Kathleen said, taking a swig from her water. We were waiting in the airport, along with most of the other members of the clan. Those who had been exposed to the fire or smoke had been examined by Sophia, the park medic, and everyone had been fine—except for the one casualty we had suffered.

Knox had cleared all park employees to have the week off. He had told the clan we'd begin our restoration efforts the following Monday, thinking a week would be long enough for the fumes to clear and for everyone to be able to be safe in the area again. The park was closed until further notice, and a clip from the helicopter camera was sent to news stations around the world. However, it was being broadcasted as a random forest fire, of course; not one deliberately set by an arsonist taking orders from the government, which pissed off a lot of us.

The hotel by the airport was very gracious in housing everyone who had been evacuated, and JetBlue had offered flights to all of those involved, as long as they could prove they had family living where they wanted to go. If someone did not have proof or they wished to stay in Bar Harbor, the park had emergency housing vouchers for everyone to stay in the hotels. They would have to stay two to four in a room, and couples would get to request to stay together.

"Do you want to go back to your hotel room?" I asked Kathleen.

"I doubt I still have one," she snuffed.

"Well, what I meant is that I could use the housing voucher on your room, so you could keep it and we could stay there for the week. It's a single, right?"

"Yeah, it's a single." Kathleen smiled up at me. "Good idea."

I called the hotel and arranged everything, but when I got off the phone, Kathleen's eyes were glued to something. She looked as if she had just seen a ghost.

"Kathleen? What's wrong?" I squatted in front of her, but her eyes never drifted from where she was looking. I followed her gaze to a thin man sitting across the airport wearing square-framed glasses, packing a box of Marlboro Reds. "Do you know him?"

"That's him, Drew! That's the guy who started the fire!" she whispered.

I was immediately filled with rage. That was the piece of shit who almost killed the woman I loved. He agreed to start a forest fire in an attempt to wipe out my entire clan and had destroyed our home. And I was going to kill him.

"Please, Drew! Don't rush at him! He'll see you coming!" Kathleen pleaded.

"Oh, don't you worry. I've got this."

I walked over to Knox and Trent, who had been talking about where they were going to stay for the next week, and told them I had the arsonist in sight. They both nodded and we casually walked in his direction, talking idly as to not startle him.

When we were only a couple of feet from him, he laughed as he continued to pack his cigarettes. "What took you pussies so long to get here? Run into a little traffic along the way?"

We pounced, all grabbing him at once. Even though Trent had gotten the asshole's hands clasped behind him, I could not hold back my rage. I wailed on him, punch after punch, hearing bones crack with every contact of my fist.

Knox placed a hand on my shoulder and I stopped my fist in midair. "Hey, hey...that's enough, Drew. I think he got the message."

When I looked at the bastard's face, I realized Knox was right. I had broken his nose for sure, and the skin around his left eye socket had split, gushing blood everywhere. My breathing was ragged as I stepped back and allowed Trent to haul him away.

"Don't worry, Trent will take care of it. I already sent a mental note to everyone, telling them he was the arsonist who started the fire, so everyone watching is with you."

I finally took notice of the crowd that had formed around me and realized they were my fellow bears, who had blocked the fight from everyone else's view. People were nodding in approval and clapping as I caught my breath. My knuckles were bloodied, and my hands were tired, but I was filled with elation.

"I would have done it myself it you hadn't, big guy," Knox chuckled, patting my back. The crowd slowly dispersed, and I could see one person still standing with her eyes fixated on me. It was Kathleen, and she was smiling, a tear gliding down her cheek.

I walked over to her and held her, doing my best to avoid getting any of the prick's blood on her.

"Thank you, Drew. For saving me; for everything."

And in that moment, I knew she was the one. I would kill anyone who tried to lay a finger on her. She was mine.

"I love you, Kathleen. I'll never let someone get that close to hurting you again."

"I love you too, Drew."

Just then, Kathleen's phone rang. She looked at it and she seemed afraid to answer the call.

"It's Hanson..."

"My promise includes *him*, too. You don't have to feel intimidated by him any longer," I assured her.

And I meant it. I would do everything in my power to make sure she wasn't hurt again. I dared him to try.

"Wait, when I hacked into the NCPD-CID's systems to get the intel for you guys, I also hacked their security camera backup files and made a copy of the footage from when I was captured and threatened. I wanted proof in case you guys didn't believe me. His technician was probably so busy addressing the message board hack that he didn't realize I was hacking their video backups, too. The message board hack would have been the event that would set off the alarm. And if Hanson knew about it, he would have told me over the phone when he thought I was going to die. He gloated about everything except that, so he probably doesn't know about it! I emailed it to myself, so I know I have it, and my email has some serious encryption, so I doubt he would be able to hack me." Kathleen's lips spread into a smile.

"Use it against him! Threaten to expose him!" Her phone was ringing again, but this time, she answered it with confidence and put him on speaker.

Hanson was fuming. "You little bitch. I will end you! No one will even know you ever existed. You can't cheat death twice."

"You must have seen the news, then? Your *awesome* plan didn't work. Acadia will be fine; a plane is on its way to put out the fire, and there's nothing you can do about it."

She smirked and I beamed with pride as I watched her stand her ground.

"Oh, killing you will make up for that, so don't get too comfortable with your boyfriend over there because I'm sending someone for you. Right now."

Hanson's tone was menacing and it infuriated me. I wanted so badly to speak up, but I knew Kathleen could handle it.

"Oh, please do. Because I have all the surveillance footage and audio recordings from our friendly little meeting in your office. Tell your rookie technician he should have been on his guard. While he was busy trying to handle my message board hack, I deleted every pixel of satellite footage that would expose these shifters and waltzed my way into your office camera's backup files. Send someone to kill me, and I send that footage of you to every news network in the world. In fact, maybe I'll send it right now for good measure. What do you think? That way, if I *do* die in the process, it won't be in vain. Oh, I can just see the headlines now...'Government Official Eric Hanson Charged With Kidnapping, Blackmail, Misappropriating Federal Funds And The Destruction Of Acadia National Park'...That would give your career a nice boost, wouldn't it?"

"Wait, wait! Don't do that! We can work something out. Come on, Kathy; let's not do anything rash!" Hanson had gone from angry and devious to a spineless piece of shit in less than a minute.

Kathleen paused, her eyes narrowing.

"I told you not to call me Kathy."

"Wait, please don't! I won't send anyone; I was just kidding—"

And with that, she ended the call. As soon as she hung up, I grabbed her and kissed her passionately. This woman was amazing, and she was all mine.

"Does getting payback turn you on?" she teased when we pulled apart.

"Just a little."

"Well, then let's go to the hotel room and do something about it." She winked and ran to the exit of the airport and I chased after her, the happiest I had been in a long time.

10

KATHLEEN

EPILOGUE

"Come on, Kathleen! We're going to be late!" I heard Drew's voice call up to me, but I was already headed down the stairs. When he saw me, wide grin spread across his lips. "You look gorgeous. You'll have an easy time upstaging the brides in my eyes."

I giggled a little and grabbed his hand.

"You don't look so bad yourself, handsome."

Drew was wearing a black and white tuxedo with a pocket square. We were on our way to Ramon, Trent and Knox's triple wedding, and as Drew's girlfriend, I had been invited. I was flattered and tried to get a dress that coordinated with all their colors. Hannah, Knox's fiancé, stayed with a traditional black and white theme. Blanca, Trent's fiancé, decided to go with fuchsia accents, while Min, Ramon's fiancé, chose robin's egg blue.

To encompass all their wedding colors, I went with a flowy, knee-length floral print dress. It was a lightweight wrap style that I paired with gladiator sandals, which I thought would be perfect for their wedding at Sand Beach in Acadia, a small beach nestled between two mountains. I had been helping the brides prepare for days and was there only hours ago, helping Sophia set up the chairs and decorations for the three o'clock wedding. We raced there in Drew's car and ended up arriving just in time to see the brides walking down the aisle.

All of the men were standing up front, wearing traditional black and white suits with pocket squares and vests in their designated colors. I'd heard it had been a nightmare to find a fuchsia vest for Trent—and to get him to actually wear it—but he ended up pulling off the color well.

Min came down the aisle first from the left, wearing a white sheath dress with a robin's egg blue lace overlay, which plunged low down her back. I had learned that Min was a simple girl, but she was beautiful, and her dress reflected that in every way. Her bob had been pulled behind her ear on one side with a jeweled hairclip. She was carrying a bouquet of forget me nots and Ramon was beaming as she approached him. They were one of the most fun filled couples I had ever been around, and I knew that would help them have an amazing marriage for years to come.

Blanca was next, coming from the right, wearing a white chiffon V-neck dress with a full, ruffled skirt. The waist of the dress featured a fuchsia satin belt and a long, sheer train trailed behind her. She carried a plump, white hydrangea bouquet with fuchsia ribbon wrapped around the stems and her hair was styled in beach waves. Trent grinned widely when she walked up to him and he looked like he could jump for joy at any moment. Their happiness filled me with warmth.

Hannah was the last to walk down the aisle, straight down the middle, and wore a white dress with a low back and a tulle skirt with at least one black layer peeking out from underneath. Her bouquet consisted of stephanotis blossoms with tiny pearl-headed pins peeking out from the center of each, and her hair fell in large waves that cascaded down her back. At the bachelorette party, she had boasted that the dress had cost her twelve hundred dollars, and it looked like it was worth every penny. She wore a beautiful pearl-studded hairband and all the brides had decided to walk barefoot in the sand to meet their husbands.

Knox was serious, but proud when Hannah joined him at the altar. I felt like Hannah brought out the best in Knox, and I knew I was right because as soon as Knox caught sight of Hannah's bright smile, he couldn't help but return the gesture.

Everyone was so in love and I was so happy to be a part of such a special day. One justice of the peace wed them all; he had a microphone and stood a few feet behind Knox and Hannah.

When the vows were exchanged, the couples went in the order of the brides' processions. Min and Ramon's vows were playful. Trent's vows were filled with jokes while Blanca's were sweet and sincere. When it came time for Hannah and Knox, they shared some of the most serious and heartfelt vows I had ever heard in my life. Granted, I only had heard vows in the movies, since I had never been to a wedding before, but by the end of their exchanges, I was crying my eyes out and Drew rubbed my back in soft circles.

"By the power vested in me, I now pronounce each of these three couples husband and wife. Men, you may kiss your brides!"

I stood and clapped with everyone else, dotting my eyes in between as the couples kissed. A moment later, the recessional music sounded, cueing the newlyweds to march down the center aisle.

Min and Ramon even skipped.

The reception was hosted by Fox Fields Farm in Bar Harbor, which was held outdoors underneath several large white tents. It was such an amazing time; we all had a blast dancing all night, drinking champagne and dining on the most fabulous surf and turf I ever ate. When it came time for the couples to be on their ways, the brides asked all of the unmarried women to gather around so they could throw their bouquets. Turning their backs to the crowd, at the count of three, they tossed their nosegays over their heads in unison. Blanca's bouquet was caught by Sophia, another she-bear caught Min's, and to my surprise, I caught Hannah's. I gasped, and Hannah turned and winked at me. I looked up at Drew and he just smiled back.

"I want our own wedding, though!" I warned. "I don't want to share our spotlight with anyone."

Drew laughed because he knew I was half teasing, but half serious. We lined up along the cars as they pulled up one by one, whisking the couples away while everyone threw rice at them.

As Drew and I made our way home, I realized it had been a month since I forwarded every shred of damning evidence against Hanson to all of the media outlets in the country. He was quickly detained, rotting away behind bars as he awaited his trial. We'd never hear from the bastard again. And as it turned out, the client who'd hired me to hack into the NCPD-CID's files in the first place was one of their own: an anonymous whistleblower, looking to put an end to Hanson's mad plans once and for all. After the fact, I wondered if he was a shifter himself, but of course, I'd never know for certain. Because of this loophole, there's no way I'd ever be faced with charges for any of the hacking I did for him.

As for the fire, the 747 Supertanker had made quick work of it, and after a week, the park had the air quality tested and found the levels had returned to a safe range once again.

Everyone chipped in and helped patrol the area, cleaning up anything they could. Trees that had been scorched by the fire had to be taken down and their roots were dug up. Acadia decided to cancel their peregrine falcon nesting program due to the extensive damage to their nesting area, so when the falcons returned, they were caught and brought to the White Mountain National Forest in Lincoln, New Hampshire.

When the trees had been completely cleared, enough fresh topsoil had to be mixed with the old to make the areas fertile again. I helped with that aspect, planting new trees in the former nesting area so the park could eventually rebuild the program. Unfortunately, even with great care, the trees wouldn't be fully grown for another ten years, so the program would be delayed for a long time. Once we finished planting the new saplings and had closed off the nesting area from the general public, the park reopened, allowing the public to revel in its magnificence once again.

And for the first time since I was a child back in Ireland, I felt like I finally had a place I could call home.

Living with Drew had been so incredible. On his days off, we took long hikes, hung out at the beach and picnicked by Acadia's many lakes. We had already eaten at virtually every restaurant in Bar Harbor and had chosen a few favorite date spots. Usually, though, we just cuddled at home and talked. And had sex. There was definitely a lot of sex.

Life was good for us. I couldn't imagine living without him; it was as if the difficulties of my life before him had been erased and I was born anew, ready to start my new life, with him.

"Do you think I could meet your bear?" I turned to Drew who had just pulled into the driveway of our home.

"Today?"

"Yeah, why not?"

"Here? Right now?"

"It doesn't have to be right now, but if you're up for it, I am. I love you.

And if I'm going to be with you and your clan for the long haul, the full moon is coming up, and I feel like I should see—"

"You won't be there for our full moon get-togethers. We only allow shifters to participate, so you don't have to worry too much about it. Hannah, Min and Blanca usually have sleep overs during it, and they already invited you."

"Still. I want to see..." He stared at me with unsure eyes, but I was confident.

"Okay, let's go." He smiled and grabbed my hand, leading me through the back of the house to the forest. When we were out of sight, he sat me on a log and stepped back.

I watched his limbs elongate, fur erupting all over his body as he grew taller and wider, and before I knew it, a majestic black bear was standing where his human form once stood. The bear was on his back legs, but came crashing down to the ground on all fours, causing my eyes to widen and my jaw to drop.

His bear approached me slowly with worried eyes. I reached my hand out tentatively and he paused, waiting for me to be comfortable enough to reach out to him on my own. As I made my way toward him, my hands felt his shiny fur; it was the softest coat I had ever felt in my entire life. Overwhelmed by the magic of it all, I nestled my face against his fuzzy neck and smiled.

"You're beautiful, Drew. I love you." And in that moment, I knew I was fully ready to start a new life with Drew, one filled with magic and love that transcends all.

ALPHA'S SECOND CHANCE

SHIFTER NATION: WEREBEARS OF THE EVERGLADES

1

OWEN

I STEPPED OUT INTO THE BRISK MORNING AIR WITH MY BARE FEET, stretching tall as I filled my lungs. The sun peeked over the tree tops, lighting the morning fog in oranges and pinks. From where I stood on my cabin's porch, I could just make out the glint of Shark River off in the distance. *Perfect morning for a run.*

That time of year—the wet season in Everglades National Park—the air was full of bugs in the heat of the day, but before the sun came up, the swarms were fewer and the air tasted cleaner. The temperature was just below 70, but in a matter of hours, the hot sun would raise it closer to 90. With the bugs, running would be unbearable, so I chose early mornings or late nights to tear through the forests.

I pushed down my shorts and boxers, stepping out of them both in one swift move. My feet touched dew-ridden grass for only a moment. Seconds later, my thick, hairy paws were trampling the wet blades in their place. I shook out my black fur and stood tall, roaring louder than any natural bear would dare.

Owen! Ezra signaled to me through our shared mind link, *Up already, chief?*

Surprised to hear you rumbling around, Ezra. I didn't think you got up this early unless there was tail to chase.

There's always tail to chase, man.

I could almost hear the wink in his words. *Who else is around?*

We both paused, waiting for another voice or two to chime into our mental conversation. All was quiet in the clan.

Just you and me, Ezra said. *Though, I should clarify. I'm not up early.*

I laughed. *If you stay up all night until the sunrise, I think that crosses the line from up late to up early.*

Whatever makes me look better. Where are you at, anyway?

I crossed the edge of my property into the boundary of the park. No one was technically allowed to live on park grounds, so my hand-built cabin sat just over the line. It felt like park living, but without the legal hassle.

Touring the park before heading toward the office. You?

Umm, you think you'll need me today?

I rolled my eyes. *You are the most unreliable ranger I've ever met.*

Hey! he said back, *I didn't earn my place as your second in command by slacking off. Maybe you should ask me why I haven't slept.*

Okay. Humor me.

The cool air rustled through my fur and my nose filled with the scents of various animals. The small family of key deer who lived nearby were out foraging, it seemed. I sent a scattering of herons into the sky as I ran too close to their nesting place. Their wings stretched out far, letting the large birds glide peacefully. Smaller game bolted when they heard or smelled me, and I wished I could've assured them all, "It's okay, it's just me. I'm actually a really nice guy and I won't hurt you." Well, unless the full moon was out. Though I tried to not hunt in bear form too often, it was sometimes necessary.

Ezra took a mental breath and began his tale. *Okay. So, it started out innocently enough. I was out with some of the clan last night, Mason and Conner, and we were minding our own business, having some beers. Then this asshole croc came up to us and started some shit—*

Wait, wait, I interrupted. *Which croc?*

Dunno. I've seen him before, though. He's local. Anyway, he was all like, "Pfft. Looks like you bear boys could use some company." While he had, like, a chick on each arm. Whatever. We weren't trying to pick up any ladies. So, we were all just kind of like, "Whatever, prick," and rolled our eyes. The place was crowded, you know? And he was just calling us bears in the middle of the joint.

grass in many places, but water hid beneath. If you didn't know and walked too far, it was nothing but mud and muck. And this kid had walked too far.

His hiking boots were barely visible in the mud. He looked terrified and could only be about eight or so. I walked as close as I could to him without getting stuck myself.

"What's your name?" I asked.

"Robbie."

"Okay, Robbie. The first thing I want you to do is stay calm, okay? Worst case scenario, we just untie your boots and your mom and dad get mad at me for losing them in the mud."

He nodded and kept his eyes on me.

"Now. Take this rope and wrap it around your waist."

I held the end of the rope out to him and he did as he was told.

"Now, I'm going to get in my UV there and press the gas real slow, but it will give you enough of a lift that you'll start to feel yourself being pulled up and out. When you feel that, don't panic and don't fight it. Just hold on tight and let the rope do its thing, okay?"

Robbie nodded again and held the rope tightly enough to make his knuckles white. I walked back to the big bear, where the other end of the rope was attached to the back roll bar.

I watched in the rearview mirror as I slowly pressed on the gas; soon, I saw Robbie pop free and splash into the wet, swampy grass. When I got out to check, he was still mostly upright from hanging onto the rope, and he still had both shoes. I stepped into the water and scooped him up, then handed him to his grateful mother.

"Oh, thank you, thank you!"

The boy vanished from sight in a flurry of hands and arms making sure he was okay.

"Thanks," Pete said, still looking flustered.

"I want a full report by noon," I said and drove off, heading back to the station. I'd need a few more cups of coffee if the day was going to start like this.

2

ADDIE

I STRETCHED MY ARM OUT THE WINDOW, LETTING THE WIND BLOW OVER MY skin and weave through my fingers. I looked at Emma behind the wheel and smiled. “This is going to be an amazing vacation!”

“Yay-ya!” Emma shouted.

Julie chimed in from the backseat. “Whooo!”

“I’m just glad to be done with finals,” Emma breathed. “All those hours of studying were starting to make my brain turn to mush.”

“Actually,” Julie countered, “You were building stronger neuropathways that increase brain matter, not decrease it.”

Emma rolled her eyes.

“Come on, now,” I said. “If it weren’t for the medical geek’s wisdom, you wouldn’t have made it through finals in the first place.”

“True.” Emma looked in the rearview mirror and stuck her tongue out at Julie. “It’s still annoying though.”

“Say whatever you want,” Julie snickered. “Just remember that when you get struck by lightning, I’ll be the one fixing you up.”

I laughed. “I don’t think she’ll have to worry much about that being a weather girl.”

“Hey.” Emma gave me a mock glare. “A degree in meteorology, *Adeline*, gives me a lot more opportunity than just being in front of a camera.”

I was in trouble if she was using my full name. "You'd make a perfect weather girl or anything else your heart desires. I'm just looking forward to getting out in nature and using my degree to explore," I said. "And you can let us know if the weather is going to be bad."

"Maybe you'll actually figure out what you want to do this week?" Julie asked me.

I sighed. I had known my whole life that I would study animals and the environment. The only problem was, now that I had, I couldn't decide what I wanted to do with my brand-new bachelor's degree in ecology. The options seemed endless—zoologist, field biologist, ranger. They all sounded amazing, too. I hoped this vacation to Everglades National Park would help me get into nature and figure out a direction to move in.

"I can always work in a pet store," I said.

Emma dropped her head to one side. "I did not just spend the last four years studying with you and correcting your papers so you can go sell cuddly kittens to little girls all day."

"I know," I said. "I'll figure it out. We just graduated. I have time."

"Should have gone into the medical field," Julie said. "I'd give you one of my *three* job offers, but, you know, ecology doesn't really work in a hospital."

"Unless it's an animal hospital," Emma said. "Maybe you should be a vet!"

"That's an entirely different field of study from ecology," I said.

"It's still animals," Emma replied.

I laughed. "Right."

"Hey," Julie said. "We just spent four years studying and focusing on school, as Emma pointed out. Can we, like, not talk about that stuff for just this week, please? I want to enjoy this time before I have to join the real world."

"I agree," I said. I didn't need the stress of trying to figure out the rest of my life when it was only just beginning.

"Yes, yes," Emma said. "It would be a lot easier if we'd gone to the beach with the rest of our classmates. Just saying."

"Who needs all that sun?" Julie said. "The rates of skin cancer have been increasing exponentially over the years. You do know that, right?"

"And the sand gets everywhere." I wrinkled my nose.

"Worth it," Emma said. "On both counts."

"Next time," I said. "That was the deal."

Emma sighed. "Just promise me that at least one night we'll go out and get trashed."

"Umm, yes," Julie said.

"Of course," I said.

The drive only took about an hour, but when we got closer to the Everglades, it felt like entering a different world. Miami was so built up with businesses and houses and people. The Everglades was the opposite. Few buildings and they were all part of the park. No homes or tall structures to break up the skyline. Trees and clouds and chirping birds. The air smelled cleaner and fresher. The greens were brighter, the sky bluer.

This was why I'd chosen a degree in ecology. I couldn't get enough of the outdoors. I loved to be in nature, letting my inner animal run wild, experiencing all that the natural world had to offer. It refreshed and invigorated me. I'd been in desperate need of some nature after years of college, and this was why I'd chosen the Everglades as our vacation destination. Emma and Julie had bargained for other locations when *my* vacation became *our* vacation, but I'd stuck to it. The beach was nice, but there were way too many people and not enough trees. In the end, they'd agreed, but only under the agreement that our next getaway would happen at the beach.

When Emma stopped at the check-in station, I hopped out and went inside. "Reservation under Pearson." I bounced on my toes, the excitement filling me, as the woman searched for our reservation.

The woman handed me a tag for the car. "Site 382." She pointed to a spot on a map and circled it. "Right here."

"Thank you!" I dashed out to the car with the tag and map. "Okay," I said as I buckled my seatbelt again. "Turn left up here."

I navigated to our spot. When we found site 382 and parked, I got out and stretched tall, taking in a nice long breath of Everglades air.

Julie and Emma joined me. We stood together, looking out at the trees and greenery.

"This was a good choice," Emma said.

"My hiking boots are calling my name," Julie said.

"Oh!" I ran back to the car and got the map. "There are lots of trails. Look!"

We checked over the map, noting the hiking trails and other sites to see.

"Let's try this one first," Emma said, pointing to a colored line on the map.

"We better set up the tent first," I said. I'd set up tents in the dark or near dark before and it was always so much easier with full daylight.

We pulled our bags out of the car and I heaved the tent into the middle of the site. I opened the bag and started pulling out stakes and poles and other pieces of tent, and Emma and Julie grabbed pieces and helped me. I'd set up this tent enough times to have each piece's location memorized. I directed and they followed, and within minutes, the tent was standing tall and proud in the middle of our site.

We spread out our mats and sleeping bags inside, chose a spot to set our bags, then changed into our hiking gear. I packed my small backpack full of essentials; my pocket knife, flashlight, map and compass were all tucked in their spot in my bag. I added a bottle of water and was set.

When my friends were ready, we set out toward the path. There weren't a lot of other tents set up. Being May, maybe it was still early in the season for camping. It was plenty warm and the perfect weather for camping, I thought. Later in the year, it would be unbearably hot, muggy, and buggy. July and August were difficult months for me. I wanted to be outside all the time, but I could only stand it for so long before my hair was wet with sweat and sticking to me annoyingly. Thank god my apartment complex had a pool.

"Already a half mile," Emma announced.

She was watching her fitness app and anytime we walked anywhere, she would give updates on how far we'd gone, how fast we'd walked, and how many calories we'd burned. She might claim she wasn't interested in being a TV weather woman, but she sure cared about her physical appearance as if that were her goal.

Emma was concerned about the exercise aspect and Julie was, too, of course. It wasn't that I didn't care as much about that part of it, but I got plenty of exercise. I was more interested in studying the plants and animals, seeing what sort of things lived here and what their environment was like.

I watched two squirrels tangle through tree branches, feeling complete delight at seeing them in their natural habitat. Several times, Julie or Emma called out to me to catch up. They wanted to keep a good pace so their heart rates stayed elevated, but I just wanted to appreciate everything my gaze fell across.

As we walked, our footsteps were quiet on the well-worn dirt path. We didn't make much sound, so when I heard a strange noise, I stopped immediately. It was a sort of whining chirping sound. A bird, maybe? Whatever it was, it sounded distressed.

"Guys," I whispered to my friends.

They walked a few steps back to where I'd stopped.

"Do you hear that?" I asked. "I think there's a hurt animal."

Emma took a step away. "Don't animals attack when they're hurt?"

"Only if they think you're going to harm them further," I said, trying to locate the sound.

"Here," Julie said.

I walked to where she was holding back a patch of tall grass. There, sitting hidden in the brush, was a white ibis. As it made the distressed sound again, I became more concerned; this was bizarre behavior for a bird like that.

I crouched down and got on my knees, making soft cooing sounds in attempt to let the bird know it was okay. I slowly moved closer, not wanting to scare it. Emma was right about one thing: if this bird were afraid of me, it would at least peck my hand if I tried to touch it.

I watched it for several minutes. Its wings were tucked around it as I would have expected, so perhaps it hadn't hurt its wing. Could it be sick? I moved my hand closer until I gently touched the bird's head, and to my surprise, it didn't attack me or flinch.

"Addie! What are you doing?" Emma hissed. "That thing is going to eat you."

"Shh," I said. "Ibises don't eat people. It's fine."

The bird let me run my fingers over both wings; those couldn't be the source of the problem, then. It then made a sound and fluffed its wings, and I noticed that it tried to stand, but couldn't. I carefully lifted one wing, and when I lifted the other, the bird pulled back.

Then I saw the problem: one of its legs was twisted in an unnatural way. It must've landed badly or something had hit it and broken its leg.

Even if it could fly, the bird needed help. It might sit there for too long and end up starving or being attacked by something else in its vulnerable state.

I stood up and took out my phone.

"What are you going to do?" Julie asked.

"The same thing you would do if this was an injured person." I dialed the number for the ranger station located closest to our location. Good thing I'd thought to bring the map. Not only did it have trails and other places of interest marked, it had a list of numbers to call if there was a problem.

When someone answered, I explained the situation.

"I'll send someone out to you right away," the man on the other end said. "Will you stay in the area to guide our ranger to the injured animal?"

"Of course," I said. "I couldn't possibly leave this bird alone to be attacked."

I gave as much detail as I could about our location, then hung up and waited. I tried to find bugs and berries to feed the bird, but it wouldn't take anything. We heard an ATV in the distance and watched for the ranger.

When the vehicle came into view, we waved to get the ranger's attention. Two rangers rode in the ATV, wearing their khaki uniforms.

"Hi there," one of the men said. "Were you the ones who called about an injured bird?"

I opened my mouth to answer yes, but nothing came out. I stared at the other ranger, and he returned the gesture, both of us standing there in complete shock.

"Owen?" I nearly choked on his name.

"Addie."

I looked into the eyes of my high school boyfriend. It'd been four years since I'd seen him. He looked the same, but somehow, even better. He'd always been gorgeous with his black hair and blue eyes, but he'd gained some muscle over the years and the stubble across his chin was not something he'd had during our high school years. He looked much more mature. And, if I were being honest, he was downright hot.

"Good to see you," I said. What else could I say? It wasn't entirely a lie, but he'd broken my heart. If I'd had to choose any person in the world to run into, he would have made the list, but wouldn't have been high on it.

"You, too." He nodded slowly. He seemed to be thinking hard, but didn't say anything.

Finally, I broke the silence. "So, the ibis is right over here."

I pointed to where the patch of grass hid the bird, and the other ranger went to it immediately. Owen hesitated, then followed him over.

I stood back to let them do their jobs. After a few minutes, Owen picked up the bird, and I was impressed. He must be very good with animals if he'd gained that much trust in such a short time—and from an injured bird, at that. He tucked the ibis under his arm and carefully got back into the ATV.

"Thank you for calling us," the other ranger said.

"You think it'll be okay?" I asked Owen.

He nodded. "We'll have our vet take a look. I think it's just a broken leg." He stroked the bird's head. "She'll be up and flying in no time, thanks to you. If you hadn't called, she would probably have been attacked."

"That's what I was worried about."

He pressed his lips together and nodded again. "Good to see you, Addie."

"You, too."

I watched them drive off, feeling a bit saddened by the exchange. Emma and Julie turned to me with wide eyes.

"Let's hear it," Emma said.

I let out a slow sigh, then resigned myself to reliving this painful story one more time.

3

ADDIE

"From the first day we met, it was like magic," I said. We started walking again, more slowly this time so they could listen to my tale. "I was lost in my giant, new high school and dropped my books while I was trying to find my class. There were so many people that I kind of freaked out a little. I was picking up my books and he stopped to help me, and he ended up walking me to my class, even though it made him late for his."

Owen had shrugged when the bell rang. "It's the first day. They won't care."

"Thank you again." I held up my schedule. "And for pointing out my next class." I smiled and dashed into the classroom. I'd sat quickly and glanced back to the door, surprised to see him still standing there.

He smiled at me and my face grew hot. He held up a hand to wave, his smile spreading even wider, before he finally walked away. When class ended, I'd looked up and down the hall for him, but didn't see him.

I knew where to go next, thanks to him, and when I got to my next class, he slid into the seat next to me. My heart jumped.

"Glad you didn't get lost on your way here," he said. "I'd hate to think I'd miss out on one minute of being this close to you."

"He did not say that!" Julie said and they both giggled.

"We were only fourteen," I reminded them. "And his brother used to teach him to say all these cheesy lines. It didn't matter, though; I fell for all of them. And he meant them, too. Those things only come off as cheesy when the person saying them isn't sincere."

"Okay, okay," Emma said. "So, it was love at first book drop. What happened next?"

"We would talk before and after class. Usually, he would walk me to my next one. Then, one Friday, he handed me a note with his phone number and he asked me to call him over the weekend. I called that day after school, and he asked me to go to the mall with him that night."

"The mall?" Emma asked, flabbergasted.

"Yeah, the mall. Hello? Fourteen," I said.

"That's where we spent, like, all of our Friday nights, Em, and you know it," Julie said. They'd gone to a nearby high school and had been friends before college, where they met me.

"Ignore her," Julie said. "Did he hold your hand as you walked around?"

"Of course," I said. "He bought me an Orange Julius and everything."

"This story could only be cuter if you'd shared a container of fries from the food court," Julie said.

I pressed my lips together and stifled a laugh.

"You did, didn't you!" Julie said.

"I feel like I'm stuck in a teen drama," Emma said.

Julie shoved her lightly.

"We shared fries and a slice of pizza," I said. "And that was it. From that moment on, we were inseparable. We talked on the phone all night, went to the mall and roller skating and all those things we used to do when we were young teens."

"So cute," Julie said.

"Yeah, cute," Emma said. "So where did it all go wrong?"

"Well..." I blew out a hard sigh. "We dated for years. All through high school. We went to proms together, homecomings, all of that."

"Wait a minute!" Emma grabbed my arm and turned to face me. "Was he your first?"

"Yes," I admitted. "And I was his."

"This is the cutest story ever," Julie said. "I'm quite jealous."

"And then he broke my heart," I said.

"I knew it," Emma grumbled.

"No!" Julie said in a whiney tone. "He's so cute! How could he?"

"He got into a college out of state and wanted to get away from everything. So, that summer, when he told me his plans, he said he wanted to end things. He thought a long-distance relationship would be too difficult to maintain, and that it would hinder our studies."

"Boo," Julie said.

"I know," I said. "It was horrible. I cried for weeks. Then I swore off men."

"Until Sam," Emma said.

"Yeah well," I said. "I should have sworn him off, too. Jerk."

"Let's not have a Sam moment, please," Julie said. "You're done with him, and let's stay done."

"Yes, please," Emma said.

"I think part of the reason I ended up staying with him for so long was because of Owen," I said. "I just wanted to be dating, you know? After four straight years of being with the same person, it was weird to not have a boyfriend. But, I have no desire to talk about or think about Sam."

Except that now that he'd been brought up, my mind drifted toward Sam. It had been a complete disaster of a relationship. I'd expected something like what Owen and I had. A relationship that was fun and easy with someone enjoyable to be around. Owen made me laugh. Sam made me worry. He was so intense, I had never been sure where I stood with him or what was going on in his mind. The year we dated was fraught with frustration and confusion.

If being in a relationship was going to be like how things had been with Sam, I never needed to be married. I didn't want that kind of drama surrounding me all the time. In a relationship that was meant to last a lifetime, I would need someone more like Owen. Well, like Owen but with enough dedication to want to attempt something as common as a long-distance relationship.

Maybe Owen had set the bar too high. After Sam, I started to wonder which one was a more accurate representation of what marriage would be like. The best I could hope for was something in the middle.

"Maybe this will be good," Emma said. "Maybe you can remember a relationship other than Sam and can actually have someone who's good for you."

"I think the bigger problem is, I never really got over Owen."

They stopped and looked at me.

"After he broke your heart, you still have feelings for him?" Julie asked.

I shrugged. "That's the only thing he ever did to hurt me, though."

"Well, it was a pretty big thing, don't you think?" Emma said.

"It was," I admitted. "It's just hard to hate him when all my memories are good ones."

"And when he's that hot," Emma added.

"Not helping," Julie said, nudging her.

I scrunched up my face as if I were in pain. "The worst part is, he looks even better now."

Emma sucked in a breath. "Oh. Sorry."

"You should date him," I said to Emma.

"Are you crazy?" Emma said. "First of all, no. Second of all, he's your ex. Third of all, you just said you still have feelings for him! I may not be the best friend in the world, but I'm not that evil. Or stupid."

"No one's dating Owen," Julie said.

My face fell into a frown. No one was dating Owen, and none of us ever would be. He probably had a girlfriend anyhow. Maybe even a fiancé. I didn't want to be hung up on anyone, especially not my ex from high school who I hadn't seen in over four years. It was about three and a half years longer than it should have taken me to get over him. Yet, here I was, my heart still racing from our brief encounter, my mind still full of his face and voice.

I shook my head. No. "Okay, stop." I held up my hands and we all stopped walking. "I can't do this. If I'm going to get over him, I can't think about him. Or Sam. Or any other disaster in my life. I want to enjoy the fact that I just earned a degree after four years of very hard work, and so did the both of you. We made it through college, and we're ready to start our new lives. I'm not going to do that being stuck in the past. From this point forward, I am in love with no one!"

Julie pumped her fist in the air. "Down with love!"

Emma raised her eyebrow at us. "Um, how about not 'down with love' so much as, yay for strong women who don't need a relationship or a man to feel whole!"

"And that!" I said, raising my fist high to match Julie's. "Here's to focusing on our careers!"

4

OWEN

THE IBIS TUCKED UNDER MY ARM NUZZLED ITS BEAK INTO THE CREASE OF MY elbow. It was warm at my side.

I should be thinking about what needed to happen for the bird now. How I should have already radioed the vet to be ready. How I would help him set the leg and hold the bird while he worked. But my mind wouldn't stay on the white-feathered creature for long; it was stuck in the place I'd found the bird.

The place where I'd seen *her*.

I don't know if I'd ever had more of a shock in my life. She had gone to college an hour away, in Miami. I didn't want to attend the same school and risk running into her or having a class with her. It couldn't be like high school. I'd never survive if there was a possibility of seeing her anytime I walked around campus.

I thought I'd chosen well with the Everglades. I could have moved to another state. Chosen another park. Joined another clan. But this had been home, and my clan was my family. I didn't want to leave the land or the shifters I'd come to rely on. Before we broke up, she'd been dreaming of mountains and snow. I expected her to go up north, fall in love with the cold, and never return.

And then, there she was.

I often thought I saw her places. I'd see a woman with the same long hair, those medium-brown locks that glinted gold in the sunlight, the way it swept over her neck. Of course, I had no idea if her hair would still be the same after so many years, but after today, I knew it was. When we first pulled up to the group of ladies, I thought it was her. But in the same way I always thought I saw her, I blew it off and refocused. Except, this time, it really was her.

When I saw her face and her shocked eyes met mine, it was as if the world had vanished. Suddenly, we were back in high school and I'd just seen the most beautiful girl in the world drop her books all over the floor. Back then, I'd been able to step in and rescue her. Saving the day made me her hero and it was easy to win her over. I wanted to save her again, but she didn't need me now.

She was her with her friends and had found an injured bird. She was not the one in need, but I still wanted to impress her. But Addie hadn't seemed to notice.

It was all I could do to walk away from her. From the moment I saw her and got a whiff of her scent, I wanted to run to her, scoop her into my arms, and never let go again. I'd let go of her once and it had been the most difficult and stupid thing I'd ever done. If I had the chance, I'd keep hold of her so tight, there'd be no danger of us ever being apart again. My blood boiled with wanting her, with missing her, with loving her.

"Whoa, man, you look worse than me." Ezra strolled out of the ranger station as we pulled up.

"I've never seen him so quiet," Zack said. "He must be *very* worried about this bird."

Zack smirked at me and disappeared inside the station.

Ezra gave me a questioning look. "Did you see a ghost out there or what?"

"Something like that," I said, walking past him into the building.

Luckily, Zack had been in his right mind as we headed back, and he'd called the vet to meet us. I carried the bird into the exam room and held it while the vet did his thing. I sensed the animal's distress and did my best to calm it, but I was more than distracted.

Our four years together played through my mind, followed by the four years without her. Hardly a comparison. After the vet got the bird's leg fixed up, I sat in my office, trying to work, but the words on the reports didn't make any sense. I read the same page over and over, but finally stopped, setting the papers down and heading to the window, looking out over my view of the park.

Ezra came in and perched on the edge of my desk, as he often did. This was why he was my second: he knew me too well. Any time I acted out of character, he was immediately on alert.

"So, it's quiet right now," Ezra said. "I think everyone is out doing the day job thing. How about a short run?"

He knew he'd be able to read me more easily when we were in bear form. Our thoughts would be linked, but it was more than that. Just like I could sense other animals, even while in my human state, I could sense my clan even better when we were all in bear form. I wouldn't have to tell Ezra how I was feeling, he would feel it.

But I could have used a run; I thought it might help distract me. "Yeah," I said. "Get in the small cat."

I let Rachel know we were heading out on patrol, then slid into the seat beside Ezra. We drove to a spot out of the way where we could leave the UV, parked and stripped down on either side of the vehicle, roaring loudly as we changed. I stood tall on my furry legs and stretched, then bounded through the woods, the wind rustling through my coat.

I don't usually have to drag things out of you, Alpha, Ezra signaled to me. *What's going on?*

There was little point in trying to change the subject or deny it. When my mind was so full of her, it'd slip even if I tried not to think about her. Better to just get it out.

I saw an ex-girlfriend today.

Ouch. Bummer. Did she break your heart?

I almost laughed. How I wished that were true. *'Fraid not. I broke hers.*

Oooh, even worse. She just won't stay gone, eh?

Nothing like that. I never wanted to end things with her. I was crazy about that girl.

Ezra didn't respond right away. He jumped through the trees, bouncing with too much energy. He was worse than a cub with his exuberance. But when he spoke again through our mind link, his words were full of maturity.

You're still crazy about her. What happened? Why'd you break up?

I didn't have a choice. Thinking back to that time still made me ache. I had no idea how hard it had been for Addie; I hadn't talked to her after I ended things. But I had been a wreck for weeks. So much, that my mother pleaded with my father, but he wouldn't relent. And he couldn't. I knew that, and it made everything worse.

When I came of age, my parents stepped in, I replied. *They didn't mind who I dated in high school. They always liked Addie. But she's not a shifter.*

Ohhhh. Sadness colored Ezra's thoughts. He got it.

Yeah. So, I hit eighteen and was about to graduate high school. They sat me down to have the talk. Shifter responsibilities. What we have to do for our clan, all of that. And, Addie. They told me it was better to end things. They said I could go to school further away and frame that as the reason. It was normal, they said. High school couples often broke up when they went to college. They thought that if we had no future together, there was no reason to keep dating. And they were right. I wanted to marry her. I would have. But that's not how shifter life works. At least, in our clan.

I know this too well, my friend.

You're not bound in the same way I am.

If I want to remain your second, I am.

The rule about marrying a shifter only actually applied to the Alpha of our clan. When my dad stepped down and I took over, that meant taking on everything that came with the duties of an Alpha, including the marriage rule. No one else technically had to follow this rule; marrying a non-shifter was perfectly acceptable, unless you were the Alpha. Or, in Ezra's case, a second who actually took the job seriously enough that he held himself to the same standards.

He could marry a non-shifter, but that would create a problem. In the event I could no longer lead, he'd have to become Alpha, and he couldn't if he'd married a non-shifter.

The rules made sense. An Alpha had to keep his blood pure and needed to be connected to shifters and his clan in all ways possible. A spouse outside of the clan would be a distraction to a leader. But it wasn't an easy decision. I'd almost considered giving up the Alpha position just so I could marry her. I'd almost considered leaving the clan since not all clans had rules like ours. Most didn't care if the bloodline was mixed. But some great, great, great, great grandfather of mine decided our clan would live a more pure life, so the rule had been created, and we all had to live with it.

I must've let my memories drift too far into my thoughts; Ezra heard.

This is serious, then. I can't believe you almost gave up Alpha and the clan for this girl!

She's far from a girl now. I tried not to picture her too hard. Ezra would see, and the lust flooding my veins wasn't something he needed to witness.

You need a hot piece of tail to take your mind off this human girl.

Right. Like that would happen anytime soon. Seeing her brought all these thoughts and feelings rushing back. It had taken me a long time to get to the point where I didn't ache for her constantly; I didn't want these feelings to return.

This is why you've never seriously dated? Ezra wondered. *You never got over Addie?*

That's why. I put everything into my work and my role as Alpha.

The right female will change everything. What about Hailey? I think she likes you.

She does. She'd been pretty obvious in her flirting. Hailey was beautiful and a really sweet woman. I probably should date her. At least see if anything was there. But how could I when my heart was so stuck on Addie? It wouldn't be fair to Hailey.

She's a cool chick. You should give it a shot.

Maybe someday.

Man, you've got it bad. Maybe go talk to this Addie and see how much she's changed. Maybe it'll kill your feelings for her. You've probably built her up in your memories and the real deal doesn't hold up anymore.

Yeah. Maybe.

But I didn't think that was true. Unless she'd become a totally different person in college, there wasn't a bar that could be raised high enough to match what Addie had been to me.

Well, facts are facts, man. Unless you're still thinking of giving up Alpha, nothing has changed. You can't be with her. So, let's find a way to move you on.

Thanks. I appreciated his concern, I just didn't think it would work. I'd been trying to get over Addie for four years. The guilt was still there for how I'd ended things between us. The pain of missing her was still there. It had moved to the background of my mind over the two years I spent in college. And as I threw myself into my work, I was able to go days without thinking about her too much.

It was always there, though. I'd see a happy family or couple walking through the park, and a little prick with her name on it would spike my heart. I avoided stores when Valentine's Day was near, and every time July 20th came around, I wondered how she was spending her birthday.

If she'd found someone who would love her as much as I had.

We finished our run and headed back to the ranger station. I checked the reservations and found that Addie would be there all week. Maybe I'd take some time off so I didn't have to worry about running into her.

5

ADDIE

"How about a boat ride?" Julie asked. "We'd get to see lots of wildlife."

I nodded. "Sounds good."

"Ugh, come on, Addie. You can't just bum around over this Owen dude. He ended things. It's time to move on."

"I'm not bumming over him, Emma," I countered, getting a little defensive. It'd been a day since we'd run into Owen and I hadn't been able to stop thinking about him, but I thought I'd done a fairly decent job of hiding it.

"Then let's go on this boat ride so you can prove it," Emma replied.

"Sounds great." I tried to sound enthusiastic, but probably failed.

By the time we arrived at the dock, I was feeling hopeful. I had my camera in tow, ready to photograph every animal and interesting plant I came across. *This is why we came here*, I reminded myself. *To spend time in nature and unwind after graduation. Not to spend the week being hung up on ex-boyfriends from high school.*

I'd spent enough time grieving over Owen. This time was for me.

We waited with a small group for the boat to be ready. Water lapped against the dock, and the air was cooler here. A large fan was positioned at one end of the boat, then several benches of seats. I'd never ridden an airboat before and, judging by the headphones resting on each seat, it would be loud. Perfect for drowning out my thoughts and making me focus on what was ahead, not behind.

A man walked over to the waiting group. "Hello there, folks." He waved to get everyone's attention. "I'm Aiden and I'll be your tour guide today. If you'll make your way to the boat, we can go ahead and get started on our tour."

He gestured toward the boat and the group started to trickle on. As we neared him, he smiled. "Hello, ladies."

I smiled back. "Hello."

He leaned close to me as I passed. "Be sure to grab a seat near the back. It's the best." He winked and continued greeting the other passengers.

When the three of us sat—near the back, though I honestly hadn't been trying to sit there—Emma and Julie converged on me.

"He totally flirted with you!" Emma teased, giggling.

"He's cute," Julie whispered. "Maybe he could take your mind off Owen."

I rolled my eyes and shushed them as Aiden took his place at the back of the boat, next to the large fan.

Aiden stood to address the crowd. "As we take our ride today, expect to see a nice sampling of the variety of wildlife the Everglades has to offer. We should see some gators, herons or ospreys, and maybe even a wild bull, believe it or not. Never know what's around the corner in these parts."

He smiled at me again as he took his seat. He dropped his voice to speak only to us. "If there's anything you ladies want to see, you let me know, okay?"

Emma and Julie agreed happily. I just nodded. Maybe he was sort of flirting, but it was nothing I was going to get excited over. Sure, he was cute. Lots of guys were cute. If my attraction to Owen had been purely physical, maybe that would have been enough to distract me. It was so much more than looks, though.

The large fan started up and we all placed our headphones over our ears. It was loud, but Aiden paused the boat every once in a while to explain what we were seeing or tell us something about the body of water we were riding through. He got very excited when we came across a baby alligator.

"It's very rare to see a baby out sunning like that," he said, pointing. Everyone took numerous photos and exclaimed over the sight. "I see a baby like that maybe once in a hundred rides. You folks must be very lucky." He leaned closer to us and smiled at me once more. "Or maybe I'm just the lucky one."

My face warmed and I tried to ignore it. I snapped photos and let my touristy side take over. I wasn't here to flirt or be flirted with. I was here for taking in the sights and to spend time with my friends. That was it. I turned away from the guide back toward the front of the boat.

Unfortunately, he turned out to actually be funny. Several times as he was giving commentary, I found myself chuckling at his stories. I *did* like guys who could make me laugh.

The ride ended, and as we got off the boat, he watched us file off. Emma and Julie glanced back at him.

Emma sighed. "Bummer."

"Yeah," Julie agreed.

I was confused. "What?"

"I thought maybe he'd ask you out," Emma confessed.

"Me, too," Julie added.

We walked into the building and weaved our way through the gift shop. As we made our way along the aisles of items for sale, we paused now and then to look at some trinkets and souvenirs. Emma bought three postcards and stamps.

"Here." She handed us each a postcard as we stepped out of the gift shop into the bright sun. "We'll send these to someone so we can feel like we're really on vacation."

"We *are* really on vacation," I said.

"Then why haven't I been drunk yet?" Emma asked.

I rolled my eyes. "Because enjoying nature is more interesting."

"What if you could have both?"

The three of us turned at the sound of the male voice. Just outside the gift shop, Aiden leaned against the railing. Had he been waiting for us? "There's a place out in the woods that friends of mine own. They're having a party tonight. Plenty of wild animals. Plenty of beer." He raised an eyebrow and looked at me expectantly.

I pressed my lips together. "I'm sure you'll have a good time."

"I'd have a much better time if you joined me."

My eyes widened and I felt heat rush up my neck. When Emma had said something about him asking me out, I'd been relieved that he hadn't. So much for that.

"Oh, I, umm… am on vacation," I said. "With my friends. We're doing things together this week."

"Even better. Bring them along."

I glanced over at them, which was a mistake. Both of them were pleading with me. Pleading to say yes. We hadn't been out yet. Of course, it had only been one night so far, but they were itching to let loose, and I didn't want to stop them.

"Okay," I said. "The three of us will meet you there."

"Excellent." He handed his phone to me. "Why don't you save your number in my phone and I'll text you the address."

I took the phone reluctantly. I didn't like giving out my number to someone I barely knew, but I guessed I could just block him if I had to. I saved my number and handed the phone back.

"Addie," I told him.

"So glad to be your tour guide today. I look forward to seeing you tonight, Addie." He nodded at us, smiled and turned away as he headed back into the building.

Emma and Julie squealed as we walked away.

"Thank you! Thank you!" Emma said. "Party in the woods, woot!"

"Awesome," Julie said. "And, this will be perfect. We'll get there, find your man, and conveniently disappear."

"No! You will not leave me alone with him!" I demanded.

"He asked *you* out, remember?" Emma said. "He let us come along."

"That's because I would have said no," I insisted. "I'm not going out alone here with some guy I don't even know."

"That's how you get to know people," Julie said. "How will you ever meet someone if you don't ever go on dates?"

I shrugged. "I haven't been too worried about it."

"Right," Julie said. "Owen? Still?"

"And Sam," I added, getting a little defensive. "Owen broke my heart, but Sam confused me. I have no desire to be in any sort of relationship right now."

Julie frowned. "You're going to give him a chance, aren't you?"

"He *is* cute!" Emma gushed. "And he's funny. That was a good tour."

"It was," Julie agreed.

"Just give him a chance," Emma begged. "If it doesn't go anywhere, then it doesn't. But you won't know unless you get to know him a little."

"Just talk to him," Julie added. "And drink a beer or two while you're at it."

I rolled my eyes. "We're going, aren't we? I told him we'd go, so we'll go. And I will talk to him, but I'm not going to be off alone all night. I'm going to spend time with you guys, too."

"We'll be with you all week," Emma said. "Talk to him. Maybe have a make out session." She made a kissy face.

"No," I narrowed my eyes. "Not on the agenda."

"Keep your mind open," Julie said. "No expectations. No assumptions."

Emma laughed, pulling the car door open. "You never know; he could be the one."

I shook my head as I climbed into the backseat. "I highly doubt it."

"You won't know unless you give him a chance," Julie pointed out.

"Fine. One chance," I said. "I'll talk to him. Didn't I already agree to that anyway? Give me a break, guys!"

"But we want you to take it seriously," Julie said.

"I take it very seriously. I will have a serious conversation with the cute airboat tour guide. Then I will seriously move on with my life."

"Unless you like him," Emma chirped.

"If he turns out to be the man of my dreams, you can both remind me that I was wrong every day of my happily ever after."

6

ADDIE

I HADN'T PACKED MUCH FOR GOING OUT. I THOUGHT WE'D BE HIKING around the area and camping. Silly me; I should have known better. Emma and Julie had plenty of cute outfits with them, so they kindly helped me supplement. A top from Emma and cute, strappy sandals from Julie and we were on our way.

Aiden had texted me the address, as promised. When we looked it up, the place was about a half hour away. So much for getting away if we were just going to head halfway back to Miami. But I said nothing and rode along, knowing that if nothing else, they were happy we were going out.

We knew were getting close when the cars started to appear, parked along the side of the road. We pulled into a dirt parking lot and were lucky enough to find a spot that didn't require us to walk a quarter mile along the dark road. I felt nervous and looked around anxiously; I hoped he wouldn't show. Then I'd have had held up my end of the deal, and my friends couldn't complain that I hadn't given him a shot. I could whine all night about being stood up and make them feel bad for me.

We walked in the direction that some of the crowd meandered toward and came to something of a clearing. There was a large fire, a few kegs of beer, and someone's Bluetooth speaker playing a playlist of country rock songs. Not really my thing, but I wasn't there to complain.

"We beat him here," Julie said.

I shrugged. "Maybe he won't show."

"Not a chance," Emma quipped.

We each got a beer and then stood off to the side. It didn't take long for the guys there to notice that three single ladies had just walked in. We were like a target, much to my dismay.

Two guys walked over and started talking to us. I tried to ignore them, but Julie and Emma chatted away, laughing and smiling where appropriate until Emma went off to dance with one of them. The other walked off to get a beer and found himself caught up in a conversation.

"That didn't take long," I said, glancing at Emma and the guy she was now dancing with.

Julie nodded toward the other guy, who had now wandered off, out of sight. "He was into you."

"Nah." I sipped my beer and glanced at the small group trickling toward us through the trees.

"You really didn't notice?" Julie asked.

"I wasn't really paying much attention."

She nodded. "So that's it. It's not that no guy has shown interest. It's that you don't pick up on it."

I shrugged again. "I guess I don't really care."

She blew out a sigh, then grabbed my arm. "He's here!"

I turned and saw Aiden walking toward us. Great. I forced a smile as he approached.

"You're missing one," he said.

I pointed to Emma.

He saw and nodded. "Glad you could all make it. I'm sure you're used to fancy nightclubs and all, but this is what us locals do to unwind. You from the city?"

"I guess so? I mean, we went to school in Miami, but my family is from the outskirts. I've always considered myself more of a suburban girl than a city girl."

"Well," he said, letting his smile spread across his face, "that's just my sort of girl. Woman, actually. You're no girl."

My face warmed and I glanced down at myself subconsciously. I turned toward Julie, and that's when I noticed that she had ducked out of the conversation. I met her eyes from several feet away as she poured herself another beer and pretended to be enjoying some conversation with a few people by the kegs. She gave me an encouraging smile and turned her attention back to her new group.

I was on my own.

"So, you're...from around here?" I asked.

"You could say that. Born and raised just a few miles down the road. My family and I are pretty tight. We stay close to each other and near the area."

"That's nice."

Why was I so bad at these sorts of conversations? At dating at all? Must have been because I had no practice. Dating was much different in high school, and in college, I had already known Sam before we were alone together for any length of time. This whole concept of going out with someone I didn't know had me baffled. Relationships really started out like this?

"What made you decide to take a boat ride today?" he asked.

"My friends and I are here camping at the park, celebrating our graduation. We wanted to do something that would give us a chance to see animals that we haven't noticed around the park."

"I love the Everglades. We're so lucky to be so close to the park. I just wished I was more accepted there."

I drew my eyebrows together. "You're not accepted at the park?"

"Well, you know. Some of the rangers there don't like the local folks very much."

"Why would that be?"

"I don't know. Technically, the boating company isn't part of the park, it's just off the property. We have permission to ride through the park, but the company is privately owned by my family. Maybe they don't like the noise; who knows."

That seemed strange to me, but what did I know of the area's politics? "Oh," was all I could say. It made sense. The rangers probably didn't like how the boats disturbed the water and animals.

"Have you met any of the rangers?"

I lifted one shoulder. "Not really. We've just hiked and kept to ourselves for the most part."

"There's this one ranger in particular." Aiden shook his head. "Owen something. He hates me."

My heart jolted. He couldn't be talking about the same Owen, could he? "Owen Bailey?"

Aiden straightened up. "I think that's his last name. Do you know him?"

"I knew him in high school, but I haven't seen him since—well, I saw him at the park, but I haven't really talked to him in years."

"I see. So, you know what I'm saying then. How much of a jerk he can be."

"Oh, I… guess so. I don't know." Could he be a jerk? I didn't know Owen now. People changed a lot in college. Maybe it was true.

"How well do you know him?"

"Not at all. We dated in high school, but like I said, that was years ago."

"Do you know about his family and friends? His brother?"

This conversation was going to a strange place, and I didn't like it. "I guess? I've met his brother."

"What about his friend, Ezra?"

"Uhh… I don't recall him having a friend with that name."

"Do you know where he lives?" he asked. "Someone said he has a cabin just off the park's land."

"When I knew him, he lived outside of the city. I really don't know."

He nodded, thinking for a moment before he kept talking. "Guys like that just get to me, you know. I get that he's a ranger. Or the main ranger or whatever his title is. I get it. I don't have a fancy degree or anything. I just know the land from growing up here. They must not like it when locals know more than they do."

I nodded absently; I really didn't know what else to say. I didn't want to be on a date, if that's what it was, talking about Owen. And not in a way that was putting Owen down. He might have been a jerk, I didn't know. But the Owen I knew wasn't, and I didn't want to think of him in that way, even if he had broken my heart.

"Have you been doing the boat thing long?" I asked. Maybe a different subject would be better.

"My family has had that business for over twenty years," he said. "No thanks to the rangers who want to shut us down. Do you know that one time that Owen guy approached me and tried to stop me from coming onto park land?" He shook his head. "I say live and let live, you know?

Why should he care if I want to make an honest living? Isn't that what we all want to do?"

"That's what I'm trying to do myself. This week, I'm hoping to figure out what I want to do with the rest of my life."

"Right. For me, it was easy. My family has this business, so if I wanted it, the job was mine. I like giving tours, meeting people, showing off the area. I grew up here, so this is all home to me. I don't think I should be chased out of it just because someone doesn't like me."

"No, I guess you shouldn't."

"So, you agree. This guy is a total jerk, and he needs to back off."

"I..." I didn't want to agree, but I also didn't want to argue with the guy. Clearly, this bothered him. "I don't know enough about the situation to make that call."

"Well, if you see this Owen again, you tell him to let me be. I never did anything to get in his way. I just want to run my tours and that's it. Meet a nice lady, which I may have already done, have a nice life with her." He smiled in a hopeful way.

"Right. That's what we all want, I guess."

"It doesn't bother you that I don't have a college degree, does it?"

"No. You have a livelihood. Seems like you enjoy it. You're good at it, so..."

"Thank you. I like to think so. What was your favorite part?"

"Umm..." I really wished Emma and Julie hadn't gone off and left me here. "I guess the baby gator. That was neat."

He nodded. "It is quite rare. That wasn't just tour talk. You're lucky; you brought me luck."

I picked at the edge of my cup. "I haven't had too much luck lately, so that's good."

"I find that hard to believe. I almost didn't work today, but something told me to just show up, that it would be good. And then you and your friends came walking along, and I knew I'd made the right call. Who needs a day off when you can spend time with a beautiful woman?"

I looked over the crowd, trying to locate Emma and Julie. I at least wanted to have an idea of where they were if I needed a quick getaway.

"Yeah, my brother and I—I have four brothers, if you can believe that —we all work on the boats. Giving tours, fixing them up, whatever needs to be done. My oldest brother even learned how to work the web site and all. We're high tech now. Did you know you could book a tour online?"

"I didn't, no."

"You can. And there's pictures, too. I took most of them. I like to think I'm somewhat of an amateur photographer. I noticed you taking a lot of photos today. That camera of yours is nice."

"Thanks. I don't really know much about it."

"I've worked with cameras for a long time. I have one like yours—the newer model, but it works pretty much the same. Great for low light. I have some of the most gorgeous sunrises and sunsets."

"I can imagine."

"I'll have to show you my collection. I have lots of photos framed and hanging in my house."

"Nice."

"I even had one printed in a local magazine," he said. "Have you ever had a photo published?"

"I have not."

"It was just a local thing, no big deal. But people around here thought it was a pretty big deal. I've sold a few copies of the print."

"That's...cool." He went on talking about himself *non-stop*. His family, the business, even his ex-girlfriend. Like I wanted to hear about her. After about twenty minutes, I was ready to get out of there and never talk to Aiden again.

What was it Emma and Julie had said about me liking him? About him maybe being 'the one?' Were they high? There was no way I even wanted to spend another half hour with this guy, let alone go on another date. I finally spotted them across a crowd.

"Well, I should get back to my friends," I said when there was a pause in conversation.

He glanced to see where I looked. "Already? I'm having such a good time talking with you. I thought we had a good thing going."

"It's just that we came together and, like I said, we're on girls' trip, so I should spend time with them."

"Well, I have your number. Maybe once your vacation is over, we can go out on a real date."

I nodded absently. "Umm... maybe."

"It's fate, don't you think?" He smiled. "I'm Aiden, you're Addie. Our names go together. Just like we should."

"Yeah... I guess they do kind of go together..."

"I think you're a really special lady." He put his hand to my cheek and stepped closer.

Shit. I didn't have time to step back. He leaned down, coming in for a kiss, and I pulled my head back suddenly before his lips could touch mine.

"I—I'm sorry, I just can't," I said, taking several steps back.

"What the hell?" his face broke into anger. "I thought we had a good time. You've been leading me on, and now you won't even kiss me?"

"I just need to get back to my friends."

I hurried away and almost ran to them.

"Here she is!" Emma held up a cup and whooped.

"Can we go? Now. Please?"

They saw my expression and exchanged a glance.

"Yeah, sure," Julie said.

"Did he hurt you?" Emma asked. "Or get rude in any way?" She put her hand on her hip and glared in his direction. "I'll kick his ass."

"Nothing like that. I'll explain. Let's just get out of here. Please."

With one of them on each side of me, we hurried back to the car, hopped in, and sped off.

7

OWEN

I SHOULDN'T HAVE GONE. I GET THAT NOW, BUT ALL I COULD THINK AT THE time was, not him. When Conner told me he saw Addie talking with Aiden Harvey and he asked her out, I was pissed. I hated to think of her spending time with that asshole, but it also meant I'd let her into my thoughts too much. My whole clan knew her face now, knew my feelings for her, knew everything. More than I wanted them to know. But it was too late.

Conner had been out on some kind of work errand and had been shocked to see the woman whose face had consumed my thoughts lately. Then he'd heard Aiden talking and the two of them making plans. He'd told me about it, not so much because he wanted to or thought he should, but because he'd been bothered enough by it that his thoughts reflected something. I'd had to convince him to give me details, and as the Alpha, he didn't have much room to disobey. As my friend, he wouldn't have held back information, either, if he'd thought it would help me. He hadn't been so sure it would be good for me to know this, however.

So, I'd gone to the party. I knew about these get togethers; they happened all the time. We never went, though. We liked to hang out and party in the woods, sure. Who didn't? But we didn't do it with a bunch of locals. Bear clans tended to be tight knit and kept to themselves. Crocs, on the other hand, loved to be around people, scamming them however they could, taking full advantage of the people passing through.

Even the airboat gig was somewhat of a scam. Sure, people got to tour the Everglades by water, but the Harvey family who ran it charged far too much, and most of the animals seen on the tour were staged. Either put there on purpose or faked. I'd even heard rumors that they had a baby alligator statue that they put in the water, then claimed it was a rare sight and that group was extra lucky for seeing such a "rare" occurrence. I came across baby gators all the time; you just had to know where to find them. And it certainly wasn't in an area where loud airboats passed through all day.

The rivalry between the crocodiles and bears of the Everglades was long standing, going back more years than either clan knew. Both wanted complete control over the land, though for different reasons. Each despised the other, though again, for different reasons. The bears had had their grasp on the park for decades and the crocs were all around it, just hovering outside the borders, waiting for their moment to slither in and wreak havoc. The conclave, which consisted of delegates of shifters of all types, helped keep both sides in check and stepped in if one side went too far.

There had always been issues with the crocs—usually not enough to go to the conclave over, but annoying, nonetheless. The day Addie showed up had started with Ezra telling me about their run-in with them the night before at a local bar. I was about ready to tell my guys to not even go out in public locally, but I wouldn't punish my guys for something the crocs did. I chose not to go out often because I didn't want to deal with it. And until now, my dealings with them hadn't been too personal. Of course, messing with the member of one clan is like messing with all the members, but none had ever gone after something so precious to me.

I didn't know if Aiden had any idea who Addie was to me. I didn't know how he could, but it didn't really matter why he was going for her. It only mattered that he was, and that she'd gone for it. She'd gone to the party with her friends and wandered off to spend time alone with Aiden. It even looked like he kissed her. Maybe they had a second one planned. Maybe they'd fall in love and get married, and everything I ever wanted out of life would be his instead of mine. Maybe I'd lost my chance forever.

How about getting a bite to eat? I'm starved. Mason, third in the chain of command within the clan, thought to me.

Then go eat, I responded. *I don't need a babysitter.*

When they realized what I was doing, I'd found myself surrounded by the thoughts of my clan. They wouldn't come to where I was unless I needed them to. Even my guys didn't love partying so much that they'd subject themselves to an event thrown by crocs. They were worried I'd do something stupid. And so Mason had been assigned—probably by Ezra and Conner—to keep an eye on me through the night and make sure I didn't start something they'd have to finish.

I just want to know you're okay.

I'm fine, thanks. I'm going home to sleep. I ran up to my cabin and stood out front to stretch. *Just got home, actually.*

And you're staying there?

That's the plan.

I'm heading off to bed, too. Hit me up in the morning. I'll do a perimeter run before work if you want.

That's not a bad idea. I shifted back to human form and dressed. But as I sat in my cabin, trying to concentrate on the piece of wood I was whittling, I couldn't stop my mind.

Addie didn't know Aiden. She didn't know all these croc guys were bad news. Wouldn't she want to know if she were getting herself mixed up with a bunch of assholes? The Addie I knew wouldn't have wanted to be around people like that. I thought I should just go tell her. Just as a concerned friend. To let her know what the truth was.

I got up and paced the room. Would I come off as too...controlling? I had no right to tell her what to do. If I went to talk to her and warn her of her new boyfriend, it would seem like I was just being jealous, trying to keep her from being happy. I needed a way to tell her that wouldn't make it seem like I just didn't want her to date. *Maybe I could fix her up with someone.*

As soon as I had the thought, I shook it from my mind. Okay, so I was jealous. There was no denying it. That wasn't the reason I didn't want her around Aiden, though. *Maybe admitting that to her would be enough,* I thought. *I could just say, "Yes, I know this comes off as a jealous ex-boyfriend thing, and I am jealous, but trust me, he's bad news." Maybe I could convince her.*

Without thinking too much more about it, I found myself outside, walking. If I happened to be strolling in the direction of her tent, then okay. It wasn't like it was close. If I went to her tent, there would have been many miles of ground to cover. But if I ran there...

I stepped out of the shorts I'd pulled on and shifted back into bear form. When my bones settled and muscles were ready, I leapt into the air, running fast until I was close. I slowed to a walk as I neared the camping area, though; I didn't need to take calls all day about some bear running around the woods, scaring the campers. I kept my ears open and crouched as I moved in closer.

I really hadn't thought this through. If my plan was to talk to her, I should have come in human form. Or at least carried a sack of clothing. Maybe it was better that way.

Just don't break the ultimate command, whatever you do.

I almost rolled my eyes at Mason. *There's no chance of that.* Like I would show her my animal form and break the rule that kept all shifters from telling humans of our existence. This one secret, this one universal command, was true of all shifters. Even if sometimes the crocs danced on the line, their way of life would be severely hindered if the world knew the truth about them. It would be for all of us.

Maybe telling Addie wouldn't start some massive, riotous outbreak that would ruin all shifter life forever, but why take the chance? Even if I could tell her, I wouldn't want to; it would scare the shit out of her and she'd think I was a freak. I didn't really have a chance with her at the time, and it was my own fault, my own family and position that kept me from being with her. I still didn't want to taint my image in her eyes. It was bad enough she probably hated me for ending things how I did; I didn't want it to be any worse.

I froze when their tent unzipped and the three of them stepped out. I didn't know these friends, but I thought she'd called the blonde Emma. Conner said the other one was Julie, who began to pull a bottle of orange juice from the cooler.

"We have plenty," she said.

"Thank god," Addie breathed, setting a large bottle of vodka onto the picnic table.

Emma came over with a few red plastic cups and held them in place as Julie poured.

"To friends only," Addie said, raising her cup for a toast.

Emma sighed. "To friends, and *good* guys."

"Like I said, *friends only*," Addie countered.

Julie rolled her eyes. "It couldn't have been that bad."

"Just be glad you walked away when you did," Addie mumbled, taking a long sip of her drink. "You were spared his long tale of life as a tour guide. Even Sam wasn't as arrogant as Aiden. He talked about himself the whole time!"

"It is quite a feat to be a bigger asshole than Sam," Emma laughed.

I had no idea who this 'Sam' was. An ex of Addie's, I assumed, by what they were saying. The jealous spark flickered. *Think about what they're saying*, I reminded myself. *Calling him an asshole. Obviously, Sam is not on their good side.*

"Why is it always the cute ones?" Julie asked. "You either find a good guy or a good-looking guy, but never both."

"That's not true," Addie pointed out. She looked off into the distance and sighed.

Emma groaned. "If you say Owen one more time, I'm going to scream."

My heart jumped. What? Had they talked about me? Addie was talking about me? My ears twitched to hear more.

"Sorry," Addie muttered.

"Hey, you know what?" Julie put both hands on Addie's shoulders and looked her square in the eye. "You took a step. You met up with a guy and you talked to him. You had a date, Addie! A date! And so it didn't go well. That happens. The point is, you did it. You're moving on. You're over Owen. You're over Sam. Now we just need to find your Mr. Right."

"I second that." Emma held up her drink and they all tapped their cups to hers.

Addie took a sip and paused. "I just wonder sometimes..."

"Don't do that," Emma said.

"But the thing is," Addie continued, "the only reason Owen ended things was to go to school. And, okay, so we were many hours apart, and that would have been hard to manage. I get it. But we're out of school now. He works here in the park and I live an hour away. That's not exactly long distance anymore—"

"To be honest, Ad," Julie interrupted, "I don't know if that was the real reason. He might have said that. He might even have thought it at the time, but guys don't want to be stuck with the same woman forever. Not right out of high school. They like to sleep around and explore, try new things—"

"And new women," Emma added.

"Exactly." Julie set down her empty cup. "He had oats to sow, and he used that as an excuse to break things off. Any guy who does that isn't worth it. It was more important to him to date other women than it was to make things work with you. And that's the truth."

I wanted to scream. My claws dug into the earth, tearing grass and breaking twigs. I could have stood up and roared. I could have charged at them and showed my fury. But it was no use.

You okay, Boss?

Not now, Ezra.

I tried to calm down. The last thing I needed was Ezra chirping in my ear.

I knew, on some level, it wasn't Julie's fault. Or Emma's. They didn't know me, and they were going by what tabloid magazines and Hollywood told them about men. I'd even guess, based on my friends at the time, that what they said was true in many cases. It just wasn't true for me.

I'd had my eyes set on a great school, just a few minutes' drive from where Addie had been accepted. I knew I wanted to work in the park, and I had an easy in with so many of my clan working in and around the area. I was never going to leave for good. And I didn't want to. I had my family and clan, I had my career picked out and was excited about it. And most of all, I had a woman I adored, who was everything I could have imagined in a mate.

I'd also had my eyes on a shiny ring I thought she'd like.

I had a plan. We'd take a midnight stroll through the park, sneaking into the area closed at night. There was a certain spot I loved. In the middle of one of the rope bridges, if you paused, you could look both directions on either side of you and see over the water to the horizon. I'd tell her that one side was our past, full of joy and happiness, and one side was our future, stretched long ahead of us. Sometime between proposing and our wedding day, I'd sit her down and tell her the truth about me. That was the only time most of us made an exception and told a pure human—when wedding bells were ringing. Or, in the event that a child was created out of wedlock. Obviously, the mother would have to be told that her baby had a 50% chance of becoming shifter. Addie would have understood and accepted me, I just knew it.

My plan was perfect. I was so excited the day I told my parents about it over dinner, how I was going to talk to Addie's dad the next day and ask for his permission. Then, my parents dropped the news on me. I hadn't known about the marriage rules in our clan. Why would I? Other clans were allowed to marry non-shifters. Even within my own clan there were mixed marriages. But in our clan, the Alpha rule stood on some ancient desire for purity or some bullshit. My father felt strongly about it; he didn't want to upset the ancestors.

I'd been heartbroken—and angry. I tried to think of ways to get around it. I'd gone as far as packing my bags, planning to leave my family or the area, or the clan altogether, if that's what it took. But my mother must've sensed it in me and came to talk to me, sitting beside the packed duffle bag on my bed.

We talked for hours, and by the end of it, I saw my duty. I understood my dad's reasoning, and though I didn't agree with any part of it, I felt compelled to go along with it. I wished I could tell Addie the truth, that I hadn't wanted to sow my wild oats as Julie had suggested. That I missed her every day.

That I still loved her.

As I listened, watching Addie and wanting to be close to her, she said something that made me completely unravel. I walked away, heading back to my cabin, her words still ringing in my ears.

"The truth is," she'd said to her friends, "I'm not over Owen, and I don't know if I ever will be. I want to talk to him and see if there's any chance of us trying to make this work."

I hadn't stayed after that; I didn't want to hear her friends convince her it was a bad idea. She still had feelings for me. She wanted to get *back together*. If anyone had been there, they might have expected me to be ecstatic over this.

But sadness weighed me down. It took a long time to get back home, and when I did, I crawled into bed, still naked, and wiped away a tear. It didn't matter that she still wanted me. The rules hadn't changed; there was no way I could be with her.

The day before, I would have said that was the best news I could have ever heard, but in that moment, it felt like a dagger to the heart. It was easy to want something when it seemed far out of reach. Having her there, knowing what I knew, meant that I'd have to do the hard part. If she did come to talk to me, I had to be the one to send her away. I had to reject her. Again. I had to watch her walk away, knowing we wanted each other more than anything.

I'd have to break her heart.

Again.

8

ADDIE

I WOKE UP DETERMINED TO DO IT. WHATEVER HAD HAPPENED LAST NIGHT, and whatever my friends had to say about it, I was going to talk to Owen. I couldn't live with myself if I didn't at least see. Maybe nothing had changed. Maybe they were right and his reasons hadn't been as pure as he claimed.

Whatever the case, I needed to know.

We got up late after our long, boozy night and it was already afternoon by the time we'd all showered and dressed for the day. We ate lunch around the fire, and that's when I announced what I'd decided.

"Before either of you say anything, just know that I've thought a lot about this," I started. "I'm going to talk to him and see what the deal is. Who knows, he might even be seeing someone. After I talk to him, I will move on. I will get closure, and while it certainly won't be with Aiden, I will get out and date and find someone. Or attempt to."

Emma shoved a piece of bread into her mouth and spoke with garbled words. "Go for it."

"Really?" I'd expected much lashing back and convincing against.

"You know, I agree," Julie said. "If this is what it'll take, then go for it. Talk to him. Find out what you need to find out. Then say goodbye to him forever."

"And if you need to cry, we'll be here," Emma added, hugging her arm around my shoulders.

"Just remember that he didn't come talk to you. You're going to him. Again."

"I know," I said. "And I've considered that, too. I really have thought about this for days."

"I believe it," Emma mumbled.

"I'm not making a snap decision and rushing into this."

Julie popped a chip into her mouth. "We never said you were, Addie."

I huffed. "I just thought you'd be trying to talk me out of it. I had all these arguments planned and everything."

Julie raised an eyebrow. "Do you want us to talk you out of it? Because that alone is a sign—"

"No, no," I said. "This isn't like that. I should have talked to him years ago. Seeing him again made me realize that I'm really not over him. And I need to be. You guys are right. And this will help."

Emma smiled. "Then I vote 100% yes."

"Me, too," Julie added.

I let out a long breath. "So, now I just have to go do it. What do you want to do when I get back?"

"Whatever you want to do," Emma said.

"We'll go for a hike if you need to talk. Or we can go out and get you drunk if it goes badly," Julie shrugged.

"And what if it *doesn't* go badly?" I chewed on my lip. "There's only one possible outcome, I know that. And I'm not getting my hopes up, but..."

"Then bring him back here for us to meet him," Julie chirped.

"Okay." I took several breaths, psyching myself up. "I'm going to talk to him."

They both gave me quick hugs, and I hopped in the car, headed for the ranger station nearby. It was the same one we'd called when I found the ibis, so I hoped this was the one he worked out of. The park was so huge and there were so many ranger stations, he could be anywhere.

I parked and ascended the steps, then approached a woman sitting behind a desk. Her name tag said Rachel.

"Hi, Rachel," I smiled. "I'm looking for a certain ranger, and I'm wondering if he's here."

"Sure. What is this in regards to?"

I had my excuse ready to go. "I found an injured bird a few days back. The ranger said to call or stop by to find out how it was doing."

Part lie, part exaggeration, close enough.

Rachel nodded. "Who you looking for?"

"Owen Bailey?"

"And your name, ma'am?" she asked.

"Adeline Pearson."

She scribbled something down, then looked up at me. "I'm afraid he's not here today, Ms. Pearson."

"Oh." Disappointment washed over me. "Do you expect him in tomorrow?"

"He's off for the rest of the week. But let me make a call. I can get you an update on the bird."

"Oh, great; thanks." I forced a smile. I couldn't very well walk away and say I didn't care anymore. Even if it was an excuse, I did wonder about the bird. Wouldn't hurt to stick around to hear something about it.

Rachel disappeared into another room and came back after several minutes. "Ms. Pearson?"

"Yes." I turned from the rack of brochures and walked back over to her desk.

"I spoke with Owen briefly. He says if you'd like, you can stop by his cabin to talk about the bird, or he can have the vet give you a call if you'd prefer that."

"Oh." *His cabin? Hell yes! Yes!* I tried to act indecisive. "I'm not really sure where his cabin is."

"Well no, he wouldn't expect you to. That's why he had me write down directions for you." She handed me a piece of paper. "It's just off the park grounds, but it can be a little tricky to find."

I took the paper and tucked it carefully into my pocket. "Thanks. We're old friends, so he probably just thought we could catch up." I tried to laugh it off.

She gave me a little smile that seemed to hint that she knew what I was up to. "If you get lost, his number is there on the bottom."

"Oh. Great, thanks."

I got back into the car and pulled out the paper. *I have his address and phone number? This information could be dangerous.* As long as I did what I planned to do and just talked to him, it'd be fine. As long as I didn't save his number to my phone and text him the next time I was drunk, or drive by his house when I was bored or suspicious, it'd be fine.

I sucked in a few breaths to steady my nerves. Once I convinced myself that I wouldn't do those sorts of things with this information, I read over the map and drove off.

I did miss one turn, but I found my way easily enough. I tended to have a good sense of direction just by taking a moment to orient myself if I became confused. When I saw the little cabin sitting there, unassuming, my heart jumped. His Jeep was there; the same red Jeep his parents had bought him for graduation. I'd ridden in it twice: once, the day he got it, and again the following day, when he took me to the park to break up with me.

Before I even got out of Emma's car, he stepped out onto the front porch. Weird that even when he was off, Rachel—whatever her position was—called him. Maybe he loved his job that much. I couldn't blame him. I would've loved to work in a national park, too.

He waved when he saw me and I raised my hand in return. Now that I was here and was about to talk to him, I wanted to leave. To turn around and keep things as they were. To not hear again that he didn't want to be with me. But it was too late. I kept walking.

9

ADDIE

"I HEARD YOU WANTED TO CHECK UP ON YOUR BIRD," OWEN SAID.

Right. The ibis was why I was there. "Is she doing okay?"

I reached his porch and we stood facing each other, several feet between us.

He leaned against the railing. "She's doing great. She did have a broken leg, but the vet got her fixed up."

"Good. I was worried."

Silence fell between us for a moment. Since my big cover reason for being there had been resolved, I didn't know what to say next.

"Why are you really here, Addie?" he asked after a long while.

There seemed to be no further reason to try and hide it. "Umm, I guess just to see you again...I don't know." I sighed. I wish I could just come right out and say it. *I love you Owen. Why aren't we together?* Instead, I lifted one shoulder and gave him a tight smile. "The bird seemed like a good excuse to talk to you."

"I didn't think you'd want to talk to me. Ever again."

"Yeah. I could see that."

He laughed. "Yet, here you are."

"Here I am." I looked around, appreciating what I could see of the cabin. "Nice place you have here. Feels like it's part of the park."

"But it's not. Believe me, there was a lot of paperwork to prove it's not."

"Makes sense. I wouldn't want just anyone to be able to build on park land."

"Right. We have enough trouble trying to keep the environment in its original state in these parts."

"Yeah. Then you get idiots with loud airboats driving all through the waterways, disturbing everything." I shook my head. Whatever had happened with Aiden didn't change the fact that the airboat tours really weren't doing much to keep the natural environment as it was.

He laughed. "You've had the pleasure of meeting the Harveys."

"I wouldn't say it was much of a pleasure."

"Yeah. I heard."

I gave him a surprised look. He heard what, exactly?

"A friend of mine saw you talking to Aiden the other day."

His friends knew who I was? That seemed a little strange. 'Why' kept coming to my mind. Did he talk about me? Have photos of me somewhere? That could be a good sign.

"He invited me and my friends to a party," I said. "It wasn't really my kind of thing."

"Probably for the best. They aren't known for being the most... upstanding? They cause us some trouble. And I'll be honest, I was concerned when I heard you were dating him."

"Whoa." I held up my hands, my face growing hot. "I don't know what your friend told you, but I'm certainly not dating him. He invited us to the party and we went. I talked to him while we were there, and that's about it."

"That's all I meant," he said. "Those parties get shut down all the time. Aiden is..."

"A complete asshole?"

He laughed again. "Something like that."

"You know what's weird? Besides the fact that he tried to kiss me when I gave him no indication that I wanted him to? He asked about you."

Owen drew his eyebrows together and stood up straighter. "He asked about *me*?"

"If I knew you. He said you didn't like his family being in the park and they weren't accepted here or something. He wanted to know about some guy named Ezra who's a friend of yours, he asked if I'd seen you and said you were a jerk."

His eyes narrowed. "What did he ask about Ezra?"

"Just if I knew him. He wanted to know where you lived. Oh, and he asked if I knew Noah, too."

"Really."

This did not seem to make him happy, and I couldn't blame him. If someone I didn't like was asking around about my family and friends, I'd be bothered, too.

"How is your brother, anyway?" I asked.

"Doing well. Just got married."

"Little Noah?" I shook my head. I sure didn't think Owen's little brother would be married before I was.

"Yup. Do you remember Tori who was in his class?"

"Mmm, maybe?"

"Really long black hair? Was a cheerleader?"

"I think so."

"Well, anyhow," he said, "she's my sister-in-law now."

"Nice. Good for them."

Awkward silence again.

"So, what's the deal with Aiden?" I asked. "Is he trying to start something with you?"

"I'm not sure, but I hope not. I would just ask—I know I don't have any right to—but please stay away from him. For your own sake. I know I might come off like a jealous ex-boyfriend or something, and I wanted a way to say something without sounding like that, but I really just want what's best for you. And I know too much about him; I don't want to see him hurt you."

"You don't have to worry about that. I want nothing to do with that guy. I already blocked his number on my phone."

"Good."

"You were going to say something about me going out with him?"

"Uh." He scratched the back of his neck. "I considered it. But I figured it wasn't my place."

"We're still friends. Aren't we?"

"Sure. I'd like to be."

"And friends look out for each other."

He nodded. "That they do."

"So, as a friend, since we're friends now, I was wondering how things are going for you. Did you find a special lady, too?"

"Nope."

"I guess you know I'm single. I dated someone for about a year in college, but that turned out to be a nightmare."

"Sorry to hear that. I hoped you would find happiness; a good man to love you like you deserve. Someone to marry and have kids with, to grow old with."

I chuckled. "I always thought that would be you. Maybe I'm just not meant to be married."

"Don't say that. Of course you are—I mean, if that's what you want. I don't think I'll ever marry, but I want you to have everything you want."

"Is that it?" I asked. It seemed like the perfect—maybe my only—opening to finally ask. "Is that why you ended things between us? You never wanted to get married and you thought I did?"

He put his elbows on the railing and rested his chin in his hands, thinking. "No," he said after a long while. "Not entirely. I thought we'd be married once, too."

He had a far off look in his eyes and stood back up, looking past me into the woods. I waited, wanting to hear more.

"I just thought with us being at schools so far away, that it would be too difficult. I didn't want to hold you back. I thought you'd find someone in college and fall madly in love."

I swallowed hard, my throat thickening despite myself. "I did," I whispered. "I fell madly in love with you. All I wanted was for us to have a happy life together."

"How many people actually marry their high school sweethearts? I didn't want you to feel trapped like I have at times."

"You felt trapped in our relationship?"

"No, that's not what I meant. I've felt trapped, yes. Not by you. Just by...life, I guess. By my family. We all have things expected of us. Sometimes it's more than we'd like to have to bear."

"I didn't feel like I was trapped with you. I wanted to tie myself to you in every way possible. You were my first love. My first...everything. My... only love."

It took several long seconds before he would meet my eyes. When he did, his expression looked pained. A tear ran down my cheek and I swiped it away.

"I wish I could say I was over you, Owen, but I'm not. You asked earlier why I was really here. That was it. Closure, is what my friends are calling it. I just wanted to know if the distance was the real reason you ended things. The only reason. Because if that was the only reason, and if we're both still single, and now we're closer and maybe it's not a reason anymore, then..."

"Addie," he whispered.

His expression looked conflicted. I couldn't remember ever seeing him look so troubled, except for when he broke up with me. This was the exact face he'd made then, too. Right before he told me he could never see me again. I expected him to say the same now.

He took a step closer and reached out to take my hands in his.

"I'm so sorry I hurt you. Believe me when I say it was the last thing I wanted to do. I did what I had to do, but there isn't a day I don't regret it and miss you."

I fell into his arms, letting the tears flow freely down my cheeks. It was everything I ever wanted to hear him say. I looked into his eyes and made my move, leaning forward until our lips touched.

When our mouths met, it was like none of the last four years had happened. We fell immediately into the same familiar pattern of moving our lips together, his hand at the back of my neck, my hands rubbing his back.

This was how things should be. Everything felt right in the world as I kissed him. I could feel the love behind it, the delicate way his tongue slipped into my mouth, caressing me. I grew warm all over. I'd spent years wanting him and finally, there we were.

Our kissing grew more intense and I couldn't get close enough to him. I pressed my body against his, my arms squeezing tighter as he squeezed me back. I ran my fingers through the soft spikes of his hair, the texture coarse but soft, just like I remembered it. He smelled good, too. It was a different cologne than he'd worn in high school, but the smell of him made me wild. I wanted to devour him.

I felt myself getting lost in him, wanting to fully merge with him in every way. Wanting what we'd had before. It might have been young, high school sex, but we'd always enjoyed ourselves. He was a good lover, and I needed that. I needed him.

I ran my hands under his shirt and along his back. He was clammy with sweat and his skin felt as if it were almost on fire. Or was it my skin that was so hot? I couldn't tell anymore, but it was all I could do to keep from biting his neck when his fingers circled the back of mine. Chills ran through me everywhere he touched.

"Owen," I breathed in his ear, breaking our kiss for the first time. "I want you."

He made a growling sound and picked me up, wrapping my legs around his waist as he carried me inside. He lay me down on the couch and pulled off his shirt. I sucked in a breath and looked him over.

He was even more muscular than I'd thought. His biceps popped as he leaned over me, and his pecs stood out over his washboard abs. The hint of hair he'd had years ago had darkened and spread to accent his chest in all the right places. I liked the changes.

I pulled my own shirt off, letting him look all he wanted. He kissed down my neck to my chest, stopping to cup my bare breasts and take my nipples into his mouth. The feeling made me dizzy with desire, and I pressed my hips up against his.

He was hard and pushed back against me as he resumed kissing me. His hands made their way down my stomach, unzipping my jeans and sliding further down, rubbing me over my panties. I let out a low moan of pleasure; It was like torture to wait, so I reached down to unzip his jeans.

When I reached beneath his boxers to feel his warm, smooth hardness, he closed his eyes and sat up. I thought he was just moving to enjoy it more, but he stood and zipped his pants.

I was still breathing heavily, and now I was confused. I looked down at my half-naked body. Had I done something wrong?

He stood beside me and reached down to squeeze my hand. "I'm sorry. You should go."

"What?" I sat up and smoothed my hair down. "Is something wrong?"

"I can't do this, Addie. I'm sorry." He put his fist to his forehead and let out a frustrated growl. "I'm so, so sorry."

I picked up my shirt and pulled it on, stunned. I sat there on his couch, taking just a second to glance around. It was nice inside, too. Clean and orderly. But in that moment, I couldn't have cared less.

"I don't understand," I stammered, getting to my feet. I slipped back into my flip flops. "I mean. You said..." My hand extended toward the porch, indicating everything he'd told me before we started kissing.

"I know, and it's all true. But I can't be in your life. I'll complicate things. I...I just can't."

"Owen," I pleaded, "don't do this to me again. Please. I love you."

"I know," he whispered. "And you deserve better than what I can give you."

"How can you say something like that? After all this time. After the last few minutes? You said—"

"I'm sorry." He walked back out to the porch.

I sat for a moment, trying to stop my mind from spinning. I'd gone from being nervous to overjoyed, thinking I was about to have sex, to confused. And rejected. Again. How was this possible?

I collected myself and walked out on the porch to join him. "Maybe someday, you'll tell me the truth. Why you really ended things. Why you're doing this now. Because your old reasons don't make sense. I want to be with you, Owen. I love you. I've only ever loved you, and I can't picture myself with anyone else. If you don't want me, then okay. At least I know. We had a final...whatever that was, and okay. I'll leave you alone. I'll tell myself whatever I have to in order to get over you. Somehow."

He looked down at his hands. His voice was tight. "I hope you can."

So that was it. He had feelings for me. He regretted ending things. But he still didn't think he could be with me.

"You're wrong, you know." I walked down the porch steps and looked over at him one last time. "You think I deserve better than you, that somehow you can't give me everything I want. Well, all I want is you. So, you're wrong if you think somehow that's not enough for me. There is no one better than you. All of the disasters I've been involved in since you have proven that. I attract men who...are not you. You were the best thing that ever happened to me."

He walked inside and closed the front door softly. I stood there for a moment, but when it was clear he wasn't coming back outside, I got in the car and left. I had no idea what I would tell my friends; this was the opposite of closure. Maybe they'd have some insight to share, some glaring reason I couldn't see that would explain why he wouldn't be with me. I wiped the tears falling from my eyes as I drove back to the site.

10

OWEN

I HEARD MY PHONE BUZZ AND GROANED. I'D TOLD THEM ONLY TO TEXT IF there was an emergency—something no one else could handle—and now my phone was going off again. I didn't even bother to look at the screen. I reached my hand out from underneath my blankets and pushed my phone off my bedside table.

All day, it'd been the same.

"Just checking in." Ezra.

"Making sure you're still alive." Mason.

"Hey, the guys said you're sick or something? Won't get out of bed? Call me." Noah.

I'd heard from every member of my clan; the ones closest to me, more than once. I got that they were worried. But they didn't get that sometimes, even the Alpha needed a few days to himself. To drink himself into a stupor. To deeply regret all the decisions he'd ever made in his life. To stay in bed sleeping all day, if that's what he wanted to do.

The light outside my window told me it was nearly evening. Again. I wasn't even sure how many days it'd been anymore. I'd taken a few days off from work to stay away from Addie. I'd done the right thing. I hadn't gone to talk to her, using the Aiden thing as an excuse. But then she'd shown up. Checking on the ibis. Yeah. Good one. Okay, so she did have a degree in ecology and a genuine interest in animals and the environment, but who would drive over here just to check on a bird with a broken leg? *Addie would*, my mind answered. And Addie did. Even if she had other reasons to talk to me, she might have called for no other reason. That's just how she was. She was perfect.

I reached my hand out again, this time to grab the bottle. It was almost empty, but I swallowed the last bit of whiskey and sat up. I rubbed my eyes and let them adjust to the room. Clothing sat in piles on the floor. Empty beer bottles littered the side table, along with wrappers and boxes from take-out food and delivery. I picked up a half-eaten burger and sniffed it, then put it back in its wrapper.

That had been the one interruption I hadn't minded as much. Ezra and Mason had stopped by, which annoyed me, but they'd brought me a huge bag of greasy food. And they just left it when it was clear I didn't want to talk or run. I couldn't shift when I was like this; it would be too easy for them to pick up on everything I was feeling. I had to get control over myself before I could let them in like that.

I trudged to the kitchen, wondering what beer I had left and what food was in the freezer. My walkie, which sat on its base near where I kept my keys and jacket, crackled.

"Earth to Owen..." Ezra said.

I snatched the walkie off its base and held down the button. "Do not use work equipment for personal communication."

"Owen! This isn't, man. We need you."

I set the walkie back down and returned to the kitchen. They didn't need me. There were plenty of well-qualified rangers employed by the park. Any of them were more than capable of handling any situation that might arise. Tonight was the last night of Addie's reservation. I'd be back at work tomorrow, after check out time. After I was sure she was gone and I'd never see her again.

"Owen!"

I heard him all the way in the kitchen.

"I know I've been bugging you when you said not to, but this is an actual emergency!"

I shook my head. Like I hadn't heard that one at least twice over the last few days. It was an emergency that no one could find Conner—until they'd realized he'd left his phone at home. It was an emergency when a fellow ranger called out sick, leaving a gap in the schedule. Until they'd called another senior ranger and got him to cover. Whatever "emergency" it was this time, they could figure it out without me.

I snapped open the top of a fresh can of beer and took a gulp. I had just enough beer and alcohol to get me through one more night before I needed to restock. If it was already getting dark outside, then I was already behind schedule. I took another long sip.

I heard the car door first. Cursing under my breath, I went to look out the window. *Ezra.* Did he never learn? Maybe it was time to get a new second. Mason could be moved up in the ranks; that might not be a bad idea.

I made him pound on my door for several minutes before I finally opened it. "If someone isn't dead or actively dying, you are turning around immediately and leaving."

Ezra hesitated. "Even if it involves Addie?"

"*Especially* if it involves her." I couldn't even say her name out loud. It'd been the only word I'd been thinking for days.

"Okay…" Ezra turned on his heel and took a few steps away.

He knew me too well. "What?"

He shrugged and didn't turn back. "I thought you might want to know about this, but you're right. I'll get someone else to handle it. Have a good night."

I narrowed my eyes and watched him get in his car. What was this game he was playing? I didn't want to give in, but if there was some kind of emergency with Addie, I did want to know, despite what I said.

"Ezra!"

He rolled the window down and stuck his head out. "Yeah?"

"What's going on with Addie?"

He gave me a smug smile before getting back out of the car. "Well, it's not directly about her, exactly."

I gave him the finger and turned away, slamming the door shut behind me.

"There's been an attack!" He shouted through the door. "I saw croc tracks. Got a turtle nest. Horrible damage. Killed a mother and destroyed her eggs."

Okay, this sort of thing happened. It angered me, sure. The crocs knew better and this was a serious crime. I'd be calling the conclave if it was found to be true that the crocs had done it. But it wasn't exactly an emergency if the turtle nest was already destroyed. If any turtles had been alive, the emergency would have been getting them to the vet, and he'd made no mention of that. So, what did it have to do with Addie?

"Not hearing any sort of emergency," I said. "And you've been demoted. Tell Mason he's my new second."

"Hey! I'm just doing my job here, man! But fine, whatever. Maybe I don't want to serve an Alpha who's such a heartless jerk."

I rolled my eyes.

"Well, anyway," he said, undeterred. "I thought you'd want to know since there was a word written in the mud near the nest. A name. After all that's happened, I wouldn't just ignore it."

"A name?"

"Addie. Whoever did it wrote 'Addie' in the mud near the nest. We don't know if they were trying to set it up to make it look like she did it. I mean, it's pretty stupid if they were because obviously, there are crocodile tracks and who would write their name where they committed a crime? Most of us think it's a threat. To you."

He waited, then continued when I didn't say anything. "We also got a call from the conclave. The crocs are complaining that bears are coming on their land. Named you, specifically."

Of course. When I'd gone to the party, I hadn't been careful. I'd gotten close and they'd picked up on my scent. But crocs went places they weren't meant to and we went places we shouldn't all the time. No one ever bothered to say anything unless something happened. Nothing happened when I went to the party except I saw Aiden and Addie together. Maybe her rejecting him pissed him off and somehow, they connected her to me. If they'd been asking her about me, then there was some connection happening.

I pulled open the door. "Show me."

Ezra nodded and pulled off his shirt. We shifted and ran through the woods. Almost the moment I changed, there was clatter in my head.

Owen! How are you? Hailey.

Glad you're back, man. Mason.

Me too, Conner chimed in. *Ezra can't run this clan. Don't ever die.*

Hey! I'm here, too! Ezra added.

I'm only here to check on the situation, I thought back to them.

Let me know if you want help. Mason again. Good guy. He made a good third.

Ezra led me to the site of the attack. Sea turtles were highly protected in the park; all animals were protected, of course, but some who were close to being on the endangered list were protected differently. In this case, no one was allowed to disturb a sea turtle in any way. All the clans in the area knew this. This was a blatant attack, and a horrible sight.

Sea turtles made what we called a nest, but was really just a hole in the muddy sand near the water. They dug the hole, the females laid their eggs, and they stayed to incubate them until the eggs hatched. Whoever made this attack killed the mother turtle, smashed and feasted on the eggs, and left the hole of the nest decimated. And, just like Ezra had claimed, near the nest in the mud was written "Addie," deliberately surrounded by crocodile tracks. It had to be shifters who did this.

I'm going to kill that asshole, I thought. *Has anyone called the conclave yet? This is a punishable crime.*

Not yet, Ezra thought to me. *We were waiting for you. We thought it'd be better if you contacted them.*

He was right. It was part of an Alpha's duty to do those sorts of things.

Maybe in this case, seeing as how it's so personal and all, I'll just handle things on my own, I said.

On your own, with me to help, Ezra corrected.

No. Stand by, but I'm going to find that jerk. He wants a piece of me? He wants to taunt me like this? Then I'm going to take care of it myself.

I took off running back to my cabin. I could feel that Ezra was following me. I could feel the questions coming from the linked minds of the clan and Ezra's gently urging of them to wait. Fine. He could take care of the clan.

And I'd take care of that asshole, Aiden, once and for all.

I dressed, put my gun in its holster at my side and slid my knife into the top of my boot. Then, I got in my car, took a moment to pound on the steering wheel to release my anger, and took off. Wearing only his shorts, Ezra stood on my porch and watched me leave. He'd probably follow me; a good second would. I wouldn't stop him, but I also wasn't going to get him involved in this fight. This was between me and Aiden, and it would be coming to an end that night.

I drove to the bar where Ezra, Mason and Conner had encountered the crocs many nights back. When I didn't see Aiden, I asked around. How convenient that no one knew where he was. I then drove over to the airboat dock and had much better luck. As I pulled up, I saw Aiden walk toward the building.

It seemed that their tours were over for the day. I guessed it was hard to convince people they were seeing a rare sight if it was too dark to actually see. Night hadn't quite fallen, but it was close.

I slammed my door shut, which made him look my way. Aiden paused with his hand on the door, watching me.

"We need to talk," I said.

He laughed. "Oh, do we?"

"Was it you?"

"You're going to have to be a little more specific if you're going to accuse me of something." He took his hand off the door and crossed his arms as he turned to face me.

"Did you come into the park and destroy a sea turtle nest?"

He put his hand to his chest and made a shocked face. "Why in the world would I do a horrible thing like that? They're protected, you know."

"To get back at me?"

"I'm sorry." He laughed. "I don't even know your name. I'm Aiden Harvey. Nice to meet you." He stuck out his hand as if I were actually going to shake it.

"Cut the shit, Harvey. You wrote Addie's name by the nest. You asked her about me. What exactly is the problem? Aside from you being a sketchy croc."

"Hey now," he said. "Let's not go calling people names. I'm sorry your little turtles had their nest destroyed. I truly, truly am. Wish I could get a sea turtle to stay over here where my adoring customers could appreciate it for all its glory. But you know, they just won't nest here. Funny thing."

"Maybe it's because your operation is a big scam. I'm surprised you don't have a sculpture of a sea turtle to go with your 'baby gator.'" I made air quotes around the phrase.

"Well, now." He shook his head. "I didn't want to believe it when people told me you were a jerk. But coming over like this, calling me names, accusing me of things? That just won't do. I never did a thing to you. I'm sure the conclave wouldn't be happy to hear that you came over here, ready to attack me for some little grudge you're holding on to."

"I am going to say this one time, Harvey." I was close enough to poke his chest, hard. "Stay off the park land. Stay away from those turtles. And most of all, stay far, far away from Addie. Do you understand me?"

He smirked and took a step back. "Oh sure. I understand you're a sorry excuse for an Alpha. I understand that the conclave will be surprised by your actions here tonight."

"You want to call the conclave? Go right ahead. You should know, they take attacks on protected species much more seriously than anything you'll try to tell them about me."

Aiden glared. "You have yourself a good night and just remember, I didn't attack you."

"Am I supposed to be thankful for that?"

"One day, the bears will not run this park, you mark my words. The crocs will. And when that day comes, your ass is mine, Bailey. You just remember this moment as the moment you screwed over your whole clan. And Addie? She'll see the truth, and she'll come around. Then she'll be mine. All you have will be mine."

I shook my head and gave him the finger, then got back in my car and sped off.

11

OWEN

When I got back home, Ezra had left. If he'd followed me, I hadn't seen him. I slammed the door shut behind me and stripped off my clothes. I grabbed a fresh beer from the fridge and carried it into my room, drinking half of it before sliding under the covers and going back to sleep.

Apparently, sleep was not something I'd be enjoying tonight; the pounding on my door was incessant. I dug my phone out of the pile of clothing and glanced at the time. It was late, almost midnight, and I had many missed calls and unseen texts.

As I pulled myself out of bed, I heard someone come around to my bedroom side of the cabin and knock on the window.

"Owen, come out! It's Addie!" Ezra shouted with his hands cupped to his mouth.

I growled and stormed over to the window, pushing it up with a loud bang. "What the fuck are you doing?"

"Dude, this time it's serious. You've gotta get over to her tent. The crocs..." He stopped to breathe, putting his hands on his knees like he'd been running. "The crocs are up to something. I think she's in danger."

I was ready to rip him a new one until he said "Addie" and "danger" in the same sentence.

I slammed the window shut and hurried out the door. I was already undressed, so I jumped from my porch, shifting in mid-air. As soon as my paws hit the ground, I was running.

Ezra caught up quickly. *One of the crocs called Mason. Told him that something was going down. Named you and Addie.*

No one went to check on her?

I came to you first. We thought you'd want to take care of it personally.

Right. Thanks.

The distance passed quickly. I ran hard, not caring if I lost Ezra or not. I would take this guy down all alone if that's what it came to. And I wasn't worried about losing the fight. Aiden had nothing on me and my rage where Addie was concerned.

I saw her tent in the distance as we neared the camping area, and then, I smelled them. There had to be several crocs in the area. I slowed and made sure Ezra caught a whiff of them, too.

Stinks, he said.

On alert, I signaled to my clan, *we may need backup.*

I heard several confirmations in my mind as others shifted and headed our way. I wasn't worried about losing a fight between Aiden and me. But I was worried that if there were a lot of crocs, I wouldn't be able to protect Addie well enough.

They must've heard and smelled us. The crocs moved as we closed in.

From what I could see, there had to be at least ten of them surrounding Addie's tent. I didn't see her or her friends; hopefully, they were sleeping soundly and had no idea any of this was going on. I did see the car Addie had driven over to my cabin. Damn, I wished they'd chosen to stay out late that night.

I heard a rustling behind us, and when I turned my head, I smelled the crocs more sharply. They had us surrounded along with Addie and her friends.

I'm going to shift back to talk to them, I signaled to my second in command.

Ezra stayed at my side in bear form. He would need to communicate with the clan, and I needed him to be a second ahead of me if something went down. It didn't take long to shift, but it was long enough when teeth and claws were coming at you.

I shifted to human form and stood tall. "Aiden, I assume?"

I watched the crocs, waiting. I ignored the fact that I was naked and standing in the park surrounded by crocodiles. It was a bad position to be in, but I couldn't show any hint of fear or worry.

As I watched, one of the crocs whipped its tail, then shifted into human form. It was Aiden.

"We meet again," he said.

"You want to tell me what all this is about?"

"It's about time, Owen. That's what this is about."

I glared at him and balled my hands into fists at my sides. At least I knew that neither of us had traditional weapons. We were both stark naked in the moonlight.

"The crocs have lived under bear rule for long enough," Aiden said. "We're sick of it. You all think you run this whole area. You show up at our bars, you take our women, you try to control us, to keep us out. You're affecting our business. We all just want to make a decent living, and yet, you and your bears won't allow it. I don't think we're asking too much."

The crocs around him hissed in agreement. Ezra let out a low rumble of a growl.

"The only problem is," I started, "you think you own the bars that we all go to. You think you own some female that my bear hooked up with? Well, I guess she made her choice, didn't she? And she saw that bears are the better option. We're not in the way of your business, if you can call it that. I don't like people getting scammed, and that's all you do. But still, we've had a peaceful existence here, both of us living in the area. Well, that was until you killed a member of an endangered species and her nest for no reason. Until you got Addie involved in this mess. She has nothing to do with any of this."

"Oh, yes she does." His mouth stretched into a broad, toothy smile. "She's our ticket to getting you to cooperate. You should know that right now, I have my entire clan of crocs surrounding her tent. It will take only seconds for them to move in, tear it down and devour her and her friends. Unless, of course, you want to give up your territory. Give up control of the park and let us run things. Then, your precious girl will be left untouched."

"I'm not giving anything to you."

"Then we have no choice."

Aiden raised his fist in the air. He watched me, giving me every chance to change my mind. When his fingers started to open, I shouted to my clan, *Now!*

12

ADDIE

At first, there was just a rustling sound. I groaned. Had we left the trash or some food out for a raccoon to get into? I didn't worry about animal attacks, especially not from such a small animal, but I didn't want our things to be destroyed. And I'd hate to think we'd attracted bears or something big to the area where other people might be endangered.

I felt around for the flashlight. When I couldn't find it, I crept to the edge of the tent.

"What's going on?" Emma asked, half awake.

"Might be a raccoon outside. I'm going to check."

"You're crazy," she mumbled, then fell back asleep.

The rustling had become louder in the time it took me to move closer to the tent door. I thought I heard voices, too. Maybe campers were setting up a tent nearby. Or someone out hiking had gotten lost.

I peeled down enough of the zipper to peek out, just a tiny bit since I didn't know what awaited us. If it were something big, like a bear, that would require different actions on my part versus a raccoon. And if there were people out there...

I grabbed my knife and stuck it in my sock. When I pulled down the flap, I squinted in the darkness. Then I saw eyes. Many eyes.

Everywhere I looked, I saw crocodiles. I sat back down, my mind spinning. This was not right. Crocodiles didn't group like this. They didn't move into areas and surround people.

I heard the voices again. Were people out there with all these crocs? My heart raced as I peeled the tent flap back again. There was one voice I'd know anywhere. I'd spent years listening to it and years thinking of it. Owen's voice spoke into the night.

I couldn't make out what was being said, but he didn't sound happy. Someone else was with him, someone he was arguing with.

"What are you doing?" Julie asked.

"Stay here. Something's going on."

"Don't go out there!" she insisted.

"No, it's okay. It's...Owen."

"Oh." She fell back down on her sleeping bag. "Have fun."

I'd been sleeping in sweatpants and a t-shirt. My flip flops sat right by the door and I quietly moved to slide my feet into them. Then, I unzipped the door even more, going very slowly. I didn't want to wake Emma and Julie again, and I didn't want to alert these crocs that I was here and awake.

As I stepped out of the tent, many scaly heads turned my way. I couldn't count all the crocs surrounding me. My heart raced. What was going on? What would make them act this way?

Then, two men turned to face me, Owen and Aiden. What the hell?

"Owen?"

He looked terrified. Then I noticed that he was naked. And so was Aiden.

In that second, something clicked in my mind. I drew in a slow, deep breath, letting my instincts do their thing. I'd been stupid before. I hadn't noticed. How could I not have noticed what was going on with Aiden?

Everything made sense now—well, not everything. But one thing was for certain: Owen and I were in a bad position. I didn't know if I could protect us both. I knew I could take down many of the crocs myself, but I didn't know if it would be enough.

Owen didn't make sense to me at all in this moment. Why was he naked? He couldn't be part of this. I'd offended Aiden, that was clear. Maybe he and Owen had had words after I talked with Owen and they were coming to confront me.

Aiden held out his arm to me, smiling. "Here she is."

I glared at him. I looked at Owen for some explanation of what was going on. He mouthed, "Run!"

I had a decision to make, and many things ran through my mind in that split second. Several sides to consider, several people I might anger, depending on how I chose. Several lives I might endanger.

I could do as Owen said and run. That would leave him there to fight the crocs and would leave my friends in peril. If I followed my instincts, I could protect everyone—or try—but I would risk something much bigger falling apart.

I looked at Owen's face, stretched in terror, and made my choice.

I threw myself forward, toward the ground. Before my hands landed palms down in the dirt, everything changed. My spine expanded, my limbs twisted, hair sprouted, and I stood tall, not roaring, though I wanted to. I didn't want to wake my friends or scare anyone.

And I was most definitely scary in bear form.

I leapt at Aiden. My hind feet hadn't hit the ground yet by the time he shifted. A dirty croc; I'd missed the scent. I must've attributed it to him always being on the boat and around all sorts of water animals. I was so new to this life, and much of it overwhelmed me. I thought I was better at recognizing fellow shifters, and I knew the members of my clan well, but when it came to other shifters, especially of another species, I'd missed it.

Aiden probably hadn't, though. He must've known from the start that I was a shifter. That's why he'd chosen me over my friends. He could sense the animal in me.

I spun and swatted at Aiden. No time to regret my lack of skills now; there was a fight. I didn't know what it was about, but I wasn't about to let Owen get injured by these crocs or because of me. He knew nothing of this life. I might have just endangered him by shifting in front of him. At least Aiden had, too. It wasn't only on me.

Aiden ducked my swat and his tail came flying around him, whacking me in the side with a hard thump, and I let out a whimper. Behind me, a sudden, mighty roar rent the air.

My head snapped to the bear standing behind me; the bear that had been where Owen was a moment before. For a wild instant, I thought the bear had attacked Owen. He was nowhere in sight. Then, I took a long sniff in his direction.

No. My mind seized and my body froze. Owen. Owen *was* the bear. The bear was Owen. Owen was...a shifter? Like me? We were both bears?

It took me too long to recover. In my shock, Aiden jumped on me. I felt his hard scales pressing against me, his teeth at my neck. I stood, and my height alone gave me an advantage against the smaller creature. With my claws extended, I swatted and caught his underbelly. Owen jumped at him, knocking him off me, and Aiden landed with a whine.

But he wasn't the only croc attacking. The others converged, snapping their jaws and swatting their tails. Owen moved in front of me, protecting me. I wanted to cry, but I turned my back to him, pressed against him, and faced the danger from behind. Back to back, we fought.

I swatted at a croc who advanced. I heard Owen whimper and gashed my claws across the croc's side. The croc let his jaw open and tried to bite Owen's foot instead. I reached to claw the croc again and felt teeth at my own foot.

Then I heard two screams. Emma and Julie were awake.

After the screams, I heard roars. I allowed one second's look away from the fight and saw a group of bears bounding toward us.

Owen stood tall and pounded his chest, and the bears immediately fell in line around us, forming a circle with me at the center.

I felt helpless watching them. I tried to move to the edge to help, but each time, a bear moved me back. They fought hard, and all the while, I kept my eyes on Owen. Even if they wouldn't let me fight, I wasn't going to just sit back and watch. I fought my protectors, punching through their legs and reaching past them to claw a croc.

Owen still fought Aiden. Right then, Aiden's scent was clear as day to me, and I kept my gaze on him. Owen had injured him; I saw him bleeding and he began to limp. But Owen had been injured, too, bleeding from a wound on his back.

I didn't hear any more screaming, and I hoped that Emma and Julie were okay. I couldn't get to them, nor could I see them. Their scent lingered in the air. I didn't pick up a hint of extreme fear or sweat, like they were running or fighting, but I didn't know for certain if they were okay.

I let out a small whine and craned my head toward them, trying to see. I didn't know how to communicate with bears like this. My clan was linked through thought when we shifted. But I couldn't hear Owen or his friends.

I hoped they would understand what I wanted. When I made a move to try to break out of my circle of protection, to go to my friends, they blocked my way.

I heard Emma call my name; she sounded terrified. Owen and I both looked in her direction when she called for me, and it was just enough for Aiden to pounce and get his teeth on Owen's neck.

The rage in me lit up. Not this asshole; he wasn't going to kill the man I loved. I jumped more highly than I'd ever jumped in my life, sailing over Owen's shoulder. I knocked him down with me as I hit the ground.

The three of us landed in a heap and I brought my claws down hard. I swiped a gash in Aiden's stomach and he let go of his hold on Owen. I could have let it go at that, but I didn't. I let loose, slashing and clawing at Aiden until he stopped moving.

I put my head near his; I couldn't tell if it was just my heavy breathing or if he still lived. I wanted certainty, so I drove my claws into his chest and pulled down, tearing him open. When I moved back, my paws covered in croc blood, he was still.

The crocs around me chomped. Owen picked up Aiden's lifeless body with one paw and held it high, and the bears roared together and lunged. A split second later, the crocs took off running.

As they ran, the bears chased them, but Owen stepped in front of me to stop me from following them. I looked back and saw that we were alone.

"Addie? Where are you?" Julie sounded as scared as Emma had.

I whined again and lurched toward them. Owen stepped in front of me again, running his nose along my neck and nuzzled into me. He circled me, sniffing. Where he found blood, he licked the wound clean. Then, he started licking me all over. From head to paws, he groomed me.

I stood very still, the shock of the event washing over me as I forced my brain to catch up and realize what was going on. Owen, in bear form, was grooming me, in bear form. It was unreal.

I put my head down into my paws; I needed the forest to stop spinning around me. I stumbled over to a tree and threw up for the first time in bear form. Although it was less violent and disgusting than doing so as a human, it was still a strange sensation.

Owen put his bear arms around me and pulled me close to him, his hair enveloping me in warmth. It was even better than a human hug with sharp joints and smooth skin. This was like falling into a huge, cuddly teddy bear of warmth and happiness, and I let my eyes close and didn't move.

13

OWEN

Got him!

Over here!

One more down.

I listened to their fight from a distance. They were doing fine; they didn't need me. More than that, they knew better. They knew I wouldn't leave Addie.

They'd all been there, linked to my mind the moment I'd seen it, and the shock crashed over me like a wave. They said plenty when it happened, but I didn't hear a word of it. My ears were ringing.

When Addie shifted into a bear, my entire world turned upside down. Nothing was what it should have been; I was suddenly in a dream. I thought they'd killed me so quickly, my brain hadn't caught up yet. I thought anything except that what I saw was real.

Ezra, thank god, had snapped me out of it. He'd said something like, "Dude, you're an idiot." The insult had made me see it. All this time, Addie had been a shifter and I hadn't known? Yeah, I was most definitely an idiot.

As the fight moved and I was left there alone with Addie, the thoughts started to sort themselves out in my mind. How in the world could I have missed this? I took a long sniff of her. Usually, I could tell in an instant when another shifter was near. No matter if it was one of my clan, another bear, or any other shifter species. There was a certain scent that came with shifters. A sort of animal smell, but different: clean and subtler than a wild animal.

Addie's scent was too familiar; that was the only thing that made sense to me. When I'd first become old enough to shift for the first time, when I'd learned about the shifter life and all that came with it, when I trained and learned what smells were what...all of that had happened when I was already with Addie. Whatever scent she had was something my nose had bypassed. Her deep spice was more like the smell of love to me. The scent of...my mate.

When we'd had sex in the past and the animal was stronger in the air from our sweat, I'd always thought it was me. God, I'd been so stupid. I was too new at it all to pick up the difference in the smell. I'd been too embarrassed, rushing to put on deodorant or take a shower, that I'd never stopped to really smell the scent and learn it and recognize it.

Even after spending so much time apart, she smelled the same to me when I saw her again. That hint of animal that I picked up on her, I'd mistaken for pure lust. Nothing more. I almost laughed at myself, thinking back on it. I thought she wanted me so badly that her lust smelled that attractive to me.

I sniffed every inch of her now, programming my mind to associate this scent I knew so well with a bear. To relearn what I knew of her body. When I put my nose to her neck and inhaled, at first, my bear brain said, "Want." My body reacted in a lustful way. It was no wonder I'd thought that was all it was. But I forced myself to look at her, to feel her hair, and to keep smelling until my brain corrected itself.

Now, I smelled her sweat. Her bear sweat on her bear skin under her bear hair. And her human was there, underneath it, taking the more subtle place while in this form. I smelled the blood and dirt and cleaned her. I sniffed until I knew every inch of her in this way.

It's over, Ezra reported. *They all took off.*

My clan returned to where we sat.

Emma and Julie are fine. I'd had Hailey watching them the whole time. *Freaked out about the bears and because they can't find Addie, but they're unharmed.*

Thank you, all, I said. *I...*

We know. Ezra sent a wave of warm thoughts to me.

They were all happy, but surprised, to say the least. Everyone was still charged from the fight, but we'd won. The crocs had taken off and none of my guys had been injured too badly; the only one dead was Aiden. The conclave would get a full report and there would be an investigation. There was much to be done, but I wasn't going to be a part of any of it.

Let me know if you need me. I'll...be a while.

One by one, they sent me their congratulations. They'd witnessed too much of my despair over the last week to not understand what this moment meant to me.

I shifted back to human form slowly. For a moment, I held Addie, still in bear form, and then she shifted back, awkwardly sitting in my lap. We were both naked.

I pulled her close and hugged her tightly, letting the tears flow down my cheeks. The complete relief of it all washed over me and I kissed her. I kissed her and didn't want to ever stop.

I was vaguely aware of the bears leaving. Not long after I shifted back, they started to drop off, returning home and back to whatever they were doing before I'd called them.

She cried, too and returned my kiss.

"Your friends are worried about you," I said after a long while.

I hadn't let her go to them before. It wasn't safe, but now, they needed to know their friend was alright. If for no other reason than if they called the ranger station, someone would come out, and things would get complicated.

"My clothes..." She'd torn everything when she shifted.

"They don't know?"

She shook her head.

"Give me a minute." I shifted back and called to Hailey in my mind, who responded quickly, so I shifted back and waited. A few minutes later, Hailey came walking out of the woods, a tote bag between her jaws. She dropped the bag and took off running back into the woods.

"It's convenient having a clan near you," Addie said, pulling the clothing over her human form.

I had so many questions. So much to say. "Addie." I reached up to take her hand. "I love you."

She smiled and got to her feet. “I'll be right back.”

I sat naked in the dark for a long time, alone with my thoughts and feelings. I'd lost track of how long she was gone for, but when I heard rustling and smelled her—that scent that was more real to me now than my own—a smile took over my face and my heart flooded with joy.

14

ADDIE

Julie and Emma were in a state when I found them. They'd seen animals all around and couldn't find me. They knew I'd gone out into the night to see what was out there.

"We thought you were eaten by a bear!" Emma exclaimed.

"I'm fine. I'm sorry you were worried."

"You could have at least said you were going to find someone," Julie said.

"I thought you were still sleeping. I wasn't going to wake you up just to tell you I was going to call the ranger."

"Well, leave a note next time!" Emma snapped.

"Or at least take your phone." Julie held my cell out to me. "Why didn't you just call the ranger?"

I shrugged. "I was half asleep and saw a croc. I didn't think much about it and just ran. I guess I thought it would come at me?"

I tried to get them settled as quickly as possible. All I could think about was Owen alone in the woods, naked, waiting for me. Finally, I decided to play the one card they wouldn't argue with.

"The thing is," I said. "I wanted an excuse to find Owen. And I found him. He wants to talk."

They looked at me with surprise.

"Where is he?" Julie asked.

"Back at the station. He had to make some calls or something. But he asked me to come back to talk to him."

"You sure that's a good idea after the last talk you had?" Julie arched an eyebrow.

"I don't know," I admitted. "Maybe it was because of that that he wants to talk."

"Well, give me the full report in the morning." Emma slid down into her sleeping bag. "I'm not waiting up."

Julie slid back into her bag, too. "Take your phone this time. Please. Call if anything happens. I don't want to wake up and find you dead because you got mauled in the night by bears or crocs or any other animal out there."

"I will." I made a show of putting my phone in one pocket and my knife in another. "I'll be with a ranger. There's not much better protection than that."

A ranger who also happened to be a *bear shifter*.

As I exited the tent, I pulled my blanket out with me; better than sitting on the cold ground naked. If I had any clothes that would fit him, I'd bring them, but he was far too muscular for my shirts or close-fitting sweatpants.

I walked back to where I'd left him in the dark, spread out the blanket, then sat. He crawled onto it to join me.

"Sorry about this." He gestured to his nakedness.

"That's something you should never apologize for."

He chuckled. "It's just awkward. I feel exposed."

I picked up the end of the blanket and covered him as much as possible. He pulled me back into his lap. Now I felt a little awkward. I was dressed, though not in my clothes, and he had only the blanket.

"So, Owen," I said in a forced conversational tone. "I may not have told you, since I'm bound by secret and all—but I'm a shifter. I can turn into a bear at will or in the full moonlight. What hobbies and interests do you have?"

We both laughed and he shook his head. "How is this possible?"

"I've been asking myself that question since the first time I shifted."

"When? How? I mean...I had no idea. And that's absurd. I'm an Alpha, for god's sake. I'm such an idiot."

"Ha," I said. "You think you're an idiot? I was a shifter for twenty years and didn't even know it!"

"What do you mean?"

"My parents? They're not actually my parents."

He sucked in a breath.

"You remember how I'd always say I felt like I didn't belong in my family? There was a reason for that. I was adopted. My parents are actually distant relatives of mine. My real parents died when I was just a baby, and they were both shifters. But my second cousin, who raised me as her daughter, was not a shifter and knew nothing about it. I was obviously a late bloomer, and I was in college the first time it happened. There was a party, kind of like the one Aiden invited us to. Outside, you know? And it was the night of the full moon."

"Ohh," Owen said.

"Yeah." I laughed. "So, we were at this party and it was in the woods. It would have been fine if I'd known I was a shifter at the time since there was lots of cover, but I didn't; it was the first change since my birth shift. When I stepped into the moonlight, I felt the pull. And let me just say that from what I've heard from others, shifting for the first time under full moonlight is not the best way to go about it."

"I'd say not."

"Now, I've shifted enough that it doesn't hurt me. But you remember those first shifts?"

"I was just a kid when I began to change. It was hard the whole first year, but when I started shifting regularly, yeah, it wasn't so bad anymore. I'm surprised you didn't shift by accident while you were growing up, though. That happens fairly often during times of extreme emotional distress."

"Well, I wasn't old enough to remember losing my parents. So, that night, I obviously didn't know what was happening. I thought I was sick or had been drugged; at a party like that, it wasn't the craziest thought. Being drugged seemed much more feasible than the fact that I was turning into a freaking bear. So, I kinda flipped out. I thought I was hallucinating. I started running, and I ran far. Luckily, another bear had witnessed the whole thing go down and followed me. When he realized what was happening, he stayed with me and got me calmed enough to shift back when the morning came.

"He was an Alpha. I joined his pack and he and his wife looked out for me. They were like my shifter adopted parents, teaching me everything. It was a hard time. Luckily, the guy I was dating had broken up with me just days before that, so I used heartbreak as an excuse to be hiding out all the time. I was lonely, but my new pack helped a lot. Only problem was, they all lived about an hour and a half away, on the western side of the state."

"You don't live near your clan?"

I shook my head.

"Addie, we're not meant to be lone bears. We're meant to live with our clans. In some areas, they live together in a big compound or a shared house, if it's a smaller clan."

"I don't know of any near me. And I like my clan. They were there for me when I needed them."

"I'm glad for that," he said. "I really am, but you're making things harder on yourself than they should be."

I shrugged. "It's okay. I don't go out when it's a full moon and I don't shift often. It's better for me to just pretend like that part of me doesn't exist. With the whole secret thing, it makes it easier, too. Sometimes, like tonight, it comes in handy. It did feel good to shift. I think it's been about six months since I have."

"You haven't shifted in six months?"

"Nope."

He blinked at me in shock. "I didn't even know that was possible."

"Really?"

"The instinct is so strong."

"I guess mine isn't."

"That might explain some things. Like why I didn't pick up on your shifter scent. Why you didn't pick up on mine."

I covered my face with my hand. "I thought you changed colognes."

"You have a good excuse—you're new and mostly alone. But I don't. I thought it was just lust. The best I can come up with is that we'd already been together so long when I came of age that I was too accustomed to your scent. And if you didn't know you were a shifter and had never shifted, I guess that's why my parents didn't pick up on it, either."

"We're a lot less rare than I thought," I joked.

"You're telling me." He nuzzled his nose into my neck, taking in a long inhale. "How could I have missed it? I'm such an idiot. God! I'm such an idiot!"

"It's okay. I mean, yeah it would have been better if you'd been the one to tell me and had been there in the beginning, but it's okay. I figured it out. I'm okay now. I know how to handle it better."

"No, Addie, you don't get it." He put his fist to his forehead and growled. "I can't believe this!"

"What's wrong? It's not that big of a deal, is it? I mean, I can see you being freaked out if I were a shifter and you knew nothing of this life, but you are, too. I don't see how—"

"Adeline."

I closed my mouth and looked at him expectantly.

"Our clan believes that Alphas should only marry shifters. They want to keep the leadership pure to preserve our lineage. No second will be promoted if he's married to a non-shifter and Alphas are forced to step down if they take a non-shifter wife."

I scrunched up my face in confusion.

"Addie." He put a hand on either side of my face. "My dad was the Alpha; that means I've always been in line to be Alpha. I took over for him when I finished college, and I've always believed that I had to fulfill my duty as his son. I hated the rule. I nearly left my family and my clan because of it. Addie, the only reason I ended things with you was because you weren't a shifter, and I had to marry a shifter if I was going to fulfill my duty."

His words sunk into my mind slowly. I didn't want to get excited. I didn't want to get my hopes up. I'd just done that and it had ended terribly.

"So... you're saying..."

He let out a laugh and kissed me hard. "I'm saying, I love you. Marry me?"

"What?" I laughed, too. I clearly hadn't heard him right.

"Marry me. Please. Please marry me. Be my wife. I can't live another day without you."

I shook my head. "No, you're... this isn't right."

"What?" His face fell. "What do you mean?"

"You can't be proposing to me. You just ended things again. You just broke my heart again."

"It was only because of the shifter thing. That was it. I've wanted you so badly this whole time. I've missed you. Ask my clan how much of a wreck I was after you came by to see me and I had to send you off. I thought about leaving again. I was ready to give up everything for you."

I spoke slowly to make sure I didn't miss anything. "So, let me get this straight. You're telling me that the only reason you broke up with me in high school is because you thought I wasn't a shifter?"

"No. It's because I thought you weren't a shifter, *and* I knew I had to marry a shifter. I could have kept dating you, I guess, but I could never marry you, and I didn't want you to go through that. We talked about marriage. I even had a ring picked out. I knew how I was going to propose and everything."

"And the other day when I came to see you?"

"Same thing. There was no way I could see you and never marry you. Or be with you for any length of time and not tell you my secret. I had no choice but to send you away again."

"That's the only reason?"

"That's the only reason." He stood and I was reminded of his nakedness. "Come for a run with me."

"I don't have my sneakers or running—"

"Not as a human."

"Oh." I stood up and took off Hailey's clothes, setting them in the center of the blanket.

We both shifted and took a moment to rub against each other before taking off on the run. I followed him, partly because I had no idea where we were going, and also, because he was much faster than me. We ran until we came to a long, wooden bridge.

He shifted back and took my hand, leading me to the center of the bridge. "This isn't exactly how I pictured it. I mean, I thought we'd at least be wearing clothing. And I planned to have a ring."

He turned toward the water and stretched out his arm. "This bridge looks out over two bodies of water. If you look to one side, it's like our past, stretched out long behind us. But on the other side is our future. Wide open. Full of possibilities. Going on and on forever, into eternity."

He got down on one knee and took my hands.

"I should have said this to you long ago, Addie. I love you. I've had to live without you for too many years now, and I don't want to spend another day without you. Will you marry me? Be my mate in every way, for the rest of our lives?"

I blinked in shock, then sputtered, "Yes!"

15

ADDIE

OWEN LAID ME DOWN ON THE BLANKET AND SLID INTO PLACE BESIDE ME. He'd carried me for what had to be over a mile, back to this place. He said he didn't want to waste one moment in bear form not seeing my face.

I didn't care if he was a bear or human, it just felt good to be close to him. As the hour grew later and the adrenaline faded, I felt tired. I curled into him, enjoying his warmth. Now that things had settled, another thought plagued my mind.

I hadn't let myself really think much about it, but now it's all I could think of. "What will happen to me?"

"What do you mean?" he asked.

"I killed someone. I killed Aiden. Won't I go to jail?"

"Don't worry about that." He tucked a strand of hair behind my ear and rubbed my arm.

"How can I not worry about it?"

"The rules are different for us. I don't know how it is in your clan's area, but here, animal on animal violence is a way of life. If you'd killed him as a human, you'd have to face the police. But you were in bear form. You'll talk to the conclave. They'll investigate, but with so many witnesses, not one of them would say you were in the wrong. You defended yourself. You defended a fellow bear. If we were in the same clan, it would be even more explainable. I think our history, though, will accomplish the same thing when it comes down to it."

"Accomplish what?"

"We have the conclave for a reason. It's a group of shifters who understand what it's like to be a shifter. When we're in animal form, our instincts are different. The instinct to protect and defend rises higher than when we're in human form. We're still responsible for our actions, but even if we'd all been human in that situation, you still acted in self defense. You'll be fine, I promise. And if the police come knocking, we'll bear up and never change back."

"Really?"

"Yes, but that won't happen. Besides, we have shifters on the police force and in other government agencies who make sure shifter law is carried out in questionable situations."

"We do?" I asked.

"If you lived close enough to be with your clan all the time, you'd know these things."

"I never thought it was that big of a deal."

"So, changing clans won't be difficult, Addie?"

"Changing clans?"

"When we get married, your human form will take my last name, but your bear form will take my clan."

"Oh." There was so much of this world I still didn't understand.

"Sometimes it's a very difficult transition for females. Clan loyalty is very intense, and when someone grows up in one clan, it can be very difficult to leave them."

"I'm not happy to be leaving them. They were there for me when no one else was. But I'm happy to be joining your clan, if that's how it works. They helped us. They fought with us and protected me and my friends. I don't take that lightly. And if this is part of shifter life, then my clan will understand."

"Good." He kissed my forehead. "I don't want anything else to come between us or get in our way."

"There's really only one thing standing between us now."

"What?" He pulled back, looking worried.

"This blanket."

He'd covered me up to keep me warm, but now the blanket acted as a barrier between our naked bodies. He gave me a seductive smile and slid the blanket out of the way, his hot body pressing down on mine.

"That's much better," I smiled.

"Care to pick up where we left off the other night, fiancée?"

"As long as this time doesn't end with you sending me away."

He shook his head slowly. "Never again. You are mine. My mate and true love, who is soon to be my wife. I will never let you out of my sight again."

"Unless I'm going to work or something," I laughed.

"Oh no. Not even then." He planted kisses all over my face, making me giggle. "You'll just have to get a job here in the park so I can have you by my side all day."

"Actually, I would love that."

He pulled back to look in my eyes. "Really?"

"I've been trying to figure out what I want to do with my life and my degree. You're here; I want to be with you. I want to protect the land and its animals and do the things you do. I think I want to train to be a park ranger."

He gave me a half smile. "Well, there's one way you'll be guaranteed to get that job."

"What's that?"

"Sleep with the manager."

"Hmm." My words became a moan as he kissed down my jaw to my breasts.

He moved his hand between my legs. I was wet just from kissing him and he slid his fingers around and inside me. I dragged my nails along his back, barely able to take the sensation.

"Owen," I begged. It'd been far too long since I felt him.

"Addie," he breathed in my ear.

I wrapped a leg around him, trying to pull him closer to me. His hardness pressed against me, and I rubbed up and down his shaft. Each time, at the last moment just before he slid in, he pulled away, teasing me until I could scream.

"Haven't I waited long enough?" I whispered.

"What's another few minutes?"

"You're cruel."

He chuckled, but it didn't last long. I reached down and grabbed his erection, and he moaned as I stroked him.

"I think," he breathed and closed his eyes, "I see your point."

He pushed my legs farther apart and positioned himself over me. He pressed in just the head of his dick, then sank into me.

I shuddered at the feeling of him sliding in so deep. It felt both familiar and new. We'd done this so many times, but we'd both changed over the years. As he moved in and out of me, my heart sped and the pleasure rushed over me. When I felt myself begin to shift, I sucked in a breath.

"Stop!"

"What's wrong?" he asked.

"I..." I breathed fast, trying to calm myself.

"Addie?"

"Hang on." I closed my eyes and tried not to move. The shivering sensation slowed, but it was still right there.

"Have you...had sex since you started shifting?"

I shook my head, my eyes still squeezed shut. Sam had been my last and we'd broken up just before my first shift. I hadn't thought anything of it until that moment.

"Shh," he whispered in my ear and stroked my hair. "It's okay."

When I calmed enough to keep the bear at bay, I pressed my hips up into him again. He moved more slowly, taking his time. But it didn't take long for the swell to rise again.

This time, instead of feeling my bear take over, I kept control of my body. I let the feeling of him thrusting in and out of me take over. I pushed my hips into him faster, urging him to speed up. I grabbed his ass and pulled him in deeper.

He pounded hard, but slow. I wanted him to speed up, but the slowness was sweet torture. The orgasm took its time to build, but when it flooded over me, it hit me so hard, I nearly passed out. My head spun, and I had to close my eyes and breathe slowly.

"You okay?" he asked.

"I didn't know it would be so different."

He chuckled. "Do you remember the night we went to that school play and I wanted to leave early and we ended up having sex in the back seat of my car in the parking lot?"

I thought for a moment. "I think so."

"That was my first time after. And it was so close to the full moon. I almost lost it a few times."

"That would have been...interesting."

"Right." He laughed. "I've heard stories..."

"I have a *lot* to learn about being a shifter."

"You have all the time in the world to learn it," he said. "And, you're hired."

"Whew," I said. "If we had done that for nothing..." I sat up to kiss him. "I love you. I always have."

16

OWEN

EPILOGUE

"Hey there, Alpha man."

I glanced over at the walkie sitting on my desk and smiled. Some people questioned our ability to work together and be married, but Addie and I loved it. Being in the park with her, running things here and in the clan with her by my side. Things couldn't be much better.

"Hello there, darling wife," I radioed back.

"If you're not too busy or anything, maybe you want to meet me in the clearing by our cabin?"

"What! Are you sure?" I jumped up and grabbed my keys, dashing out of my office. "Gotta go!" I shouted to Rachel as I ran past her.

"Let us know!" she called after me.

"I'm already here," Addie said.

I could hear the distress in her voice. "You should have called sooner."

"Meh," she said. "These things—take time."

"Are you okay? I'm halfway there."

"Don't rush."

I laughed. "Seriously? My first cub is about to be born and you tell me not to rush?"

"It'll be—all day."

The pain in her voice made me push on the gas.

I pulled up to the cabin. Hailey's car was there, as were Noah's and several others. I'd never really been part of a clan birth, being a male and all, but they'd told me all about it.

This was how they did it, they said. The females all came together and helped the pregnant bear give birth. The father could be there, of course, but they didn't want a bunch of males strutting around, getting in the way. Fine by me to let the ladies handle it all.

I ran to the clearing. Addie was sitting up, her hands on either knee, breathing hard. Hailey was at her side, rubbing her back.

"You need to shift," Tori said.

I saw Noah then and clapped him on the back. I guessed uncles were allowed, too.

"She wants to be human," I said, moving into place beside her.

"But it's much easier as a bear," Hailey said.

We'd talked about this. Many times, Addie had insisted on giving birth in human form. Something about wanting the woman's experience. I didn't really get it, and I didn't try to. I heard what the females in my clan said, but I had to do what my wife wanted. She was the one who carried our baby, after all, and she was the one about to give birth.

"Leave her be," I said. I stroked her hair. "What do you need?"

She shook her head. Sweat stuck her hair to her neck and face. I did my best to brush it back.

"Maybe—I should," she said, wincing as another contraction hit her.

"Whatever you want to do, honey."

She nodded and tried to pull her clothes off.

"Don't worry about that." I'd gotten over the amount of torn clothing we all went through shifting, long ago. It was why I owned so many cheap t-shirts. Didn't matter when I ripped them if I didn't have time to undress before shifting.

She shifted, and, so I could speak to her, I shifted alongside her. I did have to undress, though. For all my thoughts on cheap clothing, I still wore my ranger uniform, and they were certainly not cheap. Last time I'd had to replace one, it ran me more than $80. I took off my clothes quickly, shifted, and got into position behind her.

You're doing great, I said. *I love you.*

This sucks. So bad.

I know. But it'll be over soon. I nuzzled my body against hers.

I felt her sigh. *This is better. They were right.*

We'll tell them after. Who wants a bunch of bragging bear-wives?

She started to laugh, but the next contraction stopped her. As things worsened, I felt less and less helpful. All I could do was be there. I couldn't speed it up. I couldn't take her pain. There was no way I could protect her or our baby from any part of this. I hated the feeling.

Finally, after what did turn out to be all day, she was ready to push. I pressed myself against her as she pressed against me, pushing hard. It took many minutes, and then a tiny bear cub was sitting on the ground.

She began licking it clean, and I watched in awe. When she had thoroughly groomed the baby, she looked up at me. Smiling in bear form was different than in human, but I knew her face so well, it didn't matter. She beamed, and I beamed back. I nuzzled in closer, sweeping the baby into my arms along with her.

I want to shift back now, she said.

We shifted back and I wrapped her in one of the blankets. We stayed cuddled together for a long while, the baby now suckling at her bare breast.

"Thank you, ladies," I said. "And Noah."

He looked up from where he'd been sitting against a tree, reading, and waved. They'd all stepped back to give us space. Now they stepped closer to peek in on the newest member of our clan.

"What is his name?" Tori asked.

This was my part. It was tradition to have the father announce a cub's name after his or her birth. I said proudly, "His name is James, after Addie's real father, who she never knew."

Everyone made the appropriate cooing and awwing sounds. They stayed for a little while, helping to get things cleaned up. We made our way inside the cabin and the local midwife came by to check on the baby and make sure everything was fine.

When we were alone, the three of us sat in bed, and James slept in Addie's arms. I rested my head on her shoulder to watch him sleep.

"He's so tiny," I said.

"Yeah. Didn't feel that way, though," she laughed.

"You were perfect. Thank you for bringing our baby into the world."

"Thank you for giving him a family to come into."

I kissed her head, then kissed James. With the two of them in my arms, everything was finally right at last.

FATED ATTRACTION

SHIFTER NATION: WEREBEARS OF THE EVERGLADES

1

BRITT

THE SWAMPLAND OF THE EVERGLADES NATIONAL PARK STRETCHED OUT before me as I ran, enjoying the feeling of my long leg muscles contracting and expanding with the motion. Early morning was the best time for a run. Everything still quiet and sleepy, and no one was poking around. The sun hadn't come up just yet, though I could tell it wanted to. The sky had that pinky-orange look about it just over the horizon, so I knew the sun would be peeking up before long.

I paused for a moment to listen and sniff the morning air. I licked my thick paws, tasting the ground. I could sense there was an animal nearby; I would find it and kill it. My stomach growled and I wanted to let out a mighty roar, too, but that would scare away whatever lurked nearby. I crept through a patch of brush just tall enough to hide my crouching panther form, and the dim light helped hide me. That time of year, the end of summer, the grass had dried up, making it a perfect hiding spot for my tan coat. The critter would never know a panther was sneaking up on it, and I intended to keep it that way.

A flash of movement caught my eye and I knew I had it: a deer, drinking from a stream, not paying attention to its surroundings whatsoever. *Stupid animal*, I snickered inwardly. *You're all mine.*

I moved in closer, slinking silently until I was in pouncing range. This was my favorite game. How close could I get before it smelled me, heard me, or saw me? Deer were so slow-witted, it wouldn't matter. The instant I was spotted, I'd be on it and that bastard would be mine. I licked my lips in anticipation, thinking about my breakfast.

I was close enough now. I stepped closer, almost laughing at how easy it was going to be. But a moment later, the deer jerked its head up. It didn't look my way, though; it looked in the opposite direction, toward the east.

I'd been so focused on my prey, I hadn't been on guard. *Dumb move, Britt.* Something huge came bounding along, and as I saw a flash of black before my eyes, I smelled the bear, and rage tore through my thick chest.

I leapt and the bear sailed under me, taking the deer down, sliding them both about three feet forward with the motion—just enough that I landed hard on the ground instead of on top of my target.

The bear sank his teeth into the deer's neck, and as the creature cried out, the bear sat back, pleased with itself.

But this wasn't just any bear. If it were any random black bear, I couldn't have been too upset; it was just following its instincts, after all.

Nope. This bear was a shifter, like me.

And that meant a human was behind this.

A human male.

An *asshole* human male.

I drew in a long breath of him; I wanted to remember this scent. If I ever came across this arrogant prick again, I'd get my payback. When his scent hit me, though, it sent shockwaves right to my core. The instinct stirred in me, and my hormones were screaming, "Mate! Mate!"

But with this jerk face? No way. My body would just have to chill and deal with not getting any for right now. Business was more important.

I narrowed my eyes and jumped again, this time landing on the bear. My front paws hit his chest with a hard thud and he fell back. The idiot wasn't even paying attention to what was around him, so I bit him. Not hard enough to break skin or anything. Just hard enough to let him know I was pissed he stole my kill.

He actually looked surprised by my presence. I rolled my golden eyes at him and whacked him hard with my tail.

I heard him growl as he began to shift back to his human form and sat on my haunches to watch. *Here we go...* Admittedly, he wasn't too bad to look at. Bears had their weight and height going for them, but they were usually wimps when it came down to it. Not a one of them could outrun me, but I loved to see them get cocky and try.

This one, though... The scent of him still made me tingly, but I did my damnedest to ignore the sensation as much as I could. I wasn't about to give in to him. He stole my kill, and I wouldn't stand for it.

He held up his hands, palms facing me, and made an apologetic face. "Hey, I'm so sorry. I didn't even see you. I didn't mean to. It's yours. Totally."

He backed away, and I made it a point to not break eye contact, challenging him with my stare. I hoped it would make him uncomfortable. But if he was so obviously unobservant, maybe he didn't even notice I was a female.

"Okay?" he continued. "Are we cool?" He looked at me expectantly.

If he thought I'd be shifting to talk to him, he needed to get over that idea real fast. I was hungry, and surely, there was another deer around. I just had to find it. He wasn't doing anything interesting anyway, so I ran off.

After ten minutes of hunting, I couldn't sense other deer in the immediate area, so I circled around and came back to check on my original target. Hot anger flared once more as I realized that asshole hadn't even eaten it! Instead, there was a collection of small flowers. Tiny, white elderberry flowers arranged in a way that spelled out a word.

"Sorry."

What the hell?

Well, whatever. It was there, and I sure as hell wasn't going to let it go to waste. I sank my teeth into its neck, but the taste of my loss made it bitter. I ate until my belly was full, then swiped my back paws over the flowers, scattering the bear's apology into the deer's remains. I hope he'd come back and see what I thought of his "sorry" ass.

2

EZRA

Man. I yawned and it bled into my thoughts as I mentally reached out to my clan. *This is why I don't get up early. Not worth it.*

Mason picked up on my signal and shot back, *What's going on, Ez?*

Panther.

Yeah? What about it?

I was just hunting, minding my own business. I found a deer. Score, right? So, I did my thing and took it down. Only there was a panther standing there. She jumped on me, dude! Bit my neck. I guess she was there first, but I don't know. I didn't see her.

You didn't smell her, man?

Nah, I was too busy chasing after the deer. So, I shifted back to be like, hey, sorry, I didn't know. But she just sat there all prissy and watched me.

Mason laughed. *Fuck, man. So, what did you do?*

She ran off. I spelled out "sorry" in some flowers right by the carcass hoping she might see it if she came back.

Aww, aren't you sweet?

I huffed in my mind. *Well, hey. I really didn't see her. I wouldn't have done that. I'm not that much of a dick.*

Mason chuckled. *Sure, sure.*

I officially vow never to wake before noon again. Too much competition.

Ez, I was shocked to hear from you this early, to be honest. Or haven't you been to bed yet?

No, I did. Just woke up and couldn't fall back asleep. My stomach rumbled, so I got up and hunted. Next time, I'll chew on a leftover slice of pizza. What are you up to anyway? I'm still running. Guess I need to find a new kill.

Almost home. Heading to work.

Bummer. A minute or two passed, but I could sense him still there, running. *Hey Mas?*

Yeah?

You ever... get a thing for a panther?

Uh, not that I recall. Why? She hot?

She didn't shift. But man, her scent. I whistled in my head and brought the scent to my mind so he could sample the essence of it.

Maybe you should go find her.

Meh. I'm too tired right now. Think I need a nap before I do anything crazy like that.

Alright, man...well, I'm home now, so I'm gonna let you go.

Kay. Oh hey, wait. Want to meet up tonight? Owen is coming out and we can probably drag Conner along.

Sure, sounds good. See you later, Sunshine Boy.

Yeah. Catch you around.

I yawned again. Five hours of sleep was definitely not enough. Who in their right mind would get up that early to hunt? Too much competition, with shifters or otherwise. Next time, I'd wait until it was later and hotter. Most shifters didn't run then, so the kills would be all mine. Just one more advantage of my California upbringing: I didn't mind the heat one bit. The Everglades were cool and breezy compared to Death Valley.

If we'd be going out that night, I'd definitely need a few more hours to snooze. It was my day off; I'd been nuts to drag my ass out of my warm bed.

I bounded up to the forest patch outside my apartment building and shifted back as I ran. My stash of clothing was well hidden in a large tree stump hole. I pulled out shorts and a shirt and yanked them on before heading up to my apartment, where I flopped down onto my bed face first.

At any other time, I'd fall asleep instantly. My mother had always complained because I'd be sitting at dinner, and then boom! I'd be asleep in my Cheerios. I could sleep like the dead, she'd say. But in that moment, all I could smell was that panther. The scent of her massive paws lingered on my chest, so I bent my neck forward, closing my eyes as I drew in a long, deep whiff.

Man, was she intoxicating. Mason wondered if she was hot in her human form—and so did I. How could any female smell so delicious and even be average looking? I pictured a tall, curvy blonde at the beach. Hair down her back as she stood in the sun, her bronzed skin glistening as she came out of the water rocking a bright pink bikini.

I closed my eyes and grinned as I began to grow hard. It was a good image to fall asleep to, no doubt.

Maybe Mason was right: maybe I should try to find her. I couldn't stop thinking about our encounter, and I did feel bad. How many shifters didn't pick up on another shifter's scent until it was too late? Maybe I could explain that I was tired and out of my element, not paying attention. Maybe she'd forgive me and wrap her slender arms around my neck and kiss me and tell me I could take her kill anytime.

The grin spread. *Okay, dude. Get your ass to sleep or you'll be toast tonight. Stop thinking about that panther.* But the more I tried to not think about her, the more she overtook my thoughts. Frustrated, I stormed off to the bathroom and stepped into the shower. It would take a lot of cold water to get her scent and image out of my mind.

3

BRITT

I PULLED ON MY BOOTS AND BRUSHED THE SPECKS OF DIRT OFF MY CAMO pants before I hopped on my motorcycle to head to the bar where I would meet Dezi and Kat. *God, this place had better not be busy*, I groaned to myself. I didn't hang with those two often, but since they were the only other panthers in the area—and Gladeswomen, like me—they were about the only people I could tolerate for any period of time.

I guess these women were technically my clan, but we didn't act like it much. Sure, if something came up or some jerk in town was giving one of us crap, we'd have each other's backs. That was a no brainer. We did have the mental link that came with being in a clan, but we didn't use it much. There wasn't even an Alpha in our little tribe. We used to have a fourth member, but she was killed years ago. After that, we kind of distanced ourselves some; it would limit the number of people whose deaths would hurt us.

We did make life easier for each other at times, and that's what made our clan work. Dezi was a fisherwoman and often traded me fish for rabbits or whatever else I hunted up to eat that struck her fancy. Kat had the gator farm and she'd throw me one every now and then, but she was good at telling me where to find clusters of animals who came around, since she had the boat and lots of land. When a pack of something nasty was messing with her gators, she'd call on me to help hunt them all down.

Beyond that, we got together for a beer about once a month or so. Sometimes, life out there could be lonely. Mostly that was the point and main benefit of it, but every now and again, it was nice to see a friendly face, kick back and shoot the shit.

That night was Dezi's birthday, and I had a fresh osprey wrapped up for her that I'd hunted that day. She had a thing for flying creatures. Me? I'd hunt anything that moved, as long as it wouldn't bring the wardens sniffing around my place. Some things were protected, like sea turtles, and for the most part, we all kept to the restrictions. It was about preserving the land, after all, and none of us wanted to see some big shift in the wildlife because too much of whatever had been hunted out. But if something was causing trouble, protected or not, it would have to go—either by means of hunting, or a forced relocation.

I parked the bike amongst a cluster of others. *Crap. This place is damn near packed*, I thought. That joint was our best bet, though. Shady's had the only decent grub in the area, and they actually knew how to pour a beer. Every time we went to that place further in town, we got nothing but foam and hassle. But Shady's attracted the type of people we were used to and was usually good for entertainment. Someone was always pissing someone else off at Shady's, and that was part of the draw.

I walked in and spotted Kat, then Dezi at a table, and a pitcher sat between them, sweating and half empty. One unattended pint sat full and untouched. I walked over and tapped them each on the arm with my fist, then downed half of my beer in two gulps.

"Ladies," I said, taking my seat.

"About time you showed up," Dezi complained.

Kat jerked her thumb at her, "She's getting impatient in her later years."

"What are you now, forty?" I chuckled.

She smacked my arm. "Bitch, thirty is still far off from that."

"Not too far, though." I raised my glass to hers and we tapped them together.

"Watch it, there," Kat said. "I think you're pushing thirty, too, aren't you, Britt?"

"I've got six months left and I intend to enjoy them fully."

"Now that you're *thirty*," Kat said like it was a dirty word, "do you have any plans for the next decade?"

"Yup. Fish more." Dezi nodded once and poured more beer. "Maybe go north for a trip. Catch something different for a change."

"But no settling down?" Kat wondered.

"Nah."

Kat was the only one of us who bothered to marry. She had a few little cubs running around, who kept her busy when the gators didn't. Usually, her husband was the one out wrangling them when they acted up, though. She handled the business end of things when it came to selling the critters off.

We ordered some wings and they'd barely hit the table before we tore into them. With their crispy skin and hot, tangy sauce, they hit the spot just right. As I finished off the last drumette and picked the bone clean with my teeth, I sat back to give my stomach room to digest.

People had been coming and going the whole time we'd been there. I hadn't paid much attention, since that was just the nature of Shady's. People were *always* coming and going.

That's why I didn't see him. But I *smelled* him.

That fucking bear from this morning.

I was thinking about ordering another basket of wings when his scent filled my nose and distracted me. I jerked my head over and saw him and I turned back quickly, but then remembered he hadn't seen me in my human form.

I glanced over again. He didn't seem to notice me or recognize my scent. *God. How had he managed to survive so long with such pathetic basic instincts?*

"What do you guys know about the bears around these parts?" I asked.

"Bears? Black bears?" Kat asked. "They like to come and try to get at my gators from time to time."

"I mean the shifters," I clarified. "Are there many of them?"

Dezi shrugged.

"Why?" Kat asked.

I jerked my head toward the table where the bear sat with his three friends.

"I had a run-in with one this morning. Took my kill," I explained.

Dezi narrowed her eyes and turned in her seat to look. "Which one?"

"The one with the ridiculous boy-band hair." It was bad enough when women went all crazy with hair dye, but a man? He had medium-brown hair that was longer on top in jagged chunks, and the ends were tipped blonde.

Dezi turned back and raised an eyebrow at me. "And you couldn't take him?"

"I tackled him," I said. "I let him know what was up."

"What'd he do?" Kat asked.

I rolled my eyes and snorted. "I ran off and when I came back, he not only left the carcass for me like a jackass, but he wrote out 'sorry' in elderberry flowers."

They both broke into laughter. Kat almost spit out her beer.

"Go set him straight," Dezi urged.

I nodded to myself. "Yeah. I think I will."

I pushed back from my chair and walked over, making it known with my narrowed eyes that I wasn't there for a friendly chat.

He didn't see me coming—again. His side was to me, and he was in mid-conversation with the others at his table.

I shoved his shoulder. "Hey."

That got his attention. They all looked, and the one I'd shoved gaped at me with wide eyes.

"Umm..." he said.

"Pay attention when you're hunting," I said forcefully, almost shouting, and a hush fell over the crowd.

He looked to the others, then back at me.

Behind me, two men in the bar shouted, "Fight!"

I had to remember this was Shady's. Usually we were watching the fights, not participating in them. But any time someone showed a sign of aggressive behavior, the crowd liked to egg him or her on and push the fight. My demeanor and tone had been enough to alert the masses that something was about to go down.

I glanced behind me and noticed my girls nodding in encouragement. Most of the people in the bar had turned their chairs to watch.

He held up his hands, "I didn't mean to do it, and I said I was sorry. I left it for you and everything. Give a guy a break, huh?"

"Give a guy a break? I don't appreciate someone creeping into my territory and going after my kills."

Behind me, a chorus of "Ooooh" went around the bar.

He got to his feet and dropped his voice. "Look, I'm not trying to start something. I'm not the fighting type. What can I do to make this better?"

"You can stay out of my way, dumbass. Pay attention to what you're doing from now on." I poked my finger into his shoulder with each word: "And stay. Out. Of. *My*. Territory!"

"Okay, okay, I will. I didn't even know it was yours; I was just out hunting."

I stood there, glaring. He wasn't even going to defend himself?

Finally, he stuck out his hand to shake mine, not to push me back. "I'm Ezra. Sorry I pissed you off, but it's nice to meet you."

I hesitated. If I shook his hand, his scent would be all over me. And right then, his scent was driving me up the wall. It was the same as before. It made me wired, like I wanted to pounce on him, but not bite him. I'd thought it was just a reaction from my animal side. It was much stronger when I was in my panther form and he was in his bear form, but even as humans, my body wanted him. Craved him.

But my mind sure as hell didn't.

I glared at his hand. "Next time, you might get yourself killed."

I turned on my heel and stormed back to my table. The crowd responded with disappointment, but I ignored them. Fuck 'em; they could get their kicks from someone else. He wasn't worth throwing fists over, and it hadn't been all that much of a deal to get bloody over. He had left it for me and apologized several times. He was an idiot but not an asshole, I decided.

I sat hard in my chair and the ladies clapped for me. They sent final glares at Ezra before turning back to me.

"Hopefully, that'll get through his thick bear skull," Kat said.

"I'll remember his scent," Dezi said in agreement. "The second he shows up somewhere he shouldn't be, I'll let him have it."

"Thanks, ladies," I nodded.

But throughout the rest of the evening, I found that my gaze was being pulled in his direction. About half the time when I looked over, he'd be looking at me already or would turn to meet my gaze and I'd have to look away fast. If only he didn't smell like that. I might have to go as far as to wear perfume to keep his stench from my nose.

"Either of you own perfume?" I asked.

They looked at me, puzzled.

"You want to get dolled up for someone?" Kat asked.

Dezi knitted her brow. "What do you want that shit for?"

"Nothing like that, guys. I want to get his scent out of my head."

Kat's mouth jerked into a smile. "Oh boy. Got it bad, huh?"

I kicked the leg of her chair. "No."

Dezi chuckled. "Defensiveness is the first sign, you know."

"I'm not interested in him or any other fool in the 'Glades. He just smells...well, I just don't want to smell him is all."

Kat held up her glass. "We've got beer. Does that count?"

Dezi snorted and I shoved her.

"You stuff it," I said. "That's not what I meant. I ain't pouring beer on myself just to chase away his scent."

"Maybe you should just embrace it," Dezi shrugged. "You haven't really dated."

"There's a reason for that," I said.

"Did he touch you at some point? Brush against you or something?" Kat wondered.

"Nah."

"Then why is his scent so strong to you?"

I shrugged. "It just permeates everything. I don't know. Maybe it's time I went on my way."

"Sit your ass down and ignore your little boyfriend over there," Dezi commanded. "We just ordered another pitcher, and you ain't getting out of drinking your share."

I blew out a breath. "Fine. But if it gets worse, I'm out."

4

EZRA

I TRUDGED BESIDE OWEN AS WE WALKED THROUGH THICK BRUSH DEEP IN the park. He sprayed a neon pink dot on a tree and turned to smile at me.

"Did I tell you what he did yesterday?" he asked.

I blinked at him, trying to refocus. He'd been talking so much this morning in his excitement that I'd tuned out. My mind kept wandering that day. And the night before. I tried to deny it. They were just random thoughts bouncing along my brain, that's all.

But I could not stop thinking about that woman. All morning, she'd consumed my thoughts. And now, I was about to be found out.

"Umm..." I tried to bring back some part of the conversation, but my brain blanked. "Who?"

Owen gave me an incredulous look. "James?" He said it like I was the biggest idiot in the world.

"Oh, right." Who else would he be talking about? Since his baby was born, Owen's whole world had transformed. Now it was all about how many hours the baby slept and how much he ate and how many smiles he gave. It went on and on.

"So, did I tell you?"

"I don't think so." I wanted to say yes. Anything to get him to stop going on about the baby. But if I lied, he would ask me what I thought about it or would say something that needed a response from me, and I wouldn't be able to give one. So, I had to be honest and take whatever lengthy monologue would follow.

"He rolled over for the first time!" Owen looked at me like I should be overjoyed about this.

"Oh. Is that...a big deal?" I gave an apologetic smile. I didn't know the first thing about babies.

"It's just an important milestone. It means his brain is growing and working. Before long, he'll be pushing up on all fours and starting to crawl. Gosh, then it won't be long before he's pulling himself up on things and trying to walk." He blew out a breath and ran a hand through his hair. "I have to get the baby-proofing upgraded. It's one thing when they can't move much yet. There's not much he can get into, you know? But once he's crawling, everything in the house has to be moved or covered or protected. Do we have those corner protectors?" Now he was taking out his phone. Probably to text his wife, Addie, about whatever baby-proofing crap he was talking about.

While he was distracted with corner protectors—whatever the heck those were—I looked around, trying to accomplish what we came here to do. Some trees in the area were dying and had to be removed, so we were out marking which ones would be cut down and which would be watched. The questionable ones wouldn't get the axe just yet, but if they didn't improve in the next six months or so, they'd get the chop on the next round. I spotted a tree that didn't look too promising, gave it a good sniff to confirm, and sprayed an X with the bright green spray paint in my hand. This tree was a lost cause.

When Owen put his phone away, he smiled at me. "Addie is so awesome. She already had them, of course. I should have known she would. She was planning to put them on this week, now that he's turning over. She was thinking exactly the same thing I was today!"

I nodded. "Cool, bro."

"I never knew marriage would be like this. It's just... so much better than I ever imagined, you know?"

"I don't, actually." I chuckled. I'd had girlfriends, of course. Plenty. And more short-term hookups than I could count. But none of them had ever been at the level of Addie and Owen's relationship. I doubted he ever loved anyone besides her. They'd been high school sweethearts and everything, separated for years, now together again and forever.

"When's your turn, man?"

"Funny you should ask. I was just thinking about that."

"Oh?" He sprayed another tree.

"Thirty is coming, whether I want it to or not. Maybe it's time."

"Definitely. You find the right woman, and it'll change your world." Owen beamed.

"Obviously." I rolled my eyes, but laughed.

"Sorry. I guess I do tend to talk about Addie and James a lot. They're my everything, though. I can't help it."

"Yeah... I think I know what you mean."

"Oh yeah?" He raised an eyebrow. "Does this have anything to do with the panther from last night?"

"I can't get that chick out of my head." I shook my head like I was trying to shake her out. I didn't even have to close my eyes to imagine her scent. It had taken up residence in my brain and whatever thought I had brushed against it, bringing it fresh to me. I'd never taken so many cold showers in my life.

"You gonna ask her out?"

"I don't know. I mean, yeah, I guess I want to start thinking about settling down and all that. Find my special one. I see what you have. I'm not ashamed to admit my jealousy. I just don't think the panther is the one."

"Why's that?"

"She's a panther, dude. I mean, like, I don't have an issue with that. I fully respect other species. It's not the interspecies thing that trips me up. But Panthers are hardcore; all tough and serious. And she is most definitely 110% panther." I shook my head, remembering her reaction to my accidentally taking her kill, then how she'd confronted me at the bar. It wasn't even that big of a deal, but she kept going on like I'd murdered her puppy or something.

"She *was* pretty intense last night, I'll give you that."

"I need someone like me, chill and carefree. Someone who won't go all ape-shit over me making a mistake. Can you imagine living with someone like her? I use my floor like a second dresser. She'd probably slit my throat for leaving my socks out if I married her."

Owen laughed. "I will say, even more laidback women don't appreciate that sort of thing. Addie has complained more than once when I left clothes on the floor of our room."

I groaned. "Somewhere in all of the Everglades, there is a messy girl who's perfect for me."

"Good luck finding her."

"If you come across her, let me know. Basically, think of the panther, then look for someone who's her total opposite."

"Got it. What about one of Addie's friends?"

I stuck my lip out in a hurt frown. "You want me to marry a non-shifter?"

"You are free to marry whoever you want."

"Not if I ever need to be the clan leader," I said. "I have responsibilities as second in command."

"Unless you're planning to kill me off so you can take over, I wouldn't worry about that. I'm not going anywhere."

"You just never know. Accidents happen. I hope I never have to take over. Honestly? It's a lot of work and responsibility. But what sort of second would I be if I wasn't ready at any moment to take the lead if I had to?"

"I'm thinking that the whole alphas-have-to-marry-a-shifter thing is unnecessary," Owen said. "Other clans don't have that rule. It almost ruined my life."

"Well, you're the one who can change that, but even still. I can't handle that panther."

"Yet, you keep bringing her up."

I paused. He had me there. Had to think fast. "I just keep running into her is all. She's, like, everywhere."

"Everywhere?"

Our walkie talkies crackled, then Pete's voice spoke to us. "Hey guys?"

"Yeah, Pete?" Owen responded.

"We got a call about a shark being possibly injured."

"We'll check it out. Send me the coordinates," Owen said.

A moment later, Owen's phone buzzed with a text of the shark's location.

"Let's head out," I said. Anything to change the subject.

We hopped into the utility vehicle and drove through the twisting back paths to get to where the shark had been last seen. When we came to water's edge, Owen shut the UV off and we hopped out.

"I just don't get why her smell affects me so much," I said.

Owen stifled a laugh.

"What?"

"And you claim I talk a lot about my wife and kid? You haven't shut up about this panther since you first encountered her."

"Well, all of our encounters have been...stressful. And painful." I rubbed my shoulder where she'd poked me repeatedly the night before. I actually had a faint bruise there this morning when I woke up.

"I wonder..." He took out his flashlight, even though it was midday, and shined it into the water so we could see below the surface better.

"What?" I asked again.

"Does it feel almost unavoidable?"

"How do you mean?" I saw a flash of movement. "There!" I pointed.

"Does it feel like she's a magnet, drawing you to her?"

"Yeah, actually. That's pretty much exactly what it's like. I don't want anything to do with her, but I can't stop thinking about her. I keep running into her, and her scent drives me freaking wild."

"Fated."

"Umm, say what now?"

"It's an old folktale, but like anything else around these parts, most people believe it. Some people, and it happens with shifters especially, are meant to be together. For whatever reason, this is decided and then the two, when the time is right, are brought together."

"No, no, no. No way, man. Did you hear what I said? She's crazy. I can't be with someone like *her*. How could she possibly be my soulmate or whatever you want to call it?"

"Not soulmate. Fated mate."

I rolled me eyes. "If fate wants me with that panther, then fate can shove it. No way. No how." I cut the air with my hands to reinforce that there was no chance this was going down.

Owen shrugged. "Just saying. It's a thing. I see it!"

I followed his gaze and saw the shark. It was lying partially out of the water—not a good sign. We made our way over to it, keeping a distance so it didn't get scared. It was injured, with a slender gash along its body.

"Hey Pete," Owen said, getting on the walkie again. "Call the vet down here. We found it. Just has a laceration, but it'll need to be treated."

"On it, Boss," Pete answered.

There was nothing for us to do now but wait for the vet to show, then we'd get back to our tree marking.

"Who believes in this fated thing anyhow?" I asked.

"Are you *still* thinking about that panther?"

"No. I'm thinking about what you said about her."

Owen laughed and sat against a tree where he could keep an eye on the shark. "You've got it bad, man."

I leaned against the tree. "Do not."

"No point in fighting it, tough guy."

I slid down the tree's trunk to sit beside Owen. When I did, a smell hit me. A familiar smell.

"You've got to be kidding me!" I said, leaning forward on all fours, taking a harder sniff.

"What's up, man?" Owen asked.

"Her." I pointed to the patch of grass that held her scent. "She won't leave me alone!"

He made a tisk-tisk sound. "Told ya. Fated."

"Stop saying that! I'm not fated to her. I won't do it!"

"You can only resist for so long, man."

5

BRITT

I SLUNG MY SHOTGUN OVER MY SHOULDER AND GRABBED MY PACK WITH extra ammo, along with a bottle of water and some gator jerky. It was a work day; I'd be out for hours, until the sun got too hot for the animals and they hid, or until I killed enough critters that they had to be dragged inside and processed. I sold off the animals in a variety of ways to different folks around the 'Glades. Some wanted whole carcasses, while others were just interested in the meat or hides.

My cabin wasn't big enough to house my processing workshop, so I'd added a little building years ago to make sure I'd be able to do it all myself, right here on my land. This land had been in the family for decades, and luckily, the location of it was just right. I wasn't around in the 1940's when everything went down with landowners in the 'Glades, but boy, did people still run their mouths about it.

Especially at Shady's and other places where the locals hung out. They'd be talking about how their daddies had a hundred acres until the government came in and took it all from them. Hearing their stories, I wished I had been around back then. They made it sound so amazing; a town full of folks, all doing the same thing: living off the land, trading with each other, and most importantly, abiding by their own laws.

Shady's had a long history there. Back when the closest cops were a hundred fifty miles away, no one would show up to break up fights that got out of hand. The owner kept a shotgun or two behind the bar and, as the story went, he'd shot off more than his share of toes, trying to save his business from being torn apart by rowdy customers.

Of course, we had a decent presence of cops eventually. I didn't break the law, so they didn't bother me. And it was nice to know they were around if I had a problem. Same with the rangers. Yeah, they were going to reinforce the regulations, but they also kept us safe and protected the land.

But some shifter groups wanted to see things run differently. A group would flare up now and then, causing some kind of trouble until the proper authorities stepped in and fixed things, usually with the help of us Gladesmen and women. The one consistent headache came from those damned crocs.

The crocs caused problems for everyone who got in their way—shifters or not. They wanted full, complete reign of the 'Glades. Like a bunch of idiots who'd been dropped on their damn heads too much, they really thought they'd get things to go back to how they were back in the day. They'd run the park, kick out the police and be the authority of the land. Nothing but a bunch of dumb fucks if you ask me, and I wanted nothing to do with them.

I was just happy to be a Gladeswoman and have the skills passed down to me from my Ma and Gramma over the years. Gramma had been around back in the old days. She'd somehow—through smarts or luck—bought land that was real close to the 'Glades, but outside of park territory and wasn't subject to the government take over. If it'd been a mile or two to the east, she would have had to let it go when she passed. There'd have been no inheritance for Ma or for me. Who knows where I would have ended up if that were the case.

The men all vanished. Ma grew up with no Pa, and my Pa took off before I ever saw his face. But it was fine. We were used to it, and we didn't need no men to make things right. We were tough women, the Wilsons. Anyone who knew us would say, "Don't screw over those Wilson women, they'll hunt you down and skin you in your sleep." Gramma caused that rumor. She had plenty of stories of going after men who tried to steal from her, back before the law. I don't think I'll ever know which stories were true and which were exaggerations. No matter, though. Gramma was a master storyteller and you never cared if what she said was a total lie. It was entertaining just to hear her talk around the fire.

Gramma had taught me how to hunt, skin and process meat, while Ma made the connections that are still in effect today. Every time I sold a critter to the butcher down the way, he'd say, "Here's to your old Ma; may she be hunting in heaven." Of course, both my Gramma and Ma had been shot on these same lands, killed during a hunting accident—though with Gramma, I don't know how accidental it was. The two of them weren't panthers, either.

I guess my Pa musta been a panther and passed his shifter DNA down to me. From what I heard, if you had just one shifter parent, you had a 50/50 shot at being one. Guess I ended up on the lucky end of the inheritance.

From what my Ma and Gramma told me, I was four years old the first time I shifted, playing outside in the mud, as always. A bunny came hopping along and I went chasing after it. My little legs were too unsteady and slow to catch up, though, so I went back to playing in the mud. Well, some time later, the bunny came back, and that time, I was more determined. I ran after it, and at some point along the way, my determination went haywire. As I ran, Ma said I dropped down to all fours, screamed and then boom! I was a panther cub. That little bunny's skin still hangs over my bed today. My first kill. A proud moment.

But it was also a moment of sheer terror for Ma and Gramma, who had no clue what was going on. Gramma was a stealthy woman, though; she poked around town and eventually discovered what was going on. She got an old panther woman—Kat's gramma, actually—to come over and talk to us, telling us what to expect. She said I might shift by accident while I was a youngin', but once I came of age, it'd be happening regularly and the full moon would force me to shift if I stepped into its light. She became like a second gramma to me, and that's how Kat and I knew each other.

Dezi had become part of our tribe not too long after. The three of us had been all we had growing up. We liked it that way; that's just how things were done in the 'Glades. You kept to yourself, you did your work, and on occasion, you'd meet up at Shady's with a friend or two for a cold one.

I kissed the barrel of my gun—Gramma's gun—and put it back over my shoulder. I always took something of Gramma's with me on a hunt for luck, like her gun or knife. I walked on through the morning light, searching for a good spot to sit up high for a while. With my panther eyes, I could see farther than most and in dimmer light. My panther genes were a real benefit to me most days. Made me a good hunter.

As I continued to make my way through the swampy forest, I caught a whiff of a scent that made me stop dead in my tracks. I took a few steps toward it to make sure and I shook my head. *Yup. That damn bear again. Ezra.* What kind of a name was that anyhow? And, more importantly, how was I going to shake that loser? If he really started to get in my way, I'd have to do something about him.

It seemed he'd just been running around and landed at my hunting spot. Fine, whatever. It was part of the park and well within his rights to do so. I'd even heard he was a ranger, so it was his job to be in the park. I just didn't personally want him so close. Had he managed to recognize my scent this time? Did he know he was close to me? Probably not. Dumbass.

I followed his scent for a short time, but it went on through the trails for a while in a direction I didn't need to be heading. As long as he wasn't lurking somewhere, waiting to jump out and mess up my kill, I wasn't worried about it. He didn't seem to have been in the area at that moment, but he was there recently. The scent was pretty fresh.

As I sniffed around, I picked up another scent. And that one disturbed me more than the bear's. I had to be sure of my suspicions, so I crept closer, sniffing all the way. I saw a paw first, then the legs, and finally, the body.

A panther lay dead, half hidden in the tall grass. Not too many panthers were left in those parts. Even if I was a shifter, I still felt a very deep connection with the creatures that were completely animal. We were the same species. That dead panther was especially disturbing, however; clearly, it had been murdered.

Across its neck were long gashes. I couldn't tell specifically what had killed it, but it must have been some kind of blade. They were clean cuts, unlike the tear of a claw. These wounds were also too intentional to be a matter of defense. The typical signs of a fight were missing; evidence of foul play, the police called it.

If two animals fought, there should have been crushed plants nearby.

There would have been scrapes and wounds on the body, but they would be varied; sometimes, you didn't land a good swipe, making the gash shallow.

This crime scene was clean. It seemed like the panther had been sleeping and someone snuck up on it to slice its throat. I doubted that's how it happened, but that's what it looked like. It told me two things: one, it was not an animal attack, and two, someone was hunting panthers. No, not hunting. Hunting implied stealth and skill and purpose. I hunted for meat, for skins, for carcasses. This poor creature was left for dead. No sport involved. Pure murder of a pure panther.

Not too many things in the world upset me, but that filled me with such strong rage that I balled my fists and growled in anger, tears forming in my eyes. I would find who did this. I'd skin them alive and eat their scrawny frame while they watched. I'd pull out their fingernails one by one and watch them suffer.

I paced for a minute, trying to clear my mind. I'd be no good for anything if my head was foggy with rage, so I forced myself to calm down. I spent a bit of time sniffing all around the body; I wanted to know the scent of the killer better than my own scent.

Better than that bear's scent that kept plaguing me.

As I filled my nose with the mark of the murderer, I kept thinking of him. *Ezra.* If he really was a ranger, that would mean he knew those grounds almost as well as I did. As much as I hated to admit it, he might have been my best ally. My best chance for catching this killer and bringing him down. He'd be just as anxious as I was to get to the bottom of it. A ranger's duties are to protect and conserve, and that death broke both tenets.

But that meant finding Ezra, talking to him and working with him on some level. That meant time with him, in his presence. And that was the last thing I wanted.

Okay, Britt. Focus on what's important. Sure, Ezra is annoying and happens to be everywhere. Sure, your body reacts to his scent in ways you can't stand and can't shut off. But, admit it, he's a nice guy, even if he's an idiot and a pansy. He wouldn't hurt me, I told myself.

I sighed and went to find a place to stash my clothes and weapons nearby. I hung my things on a nearby tree's branches and shifted, then ran to the last place I'd picked up Ezra's scent and followed the trail.

6

EZRA

"I'll go ahead and file the report," Owen said once they'd left the injured shark. The vet seemed to think it would be just fine, but there was still paperwork to be done. I was happy to let him do it.

"I'll drop you at the station, then get back to the trees," I said.

Owen gave me a sideways smirk.

"What?" I demanded.

"You want to be out there where you girl's scent is? Hoping to run into her?"

"Um, no. I ran into her once and she bit me. Then I ran into her again and she poked me and yelled at me. I have no desire to run into her again. Ever."

Owen laughed. "Wait till I tell the guys about this."

"Nothing to tell, man."

We hopped into the UV and drove back toward the ranger station. My clan loved to pick on me, the kid from California who didn't grow up with a clan; pick on the one who speaks a little differently and isn't all uptight. How could they think I'd have a thing for that panther? They knew me well enough to bust on me constantly, yet they insisted I had a thing for this she-devil tormenting me.

"You know," I said, "you should know better."

He'd been looking at his phone and put it down in a hurry to keep his eyes on the path. "Sorry, you're right. Addie just sent me a picture of James. Look." He held the phone so I could see the photo of the baby on his stomach, looking at the camera.

"Cute. And no, I guess you shouldn't be on your phone while driving, but that's not what I meant."

"What then?"

"You know me. You guys all do. I've been part of this clan for like, five years now? Living and working here in the Everglades with you all."

"Yeah?"

"So, you know me," I went on. "You should know my type. And that means, you should know I'd have nothing to do with a chick like that panther."

Owen pulled over and stopped, leaning over the steering wheel, laughing so hard he held his stomach. I shoved him and he tumbled out of the UV onto the path. He lay in a ball, still laughing his ass off.

I got out and went around to his side to nudge him with my foot.

"You—" He couldn't talk, he was laughing so hard.

I stood over him, my arms crossed, glaring down at him. "Dude."

"You're friggin' obsessed!" He'd started to calm down and sat up now to wipe tears from his eyes. "This is hilarious."

"Yeah, real funny." My face felt hot with embarrassment. I never cared about their teasing; I had plenty of decent comebacks and I always got mine. But somehow, that was different. Maybe because deep down, I suspected what he said was true. Even if it was the last thing I wanted.

"Ezra, man." He got to his feet and put a hand on my shoulder. "You're my second in command. I want you to be happy. You're important to me. You're also my friend. But I have to tell you, from bear to bear, friend to friend, ranger to ranger, brother to brother—this chick is your mate, whether you want to deny it or not. Maybe just give into it and explore that. I mean, this is happening for a reason."

"What reason could there possibly be?"

"No idea. The tale goes that when the fated need each other, the universe brings them together. You don't have to believe it, but it sure seems like everything people say is true for you."

I shook my head and got back into the UV. "You're wrong. I don't need her for anything."

"Okay." He got back in and turned the ignition, then hit the gas.

"I'm with you, no matter what. You want this panther? Awesome. You don't want this panther? No problem. But when you say you don't want her, then go on and on about her? You're going to get busted on, sorry." He playfully shoved my shoulder. "Nothing wrong with being a little twitterpated. Especially since you're fated mates."

"We're not fated!" I hollered.

He held up a hand in defense. "Okay. I'm sorry. I'll let it go." Then, under his breath, he added, "For now."

"Heard that."

"Figured you did."

As we neared the station, I noticed an animal running in the grass beside us, along the dirt road.

"Hey, hold up for a sec," I told Owen.

He stopped and turned to look with me, and we got out to watch the running animal. It was unusual activity for this area and time of day. And then I knew why.

"Oh fuck," I said, slapping my forehead.

Owen pressed his lips together hard, trying not to laugh.

"Just don't, man," I said. "Why the hell is she here now?"

I saw the panther's head popping over the grass as she bounded toward us and prepared for another fight. What had I done to piss her off this time? I stood with my arms crossed, wearing an unhappy scowl on my face.

She dashed out of the grass, her paws sliding in the dust as she came to a halt. The second she stopped running, she shifted into her human form, not seeming to care about the fact she was buck naked as she stood before us.

"Hey!" She came right at us.

"What'd I do now?" I asked.

"For once, this isn't about you." She gave me a nasty look and turned to Owen. "I just came across something I thought you should know about. A pure panther. Dead. Murdered."

Owen's eyes widened as mine did. "Where?"

"Follow me; I'll show you," she said.

"One sec." Owen went back to the UV to radio the station that we had a situation to check out.

While he did that, I tried to talk to her. "What can you tell us about it?"

"Wasn't an animal," she said. "The wound is too clean. I picked up the scent of the killer, though."

"Whoa, whoa." I held up both hands. "We can't assume anything like that yet."

She glared at me. "You think I can't tell the difference between an animal murdered and one killed in a fight?"

"That's not what I meant, I—"

"Why don't I murder you and see if anyone can tell I did it?"

I let out a sigh. "Nevermind. What makes you so sure it was murder?"

She spoke slowly and pointedly, like she thought I was a complete idiot. "Did I stutter? The wounds on the animal are clean. Not from claws, but blades. The area around the panther showed no sign of a fight, and the smell is human—and male. Did you get all that or should I repeat it again for you more slowly?"

"I got it," I snapped. "You don't have to be so grumpy all the time."

"We'll see how cheerful you are when people start hunting bears."

I gave her an incredulous look. "Bears aren't protected like panthers are. We do get hunted. All the time. There's a bear hunting season; aren't you, like, a hunter or something for a living?"

She rested her hands on her hips. I'd done a good job of avoiding scanning my eyes over her gorgeous curves, but it was a lot of work to maintain my cool. I kept my gaze trained on hers and refused to look down, even as I felt my member begin to throb in anticipation.

"What the fuck is wrong with you?" she demanded.

"Aside from you showing up and hassling me over and over again?" I asked.

"Okay, whoa," Owen said, returning to us. "No time for your little fight here. And I'm sorry, Miss, what's your name?"

Owen actually stuck out his hand to shake hers and she returned the gesture.

"Britt Wilson," she replied.

"Britt," Owen continued. "Thank you for coming to tell us. Obviously, we're highly concerned about this and we'll do everything we can to get to the bottom of this. Since we're all shifters, I'd say Ezra, let's go ahead and bear up. We'll get the clan over to sniff it out so we can all work together. My third just became a police officer, so he'll be a valuable asset."

"Good," she said. "I want this person dead. Fast."

"Shall we get a move on?" Owen asked. "The sooner we scope it out, the sooner we can find the attacker. He might still be in the area."

Britt didn't answer, but promptly shifted and waited for us. Owen and I both went to the UV and yanked off our clothes, then shifted. She took off and we followed.

You have to chill out, Owen commanded. *What the hell was all that?*

What's going on? Everything okay?

Great. Now Mason was in on this, too.

Where's Conner? Owen asked.

Here, Conner answered. *Noah and Hailey are on their way.*

Perfect. Thanks. Owen explained the situation as we ran fast to keep up with Britt. *We're following her now to the body.*

Britt, I scoffed. *What kind of a name is Britt?*

Oh right, Owen said. *I forgot to mention that the woman who found the panther is the same panther shifter that Ezra won't shut up about.*

She keeps showing up! I defended myself. *I can't escape her and every time I run into her, it's a horrible experience.*

You should hear him whining and going on. Owen did a mental eye roll. *He's worse than a little boy pulling the hair of the girl he likes.*

I do not like her, I insisted. *I might actually loathe her.*

But her scent drives you wild, man, Mason pointed out.

It's so strong, Conner added, *that it makes me want her!* He laughed and the others joined him.

Whatever, dude, she's all yours.

I don't want to get in the middle of that, so I'll pass, but I appreciate your willingness to share, Conner amended.

It's kinda cute, really, Owen said. *I mean, when we're at your wedding, we'll think back to this moment and all have a good laugh.*

My wedding? I huffed. *You're taking things way too far. I don't appreciate it.*

Britt came to a stop and we halted behind her. Owen sent a mental map of our location and then we got to work.

We looked around, taking note of our surroundings, sharing mental images with the clan and memorizing scents. Britt was right. There was no way this was accidental or caused by an animal. I wouldn't admit it, but she was smart. She knew what to look for. She'd make a good ranger and was probably a pretty decent hunter.

I noticed these things about her, but wouldn't let the ideas become actual thoughts in my mind. If I did, the clan would pick up on them and would never leave me alone. I was grateful they were finally focused on something beside me for a change.

Owen shifted back and Britt followed shortly after. I stayed in my bear form to both connect to the clan and to avoid being naked around her again.

"Do you recognize the scent at all?" Owen asked her.

"No, but I'll be on the lookout, mark my words. I *will* find this asshole."

"There was a group years ago who thought the panthers should be taken out of the park for good; I hope they're not back. They killed a lot of panthers, and that's part of the reason you've become rare and protected."

"Yeah. My clanmate was one of them." She spit on the ground. "That's why I'm going to hunt this bastard down and make him pay."

"I'm sorry for your loss, and I understand your determination, but I have rangers on the way and the police are on their way, too. There will be a full investigation. We're all taking this very seriously. I wouldn't want you to be in danger."

"And that's why I'm going to hunt down the killer," she insisted. "If he's hunting panthers, obviously I'm in danger."

When she said it like that, the words prickled over me. I hadn't thought it through. Yeah, she was upset about finding a dead panther. But whoever did this would be hunting her, too, if he was hunting panthers. She was in danger.

Something in my heart alighted. Concern, I realized. I was worried about her. And the mention of her clanmate being killed? It saddened me. I growled at myself. Why should I be worried about her or sad for her? Of all people. Her? Well, no. I was a ranger, after all. I would be concerned about any citizen who might be in danger.

Keep telling yourself that. Mason ran up behind me and Conner was with him. Hailey and Noah were close, but still running.

Stop thought-dropping on my internal convo, I snapped.

"These are two more members of my clan," Owen explained to Britt.

She glanced over and nodded.

Whew, Mason whistled in his mind. *She is pretty hot, though.*

Umm hello? Female present, Hailey hissed.

Sorry, Mason said. *It's true, though.*

Dude, I said as a warning. *Not helping.*

What's the police's ETA? Conner asked. He was on my good side. For now.

They'll be here in a few. I'm going to shift to be ready, Mason replied, then dropped the sack he'd been carrying and shifted, dressing quickly.

It'll be alright, man. Conner nudged against me, then shifted back.

I took off into the woods. I wanted to be away from them, but I also thought I could do more trying to follow the scent than just sitting around getting ragged on.

7

BRITT

Once the rangers and police had left, I had more room to take on my own investigation. I had sniffed around the body all I could, but now that it had been removed, things had changed. Scents that had been under the body and somewhat hidden were then exposed. Of course, there were also the smells of many other people layered in there by that point, but I had stuck around just for this reason. I was careful, but I had made sure to get a whiff of each person who'd been there so I wouldn't be confused. Of course, I had no trouble recognizing out Ezra's scent. His was the strongest of them all, much to my dismay.

Once I had gone over the crime scene in full detail, I ran around my cabin to make sure the scent of the killer was nowhere near it. I wanted to identify any new odor marks and have a clear scent map of my home in my mind. If anything new came up, I needed to know; whether it was a bunny, a lizard or a person.

When that was committed to memory, I went back to the scene again, found the scent of the killer and followed it. I figured at some point, he got into a vehicle. Being human meant he couldn't get this far into the park on foot unless it'd taken him hours. And there hadn't been anyone found around the area. I still wanted to go as far as I could; I'd even sniff out the vehicle so I could recognize it.

I knew Owen didn't want me to get hurt or anything, and I'm sure they didn't want me interfering in their investigation. Hell, I sure didn't want to mess up their work, either. But I wasn't going to sit around, just waiting for this guy to show up and slash me, too. And if I could give them information that would help them nail the guy, even better.

Owen seemed like a much more reasonable bear than Ezra. It's probably why he was the Alpha, though naming Ezra as his second wouldn't have been my choice, if I were him.

Ezra. I drew in a long breath. It still didn't make sense why I reacted to his scent like I did. My body warred with my mind. My body wanted me to be closer to him, yet my mind wanted to stay far, far away.

As I followed the trail, I noted each scent I took in. Killer, Ezra, Owen, killer, Mason, Ezra, Owen, Ezra, killer, Conner, Ezra, Ezra, Ezra. I let a low growl rumble my chest. They'd apparently had the same idea and had followed the path. Well, I didn't want to be out of the loop. But as I went, it was like the scents were forcing me to think Ezra, Ezra, Ezra, over and over. Had he just run around in circles as they moved along, marking everything in his path?

Maybe I should talk to Kat's gramma, I thought. We still kept in touch, though I didn't see her much those days. Being up in age, she kept to herself even more than she used to. But I wanted to ask her what this Ezra thing was all about. Why was his scent so strong and permeable? Why did my body want him when my mind hated the idea? Unless I was turning schizophrenic, there had to be a reason for it.

I followed the trail until it came to an end on a road, as I suspected it would. I sniffed hard to pick out the correct vehicle scent, but lots of vehicles traveled this road, so I had to be careful. I noticed one that meshed the killer's scent with a vehicle's, and that had to be it. I spent time with the smell, committing it to memory, then took off to head back home.

8

EZRA

I sat in the ranger station with Owen after the panther's body had been removed. The clan had come and checked out the scene. The police talked to us and the report had been filed. Now that all of that had passed, my mind was left to wander. And, of course, it wandered to just one place.

Britt.

The hint of worry I had noticed earlier was becoming stronger. I kept seeing the dead animal and hearing and smelling Britt, and it all got tangled in my mind until *she* became the dead animal. It was too much.

Though we hadn't spent much time together, I had a decent sense of her personality. Gladesmen and women were the type of people who didn't mess around, didn't waste time, and definitely didn't sit back and wait for something to happen. If Britt thought there was someone hunting panthers—and there was a good chance there was—then she would be out in the woods trying to find him.

Most people would be smart about it. They'd leave the investigation up to the police. They'd wait to find out more before assuming this wasn't an accident or a stand-alone incident. And if they found out this was someone just going after panthers, they'd be smart about it: they'd sit at home where it was safe, not run out into the prime location for the killings. She would put her scent all over the place, giving the killer a map right to her.

From the scent, we knew the person who'd killed the panther was a pure human. And though we hadn't smelled another scent with him, that didn't mean that somehow a shifter wasn't helping him out. It wasn't like people and shifters weren't all around the park all day, every day. The Everglades National Park was a tourist attraction, after all. Whether local or distant, people came to the park to see the wildlife and experience nature.

Others were in danger, too, but my mind was on Britt and Britt alone, which was a problem for a few reasons. Obviously, I couldn't share this with my clan; they were riding my ass enough. If they heard half of what I'd been thinking all morning, they'd never let up. And without being in bear form, there wasn't much I could do anyway. What, walk around the area with a shot gun and hope the killer steps out onto the trail? I don't think so. Being a shifter, my human senses were heightened, but they were nothing compared to when I was in bear form.

The other problem was Britt herself. I was sure, without having to ask, that she did not want me around. If she knew I was trying to protect her, she'd probably attack me. She'd stop me somehow. I didn't want to be around her again, but I didn't want to be thinking about her, worrying, feeling trapped and helpless. I couldn't shift, I couldn't get my clan's help, I couldn't do anything as a human, and I couldn't find her to protect her. I was stuck.

"You okay?" Owen asked.

I guess I'd been quiet a long time. "Just thinking about everything."

He watched me for a moment. "You're worried about her."

Even in human form, I couldn't hide things from him. I shrugged.

"I know I've been getting on you, but man, if you're worried, there's nothing wrong with that. It's okay if you're attracted to her or you're into her."

"I don't think she's right for me though. Do you?"

"Can't say. Only one way to find out. If you're worried, go for a run. Sniff around and make sure she's okay."

I nodded. "Maybe I will. If she finds out and throws a fit, then I'll just say I was doing my job."

"There ya go. And it's not a lie. I do need you to help find this guy. We all need to be on the case to make sure we don't have another panther killing in the area."

"I hope it was a one-time thing," I said.

"Me, too."

I looked at the clock on the wall in his office. "I'm done for the day. Think I will go for that run."

"Let me know what you find, bud."

"No doubt, man."

I went out to my car and drove to a more secluded spot. Once there, I stripped down and hid my car key, then shifted. I stood on my hind legs and gave a good stretch, then took off running.

Without really thinking about where I was going, I ran back to the last place I'd had her scent. When I reached it and smelled it, the familiarity of it was comforting. I breathed her in, and it warmed my chest. And that made me pause. If I really didn't want to date her, or even get to know her, why did her scent affect me like this?

The whole fated thing that Owen kept bringing up seemed like a bunch of bullshit. Her pheromones made my body want her and go crazy with the wanting—that must have been it; it was purely chemical. If we ended up sleeping together ever, it would probably end this. And actually, that wasn't a bad idea. It might be the best means to the end of this obsession.

I shook the thought from my head and refocused. I didn't have time to get all riled up, and I sure as hell didn't have time to stop and take a cold shower. *A cool dip might not be bad, though*, I thought, so I dashed to the closest pond and jumped in, letting the water run through my fur and cool my body. I got out and shook off, then returned to following the scent.

As I went on, weaving through the mangroves and tall grasses, I got some insight on her hunting patterns; how she circled around nests of birds and slunk along the water's edge in places. She must have been very good at what she did.

I came to a cabin tucked deep in the woods, but off the park land, technically. It reminded me very much of Owen's cabin, but then again, there were many of those little cabins out there. They were the properties that had been outside the government takeover back when the Everglades National Park was established in the first place. I didn't know much about that time, but people still talked about how much land and property they lost. It seemed like a bunch of whining to me; the land in the area needed to be protected, after all. I'd hate to think about the ramifications all that development would have had on our natural resources if the government hadn't stepped in. But then again, I wasn't a Gladesman.

It was her property, though, and I wasn't about to trespass, so I didn't go any further. But I did pick up a very fresh trail leading away from the cabin. *She must be out hunting right now,* I thought. *I could make sure she's okay and see if she found anything.*

With that, I followed the trail and the scent grew stronger as I went.

Just then, Mason reached out. *Hey all.*

Just me here, I answered. *How goes it?*

Wish we were making more progress, but there's not much to go on.

For the panther killer?

Yeah. We haven't been able to pull evidence off the body. We've pretty much got nothing.

I'm running right now, I said. *Trying to follow a trail I picked up on to see if Britt knows something.* Right after I had the thought, I regretted it and mentally braced for the backlash.

She was helpful the other day, was all he said. *I bet she'll be a valuable resource in finding him. She has the motivation and the skills.* As it turned out, he wasn't going to rip on me after all. He must've picked up on my not-so-fully formed thoughts because he added, *She's cool, man. You could do worse.*

I'm not trying to do anything with her at all.

Okay, then. I've gotta shift and get back to work. Just wanted to check in and stretch my legs.

Catch ya later, bro.

Later.

When Mason shifted back and I was alone again, I considered what he'd said. Were they all just going to accept it going forward? Would they assume I was going to be with her and that was it? Well, that wasn't going to happen. They'd see it. I'd work with her the best I could to find the killer. Sure, we all would. But it didn't have to go any further than that.

I'd barely finished that thought when I heard a rustling and paused to listen and sniff. It was her. She had to be just over the hill from where I stood.

I didn't want to startle her, and I sure as hell didn't want to anger her. I walked slowly and loudly in her direction, and when she came into view, I saw her pounce on a raccoon, sinking her teeth in deep. She turned to look at me, holding my gaze for a long moment.

I stayed back, not wanting her to think this was going to be a of repeat of the deer incident. I wasn't interested in the raccoon, anyway. So, I sat down to watch her and waited until she was through.

She tore into the raccoon, eating a large chunk of its flesh, and I was content to watch. When she was finished, I'd shift to talk to her. But as I waited, she sat up sharply, then took off running at full speed.

9

BRITT

The timing couldn't have been worse. I'd just killed my coon and was having a nice snack, then *he* showed up. At that point, I wasn't even surprised. I'd heard him coming a long way off and then he just sat there. He was being respectful, for once. Just watching. Waiting, I guessed. Why would he have stuck around?

I had planned to talk to him; to show him the trail of the killer I'd found and see if the vehicle's scent was familiar to him at all. If it wasn't, I'd make him familiar with it. But then, I'd heard footfalls in the distance. I knew it was a human, from the sound of its steps. Most critters had distinct patterns as they moved, and it wasn't uncommon for me to recognize what something was before I even smelled it or saw it. This was no different.

I kept an ear out. If the person came closer, I'd make sure I wasn't seen. When people saw a panther, it tended to freak them out a bit, and I wasn't there to scare people. But then the wind brought me a little gift: a hint of the scent of the person—the one who'd killed the panther.

Well, nothing was going to stop me from chasing him down. Not some little raccoon snack, and not Ezra showing up. I would do whatever it took to get him. And I surely wasn't going to waste one damn second to shift back and tell that bear about my game plan.

So, I dropped the coon and took off. I was nearing the killer; nothing would stop me from tearing him to shreds. I ran hard as I could, but when I got to the place where I thought the sound had come from, he was gone.

I sniffed around and found a new trail—the vehicle—and picked up my pace. Running after a human was easy; I could outrun even the best sprinters without breaking a sweat. But a vehicle was different; much faster. And the smell was different, too; not like tracking a person or animal. Mammals had a warmer, stronger smell that my nose was built for. This task took a lot more concentration.

I was so focused, in fact, that I hadn't paid attention to Ezra. I didn't think he'd come after me—or be able to keep up, for that matter. And so, when I heard someone running just behind me, it threw me off.

The sound of paws pounding on the dirt made me whirl and pause until I realized it was him. I ran again, but now his scent overwhelmed my senses. I shook it off and picked out the vehicle scent again and ran to a crossroads.

When I got there, I found a slightly busier dirt road. This was one more heavily-traveled by visitors to the park, so there was an onslaught of odors to sort through; I couldn't tell which way the killer had gone. I sniffed and sniffed, running in circles, going down one direction, then another. *Fuck.*

I had to face the truth after several minutes of trying. I'd lost him. My gut sank and the anger ripped through my chest. It was all Ezra's fault.

I ran back a little ways until we were well out of human earshot or sight. I waited, and sure enough, moments later, he came bounding toward me. As soon as he caught up to me and stopped, I shifted back. And then I let him have it.

"Why do you always show up at the worst possible times? I had him, you asshole! Why won't you stay away from me?"

He blinked at me with his big bear eyes before he stood up and shifted back.

"How can you blame this on me?" he demanded. "I was following you to help you catch him!"

"But you didn't. You distracted me and I lost the scent."

"So, you got distracted and that's my fault?"

"If you would have stayed out of my way, I would have him right now." My rage boiled at the thought of it. "I could have put an end to all of this."

"Oh right, because you're going to chase a car now? You really think you're that fast?" he challenged.

I gritted my teeth together. "I would have followed the scent until I came to the vehicle, idiot."

"Then go ahead. I'm not stopping you."

"I can't because I lost the trail when you distracted me."

"So, you lost the trail and that's my fault, too?"

"Yes!" My hands balled into fists. "What is your problem? Why do you keep showing up and following me around?"

"I'm not. *You* keep showing up! I was out hunting and there you were, then—"

"Oh, when you took my kill? That time? When *I* was out hunting and you just showed up?"

"Then, you came into Shady's—"

"I was there first," I said.

"Whatever. But you were the one who took it on yourself to come over to me and start something. I was just sitting there minding my own business. Then you were the one who came to us when you found the dead panther, or did you forget that?"

"Hello? You're the ranger, not me. It's your job to find the killer."

"Exactly." His expression fell into cockiness, and I wanted to slap it off him. "And that's what I'm doing. So, actually, *you're* in *my* way. You got in the way of the official investigation."

"Oh, what are you going to do, arrest me? You don't have the authority to do that."

"Of course not." He shook his head. "You're an asset to the investigation—when you're not getting in the way. I came out here to make sure you were okay and see if you found anything."

"I don't need you to check up on me. Stay away and maybe I could find something to tell you about. Or, more likely, I'll just kill him myself and not bother you all with it."

"Right, because you're better at everything? You're better than everyone? Why would rangers have any idea how to do their jobs, is that it?"

I growled low in my chest before I jumped on him, sending him crashing to the ground. I pinned him down, my hands on his shoulders.

"Who's winning now, asshole?" I spit the words at him.

"Neither of us." He held my gaze for a long moment, then did something I couldn't forgive him for. He leaned up a few inches and smashed his mouth to mine.

I pulled back and narrowed my eyes. "What the *hell* do you think you're doing?"

"Let's just get it over with. We keep running into each other. It's obvious there's some stupid attraction between us."

The fact that I was lying naked on top of him suddenly registered in my body, and warmth rushed over me. He grew hard beneath my hips and that same feeling took over. That animalistic desire.

Maybe he was right. "So, we fuck and that's it? Then we'll be able to stay away from each other?"

"I sure hope so," he said. "Because I can't stand it anymore. Your scent drives me wild, but your attitude drives me crazy. I don't know if I should kiss you or smack you."

Just for fun, I slapped him—not too hard, but to make a point. Then, I pressed my lips against his in a hungry kiss, like I wanted to devour him. Because in that moment, I did.

He dug his fingers into my hair and pulled me closer. We kissed so hard, it hurt my mouth. My body tingled all over with wanton desire, and when I finally gave into it the feeling was so strong, it made my head spin.

He pushed up and flipped us so he was on top. His hands were on either side of my body and he lowered himself down to press against me. His skin was as hot as mine; we were fire together, stoking each other to raging. Pressing his hips into mine, his hard-on slid up and down against me; I was so wet already.

But I didn't like him being on top. I was going to show him that *I* was in control. I pushed up and tackled him again, reaching down to grab his cock. I had to make sure he was nice and ready, and I wanted this over fast.

He was hard as a rock, so I positioned myself over him and slid down his length, but as he entered me, the feeling overwhelmed me and shook me to the core. Before he was even fully inside me, I came with a loud moan. Any other time I had sex, it took much longer than that, and once I hit my peak, that was it. I came and moved on. Not this time. This was just the beginning; my body was still hot and wanting him.

I sat up, pushing him fully inside me before I bounced on him, sending him deep and shallow as I rocked. I tugged on his chest hair and he growled in response, pinching my nipples so hard it should have hurt, but instead, it sent a wave of pleasure through me.

He grabbed my hips and slammed me down, thrusting harder into me than before, and his eyes stared at me intently as he pounded me faster. This was not lovemaking. Not even close. This was fucking.

"Faster!" I demanded.

He sat up and embraced me, but it was only to move me. He put himself on top of me again and slid one arm under my leg to pin it up high. From that position, he was able to go deep, but also harder. His ass muscles worked as he thrusted into me again and again. It still wasn't hard enough. Nothing could be hard enough.

"Harder!" I insisted.

He sped up, his face red with the exertion. As he pounded, I came again, feeling like a wave had rushed over me, then out of me and all over him.

He yanked back, pulling out of me so fast it took my breath before he flipped me over on my stomach. Pulling my hips up to meet his, he entered me from behind. His fist wound into my hair and he tugged as he slammed into me.

Finally, from this position, he could do it hard enough. My ass slapped against his thighs and my wetness drenched him. That was the problem, I realized. I was actually too wet. Not enough friction.

As he sped up, putting his other hand on my shoulder to steady me as he pounded me, the friction increased a little. Before it had been just playing. Now we were getting serious.

"Fuck yes," he groaned.

I pushed back, forcing my ass into him with each thrust. His cock stroked my insides and when he cried out, I came for the third time.

"I'm coming," he announced and let go of my hair to grab my hips. He pounded me as hard as he could and cried out again. I could feel his dick throbbing inside me.

He collapsed to the forest floor, spent. I was still on all fours and dropped my forehead down to the soft ground, tingling all over. Even the soreness felt good, which seemed twisted to me, but then again, so did this whole thing. Did we really just have sex?

I faced him as he laid in the grass, breathing hard, glistening in a sheen of sweat.

"You think that did it?" I asked.

"That did something, that's for sure."

"Yeah." I got to my feet. "Now please, *please*, stay the fuck out of my way."

I shifted back to my panther and heard him calling out to me, begging me not to run off yet, but my paws sank into the soft ground as I ran.

10

EZRA

When I could finally move again, I pushed myself up. She'd ditched me, just like that? Get off, then take off? Weren't women always accusing men of doing that, calling it insensitive? She had just screwed my brains out and left.

I shook my head. How had we gone from screaming at each other to having sex? It didn't make much sense to me. But it had made perfect sense to my body. She felt so good. Even the thought made me hard again. *No*, I reminded myself. *That was it. We had sex so that we could stay away from each other.*

I shifted and took off, running back to my car and clothes. I went straight home and showered, but at least this time, I didn't have to shower in frigid water to calm my body down. I was worn out. I grabbed a beer from the fridge and fell onto the couch, but I didn't even get the can opened before I fell asleep. I knew this because when I woke in the morning, the sealed can was on the floor where I'd apparently dropped it in my sleep. At least it hadn't spilled all over the carpet.

I stretched and caught a faint whiff of her on my shirt. How that had even happened, I didn't know. I guess her scent was on me when I dressed and it had lingered. One little sniff and my cock stood at attention. *Great,* I sighed inwardly. *So much for the whole 'let's-have-sex-to-get-*

this-out-of-our-systems' theory. I already craved her. I wanted more. I wanted *her.*

I doubted there was any way she'd want to see my face again. This had been a one-time thing and probably a huge mistake. My mind was already foggy with desire and want; full of nothing but her. I scrubbed my face with my hands and hopped in the shower for yet another cold shower.

When I got to work, I went straight to Owen's office, where I found him working at his computer. I sat in the chair across from him and banged my forehead onto the desk.

"Bad night?" he asked.

"Depends on how you look at it," I mumbled, my face pressed into the cool wood. "I found her."

"Yeah? Anything come up?"

I sat up to look at him. "You could say that. We... had sex."

"What!" He coughed and spit out his coffee. "How the...?"

"I found her and pissed her off like I always seem to do. She was on the trail of the killer and said I distracted her and made her lose it. So, we got into this huge screaming match and the next thing I knew, she tackled me. What was I supposed to do? She was naked on top of me. My body went crazy. So, I kissed her. Then we..."

"Of all the things I thought you might say to me this morning, this would have been last on the list, right after you telling me you were abducted by aliens last night."

"It sorta feels like that, man." I set my elbow on the desk and slumped, putting my cheek in my hands. "It's like she's taking over my whole body."

"What happens now? Are you two going to be a thing?"

"No. The whole point was to get it over with so we can be done with each other."

"She said that?" he asked.

"No, I said that and she agreed. I thought if we just had sex, the attraction would be lessened. You know how that happens sometimes? You chase someone who's hard to get and when you get them, the interest is gone."

"I guess? I've never had that."

"Well, I have," I admitted. "It sucks. More for the female, but still.

The chase is over, you get what you want, then you want nothing to do with her, but now she's into you."

"Is that what happened?"

"No," I sighed. "I want her even more. And even less. I don't know what to do. This is killing me."

"You look like crap," he pointed out.

"Thanks."

"I don't know if what I'm going to say will make it better or worse."

"There is no worse."

"Okay. I'm sending you to work with Mason. I want you to join forces with the police to become part of the investigation." He looked at me, waiting for a response.

"Fine. If we find this guy, I won't have to be around her. She'll be safe, and I can move on."

"Can you?"

I stood and looked at him sadly. "Fuck, I don't know."

"Call me if you need anything."

I held up a hand to wave as I walked out.

I drove over to the police station to meet up with Mason and his team. They were expecting me, and when I got there, they welcomed me into the room where they had details of the investigation set up. We went over things, but there wasn't much new. I did tell them about Britt and I coming across the scent, then losing it, but that didn't help much. It did tell them that whoever this was, he was still in the area.

"Since you know the park best," Mason announced, "we'll team up to go on regular patrols." He flipped open a binder of photos and information. "These are our suspects. They've all been known in the community for speaking out against panthers.

Once they left the station to return to the park for their first patrol, Mason said, "Now that the non-shifters aren't around, I can tell you the rest. We checked out each suspect already and none of them match the scent. That doesn't mean the person who killed the panther isn't working with a group, assuming this isn't just a random, one-time attack. We have to treat it like an ongoing attack and expect another incident. We're trying to find connections at this point. See if the killer knows any of our suspects. They're not truly suspects any longer to those of us in the force who are shifters, but obviously we can't just come out and tell our non-shifter colleagues that. I had no idea this would be so tricky." He shrugged. "So, any trace of the scent that we come across, we'll follow fully. We have something of a scent database between the shifters on the force, so I want to get a good whiff of the vehicle to share with them. That way we can see who's connected to who and try to get evidence from there."

"Great," I said. "I'll take you to the scent."

We ran to the place where Britt and I had chased after the trail; I showed him the scent and he got a good whiff.

"I don't recognize it," he admitted after we returned to our human forms. "I'll share it with the guys and see if they do. Some of the cops who've been around a while might have come across the guy before. Most criminals don't expect the police to use smell to track them down." He chuckled.

"Right," I agreed.

"You okay, man? You're awfully quiet."

"Yeah, I'm okay," I lied. My mind was tangled. Being close to where Britt and I had been just the night before was like torture. The longing in me had grown out of control. Having sex hadn't quelled my interest; it only made it worse.

He narrowed his eyes slightly. He knew me too well, but didn't press. "We were also hoping that Britt would join us, unofficially of course, as part of the team to help patrol and search for the guy."

My eyes widened. "You want us to work together?"

"Unless that's a problem?"

I shook my head. The idea of having to be around her, to team up together to find this guy, to be out in the woods running around together, excited me; I couldn't deny it. My heart raced.

"I'll go talk to her about it. I'm sure she'd love to help. She's already on patrol, trying to find him anyway. This way, we can keep her safe."

Mason studied me again and nodded. "Exactly."

"I'll ask her and bring her back here so we can set up a plan of which directions we'll go in, how we'll report anything found, that sort of thing."

"I'll drive you over to her house," Mason offered as he grabbed his keys and headed off to his car.

I hesitated. I wanted to do this alone. As I was thinking of a way to tell Mason without alerting him to something more, an urgent voice crackled through his radio as I slid into the car.

Mason picked it up and had an intense conversation with the person on the other end. There were a lot of codes given back and forth that I didn't understand. "Ezra! There's been another attack," he said. "Another panther has been found dead."

I didn't stop to think about it, and I didn't let him know where I was going. He'd figure it out. I threw open the passenger door and shifted, leaving my clothes in his car, and ran as fast as I could. I had to get to her.

The run didn't take me long. I came up to her cabin and didn't stop at the edge of the property, but ran straight up onto the porch and hammered on the door.

11

BRITT

Someone was pounding on my door. If it wasn't the police, it sure sounded like them. This would usually piss me off, but after everything that had went down, it worried me. I hurried to the door, but when I opened it, Ezra was there. I didn't have time to get annoyed; the look on his face was so frantic, it shot ice through me.

"What is it?" I asked.

"Another panther's been found dead."

My stomach dropped. It hadn't been just the one; this was going to keep going after all. I'd never been so regretful of being right in my life.

My shotgun wasn't far. I spun, grabbed it from the living room where it'd been resting against the wall, and came back, ready to go after the asshole.

When Ezra saw me, he looked pained.

"What are you waiting for?" I asked. "Come on."

"I know you want to get out there," he said. "But let's let the police do their job first. They're already on it."

"I'm not going to sit around and wait to be slaughtered." Was he nuts? He wanted me to just sit there?

"Please. I'll stay here with you. The second I hear something, you'll know about it. And if we can help in any way, we will."

"Get out of my way." I reached out my arm to push past him.

I hadn't paid attention to the fact that he was naked. Again. I'd seen this guy naked more than I'd seen him clothed. But after our night together, I knew what that body was capable of. When I brushed my arm against him, it was like touching fire. It made my skin tingle and my scalp prickle.

He reached out to stop me by putting a hand on my arm. He didn't grab or pull or hold me; he pleaded. "Please, Britt."

Had I ever heard him say my name before? If he had, it hadn't sounded like that.

I turned to look at him. "You don't know what you're asking."

"I do. I really do. And that's why I'm begging you. As soon as I know the park is clear, we'll go out and follow the trail."

"What good is that going to do? I have to get out there if I'm going to catch him."

"What if it's more than one?"

"It's not."

"You mean, it *wasn't*," he challenged. "What if this time, there are a few of them? What if they overtake you? Can you outrun a bullet? Can you fight off two or three men at a time?"

"Did they shoot this panther?"

"I don't know yet. But wouldn't it be good to know that before charging out there? Mason is on the scene and so are several shifters from the force. They know the scent. I even took Mason to get the vehicle's scent. I know you know these parts really well. You're a good hunter, and I know you could find him. But you're not a cop. You're trained to deal with animals, not criminals. They know more about how people like this work and think. I don't want you to get hurt. Please."

I don't know what it was, and I may never know. But something in his eyes or words softened me. And that was a rare occurrence. Being sentimental wasn't exactly in my nature. In fact, I couldn't recall being sentimental once in my whole damn life. But as I looked at him, the trouble I saw in his eyes brought me pain.

What the hell? Why should I care what he felt or thought? I'd wanted this all to go away. That was why what he'd said the night before made sense. If we just did it, just went ahead and had sex, it was supposed to end these feelings. To take this obsession from me. It hadn't worked and that pissed me off. Being so close to him naked, I could hardly stand it. And now he wanted to sit around like that and wait?

I pulled my arm away. "Do you own any clothes?" I snapped.

I turned and went inside, letting the door slam behind me. I heard it open a moment later, as I was setting my gun back down.

"Actually, I kind of ran out without thinking. I didn't bring anything. I just wanted to get here to make sure you were okay."

I gave him a slight glare, but my heart wasn't in it. I went to my bedroom and found a pair of shorts and a shirt that I thought would fit him. When I came back out, I tossed them at him.

"Thanks."

"Beer?" In the kitchen, I pulled one from the fridge. If I was just going to sit around all day, I might as well enjoy it a little.

"Sure."

I grabbed a frosty can and passed it to him. When he popped the top, it foamed all over his hand.

I laughed. "Amateur."

"Not in everything." He winked.

I rolled my eyes. "You look ridiculous." I hadn't paid much attention to what I'd grabbed, but I realized that the shorts were on the shorter side—probably why they were stuffed in the back of my drawer—and I must've grabbed the one shirt I owned that had any sort of sparkle to it: a blue tee with tiny gems on the sleeves' edges. It was subtle, but too much for me to wear—definitely too much for him to wear.

He struck a pose and made a face like he was a supermodel. "It's all about being comfortable in your own skin." He chuckled and sat down on the couch, resting his feet up on the coffee table.

"Well sure, just make yourself at home." I flopped down next to him and took a long sip of my IPA.

"Nice cabin," he said.

"Thanks. It was my gramma's. My ma lived here her whole life, and so have I."

"Right. You said your mom was killed by a hunter years ago. I'm really sorry."

"Me, too." I took another sip.

This felt awkward. I didn't know him well enough to be comfortable around him, and I didn't do well with the whole getting-to-know-you thing. I didn't need to know anyone besides the people I already knew.

But desire still racked my body. A desire to know him, to be near him. It was starting to move from my bones to my emotions. And that meant it was getting dangerous. I had no reason to be with anyone; my life was just fine as it was. Alone. I'd never wanted any sort of boyfriend or partner, and I still didn't.

Except—and I couldn't bear to admit it—it felt like I was beginning to. He made me feel so...*domestic*, if that was even possible. Like I wanted to just get up and cook something for him; to take care of him. God, I was going soft and becoming a damn floozie. I had to stop this nonsense somehow.

"So, what's your story?" I asked. "Are you like, sixteen, or what?"

"Um, no. Twenty-five."

"Really?" I looked him over. "With that baby face?"

"I'm from California. It's different there."

"I'm sure. How you'd end up here, then?"

"My family moved away, but I was born here. I don't know. I got older and it was like the land itself called to me. I came out to visit family we still had in the area and I stayed. I found our original clan and they welcomed me with open arms. Everything just fit." He shrugged. "I may not be a Gladesperson like you, but it seems that I belong here somehow."

I snorted. "Is that why you highlight your hair? To remind yourself of California?"

He reached up to finger his blond tips. "I just like it."

"It makes you look ridiculous in bear form."

He grinned. "You don't like my streaks? I think they make me look distinguished."

"The first time I saw you, I thought it was dried mud. Then you shifted and I saw your hair and realized that even in bear form, you have those goofy blonde pieces."

"You should dye yours." He reached over and picked up the end of my blonde ponytail. It would look good blue or even with just a touch of red. Your hair has a hint of natural red in it."

I froze until he put my hair back down. Any touch from him seemed to make me begin to sweat. If I was going to keep a level head so we could chase this killer down when the time came, I'd have to keep my raging hormones in check. I couldn't just get turned on every time he brushed against me.

"No TV?" he asked after a minute of silence.

"Nah. What's the point?"

"Entertainment?"

"I make my own."

He crossed his arms. "Yeah? Let's see."

I raised an eyebrow. "I didn't say *I* was the entertainment. I find ways to keep entertained is all."

"Like how?"

"Going out and finding something to eat. Skinning it, selling it. Walking around or running through the park. Sometimes, I go to Shady's."

He raised his eyebrows. "That's it?"

"What else is there?"

"Fun? There is TV, but also movies, going out, dancing, hanging with friends, relaxing and maybe playing a game or two. Reading, shooting, bike rides, hikes, fishing, working out, running. Golf, bowling, painting, cooking. Then there's the local stuff like museums, zoos, arcades. The beach? I love the beach."

I blinked at him. "So, you are, like, sixteen."

"Dude! People do these things. Adult people. Adult people who want to have fun and enjoy life."

"I enjoy life."

"Do you? You seem kind of...unhappy to me."

"Based on what?" I snapped, crossing my arms.

He broke into laughter. "Well, that posture and that attitude, for starters. You're always so serious. Just have fun once in a while."

"There's no time for shenanigans. I do catch a good fight at Shady's now and then."

"So, watching two drunk idiots pummel each other is your idea of a good time?"

I lifted one shoulder. It had been. Until the night before. Now, I could think of at least one other way I wouldn't mind passing the time.

"Doesn't your clan get together and do stuff?"

"Sure," I said. "We were at Shady's the night I saw you."

"You were there with only two other ladies."

"Yeah. My clan."

"Your clan has only three people?"

"Panthers are rare, remember? We have Kat's gramma, too. But she's older and doesn't get around much anymore."

"Sound pretty lonely."

"It's not," I said, a little too defensively. I didn't need to explain myself to him. "So, what does your clan do? Sit around and play shuffleboard while drinking lemonade?"

"Shuffleboard." He tapped his lips. "That's one we haven't tried yet. Could be fun..."

"You're kidding."

"Yeah." He playfully shoved my shoulder. "Lots of times, we just build a fire on the beach and hang out, talking and telling stories. Or we go out and do things, like hang at Shady's. Usually Conner and I hit the gym together a few times a week. I go to Owen's for his wife's cooking. Though now that they have a baby, that's all he talks about. I go shooting or fishing with Mason. They're my best friends, but we have a decent sized-clan. There's eight of us. Well, I guess if you count the baby, it's nine, maybe soon to be ten. We think Noah's wife is pregnant, but no one is saying yet. Probably too soon to announce. We have clan picnics and get togethers regularly, and a lot of us work together. We're close, you know. Family."

Family. At the mention of the word, I thought of Ma and Gramma. God, did I miss their company; missed having people to just sit back with and bitch about the day to. But Ezra couldn't be that to me. We were far too different.

"Your life sounds overwhelming," I admitted.

"It's full. But it's happy. I figure it's about time I find a special lady and move onto life 2.0."

I chuckled. "Life 2.0?"

"Marriage, kids." He made a box crossing his pointer and middle fingers on both hands. "Dad life, you know."

I laughed again. "Did you just throw a gang sign at me?"

"It's a hashtag? Don't you get on Instagram?"

"What's that?"

He slapped his forehead. "You do have a smart phone, don't you?"

I pointed to the phone hanging on the wall. It was yellowed with age, its cord sagging to the ground. It was rarely used. If I wanted to talk to Dezi or Kat, I spoke through our clan's mind connection or just went to see them.

He went over to the phone and picked it up, then started laughing. "Oh my God, it has a dial tone and everything!"

He took another two beers from the fridge and tossed one to me as he sat back down. Brave little fucker, wasn't he, to just go around my place and do as he pleased.

"So, I'm guessing you have no computer?" he asked. "Wi-fi?"

"I don't even know what that is."

He whistled. "That explains a lot."

"What's that supposed to mean?"

"You're so secluded. You must really be a pain in the ass if you scared everyone away."

"Ha ha."

"Your life is really just hunting?"

"I have a garden, too. But I like to keep it simple."

"There's so much out there that you're missing, Britt. It's not even just about having fun. It's life. There's so much to experience, and you're not experiencing any of it."

"And I'm just fine with that."

"Don't you want more?" he asked. "Don't you want to see the world? Taste weird foods, see beautiful sights, meet all sorts of people and animals, do everything life has to offer you?"

"Nah."

"The Everglades is amazing. But there's a lot more to the world than just this little chunk of Florida."

"I don't think about it like that. This *is* my world. It's all I need." I paused, not sure I wanted to say it out loud. "Until..."

12

EZRA

I HELD MY BREATH WAITING FOR HER TO FINISH THE SENTENCE. UNTIL...SHE gets older? Until...she wants to settle down? Until...she met me? But before she answered, my phone buzzed in my pocket.

"One sec, it's Mason calling." I tapped the screen to answer and walked out to her porch for better reception. "What'd you find?"

"The scents match, so we're looking for a serial. I was hoping you had something more."

"No. I'm with Britt at her cabin."

"Oh." Long pause. "Good. Is she up for helping?"

"Definitely." She was inside, but she could hear me talking. "We're just waiting until it's clear so we can run."

"Until it's clear? What do you mean?"

"Um..." How could I say this without Britt finding out? "When it's safe for panthers to be in the woods?"

"You're keeping her home to keep her safe."

"Of course. That's my job."

"Uh huh... Then I guess I'll let you know when we know more."

"Thanks, man. Stay safe."

He snorted a laugh. "You too, man. You, too."

I went back inside and found Britt waiting for me, looking anxious.

"Anything?" she asked.

"He just called to make sure we were both okay. They're a caring bunch, my clan." I smiled. "He'll call when they know something."

"It seems like it's taking a long time. Let's run over to where the body is at least. I want to know if it's the same guy or not. He didn't know if it was the same guy?"

"Oh..." I scratched the back of my head. Why hadn't I foreseen this? "He didn't say."

"He didn't say." She leveled her gaze at me. "He does know the scent of the first killer, right?"

"Right."

"And he's there now at the second body?"

"Uh...I think he's there. He didn't say. Maybe he's still at the station."

She narrowed her eyes at me. "Don't you think that's kind of important?"

"Well, yes, sure. But right now, they have to gather evidence. Find fingerprints, footprints, fibers, that sort of thing. DNA, you know?"

"We don't need any of that! We need to get out there." She stood and headed for her gun again.

"We have to wait. There are a lot of cops over there right now. Non-shifter cops. Mason said once they're done, the shifters will move in. It's complicated, I guess, being on the force where some are shifters and some aren't. They can't give up the secret, so they have to let them do things the human way."

"The human way is going to get more panthers killed."

"You know, maybe we should have your clan come over here and hang out. Until we know it's safe."

She huffed. "Kat has a family and a gator farm to run. Dezi is out fishing, as always."

"Do they know what's going on? Did you use that"—I pointed to the ancient phone on the wall—"to call and tell them?"

"I didn't use the phone, but they know. I gave them the scent. Can't pass a scent through the phone."

"Good point," I said. "Got a deck of cards?"

"For what?"

"To play?"

"There's a killer running around, panthers are in danger, and you want to play cards?"

"Yes." I nodded. "That's how you stay safe. He's not going to come into your cabin and kill you. Not with all your guns and me here. Maybe we can lure him close and get him."

Her head whipped to me as if she had a sudden thought. "The second panther was a pure panther, right? Not a shifter?"

"Not a shifter."

She visibly relaxed.

"Call your friends," I suggested.

She stared off into space for a moment. "Yeah..."

She went into the kitchen and made two calls, returning much sooner than I'd thought she would. When she returned to the living room, she looked distraught. I wanted to pull her into my arms and hold her, but I wasn't sure if that would be okay. After our night together and the way it had all happened, I didn't know where we stood, if anywhere.

"You okay?" I asked.

"Sure." She dropped a pack of cards on the table.

"You updated your friends?"

"Yup."

I shuffled the cards and dealt. She sat across from me at the kitchen table, but seemed to be lost in her own world.

"So, you do care about something," I said.

"Of course, I care about something!" she snapped.

"Well, you act so tough all the time, like you don't need or want anyone, like nothing bothers you."

"I don't need anyone. What are we playing?"

"Texas Hold 'em?"

"Fine."

I dared to ask, "So, do you care about *me*?"

"I care about beating you." Her mouth quirked into a half smile.

"I'll take it."

She actually relaxed a little as we played. I don't know if it was the beers or if she was getting comfortable with me. She seemed to laugh more, and every time she did, it lit me up inside. I felt myself falling—try as I might to resist it. And I thought, just maybe, she was starting to like me, too.

I thought about kissing her. Or even starting simpler and just taking her hand. I didn't want to move too fast, but we had already slept together, so was it moving fast at all? I didn't know how to handle it, and I didn't want to mess it up.

As I was considering whether I should try to beat her or let her win the game, we heard a noise outside; a rustling of leaves and twigs. Our heads snapped to attention at the same time, then I looked at her. "Doesn't sound big."

"No, it doesn't." She narrowed her eyes.

"Probably just a coon. If you hunt them often, they'd smell it and come around. They come around here a lot, don't they?"

"No, they don't. I have several small game traps set. Something small as a coon shouldn't make it within fifty feet of this cabin."

"Guess we'd better check it out then."

We walked out onto the front porch and listened. The rustling stopped for the moment, and I could have sworn I smelled a raccoon.

She pulled off her top and dropped it on the porch, then stepped out of her shorts. Just like that. I took off the clothes she gave me and followed. There's no way I'd let her shift and run off by herself. She roared into her panther form, and I leapt into my bear, showing off with a twist mid-air.

She glanced at me, rolled her eyes, and began to run.

13

BRITT

I TOOK OFF RUNNING, LOOKING BEHIND ME TO SEE HOW CLOSE HE WAS. *A coon. So what if there was a damn coon out there?* I laughed to myself. He'd fallen for it. I just wanted to get out and run, so I came up with the perfect excuse. They didn't bother me none; it was probably just stuck in my trap.

I wanted to mess with him, so I stopped short and ran in the opposite direction. He seemed confused, but came running after me, leaping like the goofball he was as he went. We were running parallel, and without warning, I darted to the side, crashing into him. He tackled me as payback and I let him—but only for a moment. I used my strong back legs to push him off me, then bolted again.

I almost forgot about the raccoon. It was fun, running and playing around like that, but of course, I kept my nose on alert at all times. I didn't want to be taken off guard. But running with Ezra meant I had backup, something I didn't usually have. Not that he was the sharpest shifter around, but he was another set of paws and claws, should it come down to that. And really, he wasn't as dumb or slow as I'd thought initially. The more I got to know him, the more comfortable I became—and the more I'd respected him.

It was strange to feel this way; I'd never had this happen before. Not even with Kat and Dezi did I have the desire to just play around. It wasn't something I did as an adult, which was made even more obvious by all his damn questioning of me. Maybe he had a point. My entire life had been 100% 'Glades, all day every day. Was I missing out on the world? On relationships? I sure never thought I'd enjoy being around someone like Ezra, a goofy, blonde-streaked bear.

I fell back slightly to put him in front of me. When he was ahead, probably thinking he was beating me, I dashed forward and grabbed hold of his little nub of a tail with my teeth, causing him to whirl around in shock. I let go immediately, but it was enough to get his attention.

He jumped on me and pinned me to the ground. I started a laugh, which I'd never even attempted in panther form before, and it came out like a barking rumble. He licked up the side of my face, and I tried to move out of the path of his long tongue, but it was no use. He licked me all over, and when he was through and let me up, I rubbed my wet face against his coat.

He was much softer than I thought he'd be. He was warm and humming, making a sound similar to a cat's purr. Comforting.

He stuck his nose in the air and sniffed. *Right. The coon. We're out here to get the coon,* I reminded myself. Nothing else was around at the moment.

I dashed back toward my cabin to where the trap was, and sure enough, he was in there, struggling to get free. I sat back and gestured at the coon with my paw, letting Ezra have it, and he tore it free from the trap with his teeth. The coon was dead in a second in his strong jaw; he shook it back and forth and then set it down at my feet.

The action filled me with a sense of...I didn't know what, exactly. It felt warm, and I appreciated the kind gesture.

I put my paw on the coon and sank my teeth into its body, pulling so I could tear it in half. I gave him the bigger piece. He'd earned it. Plus, that boy needed to gain a few pounds. He worked out a few times a week? With what, jump ropes and wrist weights? I'd have to show him what a real workout was like. My body grew hot at the thought of us sweating together, and as excitement flooded through me, he looked up at me.

Damn pheromones. He must know what's on my mind. I had to keep my emotions in check unless I wanted to broadcast to the world that I wanted him.

I finished off my snack and took off running again, wanting to clear the air of my scent—and clear my head—while I was at it. I decided to do a perimeter run, circling the cabin. I did this at least once a day just to stay familiar with what was going on. If I detected any new scents, I'd investigate them so I didn't have any surprises popping up.

I ran light and easy. I even added in a little bouncy skip now and then, just to feel my paws' pads press into the earth then leave it. I realized then what that new feeling was. Happiness. I never even realized I wasn't happy before, but now that I had that warm glow about me, now that I was enjoying myself in new ways and with this bear, I liked it. It felt good and I wanted to be around him. And right then, I made my decision.

There was no reason to fight it. If I liked being with him, fine. If the sex was great, even better. If he wanted to hang out with me and enjoyed himself while doing it, then okay. I had no plans or expectations. It wasn't like I was saying I was in love or anything. In 'like,' maybe, if that was a thing. I just knew I didn't mind his company.

He stopped running and called out a little bark to get my attention. I circled back to him and he changed.

"This would be so much easier if we had a mind link like I do with my clan," he said.

I shifted back, too. "Something going on?"

"Yeah. I was just talking to Mason. He says they're going after the guy."

"The killer? They found him?"

"Kind of. They identified him. Some local guy trying to stir up trouble against the panthers, claiming all sorts of attacks and things. I guess they're going to get him now."

Something wasn't right. "So, was it the same guy or not?"

"Oh." His face fell into surprise for a moment, then he recovered. "Oh, yeah. It's the same guy."

I narrowed my eyes at him. "Did you know that already?"

His face turned red and his eyes widened. "Didn't we all assume it was?"

"Stop fucking around. Did you know for sure it was the same guy who killed both panthers or not?"

He hung his head. "I did. I just thought if I told you, you'd go out trying to find him."

"Obviously! He needed to be found. Why would you lie like that?"

He raised an eyebrow at me. "Why? You don't know why?"

"I can only imagine what sort of logic goes through your little pea brain. Why don't you spell it out for me?"

I thought hurt flickered across his face, but I wasn't sure. "I wanted to protect you. I didn't want you to be running around, trying to find the guy on your own. I thought if we went out together, that'd be okay, but then if we didn't find him, you might go when I wasn't around. I've been worried about you." He held up a hand before I could protest. "I know you can take care of yourself and you don't need me to protect you. But that doesn't mean I wouldn't worry something might happen."

I pressed my lips together. "Well, now what?"

"They know who it is. I guess someone recognized the scent. Right now, they're all going to arrest him. They had to find some kind of evidence so they could. You can't just stroll up to a human and tell him you sniffed his scent at a crime scene."

"Yeah. Sometimes, our secret's a little inconvenient. Most times not, though."

"Right. So, I guess that's it. It's over."

"Now I'm allowed to run around without you worrying about me?"

"I would never stop you. But you can't stop me from worrying, either."

I sighed. "Okay, whatever. I could use a long run. You up for it? We've been cooped up inside all day."

"All day?" He laughed. "It was a few hours."

"It seemed like all day. Come on!"

I shifted back and took off, and he was right behind me. I ran hard. This was more for exercise than anything else. I didn't know what to feel about the killer being found. It was a relief, but I was slightly disappointed I hadn't gotten to help at all. I felt responsible as a member of the same species to pay this guy back for what he'd done to my fellow panthers, shifters or not. As long as they got the guy and he paid for what he did, I couldn't be too upset. At least the park was safe again and Ezra wouldn't have to worry.

I tried not to feel smug that I'd made him worry. It was sweet. He had lied and that pissed me off; he'd better not do that shit again, but at least he had a good reason. It wasn't a lie to cover up something slimy he did; he was only trying to protect me. Couldn't be too upset about that, either. It seemed that things were kind of coming together, in a way I'd never expected. *But new doesn't have to be bad*, I reminded myself. *This is all new to me, but as long as it's enjoyable, I'll go with it.*

As I ran, a familiar scent hit me like a slap in the face. I stopped so abruptly that the ground shifted and piled under my paws. Ezra bounded past me, then halted and spun to double back. He moved his nose, sniffing the same scent.

He shifted to human. "It's fine," he explained. "This is one of the trails they followed to get the killer."

I shifted back, too, so I could talk to him. "You sure? It's pretty fresh."

He nodded. "I checked with Mason before shifting back. He says the area is clear. The killer wasn't at home, but they have information on his location."

"So, he's still at large. He could be anywhere." I looked around as if he'd come walking out of the woods behind me.

"Nah. So many people are looking for him, and there are patrols all over the park. He's human, so it's not like he could just run by someone who didn't know. Every vehicle coming or going is being checked."

I raised an eyebrow. "You know just as good as me that there are plenty of other ways into this park."

He pressed his lips together. "Maybe we should go back then. Just to be safe until they have the guy behind bars."

"It felt good to run while we could."

"Yeah," he agreed. "We'll get to run back."

"Care to race?"

He chuckled. "No. You run faster than me all the time. It's not a fair contest."

I pulled my mouth to the side. "Okay, then. Let me prove that I can have fun."

He tilted his head. "I'm listening."

I let the playfulness show in my eyes. "A game of shifter hide and seek?"

He grinned. "You're on."

"Close your eyes and count to five."

"Five? How about like ten or twenty, at least."

I put my hands on my hips. "Didn't you just say how fast I was?"

"Fast. Not silent. And I can smell, you know."

"Fine. Ten, but when it's too hard, just remember, I tried to help you out."

He laughed again. "Okay."

He shifted back and put his bear head down on the ground, then covered his eyes with his paws. The sight of a bear doing something so human made me crack up. I laughed at him for several seconds, until I realized that his little barks were numbers. He was already counting while I stood there laughing.

I shifted back and sprinted away. I had the perfect place in mind: in a little hollow near the water. The dampness would help hide my scent and I could roll in the mud or jump in the water if I needed to really make it tough for him.

I ran fast, focused on getting there before he got too close. My eyes were trained on the spot where I headed, but not on the ground in front of me, like they should have been. I ran that way when I chased prey, but any other time, I was careful to check the grounds and take care with my footing. There were hollows that could twist an ankle—human or otherwise. And there were traps. Some were my own.

I stepped into a small hollow and felt my footing go, and my heart jolted at the feeling. I yanked my leg back to avoid falling and felt the hard jaws of the metal trap close around my foot, crying out in a whimper of pain.

This was not my trap or any other I was familiar with. I couldn't even see all of it since it was down in the hole. I let out a howl, hoping Ezra was close and hadn't run off in the opposite direction. He had to have followed my scent, right? He had to be close.

I let out another howl, panting from the pain, and searched for any sign of movement that might be him.

14

EZRA

I HAD BEEN RUNNING, FOLLOWING HER SCENT. I DIDN'T THINK SHE COULD have gotten too far ahead of me; she wasn't *that* much faster.

But then I heard her howl. And it tore through me like I'd jumped into ice water.

I ran faster. I ran so hard, I thought my heart would explode. I had to find her. I kept thinking that was it, the killer got her. We shouldn't have been out there. We should have been more careful.

My throat burned and I pushed harder. When she came into view, she was whimpering, but perked up when she saw me.

At least she hadn't been stabbed or shot, but the situation was still dire. Britt wasn't able to disengage the trap, and neither could I, not without someone else to help provide leverage. I smelled the scent of the killer and, of course, she had, too. With a look of sheer terror in her eyes, she whimpered again. I took a long sniff; the scent of the killer didn't seem too fresh. He probably wasn't nearby right at that moment.

I tuned back in to my clan. I had blocked them out because they were all going after the killer. They were talking to each other, discussing locations and details, and I hadn't needed to be a part of it. I'd been too busy goofing off with Britt, which seemed incredibly stupid in retrospect—though honestly, I didn't regret a moment of it.

You guys find him yet? I didn't think they had, but I wanted to confirm.

Britt whined.

He's not anywhere he's supposed to be, Conner replied angrily.

All of our information has been wrong or too late, Owen added.

We're not out of options yet, Mason said, *but we've been after him a long time. We're going to have to start relieving some of the guys out there so they can get some rest.*

Britt whined again, more insistent this time, and batted at me. I lifted a paw to my temple, trying to show her that I was in communication with my clan. I rubbed my nose against hers, trying to give her some comfort, then licked her face.

I have a situation here, I told them. *Britt is trapped.*

Trapped? Owen asked.

Yes, her foot is caught in some kind of trap. And the killer's scent is on it, but it's not recent. I'm not going to leave her. Have any of you guys been able to open a large jaw trap?

There was some discussion back and forth, then Conner said, *Mason and I will come and check it out. Between the three of us, we should be able to get it open.*

I sent them a mental image of our location.

Where is that? Mason asked.

I wasn't really sure. We were far from Britt's, in a remote part of the park I wasn't as familiar with. I tried to give them a better sense of where we were stuck.

We're on our way, Conner said, *Hold tight.*

I shifted back and cupped Britt's face in my hands. "I was talking to my clan. They're on their way to help us."

She nodded once, but locked her terrified eyes on mine.

"Can you shift back?"

In a moment of extreme stress like this, it would be very difficult for her to revert to her human form. If she could manage it, that would be a good sign. Staying calm was always best in these situations, and if we needed an ambulance or other help, there would almost surely be a few humans coming to our aid, too, so being a panther meant staying panther. It also meant she'd be treated by a vet instead of at a regular hospital until we could get her away from humans. It would be much better all around if she could become and stay human.

She closed her eyes and concentrated. Sweat broke out on her forehead, but eventually, slowly, her coat melted into her skin, her snout sunk back and reformed as her nose, and her ears slid down into place.

She looked up at me, tears in her eyes. "It...it hurts."

"I know, I'm so sorry this happened. Some of my clan will be here soon to help."

"Which ones?"

"Mason, who's the officer, and Conner. He's part of the search and rescue team, so this type of thing is his specialty."

She looked at me hard. "This isn't just someone stuck in a hole, I'm caught in a trap. We have to get this off. It punctured deeply, maybe even to the bone, and it smells like..." She gulped hard and closed her eyes, sending a tear down her cheek.

I leaned in closer and took a hard sniff. There was something there that didn't belong. Besides the odor of the metal and her blood, fear and sweat, along with the scent of the killer—now more vile to me than anything I'd ever smelled before—there was a musty, earthy scent that I didn't recognize.

"What is that?" I asked.

"I don't know for sure, but I've smelled it before. My gramma had some once. Some kind of poison."

"What?" I breathed.

"If it's the one I think, it's not meant to kill. Just slowly incapacitate."

I closed my eyes and swallowed hard. How was this possible? How was this happening?

I squeezed her hand hard and shifted back to check in on the guys. *Where are you guys?*

Almost at the park entrance, Mason said.

We have a problem. There's some kind of poison on the trap. Britt says she thinks she's encountered it before, though she can't recall what it is. She thinks it's only meant to sedate, but we can't be sure.

Can you at least try to get the trap off? Mason asked.

Send me an image of it if you can, Conner added.

I looked down at it, but with my clumsy bear paws, I couldn't do a thing. I sent what I could see, but it wasn't a good view since the trap was in the hole and blocked by Britt's body. *I'm going to shift back for a sec to see what I can do.*

In human form, I could get my head closer and get a better look.

"Okay," I said to Britt. "You trap all the time. You sure you can't tell me how I can get this off?"

She shook her head. "I don't use traps like these." She blinked and another tear ran down her cheek. "They're too inhumane. Too painful to the animal."

I didn't have my phone, and even if I did, I'd never get reception this far out. So trying to Google it or watch a YouTube video on how to open it was out of the question.

My heart raced so fast, it was clouding my thinking. I got my hands down in the hole with her foot, and I tried to pull open the jaws of the trap, but they didn't even budge. They were locked tight, lined with sharp teeth that sank into her skin. I rubbed my finger around the teeth and took a sniff of the poison to get a stronger scent.

"What are you doing!" she cried. "Get that off your skin!" She shook her head and muttered, "Dumbass."

At least she was still herself.

I wiped my fingers in the grass and mud. "I need to shift back to tell them." I pressed my lips to hers hard and fast, then shifted.

This is the poison, I told them, and sent the impression of the smell. It wouldn't be as strong as smelling it firsthand, but it was something. *Recognize it?*

No, they both answered.

Even the other members of my clan paid attention, and I felt them trying to place the scent.

Then I heard Hailey react. *It's hemlock,* she said sadly.

I wasn't familiar enough with it to know what it did. *What does it do?*

She could die. Hailey's words were somewhat choked. *Do you have any idea how much she was exposed to?*

It's on the trap, I said. *I don't know, but it obviously broke the skin.*

Is she having any symptoms? she asked.

I don't know what the symptoms would be.

Conner spoke up then. *Look for drowsiness and swelling, increased saliva, severe muscle pain. Later stages are loss of speech and consciousness before...*

Before what? I asked.

You have to get her to the hospital right away, Hailey said, and I could hear the panic in her thoughts.

We're trying to find you, Conner said, frantic. *Where the hell are you guys?*

I stuck my nose in the air and sniffed and listened. There was no sign of them, so I sent the mental image again.

Not helping. I could hear the physical strain in Mason's thoughts. They were running hard to get to us. *I don't know where that is!*

I don't either, I said, and my own throat grew thick. I looked at Britt, and she had her head down, resting. Was this the drowsiness Conner had mentioned?

I shifted back and took Britt's hand. "They can't find us. Can you tell me where we are?"

She looked up at me, forlorn. "Run south and go find them."

"I am not leaving you."

"You have to. Unless you want me to die here."

I clenched my jaw and took a deep breath before I kissed her, then shifted back to bear form. I'd never shifted back and forth so much in a short time. It was making me tired, sick to my stomach, and achy. *I'm going to come find you. She told me to run south.*

15

BRITT

I CLOSED MY EYES WHEN EZRA WAS OUT OF SIGHT. I HADN'T WANTED TO CRY in front of him, and it was bad enough he saw me shed a few tears. Now that he was gone and no one else was around yet, I let the tears flow.

The pain was intense. Not just from my foot, which had to be broken, but from whatever the poison was. I could feel it seeping into my body with each second that passed. I felt heavy all over, my muscles burning. If they didn't get there soon, I'd die. Even when they did get there, I didn't know what good it would do. I couldn't run in my condition. Even if there hadn't been poison involved, the trap had done too much physical damage. I'd say, depending on how crushed the bones were, I might even be permanently injured. I tried not to think about what that meant. If it would affect my shifting, if it would stop me from running or hunting. That wasn't the time for 'what ifs.'

I just hoped he was fast. My body was in an awkward position and I was naked. I couldn't decide if it was better to stay human or be a panther, but Ezra had said human. My mind was foggy and I couldn't think straight. I didn't like being trapped there, naked and defenseless. All it would take was one slimy man to come upon me.

I decided to change back; I needed my panther senses anyhow. I set my head down; it was becoming too heavy. It was easier to shift to panther than it'd been to shift to human. Deep inside, my core was more animalistic when under duress, so the animal side usually won.

When I shifted back, though, I realized I'd made one mistake: my human calf was thinner than my panther leg. When I'd become human, the trap had closed a tiny bit more. Shifting back, I'd forced the muscles of my leg further into the teeth of the trap. It was even tighter, sending waves of hot pain through me that were so intense, I passed out. I'd never experienced pain like that in my life. The trap was bad enough, but the poison felt as if someone had injected acid into my muscles.

I had to keep spitting, too. I was starting to think I was wrong. I couldn't recall what the plant had been that Gramma made her poisons from, but the symptoms weren't matching up. *Could I have rabies? That would mean certain death.* But no, that wasn't right. Rabies wasn't that fast-acting. I knew better, but my brain wasn't pulling its weight.

I tried to keep my attention focused on the world around me, listening and sniffing like always, on alert for any hint of a predator or, in that case, help. But the pain blocked me. My mind was sludge. I put my head down again and closed my eyes, but I didn't want to drift off. Without knowing what the poison was, that could make everything worse. But I just couldn't keep my head up or my attention focused.

I must've dozed off anyway, because I felt the sudden jolt into consciousness. A noise had woken me. I sniffed first, mostly because I didn't want to pick my head up to hear better. It wasn't Ezra or any of his clan members. My heart raced and I forced myself to pick up my head to look in the direction of the sound.

Footsteps. Two men are coming toward me.

I was so very grateful that I'd shifted back to panther and wasn't lying there naked as these men approached. Their sent was vaguely familiar. As I drew in a few long breaths, I realized that their scents were on the trap, too. It wasn't just the killer who'd set it up; those men must have been working with him.

One of them began to laugh, then they stepped into view. They looked like the local scum that ran around being assholes and starting trouble. Thick boots, dirty overalls, greasy hair, too long and scraggly, with beards that hadn't been trimmed in months.

I was in a terrible position to fight back. With one leg down the hole,

I couldn't stand. I could use my front paws and maybe my one free back paw. I had my teeth, but could only use them if they got close enough.

I kept my eyes on their every move and tweaked my ear every so often in the direction Ezra had gone, listening for his return. I wanted to let out a loud howl to alert him if he was close enough to hear. I didn't think I had the strength, though. My mouth was full of saliva. I couldn't spit with my panther mouth, so the excess ran over, my drool puddling under me on the ground.

I'd seen these men before around Shady's and around town in general. Those fuckers were always up to no good. They were humans, and most likely, not the type who'd know about shifters. The only humans allowed in on our secret were mates of shifters and family members who could be trusted with our secret.

But not these two. I had to stay panther at all costs. It would be easier to stay in my condition, but I didn't like being forced into it.

"Well, looky here, Chuck. Got us a real nice panther indeed."

Chuck, I assumed, nudged his elbow into the other man. "That makes three! At this rate, we'll have the Glades pantherless by the end of the month." He then curled his lips back and muttered, "Damn vermin."

I let out a low growl. I wanted them to know I knew. I wanted them to be afraid. I wasn't used to humans walking up to me while in my animal form and being so calm.

I searched through the fog in my mind for the bit of information that kept trying to break free, and when it did, I sucked in a breath. Now I remembered. These men had been seen with some of the croc shifters in town, so maybe they were keen on our secret after all. The crocs themselves were a sketchy bunch. Always causing trouble. Always scheming.

"Aww, nice kitty," Chuck said.

The other one came over and petted me like I was his house cat. I snarled and snipped at his hand. He pulled it back before I sank my teeth into it.

"Mean kitty," Not Chuck said.

"Well, that's alright." Chuck set his shotgun on his shoulder and aimed. "Dead kitty, soon."

I pleaded with my eyes for them not to kill me. I begged the heavens for Ezra to show up; for anything, anyone, to stop this.

Then my prayers were answered. Almost.

A third man walked up. "I told you fools to wait."

He smacked Chuck on the back of the head, and Chuck lowered the gun. "Ain't no one around, Jimmy Bob."

"How would you know? Do you even know what she is? No, you don't." He shook his head.

The new guy, Jimmy Bob, looked a lot like the others, as far as his levels of cleanliness and tidiness went. He was younger, though, with blonde hair. But something didn't make sense. When his scent reached me, the resulting growl was automatic. He was indeed the killer, but something was off. The killer hadn't been a shifter like that croc was; I knew that. Even right then, he didn't smell like a shifter.

Jimmy Bob walked over to me and crouched down, smiling right at me. He put a hand to the side of my face, then slapped me.

"No boys, this here is not just any old panther. This girl's a real, live panther shifter."

Their eyes widened. Not Chuck got a creepy grin as he continued to chew a wad of tobacco. "Huh. She a female?"

The croc nodded. Not Chuck rubbed his hands together, and my stomach turned.

When he was that close, his croc odor became an overwhelming stench. As I sorted through the details of it, I figured it out. The croc smell was there; I was also able to smell the shifter in him with no problem in that moment. But I picked up on something else that wasn't his natural scent: some kind of neutralizer or scent cover that blocked it.

It was nothing I recognized, like deer piss, but he had something on, and it had worked. It'd thrown us all off so we'd thought the killer was human. I wondered if they had been chasing after the wrong guy the whole time. Good chance of it. Well, now I'd found him—or, more accurately, he'd found me.

"I'm gonna check the area, like I told you two assholes to do before we kill her. Can't take a chance of someone coming around, especially if she's called her clan."

With that, he stood and pulled off his shirt before dropping his pants, and Chuck twisted his face in disgust. "Aw man, ya coulda given us a little warnin'. I ain't into seein' yer naked ass." Not Chuck shook his head and raised his eyes to the canopy of the forest.

Jimmy Bob shifted to croc form and scampered off in his stupid lowdown run. Crocs looked like such idiots when they ran, like they just weren't made to move like that. No wonder they got taken down so easily on land. I could pounce on one in a heartbeat and crush the bastard good.

I still didn't see or hear Ezra. Where the hell was he? I wanted to scream and cry. The one time I'd let myself need someone, and he was letting me down.

A minute later, the croc came scurrying back, but didn't stop when he got to me. He charged toward me, and I sat up the best I could to swat at him with my sharp claws.

He had the advantage on me, obviously. Having me trapped and poisoned was the only way he could. When he swiped back, his black claws slashed my skin and I howled; there was no reason to hold back by that point, and I couldn't have controlled it if I wanted to.

I swatted and swatted, wildly waving my paw as I tried to slash him hard. I gave him a good gash across his neck. Blood poured from the fresh wound and he backed up, panting.

"Enough of that!" Chuck yelled out and picked up his gun again.

Fuck! This is it, I told myself. I couldn't stop a bullet, and I couldn't leap forward and bite him.

He pointed the end of the barrel at me and cocked the gun.

16

EZRA

WE ALL HEARD IT AT THE SAME TIME: THE HOWL, FOLLOWED BY THE SOUND of animals fighting. We didn't have to say it; we all knew what was going on. Britt must have shifted back, and if she was stuck in a trap, half drugged, she'd have no chance.

We'd been running fast, but now we sprinted, spending every last bit of energy we had to push harder and faster. I pulled ahead. It had to be the adrenaline because I'd never outrun Mason or Conner before.

I wished, for the hundredth time, that I could communicate with her mentally like I could with my clan. It was so hard being in animal form and not having the human level of communication we were used to.

More help was on its way behind us, but it would take them a while. Still, I felt some comfort in knowing that in a short time, the place would be swarming with police and rangers, all there to help Britt. But the comfort was minute compared to the extreme panic I felt. What if we were too late?

It seemed to take ages to get back to the place where I'd left her. I saw the tail of a croc first and a snarl ran up my chest. The croc turned and I pounced on him, noticing in my peripheral vision that two human men were there with him. This was an uneven fight. Two humans and one shifter against a helpless panther was too easy. But three bears on two humans and one croc? Even if they did have a gun, they'd get theirs real fast.

As my paws landed on the croc, my weight pressing him down, and I picked up on the killer's scent. *This bastard is the one,* I realized. I bit into his neck and he thrashed around, but my sheer size and weight were more than he could fight against. I punched his spine. The bony, scaled ridge of his back hurt my paw, but it was worth it when I felt his bones crack and he went still. I opened his soft throat with my claws to speed things along, and when I was sure he was dead, I turned back to the others.

The humans were pinned down, looking properly terrified—and very immobile. What the hell were we going to do with them? Well, they weren't my primary concern in that moment.

I ran to Britt. I wasn't sure what made her change back to her panther, but I guessed it had been a good thing. She was dirtier than she was when I left her, bleeding from a fresh gash across her muzzle.

I began licking her. The blood and her animal sweat all tasted alive to me, and I felt relieved. But we weren't clear yet. She was barely conscious, hardly able to move. I didn't know if it was because of the poison or the attack.

Before I shifted, I asked, *How long until someone gets here?* There was hesitation. *What?* I demanded.

There's no way a crew can get in here, Conner said. *Or maybe they can, but it would take too much time. We have to carry her out.*

How? There's still the trap.

Mason looked at the human he was holding down. He slammed his paw into him hard, knocking him out. Then he shifted and came over to the trap.

Conner shifted back and pulled off the pack he'd been carrying in bear form. He pulled out zip ties, flipped the man over, and secured his feet and hands behind his back. He put his face close to the man and growled, "I don't know why that croc decided to tell you and your buddy over there about us shifters, but you need to forget everything you've seen. If you breathe so much as a fucking word about our existence, mark my words, you *will* be destroyed. Do you understand?"

The man gulped and nodded. "I ain't seen nuthin', man."

When the guy Mason knocked out regained consciousness, Conner secured him after making a similar threat and joined us.

I'd shifted back and sat at Britt's head, cradling her and talking to her. "I know it's hard, but you have to shift back."

Her eyes closed and her head went still.

"Britt! Don't close your eyes!" After all that, I wasn't about to lose her.

Her body moved as Mason and Conner worked to get the trap free.

"There's no chain," Mason said.

"Small miracle," Conner added.

They dug at the ground, and in a few minutes, they had freed the trap from the hole.

"Britt, just stay still," Conner explained. "We're going to lift the trap out of the hole so we can get it open."

She nodded once and I watched them as they struggled to pull the heavy trap from the small hole while trying to not hurt Britt, but she twitched and winced in pain.

"Do you have other injuries?" I asked. "Something we can't see?"

She just looked up at me.

"Please shift back. I don't know what you're saying. I need to be able to talk to you." I felt the tears run down my cheeks as I pleaded with her.

She closed her eyes, and I thought she was either passing out or falling asleep, but then, I saw her tail twitch and begin to shorten. Mason and Conner worked at the trap.

Patches of her skin changed so she became splotchy with panther fur, skin and mud. Her skeleton seemed to change bone by bone, and I couldn't imagine what pain it must have been causing her. Every shifter perfected the art of changing as fast as possible; that was the only way to keep the pain at a minimum. It got so I barely noticed it anymore. But shifting slowly would hurt like someone was twisting and wrenching each limb, forcing it to break and morph forms.

"Just do it real fast and it'll be over," I said, rubbing her nose and head. I wished I could do it for her; wished I could give her my strength, my energy.

It took time, but finally, she looked up at me with her human eyes. I kissed her and stroked her golden hair while they worked.

"We need to get it flat on the ground to do it," Mason said.

Conner cursed and looked at me.

"What?" I asked.

"We have to move her so that her leg can bend. We have to be able to stand on these springs to get the trap to open," Conner explained.

They'd have to use a lot of weight to push down on the triangles, making them into flat pieces stacked on top of each other, so that the trap would release. With Britt lying down, the trap was on its side.

"Okay," I said, taking in a deep breath. I looked down at Britt. "Did you hear that? We have to turn you onto your back so your foot is flat on the ground. That's the only way they can get it off."

She closed her eyes. With their help, we turned her as gently as possible. Once she was in position, it only took a minute for them to stand on the trap and get it to release.

Her foot came free and fresh blood poured from the wound. Conner went to his pack and pulled out a roll of bandages, promptly applying pressure and wrapping the wound.

"I think our best bet is to carry her out," Conner said. "We'll have the EMTs meet us wherever they can get to."

"We're all going to walk out naked?" I asked.

They exchanged looks.

Mason said, "Actually, it might be better if we're bears. We can lay her across our backs."

"Take my pack," Conner said. "There are some clothes in there. Put whatever you can on her and you. We can get back to the car. We have more stuff there."

They shifted back as I grabbed the pack and slung it over my shoulder. In case any of us had to shift again, I'd wait to get us dressed. We couldn't afford to lose these clothes and we wouldn't have time to undress if something came at us.

Mason and Conner stood side by side, and I squatted down and slid my arms under Britt. She was sturdy and muscular, but the adrenaline still pumped through me, giving me just enough of a boost to easily lift her.

I set her carefully across their backs. "Try to hold on," I told her.

She dug her hands into their coats and they started moving, slowly at first, until they knew she wasn't going to slide off. They picked up speed and I walked fast to keep up, watching to make sure she wouldn't fall.

As bears, it would have taken only a few minutes of running, but at human speed, it was taking much, much longer.

"This is taking too long," I said. "Put her on my back."

I shifted and held the pack in my mouth while Mason and Conner helped move Britt onto my back. She wrapped her arms tight around my throat. It almost choked me, but I welcomed the pain; it made me move faster.

Once I was sure she was on securely, I took off running as fast as I could while carrying her, and Conner and Mason ran with me. It wasn't as fast as my usual bear speed of course, but I could cover more ground a lot more quickly than I could on human legs.

They're here, Conner said. He showed me where the ambulance was parked. It had come as close as it could and the EMTs were standing by, waiting.

Just before we got to them, I stopped and eased her to the ground.

See you at the hospital, I told them before shifting to my human form.

I hurried to get some clothes on us both, and once we were decent, I picked her up again and carried her out of the woods.

I'm sure Conner could have explained exactly what happened at that point, but all I remember is that once they saw us, the EMTs swarmed. They took her from me and got her on a stretcher, then loaded her into the ambulance, where they got an IV line running, gave her oxygen and began cleaning her wounds.

They asked her questions, but she couldn't answer, so I gave them all the critical information I knew. They asked her more questions, and at first, I answered for her, but then the EMT looked up at me.

"I need to assess her cognitive awareness."

"Sorry." I shut up and just sat beside her, holding her hand.

Just before they shut the ambulance doors, Conner hopped on. He got the report from one of the EMTs, then he did his own assessment and gave them more information as the ambulance took off.

They could have been speaking another language, for all I knew.

Conner told the driver, "Straight to the poison center."

I watched her carefully, hoping she'd just open her eyes and start talking to me and be fine. Conner sat beside me, still checking her vitals and doing things I didn't understand.

He put his hand on my shoulder. “You did good, man. I think you saved her life.”

“You *think*?”

“She’ll live. I don’t know what damage has been done, but she’ll live.”

That was all I could ask for. I set my jaw and nodded.

17

EZRA

When we got to the hospital, I had to sit in the waiting room. I still didn't have my phone, so I couldn't call anyone. But they all knew. In ones and twos, my clan trickled in.

Mason told me, "The humans are under arrest in jail, and the body of the croc is being processed by our guys."

By "our guys" I assumed he meant shifters.

When they finally let me in to see her, I refused to leave her side. I spent the night in the ICU with her, and in the morning, the doctor said she could be moved to a normal room. Progress. They kept her one more night for observation, then I was able to drive her home.

"I don't want you arguing with me," I said as I helped her inside. "I'm staying here and taking care of you."

She hadn't been speaking much over the last few days; she'd been in and out of consciousness as they worked to get the poison out of her system. Then she'd been groggy on pain killers. She'd finally started to seem more like herself on the ride home.

"I want you to stay," she said.

I helped her to the couch and got her a glass of water so she could take her medication, then sat in a chair by her side.

"You scared me to death," I said. "Do you know that? I thought you were going to die."

"*I* thought I was going to die. When those assholes showed up…and that croc." Her jaw tightened, and I put my hand on her shoulder.

"Easy," I said. "He's dead now. You took a swipe out of him, and I finished him off. We killed him together."

She pressed her lips together. "I know. I watched you do it. I was cheering you on in my mind."

"Thanks." I chuckled.

"No." She shook her head. "I need to thank you." She looked at me with tears in her eyes. "What you did for me, saving me and protecting me the way you did…no one's ever done anything like that for me. I don't even know if anyone would."

"I'm sure your clan would."

"I don't know," she admitted. "We keep to ourselves for a reason. If they saw I couldn't get away and three guys came with guns, they might have taken off, thinking I was a lost cause."

"Well, those aren't very good friends."

"We're just not like you all. We're together for convenience. I don't doubt they'd try to help me, sure. But if it was me or them, I'd be dead right now."

"I could never treat you that way."

"I know." She gave me a thin smile. "That's what made me fall in love with you."

I sucked in a breath. "What?"

"I…I love you, Ezra."

I eyed the bottle of pain pills. "I'll believe that when you're not high."

She slapped my arm. "I knew it before the attack, you damn idiot."

I laughed. "Britt, when I thought I'd lost you, it felt like my life was over. I can't imagine my life without you. I love you, too." I kissed her and smiled widely.

"We don't need to get all sentimental about it," she said.

"Then what should we do about it?"

"There's one thing I've been thinking of a lot."

She sat up and pulled off her shirt. She wasn't wearing a bra and her bare breasts shown in the room's dim light.

I raised an eyebrow. "Yeah?"

She pulled my head to hers, forcing me into a kiss. I didn't fight back; I wanted her just as bad.

I pulled my shirt over my head and climbed carefully on top of her. Her foot was in a huge cast, but she had it resting on the floor, out of the way.

"I don't want to hurt you," I said.

She huffed. "You really think you could?"

I raised an eyebrow. "You've been in the hospital with severe injuries and poisoning. Yes, I think you're maybe not quite 100% right now."

"Pfft." She pushed down her shorts, trying to wiggle free, but my weight stopped her.

I lifted myself and helped her get her bottoms off, pulling them awkwardly over her cast, then stepped out of my pants and resumed my position.

I was careful to hold my weight off her, though I let my hot skin touch hers all over. We'd spent so much time together being naked, but this was for a different reason. Now, I took the time to caress her breast and suck her nipple, enjoying every inch of her body.

I moved down slowly, kissing a trail to her stomach, then lower. I pushed her leg over to spread her wide, and when I slid my tongue between her folds, she let out a moan. I sucked at her clit, moving my tongue inside her, then back to her sensitive nub. She moaned and rocked her hips, then grabbed my hair and pulled my face closer. I almost couldn't breathe, but I kept at it, sucking and flicking until she cried out and her body tensed with pleasure.

I smiled up at her and she made a pleased murmur in response. I climbed back up, laying my head on her chest and listened to her breathing.

"What the hell do you think you're doing?" she asked.

I picked up my head to look at her. "What do you mean?"

"We're not done."

"Oh." I laughed. "I didn't want to push you too hard."

She narrowed her eyes at me. "I want you inside me. Now."

My eyes widened and I couldn't help but chuckle. "Well, yes ma'am." I saluted her and started kissing her again.

It didn't take long for my cock to stiffen right up again; around her, it happened without me even trying. She had me hard all the time, my thoughts consumed with her and how to please her.

I circled my fingers around her clit, making her moan more before I slipped my finger in and out of her, spreading her wetness around.

"Come on," she said.

I raised an eyebrow. "Patience."

"I've been waiting weeks. I can't wait any longer."

"No?"

I kissed along her neck, and when she reached down to stroke my shaft, I pulled my hips back, out of her reach. I kissed down her stomach, gave her a few flicks with my tongue, then kissed my way back up.

"Ezra!"

I gave her a wicked smile. "You'll have to be nice if you want me to give you what you want."

"I don't *do* nice."

I kissed her breasts and pinched her nipples, and she tugged on my hair to bring my face back to hers. She kissed me hard, biting at my earlobe and neck, like she was going to tame me into submission with her tongue and teeth.

I was going to draw this out and tease her as long as I could. After a lot of kissing, I rubbed the tip of my cock against her clit, slipping in the wetness. She tried to buck her hips to guide me inside, but I didn't let her.

She grabbed my hair and pulled my face close to hers. She breathed, "I need to feel you inside me. Right now."

I almost obeyed her, moving the tip down to her opening. She shot her hips down, but I only allowed the head to slip in.

She cried out in frustration. "Ezra!"

This was too good to rush, though, so I pushed in slowly. Before I was fully inside her, I pulled back out. She tried to reach down to grab my ass, but the couch wasn't the place for that sort of thing. She did not have the advantage, and her cast made her even more at my mercy. That probably pissed her off the most.

If we were in her bed, she would have flipped me over, tackled me, and sat on me to get what she wanted. This might be the only time I could tease her, and I was going to make her work for it.

"What do you want, Britt?" I cooed in her ear. "It's right there." I pressed in again a little, then pulled it back out.

"Ezra," she whined. "Please."

"Oh, I like it when you beg." I smirked.

"Please," she said.

I pushed in halfway, then stopped.

"Please," she moaned, "You're killing me."

When those words left her lips, I closed my eyes and slid in all the way. I wanted to give her everything she wanted.

"Is that what you want?" I asked.

"Yes!" She managed to get one hand on my ass and gripped my cheek to pull me closer.

Her free leg wrapped around my waist and she bucked her hips as I moved slowly in and out. I still didn't want to rush things; I didn't want that lust-filled sex we'd had before.

But as I moved in and out of her, I couldn't hold back. My own hormones kicked in and my body yelled at me for being a fool. I sped up, thrusting in harder, and each time she moaned, it sent a shot of pleasure through me that made me move faster and faster.

"Yes, yes!" she shouted. "Harder!"

I pumped into her as fast as I could, my ass muscles squeezing and working. I slammed her hard, making her breasts jump and her face twist in pleasure.

"Yes!" She grabbed my ass and wrapped me tighter and snapped her hips into me as she tightened around my cock. Her squeezing and throbbing as she came pulled the pleasure out of me, and I thrust hard a few last times as I came.

"Asshole," she muttered as we lay still.

"Oh, you love it," I said, breathing hard and enjoying the feeling of our sweat-covered bodies sticking together.

She sighed. "Yeah, I do. But next time, don't you keep me waiting like that. If you don't think there'll be payback, you're dumber than I thought."

"Really?"

"Yes."

"The thing is..." I lifted my head to look in her eyes. "I was smart enough to pick you."

She pressed her lips together. "Fine. You're smart as a damn whip."

She paused, then said, "Whip. Hmm. That could be fun. Maybe I might just cuff you to the bed and whip you, see how you like to be tortured."

"I might like that very much," I said.

"Yeah, yeah, Mr. I Love Life And Everything About It."

"I love everything about *you*." I kissed her. "And I will make you love life like you never knew you could if it's the last thing I do."

18

BRITT

One Year Later

I CAME UP TO THE CABIN, DRAGGING A CROC CARCASS BEHIND ME AS I approached the door. I'd made a point of hunting more crocs since my quite unpleasant experience with the one who tried to kill me and had killed two of my kind.

Something wasn't right, though. The door was open a crack and lights were on inside. I'd left in the middle of the day, so there was no way I'd left any on. Ezra was working and wouldn't be over until much later.

My heart raced and I started my sniffing investigation. This felt too familiar. Was someone in my place? After me or panthers again?

I pulled my handgun from my side holster and pulled back the slide to load a bullet in the chamber. If someone was in there, I wasn't going to wait for them to explain.

I crept up the porch, my gun at the ready, and aimed in front of me. I kicked the door open wider as I jumped back, out of sight in case someone was right there. When I leaned my head forward slightly to see inside, I dropped my gun and rolled my eyes.

"What the hell?"

In the center of my living room sat a trap. It looked a little like the one I'd nearly lost my foot in a year before. That one, though, happened to be covered in pink fur, and rose petals were strewn around it. The trap was only plastic. A toy.

A note sat beside it that read, "You've trapped my heart."

"This is the worst damn joke I've ever seen," I called out. He was there somewhere. I walked over and shut the door, then locked it.

Candles formed a circle around the trap, flickering in the gentle breeze. The candles formed a trail that I guessed I was meant to follow, so I walked back to the bedroom.

When I pushed open the door, I laughed. The candles formed another circle. This one had Ezra in the middle, down on one knee.

I crossed my arms. "What are you doing?"

He shrugged. "I just thought the candles and rose petals would be a nice touch."

I let out a sigh. "Well, let's hear it then." But I was laughing. This was cute.

"Britt," he started, taking something from his pocket. "You've been a pain in my ass since the day I met you, when you tackled me and almost attacked me."

I shook my head, remembering our meeting, and laughing.

"Since that day, we've gotten on each other's nerves, we've driven each other crazy, we've killed together, almost died together, and made some good sweet loving. And all that was before we even really started dating. Someone—fate, maybe—brought us together to form this wacky balance of love that we have going on. But at the end of the day, there's no one I'd rather be annoyed by than you. Your insults are like the sweetest compliments."

I snorted. "Oh, Lord, this is getting thick."

He laughed, too. "You've made me see life completely differently, and I think I've done the same for you. There is no one—not even close to anyone—on this earth that I would rather annoy the piss out of for the rest of my days than you."

I put my hand to my forehead. "Is this supposed to be a proposal?"

He smiled, but turned serious. "A year ago, I almost lost you, and it felt like the world would never be right again. I don't want to go one day without your laugh or smile or quick wit. Be my hunting partner and mate forever. Britt, will you marry me?"

He held up a ring. But it didn't look like the typical diamond ring. I squinted and moved closer to look at it.

"Now, before you go having your fit, this is not a diamond. I didn't think you'd want that."

I gasped. "Is that—"

"I talked to Kat and Dezi and Kat's gramma and they assured me—"

"You didn't!"

"—that this was the only ring you'd want."

"Ezra!"

He stood and slipped it on my finger.

"Is that my gramma's jade?"

"Yep. And the band is made from your ma's necklace, melted down."

I squealed and wrapped my arms around him. I'd never been into typical jewelry, it was true. If he'd given me a gold band with a diamond, I'd wear it, but I'd try to get out of wearing it whenever I could. I just didn't like that sort of thing. But this ring? I couldn't have designed one more perfect.

"I think I'd have to say yes just because of the ring."

"Really?" He sagged with relief. "I was worried you might be pissed that I ruined two pieces of jewelry that were both super important to you."

"I can see why you'd think that. And if you'd screwed it up, I would be. But it's perfect." I pulled back to look in his eyes. "I had no idea I could love someone like I love you. You were totally unexpected and not at all who I ever would have pictured spending my life with, if I had pictured that at all. But somehow, we're perfect together."

"We are, aren't we?"

"We are." I kissed him hard. "Now come help me skin this croc."

He laughed. "I love you."

"I love you, too." I took his hand and we blew out the candles as we went, starting out on the path to our forever.

NANNY FOR THE SOLDIER BEAR

SHIFTER NATION: WEREBEARS OF THE EVERGLADES

1

CONNER

FROM SOMEWHERE UNDER MY WARM BLANKET, I HEARD MY RADIO CRACKLE. My ears perked and I was sitting up before the alert tones even finished.

"Search and rescue team, respond. Recovery needed."

I grabbed my walkie and pressed the button as I pulled on my pants with one hand. "Conner Griffin responding. En route."

I tossed the walkie aside so I could finish dressing, but as I pulled on my shirt, I shook my head. *No, this isn't right. I should be running.* My pants came back off, and I snatched my "go" bag from the floor by my bed, tossing my shirt and pants inside.

I was barely out the door before the familiar popping and snapping of my bones coursed through me. My skin broke out into thick, black fur, my nails extended to claws and my teeth sharpened to fangs. I roared and took off running in bear form with my pack of necessary items slung over my back. I was much faster on four feet than two.

My paws hit the forest floor, the grass still damp with dew, the morning just starting to lighten. The sun would be peeking over the horizon in the next hour or so, but for now, the hint of dawn made the world a dull orange.

At least a few members of my clan are likely up and about, I thought, bounding onward. Owen, our Alpha and head Park Ranger, would've probably known what was up if the rescue was on park grounds. That meant Ezra, who was Owen's second in both the pack and as a Ranger, might have, too—unless he was fast asleep, which was just as likely. Mason was a Ranger Officer in the area, so the situation might have involved him as well.

I tuned my thoughts into our clan's mental link. *Checking in.*

You on your way? Owen asked. *I'm on site and Mason is driving in.*

I'm running. What details do you have? I couldn't hear my walkie while running since it was in my pack, but Owen would've heard the same call go out as I had.

Looks like a body in the swamp. Suspected murder.

Murder? Mason will love that. I chuckled. He'd been in on a big case recently, but it involved animal deaths, not people. Being new to the force, this might have been his first big shot at proving himself.

He seemed very serious.

I expected that. Mason was fun, and when we got him drunk, he was a blast. But when it came to work, he was 110% business. Important for a cop. Couldn't say I blamed him. My clan complained that I was far too serious and needed to lighten up all the time. Whatever; some things *should* be taken seriously. Life couldn't be all fun and games, no matter what Ezra said.

Exact location? I asked.

East swamp, by the northbound path. Follow my scent. Shifting back now.

Getting close. I could hear the general murmur of people moving around, talking, turning car radios on and off; life sounds.

When I got close enough to smell Owen, I stopped running and shifted back to human, then quickly dressed myself. Until I knew for sure who was around, I couldn't make myself known as a shifter. Plenty of us who worked in emergency services in Everglades National Park were shifters, and it aided us greatly, but it was a colossal secret, a great divide of us versus them. The shifters knew who was human and who wasn't, but we had to make sure the humans had no clue about our existence. It made things tricky at times, but was wholly critical for our survival. The world wasn't ready to believe that fairytales were real.

When I walked up, I saw that everyone present was a shifter; that was a bad sign. When a situation that involved shifters happened, those in charge made sure only shifters were sent to respond. Owen and one of his Rangers were there, Mason was there with his partner and two more cops, along with two other members of my team, Seth and Jamari.

I nodded to the others as I approached my team.

"Full-on murder," Seth announced.

"They suspect crocs," Jamari said.

My eyes instantly narrowed. How long were these crocs going to cause trouble? We'd been dealing with them for years by that point. They thought they were the superior shifter group. It didn't matter that the Everglades was home to bear shifters, panthers, wolves and tigers. No, only crocs should be allowed to live there, they believed. And they constantly tried to move into positions of power to take over. The rest of us all got along and worked together. That was how we'd kept them out so long, but it was getting to the point where we might have to ban the crocs from the 'Glades once and for all.

"As soon as the police are done taking photos of the scene, we're going in," Jamari added.

I stood back with them to watch. A few other rescue workers showed up, and finally, it was our time to get in the water and retrieve the bodies. It was easier in animal form, so we stripped down and shifted, then jumped in the water.

As soon as I was in the swamp, I started searching. Being in animal form gave us many advantages, especially in the water. We could see, hear, and smell better than humans. I picked up on the scent of blood, distinct, sharp and iron-rich; few other things smelled like that. I swam in the direction and noticed a figure at the bottom of the murky water.

I made the gesture we used to let each other know we'd found something, and my teammates swam over to me. Together, we got the body free of the tangles of the grass and I grabbed hold of the shirt. *Female*, I thought.

As I swam with her toward the surface, another scent hit me; this one was much more familiar, sending a panicked jolt through me. I broke the surface of the water, then coughed and almost lost her. Adjusting my grip, I dragged her body over to the side where two members of the paramedic team were waiting.

They pulled her out as I nudged her from behind, and when they had her, I emerged from the water and shifted back immediately, sputtering and choking.

"You okay, man?" Owen asked.

I couldn't answer. I just stared at the body, inhaling her scent. Now that she was out, there was no denying it.

I had just rescued my lifeless sister-in-law.

When Owen looked at the body, he gasped and covered his mouth. Alaina and my brother hadn't been part of our clan, but they were also shifters and had come to many of our get togethers. I stood by her side, not believing the sight before me. How could this have happened? And where was my brother? Did he have any clue?

"Alaina," I whispered.

"You know her?" one of the paramedics asked.

I nodded stiffly. "My sister-in-law."

I heard a commotion behind me: Seth surfaced with another body. We had only been expecting one. My lip trembled as I saw the last thing in the world I wanted to see.

My brother, Logan, dead; his lifeless body being pulled from the swamp.

My stomach dropped and everything around me spun. I felt my knees hit the ground. Sounds turned to echoes ringing in my ears, and I turned my head and puked in disgust. My memories were fuzzy after that, but all I remember is scrambling to my feet, shifting and taking off.

"Conner, wait!" Owen called after me.

A moment later, I felt his presence as he shifted. *Oh my God, I am so sorry. I can't even... Be safe. Check in. We're here for you, brother; we're on this. We'll find the bastards who did this and fucking end them.*

Then he was gone and it was just me. Running. From something. *To* something. To what, I didn't know; I just ran.

2

JESSIE

I GLANCED AT MY PHONE AGAIN. WHERE WAS IT SAYING TO TURN? I SIGHED in frustration, felt the anxiety increase in my chest, and made a turn. My phone's screen said, "Rerouting."

"Ahhh!" I growled and banged the steering wheel.

Though my sister, Nikki, assured me that Homestead was a far cry from a massive city like Miami, the area was still much bigger than our tiny little home town, which was all I knew. Of course, that was also the very reason I was moving.

Living in a town with just one elementary school and one high school, there were no nearby teaching jobs available out of college. After being turned down for the only two available job positions in the area, I ended up waiting tables at the local diner, paying huge school loans on skimpy tips. Not exactly what I had pictured for my future.

Nikki, on the other hand, had been ready to get out from the start. She went to school in Miami and moved to Homestead—right near Everglades National Park—after she'd graduated. Nikki had a stint as a waitress, too, though in a high-end restaurant that brought much higher tips. But shortly thereafter, she was able to land a position in her given industry—medical imaging—in a fancy hospital with a big fat paycheck. It had only taken her a month to find that job, and there were many hospitals and facilities within a half-hour range that she could transfer to if the first gig didn't work out.

"Jess, you have *got* to come. There are *tons* of schools out here; you'll definitely find something."

After a particularly difficult double shift, where the customers had been extra grouchy and my tips extra light, I finally decided to give it a go. What did I have to lose?

I picked up my phone again, trying to see where the little blue line was leading me. I set my phone back down and returned my gaze to the road—just in time to see a flash of black streaking in front of me. I slammed on my brakes. *A...bear? Was that a bear that just ran out in front of me?*

Once my heart stopped pounding, I drove on. I finally seemed to be getting the hang of my GPS. I'd never needed to use it before; I knew all the roads back home and ten ways to get anywhere. But driving in that neck of the woods was like being in a foreign country.

I saw flashing lights ahead and slowed. When I got to the intersection, I noticed a swarm of cop cars, an ambulance and a firetruck. Someone was directing traffic, so since I couldn't turn where I needed to, I pulled up to the officer and slid my window down.

"I need to go that way," I said, pointing left.

"Sorry, Miss. Road's closed."

Taking a deep breath, I drove straight through as directed. My GPS told me to turn around and go back the way I couldn't, and at that point, I felt like just turning around and going home. Old Miss Judy would have probably been retiring soon; I could have just gone back to the diner long enough to wait her out, or maybe sub or tutor in the meantime.

3

JESSIE

By the time I pulled into Nikki's driveway, I was completely flustered. It had taken me twice as long to get there as planned, and I'd gotten lost at least three times. Nikki came bursting out of the house before I had my seatbelt off.

"You made it!" she exclaimed as she ran to greet me.

I got out, and we wrapped each other in a tight hug.

"Let's take your stuff in."

Four trips later, several boxes and suitcases sat in her spare bedroom. I'd brought everything except furniture from my small room back home. I'd opened one suitcase and started to unpack my clothing when Nikki called to me, "Leave that! Come have tea!" I could unpack later.

We sat at a small, round table with mismatched chairs. Her place wasn't big, but it was all hers. I was a little jealous, though the cost of her rent terrified me. "It's all relative," she'd said. "I made three times what you did waitressing alone, and my new job pays even more. You'll see."

I certainly hoped so, sipping at my tea as I tried to relax.

"I thought I'd show you around a bit tomorrow," Nikki said.

"Sure. As long as *you* drive."

She laughed. "Of course." She slid a newspaper over to me. "Most places post their listings online, but I thought you'd want to check these out, too."

I looked at the circles she'd made around several listings for teaching positions on the page of classifieds, and my hope rose a little.

"There'll be lots more online," she promised.

We chatted about Mom and Dad and life in general. She was loving her job and had made great friends over the last two years since she'd been in the area. As we were talking, her phone rang, and she glanced at the screen and smiled.

"It's Alaina. You will *love* her." She tapped the screen to answer. "Hey gorgeous!" But moments later, her face abruptly fell into confusion. "Oh, sorry," she said. Then, "What! When?" She put her hand to her mouth, nodded and listened for a long while. "W-What about Peyton?" Her voice wavered when she said, "Thanks for letting me know."

Setting the phone down, Nikki looked at me, her face pale and shocked.

"What's wrong?" I asked, my own heart racing at her expression.

"Alaina. She's...dead."

"Your friend?"

She nodded slowly. "And her husband, Logan. Both dead. Murdered."

"Murdered?" I screeched.

"They have a daughter. Peyton. She's just six."

"Oh my god! That's just awful."

She burst into tears and I did my best to comfort her, but the news was nothing short of horrific. She was mid-sob a few minutes later, and her expression suddenly changed. "Wait; you can help them." She became determined. "You have to help them, Jessie!"

"What are you talking about?"

"The person on the phone told me Peyton's staying with her uncle, but he needs a nanny. Desperately. He's a single guy and needs help; I mean, his brother just died, and he has zero experience with kids. This is the perfect job for you."

I shook my head. "I don't know, Nikki. That's not really what I'm looking for."

"Jessie! You need a job and he needs a nanny. This would be one less thing he'd have to deal with. He'll need someone good for Peyton; someone he knows and can trust."

"But I don't *know* him."

"Yeah, but you know me. That's better than hiring a stranger from a service."

I shook my head. "I have no experience as a nanny."

"But you have experience with kids. Come on, even if it's temporary; please, Jessie." Her tears spilled over and whatever shock had kept her from crying before vanished. She burst into sobs. "I can't believe this. I just saw them! I just saw them, and now..."

I got up and went to her, wrapping my arms around her and holding her close. "I know. It's horrible."

"Help them," she sputtered. "Please. Peyton is so sweet; you'll just love her. And now she—she—doesn't have parents!"

I let her sob on my shoulder for a long while, my shirt damp with her tears, her face red and splotchy. She kept saying over and over, "I just can't believe it. I can't believe they're both gone."

After mulling the thought over in my mind, I began to reconsider. *How hard could this really be, anyway? It's not like Peyton's a baby; she's six. And I do need a job...* "Okay, I'll do it, Nikki. I'll do whatever I can, even if it's just for now."

That night, I lay in bed, wondering what I had gotten myself into. It was only my first day in town; my sister's friends had been murdered, and I was going to be a nanny? Home and the diner were looking better every hour.

4

CONNER

I KNEW MASON WAS BESIDE ME. I KNEW OWEN WAS THERE, TOO. I HAD A vague idea of where I was—in a church somewhere—and I knew the most important fact. The one undeniable, inescapable fact. I was at a funeral for my brother and sister-in-law. They were both gone. And I was about to become the guardian of their daughter.

My stomach turned and I closed my eyes to stop the room from spinning. The medication wasn't helping. The nightmares still came. The flashbacks still came. Things were getting tangled up in my mind. The years I spent on deployment in the Marines, the deaths I'd seen there, the deaths I'd seen here. Faces moved and morphed. My commanding officer was pulled from the swamp, then he became my brother, then my fellow soldier.

I woke up night after night in a sweat, reaching for someone. I hadn't been able to save Zeke when he'd been shot. I hadn't been able to save Logan and Alaina, either. I reached for them; I reached for them every damn night. And I woke up feeling inadequate with a heavy pressure on me, telling me I'd failed them all. My therapist prescribed a pill that was supposed to keep the nightmares away, another to calm my racing heart, and yet another to help quell my depression. I don't think any of them did a damn thing.

I'd been given time off from work, but the last thing I wanted to do was sit at home with my thoughts. I wanted to be out there; to be out saving people. At least let me save *someone.* Let me find some way to relieve the guilt and stress.

The service had started at some point. I hadn't noticed exactly when, but some minister began to speak. Who was that guy? Who had chosen him? He was talking about my brother. He walked over to a small CD player and pressed a button. The sound emanating from the speakers was tinny—and too quiet, yet too loud at the same time—but the melody hit me like a bullet to the chest. A sudden flash. *Logan. Me. Screaming along to this song. Goofing off. Driving too fast. Drinking too much. Dancing our asses off at his wedding.* He loved that song. And I'd never be able to listen to it again.

I stood up when the wave moved to my stomach. Hurrying out the back, I saw the bathroom sign, rushed in and heaved up the contents of my stomach. I hadn't stress puked like that in years. That was one thing my therapist had helped me with, though, the bottle of whiskey I'd guzzled down the night before probably wasn't helping, either.

Just then, I heard the lawyer's voice again. "It means that you're Peyton's legal guardian."

How was it that neither Alaina nor Logan had any other capable family members? My mother was still alive, but she was far too ill to take care of a six-year-old. She'd barely made it to the funeral, requiring the assistance of a home nurse to leave the house. "There is no one else," the lawyer said. "The will specifies you, Mr. Griffin."

If my brother's death wasn't enough to cope with, I was going to be a fucking father, too? I mean, don't get me wrong, Peyton was adorable. The times I spent with her, she always seemed to have fun, but seeing me once a week for a few hours wasn't exactly the same as living with me. What would she do at my house? I didn't have a pink room or dolls. I didn't have toys. I probably didn't have anything a child would need. And how could I? I had no idea what kind of stuff kids need to have around.

"The house is yours, too," the lawyer said. "Well, technically, it's Peyton's, but it's yours until she's eighteen. There are funds allocated for her care and education."

I figured we would stay at their house; at least she'd have everything of hers there. It would already be childproofed or whatever parents did to a house to make it safe. It would have her memories. But that meant

I'd be sleeping in my brother's room. Looking at his clothes, his razor in the bathroom and his boots by the front door. For the time being, that was the plan. But I didn't know how long I would be able to take it.

Admittedly, I'd tried to get out of it. "If you don't take her, she'll go into foster care," the lawyer warned. God, I was such a selfish asshole. Peyton was part of my brother. She was the most important person on the planet to him besides his wife. How could I have abandoned her? I couldn't. And coming from shifter parents—and being a shifter herself—she couldn't be safe just anywhere; it's not like there was a shifter adoption service in the area. I didn't have a clue what I was doing, but I would have to step up and figure it out. If not for Peyton, then for my brother. That was the only thing I could still do for him at that point.

I splashed water on my face and stumbled out the door, trying to compose myself. In the lobby, a woman sat on a bench near the bathrooms. I didn't recognize her, but her curves caught my eye, making my inner bear groan. But I noticed she was on her phone, and for some irrational reason, it caused me to rage out. How dare she sit there all casual, chatting away, while my brother and his wife were lying dead in the next room?

"*Who* are you?" I barked at her.

She looked up, shocked, then glanced around. "Who, me?"

"You." I walked over to her and crossed my arms. I wanted to yank her off the seat and throw her phone as hard as I could, watching it shatter into millions of tiny pieces.

"I... uhh..." Her face turned red and she swallowed hard. "I'm here for my sister?"

"Is that your answer, or a question?"

Her face reddened. *Good,* I thought. *She should be ashamed of herself.*

"I'm... here for my sister."

"Who's your sister?"

"Um...Nikki?" Her eyes widened slightly and she said, "Nikki. She was friends with Alaina."

"But you weren't."

"I'm new to town. I came for her, and to meet the brother of...the deceased."

"Logan," I seethed. God, she could've at least had the decency to know whose funeral she was crashing.

"Right. I'm sorry. I didn't mean to upset you, I just didn't think it would be appropriate for me to be in there since I never knew either of them. But, Logan. I understand his brother needs a nanny for their little girl, so I'm here to meet him."

"So you're a nanny?"

"No, but I have a degree in elementary education and I'm available. Nikki seemed to think that since I'm her sister and she was friends with Alaina, I'd be a good fit." She shrugged. "I need a job and he needs a nanny, so I guess it could work out."

I reassessed her from a new angle. She was dressed modestly and her mousy brown hair was pulled back. Not too much make up on. Not that any of those things meant she was capable, but it seemed like the way an elementary school teacher would be. And she was right about one thing: I needed someone immediately. I didn't know this 'Nikki,' but I knew Alaina, and if Alaina was friends with her, then Nikki must have been a stand-up person.

"384 Olive Street. Sunday at 10." I turned from her and started to walk away.

"Wait! Are you...?"

I looked back over my shoulder. "Logan's brother. Conner."

Her mouth was still hanging open as I walked back into the sanctuary.

5

JESSIE

"NO, NO, NO," I INSISTED. "NIKKI, HE WAS A COMPLETE JERK! I DON'T EVEN think Peyton should be subject to him; I'm certainly not going to deal with that asshole every day. Thank you for setting this up for me, but I just can't do it."

We were back home after the funeral and Nikki put her hands on my shoulders. After my encounter with Conner, I had been in shock at first, and then, was angry. Who did he think he was talking to me like that?

"Please," she begged. "I know he can be a little..."

"Of a dick?"

She winced. "I was going to say rough around the edges, but he's been through a lot."

I sighed. "I know. But I'm not ready for something so difficult. It's hard enough moving here to a new place, leaving all my friends and Biscuit and Muffin with Mom and Dad." My throat thickened when I thought about home. My parents, my cuddly cat, Biscuit, and my loyal and loving dog, Muffin, were all there waiting for me. I came to the area to be with my sister, but she was all I had there. My whole life was back home. I sat down on her couch and covered my face, sighing.

Nikki sat beside me. "Jessie, I know you're a compassionate person. I also know you're an awesome secret keeper, so I'm going to tell you something about Conner." She drew in a deep breath. "He was in the

Army, and he saw some of his friends get killed. Alaina said that he has nightmares and PTSD from it and that he blames himself. He has some issues, and this is obviously making everything so much worse. That's no excuse for his behavior, but give the guy a break. He just lost his brother and sister-in-law and became a dad out of nowhere. That's going to be hard for anyone, on top of his other struggles, so you can't blame him for being in a bad mood."

My sister knew me too well. Her words tugged on my heart strings and made me feel sorry for him—and for Peyton. If he was having this trouble, the little girl would need someone to be there for her; someone who had the wherewithal to be compassionate and patient.

"Just try it for a little while," Nikki continued. "Let him get settled and get back to some kind of schedule. Let Peyton adjust as much as she can. Look, you don't have another job, anyway; any time you could devote to them would be such a help to him and Peyton—and really, to Alaina and Logan, too. They would want someone amazing to take care of their daughter, and you're just that someone."

I chewed my lower lip.

"You can always bail," she went on. "You can always find something else. But don't do either until you give it a chance. I mean, attitude aside, you've gotta admit, Conner's pretty hot." She gave me a grimacing smile.

I rolled my eyes. "Like that matters."

"He's nice to look at, is all I'm saying. I wouldn't mind having a live-in boss who looks like *that*."

"Too bad he's a complete jerk."

"Not a complete jerk. Just a...situational jerk. Once he heals a little, he'll get better. It's a lot to deal with all at once."

"Yeah." I let out a slow, long breath. "I suppose it is."

6

CONNER

"WHAT DO YOU WANT TO DO TODAY, HONEY?"

Peyton sat on the couch and I was on the floor so that my face was close to her level. Somewhere, someone had told me you had to get down on their level so it didn't seem like you were a big giant to them. A pain struck my chest when I realized it had been Logan.

Peyton didn't respond to my question. She just looked at her hands.

"Do you want to...watch TV? Read a book? Color?"

She lifted her shoulder the tiniest bit.

"How about we take a walk?"

She shook her head slightly. I blew out a hard breath. Weren't you supposed to talk to kids and get them to do stuff? If she were old enough to be more in control of her shifting, we could go for a long run; I know it helped me deal with the pain. But she'd been spontaneously shifting as she dealt with the stress of everything. She was still in that childhood phase of being a shifter where you couldn't control it easily, and when it happened spontaneously, it was the result of an extreme situation. Like finding out your parents were dead.

"Do you have any homework?"

"We don't get homework," she mumbled.

It took me a second to work out what she'd said. "You have to get homework. All kids get homework."

"We don't."

I narrowed my eyes at her. Even in kindergarten, I was pretty sure there was homework. I'd have to...my first instinct was to talk to Logan about it. But obviously, I couldn't do that. I guess I'd have to talk to the teacher. Whatever homework she might have had would have been due days ago; before all this. How much school had she missed so far? Lord. How in the world was I going to do this?

I got up and went to the kitchen. My half-finished beer sat on the counter, slightly warm by then, and I guzzled it down; it wasn't strong enough to deal with the day I'd been having. *How much have I had to drink so far this morning?* I rubbed at my face, looking at the cans piled in the recycle bin. *When was the last time I'd emptied it? How many days' worth of drinking was that from? What day is this?*

My eyes burned and my head felt light and spun a bit, just the way I liked it to. *Has the kid eaten yet today?*

"You hungry?" I called into the living room. No answer. "Peyton. Are you hungry?" When she didn't answer again, my anger flared. *This kid had better start listening to me.* I stormed into the living room. "Hey! I asked if you were hungry, and when I ask you a question, you need to answer it, okay?"

She looked at me and her lip quivered. She shook her head.

"Fine." I stomped back into the kitchen. What was I supposed to do with a kid who didn't talk and wouldn't do anything? She was supposed to be getting into therapy; my own therapist had suggested that, but the sessions hadn't started yet. In the meantime, I was losing my mind trying to get her to do anything at all. What six-year-old didn't even want to watch TV?

A little voice in the back of my head told me, *one who just lost her parents, you asshole.*

Yeah. I wasn't cut out for this. I was failing her already and it was making us both miserable. It'd been days since the funeral—and that meant it'd been days since we were left there, alone, in her parents' house. She obviously didn't want to be there with me and, truth be told, I didn't really want to be there with her, either. I wanted my own house. My own shit. My own space that wasn't full of memories and chick decorations. *God, what a nightmare it would be to have a wife*, I thought. I couldn't take it. I'd never marry. But,

I'd never planned to have kids, either, and look how that worked out.

My head swung to the side as someone knocked on the door. People had been dropping off food and stopping by. The food wasn't bad, but I hated drop-bys. Who just showed up and didn't call first? Rude. We weren't expecting anyone, and I was tempted to ignore it. But after the knocking came again, Peyton got up and went to the door.

"I'll get it," I said. Kids weren't supposed to answer the door, were they?

I opened it to see someone vaguely familiar standing on the front steps. She must have been at the funeral or something.

"Yeah?" I said.

"Hi, um, I'm Jessie?"

I narrowed my eyes at her. "Is that a question?"

She clenched her jaw. "I'm Jessie."

"Well, what do you want? I have things to do."

"You...told me to come today..."

I tried to remember. Why in the world would I have told her to come over? I mean, she was a hot piece of ass, but... "What for?"

"I'm the nanny?"

I managed to keep myself from rolling my eyes. Why did people insist on making statements into questions?

"The nanny," I repeated. Then I recalled a moment at the funeral. Outside the bathroom. Right. "Yeah, okay. Come in then, I guess."

She walked in and looked around. I gestured toward Peyton in the living room.

"She's over there. If you can get her to talk or do anything, the job is yours." I went back to the kitchen and cracked another beer. I didn't want to make it obvious I was observing her, but I needed to know what was going on in there, so I stayed within earshot. It seemed like something a responsible parent would do. Not that I was neither responsible nor a parent.

I heard her soft voice speaking to Peyton. "Hi, I'm Jessie. I'm going to be spending some time with you, I hope. Maybe before and after school, to help out a little. Does that sound okay?"

I didn't hear Peyton respond. Of course she wouldn't. This Jessie girl had her work cut out for her.

"You're Peyton, right?"

I snorted. This girl wasn't sure of her own name or anyone else's.

"That's such a pretty name. Do you have a middle name?"

To my shock, I heard Peyton reply. "Rose. After my grandma."

"Oh, I love that name!" Jessie exclaimed. "Does that mean roses are your favorite flower?"

No response again. I smiled smugly.

"I love roses," she continued, "but do you know what I love even more? Tulips. Bright yellow and red tulips. They're so colorful and cheerful. I like to rub the soft petals between my fingers. Have you ever done that?"

Peyton either didn't answer or made a head gesture, but I didn't know for sure. Staying in the kitchen wasn't going to work; I needed to see what was happening. I moved a few steps forward until I could peek into the living room. Jessie was kneeling down in front of Peyton, who still sat on the couch. *Yeah, I did that getting down to their level thing, too,* I thought. *Didn't help.*

Then she said, "This is a really hard time for you, isn't it?"

I almost laughed out loud. Was she serious? Of course it was!

But Peyton nodded sadly and said, "I miss Mommy and Daddy."

"I know you do, sweetheart. I'm sure Uncle Conner misses them, too. I know a lot of people loved your mom and dad, and everyone misses them."

"Did you know them?" Peyton asked.

"No, but I wish I had. My sister was friends with your mom. Her name is Nikki."

Peyton nodded. "She came over lots of times, and sometimes, she would paint my nails."

"She painted mine last night!" Jessie wiggled her pink nails at Peyton. "I'm not as good as she is, but maybe we could paint nails one day. Would you like that?"

Peyton nodded.

"What else do you like to do?"

Peyton gave a little shrug and didn't answer.

"Yeah, I get that," Jessie continued. "Nothing seems fun anymore, does it?"

Peyton shook her head and a tear ran down her cheek. Great. She had been there, what, twenty minutes? And already, she was making the kid cry. I was about to walk in there and put an end to it. But then Peyton did something. She leaned forward and nestled her head into Jessie. She started to cry and Jessie rubbed her back and spoke softly to her. I couldn't hear what she said and that aggravated me. What were you supposed to say to a crying kid?

After a few minutes, they got up. Peyton stuck her hand right in Jessie's as she slid off the couch. I thought they would come to find me, but instead, they walked down the hall and turned into Peyton's room. I inched closer to listen in.

Peyton was showing her around, telling her about her toys and stuffed animals. Actually talking. And then I heard something I couldn't even believe. Jessie must've done something with a stuffed animal; I don't know what, but it involved a goofy voice. What it did to Peyton was magic. She laughed. She actually laughed.

I shrugged and went back to the living room with my beer and sat down. In under an hour, Jessie had done what I'd tried to do for days. What a fuck up I was. I had no clue. I would've messed this kid up pretty good, though. Made sure she had all sorts of issues like me. Made sure she grew up drunk and miserable. Like me.

I sat for a while, hating myself, and both despising and loving Jessie at the same time. Either the pills or the alcohol—or the combination of both—started to kick in and my eyes drooped. I might have slept for a whole hour or two the night before. I had to take sleep when it came, and if it was coming, then I was going to get every minute I could.

I went to Peyton's door and knocked on the frame. They were engrossed in some game and both looked over at me.

"You can start now," I muttered.

In a daze, I padded off to my room, which was actually Logan and Alaina's, flopped onto the bed and passed out.

7

JESSIE

"WHAT IS THIS ONE'S NAME?" I ASKED PEYTON, HOLDING UP A DOLL WITH long, pink hair.

"Strawberry. Mommy named her." Her face fell and she let the doll fall to the ground. She looked at the carpet.

"Do you want to have Strawberry come and play with *this* doll?' I held up another one.

Peyton shook her head and tears ran down her cheeks.

"Hey." I was sitting on the floor and she stood in front of me. I took both her hands in mine. "You can be sad. Be mad. Be whatever you want to be. It's okay. You can cry whenever you need to."

Her little chest had started hitching. "But—Uncle Conner—doesn't like it—"

My chest squeezed, and I almost cried myself.

"Can I tell you a secret?" I whispered. I moved closer to her, and she tilted her head down to me. "I don't think Uncle Conner knows what to do when you cry. He doesn't know how to be a daddy yet, and this is hard for him, too. We have to try to remember that, even when he's being mean, okay?"

She nodded and wiped her cheeks.

"Don't ever be afraid to cry and let your emotions out," I told her. "Especially not when you're with me. Okay?"

She nodded again.

"Are you in kindergarten?"

Peyton nodded.

"Do you like your teacher?"

"She's nice."

"That's good. What's the best part of school?"

Peyton thought for a moment. "Recess."

I chuckled. "That was my favorite, too. And gym. I liked to run around."

"Me, too."

"What games do you like to play?"

"Tag. I'm good at tag."

"Oh, that sounds fun. We'll have to play sometime. Would you like that?"

She nodded.

I was relieved. In all my training to be a teacher, there had been plenty of child psychology courses and instruction on how to connect with young children. If I did end up teaching one day, at least I knew the techniques I studied worked. Peyton seemed to have no trouble talking to me. I wasn't sure, though, how much was due to my asking the right questions and how much was due to her having such a difficult uncle to live with. If I had been in her place, I might open up to the first person who didn't snap at me, too.

Hours later, Conner stumbled out of his bedroom and stood in the doorway of Peyton's room. His t-shirt was crumpled and his shorts were hanging a little too low on his hips. Even like that, with his scruffy, week-old beard and tousled hair, he still looked hot. Nikki was right about that. I didn't mind the look of him. It was everything else about him that drove me mad.

"You guys okay?" he asked.

"Yeah, we're great," I said.

Peyton looked at him, wide-eyed.

"You okay?" he asked, looking directly at her.

She nodded and inched closer to me.

"You hungry?" he asked.

Peyton nodded again. He walked away; to the kitchen, I assumed, and I stood.

"I'm going to talk to Uncle Conner for just a minute, okay? I'll be right back."

Peyton resumed our game by herself.

Enough hours had passed that I was getting hungry, too. I wasn't sure what the plan was, how long I would be there, or anything, really. I found him in the kitchen, standing in front of the open fridge with a beer in one hand and a bottle of whiskey on the table.

"So, I was just wondering...what's the plan, here?"

"Leftovers." He didn't look at me. "People keep bringing trays of food over. We have way more than we can eat."

"I mean for me. How long do you want me to stay, and when do you want me come by to stay with Peyton?"

"Oh." He closed the fridge and turned to me. "Um. She has school in the mornings. So, I guess before school and after school?"

"Do you want me to come every day or just on school days? When do you need me?"

"Whenever I work."

"And when is that?"

He pointed to a calendar hanging on the wall. Beside it, a piece of paper was taped up. I glanced at it. It listed a number of days off for bereavement, but I didn't see any sort of work schedule.

"So, you don't need me the next few weeks? You're not working, according to this."

"Just be here every day. Before school. After school. Weekends. Whatever the usual wage is, I'll add 15%."

I had no idea what the usual wage was, but I threw out a number that seemed within reason.

"Fine," he replied. "Well, are you hungry?"

"Um, sure, I could eat, if you don't mind."

He turned and took a few steps, reaching up into a cabinet for plates. But then I saw that he was stumbling, barely walking straight or standing still.

"Are you drunk?" I accused.

He set the plates down hard. "What if I am? What are you going to do? Call the police? I know all the cops around these parts."

"No, I just...well, I'll stay then. To make sure Peyton is okay."

"Yeah." He picked up a plate and glared at me. "You do that."

Maybe I should have asked for a higher rate for dealing with his bullshit. "Look, I know you're going through a lot right now, but that doesn't give you an excuse to be so mean. People might actually like you if you were nicer." I turned and went back into Peyton's room, but when a half hour had passed and there didn't seem to be any food coming, I went back to the kitchen. I found Conner passed out at the table, hunched over his bent arms, his face smeared across the wood surface. Food sat on the counter in plastic containers, unopened.

I searched through the fridge, pulling out several other items and began to heat up some of the leftovers. He must've woken from the noise or smell because as I was setting plates on the dining room table, he sat up.

"I think you'd better eat something," I told him before going off to get Peyton and have her wash her hands.

When we returned to the dining room, his plate was already half empty. He couldn't even have waited for us? I shook my head, but we sat with him anyway. Peyton and I ate together; she was quiet, though, and it was clear she didn't want to speak in front of her uncle.

After dinner, I rinsed the plates and loaded them into the dishwasher. Conner stretched out on the couch while I gave Peyton a bath and put on her pajamas.

"What do you and Uncle Conner usually do at bedtime?"

She shrugged and climbed into bed.

"Do you read a story or say a prayer?"

She shook her head.

"Anything like that at all?"

She shook her head again. "Do you want to read a story?"

She nodded enthusiastically. I picked out a book and sat beside her on the bed to read. By the time I was at the end, her eyes were drooping and her head drifted forward, so I laid her down and tucked her in tight.

"I'm really glad that I get to spend time with you," I whispered and kissed her on the forehead.

"Me, too," she replied, smiling and closing her eyes.

8

CONNER

I WOKE UP SOMEWHERE IN THE DIM HOURS OF THE MORNING. MY HEART raced, and it took a moment for me to recall where I was: in the living room in my brother's house. Not lying in a ditch in the deserts of Afghanistan. I breathed slowly, using the exercises my therapist taught me. When I had calmed my heart and anxiety, I rubbed my eyes so that I could read my watch.

4 am.

I jumped up. I'd slept enough that I was sober again, and now that I realized where I was, the night started to come back.

Where was Peyton? Where was Jessie? I glanced outside; Jessie's car was gone. I walked quietly down the hall and peeked into Peyton's room. She was in there, fast asleep. In the kitchen, the leftovers had been cleaned up, neatly put away in the refrigerator, and the dishes had been rinsed loaded into the dishwasher. The bathroom smelled faintly of Peyton's strawberry shampoo, and a damp towel hung on the back of the door. I noticed Jessie had left her jasmine hand lotion on the counter and I slowly inhaled the sweet scent. *Damn, she's beautiful.* I had to put that out of my mind, though. She worked for me, and it wasn't appropriate. But I couldn't deny that my inner bear rumbled at the thought of her lying beneath me.

I tried to shake off the thought and go back through the day, but there were a lot of holes. One thing I knew for sure is that I'd been a little harsh on Jessie, and she didn't deserve it. I'd tried to get dinner going, but when I'd passed out at the kitchen table, she had picked up the slack for me. She'd gotten Peyton cleaned up and into bed. She'd been there all day. I didn't know if she'd had any plans or other things she needed to do; frankly, I hadn't cared enough to ask. I'd been more concerned with drinking my feelings away. *What a selfish prick you've been,* I told myself.

With that realization came another, and a lump began to form in my throat. Jessie reminded me of family; of home. My mother was like her, always making sure Logan and I had food to eat—good food, too—making sure we had clean clothes and school supplies, making sure we'd actually done our homework and had managed to shower. She took care of my father, too. He worked long hours to provide for us, and she did everything she could to support that, whether it was pressing his shirts and making him coffee early in the morning before he left for the day or taking dinner to him when his hours grew long. Mom had that quiet, gentle, caring nature that I missed. And I saw it in Jessie.

My family was mostly gone by that point. My father died years earlier; heart attack, of course. He'd always worked too hard and hadn't shifted and run enough. My mother was so ill, she needed around-the-clock help, so a live-in nurse took care of her. Logan was dead. And Me? I might as well have been. I was worthless to everyone. How was it that I, the most unreliable of all the Griffin men, was the one left standing? It should have been any of them but me.

Logan, too, had the same dedication as my father, yet he'd managed to temper it a bit with some of my mother's nurturing. He was the kind of dad who woke up early on Saturday mornings after working all week and made pancakes before mowing the lawn. Or who took his daughter out for ice cream in the evening so that Alaina could have time to herself or with friends. He should have been the one to live, not me. Those croc assholes should have killed *me*.

I got up and took my meds, hoping they would lift the weight off my chest. It was so hard to breathe those days. As I set my empty glass on the kitchen counter, I looked at my printed work schedule hanging by the calendar. My boss had told me to take as much time as I needed, and at that point, I think I'd taken quite enough. I wanted to know what was going on with the investigation. I had to find a way to be active and do something about it. Sitting there all day only made things worse, and now that I had Jessie, I didn't have to.

It was well after 5. I remember telling Jessie to come before school, but I didn't think I gave her a specific time. Peyton got on the bus at 8:30, so what time would she arrive; seven, maybe? It would be at least another hour before she was there and about an hour before Peyton woke up. I changed my clothes and headed down to the basement, where Logan and Alaina had built a pretty sweet home gym. Most shifters found the need to work out hard to keep the animal instincts under control, and I was no different.

I spent an entire hour pushing my body to the limit: pushups, sit ups, pull ups, weighted squats, thrusters, bench presses; anything I could do with a barbell, I did it. I rowed and biked. I went for a three-mile run on their treadmill. After an hour, I was wet with sweat, but felt better. I had to remind myself that what my therapist said was true: exercise helped with depression and anxiety, and even kept PTSD tempered, somewhat. It was like all those emotions were somehow stored in my muscles, and when I worked out, it forced them all out of me.

I took a quick shower, brewed a fresh pot of coffee and started to make breakfast. As I was cracking eggs, there was a knock on the door. I opened it to see Jessie.

"I'll get you a key today," I said, stepping aside to let her in.

"Oh. Sure, yeah, that would be great."

"Did you eat? I'm making eggs, and there's coffee."

She gave me a surprised expression. "Coffee would be great."

I poured her a mug and set it down. "There's milk and sugar and everything." I drank mine black and took a long sip as I gestured toward the cabinet where the sugar was stored.

"I drink it black, thanks."

I raised an eyebrow at her, and she gave me the same look back.

"What?"

"You look...surprisingly well rested," she said.

"You mean sober?"

She lifted a shoulder. "You were looking at me weird, too. What was that all about?"

"I'm just surprised you drink black coffee. I figured you'd have it extra light, extra sweet, for whatever reason." I shrugged and began to whip the eggs with a fork. "I'm going to work today."

"I guess we surprised each other this morning, then. I thought I'd find you passed out on the couch and would have to poke you with a stick to get you to wake up."

I wondered if she meant it to be some kind of joke; some kind of hint that she knew about me with the whole cliché of poking a sleeping a bear. But she couldn't know. Jessie wasn't a shifter and neither was her sister. I'd given them both a good sniff to make sure. If they knew, that would mean that Alaina, or possibly Logan, would have told them. They wouldn't have dared to break the shifter code and tell someone who didn't need to know, would they?

No, that was crazy. Jessie was definitely not the type to be okay with the concept of bear shifters. If she had any idea, she'd never set foot inside that house. *Not only is she working for me, she's a full-blooded human. Just one more reason to keep her at a distance,* I thought. I knew shifters that went through the process of telling their human girlfriends or boyfriends the truth. There was a point when that would be acceptable and eventually, necessary if you were going to marry or have children with a non-shifter. But that conversation terrified me. It was the reason I'd never even considered dating a non-shifter. How would you say something like that in a way that didn't make you seem crazy or scare them out of their minds? It wasn't something I didn't have the skill to pull off.

"Peyton's bus comes at 8:30," I said. "I have to get dressed."

Jessie nodded and set down her coffee before going toward Peyton's room. I heard them talking; it was muffled but sounded friendly. Cheerful. By the time I headed back into the kitchen in my uniform, Peyton sat at the table, fully dressed, almost smiling, and Jessie was braiding her hair. The kid looked cuter than I'd seen her look since I had to start dressing her; she looked like she did when Alaina had gotten her ready for school. My heart ached, but I forced a smile.

"You look very nice today," I said.

"I like your uniform, Uncle Conner."

Jessie nodded. "Very handsome and official looking."

Was she making fun of me? I looked away from them and returned my attention to the eggs I'd been scrambling in a bowl.

"I can make those if you like," Jessie said. "I wasn't sure what you had planned there."

"I've got it." I dumped the mixture into the pan and pushed them around over slow heat until they were fluffy. I knew how to make scrambled eggs, for Pete's sake. Did she think I was a total idiot?

I scooped eggs onto three plates, and we sat at the small kitchen table to eat. That was how Logan and Alaina did it. Smaller, faster meals like breakfast and lunch were at the kitchen table, but dinner was in the dining room. Didn't matter to me, but I was trying to keep things as much the same for Peyton as they had been.

"Would you like to say a prayer?" Jessie asked Peyton.

Peyton's eyes widened. "I don't know how."

"I can say one," Jessie offered.

I bowed my head obediently. That was different. We had never really prayed. I wasn't opposed, though. We needed whatever help anyone would give, God included. After she prayed, we ate quietly at first, then Jessie started asking questions.

What would Peyton do in school today? What was her favorite subject? What was my job like? What time did I usually get home? What time did Peyton get home? What should she plan for dinner? Did anything need to be done in the house before she left or when she returned later?

I had answered the best I could, but by the time we were finished eating, I couldn't think anymore. I was used to rolling out of bed, guzzling down some coffee and waking up on my drive to work. The entire process of getting a kid up and eating breakfast together—with Jessie—would take some getting used to.

After we ate, Jessie automatically got up and cleared the table, scraping any bits of food off before rinsing the plates, then put them in the dishwasher. By the time I came back out of the bedroom with my shoes and gear, Peyton already had her backpack on, shoes tied, and was waiting at the door. I was impressed, but then I noticed Peyton begin to cry. Jessie was crouching down, talking to her.

"What's going on?" I asked.

Jessie stood and gave me a sad smile. "It's just a little hard going back, is all."

I hadn't even stopped to think about the fact that this was Peyton's first day back since everything happened. The days had been blurring together. How many had passed since Logan's death? Ten? Fifteen? It was my first day returning to work, too, but was Peyton ready to get back into the routine? *Should I be sending her to school today or not?* I wondered. *I can't make decisions like that. I don't know what's best for a child. I'll see what Jessie's thoughts are.*

"Do you think...?"

She put her hands on Peyton's shoulders. "We're going to be extra brave today and tell the teacher if it gets too hard, right?"

Peyton nodded and wiped away her tears, and Jessie wrapper her arms around her, giving her a squeeze.

I knelt down and gave her an awkward hug. "If you need anything, just tell Mrs. Robinson to call me on my cell, okay? Uncle Conner loves you."

She gave me a half-smile and nodded again.

We stood in the doorway until the bus turned the corner onto the road. With a final quick hug from each of us, Peyton took a deep breath and walked toward the end of the short driveway where the bus stopped.

Jessie waved enthusiastically, and I held up a hand as the bus drove off. When she turned back to us, she had tears in her eyes. "Poor little thing. This must be so hard for her. I can't imagine."

"Yeah," I muttered, running my fingers through my hair. "Guess I'm off, too."

"Do you want me to pack some of the leftovers for you to take for lunch?"

I blinked at her. In that moment, I had the thought, *I haven't just hired a nanny, I've hired a wife...* My chest constricted and the air around me became thin as my bear threatened to make an appearance. "Oh no, thanks, I'll just get something later."

"Then, I guess I'm off until after school. Do you have a key, or...?"

"Oh yeah." I went to the junk drawer in the kitchen and pulled out the extra key, which was on a ring with a plastic Disney World keychain. They must've gotten it when they went there as a family the summer before. I swallowed hard and handed it to her. "Just use this for now until I get another made."

She tucked the key into her purse. "Hey." She smiled at me with her hand on the door. "Good luck today. I know this must be hard for you, too."

I nodded and watched her leave. I stood there for a moment, the emotions rushing over me. Tears pricked my eyes, but I refused to allow them to flow. I had work to do; whatever thoughts or feelings I had toward Jessie, I had to ignore them.

She was Peyton's nanny, and nothing more.

9

CONNER

As I drove to work, I tried to focus. I kept having flashes of that morning and the night before cycle through my head. And each time, a wave of pain and longing came.

I could not let Jessie in. I could not get close to her. When I got too close to people, they died.

That was why I kept my clan only as close as I had to, and they didn't get inside my head more than our mental clan link would allow. Even then, I'd worked hard to build my own walls. They couldn't get in. No one could.

I pulled into the station, hoping no one would make a big deal about the fact that I was back. That was precisely why I hadn't told my supervisor I was coming in that day. I took a deep breath and headed inside.

As soon as I walked in, three heads snapped in my direction. There was a chorus of "Conner!" I nodded and headed upstairs to my supervisor's office. His door was partly opened, but I knocked and waited for his response.

"Yeah?" he called.

I pushed the door open and stepped in. "Hey."

"Oh." He sat up straighter and set down his pen. "You're suited up. You working today?"

I nodded. "Any updates?"

"On?"

I had to remind myself that my brother's rescue wasn't the only mission my team had had that month. It might have been the only one that mattered to me, but my boss would've had plenty of other things going on while I was out.

"Thought maybe you'd heard from the police on my brother's case."

He nodded. "We've been working with them as much as possible, but they haven't needed us. I guess they have all the evidence there was, and now they're following up on leads. Mason would have more information; I'm sure he can give you a better update."

I nodded. I hadn't been in contact with my clan much; not that they hadn't tried to reach out, but I wasn't up for visiting or talking with anyone. I hadn't even wanted updates on the case until that day. But once I'd decided to get back to it and get something done, I wanted all the details.

"I think I'll head over to the police station," I said. "See what's going on, and if I can be of any use."

"Sure, man. Whatever you need."

My eye twitched. "What I need is to find the bastard that killed my brother and his wife, and to get back to work so that I can have some semblance of normalcy again."

"That's a good plan. You just tell me how I can help you do that."

"By not acting like I need special treatment."

He nodded and sized me up. "I get that; I do. But I also need to know that you're up for any mission I send you on. I can't have you going out there before you're ready and letting the team down."

My hands curled into fists. "I'm ready."

"Then if you don't give me a reason to question that, I'll see to it that things resume as they were before you left. Go on now and head over to the precinct. Report back with any updates."

"Thank you, sir." I turned and left, my anger slowly fading.

When I pulled up to the police station, I saw Mason's car. At first, I was relieved, but a shot of anxiety rushed through me as I parked. He might make a thing of this. I hoped he was smarter than that, but I'd been kind of MIA lately.

I nodded at the officer at reception and walked over to Mason's desk. "Hey."

He looked up, and the shock was obvious on his face. "Conner." He set down the papers he'd been looking at and turned to me. "Back to it?"

"I'm here for an update."

"Sure thing." He pulled open a file cabinet and took out a folder. "I wish I had more to tell you. It's been infuriatingly slow going."

I sat in the chair opposite of him. "What can you tell me?"

"Besides knowing it was a croc, not much else. The swamp eliminated most of the evidence, including scent. It had been raining the night it happened, which weakened the scent around the area and washed out prints. We've been carefully questioning all those we could, but you know how it is when it's a shifter thing."

I did. Resources were limited and things had to be done more carefully. Part of the police force didn't have all the details, and they never would.

"What's being done about it?" I asked. "We had the incident with crocs killing panthers, and now this. How much further does it have to go? What do we even have a conclave for if we're never going to get them involved?"

"We are. I'm not sure exactly why Owen didn't think the panther killings were worth getting them involved over. If it were up to me, I would have, but it wasn't. I guess he thought we'd handled it."

"Or his pride got in the way," I added.

Mason shrugged. Owen was a good guy and a great leader. I probably shouldn't have said it, but dammit, that was what the conclave was for—adjudicating shifter-on-shifter crimes—and if he thought we should handle it on our own, then I'd have to talk to him myself.

"Like I said," Mason continued. "We are going to them. We had a meeting the other night. We did text you about it."

I pressed my lips together. I'd gotten the text, then ignored it in my drunken haze.

"Well, we discussed it," Mason said, "And we are going to them to get them involved. The crocs have been running amuck and causing too much trouble."

"Good. I want them out." I punched my open palm. "*All* of them."

"It's not that simple, and you know it. We can't just demand their removal."

"I don't see how we can't. First, they attacked Owen's girl, then they went after the panther population, now they're murdering bears? Have many more innocent bystanders have to die before someone steps up and does something about these assholes? They act like they own the 'Glades, and they won't stop until they do."

"Keep your voice down," Mason whispered. "There are humans here. I hear you. I wish we could, but they have just as much right to be here as any other shifter group."

I clenched my teeth and kept my voice low but hard. "No other shifter groups are killing."

"And that's why we're going to the conclave. Talk to Owen. You should really be there when he goes."

I nodded. "Yeah. I want to make sure this is taken care of and not just sugarcoated."

Mason glared at me. "Do you honestly think Owen doesn't care about what happened? Do you think that just because Logan and Alaina weren't part of our clan, that he cares less about them? He doesn't, Conner, and you need to get past your own pain long enough to see that. He's doing everything he can. He's going out of his mind trying to solve this, and so is the rest of the clan. If you'd come around once in a while, you'd know that."

"Been a little busy."

"I know. And we're all hurting for you, but we can't help you if you shut yourself out. Talk to us. Let us know what's going on with you. Let us help you."

I slammed my palms on his desk and pushed the chair back as I stood. "I don't need your fucking help; I don't need *anyone's* help. I'll handle my shit the way I handle it. As for the investigation, let me know the second you have something. That is, if you actually decide to do your job anytime soon."

Mason's face hardened, and he set his jaw as I turned from him. I slammed the door on my way out and peeled out of the parking lot so fast, my tires spit gravel.

10

JESSIE

"So," Nikki said, curling up on the couch with a pint of ice cream, "I've noticed you haven't been complaining about Conner as much lately."

I set my purse down and sat beside her, then reached for her container of chocolate peanut butter swirl and took a generous spoonful. "I guess it's getting better. Peyton's doing well in school. I think she needed the distraction, honestly. And Conner...I don't know. I mean, he pays me well and all. But I really like Peyton. We're getting closer, and I think she feels comfortable telling me things she won't tell him. I guess that's a good thing?"

"It is." Nikki took the container back. "She needs someone to talk to. I'm sure you remind her of her mom in some ways. You're there every day, making sure she gets to school, does her homework, eats, bathes and all that. She needs that sort of caregiver, and I don't think Conner is able to be that yet. Do you?"

"I've tried to make suggestions to guide him. Like, 'Hey Conner, why don't you and Peyton go wait for the bus at the end of the driveway together?' Little ways he can spend time with her and show her he cares. But he usually just says that he wants to do things how they've always been done. I guess he's trying to keep things as consistent as possible."

Nikki sighed. "He's clueless. And it might be doing more damage. Things will never be the same for Peyton. How can he not get that?"

"I don't know. I'm trying to reach through to him. He needs time, too, and I get that. But I think we're getting somewhere. It's been, what, almost three months now, and he's finally starting to treat me like a person instead of hired help. He's been...nicer. It's been slow going, but he's just a tiny bit nicer every day." I took the ice cream container back and stuffed another spoonful in my mouth.

"Good. He's seeing someone, isn't he?"

"What?" My heart lurched, and I was surprised at my reaction. "Oh, I don't know. Is he? He hasn't brought anyone home or mentioned anyone."

Nikki raised her eyebrows and set down the container. "Whoa. Okay, what did you think I meant? Seeing someone like a girlfriend?"

My face felt hot, and I tried to play it off like nothing. "Isn't that what you meant?"

"No. I meant seeing a therapist. To deal with all this."

"Oh. He said something about that, yeah. Peyton's been going every week and they have a session coming up where he'll be going with her. I think that will be good for them both."

Nikki sat back and crossed her arms. "What I really want to talk about is the way you reacted when you thought he was dating someone."

"I was just surprised because he never said anything, and he doesn't seem...ready for that."

"You have feelings for him," she accused.

"I do not!" But even I heard the panic in my voice. "He's my *boss*, Nikki."

"Exactly. Your super-hot boss who pays you to basically be his wife."

"He does not! I'm there for Peyton, and that's it."

Nikki gave a smug smile. "Are you still applying at other places?"

"No," I admitted. "But only because it's been going really well. Like I said, the pay is good, and things are getting better, and I...I feel like they need me."

"Oh, god." She shook her head.

"What!"

"You totally want him."

"I do not." I took the ice cream and refused to give it back until I'd finished it off.

"I don't blame you. I knew him before all this happened, and he was a great guy. He'd actually be good for you."

I shook my head. "He is not my type *at all*, and again, he's my boss. I don't want to get mixed up in something like that, and I think it would confuse Peyton."

"So, you *have* thought about it."

I let my head fall back and growled in frustration. "Don't make me say it."

"Say it!" Just like she used to do when we were kids, she started tickling my ribs—which I *hated*.

"Okay! Okay!" I squealed. "I'll admit it! He's fucking hot!"

She sat back down with a satisfied smile. "I knew it."

"Doesn't change anything."

"Maybe not. But maybe it will. You never know."

"I just wish I knew how to help them both better. I'm a teacher, not a psychologist. I just feel like I could be doing more."

"I wouldn't worry about that." Nikki patted my hand. "They both have therapists for that, and it's not your job. You're there to take care of Peyton. And maybe Conner a little, too, but who's keeping track?"

I rolled my eyes. "Nannies do that. They take care of the household."

"Not as much as you do. You're like his housekeeper and nanny in one. I mean, it's like you're his wife already, so you might as well sleep with the guy and get the full benefit."

"God, would you let it go already?" I slapped her arm.

She laughed. "Just saying."

"Well, I'm done with this conversation." I got up and threw out the ice cream container, then dropped the spoon in the sink. "I'm off to bed."

"Have sweet dreams!" she called to me. Then added, "About Conner!"

I tried to put her words out of my head as I dressed for bed, but I couldn't. Most of them were true, and that was why the whole thing bothered me so much. I *did* like him. He'd become a lot more pleasant to be around over the last few weeks, and I began to actually look forward to seeing him. I tried to talk to him and take care of him the best I could, which, yes, did involve more housework than I initially signed up for, but it was my choice. I had student loans to pay, and the extra cash he offered for doing his laundry and mopping the floor made it well worth it.

But there were days, especially when I folded his boxer briefs and tucked them away in his drawer, that things felt a little...intimate. Maybe too much so. I felt like a wife in some ways: taking care of Peyton, preparing dinner, looking out for Conner, cleaning up...but for as much as I did around the house, any emotional connection with Conner was nonexistent. He didn't talk to me like a girlfriend, or even like a close friend. More like a coworker that he spent a lot of time with and got to know by proxy.

And of course, there was zero physical interaction between us. He didn't even seem to like it if I casually touched his arm as we spoke. The first time he'd yanked his arm back from me, I'd learned to give him more personal space. I didn't know if he just didn't like being touched or it was related to his PTSD, but I wasn't about to ask.

It's just a job, I told myself as I slid into bed. *Just a job that I'm doing for the time being.* I wanted to make sure Peyton would be okay and that they were settled. Maybe one day, I'd move on and find something in the teaching field, but right then, I was happy to take care of them and feel needed.

11

CONNER

From the moment I woke up, I couldn't deny the date. As much as I tried to put it out of my head and not think about it, I couldn't. There was a notification on my phone. It was marked there on the family calendar hanging in the kitchen.

That morning, I hadn't said much at breakfast. Jessie had made pancakes, but I'd only been able to get down a bite. When she asked, I assured her they tasted fine and that my stomach was just upset. Of course, then she'd gone off to get me some antacids and a glass of water. I drank it, chewed the chalky tablets and thanked her, but I knew it wouldn't be enough to quell the wrenching ache in my gut; it was the familiar, deep down in my bones, surging through every part of me ache that nothing would fix.

Except maybe some vodka—and I made sure I had plenty around for the occasion. I'd been doing a little better, drinking less week by week. But that night? Not a fucking chance.

I checked in with Mason, as was my normal morning ritual. As usual, he answered my text with, "Nothing new. Sorry." All their leads had dried up. They were useless, as far as I was concerned.

The conclave wasn't much better. When we'd gone to talk with them, they were deeply concerned. They had representatives in the area who would be doing their own investigation, but they hadn't accomplished much, either. It seemed that everyone was content to just let it go and move on with life. Everyone except me and Peyton. We were stuck in the misery of missing two people no one seemed to give a damn about.

I made it through the day in a daze. The only mission we'd had during my shift was a simple one: rescuing a boy who got himself stuck in a tree. I watched as Jamari climbed the ladder to bring him down and made sure the EMTs were on their way to treat his wounds.

When I got home that evening, Peyton had already finished her homework and was playing a game with Jessie while dinner was in the oven. Even if I didn't think I could eat, I appreciated how good it smelled. I'd gladly pay extra if it meant she'd keep making amazing meals like she had been. They greeted me with a hello, but I walked straight to the refrigerator and pulled out a beer, gulping it down before Jessie came into the kitchen.

"I have some chicken baking," she said.

I nodded and poured myself a drink with a lot of vodka and a splash of orange juice. "I don't think I'm going to eat, but thank you."

"Oh." With concerned eyes, she watched me down a huge gulp of the drink, then top it off with more vodka. "Are you okay? You seem...out of it today."

"I'm fine."

Did she not bother to check the calendar? Did she have no idea what day it was?

"Well, I'll let you know when dinner is ready in case you change your mind."

I nodded and took my drink to the bedroom so I could be alone. I'm sure she judged me or thought I was an asshole, but I didn't care. I turned on the TV and flipped though the channels until I found something that occupied enough of my attention.

Jessie knocked on my door a little later. "Dinner is ready. Do you want to come eat?"

"Nah," I muttered.

"Do you want me to bring you a plate?"

"No, I'm good."

I heard her walk away and felt a twinge of guilt. It wasn't her fault; apparently, she didn't realize what was going on. *Whatever,* I breathed, swigging back another gulp.

I hadn't been paying much attention to the time, so I was surprised it had gotten so late when Jessie knocked again.

"Is it okay if Peyton comes in to say goodnight?" Jessie asked.

I groaned but pulled myself out of bed, stumbling to the door, and opened it. Peyton stood there, looking a little shy. I bent down to hug her and kiss the top of her head.

"Night, honey," I slurred.

She answered with a sweet little, "Night," and turned to take Jessie's hand. They walked toward Peyton's bedroom, and I closed the door.

Seeing them walk away like that gave me a sudden pang of loneliness. What the fuck was I doing? I wanted to be with them, but more than that, I wanted to be part of the relationship they were building together; not just the third-wheel drunk uncle who couldn't take care of his niece.

As wasted as I was, it hadn't dulled the pain; it flared in me hot and demanding. I heard the door to Peyton's bedroom close and the thought of Jessie leaving, of being alone in the house with Peyton sleeping, choked me. I struggled to suck in a breath and hurried to open my door.

Jessie turned to me and we looked at each other for a long moment.

"Um, did she get to bed okay?" I didn't know what else to say.

"Yeah, she's okay, I think. We talked some."

My eyebrows drew together. "Is something wrong?"

She glanced toward Peyton's door and I realized we were probably talking a little too loudly. She motioned for me to join her in the living room, and I waited for her to turn around before I moved down the hall so that she wouldn't have to see me stumble.

I sat beside her on the couch and waited for her to speak.

"Peyton was a little sad today because it's her dad's birthday. I'd seen it weeks ago on the calendar, but I thought it was better not to bring it up. I wasn't sure what it would be like for either of you, to be honest, and I didn't want to make it worse. But, this morning she told me and said she was going to draw him a picture at school."

"Did she?" I asked, my voice breaking and my throat thick. She had noticed after all; she'd known the whole time.

"She did. It was very sweet. She was..." Jessie scratched her neck and looked down.

"What?"

"She wanted to take it to his grave today. But it seemed like you needed some space, and I didn't want to bother you with it. I didn't think it was really my place to take her, either, so I said that maybe we could talk to you and see if you could go this week some time."

I put my head in my hands, but it was the wrong move. A wave of nausea rushed over me and I hurried to the kitchen; there's no way I would have made it to the bathroom. I threw up in the trash and when I lifted my head again, I found Jessie holding a glass of water out to me.

"Thanks." I took it and drank it too fast.

"Do you want me to heat up some of the chicken? It can't be good for you to have been drinking all night on an empty stomach."

I wanted to hate her for it. I wanted to scream at her to get away from me and never come back. I wanted to stop her from caring. Instead, I nodded once, numbly, and sat hard at the kitchen table to watch her pull the food out of the fridge and prepare it for me. I ate slowly, and by the time I'd finished and she took my plate, I was already feeling a little more sober.

"Thank you," I said. "It definitely helped buffer the vodka."

She chuckled. "I guess that's good. Unless you were trying to numb your pain."

"That's what I'm always trying to do."

She gave me a sad smile. "I'm sorry that there's so much of it."

"Me, too." I looked at her for a long while, then dared to ask her what I'd been longing to. "Will you...stay a little while? I...I don't want to be alone right now."

She pulled her lower lip into her mouth. "Sure, I could stay for a little longer."

"Would you like a glass of wine?" I pulled a bottle of my favorite red from the cabinet.

"Are you sure you should...?"

I paused for a moment. "Yeah, you're probably right. Iced tea?"

"Perfect."

I poured two glasses and handed her one. I tapped mine to hers and said, "To the best nanny on the planet."

She smiled shyly and looked down. "Thanks. I don't really have any experience, so it's good to know that I've been helpful."

"You have been. I don't know what I'd do without you. I think it's pretty obvious that I have no idea what I'm doing."

"Kids aren't all that hard. You just have to be in the present with them."

"And I'm not." I walked into the living room and flopped down on the couch. She followed and sat beside me.

"You've been through a lot, and having Peyton is a big adjustment in your life. I haven't known you that long, but...I'm sure with your therapist and everything, you're making progress."

I laughed. "How could you possibly know that?"

"Well, honestly, I don't." She sighed. "I just...never know *what* to say to you. I'm certainly no therapist. I was taught how to connect with kids in school. But when it comes to men, I just don't—"

"I'm sure you were able to connect with boyfriends that you've had."

"I haven't really had any."

"Oh, come on," I said. "Don't do that innocent little schoolgirl act where you pretend to be all pure and innocent."

Her face grew redder than I'd ever seen it. I felt the embarrassment like hot fire run up my chest. God, could I say anything right to her?

"I'm sorry," I said quickly. "I didn't mean...it's just that...you're so..."

"Naive?" she offered.

"That's not what I was going to say. Beautiful. Selfless. Caring. Surely, someone in your life noticed and tried to get close to you. You must've had boys falling all over you."

"I have had dates. And I guess I could've called a boy or two from high school 'boyfriends.' But I've never been in a long-term relationship. In college, I studied hard and was the boring girl who would rather read than party. Sorry. It's lame, I know."

"I'm just surprised that no one tried to ask you out."

She shrugged. "When you stay in your dorm room and don't go anywhere except class, you don't meet people easily. I only went on a few dates. But why are we talking about this?"

"I didn't mean to bring it up. It just illustrates my point that I can't effectively connect with not only kids, but anyone. I'm always putting my foot in my mouth."

She took a sip of iced tea and gave me a sympathetic smile. "Hey, don't worry about it."

"Sorry, I shouldn't have said anything. It was stupid." But at least then I knew she was single.

"How's today been?" she asked.

"Difficult. Mostly a blur."

"Does it help? To drink it away like that?"

"For a time. But it always fades. Then the pain is usually worse."

"Why do you do it?"

I gave a half smile. "I don't know what else to do."

"Is therapy helping? I'd think talking about it would make it better."

"Why do people always think that?" I challenged. "Talking about it makes it more real, and that usually makes it more painful. After therapy, the pain is so much worse."

"But doesn't it help in the long run?"

"Doesn't seem to."

"Then why do you keep going?"

"I don't know what else to do." I set down my glass and ran my fingers through my hair. "Therapy, medication, self-medication. What else is there?"

"Having fun, spending time with friends and family, finding a purpose in life."

"Purpose." I huffed. "Who on this planet has managed to find that?"

"Lots of people."

"Have you?"

She took a moment to respond. "Partially, I think. I got into teaching because I wanted to change lives and help kids—that's a purpose. I'm trying to do that now with Peyton."

"Maybe that's my problem. I'm not living for much."

We continued to talk, getting deeper and deeper. Deeper than I had gone with anyone in a long time, including my therapist. By the time Jessie looked at her phone, it was already 5am.

"You know, maybe you should just stay," I offered. "You're going to need to get Peyton up and ready for school soon."

She started laughing. "Look at all these texts! I didn't plan on staying so long. My sister must be freaking out wondering where I am."

"No doubt. You're gonna be grounded, for sure."

She continued to laugh and put her hand on my arm as she doubled over. "You're probably right. I'm in deep shit."

Her touch sent a flood of warmth through me, driving my inner bear wild. I wanted to pull back, but I needed to feel her close. She stood and looked in my eyes and I held her gaze for a moment. Something in what I saw there made me inch closer to her. Before I stopped to think about it, I pressed my lips to hers.

She pulled back and gasped, blinking at me. “I’m sorry, I just...wasn’t expecting that.”

I walked past her toward the hall. “I’ll set up the bed for you. I’ll sleep on the couch.”

I went to the bedroom and attempted to make things look somewhat tidy, trying to not to think about the kiss. I don’t know why I’d done it, and I didn’t know how to interpret her reaction.

She stood in the doorway, watching me as I picked up my dirty clothes and straightened the pillows.

“Sorry,” I said. “It’s a mess.”

“Mine is messy, too.”

“I doubt that.”

She leaned against the doorframe and gave me a sly smile. “You know, I’m not as sweet and innocent as you think I am.”

“No?” I walked back over to her. I stood just feet from her and considered my next move. It could have gone so many ways. But I had to know.

I took her face in my hands and kissed her again, harder this time, letting my desire for her be known. That time, she let me kiss her—and she even kissed me back. But then she put her hand on my chest and broke away, looking down and resting her head on my shoulder.

“Conner,” she whispered. “This...isn’t a good idea. Peyton’s right in the next room, and I work for you. I just think it’s better if we don’t do this.” She met my eyes, and she looked sorry.

I was sorry, too, and took two steps back. “Well, do you have everything you need?” I asked.

She nodded and bit her lip.

I nodded and gently shut the door. In the living room, I shook the blanket from its folded square and lay down, pulling it up over me. But as soon as I reclined, the wave rushed over me, so I sat back up and put my feet on the floor.

The anxiety hit me first; then, a wave of sadness. The loneliness burned hot, right beside the rejection, making the perfectly terrible end to a perfectly terrible day. I put my head in my hands and tried to breathe.

It worked for a while. My heart slowed, my throat relaxed; I felt like I could breathe again. Then, the memory of last year on this day came to the forefront of my mind: me, Conner and Alaina, out for a night of fun. Peyton had been home with a babysitter; it might have been Nikki, in fact. Even if things hadn't gone so wrong, Jessie still might have found her way into my life.

My recollections of last year mixed with the memories of the last hour and created a perfect storm in my heart. I felt more alone than I'd ever felt in my life. I'd taken a chance with Jessie—and things had gone terribly wrong. Who knew what would happen next. Maybe she'd quit. Maybe she'd hate me. Hell, maybe she'd even fall for me. I wasn't sure which option would be worse.

I wallowed in the pain for a while, letting the thoughts and emotions take their turns wreaking havoc on my mind. When it became too much, tears filled my eyes. I let them fall, wanting to be rid of them once and for all. Weren't women always saying to just cry it out and that a good cry was all they needed? Maybe there was something to that. So, I decided to take a chance and just give in.

I found myself sobbing and then a creak of floorboards caused me to look up. Jessie stood there watching me. I quickly wiped my eyes and swallowed my tears, burying my feelings; she couldn't see me like that.

"Conner, I'm so sorry," she whispered. She made her way over and sat beside me, putting her hand on my shoulder. "Did I...make things worse?"

"I'm fine," I said. "I was just thinking."

"It's okay." She rubbed my back, and it was as if her hand radiated comfort, rubbing circles of warmth to my soul.

The tears threatened to continue, but I swallowed them down.

"You can cry," she said, leaning in and speaking into my ear.

Her closeness and warmth made it almost impossible for me to keep the tears from falling. I blinked fast and looked up, hoping they'd dry.

"Conner," she soothed, "Let it out. It's always better that way. I would never tell anyone. I would never do that to you. You're safe with me. I'm here for you."

She put her arm around me and rested her head on my shoulder.

She continued to rub my back, and when I closed my eyes, I felt the comfort from not only her touch and words, but from her scent. She smelled like peace, kindness and—most importantly—hope, and I could hear the purring of my inner bear as he reveled in her essence.

I let my shoulders fall and leaned into her. I did as she asked; I let it go. All of it. I sobbed into her and she held me, smoothed my hair and offered reassurance.

She was just *there*. I'd needed that so badly and I hadn't even known it.

I cried until I felt empty. And then, to fill myself back up, to get something that resembled peace, I looked up at her. I stared into her eyes, seeing everything I needed. I leaned forward and kissed her.

That time, she didn't pull back. She let me kiss her, and she returned the gesture just as strongly. Her fingers wound through my hair. I grew hard at her touch, and my bear begged to be closer to her, so I picked her up and carried her to my bedroom.

12

CONNER

I GENTLY LAY HER DOWN ON THE BED AND SLID INTO PLACE OVER HER. I DID nothing more than kiss her for a long time, just wanting to be close to her, to share affection with someone who cared for me. I didn't need things to go further.

She rubbed my back and played with my hair. Her fingernails danced along the back of my neck and sent chills through me. *I could love her*, I thought. *I could. I could make her mine.* Why not? Didn't I deserve happiness, for once? She was there and willing and wanted to be with me. Didn't she? I knew she did. Her whole body told me so, and she certainly wasn't trying to stop me.

I kissed along her neck, inhaling her scent, moving my hand slowly under her shirt. She'd removed her bra and her breasts were firm, soft as silk. I caressed them, feeling their weight in my hands as I rubbed my thumbs over her nipples, and she let out the softest moan. That moan sent tingles through my entire body, and I felt myself stiffen. God, she was perfect. Gorgeous body with curves in all the right places. I let my hands explore under her shirt a little more and she responded to my touch, nibbling on my ear and running her hands along my spine.

Her hips lifted to press into my erection and my head swam with the feeling. She wanted me. It was clear. I didn't know how far she wanted to go, and I wouldn't push her. If she didn't make it clear that she wanted more, I wouldn't try it.

Her hands found their way under my shirt, and she pulled it up and over my head. She pinched my nipples gently and played with my chest hair. Her hands felt so good; it didn't matter where she touched me or how. Her presence alone was so enjoyable, I wanted that moment to last forever.

Pulling the hem of her shirt up and off her body, I planted a trail of kisses down her neck to her breasts. I took her stiff peaks into my mouth, one by one, and she let out a soft "oh," moving her hips in response.

She wiggled her hands under my shorts and squeezed my ass, and in return, I slid my fingers over the front of her pants, gently rubbing slow circles against her, and she moaned again, pressing into my hand. I slid her pants down and let them fall to the floor. Feeling the dampness of her panties, I slipped a finger underneath and explored her wetness.

She was soaking with desire, so I slipped a finger gently inside her. She let out a loader moan—still quiet, but more insistent—and moved against me as I slid my finger in and out of her entrance.

"Yes," she whispered.

I hooked my fingers in the lace waistband of her panties and guided them over her hips, letting them pool at her ankles, and got on my knees to work her with my mouth. I kissed along her thigh, then let my tongue flick over her sensitive nub and between her folds. I reinserted my finger and moved it in and out as I sucked her into my mouth. She swiveled her hips, moaning with the pleasure of the feeling.

Letting out a more fervent cry, louder than any of the others, I felt her tighten around my finger and she came, her juices flowing over my hand as she dug her fingers into my hair. Her body shuddered as the rush of her orgasm pulsated through her, then she went still.

She breathed more slowly, recovering. I came back to her, kissed her again, and lie beside her. She flung her leg over me and pressed herself against me, sliding her hand under my shorts and pushed them down, along with my boxers. I helped her get them off as she took my stiff cock into her hands and stroked me. I was hard as a rock and every movement of her hand sent waves of pleasure through me.

I wanted her so badly; to just lay her down and thrust inside her, but

I held back. I didn't want to pressure her into anything she wasn't ready for.

I was close to the edge when she suddenly stopped.

"Conner," she whispered. "I want you."

"Are you sure?"

"Yes. Please. Make love to me."

I closed my eyes and swallowed. There was no way I could say no to that. I moved back into place on top of her and pushed her legs apart, rubbing her slickness onto my throbbing member. I pressed my head at her opening and moved inside her gently.

Pushing back against me, she gasped as I filled her to the hilt. "Oh god, Conner."

I plunged into her slowly at first, but as I sped up, she bit her lip. She let out a moan and I found a rhythm that seemed to feel good to her. Lifting her hips, she pushed me in further; harder. She slammed into me, and as I picked up my tempo, she moaned and gripped my ass, pulling me into her even deeper.

I responded with harder thrusts and faster movements. If she could handle it, I could give it. When she started to moan, I went as hard and fast as I dared. She cried out and pulled me in, contracting around me, and I came, slamming into her hard with each thrust. She tugged my hair hard and cried out, more loudly than she had before.

She shuddered again and breathed heavily into my ear. When I had emptied myself into her, I panted and set my forehead on her shoulder.

"My god," she said. "Wow."

I laughed once. "Good." I slowly pulled back to slip out of her, then lay beside her.

"That was amazing."

I kissed along her neck and jaw, nuzzling my head into her. Her warmth soothed me and I fell asleep almost instantly.

13

JESSIE

I WOKE HAPPY AND WARM IN CONNER'S ARMS. I LAY STILL FOR A LONG moment, just soaking in his closeness. It felt good to have him around me, and what we'd done the night before had felt incredible. I stifled a laugh and bit my lip. My sister was going to flip when she found out that I'd just had sex with Conner. I could hardly believe it myself. But it had been everything I'd wanted it to be; maybe, even better.

I checked the time and felt a rush of panic at the thought of Peyton finding me in there, naked, with her uncle, so I slid carefully out of bed and got dressed. She would probably notice that I was wearing the same shirt, though. I glanced in the closet and saw Alaina's clothing hanging there. *Not happening.* But then I spotted a few items I'd seen Conner wearing; the messy shirts on hangers at the end of the closet had to be his, too, so I chose a button down and hoped Peyton wouldn't recognize it.

I tied the shirt in a knot at the side to make it fit better and padded off to the kitchen to start the coffee and make breakfast. Peyton would just think I'd gotten there at my usual time and would have no reason to believe otherwise.

I woke her, and as I helped her into the outfit we'd picked out together the night before, I heard Conner head into and shower. A few minutes later, we met in the kitchen and ate together, as usual.

I had to hold back my grin; I didn't want Peyton wondering why I was on cloud nine, and it didn't seem right, given the difficulty of the day before.

I couldn't read Conner. He was usually quiet in the morning and often appeared grumpy. That morning, he was much the same as always, although to be honest, I'd hoped he would have been a little happier. He looked well-rested, but his mouth didn't twitch when I snuck him a smile behind Peyton's back. He looked away when my eyes met his.

Once we'd gotten Peyton on the bus, we came back inside. I went to him to wrap my arms around him, but he stepped back, shaking his head.

"You have to go," he said.

I winced in confusion. "What? What are you—"

"You can't be Peyton's nanny. I have to find someone else."

My heart skipped. Did he want something more, then? To start a relationship? Perhaps, like I had, he thought it wasn't appropriate for us to be sleeping together while I worked for him.

My mouth fell into a smile and I opened my mouth to say something, but he cut me off.

"I can't be with someone like you." His words were cold and hard.

My heart sped even faster and tightened. "What do you mean?"

"I have too much baggage and—"

"We all have issues, but after last night, I thought that—"

"Don't ever mention last night to me again." He glared at me and set his jaw.

I took a step back, shocked at his sudden harshness. "I told you I would never tell anyone, and I meant it. What happened between us—all of it—was special, and I—"

He started to laugh. "Special? You think that was special? You let me sleep with you after I made a fool out of myself and made you feel sorry for me."

"That's not what happened." My face grew hot and my jaw ached from clenching it so tightly. "You needed someone to be there for you, and I was." My words came out choked as the tears filled my eyes.

He rubbed his face with his hands. "Look, I wasn't even trying to manipulate you, but I did. I'm a fucking asshole—and a mess. And that's why you have to leave. Now. And don't come back."

I gasped. He couldn't mean that. "But Conner..." My arm trailed helplessly through the air. "I can't just leave; I can't do that to Peyton. At least let me talk to her after school so I can explain what's going on."

"Give me your key."

I blinked at him for a moment, then went to find my purse and fished out the Disney keychain. I handed it to him and he snatched it from me.

"And take my brother's shirt off. What right do you think you have to wear that?"

I glanced down at it, mortified. "I thought it was yours. I'm sorry. I didn't want Peyton to—"

"Take it off!"

His booming voice made me jump. I unbuttoned it as I hurried to the bedroom, pulled it off and hung it back where I'd found it before yanking my own shirt over my head. I did a quick sweep, making sure I had everything of mine. My head spun; I couldn't believe what was happening.

"Conner, please, can we talk about this? I'm sorry if I did something to upset you. I never wanted to hurt you." Tears ran down my face.

"Just go." He closed his eyes and pointed to the door.

"Conner..."

"Go."

I didn't know what else to do, so I did as he asked. Picking up my purse, I closed the door behind me. I got into my car and drove halfway down the street before the tears became too much.

I fumbled for my phone, trying to call Nikki, but after almost crashing into a curb, I decided to wait. I drove home as quickly as I could, and when I got there, I ran inside and called out for her. She popped her head out from the bedroom; when she saw the anguish on my face, she rushed over to me.

"What happened? Are you okay?" She looked me over and wrapped me in a hug.

I could barely speak, but somehow, I managed to tell her most of what happened: that we'd had what I thought was a long, amazing talk, we'd slept together, and then that morning, he kicked me out and fired me.

"He did *what*?!" The rage was obvious in her eyes.

"I just don't understand," I stammered, the tears still flowing. "What did I do wrong?"

"Nothing at all." She paced the room in tight circles. "That asshole. I'll kill him. I'm going over there right now, and I'm going to fucking kill him."

She stood, and I grabbed her arm. "No. That would only make it worse."

"He can't treat you like this!"

"I know he has issues; we both know that. Something must've just... set him off. I don't know. Maybe he's embarrassed. He did say never to mention last night to him. He really opened up to me, and maybe he regrets that."

"Well, fine. He can regret that, but he doesn't get to sleep with you, then treat you like this. It's such complete bullshit!"

Her words made my tears flow harder. "I know. And Peyton. What's she going to think? I hope he doesn't tell her that I ran out or quit suddenly or something like that. I don't want her to think I abandoned her. It kills me to leave her like this. I didn't even get to say goodbye! She'll come home and I'll just be gone. Just like her parents. Doesn't he see what that will do to her?"

"He shouldn't have her. I think we should call Child Protective Services."

"No!" I swatted her arm. "Are you crazy? And have Peyton get stuck in the foster care system for the rest of her life? Conner's far from perfect, but he's her blood relative. He wants to take care of her. He loves her; he just has a lot to learn. Being taken from him would be so much worse. And removed from her own house like that? No, no."

Nikki sighed and sat back down, hard. "You're right; that would be terrible. But he can't do this! It's not right."

"It's not," I agreed. "But there's nothing we can do."

She huffed and crossed her arms. "Well, there is one thing that might make this whole situation a tiny bit better."

"What's that?"

"Yesterday, while you were at work, someone called. They want to interview you for one of the positions you applied for."

A tiny shred of hope wiggled its way into my chest and I sighed. "Well, that's good timing."

14

CONNER

I WATCHED UNTIL SHE PULLED OUT OF THE DRIVEWAY, THEN DREW THE curtain shut. Pure anger ripped through me, and I balled my fists and screamed. I wanted to punch something. I *had to* punch something. Luckily, I had a scrap of sense left and dashed down to the basement. I stood in front of the punching bag and let loose, throwing fist after fist into it until I'd worked up a sweat and the knuckles of both my hands were covered in blood.

But it wasn't enough. I tore off my clothes, barreled up the stairs and shifted as I made my way past the back yard. *Let the neighbors see. I don't give a flying fuck.* I ran hard, sprinting for as long as I could. I refused to think about anything except pounding the ground with my heavy paws, faster and faster.

I'd gone miles; so far, that I was getting into territory I didn't know well. I slowed to a more leisurely pace and let my mind release from its tight place of rage. And then, I realized I wasn't alone in my head.

Is there something I can do for you? Owen asked.

Leave me alone.

We're worried.

You should be.

I felt him leave the mind link. Good. He was listening and giving me space. I sat down and let myself really think about what the hell was going on.

I was freaking out. I could feel myself losing it; feel that reality was slipping away.

Feel myself going batshit crazy.

I'd let Jessie not only see me cry, but I'd sobbed in front of her like a baby. I'd told her far too much about me, but still not the worst parts. She'd been so perfect. Just thinking about it made my eyes sting. She'd been everything I wanted, everything I could have dreamed. She'd shown me more care and love in those hours than anyone had in a long time—more than I'd *let* anyone in a long time.

And that was the problem. Not only had I given her all I could in that moment, she'd taken all of me. Willingly. After all I poured out to her about my nightmares, my guilt, the horrible things I'd seen at war and on my job. The way I had to save people or I felt like I couldn't breathe. She knew more about me than my therapist or my own mother. All parts of me were opened to her.

But she still didn't know my biggest secret.

I looked down at my bear paws, hating them for the first time. Jessie could accept me as broken. She already had. But she wouldn't be able to accept my bear. If I tried to tell her, she'd be scared. She'd look at me like I was a freak. A monster. And I couldn't stand the thought of it. Just picturing how she might look at me, the raw rejection she might give me in that moment, made me want to tear my fur out and pull out my claws. Made me want to never shift again.

I'd fallen for her. Like an idiot, I'd let myself love her. A *human.* So then, I had to make sure I never saw her again. I wasn't boyfriend or husband material. I wasn't father material, either. *Peyton. God, what am I going to tell her?* I had to find someone else to care for her. I would hire the best person I could, and I'd leave. Or maybe I could send her to one of those fancy schools where the kids all stay there. I'd tell her it was like Hogwarts, but without the magic. She could make friends; be away from all the things that reminded her of her parents. Being in that house had to be making it worse, right?

Jessie had left. Just like that, she walked out. Of course, I'd yelled at her first; I'd had to. It was the only way to make her leave. I'd wanted her to go. But I'd wanted her to refuse. Some desperate, twisted part of me wanted her to fall at my feet and beg me to let her love me. To let her stay. I wanted to hear her say she would refuse to leave because she refused to give up on me.

But she'd left. After just a few harsh words, she'd left, taking every remaining piece of my heart with her.

The pain was so sharp, it made my head spin. I threw up. I was shaking and collapsed on the ground, my face much too close to the vile things that had just poured out of me. I deserved it. I deserved to drown in my own disgust and take myself away from the world so I couldn't hurt anyone else. Surely, I'd hurt Jessie; probably badly. What would that do to a woman? Giving herself away like she'd given herself to me, then to be turned away like that?

Did she feel used? Manipulated? Did she feel like I'd violated some part of her heart? She must have hated me; she should've. *I* hated me. I hated Logan and Alaina for dying. I hated the world for letting it be them. Most of all, I hated the croc who was responsible for their deaths. When I found out who it was, I would shred his skin and make him suffer. *Maybe I'll just start killing all the crocs*, I thought. Eventually, I'd kill the guilty one. And in the meantime, we'd be rid of our croc problem forever. Yes. That was the plan. What had Jessie said? Purpose.

I'd finally found my purpose: I would rid the Everglades, then the world, of every last crocodile shifter I could find. With my newfound sense of determination, I rose to my paws and started running back. I'd stay in the park for as long as I could and pick them off, one by one. I had tons of energy that day, more than I'd had in a long time. I could've gone all day.

But as I ran, it hit me: I hadn't had a nightmare the night before. *No, that couldn't be right,* I thought as I mentally flipped through the ones that often recurred. None of them had played in my mind; I had slept all night without a single nightmare. That might have been the first time it'd happened since I'd been in Afghanistan. Then, I thought of Jessie's soft body curled up against mine as we slept. *Pfft. Must have been a coincidence,* I told myself. *She couldn't fix me. No one could.* I stood tall on my hind legs, roared, and beat my chest.

We're here. It was Owen. And then suddenly, damn near all my clan was there.

Where are you? Mason.

We want to help you. Ezra.

We'll come to wherever you are. Noah.

Please, Conner. Don't do it like this. Hailey.

I'll head over to your place and be there when Peyton gets home. Addie. *Take your time and deal with whatever is going on. Please. For your sake, for Peyton's sake. For the clan's sake. We can't watch you do this anymore.*

Is this a fucking intervention? I demanded.

If that's what you want to call it, fine, Owen answered. *But we're not going to let you suffer. You have to talk to us.*

I talked to someone. And it was the worst thing I could have done.

What happened? Ezra asked. *Was it something with Jessie or Peyton?*

Where are you? Mason demanded. *Don't make me get the force and your own team on the case to search your ass out.*

Why didn't you show up for work? Ezra asked.

In a brief flash, I received a mental image of Owen and Addie at my house. Their little boy, James, was with them.

I growled. *Great. Now I can't even go home.*

Yes, you can, Owen said. *Please, man. What's going on with you? Do you want me to call your therapist?*

Do you need something more? Mason offered. *An inpatient stay somewhere? This is worse than it's ever been.*

I stopped running. There was only one way to escape of all the chatter: I shifted back.

I walked through the woods, naked. It took a long time to get home on human feet; long past the time Peyton would have been off the bus. I hoped Addie and Owen had stayed to bring her inside; I'm sure they had. I'm sure, too, that people were looking for me. I'd be harder to find in my human form, but not impossible. It was a huge park. One and a half million acres would take them a long time to cover.

I walked in the direction of home. My mind settled some during the hours I walked, and by the time I saw my backyard—Logan's backyard—I was ready to face whatever or whoever was waiting for me.

A tan panther leapt up and I groaned internally. *Britt.* That meant Ezra was somewhere nearby. Then, I heard his footfalls and he ran at me in bear form, but quickly shifted back to human and threw his arms around me.

"Two men hugging naked outside is not the best way to keep our secret from the world," I said flatly. I pushed him off of me. "Nor is it at all comfortable."

He wiped tears from his eyes. "We've been so worried about you, man. We thought you..." He shook his head.

"You thought I what?"

"We thought you might have done something very stupid. Peyton is at Owen's. She's fine. She's spending the night there."

A spare key was hidden in the backyard under a piece of the wooden border around the garden.

"Dammit," Britt said. "I smelled nickel and thought it was the nails. Nice spot."

I glanced at her, then unlocked the door. I wanted to slam it in their faces, but they anticipated this and moved ahead anyhow.

I flopped down naked on the couch and they joined me. Britt smirked and went outside, and when she returned, she was wearing clothes and tossed some to Ezra. Then, she tossed me a small pouch.

"Herbs," she explained. "My gramma came up with this blend and it works really well. You can even put it in your beer."

"What does this blend do?" I sniffed in the bag, and my nose picked up on a mixture of things.

"It'll calm you down and help you sleep."

"Take some now," Ezra said.

I set the pouch down. "That's alright."

"Dude," Ezra insisted. "It wasn't a question or an option. Take some now."

I glared at him, but pinched a good bit between my fingers, then dropped it into my mouth and swallowed. It tasted like lavender and rosemary...and cedar sawdust.

I winced. "Nasty shit." I picked up a half empty beer bottle and washed it down.

"Said it worked, not that it tastes good," Britt admitted.

Ezra watched me, waiting.

"If this does something crazy to me, I will come after you," I threatened.

"That's fine," he said.

Britt got up and took a bag into the kitchen. I heard the microwave start. My stomach lurched, but the burning numb sensation from the herbs helped to keep the contents of my gut in place.

"You can start talking anytime you want," Ezra said.

"Nothing to talk about."

He sat back and crossed his arms. Maybe it was in my head, but I felt my heart slow. The anxiety faded and the heaviness in my chest lifted some. I blinked back tears. When Britt set a plate of fried chicken and mashed potatoes in front of me, I ate like I hadn't eaten in years.

I set the empty plate down and looked at them.

Ezra said, "Now. What's going on?"

I told them as much as I could without getting emotional. Britt was more like one of the guys than Ezra's mate, so that helped me feel comfortable saying what I had to without feeling like I was offending someone. She'd just come out and tell me if I did something stupid. They listened and nodded and didn't interrupt.

When I was done, Ezra raised his eyebrows. "Is that all of it? That's what has had you so messed up all day?"

"Isn't that enough?" I demanded.

"It's a lot," Britt agreed.

"Conner." Ezra leaned forward in his chair. "Dude. There's no reason to put yourself through this. You fell for her. It happens. It's not a bad thing. Go after her, apologize, tell her you freaked out, and get her back."

I shook my head. "It'll never work between us."

Britt laughed. "I thought that once, too. Turns out this idiot is my perfect match." She shoved Ezra and he rolled his eyes.

"You're both shifters."

"But we're different species and we couldn't be more different in every way," Ezra explained.

I waved my hand. "She couldn't handle the shifter thing."

"Oh, I thought you said you didn't tell her," Britt said.

"I didn't."

"Then you have no idea how she'd respond, do you?" she challenged.

"She's a human, 100%. I know I seem like a total idiot, but I'm actually not."

"Don't get worked up," Ezra said. "No one's calling you an idiot. If she has feelings for you, you could be surprised at what she might accept."

I shook my head slowly. "I can't take the chance. It would ruin me."

"But the thing is," Ezra continued, "you already have. You took the chance and let her in. You let yourself fall for her. That's huge. You opened up to her on an emotional level; you already did the hardest part. Talk to her and find out what she feels for you. I guess if she hates you, don't tell her, but I'll bet she doesn't, man. I'll bet she's just as crazy for you as you are for her. You won't know until you make the move and try. That's what I did. You remember how I was."

I rolled my eyes. "Good god, you were obnoxious. It was so obvious to us that you had it bad, but you wouldn't see it."

Ezra raised his hands. "Hello? Listen to what I'm saying. It's obvious now that *you* have it bad. That's why you're freaking out. Just like it was clear to you that I had to talk to Britt and get over myself, it's your turn."

"This is totally different."

"Yup," Ezra said. "Except it's not."

I narrowed my eyes at him.

"Dude! You're already miserable! You're already hurting, in pain and feeling rejected; it can't get any worse. Not really. But if you don't talk to her and find out, you'll never know. And then you'll have to live with that forever. Every time you feel lonely, every time you have a nightmare, every time you want someone to talk to or to be there, you'll wonder if it could have worked out."

I pictured it. He was right. It *would* kill me. And it was already terrible. I already felt like my insides were on fire, roasting me from the inside out. How much worse could it be?

"Fine," I said.

"Fine...as in, you'll talk to her?" he asked.

"I'll talk to her. I'll at least apologize and feel her out. Then, I'll decide from there."

"Perfect. My job here is done," Ezra said. "Now go get some sleep, man."

15

JESSIE

I HOPPED INTO MY CAR AFTER THE INTERVIEW AND PICKED UP MY PHONE TO send a text to Nikki.

It went great!

She'd been anxious to hear about it, so I wasn't surprised when she responded right away.

Awesome, I knew it would! You'll have to tell me all about it when you get home. I'll have a tub of chocolate peanut butter swirl ready for ya! xoxo

As soon as I arrived, I dropped my purse by the door and Nikki shoved a spoon into my hand. "So, what did he say?" she asked.

"He was so impressed by my education," I answered, sliding the spoon through the crisp, cool ribbon of peanut butter. "And even by my experience as a nanny! He said it would really help."

Nikki hugged me tightly. "See, I knew you could do it!"

"Thanks for helping me." I smiled as I took a mouthful and exhaled through my nose, allowing the sweet and salty flavors to melt on my tongue. I'd almost packed up and gone back home after the whole Conner thing happened, but Nikki had convinced me to at least go on that one interview. I had nothing to lose and only a crappy job back home to gain. My pitiful paycheck from the diner looked pretty sad compared to what I'd been making as a nanny. Heck, I'd thought about possibly looking for another nannying job if the teaching position didn't come through. As rough as it had been, I'd loved being there. I still missed Peyton and hoped that the transition hadn't been too hard on her.

The next day, I received a call telling me that I'd been awarded the job and Nikki took me out for dinner to celebrate. After our Mexican meal, I was stuffed, so I decided to end the night on our couch watching a cheesy romantic comedy. While I was excited to have a new job, I couldn't deny that I still felt upset about Conner and Peyton. I missed them badly. It had already been over a week since I'd left, and I didn't think I'd be seeing them anytime soon. Maybe not ever.

I had almost two weeks to kill before my job would be starting. It was like torture to have that much idle time. Curiosity got the best of me one day, and I found myself driving past Conner's house, just to see if I could catch a glimpse of them, but I saw no one. I wished I would run into them somewhere, but Conner didn't go anywhere—except for work, anyway.

I busied myself by reading and cleaning everything there was to clean. I even thought about picking up a small job in the meantime, but what could I do for less than two weeks? I found myself taking long walks, but my mind would always drift to memories of Conner. Our night together. Where I went wrong. What I could have done to make it better. I still didn't have any answers.

By the time the day finally came for me to start, I was ecstatic. Smoothing the skirt of my new outfit, I spun for Nikki. "Good?"

"Perfect teacher attire."

"I can't believe I'm actually a teacher!" I squealed. All those long years of college had finally paid off.

I got in my car and tried to stay calm as I drove to the school. Luckily, I'd been given a tour after my interview, so I knew exactly where to go. I checked in with my supervisor, then headed to my classroom. The other teacher I'd be working with was there already, and she looked up at me with a tired smile.

"Hi there," I said cheerfully, sticking out my hand. "I'm Jessie Miller, the new teacher."

"Yes, I know," she replied. "I hope you can keep that attitude past the first hour."

My smile faltered and I dropped my hand. "Well...I hope so, too. I've wanted to be an elementary school teacher for most of my life."

"Well," she sighed, "it's much less teaching than what they probably told you. Half the reason they can't keep anyone in this position is because they have a nasty habit of painting it differently from what it's really like."

I swallowed hard. "What do you mean? And I'm sorry, I didn't get your name."

"The kids call me Miss Marcy."

"Nice to meet you, Marcy."

"*Miss* Marcy," she corrected.

I flushed. "My apologies, Miss Marcy. How is it different?"

"Oh, you'll see. Just be prepared to yell a lot."

I furrowed my brow, but I didn't have time to ask her more questions. A boy rushed into the room and threw his backpack down on the floor so hard, it made me jump.

"Who are you?" he accused, pointing at me with an angry look on his face.

I took a deep breath. *Here we go.* "I'm Miss Jessie." I held out my hand to him. Instead of shaking it, he slapped it hard and ran around the room in laps.

"Aiden! Sit! Now!" Miss Marcy hollered at him, but he didn't stop. "You're losing your recess time right now."

"Ahhh!" He covered his ears with his hands and kept running.

I watched in horror. The man who interviewed me, my new supervisor, had said that I would be working with a small group of students who couldn't be in the mainstream classrooms for various reasons. "Most of them," he'd explained, "need a little extra help." He'd made it seem like they possibly had learning disabilities or special needs; I'd been prepared for that. But I had not been prepared for kids removed from class for behavioral issues.

I looked at the clock. The rest of the class would be arriving any minute. *Maybe it's just Aiden who's like that,* I hoped. *Maybe the rest of the class will be more like what I was expecting.*

But by the time mid-morning rolled around, I knew I'd been wrong. Every single one of my students was a handful—and using the term "handful" was being polite. Unfortunately, Miss Marcy had been right. I yelled more than I ever expected to yell. I'd pleaded with one girl to stop pulling out her hair. I had to restrain a boy from kicking another student and was told that sending him to the principal wouldn't do much, so not to bother. I'd tried to teach them something. Anything. But as soon as I got one settled, another would act up.

At the end of the day, I sat in my car, fully exhausted, and cried. That wasn't what I'd gone to school for, and it certainly wasn't how I wanted to be spending my days. I wasn't a teacher to those kids; I was little more than a prison warden, trying to keep them from rioting or killing each other.

My mind drifted to Peyton and Conner. My heart ached for them. Peyton, my quiet, sweet little girl. Even with her, it had taken time to get her to trust me; maybe that's all it would take with those kids. If I tried to connect with them differently, maybe I could get through. I thought of that movie where the teacher just had to find a way to get them interested in learning before she got through to them. Maybe I could, too. Maybe I could turn things around and help those kids after all.

I had planned to make dinner that night. Nikki was working a late shift and wasn't going to be home to eat with me, and after a day like that, I was tired and needed a little pick me up. Instead of cooking, I decided to treat myself to a frozen pizza instead—and maybe some ice cream. That would make the night better.

I drove to the local market and pushed my cart around slowly, the frustration of the day settling deep in my bones. I didn't want to go back, despite whatever hopes I had earlier. Even if I could eventually get them to learn something, it would take time and a lot of hard work, and I didn't know if I had the stamina or the ability to make it happen.

I ended up buying a pepperoni pizza, a tub of chocolate chip ice cream, a package of soft chocolate chip cookies—in case I decided to make an ice cream sandwich—and a bag of salt and cracked pepper potato chips. At least I could eat my way to happiness for the time being, right? But as I was heading to the checkout line, I caught a glimpse of someone from behind.

No.

My blood ran cold. The man turned to the side, showing me his profile, and I almost fainted. I held my breath and then turned sharply, careening down another aisle to avoid having him see me. Of all the times I'd hoped to run into Conner somewhere, I didn't want it to be then. All the things I thought I would say left my mind. I couldn't handle it that night.

I searched around, paranoid, as I slowly made my way to the check-out. I kept looking over my shoulder, making sure he wasn't coming. What would I say if I saw him?

To my relief, the checkout girl was quick and I hurried out to my car with a bag in each hand. I tossed the bags in my backseat and looked around one last time. I'd done it. I'd avoided him.

I jammed my key in the ignition and noticed a text from Nikki.

How was it? she asked.

I have a frozen pizza and junk food for dinner. Will tell you all about it later.

Yikes! Sounds like a rough day :(

I set my phone down and shrieked when someone knocked on my window.

Conner.

I put my hand to my chest and tried to calm down before lowering the window.

"Sorry, I didn't mean to scare you," he said.

"It's fine." *Of all the ways I'd pictured this moment going down...*I thought.

I saw you shopping and I...well...I'm sorry." He rubbed his face. "God, Jessie, I am so, so sorry for what I did, for how I treated you; all of it."

I didn't know what to say. In all my picturing of that moment, I never expected an apology, either. I imagined telling him off, screaming at him for hurting me, pleading with him to get better help...

"I don't even know what to say. I have no excuse for what I did," he continued. "I panicked. And I handled it so wrong. I miss you. Peyton misses you, too."

My throat burned and the tears didn't take long to reach my eyes. I closed them and breathed slowly. *This has to be a dream*, I told myself. *After such a nightmare of a day, I must be hallucinating.*

"Jessie?"

His voice was so raw and pained, so I decided to open my eyes. He looked close to tears himself.

"I miss you both, too," I replied. "But it was horrible to have to leave like that."

"I know. I'm the worst. Can I...Will you...go out with me? Like, on a date? We've never done that, and I'd like to talk to you. To see you again. If you'll have me, that is. If you can ever forgive me."

I opened my car door and got out, then put my arms around him in a tight hug. He squeezed me back so hard, it hurt a little.

"Okay," I said. "I'd like to talk to you. And see how you're both doing."

He sagged with relief. "Thank you for giving me a chance. I'll text you. How's Friday?"

I thought of my day and how drained I was after working. "How about Saturday?"

"Perfect."

I gave him a sad smile. "Tell Peyton 'hi' for me, okay?"

He nodded and waved as I got back in my car and drove off. When I got home, I texted Nikki.

WTF. You are not going to believe what just happened when I was leaving the market...

16

CONNER

I SAT ACROSS FROM JESSIE AT THE RESTAURANT TABLE. SOMEHOW, everything I'd wanted to say to her had left my mind. I stared at my hands, trying to think back to what Ezra and I had talked about. I never thought I would have found myself getting romantic advice from him, but he'd actually been a big help when it came to preparing myself for that night.

"How have you been?" she asked after a long silence.

"Okay, I guess." I had to be honest; I knew that much. I wanted to keep the same level of openness I'd given her that night. "Since I last saw you, I've been tearing myself apart over how I reacted. My clan's been worried about how I've been acting in general, and they're trying to help."

"Your what? *Clan*?"

Shit, I wasn't ready to go there. I would, when the time was right, but I couldn't start with, 'Oh yeah, I forgot to mention that I can turn into a bear.'

"My group of close friends. I call them my clan."

She nodded. "That's a...weird term. But it's good that you have them to lean on, regardless. I didn't realize you did."

"Yeah, they've saved my ass more than a few times..." I trailed off, trying to think of the right words to say next. "Look Jessie, I was a complete asshole to you, and I just want you to know how awful I feel about what happened. And after we...I didn't want you to think I was just using you or that my reaction had anything to do with us sleeping together."

The waitress showed up at the worst time possible. We ordered, and when she left, I returned my gaze to Jessie.

"Did you think it was because of that?" I asked.

"I honestly didn't know *what* to think. I knew that was a possibility; it happens in movies and books all the time. Sleep with a guy and he vanishes. Of course, I didn't think it would happen to me, but I guess no one ever does."

"Well, it wasn't because of that. You know that things haven't been good for me for a long time; I've been dealing with a lot of shit coming at me from all angles."

"I know. I wish there was a way for you to find peace in the midst of all this. I tried to help you; I really did."

"That's the thing. You *did* help me. That's why I freaked out. I never let anyone get that close. Jessie, I told you things that my therapist and even my own mother don't know."

She raised her eyebrows. "Wow, I'm...honored, I guess. Surprised, I mean, I don't know what I did to earn that from you, but I'm glad I did and that I was there. I hoped it helped."

"It did. I told you about my horrible nightmares."

She nodded.

"But that night we spent together? It was the first time in years that I didn't have a single one."

"That's great. How has it been since?"

I shrugged. "They came right back. But it was nice to have one night without them. At least I know it's possible. And now I realize it's *you* who made it possible."

"I don't think I really did anything. Maybe it was finally talking so much about your experience and all you've been through that helped."

I shook my head. "It's you. I feel safe with you. Comfortable. Like I could tell you any secret in the world and it would be okay."

Well, almost any secret.

"You can. Whatever happened between us, and whatever we end up being, you can call me. I'll listen whenever you want to talk."

She reached across the table and put her hand over mine. My inner bear surged and I wanted to jump across the table and kiss her right then.

"I really want you to come back. I've been relying on a nanny service and my friends to help take care of Peyton, but we both miss you so much. Please come back."

"I have another job," she said apologetically.

My heart sank. Things weren't going along with my master plan. I wanted her to come running back to me, but I had to remind myself it was my fault. *I* sent *her* away. And it'd been weeks earlier. I couldn't have expected her to sit around and wait for me to wise up.

I let out a breath. "Well, I'm glad you were able to find something. If anything ever changes..."

She smiled. "You'll be my first call."

The food arrived, and for a while, we didn't talk much. But I still had one thing left to do. I had to make my feelings clear. But how? I couldn't just blurt them out. I played around with different ways to tell her in my mind.

"You okay?" Jessie asked as the waitress brought the check. "You got so quiet."

"I'm sorry, I'm not good at this. Maybe we can go somewhere more private to talk?" I'd been feeling exposed the whole time we were there, wondering if anyone had been overhearing me.

"Sure."

I paid the bill and we walked out to our cars. "Peyton is at my friend Owen's for the night. Would you like to come back to the house? Just to talk."

She chuckled. "I guess I could do that." She flashed me a smile and followed me back to the house.

When we arrived, I got us each a glass of water and sat her down on the couch. "So, is the new job going well?"

"It's okay; I'm still getting used to it." She looked down at her glass, tracing the edge with her finger. "You know, I have to admit, not being able to say goodbye to Peyton made me feel terrible. I worried it would be like losing someone else close to her."

I swallowed hard and recalled that day. "You're right. It was the worst thing I could have done. She cried. She even yelled at me. Luckily, I have some really great friends that have been helping, but...things haven't been good. She doesn't like her new nannies."

Jessie's eyes filled with tears. "She's been through so much already..."

I reached out and wiped a tear away, then let my hand linger on her cheek. "It my fault. I'm so sorry; I ended up hurting you both so much."

I dropped my head in my shame, but when I looked back up, her eyes were full of compassion. I couldn't resist kissing her. It was short and sweet, but I had to let her know somehow that I loved her. I didn't think I could say it out loud, but I wanted her to feel it all the same.

"I do miss you," she said. "My job isn't exactly what I thought it would be. It's very hard. So hard, I actually kind of hate it." She laughed. "But I've only been there a short time. I don't think I could just quit on them. The kids I'm supposed to be teaching are very troubled. They can't keep anyone in that position very long, and I don't want to abandon them, either. But I'd love to spend time with Peyton. Anytime I'm not working, I can come."

I nodded. "I understand. I really messed this whole thing up for all of us."

She put her hand to my cheek as I'd done to her moments ago. "You're human, Conner. You make mistakes like we all do."

My bear bellowed at her touch, and the ringing in my ears served as a reminder of why things could never work between us. How the hell could I possibly explain who I really was—or more accurately, *what* I really was—to her?

"*This* is a mistake." I took her hand and pulled it from my face, holding it in my lap. "I'm fucked up—in so many ways you will never understand."

She shook her head. "What? Conner, stop. I know you have issues. But so do I. Everyone does! I'm afraid of everything. I didn't even want to leave my tiny home town because it's all I knew. I've been sheltered and allowed myself to be caged in. I can't be strong and brave like you are every day. I have my own issues. Believe me."

"You don't get it. I have secrets that would terrify you."

She raised an eyebrow. "I doubt it. I know you were deployed. I assume you've killed or at least shot people. I know awful things happen over there."

"It's not just that."

"Then what is it?"

"If I told you, I'd never see you again."

"It can't possibly be that bad. Did you kill someone outside of the military?"

I considered the question. As a clan, we had to take down animals from time to time. Some were shifters. Technically, that was killing people, wasn't it?

"Sort of," I admitted.

She breathed out hard. "Have you beaten someone badly?"

I pressed my lips together. "Yes. And of all of this is part of the bigger secret."

She narrowed her eyes. "Are you some kind of spy or government agent? CIA or FBI? Something like that?"

"No. There is an organization I'm part of, but it's not government-related."

Her eyes went wide. "The mob?" she whispered. "Are you in the mob or one of those biker gangs?"

"No. Not quite that...criminal. What we do is more just, I guess. More like when members of the military or law enforcement have to take a life in the line of duty."

"Well, that's about the worst I can think of. Unless you're going to tell me you sell babies on the black market."

"No." I gave her an incredulous look. "Nothing evil. I swear. Nothing even criminal, really."

"This is sounding like the CIA all over again." She blew out another breath in frustration. "Just tell me. I can't take this guessing. I'm sure it's not half as bad as you think it is."

"Or it's worse."

"But I know you. And after our time together, I feel like I know more of you. I can't see you being bad. Not like that. Not evil. You'd never hurt anyone on purpose, I don't think. Except for maybe whoever killed you brother, but I think most people would feel that way."

I pulled my mouth to the side. "I've never had to tell anyone this before. I'm afraid it'll come out sounding insane."

"Just say it and then explain if you have to."

"You have to promise that no matter what, you will keep this an absolute secret. Understand that if the public knows about this, it will put a lot of innocent people in danger. Thousands and thousands of lives are at stake. No matter how afraid you are, you have to promise to never tell anyone. Ever."

"It's nothing evil, you swear? Because if you're some kind of serial murderer, you can't expect me not to tell."

"I swear it's nothing like that."

"I promise. Now what is it?"

I squeezed my eyes shut. I remembered what Ezra had said. It sounded stupid now, but I had nothing else to go on and my mind was spinning. I took her hands in mine and squeezed them.

"Just know that I don't want to hurt you. I don't want to lose you. I know this will be hard to hear and if you need time, I get it. It's okay. You can freak out if you have to, but just promise me that at some point, you will talk to me again. Please."

"I promise." She already looked terrified.

"God, this is going to sound fucking crazy." I took a sip of water and looked deep into her eyes. "You've seen movies or read books that have... werewolves in them, right?"

She nodded her head slowly.

"Well, they're not completely fiction. Creatures like that exist. It's not exactly like most movies and books describe, but the basics are there. I'm sort of like that."

She closed her eyes. "Just don't tell me you're some kind of sparkly vampire."

"To my knowledge, vampires don't exist. But shapeshifters do. People who can become animals and then change back to their human forms. I'm a shifter. I can become...I can become a bear; a huge, furry black bear. I can control it completely, unless I step out into the light of a full moon. Then I have to shift, but other than that, it's under my control."

She pulled her hands back. I watched her face to see if she was freaking out.

"You can become a bear. And this isn't a joke."

"I would never joke at a time like this. In fact, when have you ever known me to joke at all?"

"Never, actually; but if this is true, *how*? How do you change into a bear?"

I shrugged. "If you're asking what made us like this, I don't know.

Some flaw in nature? Some genetic mutation? I don't know, and I don't know anyone else who does. We just have to deal with it."

She stared at the wall for a long moment. Okay, she didn't seem to be freaking out too badly. Maybe it would be okay after all. I felt the hope flicker but stamped it out quickly; it was far too soon for that.

"What other questions do you have?"

"Are you yourself when you change or do you just go crazy and eat people? Is that why you said you killed people?"

I shook my head. "I'm me all the time. It's completely under my control."

"Except during the full moon."

"In the light of the full moon, I have to shift, but I'm still me. It's slightly different. More intense, but it's still me. All the time. I don't attack people. The people I've killed...well, as you can imagine, there are plenty of politics in the shifter world just like the human world. There are different types of shifters, and when someone gets out of line, we can't just throw them in jail in the same way. We have to keep this an absolute secret. So, sometimes, we have to take the law into our own hands. Judge, jury, and execution."

She closed her eyes. "I need to see."

"No way."

"Conner, you just told me you're a creature from fairytales. If I'm going to believe it, I have to see it."

"It'll freak you out too much."

"I'm pretty freaked out already, so just do it."

I sucked in a breath. She was either holding it in or was in shock. Crap. And I thought it had been going well.

"I don't want you to be freaked out."

She gave me a surprised expression. "Did you honestly think I wouldn't be?"

"Of course I thought you would. I didn't think it would go this well, actually. What are you thinking right now?"

"Just that...I don't know what to think. But I have to see it. It won't seem real until I do."

"Jessie, please, don't make me do this."

"Conner. Do you want me to believe you? Do you want me to be okay with this or not?"

"Yes. More than anything."

"Then show me."

"Okay." With that, I stood and pulled off my shirt. "Um, shifting rips clothing so we usually strip naked first."

"Okay. I've seen you naked before, so it's fine."

"Right." I pressed my lips together and pushed my shorts and boxers down. I stood in front of her, naked, more vulnerable than I've ever been in my life. "Just know this is incredibly difficult for me."

"To shift is difficult?"

"To shift in front of you, knowing what it might do to you."

She only stared back, waiting.

"Just remember, I promise I won't hurt you." I closed my eyes, leaned forward to drop on all fours, and, as slowly as I could, shifted into my bear form. I kept my distance from her, not wanting to make it worse in any way. She breathed heavily, her chest rising and falling fast, and her hands went to her mouth. Tears streamed down her face and she covered her eyes.

I shifted back. "Jessie?"

She shook her head and kept shaking it. "No, no, no, no…this…can't be…real…"

"Talk to me. Please."

She kept shaking her head and slowly stood up. "I won't tell anyone. I promised that. I promised I would talk to you again." She closed her eyes and tears ran down her face. When she spoke again, her voice wavered and she broke into sobs by the end. "But I have to go now."

She snatched her purse and ran out my front door. She got into her car and backed up so fast, she almost hit a car driving down the road. As she turned and sped off, her tires squealed, leaving black marks in the road.

I stood there for a long while, staring at the marks left behind. I had expected this. *Exactly* this. Everything Ezra said was bullshit. They'd been wrong. They'd all been so wrong.

My phone buzzed. In my desperation to talk to her and know everything was okay, I leapt across the couch to grab it from the coffee table. It was Mason.

I threw my phone down, but he kept calling. On the fourth call, I finally answered.

"For fuck's sake, what?!"

"We got him. The bastard that killed Logan and Alaina. He's in custody right now."

I heard his words. They bounced around my mind, but I couldn't process them. "Thanks for letting me know." I heard him shout my name as I tapped to end the call. I let the phone fall to the floor and the world spun in streaks around me.

17

JESSIE

I couldn't talk to anyone about what I saw. I kept telling myself that. Not my sister. Not my parents. Except maybe Conner, if I could've worked up the nerve to. The worst part was, I'd had my own secret to tell him; something I'd wanted to say so badly. But the way he was going on about it, I had to know his first.

When I got home, I tried to sleep. I thought after a good night's rest, everything might seem different. That was often the case. But as soon as I lay down, the image of him came back: a big black bear standing in front of me. How could it be? How in the world did a human become a bear? It didn't make sense. It wasn't possible.

Maybe it was some sort of an epic gag? No, Conner didn't joke. He wasn't the trickster type. So that meant it was real. Conner could become a bear at will. And apparently, so could thousands of others. But why? What was their purpose on this earth? Why would such creatures exist? I got up and went to my computer; I had to see what was out there.

I started searching. Shifters, werewolves, were...*bears*? Anything that made sense and might have given me answers. Surely, shifters themselves were online, too. They must've had a forum where they could've chatted with each other, right? Or a shifter version of Facebook? I chuckled at the thought.

I was so engrossed in my search that I hadn't heard Nikki come home. She opened my door and asked, "You're still up?"

I shrieked and almost fell off my chair.

"Sorry," she said. "You okay?"

I rushed to shut my laptop so she wouldn't see what I was looking at.

"Um, do you suddenly have a werewolf fetish?"

She'd seen. Shit! I'd only known for a few hours, and already I'd screwed up. I gaped at her with wild eyes.

"Oh," she said. "Oh, okay. Did Conner...?"

"Did Conner what?" I snapped back.

"Tell you something tonight?"

"What do you mean?" I was aware that I was talking too fast and being sketchy. I didn't know what to do. I was panicking.

"Something about himself. A secret that you have to keep?"

I studied her. What was she saying? Did she know?

"Jessie, you look out of your mind. Did you see Conner tonight?"

I nodded.

"Did he tell you a secret?"

I nodded again.

"Did that secret have something to do with what you were looking up online?"

I nodded a third time.

She sighed. "So, he told you he's a shifter."

"What?!" I screeched. "You know? I thought it was this big secret!"

"It is. It definitely is. Logan and Alaina told me. I was so close to them, they thought I should know."

"They thought you should know that Conner is a shifter?"

She sat on the edge of my bed. "I guess he didn't tell you everything. No, they thought I should know that *they* were shifters."

"Wait, Logan and Alaina were, too?"

She nodded. "Which means Peyton is, too."

"No!" I gasped. "She's not anything like that! She can't be!"

"Shifter parents have shifter babies."

"No!" I covered my face with my hands in horror. "Don't say that! It can't be true!"

"It's not that big of a deal. Kids don't really shift much. But if you were her nanny, you should have known. I think it can happen by accident sometimes, but I'm not really sure. Conner would have to explain it."

I slowly shook my head back and forth. "No...freaking...way..."

"Jessie, relax. It's not that big of a deal."

"It *is* a big deal, Nikki!" I grasped her forearms, gripping her for support. "You don't understand. I...I..."

"Calm down. God, you're sweating and all worked up. It's okay. I'll make you a drink." She got up.

"No!"

"Okay. Sheesh." She sat back down.

"Do you remember that I slept with Conner?"

"Um, of course. So?" she replied. "Sleeping with a shifter doesn't make you one. You're not going to become a bear, if that's what you're worried about. It's not like those movies where you can be bit. There's no way to become a shifter except to be born as one."

"Exactly. Shifter parents have shifter babies?" My words were failing me. They came out like a squeak.

"Yeah..."

"Well, I'm pregnant. And now I'm going to give birth to a cub instead of a baby."

"Holy crap." She blinked at me. "Wait, are you sure? How late are you? How could you not have said anything sooner? Did you take a test? Did you see a doctor?"

I answered her slowly, hoping that the world would stop spinning around me. "I took a test just the other day. I had this date with Conner, and I thought I should tell him first. I was going to tell him tonight. I have a doctor's appointment for next week, but I can't keep it now. They'll probably do an ultrasound; what if they look and I have a tiny freaking bear inside me!"

I crumbled to the floor and broke into sobs, rocking back and forth, holding my hands over my ears like I did when I was little and didn't want to hear what was being said.

Nikki hugged me for a long time and tried to soothe me. Finally, she resulted to yanking my hands away from my ears.

"First, you have to tell him. Talk to him. I doubt you have a bear in there; I don't think it works that way. But he'll know the details. And he needs to know, anyway."

"I can't. I can't be with him. I can't have this baby. What am I going to do? I can't even give it away! I couldn't give someone a baby that might become a bear at any time! Oh, my god, I have to get an abortion, don't I? But Nikki, I can't do that! I can't kill my baby! But I can't have a bear, either! What the fuck am I supposed to do?"

I kept rocking and sobbing.

"Jessie...I don't know what to say. You have to talk to Conner. I'll support you in whatever decision you make, but I can only help you so much; I hardly know anything about shifters. I'm sorry you're going through this. I can imagine why you're freaked out; I would be, too. But Conner is the best person to help you right now."

18

CONNER

"This is all your fault!" I screamed at Ezra through my phone. "I never should have told her! I shouldn't have said anything! Now, everything's fucked up."

"Okay, man, calm down. You said you were going to talk to her again. Give her time to let this sink in. It's a lot to hear."

"You asshole! I never should have listened to you!" I stormed back and forth in my living room, still fuming from my encounter with Jessie. Once I'd snapped out of my daze, the rage had taken over. And I had just one place to unleash it. "Don't ever talk to me again."

I hung up on him. He called back immediately, and I ignored the call. He left a voicemail and I refused to listen. I wouldn't give him the satisfaction.

I did have one solution, though. There was something more productive that I could've been doing with all that fury. I stripped down and went out back, then shifted before I took off running in the direction of the jail.

Conner!

Fuck off, Ezra.

Dude, come on. Just see what happens. You don't even know how it'll turn out!

I refused to answer him.

Hey man, let's talk about this, Owen said. *I can't have you guys fighting.*

I ignored them both.

Where are you going? Owen asked.

I felt him listening to my thoughts. It was a sort of an intrusive feeling, like someone prying at your scalp.

Get out! I screamed back.

Do not go over there, Owen warned. *Conner! This is not how we do things.*

This is how I do things.

Absolutely not. I forbid it.

As the Alpha, he had that power over me. Usually. But not that day. It didn't matter what the consequences would have been. He could've kicked me out of the clan. He could've had me killed. I would've welcomed that, even. It didn't matter. I was going to tear that croc to shreds.

The conclave is meeting tomorrow, Owen said. *You'll have your chance then. There will be justice for this.*

Yup. About two seconds after I get my hands in that cell.

I wasn't that far away. I was closing in on the jail and I could almost taste the crocs's blood.

But then I smelled Owen.

He ran into me, crashing hard and interrupting my stride. I fought back for a moment, trying to get away from him. We wrestled, but in the end, I let him pin me. I gave up.

I don't want to see you get killed or be in trouble for this. Let the conclave do their job.

Like they've done so far? I barked. *Why didn't they step in sooner? Why didn't they do anything after your mate was attacked or after the panthers were killed? You thought we could handle it, that's why. And now we're handling it.* ***I'm*** *handling it.*

You're not. I can't let you do that. I know this is the worst time of your life. And it seems like it keeps getting worse. I get it and it sucks, but it will get better. It has to.

I tried to push him off me. *I don't need your patronizing words right now.*

That's not what this is, he promised. *I just want to help you. We all do.*

Look, why don't I have Addie talk to Jessie? Woman to woman. I think she can get through to her.

It doesn't matter. I'm done with her. I'm letting her go. I can't take the pain anymore. I almost choked on the words. He backed off a bit, and I could breathe better.

Don't give up yet. You love this woman. Give her a chance to get used to our world. Bring her to meet the clan. Let her see that we're all just human on some level. We're not monsters.

I lay back down and stopped struggling. *I'm hiring a permanent nanny. I'll figure out how to be a single dad, and I'll move on. I don't need her. I need to see this croc die, though. That's all I need. I don't need anyone else.*

He will face justice. I swear on my life.

If the conclave doesn't take him out, I swear on what little life I have left that I will.

If the conclave fails us like that, which they won't, I'll help you.

Fine then, I snapped.

I'm letting you up now. Don't make me regret it.

Just to prove I was the stronger bear and had let him pin me down, I kicked up with my back legs and sent him flying.

Point made, he said. *Why don't you come just hang out for a while? You and Peyton. She's having a blast with James.*

I want to be alone for a while. Can you keep her tonight?

Sure, man. But she needs you. This is a hard time for her, and you're the only family she has left.

I know.

I ran home more slowly than I had when I'd left. When I felt Ezra shift in, I admitted, *I'm sorry, man.*

It's okay, he said. *I'll pay you back next time I see you. Heard from her?*

No. And I don't expect to.

Then maybe you should hurry home.

Um, why?

Just hurry. But maybe shift before you get there.

I picked up my pace. *Could she be there? Is there any chance?* It was so late. I could see the hint of dawn breaking; she had to be sleeping. But when I got closer, I spotted her car. I shifted back and went to the shed to get an extra set of clothes I had there, got dressed and walked around to the front to meet her.

Her eyes were red and swollen. She looked distraught and as out of her mind as I felt.

"Come inside." I unlocked the door and let her in.

She sat on the couch, stiffly. Her hands were on her knees, her back straight. She looked straight ahead.

I stood in front of her, moving my weight from foot to foot. I was so nervous, I felt ready to explode. She certainly didn't seem happy.

"So...?" I dared after a long silence.

She didn't look at me. "There is something I need to tell you."

"Okay." I blew out a breath. "Go ahead."

"I'm pregnant. In light of recent developments, I've decided not to have the baby because I don't think I can handle having a bear cub, but I thought you should know."

I didn't think I was still capable of being shocked. I thought that because so much shit had happened, nothing would have phased me any longer. But that? The news rocked my world so hard, I actually stumbled. I made it to the couch and dropped down, taking a moment to replay her words in my mind.

"You're pregnant?"

"I believe so, yes. I took a test and it was positive, but I haven't been to see a doctor yet, so I suppose there's a chance the test is wrong."

"Does that happen often?"

"Not that I know of."

"Okay. Well. I mean, obviously it's mine, there's no question there, right?"

"Of course."

"Right," I said. "I know that. I wasn't questioning it. I'm sorry, I was just...I'm just trying to get my head around this."

"I would guess that this isn't quite as big of a shock as finding out that the father of your unborn child turns into a bear at will."

"I guess not. I wouldn't know; I was raised in this world. And I made a point of not letting people in who weren't shifters know so that I never had to have that conversation."

"Then that's just one more thing you've messed up, isn't it?"

Her words cut me. She never spoke like that to me. Never. Her judgment of me, of my failure, made it seem final and irrevocable. Not just a mistake, but a grave error that would scar me for life.

"I'm sorry, Jessie. I didn't plan this. I didn't plan to have my brother and his wife die. I didn't plan to become a single father. You came to me, remember? You said you'd be Peyton's nanny. I needed someone and your sister was friends with Alaina, so it made sense. But I didn't think..."

"You didn't think *what*?" She finally looked at me and began to sob.

"Just don't do this, please. Let's at least talk about this and think things through before you make a decision. I mean, that's my baby, too. That's my son or daughter growing inside you."

As I said it, the words sunk in. *My child. I had a child.* Tiny, growing, inside the woman I loved but couldn't tell.

Her body shook violently as she continued to cry. "But I'm—I'm so scared, Conner. How am I going to do this?"

My throat thickened. I needed to find the words to get through to her. "Jessie." I slid down in front of her and took her hands in mine. I pressed her hand to my cheek and let the tears flow. "I love you. I know I'm not perfect; I'm not even close. But you make me better. You make me want to be better. This baby—" I dared to put my hand on her stomach and was relieved she didn't push it away— "This baby is here now. It's part of you and me. That means something. It's a new life. In the middle of all this death, there's something new. I've never done this before. I've never been in love, and I don't know how to do it. I don't know how to be a father. I'm failing Peyton every day. You know that better than anyone. But I want to be better. You can help me do that; you already have. I can be myself with you. I can let go and be free. I feel safe with you, and I haven't felt that since I was a kid. And now... You said we all need to have a purpose. I haven't had one. But I do now. This baby, our child, us..." I looked up at her, blinking through my tears to see her face. "You're my purpose. Our family—you, me, Peyton, and this new little baby—you're my purpose."

She blinked back at me. I wanted her to say something. Anything. I pleaded with my eyes, but she just stared. And then, I had another thought: I would have to prove it to her.

"Jessie Miller. I need you more than I've ever needed anyone in my life. I love you. I want to be with you forever, and I want us to share a family and a life together. I want to raise this baby with you and be the man I know I should be; the man I can be with you by my side. I promise I will love you and sacrifice everything for our family. I will do whatever it takes. I'll clean up and get more help. I'll learn how to be a father. I'll do better. I'll *be* better. I'll be whatever you need. Please. Stay with me. Love me. Marry me. Be mine forever."

Her mouth popped open. "What?"

"Marry me. Please."

She swallowed and licked her lips, then, very slowly and softly, responded. "I will."

19

JESSIE

He bowed at my feet and cried.

My *fiancé.*

I couldn't make the word sound right. Had I just gotten engaged? Had he just proposed? I put my hand on his head. His crying became wracking sobs that shook his shoulders. I knew he needed this; he needed to let out so much pain he'd kept buried inside for so long.

I wondered if he could really do all he promised. Could he really stop drinking? Could he really learn become a good father? He seemed genuine, but I was still in shock from everything so much, that I didn't know what to think.

He looked up at me, his eyes as red as mine had been earlier. "I'm sorry I don't have a ring. I didn't realize I'd be proposing today."

"Yeah, it's kind of been a crazy day."

"To say the least. I have something else to tell you, too."

I braced myself, not sure if I could handle much else. "Is everything okay?"

"More than okay. They found the bastard who killed Logan and Alaina."

"Are you serious? That's incredible!"

"It was a shifter who did it. A crocodile. We've been—"

"Crocodile? There are crocodile shifters?"

"In the Everglades, we have crocodiles, panthers, wolves, and of course, bears."

Okay then. At some point, I'd stop being shocked by this. Just not yet. "Wow."

"Yeah." He pulled his mouth into a half smile. "Usually, we all get along. But the crocs don't want other shifters in the area, so they've been causing problems. My clan leader, Owen, had to save his now-wife from being attacked by one. We just dealt with a huge panther attack, and now this. We have a conclave—a group of representatives from all different types of shifters—that's like our judicial system. They're going to come and decide what to do with him. He'll likely be killed."

"Ah. That shifter justice system you mentioned before."

"Right."

"Wait, so is Peyton in danger? Are you? Am I?" My hand went to my stomach instinctively. I still worried about giving birth to a bear, but knowing Conner's commitment of being with me through it all made it easier to handle.

"Not that I know of specifically. The crocs are somewhat of a threat to shifters in general, but that's what we're fighting to stop. And so far, it's been just them. And once we find out why, we can end it. A lot of us want to ban the crocs from the 'Glades altogether."

I nodded. "I think I like that plan."

He flashed me a grin. "Are you okay with all this?" he asked. "You must be tired, if nothing else. It's nearly morning, and it's been a long night."

"I'm exhausted."

"Can we just go to sleep and talk more in the morning?"

"Where's Peyton?"

"At Owen and Addie's." He stood and held out his hand. I put mine in his and let him help me up, then lead me to the bedroom. "I can't wait to introduce you to my clan. You'll love Addie and Hailey. Ezra's girl, Britt, is a panther, so she's not part of our clan in the same way, but she's still considered a member and is always around. She's cool. We're all like family."

"They're all shifters?"

"In our clan, yes." He gave me an apologetic smile. "Does that make it weird?"

"What's weird about hanging out with a bunch of people who turn into animals?" I laughed.

"Right. Well, they're all very welcoming." Once we reached the bedroom, he pulled his shirt off. "Do you want something to sleep in?"

I shook my head as I unhooked my bra and slid it out from under my shirt, then stepped out of my pants. He kicked off his shorts and slid into bed in his boxers. Seeing him again—all of him—gave me that same thrill I'd felt before. His hard, muscular body, adorned with tattoos, all there for me to see. And I was going to have *that* by my side forever? I couldn't believe it.

"I hope our child looks like you." I slid in under the covers and snuggled close to him.

"Are you kidding me? I hope he or she is even half as gorgeous as you are."

He pulled me close and I melted a little. I'd wanted this so badly. As freaked out as I'd been, as angry and confused and distraught I'd been all night, what I really wanted was to be able to be close to him again. I hadn't thought it would have happened. And there I was. Not only with him, but soon to be his wife.

"Are we really engaged?" I asked. "Are you really going to marry me?"

"Are you already having doubts?"

"Yes."

I felt him stiffen.

"I can't believe this is happening," I continued. "I'm doubting all sorts of reality today."

"So, does that mean you don't know if you want to be my wife?"

"I do. More than anything. I love you, Conner. I've loved you for a while now."

"You have?" His voice wavered.

"I should have told you sooner."

"You should have. You know, no one has ever said that to me before."

"I'm sure your parents did," I corrected.

"You know what I mean. Not in the romantic sense."

"Not to me, either."

"First loves never die, isn't that what they say?"

"Who's this *they*?" I asked. "*They* also say there's no such thing as werewolves and vampires. I don't trust *they* one bit." I laughed. "Conner?"

"Yes, love?"

The pet name washed over me like a warm shower. I smiled. "Is it true that there's no way to become a shifter? Like by being bitten or something?"

"It's true. You're either born a shifter or you're not."

"Am I going to give birth to a cub?"

He sucked in a breath. "Well, there's no chance at all that the baby will born in bear form. But there's a 50/50 chance that he or she will be a shifter."

"Huh?"

"When shifter women give birth, if they're in their animal form, the baby is born in animal form. If they're in their human form, the baby is born in human form. If both parents are shifters, like in Peyton's case, it's a 100% chance that the baby will be a shifter."

"Yeah, Nikki told me about Peyton. I still can't believe that tiny little thing is capable of morphing into a bear."

"Huh. She knows?"

"She said Alaina told her."

"I wonder why. Did she tell you about us outright?"

"No, she happened to come up behind me when I was researching shifters on my laptop, and she asked me a lot of questions until I admitted that you'd told me a secret related to my search, and then she put two and two together..."

"Okay. She knows it's an important secret, though, right?"

"Definitely."

"Okay, then. Let's sleep now."

"Conner?"

He let out a sigh. "Yes, honey?"

"Will you make love to me first?"

He chuckled. "Are you kidding?" He nuzzled his nose into my neck and started to kiss me. "Tonight, tomorrow, and every night for the rest of our lives."

"Mmm," I moaned as he sent chills over my skin. "I like that arrangement."

He kissed down to my nipples and sucked on one and I reveled in the sensation. They were even more sensitive those days; I wondered if anything else would feel different because of the pregnancy.

"How do you like *this* arrangement?" he asked, yanking my panties off and making his way down to the apex of my thighs with his mouth.

"Oh god," I moaned as he teased my sensitive bundle of nerves with the tip of his tongue. "I love when you do that."

"How about this?" He slid a finger inside me. A wave of pleasure ran over me as he moved it in and out and continued to flick me with his tongue.

I answered him with a moan. I could feel my wetness as he moved his finger around, plunging it in deeper. But his finger wasn't enough. I wanted more of him.

He kept working me until I couldn't take it anymore. I didn't want to come just yet, I wanted to draw it out; to wait until I couldn't hold back any longer.

When I got too close, I gently tugged on his hair and he crawled up my body, kissing me along my neck to my jaw. He pulled my lip into his mouth and sucked gently.

"My turn," I said.

He raised an eyebrow. "Okay..."

"Lie down."

He obeyed. His cock stood at full-mast, thick, rock-hard and begging for attention. I took it in my hand, feeling its smoothness as I stroked it. I watched his face; I liked the way he closed his eyes and clenched his jaw at the pleasure of my touch.

I leaned forward and slid my lips over his member, stroking its base while I sucked him, moving my mouth up and down along with my hand. I took him as deep as I could, opening the back of my throat a bit to accommodate his length.

"Oh god," he moaned. "Yes."

He put his hand on my head, running his fingers through my hair. "Damn," he pulled back suddenly and gave a half chuckle. "You're a little too good at that. I don't want to come just yet. Why don't you come over here?"

I gave him a satisfied smile and climbed on top of him, my breasts pressed flat against his chest. I rubbed against him, letting his shaft get wet between my aching folds, driving myself mad in the process. He reached down and positioned himself at my opening and I sat up slightly, letting him slip inside me before I began to grind against his cock.

Grabbing my hips, he pulled me down harder, driving himself even deeper. I liked being on top; it gave me more control. As I rode him, every time our eyes met, his stare thrilled me.

He pulled me down close to him and grabbed my behind. "I love this ass."

I answered with a moan.

"I want to see you touch yourself," he said.

"Yeah?" I kissed him and began to buck my hips against him even faster.

I stuck my fingers in my mouth, then dragged them down my torso, reaching for my pleasure pearl. He gave a wicked smile as I started to rub myself in circles—slowly, at first, but then picking up speed to match the rhythm of his thrusts. Feeling tiny jolts of electricity beginning to tingle in my extremities, I added another finger and worked myself even harder, knowing my climax was just moments away. As I moaned out, constricting more and more tightly around his shaft, he pounded into me even faster. The sensation rushed through me so hard, it sent me over the edge, crying out loudly as he grabbed my hips, thrusting into me with full force. Seconds later, I felt his dick throbbing with his heartbeat as he reached his peak, filling me with his essence.

I lay flat on his chest, breathing fast.

"Did you like that?"

"Are you kidding?" I breathed.

He chuckled. "Good. I just want to make you feel good. Forever."

"I want to let you."

I didn't remember falling asleep, but when I felt him slip out of me, it seemed like hours had passed and the day had grown light. I nuzzled into him and drifted back to sleep.

20

JESSIE

"You have nothing at all to worry about," Conner said for the tenth time.

"But there's just so many of them," I said.

Peyton bounced in the backseat. "Clan time, clan time," she sang.

"See? Even Peyton loves them."

I glanced back at her, her pigtails bouncing as she moved from side to side.

"Yeah, but I think she's actually just on a sugar high."

In the months since I moved in with Conner and Peyton and had left my awful job, Peyton seemed to have become a different person. She was thrilled to see me again, just as much as I was to see her. We'd had a tearful reunion, followed by a long talk where Conner apologized and shared his feelings with her more than he ever had. He asked her if she wanted me to come back as her nanny. She gave him an emphatic yes and jumped into my arms.

When he asked her what she thought of me moving in, she squealed with joy. And then, when she found out we were going to have a baby and get married, she ran around the room in circles, cheering.

Conner had looked at me with wide eyes. "I haven't seen her like this in months."

We still had plenty of sad moments, and Logan and Alaina would always be sorely missed. We talked about them as much as we could. By then, I felt like I knew them in a way, from everything Conner and Peyton had told me about them and all the photos and videos I had seen. It seemed to help Peyton to sit with Conner and me and reminisce about their family trips and times together. She would always cry at some point and we would hug her; often, we cried along with her. Conner, especially, had gotten much better about letting his grief out and allowing Peyton to see him cry. The first time it happened, Peyton had looked at him and gave him such a sweet hug, it brought tears to my eyes—not that it took much those days, with all the extra hormones circulating around my body.

We were on our way over to Owen and Addie's house. I'd met them briefly a few times, but that day, I'd be meeting the entire clan, spending time getting to know them. It was both an engagement party and pregnancy celebration, they said. Addie had promised that we'd also have a baby shower when the time grew closer, where we could kick the men outside and oooh and ahh at the tiny baby clothes to our hearts' content.

Addie had emphatically told me I was not allowed to bring anything—so, I'd baked cupcakes. Once they found out that the color of the filling inside would reveal the baby's gender, I figured she couldn't complain too much.

When we pulled in, the sight of the decorations and lights and so many people made me feel even more overwhelmed.

Conner squeezed my hand. "These people are my very best friends and they'll become yours, too."

"Right. Unless they hate me."

"Not a chance."

Peyton had thrown off her seatbelt and was running toward James and Addie. We walked over and Addie came to greet us.

"Hey! What is this?" she asked, taking the white bakery box from me.

"Cupcakes. But not just any cupcakes! Gender reveal cupcakes."

Her face broke into a beaming grin. "Oh my god, how awesome! I can't wait to find out!"

She set the cupcakes down and came back to escort me around. Her own belly was quite round; she was due in just a few weeks and had already invited me to be there. It was apparently a shifter thing to have people around when you gave birth, like women used to do to help each other back in the day, but she'd assured me that no one would be offended if I decided to not do that. Most of them preferred giving birth in animal form because it was easier, so that limited the choice of venue a bit. Addie pointed to a grassy section and a tree at the edge of the yard and said that James had been born right there.

It seemed very bizarre to me. I couldn't imagine it, but I would get to see a birth before I had to decide. And Conner had told me many times that we could go to a hospital or do whatever I wanted to do.

I was introduced to all the ladies of the clan, and even though I was a little overwhelmed, I tried my best to remember all their names: Britt, Hailey and Tori. Then Conner had me meet the men, Noah, Ezra and Owen. Mason was apparently missing. They were all really great, actually. They asked questions, told me stories, and I felt like I was already accepted as part of their group. The ladies talked about married life as shifters, how difficult it was to keep clothes stashed all over the place and to find deals because things got ruined so often.

When I asked if Britt and Ezra had any kids, Britt coyly replied, "Not yet. But maybe we'll think about having a little bundle of fur soon." She'd glanced over at Ezra and made a roar face at him. He responded with a wink.

"But, you're a panther and he's a bear, right?" I asked.

"I know. Crazy, right? But we make it work somehow."

"So, would your baby be...?"

"Definitely a shifter. Interspecies couples don't happen all that often, but from what we can gather, it's about a 50/50 shot: 50% it'll be a Florida panther like me and 50% it'll be bumbling bear like Ezra."

I nodded. Such a strange world. I didn't know how I'd managed to accept it. It had taken me some time, but I finally had. Only recently had I stopped freaking out when Conner shifted in front of me. Once, Peyton had done it, sort of by accident, but she'd had a really bad day and then Conner had been a little short with her. When he'd first quit drinking, there had been a rough period when he'd been more than a little grumpy. Peyton had been upset and then she'd dropped a mug that her mother had given her, which shattered and cut her foot in the process. She'd howled in pain and misery and started to shake.

I'd screamed for Conner. I thought she was having a seizure, but he knew what was going on. He'd talked her through it as she shifted, and then shifted back a few minutes later. I wasn't sure which of us was in the worst shape that night. Conner had assured me it was rare for kids to shift until they hit puberty. He'd said it would be very unlikely that, if our baby were to be a shifter, he or she would spontaneously shift for at least the first few years of his or her life.

"I was wondering one thing," I asked them as we continued to discuss shifter life. "For us, if it's only a 50/50 chance, will we just have to wait until it happens accidentally one day or until the child is closer to puberty to know?"

They exchanged glances, seeming to decide on the answer. "It depends," Hailey finally said.

"Sorry, that's a terrible answer," Addie added.

"With my brother," Hailey continued, "his wife is human, and it wasn't long after their baby was born that he could smell she was a shifter."

"You can smell it?"

Addie nodded. "But with kids, it can be tricky. Not all of them give off the scent early. And it can be faint. Honestly, if I didn't know for sure James was, I would guess he wasn't."

"He hardly has the scent at all," Britt agreed.

"I know. Weird, right?" Addie said. "So, it might be years."

"Or you might know right away," Tori offered. "When my cousin had her baby, we all knew as soon as the baby was making his way out of her." She laughed. "Of course, that boy is a handful and a half. And he shifts a lot."

I nodded, my worry increasing with each story.

"It probably won't be years and years," Hailey said. "My friend said all four of her kids shifted when they were two, the first time they had a tantrum."

"I know someone who's baby shifted when she was just a day old," Tori added. "The poor thing had some kind of heart condition. I guess it was so much that the little thing just couldn't hold it back. Turned out to be a good thing, though. It straightened something up in her little body and she was fine after that."

"A day old?" I repeated. Conner had assured me that wasn't possible.

"That's very unusual," Addie said, putting her hand on my shoulder.

"Peyton has the scent, and since she's Conner's brother's child, maybe your baby will, too."

"Mason!" Someone shouted and I turned with the group to see a man approaching. He held up a hand to us and hurried over to Conner.

They had an intense conversation, then Conner made his way over to us. "I found out where Mason's been. Turns out that the croc who killed Logan and Alaina is dead. The shifter in the cell next to him didn't like him much, either and clawed him to death. A wolf."

I searched his face to see how he was taking it. Justice had been served, but he hadn't had a part in it.

I turned him to me and hugged him. I whispered, "You okay with this?"

"Yeah," he said in my ear. "At least I don't have to worry about him again."

By the time we left that night, our spirits were high. Peyton fell asleep in the car on the way home, having played so hard. I felt wholly accepted and thrilled to be joining the clan, and Conner had found some peace, knowing his brother and sister-in-law's killer was finally dead. The question of why it was Logan and Alaina had been answered weeks ago, when the conclave interrogated the croc. The two of them had witnessed a crime: the croc had a truckload of poison and was about to contaminate the clan's water supply. They'd been spotted, and later that day, turned up dead, conveniently before they could identify the croc who'd tried to wipe out the entire clan. Knowing that, and now having the killer gone for good, seemed to bring some sense of healing.

As we lay in bed that night, Conner tracing circles over my little baby bump, I said, "I have a confession."

"Oh yeah?"

"I'm a little jealous that I'm not a shifter. I think, if it were an option, I'd want to become one. To be more like you."

He kissed me. "You are like me. More so than some of my clan."

"You know what I mean. Especially with that mind link. Could be handy."

"It can also be a pain."

"Even still. I hope the baby is a shifter."

He pulled back to look at me. "You do?"

"I do. After meeting your clan, I know that it would be a good thing." I saw something by his ear and turned his head. I broke into laughter.

"What?"

"When they smashed that cupcake in your face, they did a good job." I swiped my finger just inside his ear and showed him the light blue frosting.

He licked it off my finger. "Still yummy."

"I can think of better places to put that finger."

"Oh, can you now?" He wiggled his brow and tickled me.

"Stop! Stop!" I laughed and tried to get away from him. "Wait! I have a name idea!"

"What?"

I pulled my lip into my mouth. "You can say no, and it's totally fine. But I thought it would be a nice tribute to name him Logan."

Tears rose in his eyes, and he kissed my stomach. "I can't think of anything more perfect."

21

JESSIE

EPILOGUE: TWO YEARS LATER

"Logan William Griffin!" I shouted. "Put that down right now!"

My toddler held a metal fork just a little too close to the electrical outlet. He was going to shove it in; I could see it in his eyes.

He stared at me, and as I moved closer, he defiantly jammed the fork into the socket and I screamed. "Don't!"

Sparks flew and he shrieked. I heard Conner's footsteps running closer and Peyton called from somewhere in the house. The lights didn't flicker, so that must have been a good sign.

"Logan!" I screeched. "Are you okay?" I turned him over, frantically scanning his body for burns. He cried loudly, and when I took the fork from his hand, he threw himself down on the ground and pounded his fists on the floor.

Conner reached us and bent over him with his stern daddy face on. "Logan, stop this right now."

"Fork! Fork!" he yelled.

As he twitched and cried, I saw his tiny body start to shake. It reminded me of when Peyton had spontaneously shifted.

"Conner..." I said. "Is he...?"

"I think so. Just give him room."

With a hideous shriek, black fur emerged from Logan's delicate skin.

His mouth stretched wide and his teeth grew into fangs. His little hands, still sticky with jelly from breakfast, lengthened and sprouted claws.

He stood there, a tiny bear cub, looking shocked and scared. Conner pulled off his clothes and shifted, then he grabbed him in a hug and held him as I watched in awe.

My son was a shifter. We hadn't been sure. For all the talk of the scent, there hadn't been much of anything either way. Some of the clan said he definitely was, some said there was no way. There'd been a pool going since he was born two years earlier, and in that moment, I laughed to myself, wondering who had won.

Peyton came to see what was going on and sat with me, petting Logan and nuzzling into Conner. After some time, Logan shifted back and fell asleep and I took him from Conner, who shifted back himself.

"Well, now we know," Conner said. "Logan takes after his namesake in more than just looks."

I smiled at my husband. "I wonder what this one will turn out to be."

Conner put a hand to my swollen belly. "I guess we'll know soon...or at least in a few years."

"I'm glad it's a girl this time," Peyton said. "Since I already have a brother."

I patted my belly, and the baby moved. "She's glad, too."

"Can we name her Alaina?" Peyton asked.

I met Conner's eyes and we smiled at each other. We'd had this conversation already and thought it would be a fine choice for a name. We'd use my mom's, Michelle, for a middle name since we'd used Conner's dad's, William, for Logan's middle name.

"I think that's a great idea," I said, pulling Peyton in close to join our hug.

With a loving, devoted husband, two amazing kids and another on the way, my family was complete. My heart swelled at the thought; I could ask for nothing more.

RELENTLESS MATES

SHIFTER NATION: WEREBEARS OF THE EVERGLADES

1

GRACE

I WALKED INTO MY FAMILY'S DINING ROOM AND PLOPPED DOWN IN MY SEAT at the table. "I'm starving!"

My dad and brother, Tyler, were already sitting there, waiting.

"Got some good steaks tonight." Dad rubbed his hands together.

A few minutes later, my mom placed our meal on the table. For the first few minutes of dinner, we ate so hungrily that we didn't talk. But, as we slowed down, conversation crept in.

"I think I found a law school," I said after my brother mentioned that he'd applied at Miami University.

I'd been looking at schools for a little while, deciding where would be the best place to take my degree in biology to the next level to become an environmental lawyer. Living in the Everglades, I saw a lot of conservation efforts going on at all times. Not all were successful, though, and I wanted a hand in helping to make sure the 'Glades were preserved.

I thought they would be happy that I'd decided; my mom especially had been asking me about it. But I noticed my parents exchange a look.

My dad set down his fork. "Grace, we've been talking."

Something in his tone made me nervous. "Okay..."

"What if you went over to the park and became a ranger?"

"Well, that's not exactly what I want to do. Being a lawyer is much different."

"But isn't it kind of the same thing?" my brother asked.

I gave him an incredulous look. "No. A ranger does the conserving and runs the park, taking care of issues that happen only there. I would be a lawyer, going to court to help clients with issues dealing with conservation. Like how the local paper plant keeps polluting the water. They just pay the fine and go on polluting. I would represent the state or the county or whoever wanted to stop them and help them to win so that the water stops being polluted."

Tyler rolled his eyes. "I know *that*. I'm not an idiot."

Before I could respond, my mom jumped in. "I think he just meant that both positions are focused on preserving the environment."

With a full mouth, Tyler said, "Yeah, that."

"I guess they are similar, but they're two very different jobs," I insisted.

"Here's the thing, Grace." My dad sat forward with his serious face on. "I'll just get right to it. We need you. The clan needs you. You're the only one of us crocs who's qualified to work in the park as a ranger. We need a presence in that park if we're going to survive."

I blew out a hard breath. So it was more than just simple conversation, then. It was planned, and they were trying to coerce me. "Dad, I know that's important, but I can do a lot of good for our clan and all shifters by being a lawyer."

"I don't doubt it," he said. "You'll be good at whatever you do. But this can't wait. Tyler is just starting school this year. It'll be at least four years until he graduates, maybe longer."

"Hey!" Tyler protested.

My dad raised an eyebrow at him. "What year were you supposed to finish high school?"

"I only flunked one year, and I've changed since then!"

My mother held up her hands. "Okay. This isn't about that right now. The point is, Grace, you're the only who can get in there now or anytime in the near future. And we need information on things that are happening."

"Things?" I asked. "What things?"

"There've been some rumors," my dad continued.

My mom got up and started clearing the table. I collected plates and took a stack over to the sink to help, and Dad followed, carrying an empty platter.

"The clan is saying they've heard of a bear attack coming. Against us crocs."

"Why would they do that?" I asked him. Sure, bears and crocs hadn't gotten along over the years, especially in the Everglades. That didn't mean they would just attack us unprovoked.

"That's what we need to find out. If we had someone in there who might easily overhear conversations, who might pick up on who is where at what times, who is friendly with whom, that sort of thing..."

"So, you want me to work in the park to spy on the bears." I gave him a flat look.

"You can think of it like that, or you can see it as a way to fulfill your desire for preservation in a more...*direct* way, while also helping to preserve your clan and very species. The more we know, the better we can protect ourselves."

"You can always go to law school later," my mother added. "Once we get this thing with the bears settled once and for all."

"And what does that even look like?" I asked. "Is it possible to settle anything with them if they're always so against us?"

"That's exactly what you'd be helping to do," my dad said. "You would get to know them and then use your future lawyer knowledge to help us all come to an agreement. Your award-winning debate skills would come in mighty handy in that case."

I rolled my eyes. "Laying it on a bit thick."

"But he has a point," my mom added. "You want to be a lawyer for a reason, and doing so well on the debate team in high school and college proves that you're good at winning debates and talking to people. You're perfect for this task, and what more important case would you have to win than one that will keep your people alive and bring the clans and the entire Everglades peace?"

"Yeah, no pressure, though," I snickered.

Could I do that? Could I really give up my dream of becoming a lawyer—or least postpone it for a few years—to become a park ranger?

"I'll have to think about this."

A few minutes later, while I was helping my mom with the dishes, there was a knock on the door. My dad got up from the living room to answer it.

From the kitchen I heard him exclaim, "Well, look who it is!"

Two sets of footsteps made their way toward us.

"Adam's stopped by to see us," my dad announced.

"Hello," my mom said and wiped her hands on her apron.

I nodded at Adam and kept at my task of scrubbing the pan.

"We were just talking about the rumor of the bear attack," my dad said. "Grace here is thinking about becoming a park ranger so that we can get some inside information and stop the attack before it happens."

Adam's eyes grew wide. "Wow, Grace. I can't tell you how much that means to the clan and to me, personally. I mean, it would give us so much information and really help us get to the bottom of this situation once and for all. You might be saving many lives doing this. I always knew you'd end up doing something grand and selfless. That's just the kind of croc you are."

I set down the pot and turned to him. "Thanks. But even if I do this, there's no guarantee they'll hire me."

He beamed at me as if I were his favorite person on Earth. "With your degree and credentials? There's no way they wouldn't."

I didn't smile back. "We'll see."

"You know, Grace, I've been watching you for a while."

He stepped closer to me and looked down at his feet. I think he was trying to look vulnerable. Humble, maybe? But it came off as somewhat creepy. Then I noticed my parents had snuck out of the room, leaving us alone in the kitchen. *Real subtle, guys.*

"Yeah?" I asked. "Why would you do that?"

"Besides the fact that you're stunning?" He met my eyes and gave me an intense stare. "Even back when we were in school together, I saw how special you were."

"We weren't even in the same grade."

"Upperclassmen know things about lowerclassmen. People talked about you. How amazing you were, and I have to agree. You do something like this for the clan, and they'll all adore you even more than they already do. I'd even say you would make a fabulous co-Alpha."

"I appreciate that, Adam. But I wouldn't want to steal your glory. You earned your role, and you do it well. You deserve to be Alpha alone."

"Well, if you were by my side as not just co-Alpha, but a partner, we would be a team—and I think we'd make a great one, you and me. We could be one of those power couples, you know?"

I had to remind myself that he was the Alpha of our clan. I couldn't say what I really wanted to because of his position. If I were just outright rude, it wouldn't have been appropriate.

"The only problem with that," I pointed out, "is that we're not a couple."

"That can be easily fixed."

He stepped closer, and I worried he might do something very stupid, like try to kiss me. He wasn't a bad looking guy, but I knew him too well and had known him far too long to have any sort of feelings or interest in him whatsoever.

I held up my hand. "Adam, I'm focusing on my career right now. This isn't the time for me to be in any sort of relationship."

"I can be patient."

"Really, I appreciate your kind words and all, and I'll go ahead and try to work at the park to help the clan. I know we can work together for the greater good of our people, but I'm just not interested in a relationship like that."

He gave me a sideways smile. "I don't mind a challenge. You let me know when you hear from that park. I'll make sure we throw you a nice party for doing something so big for us."

"Thanks." I turned back to my dishes and let out a sigh of relief when he went off to find my dad.

I could help my clan, I'd decided. Who was I to put myself over helping the entire population of croc shifters in the 'Glades? There was too much danger for me to just ignore it and go on with my plans. Maybe I'd get back to law school one day. Or maybe I'd find enough satisfaction in winning the fight, like my dad had said. I was willing to at least give it a try. School would always be there, but if someone didn't step in and put and end to these clan wars, we might not be.

2

MASON

I DROVE TO THE RANGER STATION, AS I OFTEN DID IN THE LATE MORNING. The Everglades general Park Rangers and Law Enforcement Rangers were closely tied and often worked together. Since the 'Glades took up such a massive amount of land—1.5 million acres—we always were each other's eyes and ears for whatever was going on in the park. It also happened that two of my best friends and clan mates worked as Rangers there. Owen, our clan's Alpha, was also the supervisor of all the Rangers. His second in command, Ezra, also worked as a Park Ranger. I loved being able to do my job serving and protecting while also hanging out with my friends. A real win-win.

I strolled into the Ranger Station and waved to Rachel, the office assistant. "Anyone in?" I asked.

She smiled at me and nodded. "Owen's in his office. Not sure where Ezra is."

That was typical. Ezra tended to be late or off doing who knew what. I knocked on Owen's door with our special knock.

"Hey, Mason."

I walked in and sat down across from him. "What's the word?"

He scrunched his face and tapped his fingers on the desk as he glared at his computer screen.

"Something wrong?" I asked.

"I don't know yet, man."

"Care to elaborate?"

"We hired a new ranger."

"And...?" I pulled my eyebrows together, and he kept squinting at his computer screen. "That doesn't sound like a problem unless there's an issue with the new hire himself."

"*Her*self," he corrected me. "And I don't know if there's an issue or not." He turned from his screen. "She's a croc."

I sucked in a breath. "Okay, well, you must've hired her for a reason."

"I didn't hire her, my boss did. She has impressive credentials—assuming they're all real."

"Are you questioning that?"

"I'm questioning everything at this point until I know for sure if she's a threat or a phony or just plain stupid."

"What do you have there?" I gestured to his computer, where he kept refocusing his attention.

"Searching her name and her school to make sure she is who she says she is."

I nodded slowly. "Everything checking out?"

"So far." He sounded disappointed that he didn't have a reason to turn her away.

"Maybe it won't be a bad thing. We've been trying to settle our differences with the crocs for years. Maybe she can be a bridge."

"Or a spy," he said.

I shrugged. "Or a spy. I guess we'll have to be careful until we know for sure."

"I've never dealt with a situation like this. I'm not sure how to proceed."

"Owen, you're the sharpest man I know. You'll figure it out. I'm sure you'll just keep an eye on her and an ear open. There's nothing else to do, really."

"So far, she's done nothing wrong. At all. I can't even write her up for being late. It's like she's..."

I raised an eyebrow at him.

He continued. "Trying too hard. I hate to make assumptions, but it's like she's up to something. Like she's here for a reason."

"Yeah, I get it. The crocs have not exactly been willing to intermingle on friendly terms."

"She's just so *nice.*" He made a disgusted face. "I wish she wasn't so pleasant. It's hard to hate her."

I laughed. "She's a croc. That limits her likability automatically."

His radio crackled and he pressed the button on its side. "Go ahead."

"I checked out the swarm and everything looks good." It was a female's voice on the other end.

"That's her," he said to me. Then, into the radio, "Go on and head back in then."

"Have you heard anything from the conclave lately?" I wondered.

They'd supposedly been aware of and trying to figure out our problem with the clans fighting for a while now. But they never seemed to do much to help us.

"Same as always. I report to them, they listen and take notes and file them, and that's it. Sometimes they make 'helpful' suggestions." He rolled his eyes, then looked up. "Oh hey, Grace."

I turned toward the door to see the new hire. I could smell the croc in her before I even turned. But when my eyes rested on her face, my heart jumped. She might have been a croc, but she was drop dead gorgeous. Like, model gorgeous. I swallowed hard. How could Owen work alongside someone like her? Oh, right, he had his own beautiful wife, Addie. Well, I didn't. I was single, and I'd take my time looking, thank you very much.

I nodded at her. "Welcome to the team."

"Thanks." She smiled and the sight lit up my heart.

"This is Mason." Owen gestured toward me. "He's one of the Law Enforcement Rangers here at the park. If anything questionable goes down here, he'll be on his way."

She met my eyes and her smile grew. "Nice to know we're protected."

"Indeed." I tipped my head at her.

Owen was all business. "Why don't you go on and check on the new calls that came in today. See if there are any you can handle on your own."

"Sure thing, Boss." She smiled at me again, then spun on her heel and left to chat with Rachel.

I gave Owen a wide-eyed look and mouthed, "Holy shit!"

He closed his eyes and slowly shook his head.

The moment she left the station, I was on my feet, leaning on his desk. "I'll keep an eye on her, look her up. Whatever you need."

He smirked back. "You do that, Mason. You do that."

"I will." I tapped my finger on his desk, then hurried off.

I wanted to know all there was to know about that woman.

3

MASON

OWEN HAD CALLED ME FIRST AND GAVE ME A HEADS UP. I WAS GRATEFUL because I'd planned to go out on patrol. When he said Grace was coming in for her fingerprints and background check, I parked my butt right behind the front desk, under the guise of doing research.

And, technically, I *was* doing research. I was looking up everything I could on Grace. No criminal record or history of arrests. Nice. Meant she was probably a good little croc. There wasn't even a mention of her having called the police to report anything. That could've meant two things: either she'd never been involved in anything that required a call, or she had, but hadn't reported whatever crime was going down. For the time being, I'd give her the benefit of the doubt. Her DMV record didn't have as much as a speeding ticket.

When the door opened and it was her, I tried to play it cool. "Hi there. What can I do for you?" Then I feigned a moment of recognition. "Oh, it's Grace, right? Owen said you'd be stopping by."

"Hello." She stuck out her hand and I shook it. "Grace Osborn."

"Mason Rowe."

"Nice to meet you."

I pulled my mouth into a half smile. "You, too. Ready to get started?"

"Yup."

I gestured to the seat at the desk. "The background check for new employment asks a lot of questions. Just answer the best you can."

I planned to print a copy of her information for my own purposes later, but for now, I took note of particularly interesting pieces of information. Like her birthday and the fact that she was 26, which was conveniently only a few years younger than me. She'd lived in the 'Glades her whole life, even at the same address. Her family had been in the area for a long time; old crocs. I didn't really have a concept of if the problems we'd been having were more with the newer clans or older, but it seemed like good information to tuck away.

Once that was done, I retrieved the fingerprint kit, set it up and walked around to her side of the desk. I stood close to her and took her hand to roll her finger in the ink, then pressed it down on the page. She was so close, I couldn't help but take in deep breaths of her scent. I thought the croc in her might bother me, but her scent drove my bear wild. It made my heart race; made beads of sweat begin to gather at my temples. I moved slowly, trying to make it seem methodical and careful, but really, I just wanted an excuse to linger near her longer.

When we were through, I handed her a wipe for her fingers. I perched at the edge of the desk, closer than I was when I'd been behind it.

"So, how are you liking the new job?"

"Pretty great so far. Everyone is really nice."

"Owen and Ezra are two of my best friends. They're good guys. Owen's been at this a long time. How about you? Did you dream of being a park ranger when you were a girl?"

She laughed, and the sound was like ecstasy to my soul. "Not exactly. I've actually always wanted to be a lawyer."

I let my shock show. "Then how in the world did you end up working in the park?"

"Well, I wanted to go into environmental law, so it's not too far from my original dream. I guess you could say it was family duty."

"Your clan made you?"

She glanced around, then let out a nervous laugh. "I wasn't sure if it was safe to talk."

"There are a few non-shifters on the force, but none of them are here right now."

"Oh. Well, they didn't make me, but it just seemed that staying local would be better," she explained.

"We all make sacrifices for our clans, I guess."

"Did you? Or did you always want to be a cop?" She leaned against the desk, just feet from me.

"I had no idea what I wanted to do. I spent a lot of time just running and being with my clan. I guess I did sort of the same thing you did in the end. I thought it would help keep all shifters safe, and I wanted to keep the park safe for everyone."

Our conversation came easily; naturally. I could have sat there talking to her all day. We had several things in common, I was pleased to find. Besides being shifters both working to better the park and protect and serve people, we both liked the same kind of movies and music. We even had the same favorite beer—one brewed locally by 'Gladesmen called Beast. I'd never seen nor heard of a woman liking Beast. She just laughed it off and said it was what her dad and uncles all drank, so it was the first thing she tasted when she was a kid sneaking sips just to see what all the fuss was about. I shared my story of doing the very same thing.

It seemed like every sentence of our conversation brought up something else we had in common, until the phone rang, interrupting us. I let it ring a minute, but when no one answered it, I reached back and picked it up.

"Hey," Owen said.

"Oh, hey man. Got something?"

"Was wondering if *you* had something, actually. Grace? Is she still there?"

I glanced at her. "Yeah, she's here."

"Is there a problem?"

"No, why?"

"She's been gone for almost two hours."

I checked my watch. We'd been talking for a long time. "Ah, yeah, I guess it is getting late."

He sighed. "Just send her back, please. I have things to go over with her before I can leave for the night."

"Sure thing."

I replaced the phone on its receiver and pressed my lips together. "That was Dad calling. He says you're out past curfew."

When she made a confused face, I explained.

"Owen. Wondering what's taking so long."

She looked at her phone and gasped. "Oh, my goodness." Her face turned red. "I've been gone a long time. I'm sorry, I'd better get going." She grabbed her purse from the desk and slung it over her shoulder. "I guess it's too late to try to come up with an excuse?"

"Probably."

She pressed her lips together.

"It's my fault," I confessed. "I shouldn't have kept you talking so long."

"I loved talking with you."

"Then maybe we can finish our conversation over dinner?"

"I would love to. You have my number in all that information somewhere?"

"I do." I patted her file sitting on the desk.

"Then I'll be expecting your call." She walked to the door and paused to look back at me before pushing her way through and walking away.

I sat down with a hard sigh. It felt like little hearts were floating around me, and I grinned. A date with Grace. I wondered if it was it too soon to call her right then.

4

GRACE

I NEARLY DANCED OUT TO MY CAR AS I LEFT THE POLICE STATION. MASON was so adorable and funny, and we had so much in common.

My buzz was killed slightly when I got back to work, though. I felt bad about being gone so long and hoped it wouldn't be a mark against me. My cheeks must have been red as I walked into the station because they felt like they were on fire. I went right to Owen's office and knocked.

"I'm so sorry," I blurted out the moment I entered the office.

He waved me off. "Mason can be a chatter. I need you to do the afternoon drive through and make sure all is right."

"Sure thing." I turned to leave but thought better of it and turned back around. "I really am sorry. I won't let it happen again."

He nodded and returned to his computer screen.

I hopped in the utility vehicle, grateful to be out of the station. He hadn't seemed too upset, though, so my worry faded and my buzz from earlier returned as I cruised through the park, taking in the sights of all the trees and wildlife, all the scents around me.

That night at home, the questions seemed endless.

My dad raised a thick eyebrow. "Well, aren't you in a good mood."

"Isn't that allowed?" I asked.

"Just wondering why is all," he said.

But my mom was there, and she looked at me more carefully. "Wait a minute." Her mouth spread slowly into a grin. "Did you meet someone?"

Damn that mother's intuition. There was no way I could tell them I had set up a date with a bear shifter. They'd probably disown me. They certainly wouldn't be happy, and I didn't want anything to dampen my excitement.

I quickly dropped my smile. "Meet someone? At work?" I huffed. "It was just a good day is all. I like my new job."

"What have you found out so far?" Dad asked.

"Nothing really. The bears all seem pretty nice, actually." I almost mentioned how I'd taken too long at the station and Owen didn't seem mad, but then they'd wonder what took so long, and I didn't want to have to keep lying. "My boss especially really just wants to make the park safe and enjoyable for all who visit and for the animals who live there."

My dad narrowed his eyes. "Well, you just keep your ears out."

"Of course, Dad."

That night, I was in my room going over the Ranger handbook when my phone buzzed.

Mason. I sighed and grinned.

Hey there. I know there's some man code about waiting so many days before asking a lady out, but I couldn't do it.

If you wouldn't have told me, I never would have known, I replied. *See, some secrets are better kept.*

I almost giggled as I held my phone, watching the little dots showing that he was typing.

LOL. So, when can I see you? Tomorrow?

I'd love to. Where? When?

There was a bit of a pause. *Hadn't gotten that far yet. I'll send you details tomorrow.*

He sent a smiley face and I sent one back, and I fell asleep thinking of him with a grin on my face.

The next day, work seemed to go on forever. When it was finally over, I headed home, trying not to seem too obvious about my excitement. I told my family I was going out with some friends, hoping to meet some guys. Luckily, they didn't question it much since they were twenty minutes deep into some documentary on hunting.

As soon as I got to the restaurant, I saw him. I thought he'd looked hot in his uniform, but he looked even cuter in his polo shirt and dark blue jeans. He probably looked good no matter what he wore. Then, my mind started to wonder what he'd look like if he wore nothing at all, and I had to snap back to the moment. *Easy, girl; not time to go there—yet.*

He gave me a warm hug and took my hand as we went inside and were seated. From the moment we sat down, he charmed me and had me laughing; god, he was just all-around amazing. I had felt like that once before, with my longtime high school boyfriend, but that had taken weeks. I was already feeling myself go crazy for Mason.

Halfway through our date, though, the cloud I'd been dancing on burst. Adam appeared across the restaurant and walked over to our table, and as he neared, I felt my smile fade. *Shit.* There was no way he wouldn't know that Mason was a bear; his scent was too strong. I swallowed hard and looked at Mason fearfully. He sent back a confused expression and it only intensified when Adam paused at our table, putting his hands down and bending over toward us.

"Well, hello there," Adam said.

"Hi, Adam." I tried to keep my cool. I wasn't doing anything wrong; we were just two people having a meal. I gestured to him. "This is Adam, my clan's Alpha."

Adam nodded, smiled at Mason, and they both looked at me expectantly.

Mason spoke up for himself. "Mason Rowe." He stuck his hand out to Adam, who shook it hard. "Nice to meet you."

"You, too," Adam replied, giving a phony smile. "I had no idea my Grace here needed entertaining tonight. Why didn't you call me if you wanted to go out, honey?"

I had to be extremely careful. I didn't want to upset either of them. "Uh…sorry?"

"I know you said you needed some time before we could really start dating," Adam continued, "and it looks to me like that time has come. Good to know. We can pick up right where we left off."

Adam looked over at Mason and smirked, then spoke to me again. "I know you must feel like you owe this jerk something, but you don't, honey. If he gives you any trouble, just let me know and I'll take care of it." He leaned closer to Mason. "But I'm not expecting any trouble from no bear. And I expect all of your kind will keep your distance from mine."

Mason narrowed his eyes, but said nothing.

"Mason is a police officer," I pointed out. "I don't think I'm in danger."

"Is that so?" Adam stood up and ran his tongue over his teeth. "Well, Grace, my darling, you just keep your head up and don't do anything wrong, and if he tries to accuse you of something, we'll stand by you. Don't worry about a thing."

"Thanks, Adam. I'm not worried."

I gave him a thin smile, and he leaned down to hug me before walking off.

I stared at Mason in shock and horror for a long moment. We'd finished our meal and had been just sitting, chatting.

"Can we go?" I whispered.

He nodded and slid out of the booth. Neither of us said a word as we walked outside and toward my car. When we stopped in front of it, I turned to him.

"I am so, so sorry about that. Adam...he's the clan leader, like I said, but he also has a thing for me. I've never been interested in him, and he doesn't like to take no for an answer."

Mason visibly relaxed. "That's what all that was? Jealousy?"

"Yes." I covered my face with my hands and tried not to cry from sheer embarrassment.

"Hey, it's okay."

He put his arm around me and the tension melted. I leaned into him and inhaled his wild scent.

"I'm so mortified that he would act that way. My parents would be thrilled if I ended up with him, I'm sure," I sulked.

"I have to say, this worries me a little."

I stood up and looked at Mason. "Oh, I don't think he'd come after you or anything like—"

"No, no." He chuckled. "I'm worried about *you*, silly. I'm rather well-trained to fight and shoot, and the fact that you told him I'm an officer would mean higher charges if he came after me." He put his hand to my cheek. "I just don't want him coming after you and trying to pull something. Do you have a gun? Some way to protect yourself?"

"No, it's okay. I don't need anything like that."

"Hang on." He dashed over to his car and returned a moment later. "At least keep this with you. You know how to use it?"

I looked at the small black canister and saw its little red trigger. I'd never used pepper spray before, but it didn't seem complicated. I saw where the lock was, which would prevent it from accidentally going off.

"Yes. Thank you." I tucked the spray into my purse.

"The only thing I'm sorry about is that he interrupted our night," Mason said.

"Then I guess I'll have to make it up to you next time." I gave him a coy smile and he pulled me in close.

He pressed his lips to mine. They were soft and warm, and kissing him was the best thing I'd experienced in years, it seemed. I didn't want to stop. But I was vaguely aware that we were in a parking lot and that Adam wasn't far. Finally—*regrettably*—I had to step back and break the kiss.

"Thank you so much for a wonderful night," I said.

"Thank you for tonight. And for all the nights to come." He winked and opened my car door for me, and as I drove home, I replayed his kiss over and over in my mind.

5

MASON

I WOKE UP EARLY THE NEXT MORNING FOR A CLAN RUN. IT WASN'T something we'd always done, but over the years, it seemed more and more necessary as the clan grew and our responsibilities increased. It had become like a weekly meeting, but rather than sit around in some room, we got out and stretched our legs, tearing through the park like the pack of bears we were.

Here! I announced with my mind when I'd shifted in.

I was greeted back as everyone else checked in and we all ran to our meeting point. Once everyone was there, Owen began.

Hey all. Thanks for coming. On the agenda for today is the clan picnic. We all ready?

No one objected, so he turned and took off running, with Ezra directly behind him, then me.

I think we're settled on the date, Owen continued, *but what do we want for entertainment, food, all that?*

Beer, Ezra said.

Duh, Hailey added.

I'm good with those things, but I'd also like to add a guest, I mentioned.

Who? Conner demanded.

I know who, Ezra said in a singsong sort of voice.

Wait a minute! Hailey sounded offended. *Are you seeing someone? And I didn't know about it?*

We've only been out once, but I think this could be it. As I thought of her, my chest warmed and I sighed in delight.

Oh, wow, Conner said. *Gettin' serious, bud.*

They could all sense my feelings as I thought about her.

Tell us everything! Hailey was paying close attention to every thought and feeling that came from me.

I sighed once again. *She's perfect. We have so much in common. She even works with Owen and Ezra at the park. She's funny and amazing. And stunning.*

That's so great, Hailey said. *I hope she stays awesome. You've been out with some...interesting women.*

I laughed. *That's a nice way of putting it.* I'd been in some bad relationships over the last few years. They either went crazy on me or cheated on me; I certainly hadn't been the luckiest in finding love thus far. But that was about to change.

Tell them the rest, Owen added.

She likes me back? I offered. I didn't know what he meant.

And... Owen said.

Uh? She's a great kisser, but I didn't think you'd want to know that.

Owen sighed. *Dude, she's also a croc.*

I felt silence and shock emanating from each member. Well, except Ezra, who already knew that detail about Grace.

I tried to play it off like it wasn't a big deal. *Yeah, she is, and she's dedicated to making the park great for* ***all*** *animals, just like we are.*

Wait, why is there a croc working in the park in the first place? Conner asked.

I felt my defenses rise. *Wow, prejudiced much? Are we not allowing other species to have jobs now?*

Okay, okay, Owen interrupted. *Let's not get into a thing about it. I just thought everyone should know ahead of time so they won't be surprised when you show up with a croc at the next event.*

I'm not showing up with a croc, I said, my mental voice getting snippy. *I'm showing up with my...girlfriend? Whatever she is, I'm showing up with a date. A* ***person*** *who I'm very much into. That should be all that matters.*

You're right, man, Ezra said. *Most of us haven't even met her, but I can say that so far, Grace has been great to work with. She's really nice.*

That's her name? Grace? Hailey asked.

It felt like she was looking for something to say; something that didn't come off as prejudiced or judgmental, but she was having a hard time with it.

That's her name. Grace Osborn.

There was a long silence.

Then Hailey added, *I can't wait to meet her.* But the excitement she'd had about a minute before was lost and her words sounded forced.

I just don't get it, Conner said. *With all the issues we've had with the crocs, how could you do this?*

I tried to remember that Conner had even more of a jaded position against the crocs than any of us. His brother and sister-in-law had been murdered by crocs and he'd been part of the search and rescue team that had pulled their bodies from the water.

She didn't have any part in what happened to your family, I reminded him.

Conner, we'll discuss this at a more appropriate time, Owen said. *For now, we're not going to hold anything against her that she hasn't done.*

I just don't see how this will work out, Conner said.

And I don't see why it matters one bit, I snapped. *She hasn't done anything wrong. She hasn't done a thing to you.*

Noah spoke up then. He'd been quietly listening this whole time. *You've only been out with her once?*

So far.

Okay. Then you're not too attached.

What does that mean? I asked.

If there's an issue, it shouldn't be a big deal for you to move on, he explained.

There already is an issue, Conner added.

Well, thank you all for being so supportive and understanding, I snapped.

This is why I just said we're not doing this, Owen demanded. *If there's a problem, we'll figure out how to handle it as a clan.*

I wasn't ready to let things go so soon. *You guys go ahead and judge all you want. If you want me to leave the clan over this, then that's what I'll do.*

I ran the opposite direction, away from all of them for a few feet, then shifted back. I was far from home, but I didn't care. I wasn't going to listen to their bullshit anymore. I didn't want to think badly of Grace, and I didn't want anyone else to, either. Especially since she'd been nothing but a complete sweetheart. I would hate for her family to judge me simply for being a bear.

As I walked back, being careful to stay in the shadows since I was naked, I considered that there was a good chance her family might have a problem with me. Maybe we'd have to run away somewhere to have peace if we wanted to be together.

It was a long walk back, and by the time I got home, I had texts waiting for me.

Owen: *Hey man, sorry. I'll talk to Conner. He still holds a lot of resentment toward the crocs.*

Duh. Obviously, he wouldn't get over someone killing his brother and sister-in-law, but that didn't mean Grace was somehow responsible just because she happened to be the same species as their murderer.

And Conner had sent a text, too: *This is already causing problems in the clan. You're better off just ending things now before you do something really stupid, like fall for her.*

I decided to ignore them both and talk to the one person I actually wanted to hear from.

Hey there, beautiful. How's your morning going?

It didn't take long to get a response from Grace that made me smile.

Better now, she responded, along with a smiley face.

I sat on my couch with my phone in my hand and a smile on my face, and let my clan and their drama fall away.

6

GRACE

I SET DOWN MY PHONE AFTER FINISHING MY CHAT WITH MASON. MY HEART was beating out of my chest; we had another date for that night and I could hardly wait.

I hopped downstairs to get something to eat and my mom was there in the kitchen, cooking eggs.

"That smells amazing!" I gushed.

She turned to look at me suspiciously. "You're in an awfully good mood this morning."

I shrugged. "Just happy, I guess."

She narrowed her eyes at me. "Any reason in particular?"

"I'm not allowed to just be happy? Thanks, Mom."

"Of course you're allowed, I just don't see why you are all of a sudden."

"Life is going well. I have a great job doing something good for the clan. What is there not to be happy about?"

"*I* know why you're so happy."

My heart jumped and I spun at the sound of Adam's voice as he stepped into the kitchen. Was he going to say something? I glared at him.

"Why is that?" I demanded.

"Because you're working hard for your clan, to get to know the bears and see what they're up to. It's a big sacrifice. And I see you taking your task very seriously." He raised his eyebrow slightly in a challenge.

"Right," I said. "I was just telling my mom that I was enjoying my job and knowing I was helping the clan."

"And I know you'll be a big asset." He smiled at me widely, and I noticed a hint of warning in it.

"I sure hope so." I gave him a flat smile and turned back to my mom to serve myself some eggs.

He didn't say anything about me being out with a bear, but the whole encounter had me shaken up so much that by the time he left, I went back to my room to text Mason.

Hey, so, given what happened the other night with Adam showing up, could we go somewhere tonight that's maybe less public or a little out of the area?

I hated to have to even ask him, but I didn't want to be paranoid the whole time, either. I wanted to fully enjoy every second I spent with him.

I have the perfect place in mind, he responded.

I sighed in relief. I didn't want him to think I was somehow ashamed to be seen with him; it had nothing to do with that. I'd love to tell the world about him, but the bear and croc rivalry worried me.

Later that evening, after I met Mason and we got into his car, he drove for a long time before pulling into a park.

"I thought maybe a quiet picnic in a distant park would be best," he said as he lifted a basket from his trunk.

"This is perfect. Thank you for understanding." I wrapped him in a tight hug and kissed him.

We set up the picnic together, spreading out blankets and pulling food items out of the basket. He'd brought buttery rolls, chicken salad with fresh herbs and a bottle of Merlot. He poured the wine into a pair of plastic glasses and handed one to me, then held his up to toast.

"To us," he said.

I tapped my cup to his. "To us."

"I had an idea," he said as we started to eat. "There was that incident with your clan leader. My clan isn't too thrilled about things, either, and I was thinking that maybe there's a way we can kind of smooth things over with both your clan and mine."

"How?" He hadn't told me before that his clan was unhappy about us, too. It tightened my stomach.

"We're having a clan picnic, which we often do. I was hoping to bring you along so everyone can meet you. Then they'll understand why I can't keep away from you."

He twisted his fingers through mine, and I thrilled at his closeness, but his suggestion made me nervous.

"And maybe you can take me to meet your family and clan, too," he continued. "That way, we can be sure no one will have a problem with us being together; they can just let us be happy."

I pulled my hand free from his. "I don't think that would work. I mean, my clan definitely won't be okay with it. My leader already isn't. He made it clear today that he expects me to use you to get information about the upcoming attack, and if your clan already has a problem, too, then I think...I don't know. I don't know what to do."

"Wait a minute. He wants you to use me to get information on *what* attack?"

"There's a rumor going around. It's part of the reason I got this job at the park: to get information and make sure everything was good between the clans."

"What is this rumor, exactly?" His voice started to take on a hard edge, and I could feel myself getting upset.

"That the bears are planning a big attack on the crocs."

"And you believe this rumor?"

"No, not necessarily. I mean, I guess I didn't know before. But that was before I met you and Owen and Ezra."

"You really think we would attack your whole clan?" He looked hurt.

I felt myself grow near tears. "I don't think that now. I've told them there's nothing like that going on and that all the bears want is to keep the park safe."

He shook his head and let out a long sigh. "It's working already."

"What is?"

"They're already coming between us, turning us against each other."

"I'm not against you! Are you against me? What did your clan say? You never told me anything about that."

"I was too mad to talk about it, and I wanted to talk to you in person. They're just not happy that I'm dating a croc."

"And?"

"And, that was basically it. They think that with all that's happened over the years from the crocs that it might cause problems to have you and me be so close. I guess they think you'll do exactly what your clan wants you to do: use me to somehow get information that will hurt us in the end."

I blinked and a tear fell down my cheek. "I never said I was doing that or that I wanted to. I told them I was going to work in the park to get information, but I hoped that I could get to know some bears and make things better between the clans. That I could become a mediator of some sort. I want there to be peace, Mason. So that we don't have to hide out and anger our families to be together."

"That's what I want, too. I swear, we would never plan any sort of attack. We'd defend ourselves if something came at us, of course. You can't fault us for that. And we do want to stay safe, given the fact that there have been croc attacks against us in the past, but we're not—nor have we ever—planned to attack anyone."

"I didn't believe you were." I wiped a tear and he leaned in close to kiss me.

"I don't want to upset you. Maybe it would be best if we met everyone and came out in the open. Stop hiding. Tell everyone that there is no attack and bring peace once and for all."

"I don't know. It might just start a big fight and give us more trouble."

"Maybe." He moved closer and put a hand to my cheek, then kissed me. "Maybe we can accomplish what Romeo and Juliet never could."

He kept kissing me and drew me into his lap. His body pressed against mine, warm and strong. It felt so good to be close to him. In that moment, I'd do anything to be with him freely; to not have to hide or worry about my family being angry. I just wanted to be with him and have everything be copacetic.

"I'll think about it. Maybe there's a way I can ease my family into the idea so they'll accept it."

"Good," he breathed into my ear and kissed along my jaw.

I closed my eyes and let him kiss down the column of my neck and back up to my lips. I ran my fingers in his hair, pulling him close and taking in long inhales of his scent.

"You smell so good," I murmured. My heart raced as he ran his hands along my back.

"So do you."

We kissed for several minutes, getting more and more tangled in each other. Then my phone started buzzing. I ignored it at first, but after a while, it became annoying.

"You'd better check that," he said, brushing his lips over my ears.

I sighed and turned to look at my phone's screen.

Are you with that bear right now? It was Adam. He'd sent several texts in a row. *People saw you, so don't try to hide it.*

When I didn't answer he continued, *So much for trying to get information on the bears. You're changing sides now? Do I have to worry about you?*

And finally, the last one said, *I thought I could trust you, Grace. I thought you were going to be a leader in this clan. But you're nothing more than a bear lover. Does your family have any idea where you are right now, traitor?*

By the time I had read them all, I was shaking with fear and anger. Tears sprang to my eyes. "I'd better go."

"Everything okay?" He started packing up the picnic, but I couldn't move.

"No," I said softly. "Adam is giving me crap. Somehow, he knows I'm with you. He called me a traitor."

Mason set down the basket and came to take me in his arms. "We'll figure this out somehow. I promise."

I wanted to believe him, but the pit in my stomach kept growing.

7

GRACE

I didn't know how to respond to Adam, so his text went unanswered. I said goodbye to Mason with a growing feeling of dread, and by the time I reached home, that dread had increased exponentially, then exploded when I pulled into the driveway. Adam's car was there.

I wanted to turn back and take off; to never come home again. We could've gone somewhere, Mason and I. Somewhere that didn't have clan issues like the ones we were facing. I swallowed hard and got out of my car.

My father met me at the door as I walked in. "Come on into the living room, Grace. We need to talk."

He looked pissed, to say the least. I followed him into the living room and found my mother and brother sitting on the couch, and Adam on the chair. My mother's eyes looked red from crying. Tyler glared at me. My dad gestured to the love seat and I sat obediently. My dad stood in the middle of the room, his arms crossed, facing me. The room was tense with silence. Then it felt like all the anger exploded at once.

"Adam has told us some very disturbing information," my father said.

"Please say it's not true," my mother added, her voice wavering. "You're not really dating a bear, are you?"

"Can't believe my sister is a freaking traitor," Tyler said.

Adam just laced his fingers and gave me a smug look. They all stared at me.

"The bears aren't what we thought," I explained.

"So, it's true?" my mother said, sounding pained.

"I'm seeing someone, yes. And he happens to be a bear, but—"

"Ohhh," my mother wailed and put her face in her hands. "Why, why, why?"

My father clenched his jaw. "Grace, this is *not* acceptable."

"How can you even stand the smell?" Tyler asked.

I thought of Mason's scent and how it drove me wild; how he kissed me, touched me. Suddenly, it all seemed so far away.

"How did this even happen?" my father asked. "You were there to work and get information, not hook up with one of them."

"I *did* get information. There is no attack planned," I said.

My father turned to Adam, who spoke up then. "We've got some information of our own."

"Looks to me like you've been helping them rather than us," my father accused.

"I haven't helped them!"

Adam stood and pulled a map from his pocket. He spread it out on the living room table. The map was of the park and had several places circled in red.

"Right here." Adam pointed to one of the circles where the word 'attack' was written beside it. "Is this not your boyfriend's handwriting?"

I looked at the letters closely. I had only seen Mason's handwriting a few times; not enough to recognize it. "I don't think so."

There were several other places on the map that also said 'attack' beside a circle.

Adam took another paper from his pocket: a traffic violation ticket. He pointed to several lines of writing. "This ticket was given and signed by your boyfriend. Notice how the As and Cs look exactly the same."

I looked at where Mason had written 'traffic violation' and compared the letters, and admittedly, they did look close. And there was no denying that Mason had written the ticket. His name was printed and signed at the bottom of it.

"What do you make of this?" Adam demanded.

"I…I don't know, but I'm sure there's some explanation," I said. "They wouldn't do this."

"So, even when you see proof of a pending attack, you're going to take their side?" my father fumed, his hand forming a fist.

"I'm not taking their side, I'm just—"

"How can you do this to your family?" my mother cried. "Is dating this guy worth getting people killed over?"

"No. That's not going to happen," I insisted. "Mason is not like that!"

"Yet, we have his handwriting here." Adam pointed again to the map. "You agree that it's his handwriting, yes?"

"I don't know. It looks like it, but I don't know that—"

"So, you agree that your boyfriend wrote the words 'attack' on this map near several circles?"

My mouth hung open.

"Well do you agree that's his handwriting or not?" my father barked.

I jumped in surprise. "Well, it looks like his handwriting," I admitted. "But that doesn't mean—"

"Then you have to see how highly suspicious it looks," Adam said. "He writes 'attack' on a map that has several locations circled? Do you still not believe anything's going on?"

My mind was spinning in a thousand directions, my heart racing. I was near tears but couldn't let them see me cry, especially Adam. When I looked at what he had, it did seem like proof. How could I deny that? But it didn't match with what I knew of Mason. He wouldn't do that. He wouldn't lie about it, either. Would he?

"How well do you even know this bear?" my mother asked. "How long has this been going on?"

"I've only been out with him a few times." I thought that was going to be good news, but she turned it on me.

"So, you don't know him at all! He might have you completely fooled, making you think he has feelings for you."

"He charmed you, said all the right things, and you fell for it," Dad added. "We don't blame you for that. These bears, they're masters at that. But you need to make this right. You need to end things with him immediately and never see him again."

"Well, of course she's not going to see him again," my mother said, indignant. She looked at me for confirmation. "You wouldn't dare see him again after all this proof, would you?"

"I..."

"Grace, I don't think I have to tell you how disappointed the whole clan is," Adam said. "Our leadership had very high hopes for you and your mission. We had faith in you, trusted you to do right by us. Now that you've turned and proven to be a traitor—or at least have been taken by these bears if they've managed to manipulate you—we have to think differently about you. About your whole family."

"My family?" I whimpered. "But they didn't have anything to do with it. It was just me—"

"Don't you see how this affects us all?" my father demanded. "Your actions reflect on us as a whole. On this family, on this clan, on all crocs everywhere."

"It's not like that! I swear, it's not like that." The tears broke free; there was no stopping any of it now. I tried to keep my chest from hitching as I cried and breathed through it.

"Adam needs to hear that you're not going to see this bear again," Mom insisted.

What could I say to that? How could I possibly still be thinking that dating Mason would ever work? If everyone was up in arms about it and they were coming against my family because of me, because of what I'd done, how could I put my wants ahead of what was best for so many people?

"I won't see him again," I said softly.

"Of course you won't," my father said. "Because if you do, you'll be out on the street so fast, your head will spin."

I swallowed hard and the tears kept coming.

"We're putting you on probation," Adam said. "It's not a mark against you—yet. We're just going to watch your actions for a while and make sure there's nothing questionable happening. If we do find something, some kind of proof that you've been giving the bears information, then there will be a more formal investigation that could lead to your removal from the clan. Do you understand?"

I nodded, but didn't look up. I couldn't believe what was happening. How could something that seemed so perfect and necessary just hours before suddenly seem like the most terrible thing I'd ever done in my life?

"I'll keep an eye on her," my brother said.

I sent him a glowering look.

Adam nodded. "I expect all of you to report regularly with anything you see that might be suspicious. The more we know we can trust the Osborns, the faster your names will be cleared."

"Why couldn't you just find a nice croc boy to date?" my mother hissed.

"It's not for lack of interest, I'll tell you that much," Adam said. "I've been trying to get Grace to like me for as long as I can remember, and then I see her running off with this bear. I'm starting to question my own abilities."

"Oh no," my mother said. "You are a fine-looking man and a good leader. Don't you go doubting yourself just because of Grace's poor choices."

"And I'm sure Grace will be making better choices in the future, won't she?" My father looked at me expectantly.

"Yes," I whispered. "I never meant to hurt anyone or make anyone look bad. I didn't tell him anything that would hurt anyone or give anything away."

"We know that you're the victim here," Adam said. "That Mason and these bears are the real ones to blame for taking advantage of you. But you do understand that we have to take precautions and make sure his hold on you is broken for good."

I nodded.

"Good." Adam stood and shook my father's hand. "I think my work here is done for the night."

My mother stood to hug him and whispered something to him that I couldn't hear.

"Grace, if I might have a private word?" Adam said as he walked toward the door.

I followed him out and he stopped on the front porch, waiting until I closed the door behind me. I didn't meet his eyes. He leaned in close, so that his arm was touching mine.

"Grace," he said softly, "I know this is a lot to take, and I don't want you or your family to be negatively impacted by this. Just keep your head straight, and soon enough, it'll all blow over."

"Thanks," I muttered. "I never meant to cause anyone any trouble."

"I know." He put his hand on my shoulder. "I know you've needed time, but I want you to know that if you're looking for someone who won't manipulate you, someone your family will be thrilled to have you be with, I think you know that I'm here. I want you to be mine, Grace. I think we could do great things together."

"I know."

"Okay, well, I just didn't want to leave any doubt. Think about what would make your family happy. You can fix all of this very easily, you know."

"I know."

"Grace..."

I finally looked up at him. His gaze was intense and he leaned down toward me. I turned my head from him.

"It's been a really awful night," I said. "I need to get some sleep."

"Right. You do that and call me in the morning, okay?"

"Sure."

I turned from him and ran up to my room before anyone else could say anything to me. I picked up my phone and sent the most awful text I'd ever had to send.

I'm so sorry, Mason, but I can't see you anymore. Adam told my family and the whole clan about us. My dad will kick me out of the house if I see you again, and my family might even get kicked out of the clan because of this. It's a huge mess and I can't keep bringing them harm just to satisfy my own wants. I'm so sorry. I know you'll understand why it has to be this way.

I powered down my phone and pressed my face into my pillow to sob. It was bad enough that they all knew, that I was causing all this trouble for everyone, and that the bears might actually be planning an attack. But at that moment, all I wanted was for Mason to hold me and tell me it would be okay somehow. For us to figure this all out together. But instead, I'd just promised my clan and family that I'd never see him again. The day couldn't have been any worse, and I just needed it to end.

8

MASON

I READ GRACE'S LAST MESSAGE AGAIN, FOR THE HUNDREDTH TIME. AND then the long stream of texts I'd responded with that had gone unanswered.

My first reply was, *What? What is going on? Can you call me?*

When she didn't call—and avoided my voicemails—I'd followed up with, *Grace, please talk to me. Tell me what's going on. It can't just end like this. We're adults. They can't keep us apart unless we let them.*

Later that night, I'd written, *Please. I'm going out of my mind here.*

I hoped that in the morning, somehow, things would have been better. But she still hadn't responded. Throughout the day, I'd sent many more texts, called many times, but still to no avail.

I didn't know what to do or what to think. And my clan sure wasn't being helpful. They'd all just seemed relieved that it was over.

But I couldn't let it be over.

Grace had taken two days off work and it seemed like she'd quit, disappearing from my life completely and instantly. But on the third day that she was supposed to be at work, the fifth day since I'd talked to her, she showed up.

I got a text from Owen. *She's here, but don't do anything. Just keep your distance.*

At least it was *something*. Someone I knew would have contact with her. I knew where she was, and I could figure out a way to see her and talk to her.

How does she look? I asked.

Awful. She came to talk to me to make sure I knew what was going on. She was concerned for her job and asked if I could make sure she doesn't run into you, that it would be too hard.

She did? What did you say?

Of course I agreed, he said. *What else can I do? She's still an employee of the park, under my direct supervision. I could be fired if I somehow let you see her against her wishes.*

I don't want you to get in any trouble, I replied. *I would never ask you to do that. I guess I just hoped you would defend me a little? Or find out what happened?*

It's not my place to get into personal matters.

Right. I know that, I admitted.

Maybe just give her some time. Obviously, it was a shitstorm when everyone found out. Let it blow over and maybe she'll talk to you again so you can get some closure.

Closure. That's what they all thought I needed. Well, I wasn't about to let things go and just forget her. I couldn't.

I did wait a little while. For days, I didn't text or call her. I showed up at the clan picnic and felt even more alone knowing I had wanted to bring Grace. I sat off to the side, not talking or mingling much, just sipping on a beer and wallowing in my misery.

At one point, as the day stretched into evening, Ezra and Owen came to talk to me.

"She looked better today," Ezra said. "I think she's moving on. It's best if you can do the same, man. I know it's hard, but you've gotta let her go."

"I don't think I can." I picked at the label on my beer bottle, trying not to think about the fact that Beast Brew was something Grace loved, too. "I've never felt like this about anyone before. I can't sleep; I can't stop thinking about her, and my bear is driving me up the friggin' wall. I just have to find a way to talk to her. To see her. I...I love her."

Owen put a hand on my shoulder. "I know this is difficult, but the thing is, you have to remember that she ended it. She won't text you or call you. She's asked to not have to work with you at the park. It's clear she doesn't want to see you."

"It's not a matter of you trying harder, buddy," Ezra added. "It's over. You don't have a choice but to move on."

I left the picnic early and felt even worse than I had before I'd gone. Everyone had the same sort of things to say, that it was better to just forget about her find someone else. But I couldn't, and the longer it went on, the more out of my mind I felt.

When it had been a week since I'd heard from her, I decided to do something. I couldn't just show up at her house. I knew that. I couldn't just show up at her work, either. But there was one thing I could do.

I headed to the Ranger Station, as I always did, and made it seem like I was just going about my usual business. While I was there, I checked the territories for the day. Owen broke up the park into sections, and if anything happened in a certain area, the Ranger assigned to that section would be sent to check it out.

I saw where Grace would be stationed for the day and found the best spot in that area—secluded, but with easily identifiable landmarks. I set up my tent there, where no camping or tents were allowed, then I dialed the number for the main office and used a fake voice to place the call, which I knew would be answered by Rachel, the office assistant. She knew my voice, but not well enough to notice I was disguising it. She also wouldn't be suspicious of a call like that, where Owen might be.

"I'll send someone to check on it," Rachel said.

I'd given her a description of where my tent was and called in to complain that someone had set up a tent in an unauthorized area. Then I waited. I worried she wouldn't come, or that if she did, she'd pick up my scent and take off.

I had a view of the road and watched from the tent. When she pulled up in the utility vehicle, my heart skipped. My stomach twisted into knots as I saw her get out and make her way toward the tent.

"Hello there," she called out from several feet away.

I unzipped the tent's door and looked at her, and when she saw me, she froze. I gestured for her to come closer, to step inside. She swallowed hard, took a minute to look around, then ducked down to enter the tent.

I wanted to scoop her into my arms right then and kiss her madly. But she had ended things, and I didn't know where I stood.

"I'm sorry," I said. "I was going out of my mind and I hadn't heard from you. I just couldn't take it anymore."

She sat down across from me, leaving a few feet between us. "I couldn't. It would have been far too difficult to talk to you."

She looked down and wouldn't meet my eyes again.

"Tell me what we can do. How can we make this better? There's got to be something we can do."

"There isn't. I'm sorry, I shouldn't even be here." A tear fell from her eye and she stood.

"Please don't go. Please, Grace. I love you. I want to be with you, and I'll do whatever it takes to make that happen. I don't want our clans to come between us. We can leave; go where no one cares about who we are. I just want to be with you. More than anything in the world, I want you."

Grace stopped and pulled her lower lip into her mouth. I stood and braved putting my hand on her arm, and she didn't pull back or flinch from my touch.

"You...really love me?" she stammered.

"I do. So much. This has been the hardest week of my life."

She turned to me and had tears in her eyes. "Mine, too."

I was flooded with relief by hearing those words. Tears burned in my own eyes. "Please tell me we can find a way to make this work. I can't live without you."

She fell on my shoulder, crying. I pulled her close, soaking in the sweet feel of her body pressed against mine. I didn't know if I'd ever get to feel her again, and I enjoyed every moment. I drew her scent deeply into my lungs, filling my mind with it in case it would soon be gone again.

"I don't see how we can make this work," she admitted. "Can we really just leave everything behind? Our whole lives?"

"I don't know, but if we have to, if that's what it takes, then I will. I'll give up everything for you."

9

MASON

GRACE LOOKED UP AT ME, HER EXPRESSION HOPEFUL. "REALLY? YOU'D really do that for me?"

"Of course. I love you, Grace. I'm crazy about you."

"I love you, too," she whispered. "I have to ask you something, though."

"Anything."

"All I need is for you to tell me the absolute truth."

"Okay..."

"Adam had a map." She sucked in a slow, shaky breath. "It looked like your handwriting. There were several places circled on it and by each one it said 'attack.' Do you know anything about it?"

That question explained a lot. I pulled out my phone, my emotions whirling in turmoil. Was that what they'd used to turn her against me? I scrolled until I found what I needed and showed her the image on my phone. "This map?"

Her eyes widened. "Yes."

"I can only imagine what they tried to tell you this was. I wondered where it had gotten to, but now I know it was stolen from the Ranger Station, not lost. Must've been after Owen and I marked it together. It's a map of all the places there have been croc attacks in the last few years.

All the places that *crocs* have done the attacking on either other animals or other shifters."

I pointed to the different places on the map. "This is where a dead panther was found. This is where Owen's wife Addie was almost killed and our clan fought back. This is where Conner's brother and sister-in-law's bodies were found. This is where Britt was trapped and almost killed. This is where a nest of sea turtles was desecrated, killing all the turtles, including their eggs, and Addie's name was written in the mud as a warning after Owen started digging around to investigate some crocs in the area. Did you know Aiden Harvey?"

She blinked at me and looked back to the map several times. "So, this isn't a map of where the *bears* were planning to attack? This isn't your plan to retaliate?"

"Do you know anything about the situations I mentioned? Each one was dealt with at the time. Aiden, who killed the sea turtles and attacked Addie, was killed when his troop attacked and we fought back. The croc who went after Britt and the panthers was killed in the process of him trying to kill us, and the croc who killed Conner's brother and sister-in-law went to jail, but was then killed by an inmate because he pissed off the wrong person. These are only the major attacks that affected my clan directly. There have been hundreds of reports of smaller incidents over the years. If we were going to retaliate, we would have done it long ago, but we've been busy trying to make things work, trying to keep the peace all this time."

She put her face in her hands and started sobbing again. I wrapped her tight in a hug and let her cry against my chest.

"I'm sorry," she mumbled. "I'm so sorry. They said— they told us—"

"Look, both our clans are trying to convince us of the reasons we shouldn't be together. But they're wrong."

"How can we do this?" She looked up at me with wet eyes and cheeks.

I wiped away her tears. "I'm not sure, but I want to try. We have to try. I won't just give up and let them keep us apart. Especially not because of a bunch of lies."

"I'm sorry I ever questioned you. I should have known." She shook her head.

I put my hand to her cheek and kissed her. Feeling her lips against mine again was pure heaven; I couldn't stop and neither could she.

Having been apart for days and being forced into something neither of us wanted drove us to cling onto each other desperately, and we kissed hungrily.

"I never want to be away from you again," I whispered in her ear.

"I don't either. We have to find a way."

"We will." I kissed along her neck and back to her mouth.

I sat and tugged her hand to join me on the floor of the tent. When she did, she sat in my lap, facing me, with her legs wrapped around me.

I dug my fingers into her hair, pulling her closer. She ran her hands along my back, in my hair, sending chills through my body. God, I needed her; I just had to have her.

I laid her down on her back and moved into position over her, kissing her until she pulled my shirt over my head, forcing me to let my lips leave hers for a moment.

Her nails trailed along my skin. I slid my hands under her shirt, feeling the firmness of her full breasts, and she moaned against my mouth. When I pinched her nipples gently, she reached down and tugged at my jeans. I helped her unbutton and unzip them before she pushed them down. She wiggled out of her Ranger uniform and, for a moment, I remembered that she was on the clock. Someone might have come looking for her.

"Wait, Grace, should we...?"

She pulled herself up to meet my mouth and crushed her lips against mine as she took my stiff cock in her hands and stroked me. That seemed to be the only answer I was going to get.

I moved my hand down between her legs and she opened herself to me. I slid a finger inside her, feeling her wetness.

She moaned and bit gently on my earlobe. "Please, Mason. Don't make me wait any longer."

I slid my finger out and moved my member into position, then slipped slowly inside her.

She gasped and dug her nails into my back. "Oh, god," she breathed in my ear.

I thrusted in and out of her, every second sending a wave of pleasure through me. She rocked her hips up and around to bring me in deeper.

"Faster," she demanded.

I sped up and felt myself get so close, I had to ease back for a moment. I wanted to make sure I gave her the most pleasure possible and didn't want to let things end too quickly.

"Don't slow down!"

I half chuckled into her ear. "I have to for a sec."

She reached back to grab my ass and forced me into her. Slamming into her hard several times, I came just as she cried out and shuddered beneath me. She gasped as I felt her contracting around my throbbing length.

Letting out a shaking breath, I lowered myself to my elbows. She'd felt so good, I didn't want the moment to end. But I was also faintly aware that a call had come across on her walkie. She had to get back to work.

I moved back, slipping out of her slowly, and she sighed and closed her eyes. Collapsing beside her, I was no longer able to hold myself up. I panted and she turned to lay on my chest.

"We'll have to be extra careful not to be seen or found out," she whispered.

"You sure you want to do this?"

"I love you, Mason, and if you love me, too, and want to make this work, then we have to try."

I kissed the top of her head. "I want that more than anything. I want *you* more than anything."

"Me, too. And after *that*, I have to be able to see you again."

I chuckled. "You'll get no argument from me there; that was amazing. You'd better get back to work, though. I don't want to get you in trouble or raise suspicions."

"Right." She sat up and gave me a sad smile. "When will I be able to see you again?"

"Whenever you want; tonight, even. Why don't you save my number under a different name in case anyone sees your phone, then call me and I'll come get you."

She pressed her lips into a smile. "Okay."

"We'll figure this out." I tucked a strand of hair behind her ear. "We have to end this feud between the clans once and for all. We're the ones who can, I just know it."

She nodded and pulled on her shirt. "I do have to make you aware, sir, that there is no tent camping allowed in this part of the park."

"My apologies, ma'am. I'll be sure to take it down right away."

I stood and pulled on my pants as she finished dressing. She smoothed her hair down. "Do I look obvious?"

"You look obviously gorgeous." I kissed her and she sighed as she pulled away.

"Tonight."

"I'll be counting the hours."

10

MASON

I WORKED THAT AFTERNOON AND EVENING, BUT THEY WERE THE HARDEST hours I'd ever put in. With all the turmoil of the past week on top of what had happened earlier that day, my brain was scrambled. I almost couldn't believe it had happened. Had I really seen Grace, really told her I loved her and she'd said it in return? Had I actually made love to her right there in a tent in the middle of the park? It was like a dream. And, thankfully, it would be just a matter of hours until I'd see her again.

I didn't know what the future would hold for us. How we'd keep things a secret and for how long. I didn't know how we'd end the battle between our clans. But I knew that as long as we had time together, we'd be fine. We'd figure out a way because nothing could stop our love. They'd tried and almost succeeded, but I hadn't let them and neither had Grace. We wouldn't let them do it again.

I drove around my usual patrol, watching the scenes of the evening. Every time I sat somewhere that I could see people, I watched the couples, happy and in love. I thought about Grace and I grinned.

A call came in over my radio. I picked up the receiver and held in the button to respond. "Officer Rowe here. Go ahead."

Dispatch answered with, "We just got a call. Looks a possible assault in the park."

"On it."

I started my car and headed down, following the map to the exact location as it came across my monitor. When I arrived, I saw a Ranger's vehicle there with Owen and Ezra, as expected. An ambulance pulled in right behind me, lights and sirens going strong. But then I saw Conner's crew pull up in the first responder truck. This wasn't just a simple assault, then.

I called in that I had arrived and sent for backup, then went right to Owen.

"What's the word?" I asked.

"Got a call about someone found in the woods. Possible assault. Still waiting for all the details."

"Why's the search and rescue team here?"

"Wasn't sure what we'd find."

I nodded and headed over to Conner. "Are you guys ready? Let's head in."

As soon as my backup arrived a minute later, we armed up and made our way toward the location of where the victim was to be found, with search and rescue right behind us. As we got deeper into the mangrove, we heard someone moving not too far from us.

"There!" One of the officers called out and we moved toward the sound. "I see someone. Ma'am? Can you hear me?"

The group closed in around the victim. I didn't have a clear view of her, but I listened intently for my cues.

"Let's get her out of there."

"On the stretcher," Conner said. His team moved in and loaded up the woman. "Cut the gag."

Gag? I moved to get a clear view and saw that the woman on the stretcher had her hands bound behind her back. Her back was to me. Her clothing was torn and muddy, her hair mixed with twigs and leaves. *Probably a sexual assault*, I assumed and my heart dropped. Those were the worst kind of calls. And in the park? I hated to think something like that could happen there.

"Can you tell me your name?" One of Conner's team members shined a light at her, checking her pupils. "Ma'am? Can you tell me your name?" he repeated.

She let out a sob. "I...don't know."

When the words hit my ears, ice shot through me. *No. No fucking way.*

I rushed over to the front of the stretcher, and that's when my worst fear was confirmed. I would recognize her voice anywhere. But the last place I wanted to hear it was right then.

"Grace!" I shouted and pushed through the crew working on her to be by her side.

I looked her up and down, checking for any signs of injury, already knowing I would tear anyone who hurt her to shreds.

"Are you okay? Are you hurt? What happened?" I asked, taking her hand.

Though her clothing was torn and dirty, it was still in place. The closer I looked, I thought my initial assessment of sexual assault was likely false; she didn't have any signs. *Thank god.*

She looked up at me, horrified.

"Grace? Are you okay? Talk to me." What had happened to her? Why was she looking at me like that?

I put my hand to her cheek and she flinched, so I placed it down at my side, not wanting to upset her.

The team moved through the woods to get her onto the ambulance. I jumped in behind them and tried to talk to her more while they worked on her.

"Vitals are good," I heard Conner say.

"You're going to be okay," I told her. "What happened?"

She shook her head slightly and tears formed in her eyes. "Do I know you?"

"You're probably in shock. It's okay. It's me, Grace. It's Mason." I kissed her hand and set it back down. "I'm here. I love you."

"I...I can't remember anything."

I looked to Conner, not sure what to expect. He was all business, though. Of course he would be. He wasn't going to hold anything against her in that moment, when he was there to do his job and save her life.

Conner moved into place beside her. "I'm going to ask you a series of questions that will help us determine your injuries, okay? Just answer the best you can, and if you don't know, just say, 'I don't know.'"

He shined a light in her eyes, watching how her pupils dilated. "Can you tell me any part of your name?"

She shook her head.

"Do you know what year it is?"

She thought for a moment, then admitted, "I don't know."

"Do you know where you are right now?"

"In a..." She gestured around the ambulance, but didn't seem to know the word.

"Do you know where this vehicle is located? The town, state, or country?"

She took a long time to answer, then finally said, "America?" She looked over at me, still terrified.

"Do you know the names of any family members or people we should notify?"

She shook her head again.

"I do," I offered.

Conner nodded to me and motioned for me to step off the ambulance with him.

"She's suffering from some sort of amnesia. It happens sometimes with head injuries. I'm hoping it'll probably clear up in the next few hours. If you could notify her family, that would be great."

"I..." I sucked in a breath and swallowed hard. "I can't. They hate me and they'll be pissed if they know I'm here. I'm sure Owen has contact information for her on file."

Conner nodded and walked over to Owen.

And that's when it really hit me. I couldn't ride in the ambulance with her. If her family found out, they'd be furious. She'd said her dad threatened to kick her out of the house, and her clan had said they'd kick her family out if she was found talking to me. I couldn't take the chance of making things hard for her, not when this was all so new.

Owen made the calls and I stood there, watching the ambulance pull away with a knot in my stomach. What if this was somehow related to what we'd done earlier in the day? What if someone had found out we were together? I couldn't go to the hospital to make sure she was okay. I couldn't call to check on her. I was helpless.

I turned to Owen and pleaded, "Go to the hospital and make sure she's okay, please. You know I can't go. It's killing me. I—I—" I started to breathe heavy and got dizzy. Black spots dotted before my eyes.

I sat quickly and Owen knelt beside me. "Put your head between your knees, man."

I did and it helped some, but I still felt like I could throw up at any second.

"I'll go," he assured me. "I'll make sure she's okay and tell you everything I can."

"I love her," I whispered.

"I know." He patted my shoulder. "I'm sure she'll be okay. Hang in there, bud."

11

GRACE

I WOKE WITH A SPLITTING HEADACHE LIKE NONE I'D EVER EXPERIENCED before. Looking around, I had no idea where I was. I thought I knew what sort of place I was in, but the word wouldn't come; it was whatever you'd call a place people went to when they're sick.

A nurse came in the room and did something to my arm. "Is your name Grace?" she asked.

"I don't know," I admitted. How strange to not know your own name.

Three people rushed into the room.

"Here she is!" the woman said. "Grace, honey, we're here."

She held my hand and the man looked worried, too.

"We got here as fast as we could," he said. "What happened?"

I pulled my hand from the woman. I had no idea who these people were. The nurse pulled them aside to talk to them, and the woman gasped and held a hand to her mouth. The young boy with them looked at me, then looked away.

When the nurse left, they sat in a circle around me, asking questions and discussing things I knew nothing about. They said something about us all being croc shifters, which meant that apparently, we could turn into crocodiles. That's when I couldn't take it anymore. It hurt my head and after a while, I had to do something.

"I need to sleep," I said. "This is too much." They had to be crazy, these people. No one could turn into an animal. It had to be some kind of joke, and I certainly wasn't in the mood.

They all fussed when I asked them to leave, but they left me, eventually. I felt more at peace alone. What did that mean? How could I not remember my parents, if that's really who these people had been? How could I forget my brother? But I had no recollection of them at all.

I drifted in and out of sleep on the medications they kept giving me. The doctors said I'd been attacked and lost my memory. They didn't know when it would come back, if ever.

Sometime in the night, when the windows in the room were showing only blackness, a man came into my room. I recognized him, though I didn't know him. He was the one who had been there in the woods. He'd held my hand and said he loved me.

"Hey," he whispered and slid into the seat beside my bed. "How are you feeling?"

"Scared and confused."

He nodded. "I don't blame you. Me, too."

I drew my eyebrows together. "Why?"

"Do you know who I am?"

"You were there. In the woods."

"Is that all you know?" he asked.

I nodded.

"That's why I'm scared and confused. You don't know me, and I don't know what it means, who could have done this to you. I'm worried that it's my fault."

"You think you did this to me?"

He shook his head. "Of course not. Grace, I love you more than anything, and I will protect you with my life. But things haven't been easy for us. Our clans, our families, don't want us together. We're in a sort of secret relationship. I'm worried that someone found something out and did this to you as a result."

"Why would my family not want me to be with you? Are you bad? What do you mean by clan?"

He picked up my hand and I let him hold it. Even though I didn't know him, I felt better when he was around. Not like when my supposed family was there; they'd made me feel crazy and even more afraid. But that guy…I wished I could've remembered his name. He made me feel comforted somehow. I wanted to believe him.

"I don't want to put too much on you," he said. "Do you remember any of your family or clan?"

"I don't know what you mean by clan. Am I in a cult?"

He shook his head. "We're all shifters. Your family, me, you. I'm a bear shifter, you're a croc, and that's the problem."

Tears returned to my eyes. Now he was saying this, too? This animal thing? "Yeah, I guess it is a problem that people keep telling me I can turn into a crocodile."

He put his hand to his face. "I can't even imagine what it's like to not remember you're a shifter. God, Grace, this is just terrible." He looked at me with tears in his eyes. "I'm so, so sorry this is happening to you. I wish I could stop it or fix it somehow. I swear that I will end whoever did this to you."

"Can you show me?"

"Show you?"

"That you can turn into a bear?"

His eyes widened. "I've…never shifted in front of you before. I don't know if this is the best place or time, with so many humans buzzing around."

"Please. I feel like I'm going crazy, and I don't know who to believe or what to think. If you don't want to do it, I'll change. How do I become a crocodile?"

"No, don't do that. When you get out of here, we'll work on that, but not now, not here. If you really want me to, I will."

"Please."

He got up and locked the door, then proceeded to take his clothes off.

I gasped. "What the hell are you doing?"

"Oh, sorry. I can see why that would be disturbing. When we change, our clothes don't, and since our animal bodies are bigger, it rips our clothing. If I'm going to walk back out of here and not draw attention for walking through a hospital naked, I need to take my clothes off so they don't get ruined."

"Oh." That did kind of make sense. And I didn't mind the look of him without a shirt, either.

"I'm going to change, then change right back. This is really risky to do it here like this."

I watched as he pushed down his pants then got on all fours. It happened very quickly. He was a man one moment, then sprouted fur and his body expanded into the form of a bear. In another minute, he was back to human, dressing quickly and unlocking the door.

"Are you okay?" he asked, panting.

"Why is it risky?"

"The world doesn't know about us. There are a lot of shifters, but we keep it a secret."

"So many secrets."

"It's not a secret that I love you." He sat back down and picked up my hand again. "Are you okay? I never thought I'd shift in front of you for the first time like that. I can't believe you're not freaked out."

"I am. Sort of. Like, my head is freaked out? But in my body, it's like I know that it's right, if that makes any sense. Nothing really makes sense right now, so I don't know."

"Can I show you something?"

I nodded.

He took out his phone. "Where's your phone?"

I pointed to the device on the table and he picked it up and turned it so I could see the screen. He went to the text messages on both phones and I saw that they matched. It was a conversation between the two of us.

"We use code names. Your clan, being crocs, doesn't want you to be with a bear. That's the problem. But here you can see what you've said to me and what I've said to you."

He handed me the phone and I looked over the messages, reading how I'd said I loved him and apparently had had sex with him recently and enjoyed it. That made my cheeks hot, but if I was doing that with him, and it seemed like the proof was there, then I could believe him. I kept reading back through and saw a message that bothered me.

"I broke up with you?" I asked.

"Your clan made you. Look at what it says. Your family said they'd kick you out of your house, and your clan threatened to disown your family."

"Just because I'm with you?"

"There's been a feud between the bears and crocs for a long time in this area."

"Is that why we used the code names Roman and Julie? It's like we're Romeo and Juliet?"

He chuckled. "Basically. You thought it was cute when you came up with it."

"Oh. That was my idea?"

He nodded. "Can I do one thing?"

"What?"

"Can I kiss you? If you don't feel comfortable with it, that's okay. I understand. I just want to feel you. I don't know what's going to happen with all this. It might be my last chance."

I nodded and closed my eyes. I didn't remember anything, but he knew it all and now he was going through it alone, like I was. Yet, he was there, helping me, so I wanted to do whatever I could to help him, too.

His lips touched mine and he kissed me sweetly. My heart raced and when he pulled back, it was too soon. I didn't want him to stop; it felt right, even though I couldn't remember ever kissing him before.

"Did that happen to trigger any memories?" he asked. "I've been reading all I could, and I came across something that said memories can be uncovered by certain things."

He looked so hopeful, I wanted to lie to him. "I'm sorry, no. But I liked it. A lot." I gave him a half smile. "I can see why I love you."

His smile grew and he kissed me on the forehead. "I will find a way to make this better. I promise."

"I believe you."

12

MASON

I HADN'T SLEPT WELL AND I WOKE FEELING GROGGY. IN MY TEMPORARY state of confusion, I wondered if that was what Grace felt like all the time. The investigation hadn't given me much information yet, and I was frustrated with the lack of evidence. What we really needed was for Grace to remember something that would help us find out what happened and who did this to her.

I went to work and spent hours reviewing evidence, trying to see things from a new angle. By lunch, I was out of ideas and out of coffee, so I made a fresh pot and sat down to get back to work. I checked my phone, which I hadn't done in almost an hour, and noticed a text from Ezra:

Call me right away.

I rolled my eyes. Who knew what it would be about. Probably something I had no time for. But, I wanted to get up and stretch my legs, so I called him from outside the station with plans to make the call short so I could get back to deciding who to interview next. The crocs had to have something to do with what happened.

"Got your text, Ez."

"Yeah, good. I'm glad you called back. So, I noticed a certain smell when Owen and I were out searching around the spot where Grace was found. I had Britt come and check it out because I thought she would know what it was. She's really good with herbs and all that, you know?"

"Yeah." I rubbed at my face, hoping he would get to the point.

"So, she came and sniffed around and sure enough, she knew exactly what the smell was."

"Okay..."

"It's some kind of herb that can be used to cause confusion and memory issues."

"What herb?" Finally, something that could help.

"Uh, I forget what it's called."

"Is that supposed to be a joke?" I gritted my teeth.

He laughed. "No, but that would have been a good one. It doesn't matter, man; Britt has an antidote for it, and it's almost ready. She had to distill it, or something. I don't know; that's her thing. But I thought you'd want to know."

"Yeah, of course. Can I come see Britt and talk to her about it?"

"Yeah, man, sure thing. Hey, Britt!"

I held the phone away from my ear as he shouted into it. Sometimes, I didn't know how Ezra managed to become an adult. He always came off as scatter-brained surfer, but then, when you needed him, he was there. He might have frustrated me at times, but there was a reason Owen had made him his second.

"She said it'll be ready in like fifteen."

"Perfect. I'll see you in twenty."

In just forty-five minutes from the time of my call, I had completed my interview with Britt, getting all the details she had to give, and I had a vial of the antidote. Britt claimed it would return Grace's memory quickly, but that she'd, "likely puke up her guts," as well. I was prepared for both. But now I had to wait.

I'd had people checking on her during the day—Owen and Ezra mostly, since they worked with her and had a viable excuse to be there. They'd said all sorts of crocs were in and out of her room all day long. I worried that they would overwhelm her, but there wasn't anything I could do about it.

Just when the afternoon was feeling like it would go on forever, I got a text. The name on my phone said 'Julie' and my heart skipped a beat.

Are you coming back? she'd asked.

Did that mean she wanted to see me? Or was it somehow a trap? Had they figured it out? My paranoia was on overdrive with all that had happened. I didn't want to leave her hanging, though.

I sighed and began to tap the screen with my thick fingers. *Yes, I'll stop by later.*

Thank you, she sent back.

I was happy to get the text from her, whatever it meant, but it made the hours pass even more slowly. I finished my shift with no progress on her case. On my way home, I stopped by the restaurant where we'd had our first date and picked up a slice of the peanut butter pie we'd shared that night. It would serve several purposes: one, it would be a nice treat for her since she'd loved it; two, I hoped it would bring some memories back; and three, if the antidote made her nauseous, she might want something to put back in her stomach. I also grabbed a box of crackers in case the pie made her stomach more upset, being so sweet.

When the hour finally grew late enough and visiting hours had long since ended, I went to the hospital. I showed my badge as I had before and walked right past security, then the nurses' station, to her room.

Grace was sleeping when I'd arrived; she had her phone gripped tightly in her hand. I carefully slid it from her grip and looked at the screen. She'd been reading our texts. It filled my heart with warmth, and I sat to watch her for several minutes. She looked so beautiful; so perfect and innocent lying there asleep. I hated to wake her, but I had to see if the antidote would work.

I rested my hand on her arm and whispered her name. She stirred and her eyes flickered open, and when she saw me, she broke into a smile.

"Roman," she said.

"Julie," I said back with a wink. But then I wondered, *Does she even know my name?*

"I'm glad you're here."

"Me, too." I gave her a quick kiss on her forehead. "I brought some things for you."

Her face fell. "It won't help me remember. People have been showing me things all day."

"I'm sorry. It has to be frustrating not to remember. This is different though, I hope." I took the vial out of the container I'd brought it in. "You work with a guy named Ezra. He's been here to see you a few times with Owen." I didn't pause to see if she remembered. I figured it was less stressful for her if I assumed she didn't until she told me otherwise. "Ezra's wife is a master at herbs and things like that. She recognized a smell at the spot where you were found and thinks she knows what was used to make you confused like this."

Grace's eyes widened and she sat up. "She does?"

I held up the vial. "This is an antidote. If Britt is right, it should bring back your memory quickly."

She reached for the vial, but I pulled it back.

"I should warn you, though. She also said it would probably make you sick to your stomach. We should get a trash can or something for you to throw up in."

Grace pointed to a can a few feet away. "I don't care. If it works, I'll throw up all night."

I unscrewed the top and handed it to her. "Drink it slowly."

She didn't listen, pouring the vial down her throat and swallowing the contents in one gulp. She sat there staring at me and we both seemed to be holding our breath. Moments later, her eyes went wide and she covered her mouth with her hand. I shoved the trash can right under her chin just in time.

I did my best to help hold her hair back and soothe her. When she seemed to be finished, I got her a glass of water and sat as she drank it, then wanted more.

I didn't want to keep asking if she remembered anything, but it was like torture to wait. After a few minutes of us staring at each other, I showed her the other things I'd brought her. She ate some of the crackers gratefully and said it helped her stomach feel better. A little while later, she took a bite of the peanut butter pie.

"This is *so* good," she mumbled with a full mouth. "You have to have some."

"Oh no, it's all for you."

"Wait a minute." She pointed the fork at me and narrowed her eyes. "We've had this before."

I tried not to get too excited, but my heart jumped.

"At Mason's," she continued. "We've had this before!"

I grinned and tried to contain myself. I wanted to jump for joy, though.

"Is that right?" she asked.

"Almost. Close enough, though."

"No, no. Tell me what it was, so I know. I don't want to remember things wrong."

"Well, we did have this before, on our first date. But you were *with* Mason. The place was called Antonio's."

Her face reddened. "You're Mason."

I nodded.

She slapped her hand over her face. "I'm sorry. I should know that. I knew something wasn't right about Roman, but I couldn't remember what."

"Those are codes names."

"That I came up with because we're like Romeo and Juliet and our families don't want us together." She gasped. "But we're going to be anyway, and we're going to end the feud."

I didn't say anything. It was better to sit back and watch her come to life, come back to me, and just let it happen. I watched her excitement as she recalled things and blurted them out.

"Oh, that jerk, Adam. Do you know he came here and tried to tell me that he and I were dating? I'm so glad you came that first night, because that's how I knew he was lying. I knew not to trust him, even if he is my clan's leader. I think the title of Alpha goes to his head." She narrowed her eyes. "He did this."

"What?" My hands balled into fists. "Adam did this to you?"

"Not directly; I knew them, though. It was three crocs who attacked me. They made me drink something, then they started talking to me. Saying horrible things about you. They tried to brainwash me, and they tried to make me forget you."

"Tell me everything you can think of."

"You're a Law Enforcement Ranger." It wasn't a question; she knew it was true now. "Can you take this as an official statement so I can press charges?"

"Yes." I took out a notepad that I had put in the bag of things I brought. "Write down what happened in as much detail as possible."

13

MASON

I RUSHED TO THE STATION WITH GRACE'S STATEMENT CLUTCHED TIGHTLY IN my hand. Finally, we had something concrete to go on. I had to show it to my chief to get a warrant for the arrest of these assholes. I went into his office and told him what had happened.

As he read over the statement, he sighed. "This is great, but it's not enough."

"What do you mean? Since when is the victim's statement not enough?"

"When the victim has amnesia and is highly susceptible to suggestion. You did this without any witnesses; it'll never hold up in court. I can't rightly issue a warrant. And I don't think you'd want to take the chance of them getting off on a technicality and losing the case forever."

No, I certainly didn't want that; I wanted them to pay. But I couldn't hide my anger. I pounded my fist on his desk.

"I know," he said. "It sucks. But we have to do this right if we're going to nail them. Find more evidence."

I snatched up the statement and went to my desk. I sat there for an hour, drumming my fingers on my chair, trying to think of ways to get something—anything—that would help. Could I try to track the herb somehow? Get a secret confession through Grace? I had to get some sleep, so I made myself go home and took some medicine to knock myself out. When I woke, I had a new idea.

Owen had talked to the conclave a dozen times. Each time a new incident came up with the crocs, we went to them. They were supposed to be a group of representatives from all clans of all species who would oversee and make rulings on shifter crimes and help keep the peace. They hadn't been too much help to us, at least from what Owen said.

I trusted Owen. He was our Alpha and had always been a fabulous leader. But he wasn't a cop. If the conclave was some sort of law-keeping organization, then maybe I could do more than he could. Maybe he somehow didn't get across just how bad things had been with the crocs.

I hated to do it, but I had no choice. If I was going to talk to them, I had to do it behind Owen's back. As his third in command, it wasn't my place to make that call. But I didn't think I had much of a choice. He felt there was enough peace. Each incident had been dealt with at the time, and the latest one with Grace would be dealt with, too. But as a whole, it was all too much to not do something more.

I made the call and finally got the right person on the line. After I took the time to explain the full situation—all that had happened over the years—I told him that we wanted to find a way to have peace between the clans once and for all.

He thought for a moment, then responded. "Most of the time, when there is an ongoing feud, it has to do with lack of representation. You said there are no crocs working at the park except for this new Ranger, Grace, correct?"

"Yes."

"And how about your local conclave chapter?"

Our what? "We don't have one. I didn't know we could do that."

"It's not a common thing to have. Most times, clans get along, but if this has been going on for all these years and you truly want to stop it, perhaps you should assemble one, giving the crocs equal representation. If the territory is causing so much of the issue, give the crocs a reservation, a part of the land that is only theirs, that no other shifters can enter without their permission and that no other shifters have a say over. Put the crocs in shared leadership with the bears and panthers and whatever other species you have down there in the Everglades. Have regular meetings and votes on what happens in the area."

"So, you're saying democracy is the way to answer all these croc attacks."

"That or war. Which, by the way, we would not condone or support in any way. The conclave does not believe—"

"Yeah, yeah, I know. No shifter on shifter killings."

"Peace is always better in the end. Look at the humans and their wars. They haven't achieved much, have they?"

"No, but the humans in this country also don't stand by and let violence go on unpunished. Don't you believe in justice?"

"Sure. But our definitions of justice are likely very different."

I knew I wasn't going to get anywhere with that guy, so I decided to wrap up the call. "Well, thank you for your input. I appreciate your suggestion." I wondered if he could even pick up on my sarcasm.

I hung up more pissed off than I'd been before. Give them a section of the park? So, they'd gone around attacked different species, and we were going to answer that by giving them a gift? And then by letting them make decisions and have a say over what happens in the 'Glades? When they couldn't manage to uphold the rules we already had in place? The rules we've had for decades?

What an idiot. No wonder Owen didn't see a reason to run to the conclave. They were useless, as far as I was concerned. As the day went on, though, I started to think differently about his suggestions. Maybe I was just angry over the thing with Grace and that was affecting my feelings about it all. I texted Owen and Ezra and asked for a meet up, just the three of us.

After work, we went to the small playground near Owen's house. His kids ran around, playing on the slide and swings with Conner's niece.

I told them what I had done. I expected Owen—and maybe Ezra—to be mad about my going over their heads and talking to the conclave myself.

Instead Owen said, "Well, now you see what I've been dealing with."

I explained what they'd said and Ezra had a similar response to mine.

"Reward them for their crime sprees? Yeah, okay, great plan, dude." He shook his head.

"That's what I thought," I agreed, "but I didn't know if it was just my anger getting in the way."

Owen was quiet for a moment, looking off into the distance toward where the kids were. "Well..."

We both turned to him.

"I obviously don't want to just give them part of the park and a bunch of control when they haven't handled their current business well at all." He scratched his chin for a moment. "But there is one thing that makes some sense. The rules we have now? The crocs weren't here when all that was decided; they don't have a say in what happens in the 'Glades. We've been all thinking they shouldn't because of what they've done, but maybe they've done all this *because* they don't have a say. Maybe we could have some sort of meeting with the clans and try to come to a resolution. Some kind of treaty?"

"You think that would work?" I asked.

"I don't know, but if finding peace is our goal, I don't know where else to start. With you and Grace together, maybe you'd be the perfect ones to find a compromise for both sides."

"Or it'll break you up and carry the battle on," Ezra added.

"I don't think that would happen. She's not happy with her own clan right now, anyhow."

"Then maybe it could work," Owen said. "I'd be willing to try."

Grace was released from the hospital once her memory had 'miraculously' returned. I'd put in an order to have a full legal workup done to trace any amount of the herb that might still be in her blood. I had given her one of my guns to make sure she was protected. The pepper spray I'd given her before hadn't even been on her at the time of the attack, but from that point on, I made sure she carried it everywhere she went. She also wrote herself a letter in case something like that happened again.

She was as pissed as I'd been with the legal system and decided to hire a lawyer and find a doctor to clear her and confirm that her memory was perfectly intact. She was thrilled about a possible meeting between the clans, but dreaded the thought of returning home. I suggested staying at my place, of course, but she declined. She did, however, take me up on my offer to pay for a hotel. She wasn't ready to be at home.

Now, we just had to move forward with our plan.

14

GRACE

"Grace, I wish you would just come home and stop this nonsense," my mother spat in her voicemail message.

They hadn't liked it when I said I was going to stay at a hotel for a while, but I couldn't trust them. The way the attack happened, that the crocs who did it seemed to know exactly where I was and that I was alone all seemed too obvious. I hated to think it, but they might have been in on it themselves. Even if they weren't, I couldn't have been at home; it was just too stressful. Aside from that, I wanted the freedom to be with Mason.

I responded to her voicemail with a text. *Make sure you and Dad are at the meeting tonight. A lot will be explained there.*

We'll see you there, she responded.

Perfect. Even if they hadn't had any part in my attack, they needed to hear the truth. They needed to know whose side they were taking.

When the time for the monthly clan meeting came, I drove over there feeling nervous, but determined. I had several things to cover and hadn't talked to Adam beforehand to make sure I could have time at the meeting. I would have to rush in and just take over.

I got there as people were still arriving. I took a seat and made it seem like I was just there for the meeting like everyone else, and when the time came to start, Adam walked to the microphone at the front of the room.

He said his usual greeting. "Hello, my fellow crocs. Welcome and thank you for coming."

I jumped up from my seat near the front. He gave me a confused look as I walked up to him.

I said quietly to him, "I have a few words to say, if that's okay?"

He smiled and nodded, then took a step back. Idiot probably thought I was going to thank him or some crap.

"As you all probably have heard by now, I was recently attacked and my memory was temporarily lost. I've now made a full recovery, and as it turns out, I know exactly who attacked me." I pointed to the three crocs in the crowd and called them out. "These three men followed me home, jumped me as I got out of my car, and dragged me into the woods. They bound and gagged me, and then forced me to drink the liquid that erased my memory. They tried to confuse me and turn me against the bears. They tried to keep me quiet when I found out the truth. Luckily, my boyfriend knows someone who was able to make me an antidote to restore my memory."

I let that sink in for a moment. There was a lot of murmuring and when I saw my parents, they looked confused and angry.

Adam stepped up and covered the mic with his hand. "What do you think you're doing?"

"Adam doesn't *want* you all to know about things like this," I shouted to the crowd. "Right now, he's trying to stop me from telling you the truth. I'm in love with a bear shifter and ever since Adam found out, he's been trying to break us up. He told my family, who threatened to kick me out of the house. He said my entire family was being watched and he put me on probation with the understanding that I could be removed from the clan and so could my family. Does this break that probation?"

I gave Adam a challenging look. He took his hand off the mic. "Grace has been under a lot of stress lately. We all need to understand what she's been through and how difficult it must be for her. I know that you're still having some confusion, so maybe things aren't as you think they are."

"Oh no," I said. "I have zero confusion. The problem all these years hasn't been the bears, like we've been told. We've been lied to and led astray, made to think it's their fault and that they're evil. But that's not the case at all."

I took the map from my pocket; the one that Mason and I had made that was a duplicate of the one Adam had stolen. "Adam showed me this map and tried to say it was evidence of the bears' planned attack on us. It looks like that, doesn't it?"

People in the crowd agreed and seemed to grow more concerned and agitated.

I continued, "But the truth is, these areas marked are attacks that have already happened. Attacks that crocs made on different species. Panthers, bears, even sea turtles, who aren't even shifters! These facts have been covered up and the truth has been altered."

"These are all lies," Adam said, trying to take the map from me. "I know for a fact that the bears are planning an attack."

"What proof do you have? I know the bears. Not only do I work with two of them, I'm in love with one of them. They are the kindest people I've ever met. Unlike a few members of my own clan, who attacked me and tried to brain wash me."

"I think you've been brain washed by *them*," Adam seethed. "We've seen what the bears are capable of. How many of these incidents involved the bears killing a croc? Somehow, no other species has killed crocs like they have."

"Right, so that's why I was attacked to make me keep quiet? Because the *bears* are so innocent?"

"I don't know, Grace. I don't see an arrest being made. If you're so sure you know who it was, why are they sitting here and not behind bars?"

"We're working on it," I pointed out. I should have known Adam was going to try to defend himself and make the bears the looks bad, but I didn't have a good answer for that question. It was frustrating that they hadn't been arrested.

The crowd started to turn on me. Questions were being shouted at the two of us from both sides.

"Why are crocs doing so many of these attacks?" someone asked.

"Where are the maps of all the other species' attacks? I know those happen, too!"

"How do we know Grace isn't the one lying? She's the one that's a traitor!"

I stepped back up to the mic and yelled to be heard over the chaos. "I know you have questions, and that's understandable. But the bears want peace. They want the attacks to stop. There will be a meeting between the bears and any crocs that want to come."

I turned to Adam and spoke so only he could hear. "Owen, the bears' leader, wants you to come to the meeting to talk. He wants peace and he hopes an agreement can be made to achieve that peace. I'll make sure everyone knows if you're not there, if you don't attempt to make peace with the bears once and for all."

"I should have kicked you out already," he snapped back. "But I guess that wouldn't matter to you. You'd just run off with your bears."

"I want now what I've always wanted. Peace for every clan in the area."

15

MASON

We headed to the room we'd booked to meet in. Since Owen was the head Ranger, it was easy for us to get a room at the park in one of the event pavilions. No one usually used them at night, anyhow.

Grace and I arrived first with Owen and Ezra, but it wasn't long before bears and crocs alike started to trickle in. When the time came for the meeting to start, we waited another few minutes to make sure everyone who confirmed they'd be coming was there. But really, Owen and Adam were there, and they were the most important members in attendance.

I looked over at Grace and squeezed her hand. "Ready to do this?"

"So ready."

We stood and I called out to get everyone's attention. "We're going to get started with the meeting now, if everyone would quiet down please."

Grace said, "Thank you all for coming. I think we all know that this feud has been going on too long. We all want the fighting to come to an end."

I nodded and added, "This is the first of what we hope will be a long understanding between the clans. We're hoping for a way we can all work together to make the Everglades National Park the best it can be for everyone who wants to come and enjoy it."

"Without having to worry about attacks or prejudice or anything else," Grace added.

"Is this just about your relationship?" someone in the crowd shouted.

"It is," Grace admitted, "but only a small part of it. We don't think anyone should be threatened just because they want to date someone of another species. But it's much more than that. Our clans haven't been at peace for many years. It's time the attacks and the killings and yes, the prejudices, come to an end."

"We want to make sure both sides are heard, and that both sides have equal representation," I said. "That's why we're all here together. To find an agreement between us that works for everyone."

"Are you giving us the park, then?" a croc shouted.

Grace jumped in. "That wouldn't be what's best for *everyone*. The park is a huge area and it can't belong to just one clan or another. That's why I work there now. To help balance things out."

"But you're a traitor," another croc said. "You'll just do what's best for the bears."

Grace shook her head. "When Adam came to me, with my family, and asked me to give up my dream of becoming an environmental lawyer to go work in the park, I did it. Adam was actually using me to spy on the bears, but there was nothing to find out. But when my own clan attacked me and attempted to brain wash me and keep me quiet about the truth, I knew I had to do something. I am loyal to my kind. But we need leaders who won't lie to us, and we need to know the truth on all sides."

"We have a few ideas to make things in the 'Glades more equal," I said. "It's been suggested that the crocs have a sort of reservation in the park, a sanctuary area just for them."

"So, let's give them what they've attacked us to take?" Noah shouted. "How is that what's best for everyone?"

"The crocs weren't here many years ago when the initial shifter rules were put into place," I explained. "They didn't have proper representation like the other clans did."

"That didn't help the panthers," Conner said, looking over at Britt.

"There's no denying that there have been major issues," Grace said. "The crocs have not gone about things the best way. That's why we want—"

"Why are the crocs always the ones to blame?" Adam got to his feet and marched toward us. "I've been sitting here, listening to you two go on and on about how terrible the crocs are. It's bullshit. It's nothing but lies. We've been pushed aside, pushed out, given nothing but rules and no say."

"That's exactly what we're talking about," I said. "We're trying to find a place of more equal representation."

"No, you're trying to control the crocs even more," Adam said. "You want us to feel like we have more power, when we won't. I know how the bears do it. The same way they've taken over the entire Everglades and have put themselves into all the ruling positions over the other clans. Why would they suddenly play fair?"

"We've always played fair," Owen said, joining us at the front of the room. "We've made rules that protect everyone. We've kept the park safe for all. We were one of the first species on this land and had to set things in place the best we saw fit all those hundreds of years ago. This is what our ancestors planned. And now things have changed and we recognize that."

"Bullshit." Adam stepped up into Owen's face. "This is just a trick. This whole meeting is probably one big ambush. You want us dead, and now you've planned this meeting to get us all together so you can kill us all at once."

Owen tried to respond, but it was too late. When Adam spoke those words, the crocs reacted. They were on their feet, shouting and pushing each other. The room exploded in chaos.

I waved my hands to try to get everyone's attention, but it was impossible.

Then I heard someone shout, "He has a gun!"

I couldn't tell who had said it or who supposedly had a gun. All I knew is that the next time I looked out into the crowd, I saw many guns and knives being pulled. I saw fists flying and more pushing and slapping.

I looked at Owen, who had his defensive face on, and we moved forward as the crocs came toward us. I wouldn't have thought a scene like that was possible; not amongst civilized people. But it was a war.

I hadn't heard gun shots, but as I dodged a punch, I heard someone smash a chair into a wall. There was so much shouting, I couldn't even hear myself think. We had to defend ourselves. And we had to do it in a way that didn't end up with a bunch of shifters dead.

I grabbed a man's hand and twisted his knife away from him, kicking him in the knee to drop him to the ground. He lie there, cursing me and holding his knee, but he was down and out of the fight for the moment.

My gun was on me, but I kept it holstered. It would be too easy for me to start taking crocs out, and I didn't want to resort to that; not unless we absolutely had to. I still had a responsibility to uphold the law.

A croc came charging at me and I used his momentum to send him flying into a mass of chairs. I turned to make sure Grace was still by my side, but I didn't see her. She had been right there a moment ago. Panic flooded over me, and I searched the room for her.

I stood on a chair and finally saw that she'd been pulled across the room. It looked like Adam was holding her. I pushed my way through the fray to her.

Adam pointed a gun at me. "She stays with her kind."

I weighed my options for a moment. In the end, I knew my years of training as an officer had to outrank whatever training he might possibly have, so I lunged forward, ducking, wrapping my arms around Grace's waist. When I had my arms around her, I spun, throwing my elbow into Adam's side as I freed her from his grip.

I let her go for a moment, then threw an uppercut into Adam's stomach. He bent forward just enough that I was able to twist the gun from his hand.

As Adam tried to claw me to get his gun back, someone grabbed it from my hand. I looked over and saw Grace holding the gun. She pointed it straight in the air and fired several times.

16

GRACE

THE LOUD SHOTS RANG OFF THE WALLS, CREATING AN ALMOST DEAFENING wave of sound. The room went quiet and my ears rang; I'd never shot a gun before, and it was much louder than I'd expected. I shouldn't have fired it so close to Mason, but he seemed fine. I assumed he was probably used to that sort of thing as a cop.

I waited a few seconds for everyone to look in my direction, and as I opened my mouth to speak, tears came to my eyes. I swallowed to blink them back, but they still made my voice waiver.

"This has to stop," I said. "This fighting gets us nowhere except hurt or killed. Even now, as we all come together to find peace, the crocs have acted first. Don't you see this? Adam convinced you all that the bears were lying, that they did this as some sort of ambush, when there was no proof of that at all. Where is this ambush? Where is their big attack? I see bears taking weapons from crocs and not using them. In fact, look around. Who has the weapons? Who is using them? Who is really doing the fighting and attacking here?"

There was murmuring as they looked around. They had to be seeing what I saw, that it was the crocs, once again. We'd been at fault so many times over the years. I had to find a way to get them to see it; to see that we should be grateful for any olive branch of peace from the bears.

"In the midst of all this, it was a croc, my own leader, who held a gun to my head, then pointed it at Mason to keep us apart. I don't blame Adam. I've looked into the history of our clan and I know that there's a long line of lies before him. He's been lied to by those above him, and he's believed those lies and is now passing them on to us. But know this. They *are* lies. You can choose to believe whatever you want, but look at the proof. In the last few years, there have been more than ten attacks committed by crocs in the 'Glades. Do you know how many attacks the bears have committed? Or the panthers? Or any other species in the park? If you add up all the attacks committed by non-croc shifters in the last six years, you get a big, fat zero on the other side of our more than ten. You tell me what the truth is. We've been brought here to find peace; we don't deserve that. We haven't been a beneficial part of the 'Glades; we've been a blight. Yet, the bears are still willing to go out of their way to make it better for us. Which side do you really want to be on?"

I lowered the gun and tucked it in my waistband. "Take a moment and really think for yourselves for once. Do you want the fighting to stop? Do you want things to be fair? Or do you want to keep attacking and being responsible for the killings in our homeland? Do you want to be on the side of peace or war?"

Mason pulled me in for a quick hug. "Is anyone seriously injured?" he asked the crowd. "We do have people here who can give first aid."

Noah came to the front with a cut over his eye. Then a few crocs made their way forward, too, with similar injuries. By the time we'd sorted it all out, there didn't seem to be much more than a few bruises and cuts. No one stabbed or shot. No one killed. That alone was a miracle.

"This gives me hope," Mason said loudly to the crowd. "In a room of so many people, with so many weapons, no one was killed or seriously injured. That shows me that we all want peace. We don't actually want to hurt each other, and I'm grateful for that."

Once everyone had been cared for by those shifters who worked in the medical field, Mason stood to address the crowd again. "I know it's getting late and that we've been here for many hours. But I'd like to see our leaders sit down and talk. Anyone who would like to stay is welcome, and anyone who needs or wants to go is also welcome. There may be a vote at some point."

I was at his side and couldn't stifle a yawn. We had been there a long time, and we'd likely be there much longer. "I saw my parents once after the fight. They were fine. Have you seen them again?"

He shook his head and looked out over the crowd. "Maybe they decided to go. Is Tyler home?"

I nodded. "I'll text them to make sure they're okay." I sent a quick text to my mom, and when I didn't get an immediate response, put my phone back in my pocket. They'd been fine after the fight, so there was no reason to think anything was wrong. They were probably just driving.

Mason gripped my hand and squeezed it tightly. "I thought I was going to have to call for back up for a minute there and pull the cop card."

"It was bad," I agreed. "But, like you said, no one got seriously hurt. Even if Adam did point a gun at us both."

He put his hand on my cheek. "I want to make sure nothing like that ever happens again. I'm glad my training allowed me to act quickly and not have to shoot him."

"Me, too. That might have escalated the whole situation."

He nodded. "Let's see if we can get this settled."

He pulled me back toward the front of the room. "Owen. Adam." He gestured for them to come forward. Owen came first, then as Adam realized that the crowd was watching him, waiting for him to make a move, he came to the front, too.

"Let's sit here right now," Mason said. "And hear both side's terms. What will it take for there to be peace? What are your demands to make some kind of treaty that will end the fighting?"

We pulled up several chairs and all sat in a circle. The crowd was still loud and moving around, but had settled considerably during the time that the injuries were being assessed and taken care of.

Once we all sat, they thankfully quieted even more. My throat was already aching from having to shout so much, I wouldn't want us all to have to keep straining our voices to be heard.

Mason looked at our clan leaders, taking the natural position of mediator. I loved seeing him in a place of leadership; he really excelled in the role. I wondered briefly how he'd come to be third in command behind Owen and Ezra and thought I'd have to ask him the story sometime. It would be interesting to see how the bears decided their hierarchy and compare it to our system. Our leaders were decided mostly by force under the guise of a vote. Whoever fought the hardest for it, got the votes. The candidates would usually coerce and manipulate to get votes, sometimes even threaten. Adam had been in power for two years now and had eight years left in his term, unless something changed. There had to be a better way.

Mason asked Adam and Owen, "Who wants to speak first?"

Adam didn't hesitate. "If the bears had the park for so long, we should have it now," he said.

"I'm sure we can work out some equal agreement, but we're not going to just hand over complete control of the entire Everglades to you," Owen countered. "You haven't proven you can handle it."

"You haven't given us the chance! We've always been repressed. We had no choice but to fight back."

"I'm sure it seemed that way," Owen said. "But you always have a choice. Will you agree to stop attacking? To stop coming against us in every way?"

"That depends. What will you give us to do it?"

I heard the crowd start to speak up again, but they couldn't be allowed to get involved now. It would only derail things and interrupt progress.

"Please," I said loudly. "If everyone can sit down. I'm sure there will be time for a vote, but for now, let's allow our leaders talk this through. That's why we've chosen them to lead us, after all."

Adam gave me a look. I wasn't sure what it was, exactly. Appreciation maybe that I still considered him my leader and that I was letting him take charge? I didn't care as long as they could figure it out.

"What do you think about having some kind of sanctuary for just the crocs?" Owen asked. "A part of the park that could be all your own."

"We want half." Adam crossed his arms.

"There are a lot of species who live in the 'Glades," Owen countered. "We can't just let you have half of it. I'm talking about a section where no other shifter is allowed to go. If you want a bigger role in the leadership of the park as a whole, we can work that out, but if you're going to be unreasonable, we're never going to get anywhere."

"So, you're still trying to control things," Adam snapped.

Owen put his face to his hands. "The bears are in the position of authority, currently. It is actually well within our rights to not only remove all crocs from the 'Glades, but also, given the number of attacks, to ban the crocs forever, and according to the old laws, hold the croc leadership accountable for those past attacks with their lives."

Adam ground his teeth and raised a fist like he was going to punch Owen.

"But," Owen said, holding up his palm. "We haven't done any of those things, have we? We've never done one thing that's been unfair to the crocs. We've tried to have peace, and we've defended ourselves and others when necessary. We've only killed when an attacker couldn't be brought down and out of self-defense."

Adam crossed his arms. "How much of an area are you thinking?"

"I don't know for sure," Owen said. "We'd have to find the best place for it. Somewhere with plenty of saltwater or brackish water, of course."

"And you're saying this would be our land where no shifter could come and no one could have a say over it?"

"You'd still have to obey the general laws of the land, of course, but it would be croc territory. And might I point out," Owen said to the crowd, "that no other clan or species has a sanctuary of land like that. Yours would be the first."

That seemed to finally resonate with Adam. "Okay. We'll agree to that as long as we get a nice chunk of quality land. At least a few hundred acres."

"I'm sure a few hundred acres would be just fine," Owen said. "But I want a guarantee of peace. And the understanding that any attack by the crocs will end whatever treaty we hold, including your sanctuary."

"We can't hold all crocs accountable for one croc's actions," Adam demanded.

"Then it'll be your job as leader to carefully select who gets to stay on that land; to make sure everyone knows the rules and follows them. If you can prove that you're taking action against any rumor of attack and that you're willing to reprimand your own if something happens, then maybe we can work in some conditions that would allow the uninvolved crocs to remain if there were a situation like that."

"We'll be policing our own lands for sure. I don't want anyone coming onto our territory who shouldn't be there. And I don't want anyone messing it up for everyone else." Adam glared into the crowd, daring anyone to act out.

17

GRACE

"Okay then." Owen let out a long breath. "We have Grace on the Ranger team. In that position, she speaks for the crocs in whatever decisions need to be made in the park. I would welcome any other croc who wanted to be a Ranger."

"Or to join the law enforcement branch," Mason added. "We don't have any crocs, and I suspect they didn't think they'd get hired or that we would treat them well. I think we need some crocs on the force."

"I think it'd be best," Owen continued, "if we did make a local chapter of the conclave. A group where all species can be represented equally and the decisions can be made together for the good of all. We could hold monthly meetings to discuss and decide issues."

"And the crocs would have equal say?" Adam asked.

"I think the fairest way to do it is to mirror how other branches do it, by having one representative from each species in the area. That way, each clan gets a vote." Owen looked to Adam for a response.

Adam nodded. "That would make things better. As long as it's equal."

"It will be. A true democracy," Owen said. "You decide who represents the crocs. We can set up some kind of process of voting for the candidates and let the people decide who should represent them."

Adam narrowed his eyes slightly. "You'd take the chance they might not vote for you?"

"Of course. I'm the Alpha, but in the bear clans, that's more of a born position than chosen. I think it'd be better to have someone else represent the bears in a local conclave, actually. I can't be the only one making all the calls. In fact, I might require my clan to choose someone else. Any of my clan would be a find choice to represent us all."

Adam nodded slowly. "I'll have to think about that process some. We'd get to decide how to pick ours?"

"I can't see any other way, as long as you make it fair for all crocs. If there's a dictatorship in choosing representation, I don't know if things will really improve."

"Then maybe we best set something in place for that. To decide how we'll decide," Adam said. "So that in the future, we don't end with a bad leader in place."

Owen nodded. "I could agree to that."

I wondered if Adam was thinking of his own election and all the hassle he'd gone through to win. Or maybe he was hoping to change things before the next one so that he could stay in the leader position longer. Owen had said the bears were born into it. I wasn't sure how long Owen had been Alpha, but it had been many years, and I guessed it would be for life. I didn't know if that was the best way to go, either. If you had a good leader, like Owen, it was great. But what if you had a leader like Adam, who wouldn't think twice of using his own people to suit his own purposes?

Either way, I was glad to hear that they would decide on a way to choose the clan representatives. We didn't need another pushy croc trying to gain power. I thought, depending on how it happened, if I were able, I'd likely run for the position. As one of the two driving the peace treaty from the start, who better to see it through to the next stages?

"And we can agree to peace," Adam said. "I'll make sure my people know that these are new times, and new times call for new actions. I will get to the truth of what happened in the past. I want to know what lies I've been told, too. I do take these accusations very seriously." He shot a look at me. "And I want to clear things up once and for all."

"Let's start writing all this down," I said. "Get it on paper now so we can walk out of here with a set plan."

I had a notebook with me and took on the role of secretary. Mason went over the points we'd decided on so far. That there would be a local conclave chapter and that each clan would have a single representative to speak for the species as a whole. We would decide on a process to choose that individual, by some kind of vote. The crocs would get a chunk of the park as a sanctuary, with the understanding that any attacks would end the treaty and they'd be removed from their sanctuary and possibly the park as a whole, depending on what the crime was.

I wrote all that down as Adam and Owen agreed that that was what had been decided. I wondered what Adam would do to police the new lands. I couldn't be watching it if I were doing my ranger duties for work. Sure, I'd check on it, but someone should be there at all times to watch things. I made that suggestion and Adam nodded.

"What we need are croc cops," Adam said. "But we don't have anyone who can join the force. We haven't had any crocs interested in law enforcement in a long time."

"It would be the best way to keep things equal in all areas," Mason said. "Maybe talk to some of your young men and women, some who are just going into college or just getting out, to see if anyone has any interest."

"I would like to make a suggestion as well," Owen said. "I've never turned down a croc application in the park for a Ranger. Do you have anyone who is interested in becoming one?"

Adam gestured to me. "Looking at her. And we had to convince her to do it."

"That's what I thought," Owen continued. "In that case, here's my suggestion. Since there is no other croc on staff and no one interested in taking that position, I will promote Grace to be my co-head Ranger."

I blinked at him. He wanted to promote me? To give me more leadership and power?

"Wow," I said. "I would be honored to take that position. Don't you have bosses to talk to first?"

"Not as head Ranger." He winked at me.

Mason squeezed my shoulder and smiled. I wasn't sure how that had just happened, but I'd just gotten a huge promotion. I was too shocked to even be excited about it.

"I will be sure to speak up for the crocs," I said. It was great working with Owen and it'd be great to work even more closely with him. I knew

I could learn a lot from him. He had many years of experience and seemed connected with the park as if it were part of him.

They did decide easily that when it came to choosing a representative for the conclave, the simplest thing would be to have anyone interested in the position add their name to a list, then have a simple vote. When I explained a little of how the other croc elections had gone, there were additional parameters set that guaranteed no campaigning beyond a one-time, debate-style discussion between all candidates. If anyone was found to be forcing or bribing people to vote a certain way, that person would be removed from the list and could never be a candidate again. If someone outside the candidates was forcing votes, that person would be arrested and face charges. They weren't taking any chances that a bad leader would get such an important role.

Toward the end, when it seemed that things were winding down, someone brought out a map and Owen and Adam marked the spot that would be the croc sanctuary. When everyone was satisfied, they drew the area out in thick black marker. Several people took a photo of the map on their phones.

A date was set for the vote to choose conclave reps, as well as for the first official meeting. The meeting would be a time for grievances to come out and for decisions to be made about them. It was stipulated also that law enforcement would be called in the event of an attack or criminal issue, even if the matter was taken to the conclave first.

The whole thing had come together much more easily than I thought it would have. But, it seemed that once Adam understood not only that we didn't deserve what they were giving us, but that we were getting a lot—most importantly equal say and power—he finally saw the benefit in getting along.

When everything had been written out, we turned back to the crowd for the first time in hours.

"Let's vote," Mason said. "I think we can make this simple with a show of hands."

He glanced at Owen and Adam and they both nodded.

"Anyone opposed to any part of the treaty, raise your hand now."

We all watched. Just one person raised his hand.

"Anyone in favor of all parts of the treat, raise your hand now."

Hands went up all over the room. I suspected that a few people didn't vote, and that was their choice, but the overwhelming majority was for the treaty. I did wonder who the croc was who had been against the treaty and which part he had issue with or if the whole thing was an issue. It wasn't the time to find out something like that, and it didn't matter why in the end. We had an agreement and the people had voted.

I watched with tears in my eyes as Mason handed the pen to Owen, who signed the bottom of the paper. Then Adam took it and signed as well. It was done. I would have the whole thing typed up more officially and copies given to all so that everyone was clear on the points. Someone had said we should frame the original handwritten notebook paper as a piece of history. I thought it sounded like a fine idea. I was glad to be part of making history. Glad that I had been there to not only witness it, but to participate in it and to be one of the ones who helped make it possible in the first place.

What would have happened if I hadn't agreed to work in the park? Would I have met Mason? Would any of those decisions have been made that night? Our love was strong and we needed each other. But it seemed that our clans needed us to be together, too. So much depended on us coming together. What if Mason had let me go when I'd tried to end things? The thought turned my stomach. What if I hadn't gotten my memory back?

I shook the negative thoughts from my mind. It had all happened and now there we were. There would be peace between the clans. Finally.

18

GRACE

As the meeting was coming to its end, Mason stood up suddenly. "I have one more idea." He turned to face the crowd, then turned back to me. "One more way that we can bring our clans together."

"But the treaty is already done," I said.

He gave me a wide smile and stood in front of me, taking both my hands in his. Then, he knelt down in front of me.

"Grace, from the moment I met you, I have been taken by you. Everything about you drives me wild. I know it's been hard for us to even be together, but I want to make sure that nothing ever separates us. I want us to be united forever, not only through love, but through marriage."

He reached into his pocket and took out a ring, turning the silver band in his fingers so that the diamond caught the light and sparkled.

"Grace Osborn, will you marry me?"

"Oh my god, yes!" I pulled him into a hug and kissed him.

He slipped the ring over my finger and we heard cheers from the crowd. My mother and father rushed toward us. I hadn't heard back from them after I texted them, but they must've stuck around. I was glad they had been there to see it all.

They joined us at the front of the room and I gave them a wary look. I didn't know how it was going to go down. They'd never been a fan of Mason or us being together.

I watched, as if in slow motion, as my father stuck out his hand to shake Mason's. Then my mother hugged him.

They came to hug me next and my mother said, "As long as you're happy, we're happy."

"If the clan doesn't have an issue with it, then I don't, either," my dad added.

I'd take it. They weren't trying to talk me out of it. They weren't acting unhappy. I was sure that deep down, they were a little disappointed, but they didn't show it.

Owen and Ezra congratulated us and the rest of the bears followed. A few crocs came to add their congratulations as well. Then Adam was there. He walked over and begrudgingly shook Mason's hand.

The clan was watching and he knew it. He gave me a forced smile. "I hoped we would end up together one day, but I see that you love him, and he's willing to fight for you. As long as he doesn't ever hurt you, then I wish you both happiness."

"Thanks, Adam. I appreciate it." It felt like with those words, I had my clan's permission. Whatever threats had been spoken before were long gone.

As the crowd dispersed and went on their way, I hugged Mason close. "How long have you been planning that?"

He pressed his lips together. "I got the ring right after your memory came back and I knew I never wanted to lose you again. But I hadn't decided how to actually propose until about two seconds before I did."

I laughed. "Well, it was a fine move. And it saves us the trouble of having to tell everyone. They were all there!" Though I did have a few friends out of the area and my best friend, Sophie, was still off at grad school. But that was way at the back of my mind in that moment.

I inspected the ring, watching the light shine through the round stone. "It's beautiful."

"Not as beautiful as you."

He put his hand to my cheek and kissed me, and the joy and relief of the day rushed through me. As he kissed me, I grew warm all over.

"I think we should get out of here," I said.

"Why?" He looked around, concerned.

"Because I want to celebrate and we can't do that with clothes on." I pressed my body to his and kissed him again.

"Oh." He chuckled in my ear. "In that case, why aren't we already in my truck?"

He took my hand and we said quick final goodbyes as we got into his truck. To celebrate, when we got to his house, he poured us some wine.

"To us and being one forever," he said.

"One forever," I repeated and clinked my glass against his.

I had only drank a few sips when he started to run his hands all over me. We were in his living room and I set my glass beside me on the end table so I could turn to fully face him.

"I'm thinking," he said, running his hands under my shirt and along my back. "That we both have far too many clothes on."

"Hmm. That is a problem."

He pulled my shirt over my head, and I did the same with his. He reached back to unhook my bra and then cupped my breasts in his hands.

"You are so goddamn sexy," he said. "Just perfect."

He leaned down to kiss along my chest and teased my nipples, sending tingles through me.

"We still have a problem," I whispered.

He looked up at me questioningly.

"Pants," I explained.

He unbuttoned my jeans and pulled the zipper down before pushing them to the floor. I reached for his and when we were both completely naked, he lay me back on the sofa.

"Mind if I finish my wine?" he asked.

I chuckled, but said, "Sure," thinking he was just going to gulp it down.

Instead, he picked up the glass and tilted it until the cool liquid formed a pool around my belly button, then teased me as he lapped up the wine with his tongue.

He placed the glass on the table and moved his mouth downward to kiss my thighs. I let my legs fall open, desperate for his touch. He read my mind and began to flick between my folds, and the exquisite feeling made my toes curl in pleasure.

He pressed his tongue more firmly against me as he ran his hands along my legs, and the ecstasy building from deep within my core was warming me from head to toe. Gripping the sofa cushion, I tilted my hips to position myself even closer to his mouth, and I moaned as I felt myself growing close.

I was so worked up, all it took was him slipping a thick finger inside me to push me over the edge and I came, shuddering in utter bliss, and he continued his ministrations as I rode out the ebbing waves of my orgasm.

Mason returned to meet my gaze, then planted a trail of kisses along my collarbone. "That was just the preview."

"I can't *wait* for the main attraction."

He kissed me passionately for a few minutes, but I started to grow impatient. I bit his earlobe gently. "Just how many previews are there?"

"I thought maybe you needed a minute."

"It's been more than a minute."

He reached his hand between my legs and began to rub my clit in torturously slow circles. I moaned and pushed my hips up into him.

I felt his hardness at my entrance and he penetrated me with his entire length in one quick movement, and I let out another moan as he filled me and pounded into me again and again. He felt absolutely amazing.

"This has got to be a five-star performance," I breathed into his ear.

His lips crashed over mine as he sped up his thrusts, and when I grew close to my peak again, I told him, "Harder."

He slammed into me faster, harder, until I dug my nails into his back and reached down to grab his ass, pulling him into me as I came yet again. With a few hard thrusts, he let out a moan as he reached his own climax.

He dotted my face with kisses, making me giggle from the ticklish feeling.

"I can't believe I really get to make love to you forever," he said.

"You," I touched the tip of his nose and smiled, "are a dream come true."

He continued to lie on top of me; there wasn't room on the couch to lie side by side. "Do you ever wish I was a croc?"

"Definitely not."

"Why?"

"Do you wish I was a bear?"

"No," he admitted, "but it would make things easier for us if we were the same species."

"That's no fun. If we were, maybe things would have been different. I love you just how you are, fuzzy bear fur and all."

He ran a fingertip over my hard nipple. "One of these days, you'll have to actually shift in front of me so I can appreciate that scaly skin of yours."

I slid out from under him and got down on the floor on my hands and knees. I was already undressed, so I figured, why the hell not? I felt the familiar cracking of my bones as my limbs shortened and my skin hardened.

I looked at him with my reptilian eyes and playfully snapped my jaw. He ran his hand over the ridges of my spine, then along my underbelly, feeling the smooth scales of my skin. "You're magnificent, even as a crocodile."

I waved my tail and shifted back, then sat on his lap, facing him. "We really are two vicious beasts."

"Indeed. Two, about to become one."

"Forever."

19

GRACE

I WALKED DOWN THE AISLE SLOWLY, MY LONG, WHITE LACE TRAIN TRAILING behind me. Mason met my eyes. He beamed and my smile grew wider.

Everything had turned out perfect. The flowers were beautiful in their purples and blues. The aisle had been scattered with purple petals just moments ago by Owen's boys and Conner's niece, son, and daughter. There were quite a few kids on the bear side of things, and I hoped we'd be adding to them soon. We'd just found out on the night of our bachelor and bachelorette parties that Ezra and Britt would be welcoming a little cub—or panther—of their own in a few months.

That day felt like the moment that everything was finally coming together. My side of the church was filled with crocs. My family was there, my mom teary eyed, of course, holding onto my father. Bears took up most of the seating on Mason's side, and I knew of at least one panther or two as well. There were a few humans scattered here and there, too; all close enough to our clans to be trusted to know the truth.

The first meeting of the Everglades Chapter of the Conclave had met, with the representative elections having been held just weeks before. With Mason as the rep for the bears, me as the rep for the crocs, Britt for the panthers, and a man named John for the wolves, I was confident we'd all be able to keep the peace. We were family on more than one level, and as long as we kept each other in the front of our minds, we couldn't go wrong.

Even our wedding party was a fine mix of species. My maid of honor was Sophie, who'd been my best friend in the clan since we were croc kids trampling through the swamps together. She was finally back from grad school after being gone for ages. Behind her stood Addie, a bear; then Britt, a panther; Tori, a bear; and finally Jessie, a human. With Mason was Owen as his best man, then Ezra, Conner and Noah, and finally, my brother Tyler.

I felt proud of our mix. We had four species in strong representation and had even invited John and his wife as a good faith measure, which sprinkled in just enough wolf to bring the count to five species. They were all sitting together, smiling, happy for a croc and bear to be getting married. The happy part was a feat in itself, but after the meeting and our very public engagement, interspecies relations in the area had slowly been getting better.

When I reached Mason, I handed my nosegay of lavender roses and blue delphinium to Sophie and the ceremony began. Toward the end, after we'd said our vows and exchanged rings, we had another special part planned.

We brought a small table to the center of the aisle, in the middle of everyone there, where a clear glass bowl had been placed, filled with stones that we'd collected from the park. Mason lightly cut my palm and I returned the gesture, then we dripped our blood over the stones, symbolizing the coming together of the crocs and bears forever.

We had our first married kiss and bounced down the aisle hand in hand, alight with joy, and next, it was time to party. At the start of the reception, after we'd had our first dance, we'd asked Owen and Adam to give a toast.

Owen went first. "I know it hasn't been an easy path for you two, but you worked together to overcome everything against you and found a way to be with each other. You refused to give up and even managed to end a feud between two species in order to make this day possible." He paused to look around for effect. "Nothing you'll come across in married life will be as difficult as that, so I think you're pretty much set." The guests laughed. "I wish you both all the happiness in the world and I look forward to many long years of peace with the two of you representing our clans."

Owen handed the mic to Adam and they shook hands as they did. "Well." Adam sighed. "He pretty much took my speech, so I'm not sure what to say now..." Everyone laughed again. "I'll just say that any couple who can triumph over what Mason and Grace have can triumph over anything. And I will go ahead and start the pool right now. I put my money on the first baby being a croc." He took a twenty from his pocket and slapped it down on a nearby table. "To Mason and Grace and the eternal peace between the bears and crocs."

I saw that while he was giving his toast, he kept looking across the room at a certain bear shifter in Mason's clan. Hailey was her name. I made a mental note of it as the night went on, and we ate and resumed dancing. Sure enough, over the hours, I caught Adam dancing with Hailey several times.

"I think there might be a competition for cutest bear/croc couple," I said to Mason as he held me close and we danced.

He looked to where I nodded. "Huh. Well look at that. I never thought Adam, of all people, would be next."

"Well, you know how it is. When fate leads you to the person you're supposed to be with, you don't have much of a choice."

He returned his gaze to mine and kissed me. "Thankfully, fate led me to you."

20

GRACE

EPILOGUE - ONE YEAR LATER

The pain was becoming too much for me. I knew it was going to hurt; I'd talked to all our friends who'd had babies and they'd each given me their birthing stories, so I thought I was prepared. But this was insane. It felt like my whole torso might implode at any moment.

I gripped Mason's hand so tightly, it was leaving a mark. "You're doing great, honey. I love you."

He kissed me and I wished it helped.

"Okay, Grace, I think you should change." Addie had said it, and Britt, Jessie, and Sophie agreed.

I'd always known what a group effort shifter births were; when my mom had me, she had four or five friends there with her to help. I thought it was a good way to go. They had been so supportive and helpful that I was grateful for their presence.

I shifted into croc form, and now I needed Sophie more than anyone. She shifted, too, as we'd planned; that way, I'd have an easy mental link to communicate. Mason also shifted. Though he and I could communicate telepathically since we were husband and wife, it was still easier to default to my own clan's link. And this way, I'd have him and still have Sophie. If the bear ladies had shifted, I'd have no way to talk to them at all. Mason would have to pass messages, which was just pointless. It was better for them to be humans for this part anyhow.

We had gotten a baby pool, knowing that at some point, I would probably get in it. But, being a mixed species couple, we had an added complication. If Mason was a croc, this baby would be a croc, no doubt. But there was only a 50% chance he or she would end up as a croc. Our child could just as easily have been a bear. Shifters often gave birth in their animal form because they found it easier, and if they did, that meant their baby would be born in animal form, too. Too bad that I couldn't have just laid an egg like a pure croc, though; it seemed like it would've been so much easier than delivering the baby, head, limbs and all.

Being a croc shifter, I had to try to predict which way things would go based on signals from my body. Britt had been helpful for this part. She and Ezra ended up having a bear child, and she said that when she was in panther form, she could tell something wasn't right. As soon as she shifted back to human, the baby was born with no problems and they had to assume he was a bear until he had his first shift. He smelled like a bear, though, we all agreed.

Because we were a mixed-species couple, I had the same challenge: I had to feel it out and see if things felt right or not. But that was my first baby, and I had no idea what was right and what wasn't. It hurt like hell; that's all I knew for certain. I did have the notion, though, that once I shifted into my croc form, if the baby was a croc, I should be able to feel whether or not the baby changed through my belly. Britt had tried, but a panther had too many similar parts to a human for it to be telling. That's one benefit in being so very different from a bear: there would be no denying a long croc tail and short, little legs.

When I shifted, I said to Mason, *Feel and see if you can tell.*

We'd had this discussion beforehand of course, and my croc doctor thought there was a good chance it would work. As he felt my stomach with his paws, though, he made a confused face.

I think Addie or a human should try, he said. *I can't tell with my paws. I think there's a tail?*

Sophie came over, too, and tried to figure it out. *No idea; sorry, hun.*

Britt seemed to pick up on what we were doing. I'd talked to her about the whole interspecies thing many times. "Want me to see if I can tell?"

I nodded my croc head and she felt my swollen belly with her human hands. "Um..." She made the same confused face. "Well, I do feel a tail. But I also feel an arm, I'm pretty sure."

Can a baby partially shift inside its mother? I asked Sophie and Mason mentally.

Neither of them seemed to know. But if there was a tail, then it had to be a croc. I slithered into the pool, and when the contractions were stronger and Addie told me to push, I did.

It took some time, but before long, a tiny baby croc floated into the pool and Mason scooped it up with his massive bear paws.

He cuddled the baby and told me, *Girl!*

I felt the surge of joy, but something else was happening. Something felt very wrong inside me. The pain was still there. That shouldn't be happening after I'd already given birth, should it? I let out a hiss and caught everyone's attention. What was going on?

I shifted back to human form and reached out for Addie. "Something's wrong."

"What are you feeling?"

Mason had shifted back and held our baby in his muscular arms, who was already starting to shift to her human form. When she'd come of age, she'd begin her routine shifting. That was normal, they'd all said, for a baby born in animal form to shift back quickly if he or she were to be surrounded by humans.

Mason was at my side, though, looking extremely concerned. I wanted to hold the baby, but I couldn't bear the overwhelming pain that racked my body.

"It hurts," I cried.

"Delivering the placenta shouldn't be too painful," Jessie said.

"Unless there's a problem," Britt added.

"What sort of problem?" Mason asked. "Do we need to get to a hospital?"

"Wait." I felt another contraction. A strong one. The instinct to push was there, so I did. If there was a problem with the placenta, it would be better to get it out, right?

"Oh my god!" Tori shouted. She crouched in the catching position and I felt her hands touching me. "Push again!"

I did and heard something splash into the water.

Mason let out a cry of shock. "Twins!"

"What?" I asked. There was no way we'd just had two babies.

He laughed and tears streamed down his face. "It's a girl! Again!"

"You've *got* to be kidding me."

But then Tori placed a wet baby girl on my chest. The pain had subsided and was replaced by minor contractions, which I had expected.

"We have twins?" I blinked through my tears at Mason. "How did we not know that?"

He laughed again. "I don't know."

We switched babies and I gazed adoringly at both of my daughters.

Mason closed his eyes, taking a long sniff of our second daughter and gave me a mischievous smile. "She's a bear."

Mason positioned both babies on my chest and stood back to gaze at us. "My ladies. I love you all so much."

He bent down to hug and kiss each of us. "Guess Adam won the pool, since our croc girl was first."

I chuckled. "He'll be thrilled."

I thought about what our babies meant for a moment. Twin girls. One croc and one bear. These interspecies siblings were the first of their kind.

We had truly brought the clans together forever; first, through our love, and now, through our family.

We were finally one.

ABOUT THE AUTHOR

Meg Ripley is an author of steamy shifter romances. A Seattle native, Meg can often be found curled up in a local coffee house with her laptop.

FREE BOOK SERIES!

Download Meg's entire *Caught Between Dragons* series when you sign up for her steamy paranormal romance newsletter!

Sign up by visiting Meg's Facebook page:
https://www.facebook.com/authormegripley/